Oxford excellence for the Caribbean

Book 1

STP Caribbean Mathematics

FOURTH EDITION

S Chandler
E Smith
K Chan-Tack
W R Griffith
K D Holder
L Bostock
A Shepherd

OXFORD UNIVERSITY PRESS

OXFORD
UNIVERSITY PRESS

Great Clarendon Street, Oxford, OX2 6DP, United Kingdom

Oxford University Press is a department of the University of Oxford. It furthers the University's objective of excellence in research, scholarship, and education by publishing worldwide. Oxford is a registered trade mark of Oxford University Press in the UK and in certain other countries

The Publisher would like to acknowledge the contributions of Karyl Chan-Tack, Wendy Griffith and Kenneth Holder to this series.

First published in 1987

Second edition published by Stanley Thornes (Publishers) Ltd in 1997

Third edition published by Nelson Thornes Ltd in 2005

This edition published by Oxford University Press in 2019

British Library Cataloguing in Publication Data
Data available

978-0-19-842647-9

10 9

Paper used in the production of this book is a natural, recyclable product made from wood grown in sustainable forests.
The manufacturing process conforms to the environmental regulations of the country of origin.

Printed in India by Multivista Global Pvt. Ltd

Acknowledgements
The publishers would like to thank the following for permissions to use copyright material:

Cover image: Radachynskyi/iStock

Artwork by Thomson Digital

Although we have made every effort to trace and contact all copyright holders before publication this has not been possible in all cases. If notified, the publisher will rectify any errors or omissions at the earliest opportunity.

Links to third party websites are provided by Oxford in good faith and for information only. Oxford disclaims any responsibility for the materials contained in any third party website referenced in this work.

Contents

Introduction

To the student

This new edition of *STP Caribbean Mathematics Student Book 1* attempts to meet your needs as you begin your study of Mathematics at the Secondary school level. Your learning experiences at this stage lay the foundation for future achievement in CSEC Mathematics and beyond. We are very conscious of your need for success and enjoyment in doing Mathematics, which comes from solving problems correctly. With this in mind, we have divided most of the exercises into three types of question:

Type 1 questions

These are identified by numbers written in bold print, e.g. **12**. They help you to see if you understand the topic being discussed and should be attempted in every chapter you study.

Type 2 questions

These are identified by a single underline under the bold print, e.g. **12**. They are extra questions for you to do and are not more difficult. They should be attempted if you need extra practice or want to do revision at a later time.

Type 3 questions

These are identified by a double underline under the bold print, e.g. **12**. They are for those of you who completed Type 1 questions fairly easily and want to attempt questions that are more challenging.

Multiple choice questions

Multiple choice questions have been used throughout the book to help you become more familiar with the format of your assessments at CSEC.

Mixed exercises

Most chapters end with Mixed exercises to help you advance your critical thinking, problem-solving and computational skills. These exercises will also help you revise what you have done, either when you have finished the chapter or as you prepare for examinations.

Use of calculator

You should be able to use a calculator accurately before you leave school. We suggest that you use a calculator mainly to check your answers. Whether you use a calculator or do the computations yourself, always estimate your answer first and always ask the question, 'Does my answer make sense?'

Suggestions for use of student book

- Break up the material in a chapter into manageable parts.
- Have paper and a pencil with you always when you are studying mathematics.
- Write down and look up the meaning of all new vocabulary you encounter.
- Read all questions carefully and rephrase them in your own words.
- Remember that each question contains all the information you need to solve the problem. Do not look only at the numbers that are given.
- Practise your mathematics. This will ensure your success!

You are therefore advised to try to solve as many problems as you can.
Above all, don't be afraid to make mistakes as you are learning. The greatest mathematicians all made many mistakes as they tried to solve problems.

You are now on your way to success in mathematics – GOOD LUCK!

To the teacher

In writing this series, the authors attempted to present the topics in such a way that students will understand the connections among topics in mathematics, and be encouraged to see and use mathematics as a means to make sense of the real world. The exercises have been carefully graded to make the content more accessible to students.

This new edition is designed to:

1 Assist you in helping students to

   - attain important mathematical skills
   - connect mathematics to their everyday lives and understand its role in the development of our contemporary society
   - see the importance of critical thinking skills in everyday problems
   - discover the fun of doing mathematics both individually and collaboratively
   - develop a positive attitude towards doing mathematics.

2 Encourage you to include historical information about mathematics in your teaching.

   Topics from the history of mathematics have been incorporated to ensure that mathematics is not dissociated from its past. This should lead to an increase in the level of enthusiasm, interest and fascination among students, thus enriching the teaching and learning experiences in the mathematics lessons.

Investigations

'Investigation' is included in this revised STP Caribbean Mathematics series. This is in keeping with the requirements of the latest Lower and Secondary and CSEC syllabuses in the region.

Investigations are used to provide students with the opportunity to explore hands-on and minds-on mathematics. At the same time, teachers are presented with open-ended explorations to enhance their mathematical instruction.

It is expected that the tasks will

- encourage problem solving and reasoning
- develop communication skills and the ability to work collaboratively
- connect various mathematical concepts and theories.

Suggestions

1 At the start of each lesson, give a brief outline of the topic to be covered in the lesson. As examples are given, refer back to the outline to show how the example fits into it.

2 List terms that you consider new to the students and solicit additional words from them. Encourage students to read from the text and make their own vocabulary list. Remember that mathematics is a foreign language. The ability to communicate mathematically must involve the careful use of the correct terminology.

3 Have students construct different ways to phrase questions. This helps students to see mathematics as a language. Students, especially in the junior classes, tend to concentrate on the numerical or 'maths' part of the question and pay little attention to the information that is required to solve the problem.

4 When solving problems, have students identify their own problem-solving strategies and listen to the strategies of others. This practice should create an atmosphere of discussion in the class centred on different approaches to solving the same problem.

As the students try to solve problems on their own they will make mistakes. This is expected, as this was the experience of the inventors of mathematics: they tried, guessed, made many mistakes and worked for hours, days and sometimes years before reaching a solution.

There are enough problems in the exercises to allow the students to try and try again. The excitement, disappointment and struggle with a problem until a solution is found will create rewarding mathematical experiences.

1 Whole number arithmetic

At the end of this chapter you should be able to...

1 recognise the place value of a figure
2 add, subtract, multiply and divide whole numbers
3 approximate a given whole number to the nearest ten, hundred, thousand, ...
4 solve problems involving whole numbers
5 use a calculator to work with whole numbers after finding approximate answers
6 estimate the product of two whole numbers to the nearest ten, hundred, thousand, ...
7 perform operations involving a combination of +, −, × and ÷
8 supply numbers to continue a given sequence
9 solve problems using brackets
10 identify square, rectangular and triangular numbers.

Activity

The Romans did not use symbols for numbers, but used letters of the alphabet. For example the Romans used X for ten, V for five; XV means 'ten and five', i.e. 15.

The Roman way of writing numbers is still used today. (When you write your CXC examinations, your grades are written using Roman numerals. If you study hard and do very well you will get Grade I.)

The numbers one to six are written I, II, III, IV, V, VI.

1 Why do you think I is written before V for the number 4, and I is written after V for the number 6?
2 Write the numbers that you think IX and XI mean.
3 The numbers 7 and 8 are written VII and VIII.
  The letter L is used for 50, the letter C is used for 100 and the letter M is used for 1000.
  Write the value of XIV, CLX and MLII.
4 Write the following numbers in Roman numerals: 25, 152, 1854, 2006.
5 Find LXII − XXIV and write your answer in Roman numerals.
6 In Roman numerals, the year 2019 is written MMXIX.
  Which year, written in Roman numerals, uses the most letters?
  Hint: it is in the 19th century.

You need to know...

✔ the number bonds up to 20

✔ multiplication tables up to 10 × 10.

Key words

bracket, calculator, difference, digit, estimate, even number, hundreds, magic square, magic triangle, number pattern, odd number, operation, place value, rectangular number, remainder, sequence, square number, tens, triangular number, units, vertices

Place value

You can write the number one thousand four hundred and twenty-seven in figures as 1427.

The number two thousand seven hundred and forty-one is 2741.

The same figures (or *digits*) are used but they are in different places.

In 1427, the digit 2 means 2 tens.

In 2741 the digit 2 means 2 thousands.

You can write a number under place value headings:

	hundred millions	ten millions	millions	hundred thousands	ten thousands	thousands	hundreds	tens	units
1427 can be written						1	4	2	7
205 100 can be written				2	0	5	1	0	0
1 500 100 can be written			1	5	0	0	1	0	0
999 999 999 can be written	9	9	9	9	9	9	9	9	9

Note that the place value of the next column to the left after hundred millions is billions.

Exercise 1a

1 Write these numbers in figures.

a three hundred and twenty-seven

b fifteen thousand, two hundred and thirty-four

c twenty million four hundred

2 Write in words:

a 734 **b** 9488 **c** 360 100 **d** 2 500 000 **e** 3 620 000

3 Look at the number 7 086 935.

Write the digit that gives

a the number of hundreds

b the number of thousands

c the number of millions

d the number of ten thousands.

4 Write these numbers in order with the smallest first.

a 6493, 3724, 5024, 5566

b 24 721, 8492, 6643, 17 021

c 8451, 8876, 534, 10 880

d 43 624, 734 921, 2 000 843, 933 402

> In part **a** the number with the smallest number of thousands is 3724 so 3724 is the smallest number. There are two numbers in the five thousands. 5024 comes before 5566 so 5024 is the next smallest after 3724. 6493 has the largest number of thousands so is the largest number of the four.

5 Write the value of the 4 in these numbers.

a 5047 **d** 4056

b 6403 **e** 48 976

c 3304

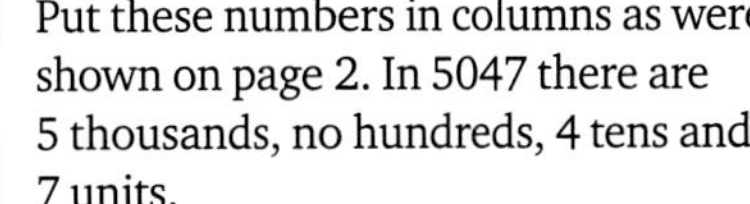

6 Write the value of the 6 in these numbers.

a 3607 **b** 9056 **c** 6883 **d** 62 854

7 Use all five of these cards to make

a the largest number possible

b the smallest number possible.

8 Use the digits 3, 7, 9, 2, 0 once each to make the smallest possible number.

9 Use the digits 4, 6, 8, 0, 7, 2 once each to make the largest possible number that is smaller than four hundred thousand.

10 Read the following two numbers. Which is the larger?

Twenty-two thousand four hundred and sixty

Twenty-two thousand and fourteen

11 Write as many different numbers as you can using each of the digits 3, 4, 5, 8 once in each number. Put these numbers in order with the largest first.

Continuous addition

To add a row of numbers, start at the left-hand side:

	Working in your head
$6+4+3+8=21$	add the first two numbers (10) then add on the next number (13) then add on the next number (21). Check your answer by starting at the other end.

To add a column of numbers, start at the bottom and *working in your head* add up the column:

$$\begin{array}{r} 8 \\ 7 \\ 2 \\ +5 \\ \hline 22 \\ \hline \end{array}$$

$(5+2=7, 7+7=14, 14+8=22)$

Check your answer by starting at the top and adding down the column.

Addition of whole numbers

To add a column of numbers, start with the units:

In the *units* column, $2+1+3=6$ so write 6 in the units column.

$$\begin{array}{r} 83 \\ 291 \\ +702 \\ \hline 1076 \\ \hline {}_1 \end{array}$$

In the *tens* column, $0+9+8=17$ tens which is 7 tens and 1 hundred. Write 7 in the tens column and carry the 1 hundred to the hundreds column to be added to what is there already.

In the *hundreds* column, $1+7+2=10$ hundreds which is 0 hundreds and 1 thousand.

Exercise 1b

Find the value of:

1 $4+6+4+2$

2 $5+4+9+1$

3 $6+7+3+5+6$

4 $4+2+5+6+1+4$

5 $6+9+4+7+8+5$

6 $5+7+3+8+8+6$

7 $\begin{array}{r} 3 \\ 7 \\ 8 \\ +6 \\ \hline \end{array}$

8 $\begin{array}{r} 4 \\ 6 \\ 7 \\ 3 \\ +5 \\ \hline \end{array}$

9 $\begin{array}{r} 45 \\ 21 \\ 30 \\ 90 \\ +32 \\ \hline \end{array}$

10 $\begin{array}{r} 60 \\ 54 \\ 34 \\ 11 \\ +43 \\ \hline \end{array}$

11 $\begin{array}{r} 73 \\ 82 \\ 20 \\ 20 \\ +85 \\ \hline \end{array}$

12 $\begin{array}{r} 67 \\ 70 \\ 33 \\ 90 \\ +72 \\ \hline \end{array}$

13 202 + 515

14 1014 + 250 + 2031

15 870 + 1001 + 502 + 3040

16 303 + 620

17 2007 + 3102 + 3420

18 930 + 2014 + 1002 + 10 201

19 206 + 436

20 4023 + 8023 + 7300

21 30 217 + 804 + 9000 + 50 413

22 1030 + 2057

23 2501 + 282 + 7043

24 90 078 + 8203 + 32 004 + 80 720

25 56 009 + 200 034

26 301 300 + 1020 000 + 915 705

27 600 300 + 27 004 + 540 100 + 300 048

28 207 + 3900 + 6010

29 64 000 + 30 021 + 49 020

30 55 000 + 920 000 + 60 049

31 5200 + 4001 + 12 120

32 4800 + 903 + 30 506

33 322 000 + 7200 + 5008 + 27 000

34 3209 + 260 000 + 76 000 + 40 093

35 250 000 + 802 000 + 71 002 + 300 500

36 670 000 + 409 000 + 2 000 000

37 30 025 + 20 000 + 50 206 + 700 002

38 602 004 + 1 000 310 + 430 000 + 5 100 605

39 20 000 504 + 8 900 007 + 303 033 + 250

40 58 000 000 + 4 000 430 + 50 505 050

Puzzle

Each disc shows three digits. Remove one digit from one of the discs and place it on another disc so that the digits on each of the three discs have the same total.

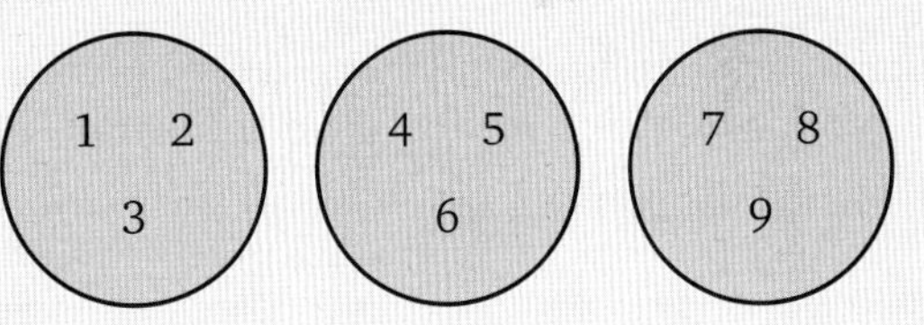

Puzzle

Copy this diagram onto a sheet of paper.

Cut it into three pieces and fit them together to form a magic square.

In a magic square, the numbers in each row and in each column and in each diagonal have the same total.

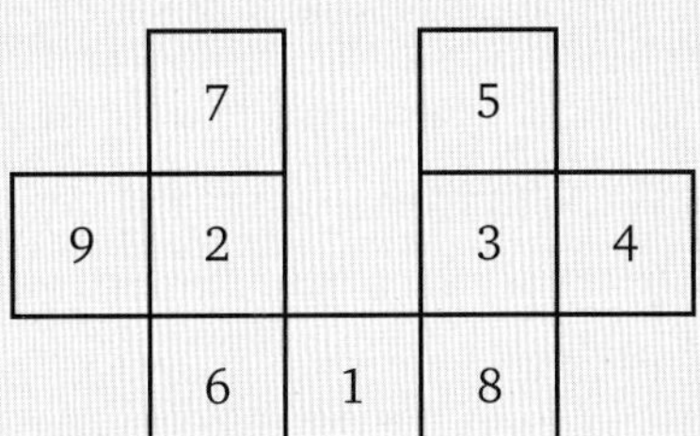

Investigation

Cassie makes up a pattern starting with 3 and 4. To get the next number in the pattern she adds the previous two numbers together. If the answer is more than 10 she writes down only the number of units.

Her pattern is 3, 4, 7, 1, 8, 9, 7, . . .

Write down the next ten numbers in this pattern. Does the pattern repeat itself? If so, how many numbers are there before it starts to repeat?

Now start with 4 and 3 and see what happens. (You need to keep going for a long time!)

Investigate some other pairs of numbers.

Exercise 1c

Find the total cost of a dining suite priced at twelve thousand three hundred and six dollars and a lounge suite priced at twenty-one thousand and forty-three dollars.

To find the total cost you need to **add** the price of the dining suite to the price of the lounge suite.

First you have to write the prices in figures: twelve thousand three hundred and six dollars means 1 ten thousand, 2 thousands, 3 hundreds, 0 tens and 6, i.e. 12 306.

Twenty-one thousand and forty-three dollars means 2 tens of thousands, 1 thousand, 0 hundreds, 4 tens and 3, i.e. 21 043.

Total cost is \$12 306 + \$21 043
i.e. \$33 349.

$$\begin{array}{r} 12\,306 \\ +\,21\,043 \\ \hline 33\,349 \\ \hline \end{array}$$

1 Find the total cost of a tin of baked beans at 675 c, a cake at 250 c and a can of cola at 325 c.

2 In the local corner shop I bought a magazine costing 295 c, a pencil costing 145 c and a packet of sweets costing 350 c. How much did I spend?

3 Find the total cost of a washing machine at \$2742, a cooker at \$1999 and a freezer at \$3358.

4 Add four thousand and fifteen, twelve hundred and sixty-eight and thirteen thousand and four.

5 I have three pieces of string. One piece is 227 cm long, another is 534 cm long and a third is 95 cm long. What is the total length of the string I have?

6 George flew from São Paulo to San Francisco, then from San Francisco to Montreal and finally from Montreal to São Paulo. The distances in air miles are:

São Paulo to San Francisco	6581
San Francisco to Montreal	2567
Montreal to São Paulo	5394

How many miles did George fly on his round trip?

7 The International Air Miles between certain cities are:

New York to London 3457, Auckland to Mumbai 7665, New York to Auckland 9118, Mumbai to New York 7841, London to Auckland 11 840, Mumbai to London 4479.

How far is it

- **a** from New York to Auckland via Mumbai
- **b** from Auckland to London via Mumbai
- **c** from Auckland to New York, first calling at Mumbai, and next calling at London?

8 Our local council have allocated \$16 000 000 for education, \$13 500 000 for the care of the elderly, \$750 000 for keeping the area clean and tidy and \$2 350 000 for all their other expenses. How much do they need to cover all these expenses?

9 A boy decided to save some money by an unusual method. He put 1 c in his money box the first week, 2 c in the second week, 4 c in the third week, 8 c in the fourth week, and so on. He gave up after 10 weeks. Write down how much he put in his money box each week and add it up to find the total that he had saved. Why do you think he gave up?

Investigation

A number that reads the same forwards and backwards, e.g. 14 241, is called a palindrome.

There is a conjecture (i.e. it has not been proved) that if we take *any* number, reverse the digits and add the numbers together, then do the same with the result, and so on, we will end up with a palindrome. For example, starting with 251,

$251 + 152 = 403$

$403 + 304 = 707$ which is a palindrome.

1 Can you find some two-digit numbers for which the palindrome appears after the first sum?

2 If two palindromes are added together, is the result always a palindrome?

Subtraction of whole numbers

Exercise 1d

Do the following subtractions in your head:

1	15 − 4	2	19 − 7	3	18 − 4	4	12 − 7	5	15 − 8
6	20 − 8	9	14 − 6	12	12 − 9	15	19 − 9	18	15 − 9
7	18 − 3	10	10 − 4	13	17 − 6	16	11 − 7	19	20 − 6
8	17 − 8	11	15 − 2	14	16 − 8	17	13 − 8	20	15 − 7

Find 1508 − 721

Here is one method:

```
 0 14
 1 5 0 8
−  7 2 1
   7 8 7
```

You can subtract 1 one from 8 ones to give 7 ones.

Move to the tens: you cannot subtract 2 tens from 0 tens so regroup the 5 hundreds so that there are 4 hundreds and 10 tens. Then you can subtract 2 tens from 10 tens to give 8 tens.

Next change the 1 thousand to 10 hundreds and add it to the 4 hundreds. Then 14 hundreds minus 7 hundreds gives 7 hundreds.

Find:

21	526 − 315	29	3090 − 2309		
22	754 − 203	30	50 076 − 27 005		
23	821 − 415	31	670 504 − 500 680	37	200 707 − 193 000
24	526 − 308	32	100 123 − 78 000	38	910 027 − 452 009
25	1495 − 369	33	808 023 − 505 022	39	730 005 − 580 006
26	2283 − 357	34	770 000 − 439 000	40	3 919 000 − 2 828 000
27	5648 − 4722	35	200 308 − 150 107	41	78 000 000 − 54 060 000
28	7384 − 3491	36	404 707 − 303 505	42	345 000 000 − 293 005 500

Exercise 1e

Cheryl had 49 marbles in her bag. Darren had 86 marbles in his bag.

How many more marbles did Darren have than Cheryl had?

'How many more' means the number that Darren has over and above 49, i.e. you have to subtract 49 from 86.

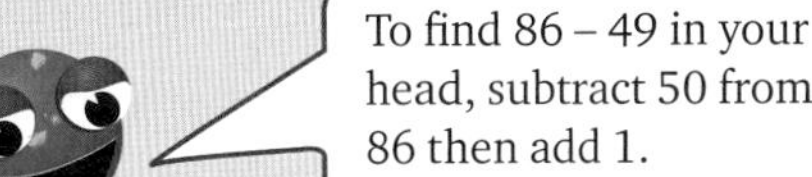

$86 - 49 = 37$

So Darren had 37 more marbles than Cheryl.

1 The club dues for last week were 297 c. I paid with a $5 note ($5 is 500 cents). How much change did I receive?

2 In a school there are 856 children. There are 392 girls. How many boys are there?

The difference is the smaller number subtracted from the larger number.

3 Find the difference between 37 007 and 29 302.

4 Take two thousand and fifty-one away from three thousand and forty.

5 A distribution centre starts with 25 750 cans of cola and delivers 8463 cans to supermarkets.
How many cans are left in the distribution centre?

6 Subtract twenty-two thousand and sixty-five from eighty thousand, five hundred and forty-eight.

7 Find the difference between 210 802 and 309 056.

8 The population of St John Antigua is 23 342 and the population of Kingston Jamaica is 937 700. How many more people live in Kingston than in St John?

9 The highest peak of the Blue Mountains in Jamaica is 2220 m.
Mount Everest is 8843 m high.
How much higher than the highest Blue Mountain peak is Mount Everest?

10 A company has allocated $2 740 000 to cover overheads and $18 500 000 to pay wages and salaries. How much more have the company allowed to cover wages and salaries than to cover overheads?

11 A book gives the populations of three countries as follows:

USA	287 365 732
Japan	152 845 756
Canada	34 815 377

How much larger is the population of the USA than the combined population of the other two countries?

Investigation

Write down any three-digit number, e.g. 287.

Arrange the digits in order of size; once with the largest digit first and once with the smallest digit first, i.e. 872, 278.

Now find the difference between these two numbers (take the smaller number from the larger number),

i.e. $872 - 278 = 594$

Repeat the process for your answer,

i.e. $954 - 459 = 495$

Repeating the process again,

i.e. $954 - 459 = 495$

These rules give us a chain of numbers. In this example we have

$$287 \rightarrow 594 \rightarrow 495 \rightarrow 495$$

Form a similar chain for a three-figure number of your own choice. Try a few more. What do you notice?

Exercise 1f

Find the missing digit; it is marked with □:

1 27 + 28 = □5

2 34 + 5□ = 89

3 5□ − 25 = 32

4 6□ − 48 = 16

5 128 + □59 = 1087

6 5□ + 29 = 83

7 □4 + 57 = 81

8 □3 − 47 = 26

9 25 − 1□ = 6

10 1□7 + 239 = 416

11 □647 + 592 = 5239

12 2943 − 16□2 = 1301

Mixed addition and subtraction

It is the sign *in front* of a number that tells you what to do with that number. For example $128 - 56 + 92$ means '128 take away 56 and add on 92'. This can be done in any order with addition and subtraction. For example,

$$128 - 56 + 92 = 72 + 92 = 164$$
$$128 - 56 + 92 = 128 + 92 - 56 = 220 - 56 = 164$$

We worked the same question in two different ways and both gave the same result.

This is ALWAYS the case with addition and subtraction.

Exercise 1g

Find:

a $7253 + 832 - 2264$ **b** $560073 - 606070 + 290050 - 70034$

a $7253 + 832 - 2264 = 8085 - 2264 = 5821$

$$\begin{array}{r} 7253 \\ +\ 832 \\ \hline 8085 \\ \hline \end{array} \qquad \begin{array}{r} 8085 \\ -\ 2264 \\ \hline 5821 \\ \hline \end{array}$$

b You can change the order of the numbers so that the addition is done first. When you do this, remember that the sign in front of a number stays with that number. So

$$\begin{aligned} 560073 - 606070 + 290050 - 70034 &= 560073 + 290050 - 606070 - 70034 \\ &= 850123 - 606070 - 70034 \\ &= 244053 - 70034 \\ &= 174019 \end{aligned}$$

By working each question in two different ways, find:

1	$25 - 6 + 7 - 9$	**11**	$95 - 161 + 75 + 34$
2	$14 + 2 - 8 - 3$	**12**	$9500 - 1010 - 2050 + 4300$
3	$7 - 4 + 5 - 6$	**13**	$1200 - 5005 - 3060 + 8400$
4	$19 + 2 - 4 + 3$	**14**	$20078 + 39004 - 40006 - 18040$
5	$23 - 2 + 4 + 5$	**15**	$107000 - 1127000 + 854000 + 231000$
6	$46 - 12 + 3 - 9$	**16**	$463002 - 650043 + 360004 - 170075$
7	$27 + 6 - 11 - 9$	**17**	$83000000 - 17000000 - 8300000 - 220000$
8	$2 + 13 - 7 + 3 - 8$	**18**	$800500 + 355000 - 390500 - 680000$
9	$7 - 6 + 9 - 1 - 3$	**19**	$10080050 - 8350000 - 550000 - 128000$
10	$17 + 4 - 9 - 3 - 5$	**20**	$76000500 + 765000 - 85000000 + 12090000$

? Puzzle

Solve this cross-number puzzle.

Across
1 $73 - 31$
4 $249 + 167$
6 $700 - 565$
7 $231 - 158$

Down
2 $77 + 166$
3 $222 - 136$
5 $78 + 79$
6 $52 + 106 - 139$

1	2	■	3
■	4	5	
6			■
	■	7	

Exercise 1h

A bottling factory had 50 000 bottles of water in stock at closing time on Monday.

On Tuesday 3150 bottles were sold, on Wednesday 12 480 bottles were sold and on Thursday 16 950 bottles were sold. Total production on Tuesday, Wednesday and Thursday amounted to 35 000 bottles. How many bottles were in stock by closing time on Thursday?

The number of bottles in stock at the end of Monday = 50 000

The number of bottles sold on Tuesday, Wednesday and Thursday is

$$3150 + 12480 + 16950 = 32580$$

Number of bottles in stock after these sales = 50 000 − 32 580
= 17 420

New stock produced is 35 000.

Total stock at end of Thursday = 17 420 + 35 000
= 52 420

1 A boy buys a comic costing 65 c and a pencil costing 55 c. He pays with $2.00. How much change does he receive?

2 I have a piece of string 7500 cm long. I cut off two pieces, one of length 1865 cm and one of length 2345 cm. How long is the piece of string that I have left?

3 On Monday 4000 fish fingers were cooked in the school kitchen. At the first lunch sitting 2384 fish fingers were served. At the second sitting 1298 fish fingers were served. How many were left?

4 Find the difference between twelve thousand, and three thousand two hundred and eighty-three. Then add on eight hundred and forty-five.

5 A supermarket has 438 kilograms of carrots when it opens on Monday morning. During the day the shop gets a delivery of 360 kilograms of carrots and sells 529 kilograms.

How many kilograms of carrots are left when it closes on Monday evening?

6 A boy has 30 marbles in his pocket when he goes to school on Monday morning.

At morning break he wins 6 marbles.

At lunchtime he loses 15 marbles.

After school he loses another 4 marbles.

On Tuesday he loses 3 marbles during morning break, wins 6 marbles at lunchtime and doesn't play after school.

a How many marbles does he have when he goes home on Monday?

b He returns on Tuesday with the same number of marbles as he went home with on Monday. How many marbles does he have when he leaves school on Tuesday?

7 Sarah gets 550 c pocket money on Saturday.

On Monday she spends 235 c.

On Tuesday she is given 450 c for doing a special job at home.

On Thursday she spends 730 c.

How much money has she got left?

8 Yesterday Keron reached his 12th birthday. Next year he will be 14. What is today's date? When is Keron's birthday?

Investigation

Follow these instructions:

Step 1 Write down any three-digit number in which the number of hundreds differs by at least two from the number of units,

e.g. 419 or 236 or 973 but not 707 or 514.

Step 2 Now write down the digits in reverse order,

e.g. 419 becomes 914.

Step 3 Subtract the smaller number from the larger number.

e.g. $914 - 419 = 495$.

Step 4 Add this number to its reverse, i.e. add 495 to 594.

The result in this case is 1089.

Now try these four steps with any number of your choice. Repeat the instructions six times for six different numbers, but do remember that the number of hundreds must differ by at least two from the number of units.

What do you notice?

Approximation

Calculators are very useful and can save a lot of time. Calculators do not make mistakes but *we* sometimes do when we use them. So it is important to know roughly if the answer we get from a calculator is right. By simplifying the numbers involved we can get a rough answer in our heads.

One way to simplify numbers is to make them into the nearest number of hundreds. For example

1276 is roughly 13 hundreds or 1300

and

1234 is roughly 12 hundreds or 1200

We say that 1276 is rounded up to 1300 and 1234 is rounded down to 1200. In mathematics we say that 1276 is approximately equal to 13 hundreds.

We use the symbol ≈ to mean 'is approximately equal to'. We would write

$1276 \approx 13$ hundreds

$1234 \approx 12$ hundreds

When a number is halfway between hundreds we always round up. We say

$1250 \approx 13$ hundreds

Exercise 1i

Write each of the following numbers as an approximate number of tens:

1 84 **2** 151 **3** 632 **4** 228 **5** 155

Write each of the following numbers as an approximate number of hundreds:

6 830 **7** 256 **8** 1221 **9** 1350 **10** 3780

Write each number as an approximate number of thousands:

11 30 978 **12** 876 434 **13** 710 256 **14** 979 797 **15** 267 262

Write each number as an approximate number of millions:

16 45 672 189 **17** 6 665 555 **18** 35 454 430 **19** 94 325 432

By writing each number correct to the nearest number of tens find an approximate answer for:

20 $153 + 181$

21 $68 + 143 + 73$

22 $369 - 92 + 85$

23 $295 + 304 - 451$

24 $63 + 29 + 40 + 37 + 81$

25 $13 + 29 + 83 + 121 + 5$

26 $103 + 125 + 76 + 41 + 8$

27 $260 + 145 - 36 - 118$

28 $142 - 89 + 64 - 101$

Now use your calculator to find the exact answers to questions **20** to **28**. Remember to look at your rough answer to check that your calculator answer is probably correct.

Multiplication of whole numbers

Exercise 1j will help you to practise the multiplication facts.

For example 69×4 can be found by adding

$$69 + 69 + 69 + 69$$

but it is quicker to use the multiplication facts.

Now $69 \times 4 = 9 \text{ units} \times 4 + 6 \text{ tens} \times 4$

$$\begin{array}{r} 69 \\ \times\ 4 \\ \hline 276 \\ \hline {\scriptstyle 3} \end{array}$$

9 units × 4 = 36 units = 3 tens + 6 units

so write 6 units and carry 3 tens.

6 tens × 4 = 24 tens

Then add on the 3 tens carried to give 27 tens, which is 2 hundreds + 7 tens.

Multiplication by 10, 100, 1000, ...

When 85 is multiplied by 10 the 5 units increases to 5 tens and the 8 tens increases to 8 hundreds. So

$$85 \times 10 = 850$$

When 85 is multiplied by 100 the 5 units increases to 5 hundreds and the 8 tens increases to 8 thousands. Thus

$$85 \times 100 = 8500$$

When 85 is multiplied by 20 this is the same as $85 \times 2 \times 10$.
This is so because $20 = 2 \times 10$. So

$$\begin{aligned} 85 \times 20 &= 85 \times 2 \times 10 \\ &= 170 \times 10 \\ &= 1700 \end{aligned}$$

In the same way 27×4000 is the same as $27 \times 4 \times 1000$.
This is so because $4000 = 4 \times 1000$.

$$\begin{aligned} 27 \times 4000 &= 27 \times 4 \times 1000 \\ &= 108 \times 1000 \\ &= 108\,000 \end{aligned}$$

Also

$$\begin{aligned} 67 \times 7\,000\,000 &= 67 \times 7 \times 1\,000\,000 \\ &= 469 \times 1\,000\,000 \\ &= 469\,000\,000 \end{aligned}$$

Exercise 1j

Without using a calculator, find:

If you can do these in your head, write down the answer. You may find it easier to write the numbers in columns. Keep units under one another, tens under one another, and so on.

For example
$$\begin{array}{r} 23 \\ \times\ 2 \\ \hline \end{array}$$

1 76×4
2 26×5
3 83×3
4 47×9
5 72×2
6 54×6
7 204×6
8 408×8
9 390×5
10 807×4
11 730×7
12 440×9
13 6400×3
14 8082×4
15 $36\,000 \times 5$
16 $705\,500 \times 7$
17 $600\,600 \times 9$
18 $2\,021\,500 \times 4$
19 $39\,500\,000 \times 2$
20 $6\,350\,000 \times 5$
21 $41\,000\,800 \times 6$
22 $70\,450\,000 \times 7$
23 $31\,500\,000 \times 3$
24 $5\,700\,500 \times 4$
25 76×10
26 26×100
27 83×10
28 47×1000
29 $72 \times 10\,000$
30 54×30
31 204×50
32 448×80
33 390×400
34 867×600
35 732×3000
36 $81\,823 \times 900$
37 $6000 \times 43\,656$
38 808×4000
39 $10\,600 \times 3000$
40 $66\,500 \times 700\,000$

Remember numbers can be multiplied in any order, e.g. $100 \times 56 = 56 \times 100$

Investigation

1 *Do not use a calculator for parts* **a** *to* **d**.

a Multiply 123 456 789 by 3 and then multiply the result by 9. What do you notice?

b Repeat part **a** multiplying first by a different number less than 9.

c Repeat part **a** again using a third number less than 9.

d Is there a rule for predicting the answer when 123 456 789 is multiplied by one of the numbers 2, 3, 4, 5, 6, 7 or 8, and the result is multiplied by 9? If you find one, write it down and test it.

2 *Now try using your calculator.* What do you notice?

Long multiplication

To multiply 84×26 we use the fact that

$$84 \times 26 = 84 \times 20 + 84 \times 6$$

This can be set out as

$$\begin{array}{rl} 84 & \\ \times 26 & \\ \hline 504 & (84 \times 6) \\ +1680 & (84 \times 20) \\ \hline 2184 & \\ \hline \end{array}$$

To multiply 1054×2007 we use the fact that

$$1054 \times 2007 = 1054 \times 7 + 1054 \times 2000$$

We set this out as

$$\begin{array}{r} 1054 \\ \times\ 2007 \\ \hline 7378 \\ 2108000 \\ \hline 2115378 \\ \hline \end{array}$$

Exercise 1k

Without using a calculator, find:

Large numbers are easier to multiply together when written in columns. Remember to keep units lined up in a units column, tens in a tens column, and so on, as shown in the example in the text before Exercise 1k.

1 43×13

2 390×90

3 556×70

4 81×3000

5 200×73

6 243×106

7 409×206

8 632×107

9 903×3060

10 6320×4200

11 1500×802

12 $40\,502 \times 5060$

13 $73\,006 \times 3080$

14 $83\,007 \times 15\,040$

15 $68\,304 \times 230\,080$

Using a calculator for long multiplication

Calculators save a lot of time when used for long multiplication. You do, however, need to be able to estimate the size of the answer you expect as a check on your use of the calculator.

One way to get a rough answer is to round off

a number between 10 and 100 to the nearest number of tens

a number between 100 and 1000 to the nearest number of hundreds

a number between 1000 and 10 000 to the nearest number of thousands

and so on.

For example $512 \times 78 \approx 500 \times 80 = 40\,000$

and $2752 \times 185 \approx 3000 \times 200 = 600\,000$

Exercise 1I

Estimate each answer and then use a calculator to find the exact answer:

1 84×36

2 55×22

3 62×57

4 59×18

5 174×46

6 283×53

7 57×636

8 68×239

9 435×122

10 276×308

11 723×803

12 440×967

13 251×663

14 773×203

15 253×704

16 706×338

17 3521×505

18 7342×706

19 1854×433

20 8093×654

21 6825×778

22 5058×765

23 2985×456

24 8462×543

25 6342×4042

26 1885×6032

27 8256×9007

28 4062×7358

29 3241×7653

30 8456×7032

31 7281×3552

32 $65\,482 \times 2543$

Exercise 1m

A library has 268 shelves. There are 124 books on each shelf.
How many books are there altogether?

To find the number of books you need to multiply the number of shelves by the number of books on each shelf.

Number of books = number of shelves × number of books on each shelf

$= 268 \times 124 = 33\,232$

1 Multiply two thousand three hundred and fifty-six by three hundred and twenty-three.

2 A car park has 34 rows and each row has 42 parking spaces.
How many cars can be parked?

3 On a school outing 17 coaches were used, each taking 49 students.
How many students went on the outing?

4 A concert hall has 54 rows. Each row has 54 seats. How many seats are there?

5 A supermarket takes delivery of 54 crates of soft drink cans. Each crate contains 48 cans. How many cans are delivered?

6 One jar of marmalade weighs 454 grams. Find the weight of 144 jars.

7 Find the value of one hundred and fifty thousand three hundred multiplied by seven hundred and forty-five.

8 During a year a school is open five days a week for forty weeks.
The students attend lessons for five hours each day.

- a How many days is the school open in a year?
- b How many hours do the students attend lessons in a year?
- c For how many minutes do the students attend lessons in a year?

9 Last year an airline pilot flew a distance of 3627 miles each way between two international cities. In the year he made 63 return flights between these two cities. How many miles had he flown between them during the year?

10 The government decide to collect 13 c tax on every bottle of a particular soft drink sold in the country. They estimate that during a year 25 455 500 bottles will be sold.

- a How much tax do they hope to collect for the sales of this soft drink? Give your answer in dollars.
- b Now give your answer correct to the nearest ten thousand dollars.

Division of whole numbers

Division is the opposite of multiplication.

$38 \div 8$ means 'how many eights are there in 38?'. We can find out by repeatedly taking 8 away from 38:

$38 - \mathbf{8} = 30$

$30 - \mathbf{8} = 22$

$22 - \mathbf{8} = 14$

$14 - \mathbf{8} = 6$ We have subtracted 8 four times.
So there are 4 eights in 38 with 6 left over.

Thus $38 \div 8 = 4$, remainder 6.

A quicker way uses the multiplication facts.

We know that $32 = 4 \times 8$

therefore $38 \div 8 = 4$, remainder 6.

To find $525 \div 3$ start with the hundreds:

5 (hundreds) $\div\, 3 = \underline{1}$ (hundred), remainder 2 (hundreds).

Take the remainder, 2 (hundreds), with the tens:

22 (tens) $\div\, 3 = \underline{7}$ (tens), remainder 1 (tens).

Take the remainder, 1 (tens), with the units:

15 (units) $\div\, 3 = \underline{5}$ (units)

Therefore $525 \div 3 = 175$

This can be set out as:

$$\begin{array}{r} 1\,7\,5 \\ 3\overline{)\,5^2 2^1 5} \end{array}$$

divisor (3), quotient (175), dividend (5^22^15)

Each part of a division has a name as is shown above.

Division by 10, 100, 1000, ...

$812 \div 10$ means 'how many tens are there in 812?'.

There are 81 tens in 810 so

$812 \div 10 = 81$, remainder 2.

$2578 \div 100$ means 'how many hundreds are there in 2578?'.

There are 25 hundreds in 2500 so

$2578 \div 100 = 25$, remainder 78.

Exercise 1n

Find 4669 ÷ 5

$$\begin{array}{r} 9\,3\,3 \quad r4 \\ 5\overline{)4\,6\,{}^{1}6\,{}^{1}9} \end{array}$$

4669 ÷ 5 = 933, r4

46 (hundred) ÷ 5 = 9 (hundred) remainder 1 (hundred).

Put the 9 hundred above the 6 in the dividend and add the remainder to the tens giving 16 (tens).

Next 16 (tens) ÷ 5 = 3 (tens) with 1 ten left over. Put the 3 above the tens in the dividend and add 1 ten to the units giving 19 units. Then 19 ÷ 5 = 3 with 4 left.

Do the following calculations and give the remainder where there is one:

1	87 ÷ 3	**9**	630 ÷ 3	**17**	3005 ÷ 5	**25**	600 340 ÷ 4
2	36 ÷ 6	**10**	701 ÷ 7	**18**	73 000 ÷ 4	**26**	180 078 ÷ 6
3	72 ÷ 4	**11**	800 ÷ 5	**19**	10 004 ÷ 3	**27**	82 000 000 ÷ 9
4	73 ÷ 5	**12**	440 ÷ 6	**20**	80 960 ÷ 2	**28**	4062 ÷ 7
5	69 ÷ 3	**13**	251 ÷ 4	**21**	6 800 024 ÷ 7	**29**	320 043 ÷ 8
6	78 ÷ 6	**14**	673 ÷ 9	**22**	5 058 000 ÷ 6	**30**	48 400 560 ÷ 4
7	85 ÷ 7	**15**	800 ÷ 7	**23**	6 290 805 ÷ 4	**31**	8 108 100 ÷ 9
8	54 ÷ 8	**16**	706 ÷ 3	**24**	8 004 602 ÷ 3	**32**	1 750 005 ÷ 5

Calculate the following and give the remainder:

33	256 ÷ 10	**36**	2783 ÷ 100	**39**	186 ÷ 10	**42**	8512 ÷ 100
34	87 ÷ 10	**37**	4910 ÷ 1000	**40**	2781 ÷ 10	**43**	3077 ÷ 100
35	196 ÷ 100	**38**	57 ÷ 10	**41**	9426 ÷ 1000	**44**	5704 ÷ 1000

? Puzzle

1 Maria has some tennis balls and some bags to keep them in. If 9 balls are put into each bag, one ball is left over. If 11 balls are put into each bag, one bag is empty. How many tennis balls and how many bags are there? Explain your thinking.

2 Write each of the digits from 1 to 9, one in each box, so that all three expressions below are correct. Each digit is therefore used once and once only.

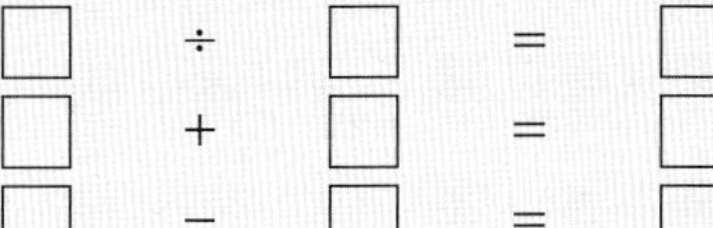

Puzzle

Copy the following sets of numbers. Put +, −, ×, or ÷ in each box so that the calculations are correct.

1 $9 \square 4 = 5$ 2 $7 \square 3 = 21$ 3 $28 \square 4 = 7$ 4 $8 \square 2 = 4$

Mixed operations of +, −, ×, ÷

When a calculation involves a mixture of the operations +, −, ×, ÷ we always do

multiplication and division first

For example

$$\begin{aligned} & 2 \times 4 + 3 \times 6 \quad \text{(multiplication first)} \\ = \ & 8 + 18 = 26 \end{aligned}$$

Exercise 1p

Find $5 - 10 \times 2 \div 5 + 3$

$$\begin{aligned} & 5 - 10 \times 2 \div 5 + 3 \\ &= 5 - 20 \div 5 + 3 \quad (\times \text{ done}) \\ &= 5 - 4 + 3 \quad (\div \text{ done}) \\ &= 1 + 3 \\ &= 4 \end{aligned}$$

Find:

1 $8 \div 2 + 6 \times 3$

2 $14 \times 2 \div 7 - 3 + 6$

3 $5 + 4 \times 3 + 8 \div 2$

4 $5 - 4 \div 2 + 7 \times 2$

5 $6 \times 3 - 8 \times 2$

6 $9 \div 3 + 12 \div 6$

7 $12 \div 3 - 15 \div 5$

8 $9 + 3 - 6 \div 2 + 1$

9 $6 - 3 \times 2 + 9 \div 3$

10 $5 \times 3 \times 2 - 2 \times 3 \times 4$

11 $10 \times 3 \div 15 + 6$

12 $8 + 7 \times 4 \div 2$

13 $3 \times 8 \div 4 + 7$

14 $9 \div 3 + 7 \times 2$

15 $4 - 8 \div 2 + 6$

16 $5 \times 4 \div 10 + 6$

17 $6 \times 3 \div 9 + 2 \times 4$

18 $7 + 3 \times 2 \div 6$

19 $8 \div 4 + 6 \div 2$

20 $12 \div 4 + 3 \times 2$

21 $19 + 3 \times 2 - 8 \div 2$

22 $7 \times 2 - 3 + 6 \div 2$

23 $8 + 3 \times 2 - 4 \div 2$

24 $7 \times 2 - 4 \div 2 + 1$

25 $6 + 8 \div 4 + 2 \times 3 \times 4$

26 $5 \times 3 \times 4 \div 12 + 6 - 2$

27 $5 + 6 \times 2 - 8 \div 2 + 9 \div 3$

28 $7 - 9 \div 3 + 6 \times 2 - 4 \div 2$

29 $9 \div 3 - 2 + 1 + 6 \times 2$

30 $4 \times 2 - 6 \div 3 + 3 \times 2 \times 4$

? Puzzle

1 Copy the following sets of numbers. Put +, –, × or ÷ in each box so that the calculations are correct.

a 5□4□6 = 3 **b** 8□3□4 = 1 **c** 3□4□2 = 9 **d** 2□1□3 = 6

2 Solve this cross-number puzzle.

Across
1 $127 - 64$
3 $44 + 73 - 58$
4 6×53
8 330×41
11 $9 \times 10 - 9$
12 The next number after 40

Down
2 $3 \times 13 - 6$
3 $464 \div 8$
5 $625 \div 5$
6 74×7
7 9×89
9 $5 \times 8 - 27 \div 3$
10 $2 \times 19 - 4$

1	2		3	
	4	5		
6				7
8	9		10	
11			12	

Using brackets

If we need to do some addition and/or subtraction before multiplication and division we use brackets round the section that is to be done first. For example $2 \times (3 + 2)$ means work out $3 + 2$ first.

So $2 \times (3 + 2)$
$= 2 \times 5$
$= 10$

For a calculation with brackets and a mixture of ×, ÷, + and – we first work out the inside of the Brackets, then the order is to do the Multiplication and Division, and lastly the Addition and Subtraction.

You can remember this order from the acronym BODMAS.

Another way of remembering is using the first letters of the words in the sentence

Bless My Dear Aunt Sally.

Exercise 1q

Find $2 \times (3 \times 6 - 4) + 7 - 12 \div 6$

$$\begin{aligned} 2 \times (3 \times 6 - 4) + 7 - 12 \div 6 &= 2 \times (18 - 4) + 7 - 12 \div 6 \\ &= 2 \times 14 + 7 - 12 \div 6 && \text{(inside bracket first)} \\ &= 28 + 7 - 2 && (\times \text{ and } \div \text{ next}) \\ &= 33 && (\text{lastly } + \text{ and } -) \end{aligned}$$

Find:

1. $12 \div (5 + 1)$
2. $8 \times (3 + 4)$
3. $(5 - 2) \times 3$
4. $(6 + 1) \times 2$
5. $(3 + 2) \times (4 - 1)$
6. $(3 - 2) \times (5 + 3)$
7. $7 \times (12 - 5)$
8. $(6 + 2) \div 4$
9. $(8 + 1) \times (2 + 3)$
10. $(9 - 1) \div (6 - 2)$
11. $2 + 3 \times (3 + 2)$
12. $7 - 2 \times (5 - 3)$
13. $8 - 5 + 2 \times (4 + 3)$
14. $2 \times (7 - 2) \div (16 - 11)$
15. $4 + 3 \times (2 - 1) + 8 \div (9 - 7)$
16. $6 \div (10 - 8) + 4$
17. $7 \times (12 - 6) - 12$
18. $12 - 8 - 3 \times (9 - 8)$
19. $4 \times (15 - 7) \div (17 - 9)$
20. $5 \times (8 - 2) + 3 \times (7 - 5)$
21. $6 \times 8 - 18 \div (2 + 4)$
22. $10 \div 5 + 20 \div (4 + 1)$
23. $5 + (2 \times 10 - 5) - 6$
24. $8 - (15 \div 3 + 4) + 1$
25. $(2 \times 3 - 4) + (33 \div 11 + 5)$
26. $(18 \div 3 + 3) \div (4 \times 4 - 7)$
27. $(50 \div 5 + 6) - (8 \times 2 - 4)$
28. $(10 \times 3 - 20) + 3 \times (9 \div 3 + 2)$
29. $(7 - 3 \times 2) \div (8 \div 4 - 1)$
30. $(5 + 3) \times 2 + 10 \div (8 - 3)$

Exercise 1r

A fleet operator needs to replace its fleet of thirty-five cars. The company decides to buy thirteen cars costing $153 450 each and the remaining twenty-two cars at $209 750 each.

a Find the total cost of the thirty-five cars.

The company is prepared to pay a total cost of eight million dollars.

b Is the total cost of the cars within the budget? If so, how much is it short of what the company is prepared to pay?

a Cost of 13 cars at $153 450 = $153 450 × 13 = $1 994 850
Cost of 22 cars at $209 750 = $209 750 × 22 = $4 614 500
Total cost of 35 cars = $1 994 850 + $4 614 500 = $6 609 350

b The company is prepared to pay $8 000 000 which is more than the cost of the cars.
The cost of the new fleet is therefore within the company's budget.
Amount below the budget = $8 000 000 – $6 609 350 = $1 390 650

1. A cake shop bought 55 bread rolls that cost 275 c each and 85 cakes that cost 550 c each. Find the total cost of the rolls and the cakes.
2. How many dresses costing $210 could a shopkeeper buy with $10 000?
3. If a bus will hold 45 children, how many buses are needed to take 630 children on a school outing?
4. Three children went into a sweet shop. The first child bought three bags of sweets costing 145 c each, the second child bought three bags of sweets costing 185 c each and the third child bought three bags of sweets costing 235 c each. How much money did they spend altogether?
5. Christine is paid the same amount every week. After 8 weeks she has earned $17 296. How much does she earn each week?
6. A cricket club started the year with 1482 members. During the year 136 people left and 289 people joined. How many people belonged to the club at the end of the year?
7. At a bank Mr Beynon pays in two hundred and five 5 c pieces and fifty-four 10 c pieces. The following week he pays in three hundred and fifty 5 c pieces and two hundred and twenty 10 c pieces. How much has he paid in altogether?

8 At an election one candidate got 1267 votes, and the other candidate got 859 votes. 37 voting papers were spoilt and 375 people who could have voted did not do so. How many people could have voted altogether?

9 Ryan can walk up a flight of steps at the rate of 30 steps a minute. It takes him 4 minutes to reach the top. How many steps are there?

10 Three brothers inherit \$487 563 to share equally among them. How much does each brother receive?

11 An extension ladder is made of three separate parts, each 300 cm long. There is an overlap of 30 cm at each junction when it is fully extended. How long is the extended ladder?

12 Janine, Sarah and Claire come to school with 320 c each. Janine owes Sarah 95 c and she also owes Claire 45 c. Sarah owes Janine 40 c and she also owes Claire 85 c. When all their debts are settled, how much money does each girl have?

13 At the bookstore Anora buys three books costing \$[illegible]5 each and one book costing \$235. How much change does she get from a \$500 note?

14 A man gets paid \$3040 for a five-day working week. How much does he get paid a day?

15 The total number of children in the first year of a school is 540. There are 50 more girls than boys.

a How many boys are there? **b** How many girls are there?

16 4000 apples are packed into boxes. Each box holds 75 apples. How many boxes are required?

17 In a book of street plans of a town, the plans start on page 6 and end on page 72. How many pages of street plans are there?

18 My great-grandmother died in 1894, aged 62. There are two years in which she could have been born. What are they and why?

19 How many times can 35 be taken away from 570?

20 A palm tree was planted in the year in which Sir Grantley Adams was born. He died in 1971 aged 73. How old was the palm tree in 2017?

Number patterns

Exercise 1s

2	7	6
9	5	1
4	3	8

This is a magic square.

The numbers in every row, in every column and in each diagonal add up to 15.

Copy and complete the following magic squares. Use the numbers 1 to 9 just once in each, and use a pencil in case you need to rub out!

1

8		
	5	
4		2

2

4	9	
	5	
	1	

3 Use each of the numbers 1 to 16 just once to complete this 4×4 magic square. Each row, column and diagonal should add up to 34.

		7	
15			
9	5	16	
8		1	13

4 Make up a 3×3 magic square of your own. Use the numbers 1 to 9 just once each and put 5 in the middle.

This is magic triangle.

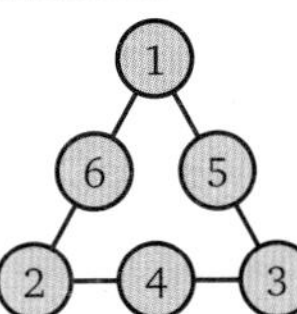

The sum of the numbers along each side is equal to 9.

In the next questions, use the numbers 1, 2, 3, 4, 5 and 6 to fill in the circles so that the sum along each side is equal to the number given below the diagram. Each number is to be used exactly once in each question.

5

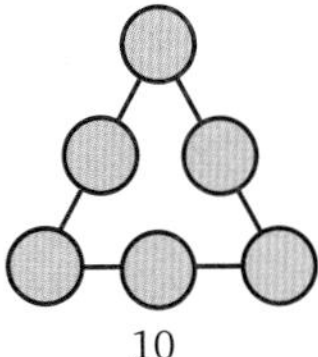

6

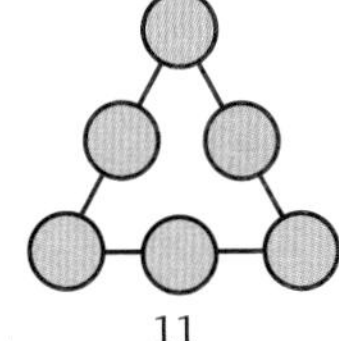

7

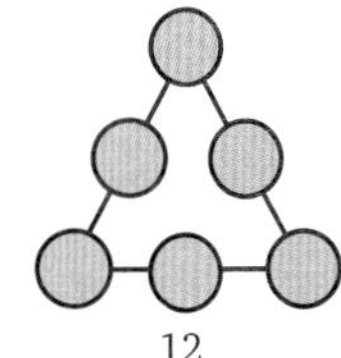

8 Use the results from questions **5**, **6** and **7**.

a Complete the table. The vertices are the corners of the triangles.

b What is the sum, t, of the digits used in each triangle?

c What do you notice about t and $3s - v$?

Sum along each side, s	10	11	12
Sum of vertices, v			
$3s - v$			

Write the next two numbers in this sequence:

1, 3, 5, 7, ...

In this sequence, the next number is always 2 bigger than the number before it.
The next two numbers are 9 and 11.

In questions **9** to **20** write the next two numbers in the sequence:

9 1, 4, 7, 10, ...

10 12, 10, 8, 6, ...

11 1, 5, 9, 13, ...

12 2, 4, 8, 16, ...

13 3, 6, 9, 12, ...

14 64, 32, 16, 8, ...

15 1, 3, 9, 27, ...

16 4, 9, 16, 25, ...

17 1, 10, 100, 1000, ...

18 81, 72, 64, 54, ...

19 3, 7, 11, 15, ...

20 5, 10, 17, 26, ...

Investigation

Try to find the pattern in this triangle of numbers.
Can you write the next three rows?
Do you know that this triangle has a special name?
Perhaps your teacher may help you to find this name.

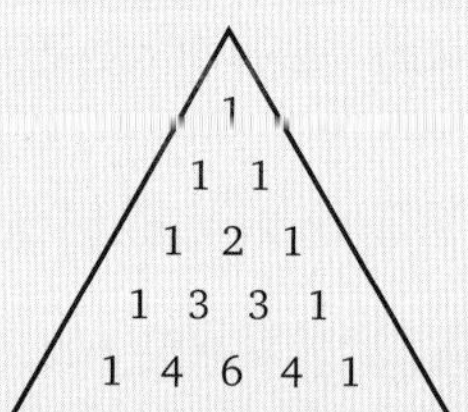

Types of number

Even and odd numbers

Whole numbers that divide by 2 to give whole number answers are called *even numbers*. For example 10, 456 and 83 450 are even numbers. Even numbers end in 0, 2, 4, 6 or 8.

Whole numbers that, when divided by 2, do not give a whole number answer are called *odd numbers*. For example 9, 389 and 997 733 are odd numbers. Odd numbers end in 1, 3, 5, 7 or 9.

Square numbers

Square numbers can be represented by a number of dots arranged in a square formation. For example 9, 16 and 25 are square numbers because they can be arranged in square formations as shown below.

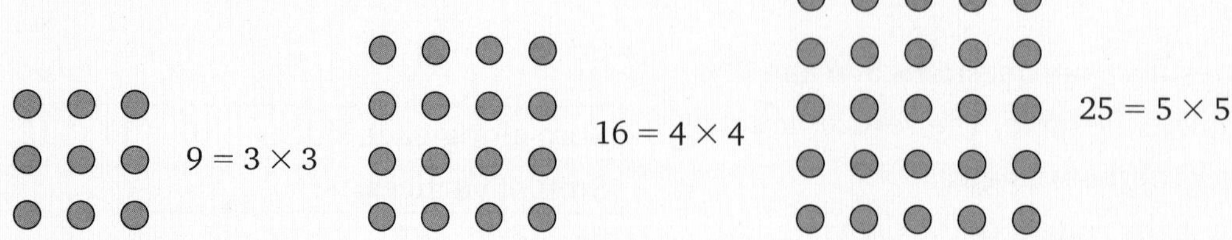

The smallest square number is 1 because $1 = 1 \times 1$.

Rectangular numbers

Any number that can be shown as a rectangular pattern of dots is called a *rectangular number*. For example, 24 is a rectangular number because 24 dots can be arranged as

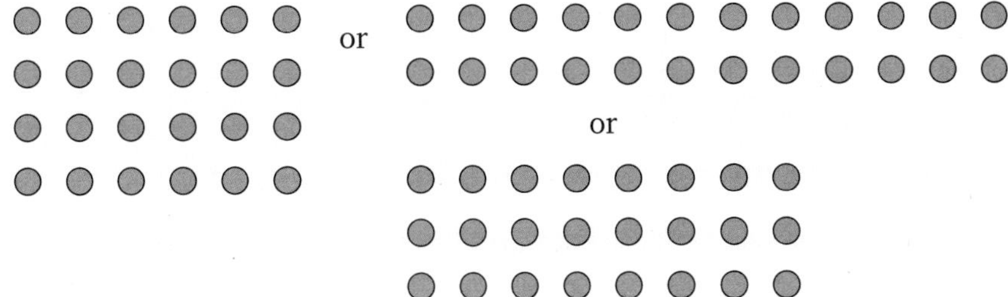

5 is NOT a rectangular number because a line of dots is not a rectangle.

Triangular numbers

A *triangular number* can be shown as dots arranged in rows so that each row is one dot longer than the row above.

These are the first four triangular numbers:

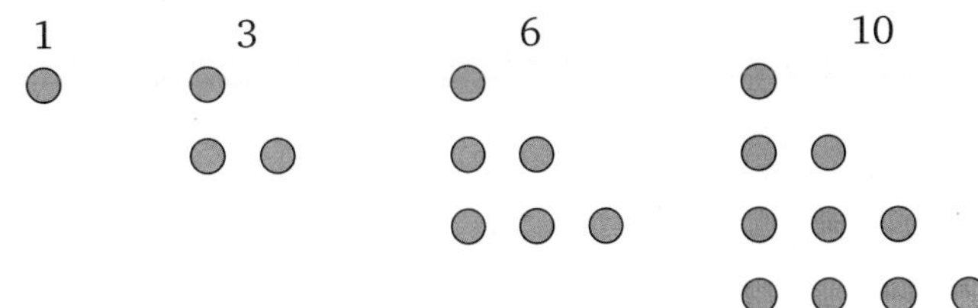

Exercise 1t

1 Consider the following pattern:

$$\begin{aligned} 1 &= 1 = 1 \times 1 \\ 1+3 &= 4 = 2 \times 2 \\ 1+3+5 &= 9 = 3 \times 3 \\ 1+3+5+7 &= 16 = 4 \times 4 \end{aligned}$$

Write the next three lines in this pattern.

Now try and write (without adding them up) the sum of

a the first eight odd numbers **b** the first twenty odd numbers.

2 Consider the following pattern:

$$\begin{aligned} 2 &= 2 = 1 \times 2 \\ 2+4 &= 6 = 2 \times 3 \\ 2+4+6 &= 12 = 3 \times 4 \\ 2+4+6+8 &= 20 = 4 \times 5 \end{aligned}$$

Write the next three lines in this pattern.

How many consecutive even numbers, beginning with 2, have a sum of 156? ($156 = 12 \times 13$)

3 Which of the following numbers are square numbers?

4, 6, 8, 9, 12, 18, 30, 36, 40, 61, 140, 169

4 Which of the following numbers are rectangular numbers?

8, 6, 11, 14, 15, 72, 91, 323, 403

Give a reason for your answer.

5 Show that 12 is a rectangular number in two different ways.

6 Show that 18 is a rectangular number in two different ways.

7 Show that 36 is a rectangular number in three different ways.

8 Draw dot patterns for the next three triangular numbers after 10.

9 Without drawing dot patterns, write down the next three triangular numbers after 28.

10 Look at the pattern.

1

1 2 1

1 2 3 2 1

1 2 3 4 3 2 1

What total do you get for each line in this pattern?

Are all these totals rectangular numbers and/or square numbers?

11 What type of number do you get by adding the numbers in each row of this pattern?

1

$1 + 2$

$1 + 2 + 3$

$1 + 2 + 3 + 4$

$1 + 2 + 3 + 4 + 5$

12 Write down the numbers between 1 and 12 that are

a square numbers

b rectangular numbers

c triangular numbers.

13 Which of the numbers between 24 and 40 are

a square numbers

b rectangular numbers

c triangular numbers?

Mixed exercises

Exercise 1u

Find:

1	$12\,006 + 50\,100 + 9708$	4	$48\,900 \div 3$	7	$624 - 468 + 2655 - 1009$
2	$8\,100\,053 - 400\,136$	5	$1350 + 78\,796 - 52\,538$	8	$220 \div (19 - 14) - 19$
3	7600×9001	6	$800 \times 60\,701 - 4\,700\,080$	9	$(7 + 5) \div (12 \div 3 + 8 \div 4)$

10 How many packets of popcorn costing 85 c each can I buy with $10?

11 An athletic club for boys and girls has 375 members. There are 23 more boys than girls. How many of each are there?

12 What is number of small triangles in each diagram?

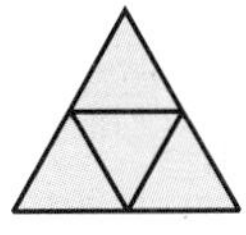
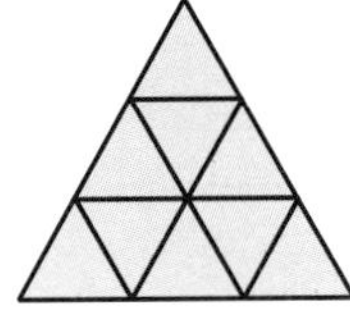

What type of number are they?

Exercise 1v

Select the letter that gives the correct answer.

1 $392 + 6250 + 307 =$

A 6409 B 6459 C 6639 D 6949

2 $54\,007 - 7450 =$

A 46 447 B 46 557 C 46 567 D 46 657

3 $(7 + 30) \times 6 - 137 =$

A 85 B 92 C 113 D 119

4 $72 \div 8 =$

A 8 B 9 C 12 D 14

5 The number of times 16 can be taken away from 200 is

A 10 B 11 C 12 D 14

6 The contents of a carton of sweets has a mass of 5 kilograms. These sweets are divided into packets, each with a mass of 500 grams. If 1 kilogram = 1000 grams, the number of packets that can be made up is

A 8 B 10 C 12 D 20

7 Ann and Ben were two candidates in an election. Ann got 441 more votes than Ben.

Ben got 320 votes. There were 34 spoilt voting papers. 293 people could have voted but failed to do so.

The number of people who could have voted was

A 1088 B 1115 C 1374 D 1408

Puzzle

1 My calculator has an odd fault. The + button multiplies and the × button adds.

a When I press 7 + 5, what number shows on the display?

b Before I realised what the fault was, I got 21 when I tried to add two numbers. What were the two numbers?

c I pressed 2 + 8 × 5. What number showed in the display?

d Find a calculation using three or four numbers for which my calculator will give the correct answer.

2 Enter any two digits in your calculator with the largest first. Now enter the same again and then once more.
For example 737 373
Now subtract from this the number you get by reversing the digits in your number, i.e. in this case subtract 373 737.
What is special about the numbers you subtract in each case?

In this chapter you have seen that...

✔ numbers are easier to add or subtract when they are written in columns (unless you can do the calculations mentally)

✔ you can do a rough check on calculations by rounding the numbers to the nearest 10, 100, 1000, ...

✔ to solve word problems, you need to read the question carefully to make sure that you understand what you have been asked to do

✔ the sign in front of a number tells you whether you add or subtract that number

✔ when you are working in columns for long multiplication and in division you should keep units under units, tens under tens, and so on

✔ brackets are used to show what needs to be done first

✔ when there are no brackets do multiplication and division before addition and subtraction

✔ square numbers can be shown as a square pattern of dots

✔ rectangular numbers can be shown as a rectangular pattern of dots

✔ triangular numbers can be shown as a triangular pattern of dots.

2 Factors and indices

At the end of this chapter you should be able to...

1 list the factors of a given number
2 write down multiples of a given number
3 use indices to write products of repeated numbers
4 classify numbers as prime or composite
5 express a given number as a product of primes
6 find the HCF or LCM of a group of numbers
7 solve problems requiring the use of the HCF or LCM of a set of numbers.

Did you know?

Wherever you are a million is always a million (1 000 000).

However, a BILLION is not always a billion.

In the USA, 1 billion $= 1000 \times 1\,000\,000$

But in some countries, 1 BILLION $= 1\,000\,000 \times 1\,000\,000$.

You need to know...

✔ your multiplication tables up to 10×10

✔ how to divide by whole numbers less than 10.

Key words

composite number, divisible, factor, highest common factor (HCF), index (plural indices), lowest common multiple (LCM), multiple, prime number, product, twin primes

Factors

The number 2 is a *factor* of 12, since 2 will divide exactly into 12 six times. There is no remainder.

The number 12 may be expressed as the product of two factors in several different ways, namely:

1×12 $\quad 2 \times 6$ $\quad$ or $\quad 3 \times 4$

The numbers 1, 2, 3, 4, 6 and 12 will divide exactly into 12.

All the factors of 12 are 1, 2, 3, 4, 6, 12.

Exercise 2a

Express each of the following numbers as the product of two factors, giving all possibilities:

1	18	**5**	30	**9**	48	**<u>13</u>**	80	**<u>17</u>**	120
2	20	**6**	36	**10**	60	**<u>14</u>**	96	**<u>18</u>**	135
3	24	**7**	40	**11**	64	**<u>15</u>**	100	**<u>19</u>**	144
4	27	**8**	45	**12**	72	**<u>16</u>**	108	**<u>20</u>**	160

Exercise 2b

List all the factors for each of the numbers in Exercise 2a.

Multiples

A *multiple* of a number is that number multiplied by a whole number. 12 is a multiple of 2 since $2 \times 6 = 12$.

The multiples of 2 are 2, 4, 6, 8, 10, 12, . . .

Similarly 15 is a multiple of 3 since $3 \times 5 = 15$. The multiples of 3 are 3, 6, 9, 15, 18, 21, ...

Exercise 2c

1 Write down the multiples of 3 between 20 and 40.

2 Write down the multiples of 5 between 19 and 49.

3 Write down the multiples of 7 between 25 and 60.

4 Write down the multiples of 11 between 50 and 100.

5 Write down the multiples of 13 between 25 and 70.

Prime numbers

A *prime number* is a whole number whose only factors are 1 and itself. For example, the only factors of 3 are 1 and 3 and the only factors of 5 are 1 and 5. The numbers 3 and 5 are both prime numbers. Note that 1 is *not* a prime number.

A whole number, other than 1, which is not prime is *composite*, e.g. 6 ($6 = 2 \times 3$).

Exercise 2d

1 Which of the following numbers are prime numbers?

2, 3, 4, 5, 6, 7, 8, 9, 10, 11, 12, 13

2 Write down the prime numbers between 20 and 30.

3 Write down the prime numbers between 30 and 50.

4 Which of these numbers are prime numbers?

5, 10, 19, 29, 39, 49, 61

5 Which of these numbers are prime numbers?

41, 57, 91, 101, 127

6 Are the following statements true or false?

a All prime numbers are odd numbers.

b All odd numbers are prime numbers.

c All prime numbers between 10 and 100 are odd numbers.

d The only even prime number is 2.

e There are six prime numbers less than 10.

Investigation

The first ten prime numbers are 2, 3, 5, 7, 11, 13, 17, 19, 23 and 29.

Two prime numbers that differ by 2 are called *twin primes*, so 3 and 5 are twin primes, and so are 17 and 19.

1 What is the next pair of twin primes after 19?

2 71 is a prime number. What is the next prime number

a smaller than 71   b larger than 71?

Hence find out whether or not 71 is one of a pair of twin primes.

3 313 is one of a pair of twin primes. Find the other one.

Indices

The accepted shorthand way of writing $2 \times 2 \times 2 \times 2$ is 2^4.

We read this as '2 to the power of 4' or '2 to the four'.

The 4 is called the *index*. We say 2^4 is the index form of $2 \times 2 \times 2 \times 2$.

Hence $16 = 2 \times 2 \times 2 \times 2 = 2^4$ and similarly $3^3 = 3 \times 3 \times 3 = 27$.

Expressing a number using indices gives a convenient way for writing large numbers. For example, it has been discovered that

$$2^{216091} - 1$$

is a prime number. This is a very large number that would fill two newspaper pages if it were written in full, as it contains 65 050 digits. Using indices we are able to write it in the short form shown above.

Exercise 2e

Write the following products in index form:

1 $2 \times 2 \times 2$

2 $3 \times 3 \times 3 \times 3$

3 $5 \times 5 \times 5 \times 5$

4 $7 \times 7 \times 7 \times 7 \times 7$

5 $2 \times 2 \times 2 \times 2 \times 2$

6 $3 \times 3 \times 3 \times 3 \times 3 \times 3$

7 $13 \times 13 \times 13$

8 19×19

9 $2 \times 2 \times 2 \times 2 \times 2 \times 2 \times 2$

10 $6 \times 6 \times 6 \times 6$

Find the value of:

11 2^5

12 3^3

13 5^2

14 2^3

15 3^2

16 7^2

17 3^4

18 4^2

19 10^2

20 10^3

21 10^4

22 10^1

2^5 means five 2s multiplied together, i.e. $2 \times 2 \times 2 \times 2 \times 2$

Express the following numbers in index form:

23 4

24 9

25 8

26 27

27 49

28 25

29 32

30 64

Place values and powers of ten

We saw in Chapter 1 that we can write a number under place headings, where the place heading gives the value of a digit.

	thousands	hundreds	tens	units
For example, 1507 can be written	1	5	0	7

These place headings can be written as powers of 10 because $10^1 = 10$, $10^2 = 100$, $10^3 = 1000$, $10^4 = 10\,000$, and so on.

You can see that the value of 10^3 is 1000 (1 followed by three zeros), and the value of 10^1 is 10 (1 followed by one zero), and so on.

So the number of zeros in the value of $10^{\text{any index}}$ is the value of the index.

Continuing this pattern, it follows that $10^0 = 1$.

	10^3	10^2	10^1	10^0
So 1507 can be written	1	5	0	7
and 210 can be written		2	1	0

The value of the digit 2 in the number 210 can be written as 2×10^2 and the value of the digit 1 in the number 1507 can be written as 1×10^3.

Expressing a number as a product in index form

We can now write any number as the product of prime numbers in index form. Consider the number 108:

$$\begin{aligned} 108 &= 12 \times 9 \\ &= 4 \times 3 \times 9 \\ &= 2 \times 2 \times 3 \times 3 \times 3 \end{aligned}$$

i.e. $\quad 108 = 2^2 \times 3^3$

Therefore 108 expressed as the product of prime numbers or factors in index form is $2^2 \times 3^3$.

Similarly

$$\begin{aligned} 441 &= 9 \times 49 \\ &= 3 \times 3 \times 7 \times 7 \\ &= 3^2 \times 7^2 \end{aligned}$$

Exercise 2f

1 Write down the value of the digit 6 in each number. Give your answer in the form $6 \times 10^{\text{a power}}$.

a 60 **b** 600 **c** 6 **d** 6000

2 Write these numbers as ordinary numbers.

a 3×10^2 **c** $2 \times 10^2 + 5 \times 10^0$

b 2×10^3 **d** $3 \times 10^4 + 6 \times 10^1$

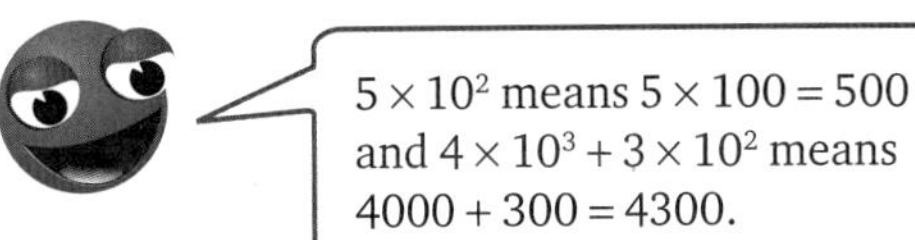

Write the following products in index form:

3 $2 \times 2 \times 7 \times 7$

4 $3 \times 3 \times 3 \times 5 \times 5$

5 $5 \times 5 \times 5 \times 13 \times 13$

6 $2 \times 3 \times 3 \times 5 \times 2 \times 5$

7 $2 \times 2 \times 3 \times 2 \times 3 \times 5 \times 5$

8 $3 \times 11 \times 11 \times 2 \times 2$

9 $7 \times 7 \times 7 \times 3 \times 5 \times 7 \times 3$

10 $13 \times 5 \times 13 \times 5 \times 13$

11 $3 \times 5 \times 5 \times 3 \times 7 \times 3 \times 7$

12 $2 \times 3 \times 2 \times 5 \times 3 \times 5$

The number of times the same number is multiplied together gives the index for that number. There are two 2s multiplied together so they give 2^2 and two 7s multiplied together so they give 7^2. You can only use an index when the same number is multiplied together two or more times. 2×7 cannot be written as one number in index form.

Find the value of:

13 $2^2 \times 3^3$ **16** $2^2 \times 3^2$

14 $3^2 \times 5^2$ **17** $2^2 \times 3^2 \times 5$

15 $2^4 \times 7$ **18** $2 \times 3^2 \times 7$

The index shows how many times the same number is multiplied together, so here 2 is multiplied by 2 and 3 is multiplied by 3 and by 3 again.

Find the value of:

19 $1^3 + 5^3 + 3^3$ **20** $3^3 + 7^3 + 1^3$ **21** $3^3 + 7^3 + 0^3$

Can you find any other numbers like these three?

Finding prime factors

The following rules may help us to decide whether a given number has certain prime numbers as factors:

A number is divisible

- by 2 if the last digit is even
- by 3 if the sum of the digits is divisible by 3
- by 5 if the last digit is 0 or 5
- by 9 if the sum of the digits is divisible by 9.

Exercise 2g

Is 1683 divisible by 3?

The sum of the digits is $1 + 6 + 8 + 3 = 18$, which is divisible by 3.
Therefore 1683 is divisible by 3.

1 Is 525 divisible by 3?

2 Is 747 divisible by 5?

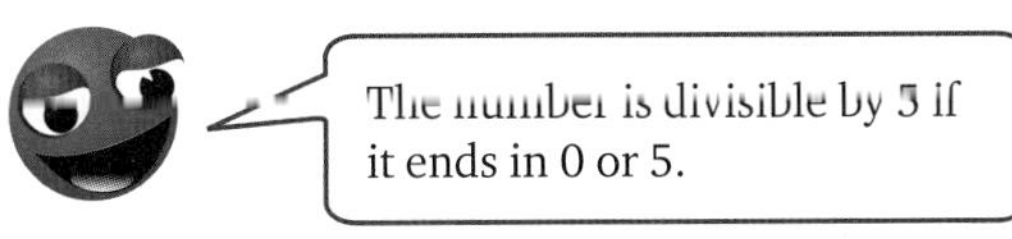

3 Is 2931 divisible by 3?

4 Is 740 divisible by 5?

5 Is 543 divisible by 5?

6 Is 1424 divisible by 2?

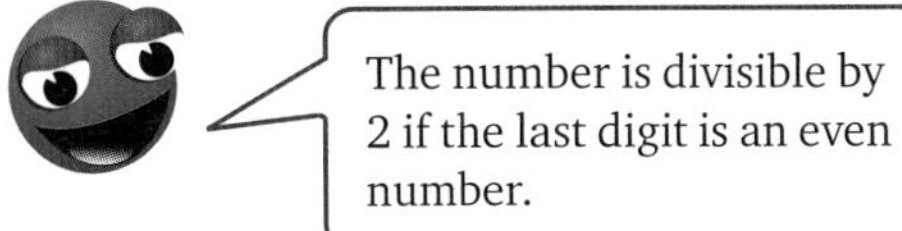

7 Is 9471 divisible by 3?

8 Is 2731 divisible by 2?

Is 8820 divisible by 15?

8820 is divisible by 5 since it ends in 0.

8820 is divisible by 3 since $8 + 8 + 2 = 18$ which is divisible by 3.

8820 is therefore divisible by both 5 and 3, i.e. it is divisible by 5×3 or 15.

15 is the product of the prime numbers 3 and 5, so you need to test to see if 8820 is divisible by both 3 and 5.

9 Is 10 752 divisible by 6?

10 Is 21 168 divisible by 6?

11 Is 30 870 divisible by 15?

? Puzzle

It is a curious fact that $12 \times 12 = 144$ and if the digits in all three numbers are reversed you have $21 \times 21 = 441$ which is also true.

Find other examples with this property.

Expressing a number as a product of prime factors

To express a number in prime factors start by trying to divide by 2 and keep on until you can no longer divide exactly by 2. Next try 3 in the same way, then 5 and so on for each prime number until you are left with a quotient of 1.

Exercise 2h

Express 720 as the product of prime factors in index form.

(Test for the prime factors in order, 2 first, then 3, and so on.)

2	720
2	360
2	180
2	90
3	45
3	15
5	5
	1

Therefore $720 = 2 \times 2 \times 2 \times 2 \times 3 \times 3 \times 5$

i.e. $720 = 2^4 \times 3^2 \times 5$

Express each of the following numbers as the product of prime factors in index form:

1	24	**3**	63	**5**	136	**7**	216	**9**	405
2	28	**4**	72	**6**	84	**8**	528	**10**	784

11 List every even number from 20 to 30 as the sum of two primes.

Highest Common Factor (HCF)

The *highest common factor* of two or more numbers is the largest number that divides exactly into each of them.

For example 8 is the HCF of 16 and 24 and 15 is the HCF of 45, 60 and 120.

Exercise 2i

State the HCF of:

1	9, 12	**5**	25, 50, 75	**<u>9</u>**	25, 35, 50, 60
2	8, 16	**6**	22, 33, 44	**<u>10</u>**	36, 44, 52, 56
3	12, 24	**7**	21, 42, 84	**<u>11</u>**	15, 30, 45, 60
4	14, 42	**8**	39, 13, 26	**<u>12</u>**	10, 18, 20, 36

Investigation

Two or more counting numbers (1, 2, 3, ...) are called relatively prime if their highest common factor is 1. For example 2 and 3 are relatively prime, so are 3 and 8.

Find as many relatively prime numbers as you can less than 20.

Lowest Common Multiple (LCM)

The *lowest common multiple* of two or more numbers is the smallest number that divides exactly by each of the numbers.

For example the LCM of 8 and 12 is 24 since both 8 and 12 divide exactly into 24.

Similarly the LCM of 4, 6 and 9 is 36.

Exercise 2j

State the LCM of:

1	3, 5	**4**	9, 12	**7**	12, 16, 24	**<u>10</u>**	18, 27, 36
2	6, 8	**5**	3, 9, 12	**8**	4, 5, 6	**<u>11</u>**	9, 12, 36
3	5, 15	**6**	10, 15, 20	**<u>9</u>**	9, 12, 18	**<u>12</u>**	6, 7, 8

Problems involving HCFs and LCMs

Exercise 2k

Mrs Walcott buys a box of chocolates for her party. She is unsure whether there will be 8, 9 or 12 people altogether, but she is sure that whichever number it is everybody can have the same number of chocolates. What is the least number of chocolates that needs to be in the box?

You need to find the smallest number that 8, 9 and 12 will divide into exactly.

First express each number in prime factors.

$$8 = 2 \times 2 \times 2$$

$$9 = 3 \times 3$$

$$12 = 2 \times 2 \times 3$$

You must write three 2s so that 8 will divide into the number and you must write two 3s so that 9 will divide into the number. The two 2s and one 3 for 12 are already there so there is no need to write them again.

The smallest number that 8, 9 and 12 divide into exactly is
$2 \times 2 \times 2 \times 3 \times 3$

i.e. $8 \times 9 = 72$

1 What is the smallest sum of money that can be made up of an exact number of 10 c pieces or of 25 c pieces ?

2 Find the least sum of money into which 24 c, 30 c and 54 c will divide exactly.

3 Find the smallest length that can be divided exactly into equal sections of length 5 m or 8 m or 12 m.

4 A room measures 450 cm by 350 cm. Find the side of the largest square tile that can be used to tile the floor without any cutting.

5 Two toy cars travel around a racetrack, the one completing the circuit in 6 seconds and the other in $6\frac{1}{2}$ seconds. If they leave the starting line together how long will it be before they are again side by side?

6 If I go up a flight of stairs two at a time I get to the top without any being left over. If I then try three at a time and again five at a time, I still get to the top without any being left over. Find the shortest flight of stairs for which this is possible. How many would remain if I were able to go up seven at a time?

7 In the first year of a large comprehensive school it is possible to divide the pupils into equal sized classes of either 24 or 30 or 32 and have no pupils left over. Find the size of the smallest entry that makes this possible. How many classes will there be if each class is to have 24 pupils?

8 Find the largest number of children that can equally share 72 sweets and 54 chocolates.

? Puzzle

1 Using the four digits 2, 3, 6 and 9 once only you can make several pairs of two-digit numbers, e.g. 26 and 93. Find 26×93.

Now pair the digits in a different way, e.g. 39 and 62 and find 39×62.

What do you notice?

Can you find another four digits with the same property?

2 The church at Arima has a peal of four bells. No. 1 bell rings every 5 seconds, No. 2 bell every 6 seconds, No. 3 bell every 7 seconds and No. 4 every 8 seconds. They are first tolled together. Investigate how long it will be before they all sound together again.

Exercise 2I

Select the letter that gives the correct answer.

1 The multiples of 6 between 15 and 32 are

A 12, 24, 30 B 18, 20, 30 C 18, 24, 28 D 18, 24, 30

2 Which of the numbers 10, 13, 17, 21, 26, 27, 29 are prime numbers?

A 10, 13, 26 B 13, 17, 21 C 13, 17, 27 D 13, 17, 29

3 Written in index form $2 \times 2 \times 5 \times 5 \times 2$ is

A $2^2 \times 5$ B $2^2 \times 5^2$ C $2^3 \times 5$ D $2^3 \times 5^2$

4 The LCM (least common multiple) of 4, 6 and 8 is

A 16 B 24 C 32 D 48

5 Expressed as the product of its prime factors 36 is

A $2^2 \times 3$ B 2×3^2 C $2^2 \times 3^2$ D $2^3 \times 3$

6 The HCF (highest common factor) of 22, 33 and 66 is

A 2 B 3 C 6 D 11

7 48 written as the product of its prime factors is

A $2^2 \times 3$ B $2^3 \times 3$ C $2^4 \times 3$ D $2^5 \times 3$

Investigation

The ancient Greeks discovered a set of numbers, each of which is equal to the sum of its factors, excluding itself. These are called perfect numbers.

For example, the factors of 6, excluding 6, are {1, 2, 3}.

$1 + 2 + 3 = 6$. Hence 6 is a PERFECT number.

Find some other perfect numbers. Consider all factors, not just prime factors.

Can a prime number be a perfect number? Explain your answer.

Investigate 496 to see if it is a perfect number.

Did you know?

The following method may be used to find the LCM of two numbers.

e.g. Find the LCM of 45 and 60.

First find the HCF of 45 and 60. This is 15.

Divide each number by the HCF, 15. We get 3 and 4.

The LCM is the product of these answers and the HCF, i.e. $3 \times 4 \times 15 = 180$.

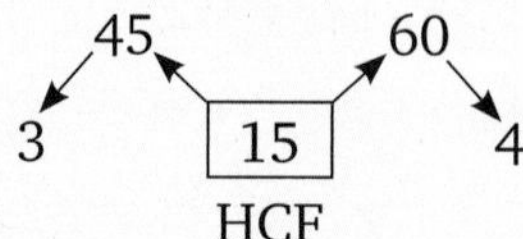

$$\text{LCM} = 3 \times 15 \times 4 = 180$$

In 1999 Nayan Hajratwala found the largest prime number known up to that time. It contains 2 098 960 digits. It comes from the calculation of $2^{6972593} - 1$.

A prime expressed in this way is called a Mersenne Prime.

This was the first-known million-digit prime.

In this chapter you have seen that...

- ✔ a prime number is any number bigger than 1 whose only factors are 1 and itself
- ✔ you can use indices to shorten the way you write an expression that is the same number multiplied together several times
- ✔ numbers that are not prime can be expressed as the product of prime factors in index form
- ✔ you can use prime factors to find the largest number that will divide exactly into each number in a group by picking out the prime factors that are common to all the numbers and multiplying them together. It is called the Highest Common Factor (HCF) of the group
- ✔ you can use prime factors to find the lowest number that all the numbers of a group will divide into exactly by picking out all the prime factors that appear anywhere in the group, each one to its highest index, and multiplying them together. It is called the Lowest Common Multiple (LCM).

3 Sets

At the end of this chapter you should be able to...

1 identify a set as a collection of objects with a common property
2 list a given set
3 describe a given set in words
4 use correctly the symbols $\in$, $\notin$, $\subset$, U, $\cap$, $\cup$
5 write statements using set notations and vice versa
6 classify sets as finite or infinite
7 determine when two sets are equal or equivalent
8 identify empty sets and use the correct symbol for such a set $\varnothing$ or { }
9 write down the subsets of a given set
10 give a suitable universal set for a given set
11 draw Venn diagrams to display given sets
12 find the union or intersection of sets
13 draw Venn diagrams to show the union or intersection of sets.

Did you know?

Charles Dodgson (1832–1899), who is better known as Lewis Carroll, the author of *Alice in Wonderland*, was an Oxford mathematician who did a lot of work on sets.

Key words

disjoint sets, element, empty set, equal set, equivalent set, finite set, infinite set, intersection of sets, member, null set, set, subset, union of sets, universal set, Venn diagram, the symbols $\in$, $\notin$, U, $\varnothing$, { }, $\subset$, $\cup$, $\cap$

Set notation

The branch of mathematics known as Set Theory was founded by Georg Cantor.

A *set* is a clearly defined collection of things that have something in common. We talk about a set of drawing instruments, a set of cutlery and a set of books.

Things which belong to a set are called *members* or *elements*. When written down, these members or elements are usually separated by commas and enclosed by curly brackets or braces { }.

Instead of writing 'the set of musical instruments'

we write {musical instruments}

Exercise 3a

1 Use the correct set notation to write down
   a the set of rivers of the world
   b the set of pupils in my class
   c the set of subjects I study at school
   d the set of furniture in this room.

You can write down any two members you can think of. For example {rivers} includes any river you can think of such as the Mississippi, and so on.

2 Write down two members from each of the sets given in question **1**.

Describing members

We do not have to list all the members of a set; frequently we can use words to describe the members in a set.

For example instead of {Sunday, Monday, . . . , Saturday} we could say {the days of the week} and instead of {5, 6, 7, 8, 9} we could say {whole numbers from 5 to 9 inclusive}.

We could write {a, b, c, d, e} = {the first five letters of the alphabet}.

Exercise 3b

In questions **1** to **10** describe in words the given sets:

1 {w, x, y, z}

2 {January, June, July}

3 {June, July, August}

4 {Grenada, St Vincent, St Lucia, Dominica}

5 {Plymouth, St John's, Basseterre}

6 {2, 4, 6, 8, 10, 12}

7 {1, 2, 3, 4, 5, 6}

8 {2, 3, 5, 7, 11, 13}

9 {45, 46, 47, 48, 49, 50}

10 {15, 20, 25, 30, 35}

In questions **11** to **15** describe a set which includes the given members and state another member of it:

11 {Anil, Kyle, David, Richard}

12 {jacket, raincoat, sweater, anorak}

13 {rice puffs, corn flakes, bran flakes, granola}

14 {hibiscus, croton, bougainvillea}

15 {*Macbeth*, *Julius Caesar*, *King Lear*, *Romeo and Juliet*}

In the remaining questions list the members in the given sets:

{months of the year beginning with the letter M} = {March, May}

16 {whole numbers greater than 10 but less than 16}

17 {the first eight letters of the alphabet}

18 {the letters used in the word 'mathematics'}

19 {the four main islands forming the Windward group}

20 {the four main islands forming the Leeward group}

21 {subjects I study}

22 {oceans of the world}

23 {foods I ate for breakfast this morning}

24 {prime numbers less than 20}

25 {even numbers less than 20}

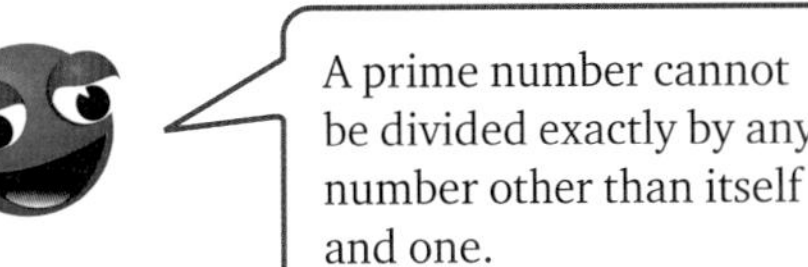

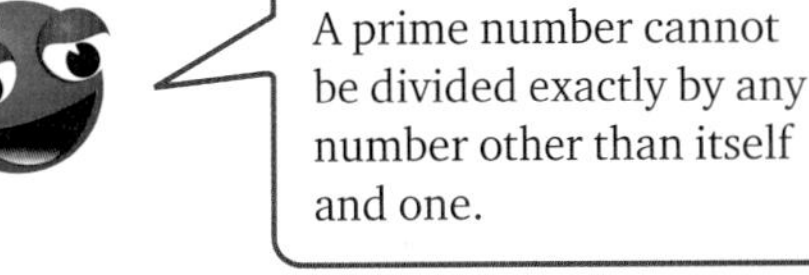

26 {odd numbers between 20 and 30}

27 {multiples of 3 between 10 and 31}

28 {multiples of 7 between 15 and 50}

29 {capital cities in the Windward Islands}

30 {Caricom states}

Puzzle

Write down a set using five odd digits whose sum is 14.

The symbol ∈

Instead of writing

'August is a member of the set of months of the year'

we write August ∈ {months of the year}

The symbol ∈ means 'is a member of' or 'is an element of'.

Exercise 3c

Write the following statements in set notation:

1 Apple is a member of the set of fruit.

2 Shirt is a member of the set of clothing.

3 Dog is a member of the set of domestic animals.

4 Geography is a member of the set of school subjects.

5 Carpet is a member of the set of floor coverings.

6 Hairdressing is a member of the set of occupations.

The symbol ∉

We are all aware that August is *not* a member of the set of days of the week.

Since we have chosen ∈ to mean 'is a member of' we use ∉ to mean 'is *not* a member of'. We can therefore write

'August is not a member of the set of days of the week'

as August ∉ {days of the week}

Exercise 3d

Write the following statements in set notation:

1 Orange is not a member of the set of animals.

2 Cat is not a member of the set of fruit.

3 Table is not a member of the set of trees.

4 Shirt is not a member of the set of subjects I study.

5 Anne is not a member of the set of boys' names.

6 Chisel is not a member of the set of buildings.

7 Cup is not a member of the set of bedroom furniture.

8 Cherry is not a member of the set of Japanese cars.

9 Aeroplane is not a member of the set of foreign countries.

10 Curry is not a member of the set of breeds of dogs.

Now write each of the following in set notation:

11 Porridge is a member of the set of breakfast cereals.

12 Electricity is not a member of the set of building materials.

13 Water is not a member of the set of metals.

14 Spider is a member of the set of living things.

15 Saturday is a member of the set of days of the week.

16 A salmon is a fish.

17 August is not the name of a day of the week.

18 Spain is a European country.

19 Brazil is not an Asian country.

Write down the meaning of:

20 Football $\in$ {team games}

21 Shoes $\notin$ {beverages}

22 Hockey $\notin$ {electrical appliances}

23 Needle $\in$ {metal objects}

24 Danielle $\notin$ {boys' names}

25 Using the correct notation write down

- a three members that belong to {dairy produce}
- b three members that do not belong to {dairy produce}.

26 Using the correct notation, write down

- a three members that belong to {clothes}
- b three members that do not belong to {clothes}.

Finite and infinite sets

We often need to refer to a set several times. When this is so we label the set with a capital letter. For example

$$A = \{\text{months of the year beginning with the letter J}\}$$

or $$A = \{\text{January, June, July}\}$$

In many cases it is not possible to list all the members of a set. When this is so we write down the first few members followed by dots.

For example if $N = \{\text{positive whole numbers}\}$

we could write $N = \{1, 2, 3, 4, \ldots\}$

Similarly if $X = \{\text{even numbers}\}$ and $Y = \{\text{odd numbers}\}$

we could write $X = \{2, 4, 6, 8, \ldots\}$ and $Y = \{1, 3, 5, 7, \ldots\}$

Sets like N, X and Y are called *infinite sets* because there is no limit to the number of members each contains. When we can write down, or count, all the members in a set, the set is called a *finite set*.

Equal sets

When two sets have exactly the same members they are said to be *equal sets*.

If $A = \{2, 4, 6, 8\}$ and $B = \{6, 4, 8, 2\}$

then $A = B$

Similarly, if $X = \{\text{prime numbers less than 8}\}$

$= \{2, 3, 5, 7\}$

and $Y = \{\text{whole numbers up to 7 inclusive except 1, 4 and 6}\}$

$= \{2, 3, 5, 7\}$

then $X = Y$

The order in which the members are listed does not matter; neither does the way in which the sets are described.

Equivalent sets

Sets are *equivalent* when they contain the same number of elements. The elements in equivalent sets are not usually the same (if they were, the sets would be equal sets).

For example $A = \{1, 2, 3, 4\}$ and $B = \{a, b, c, d\}$ are equivalent sets.

Exercise 3e

Determine whether or not the following sets are equal:

1 A = {chair, table, desk, blackboard}
B = {desk, blackboard, table, chair}

2 X = {d, i, k, f, w}
Y = {f, w, k, i}

3 V = {4, 6, 8, 10, 12}
W = {even numbers from 4 to 12 inclusive}

4 C = {i, e, a, u, o}
D = {vowels}

5 P = {capital cities of all the West Indian islands}
Q = {Roseau, Kingston, Plymouth, San Fernando}

Determine whether or not the following sets are equivalent:

6 A = {0, 1, 2, 3, 4}
B = {the first five letters of the alphabet}

7 C = {apple, orange, banana, grape}
D = {fruit sold in the local market}

8 P = {students in your school's baseball team}
Q = {students in your school's football team}

Empty set

Have you ever seen a woman with three eyes or a man with four legs? We hope not, for neither exists. There are no members in either of these sets. Such a set is called an *empty* or *null* set and is written { } or ∅.

Exercise 3f

1 Give some examples of empty sets.

2 Which of the following sets are empty?

a {dogs with wings}
b {men who have landed on the moon}
c {children more than 5 m tall}
d {cars that can carry 100 people}
e {men more than 100 years old}
f {dogs without tails}

Subsets

If A = {Andrew, Stefan, Matthew, Maria, Jay} and B = {Maria, Jay} we see that all the members of B are also members of A.

We say that B is a *subset* of A and write this $B \subset A$.

If X = {a, b, c} then {a, b, c}, {a, b}, {b, c}, {a, c}, {a}, {b}, {c} and ∅ are all subsets of X.

Note that both X and ∅ are considered to be subsets of X. Subsets that do not contain all the members of X are called *proper subsets*. All the subsets given above except {a, b, c} are therefore proper subsets of X.

Exercise 3g

1 If A = {w, x, y, z} write down all the subsets of A that have two members.

2 If B = {Amelia, Brendan, Kevin, Leela} write down all the subsets of B that have two female members.

3 If N = {1, 2, 3, . . ., 10} list the following subsets of N:

A = {odd numbers} B = {even numbers} C = {prime numbers}

4 Give a subset with at least three members for each of the following sets:

a {islands in the Caribbean}
b {rivers}
c {oceans}
d {basketball teams}

5 If X = {1, 2, 3, 5, 7, 11, 13} which of the following sets are proper subsets of X?

a {positive odd numbers less than 6}
b {positive even numbers less than 4}
c {positive prime numbers less than 14}
d {positive odd numbers between 10 and 14}

The universal set

Consider the set {natural numbers less than 16}, i.e. the set {1, 2, 3, 4, . . ., 15}.

Now consider the sets A, B and C whose members are such that

A = {prime numbers} = {2, 3, 5, 7, 11, 13}

B = {multiples of 3} = {3, 6, 9, 12, 15}

C = {multiples of 5} = {5, 10, 15}

The original set {1, 2, 3, 4, . . ., 15} is called the *universal set* for the sets A, B and C. It is a set that contains all the members that occur in the sets A, B and C as well as some other members that are not found in any of these three. The universal set is denoted by the symbol U.

For example, a universal set for {cup, plate, saucer} could be {crockery}.

We write U = crockery.

Exercise 3h

Suggest a suitable universal set for:

1 {8, 12, 16, 17, 20}

2 {vowels}

3 {rivers in Guyana}

4 {prefects}

5 {cats with three legs}

6 {sparrows}

There is no one correct answer for these. Another universal set for {cup, plate, saucer} could be U = {tableware}.

U = {boys' names}

Two subsets are {John, Peter, Paul} and {Dino, Fritz, Alec}.

Write down two subsets, each with at least two members, for each of the following universal sets:

7 U = {girls' names}

8 U = {European countries}

9 U = {African countries}

10 U = {Members of Parliament}

11 U = {school subjects}

12 U = {colours}

Suggest a universal set for:

13 {set squares, protractors, rulers}

14 {houses, apartments, bungalows}

15 {cars, vans, trucks, motorbikes}

16 {trainers, shoes, sandals, boots}

17 {golfers, football players, netball players, sprinters}

Venn diagrams

Many years ago a Cambridge mathematician named John Venn (1834–1923) studied the algebra of sets and introduced the diagrams which now bear his name. In a *Venn diagram* the universal set (U) is usually represented by a rectangle and subsets of the universal set are usually shown as circles inside the rectangle. There is nothing special about circles – any convenient enclosed shape would do.

If U = {school children} then A could be {pupils in my school}, i.e. A is a subset of U.

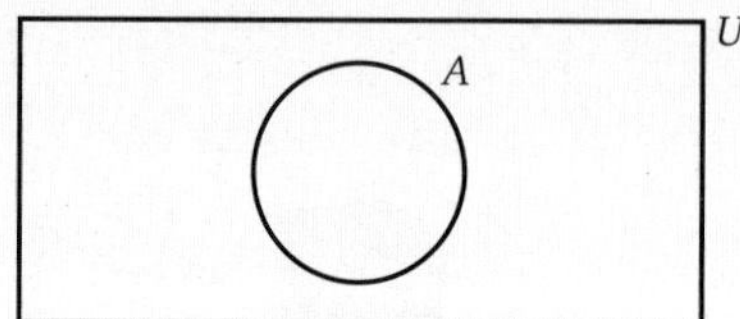

Similarly, if B = {pupils in the next school to my school} the diagram would be

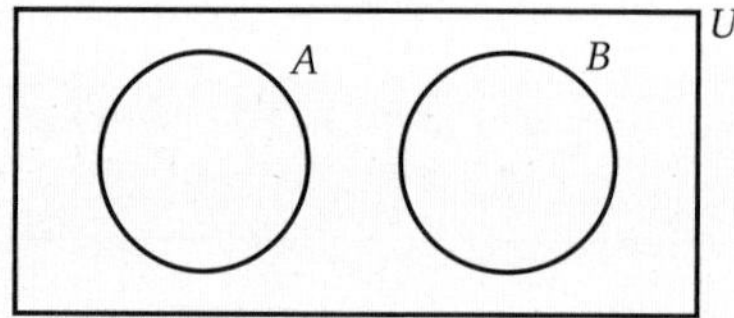

Two sets like these, which have no common members, are called *disjoint sets*.

If C = {pupils in my class} then, because all the members of C are also members of A, i.e. C is a proper subset of A, the Venn diagram is

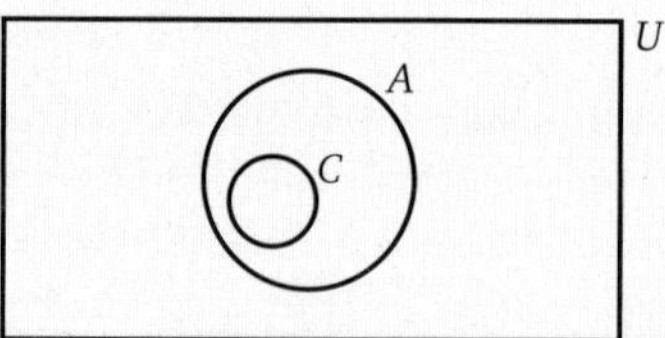

If D = {my school friends} the corresponding Venn diagram could be

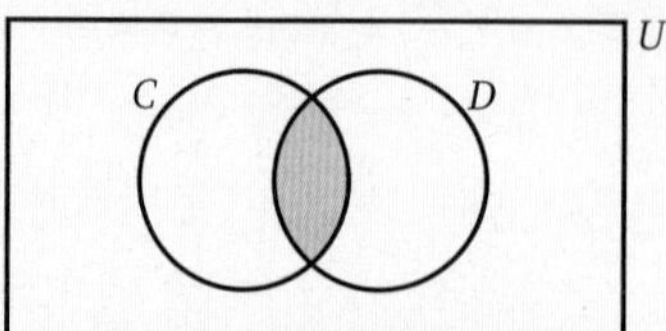

The shaded region shows the friends I have who are in my class. These friends belong to both sets. The unshaded region of D represents friends I have in school who are not in my class.

Union of two sets

In my class

$$A = \{\text{pupils good at maths}\} = \{\text{Frank, Javed, Asif, Sian}\}$$

and

$$B = \{\text{pupils good at French}\} = \{\text{Bina, Asif, Polly, Frank}\}$$

If the universal set is {all the pupils in my class} the names could be placed in a Venn diagram as follows:

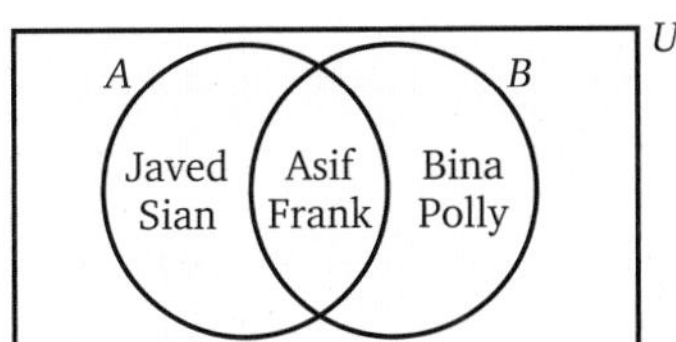

If we write down the set of all the members of my class who are good at *either* maths *or* French we have the set {Javed, Sian, Asif, Frank, Bina, Polly}. This is called the *union* of the sets A and B and is denoted by

$$A \cup B$$

Similarly if $X = \{1, 2, 3, 5\}$ and $Y = \{2, 4, 6\}$ we can illustrate these sets in the following Venn diagram:

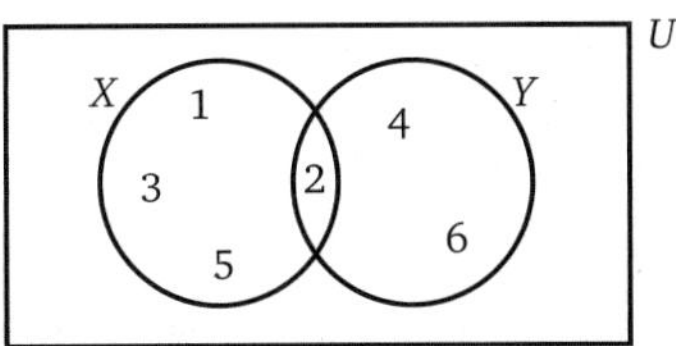

and write the union of the two sets X and Y

$$X \cup Y = \{1, 2, 3, 4, 5, 6\}$$

To find the union of two sets, write down all the members of the first set, then all the members of the second set which have not already been included.

Exercise 3i

Find the union of $A = \{3, 6, 9, 12\}$ and $B = \{4, 6, 8, 10, 12\}$.

6 and 12 are in both sets so they do not need to be included twice.

$A \cup B = \{3, 4, 6, 8, 9, 10, 12\}$

Find the union of the two given sets in each of the following:

1 $A = \{\text{Peter, James, John}\}$ $B = \{\text{John, Andrew, Paul}\}$

2 $X = \{3, 6, 9, 12\}$ $Y = \{4, 8, 12, 16\}$

3 $P = \{a, e, i, o, u\}$ $Q = \{a, b, c, d, e\}$

4 $A = \{a, b, c\}$ $B = \{x, y, z\}$

5 $A = \{p, q, r, s, t\}$ $B = \{p, r, t\}$

6 $X = \{2, 3, 5, 7\}$ $Y = \{1, 3, 5, 7\}$

7 $X = \{5, 7, 11, 13\}$ $Y = \{6, 8, 10, 12\}$

8 $P = \{\text{whole numbers that divide exactly into 12}\}$

$Q = \{\text{whole numbers that divide exactly into 10}\}$

9 $A = \{\text{letters in the word 'classroom'}\}$

$B = \{\text{letters in the word 'school'}\}$

10 $P = \{\text{letters in the word 'arithmetic'}\}$

$Q = \{\text{letters in the word 'algebra'}\}$

To represent the union of two sets in a Venn diagram we shade the combined region representing the two sets. This shaded area may occur in three ways.

a When sets A and B have some common members:

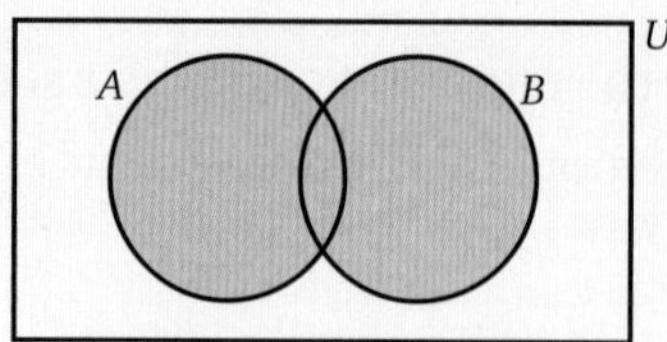

b When A and B have no common member, i.e. when they are disjoint:

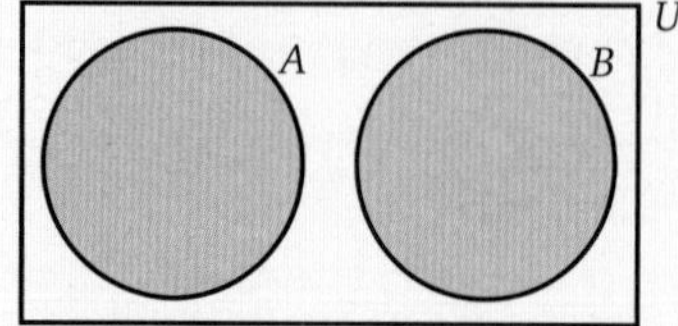

c When B is a proper subset of A:

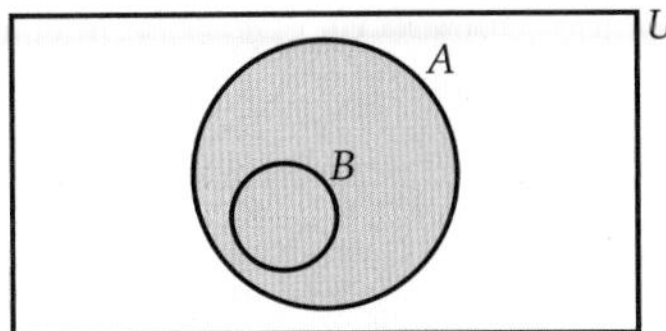

Exercise 3j

Show the union of $P = \{3, 6, 9, 12, 15\}$ and $Q = \{3, 5, 7, 9, 11, 15\}$ on a Venn diagram.

3, 9 and 15 are in both sets so these go in the overlapping part.

6 and 12 are only in P so they go in the left-hand part of the circle marked P.

5, 7, and 11 go in the right-hand part of the circle marked Q.

The union is the combination of both sets so both circles are shaded.

$$P \cup Q = \{3, 5, 6, 7, 9, 11, 12, 15\}$$

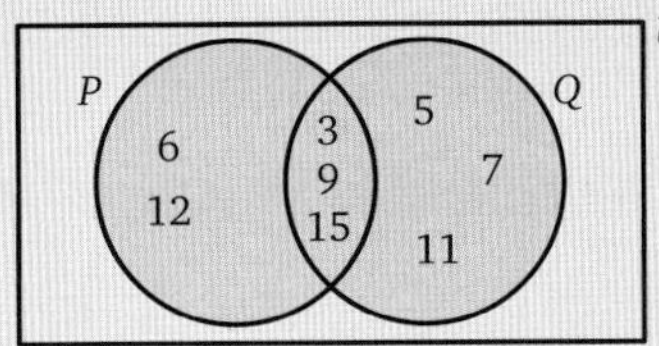

Note that we don't repeat elements in a set, so elements 3, 9 and 15 are only written once in the union of P and Q.

Draw suitable Venn diagrams to show the unions of the following sets:

1	$A = \{p, q, r, s\}$	$B = \{r, s, t, u\}$
2	$X = \{1, 3, 5, 7, 9\}$	$Y = \{2, 4, 6, 8, 10\}$
3	$P = \{a, b, c, d, e, f, g\}$	$Q = \{c, d, g\}$
4	$E = \{\text{rectangles}\}$	$F = \{\text{squares}\}$
5	$G = \{\text{even numbers}\}$	$H = \{\text{odd numbers}\}$
6	$M = \{\text{triangles}\}$	$N = \{\text{squares}\}$
7	$A = \{3, 6, 9, 12, 15\}$	$B = \{4, 6, 8, 10, 12, 14\}$
8	$P = \{$letters in the word 'Donald'$\}$	$Q = \{$letters in the word 'London'$\}$
9	$X = \{$Marc, Leslie, Joe, Claude$\}$	$Y = \{$Leslie, Sita, Joe, Yvette$\}$
10	$A = \{$letters in the word 'metric'$\}$	$B = \{$letters in the word 'imperial'$\}$

Intersection of sets

If we return to the set of pupils in my class

$$A = \{\text{pupils good at maths}\}$$
$$= \{\text{Frank, Javed, Asif, Sian}\}$$

and

$$B = \{\text{pupils good at French}\}$$
$$= \{\text{Bina, Asif, Polly, Frank}\}$$

then Frank and Asif form the set of pupils who are good at *both* maths and French. The members that are in both sets give what is called the *intersection* of the sets A and B.

The intersection of two sets A and B is written $A \cap B$,

i.e. for the given sets, $A \cap B = \{\text{Frank, Asif}\}$

Exercise 3k

Find the intersection of $X = \{1, 2, 3, 4, 5, 6\}$ and $Y = \{1, 2, 3, 5, 7\}$.

The intersection contains the elements that are in both X and Y

$$X \cap Y = \{1, 2, 3, 5\}$$

Find the intersection of the following pairs of sets:

Look for the elements that are common to both sets.

1 $A = \{3, 6, 9, 12\}$ $B = \{5, 6, 7, 8, 9\}$

2 $X = \{4, 8, 12, 16, 20\}$ $Y = \{4, 12, 20\}$

3 $P = \{\text{Zane, Gabriel, Colin, Alice}\}$ $Q = \{\text{Alice, Tyrell, Hans, Zane}\}$

4 $C = \{o, p, q, r, s, t\}$ $D = \{a, e, i, o, u\}$

5 $A = \{\text{tomato, cabbage, apple, pear}\}$ $B = \{\text{cabbage, tomato}\}$

6 $M = \{\text{prime numbers less than 12}\}$ $N = \{\text{odd numbers less than 12}\}$

7 $P = \{4, 8, 12, 16\}$ $Q = \{8, 16, 24, 48\}$

8 $A = \{\text{factors of 12}\}$ $B = \{\text{factors of 10}\}$

9 $X = \{\text{letters in the word 'twice'}\}$ $Y = \{\text{letters in the word 'sweat'}\}$

10 $P = \{\text{letters in the word 'metric'}\}$ $Q = \{\text{letters in the word 'imperial'}\}$

Exercise 3I

Show the intersection of $X = \{1, 2, 3, 4, 5, 6\}$ and $Y = \{2, 3, 5, 7, 11\}$ on a Venn diagram.

$X \cap Y = \{2, 3, 5\}$

The elements in $X \cap Y$ are in the overlap, so this is the part to shade.

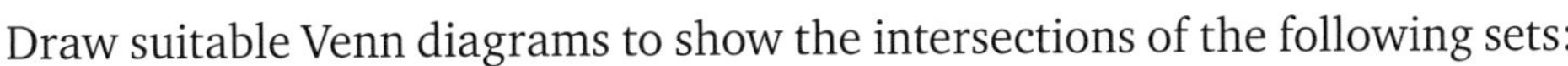

Draw suitable Venn diagrams to show the intersections of the following sets:

1	$A = \{1, 3, 5, 7, 9, 11\}$	$B = \{2, 3, 4, 5, 6, 7\}$
2	P = {John, David, Dino, Kay}	Q = {Pete, Dino, Omar, John}
3	X = {a, e, i, o, u}	Y = {b, f, o, w, u}
4	A = {oak, ash, elm, pine}	B = {teak, oak, sapele, elm}
5	X = {poodle, greyhound, boxer}	Y = {pug, collie, boxer, cairn}
6	$P = \{4, 8, 12, 16\}$	$Q = \{8, 16, 24, 48\}$
7	A = {factors of 12}	B = {factors of 20}
8	X = {letters in the word 'think'}	Y = {letters in the word 'flint'}
9	A = {letters in the word 'arithmetic'}	B = {letters in the word 'geometry'}
10	P = {prime numbers less than 10}	Q = {odd numbers less than 15}

Puzzle

The number 30 can be written as the product $2 \times 3 \times 5$.

We may write these numbers as the set $\{2, 3, 5\}$.

Writing another number as a product gives this set $\{2, 5, 7, 11\}$.

1 What is the second number?

2 **a** Write down the intersection of the two sets.

b What is the number that comes from multiplying the elements of the intersection?

c What is the relationship of this number to the first two numbers?

3 **a** Write down the union of the sets $\{3, 5, 7\}$ and $\{2, 3, 7\}$.

b What number comes from the product of the elements in the union?

c Describe the relationship of this number to the two original numbers.

Exercise 3m

Select the letter that gives the correct answer.

1 Which of the following sets are empty sets?

- **i** birds with wings
- **ii** children more than 6 metres tall
- **iii** schools with teachers but no pupils on their registers
- **iv** prime numbers greater than 3 that divide exactly by 3

A i **B** i and ii **C** iii **D** ii and iv

2 If $A = \{p, q, r, s\}$ the number of proper subsets is

A 4 **B** 10 **C** 14 **D** 15

3 A suitable universal set for the set {vowels} is

A {consonants} **B** {letters of the alphabet}

C {letters in the word 'mathematics'} **D** none of these

4 If $A = \{a, b, c\}$ and $B = \{c, d, e\}$ then $A \cup B =$

A $\{a, b, c, d, e\}$ **B** $\{a, b, c, d\}$ **C** $\{a, b, e\}$ **D** $\{c\}$

5 If $A = \{3, 6, 9, 12\}$ and $B = \{9, 15, 12, 8\}$ then $A \cap B =$

A {9, 12} **B** {9, 12, 15} **C** {12, 15} **D** {9, 15}

Investigation

Consider the following sets X and Y.

$X = \{0, 2, 4, 6, \ldots\}$, $Y = \{1, 3, 5, 7, \ldots\}$.

1 Describe X and Y in words.

2 Give the next three numbers in X and in Y.

3 Choose two numbers from X and find their sum. Is this sum a member of X? Is this always true?

4 Choose two numbers from Y and find their sum. Which set contains this sum? Is this always true?

5 When will the sum of any two whole numbers always be in Y? Explain your answer with examples.

In this chapter you have seen that...

- ✔ a set is a collection of things that have something in common
- ✔ an infinite set has no limit on the number of members in it
- ✔ in a finite set, all the members can be counted or listed
- ✔ a proper subset of a set A contains none or some, but not all, of the members of A
- ✔ the union of two sets contains all the members of the first set together with the members of the second set that have not already been included
- ✔ the intersection of two sets contains the elements that are in both sets
- ✔ when two sets contain the same number of elements, they are said to be equivalent
- ✔ when two sets have exactly the same members, they are said to be equal
- ✔ a set which has no members is called an empty or null set and is written { } or ∅.

4 Introduction to geometry

At the end of this chapter you should be able to...

1 use the correct geometrical terms

2 identify the different special quadrilaterals

3 draw tessellations

4 draw nets to make solids.

You need to know...

✔ how to use square grid paper to copy diagrams.

Key words

cube, cuboid, edge, face, hexagon, kite, line, line segment, net, parallel, parallelogram, pentagon, perpendicular, point, plane figure, polygon, prism, pyramid, quadrilateral, ray, rectangle, regular, rhombus, square, solid, tessellation, trapezium, triangle, vertex (plural vertices), 2D, 3D

Terms used in geometry

Geometry is about investigating shapes.

The terms we use in geometry are

- points: these have no width, length or depth. We cannot draw a point, so we draw a small dot.
- lines: a line can be straight or curved. A line has no start and no end. A line has no thickness.
- line segments: a line segment is part of a line between two points.
- rays: a ray is a part of a line with only one end point.

- horizontal and vertical lines: horizontal lines go across the page and vertical lines go up and down the page.

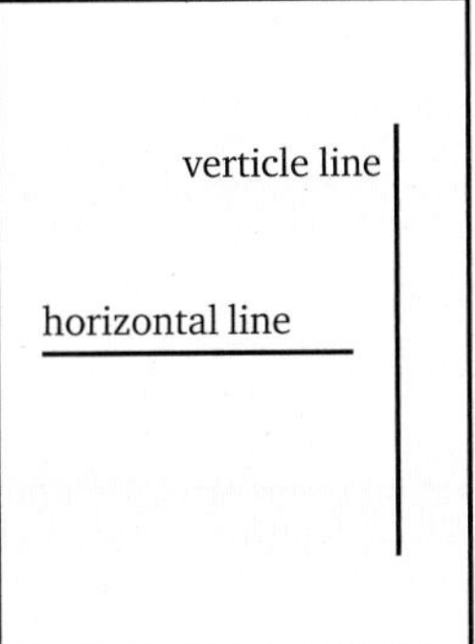

- intersecting lines: intersecting lines cross each other.

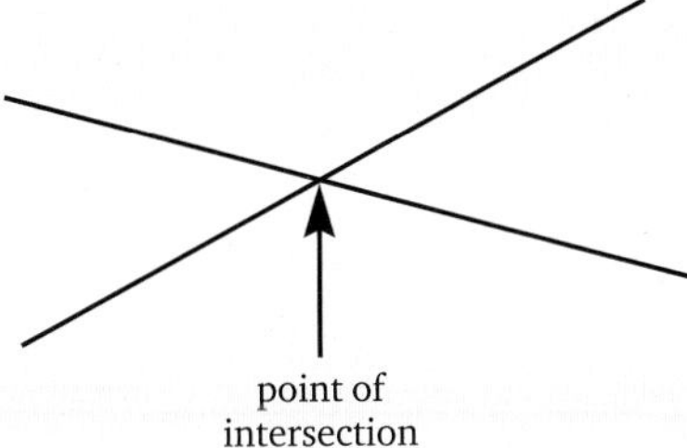

- parallel lines: parallel lines are always the same distance apart. Parallel lines are marked with arrows.

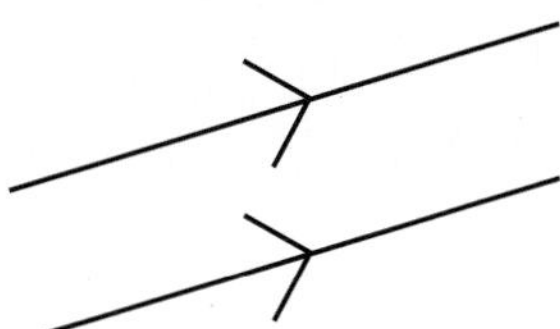

- perpendicular lines: a north–south line and an east–west line are perpendicular. The lines remain perpendicular when they are rotated.

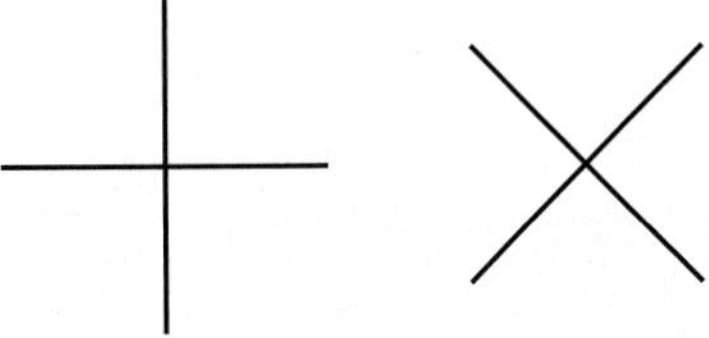

- plane figures: these are two-dimensional (flat) shapes bounded by line segments, for example a square. A plane figure is a *2D shape*.

- solids: a solid occupies three-dimensional space, for example a cube. A solid is a *3D shape*.

Plane figures

A plane figure bounded by straight line segments is called a *polygon*. Polygons have sides and vertices (singular vertex). A vertex is where two sides meet.

Vertices are labelled with capital letters and a side is named by the letters at each end. The figure is named by all the letters in order around its vertices, so the figure in the diagram is ABCDEF.

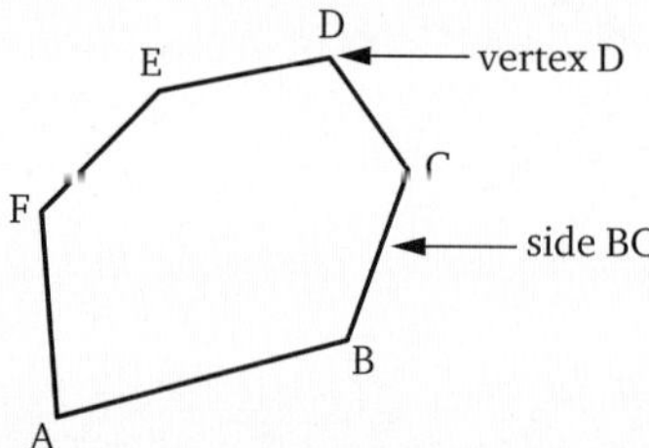

A plane figure bounded by three straight line segments is called a *triangle*.

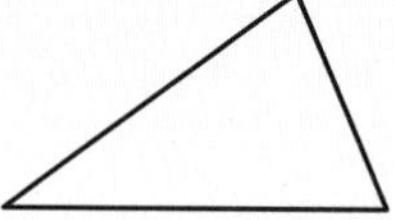

A plane figure bounded by four straight line segments is called a *quadrilateral*.

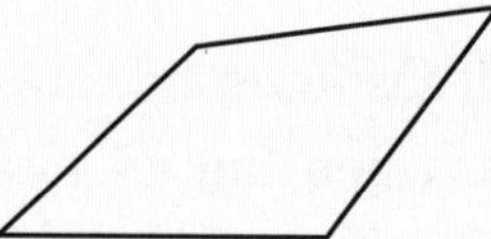

A plane figure bounded by five straight line segments is called a *pentagon*.

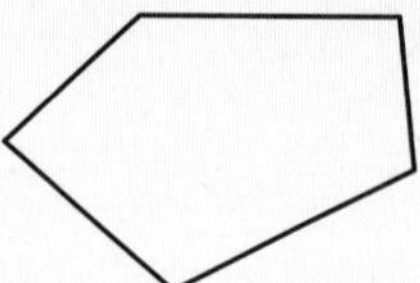

The figure ABCDEF shown here has six sides and is called a *hexagon*.

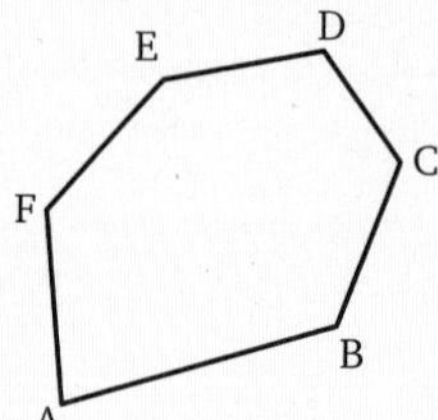

Exercise 4a

1 Each line in your exercise book is a line segment.

List three other line segments that you can see.

2 Match the correct description to each diagram.

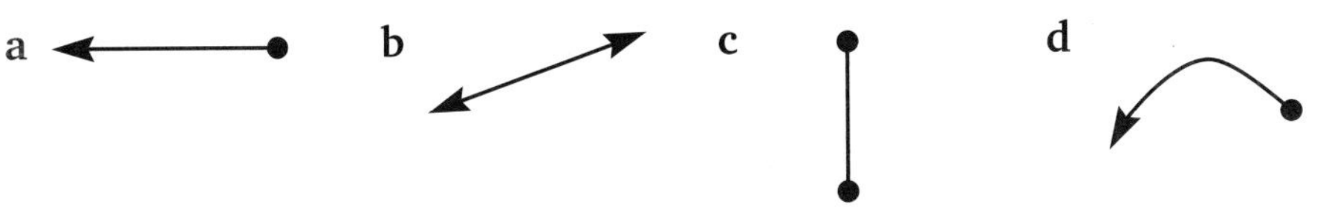

1 a straight line **2** a ray **3** a curved ray **4** a line segment

The arrows on the ends of the lines above show that they have no ends.

We do not usually show these arrows. So, in the diagrams below, we assume that the lines go on forever unless they have an obvious end.

3 C and D are two points. Describe the line in each diagram.

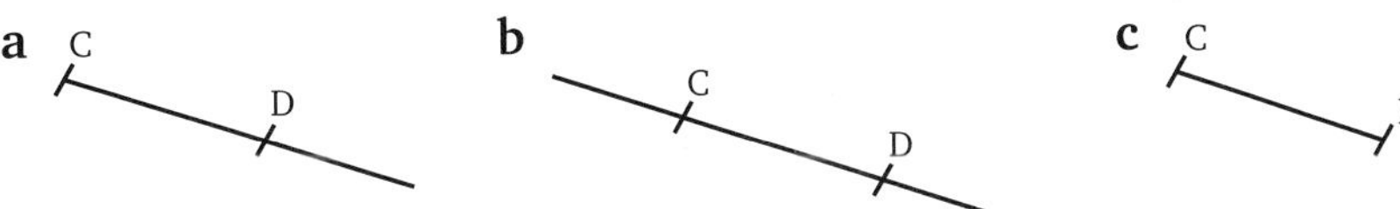

Special quadrilaterals

A *square* and a *rectangle* are both quadrilaterals.

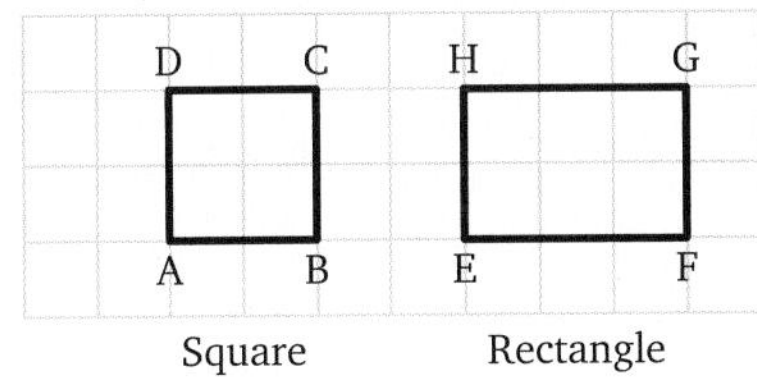

In a square

- all the sides are the same length (i.e. AB = BC = CD = DA)
- opposite sides are parallel (i.e. AB is parallel to DC; BC is parallel to AD)
- adjacent sides are perpendicular. (i.e. AB is perpendicular to BC; BC is perpendicular to CD; CD is perpendicular to AB)

In a rectangle

- the opposite sides are the same length (i.e. EF = GH and FG = HE)
- opposite sides are parallel (i.e. EF is parallel to HG and EH is parallel to FG)
- adjacent sides are perpendicular. (i.e. EF is perpendicular to FG; EG is perpendicular to GH; GH is perpendicular to HE and HE is perpendicular to EF)

The other special quadrilaterals are the parallelogram, the rhombus, the kite and the trapezium.

Exercise 4b

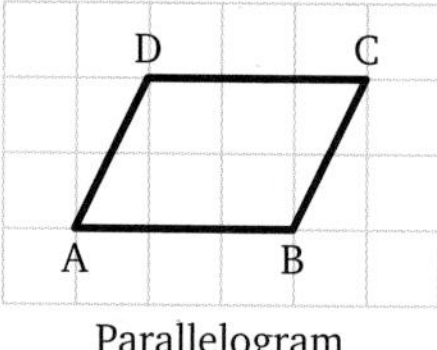

Parallelogram

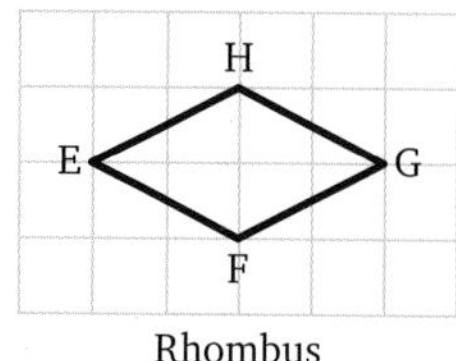

Rhombus

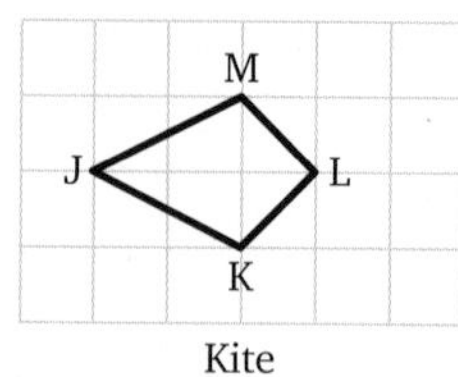

Kite

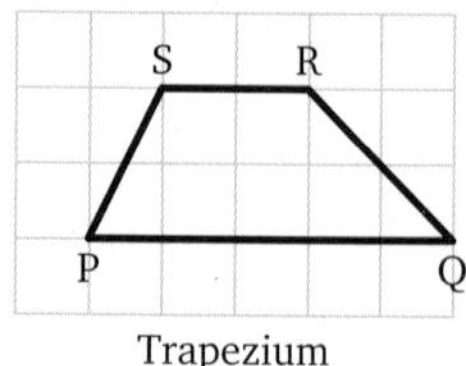

Trapezium

Each of the figures in the diagram is a quadrilateral. Copy them onto 1 cm squared paper.

For each one, name the sides, if any, which are

a the same length
b parallel
c perpendicular.

Tessellations

Shapes that fit together on a flat surface without leaving any gaps are said to tessellate. The diagram shows a *tessellation* using regular hexagons. (A regular polygon has all sides the same length, and all angles at the vertices are the same size.)

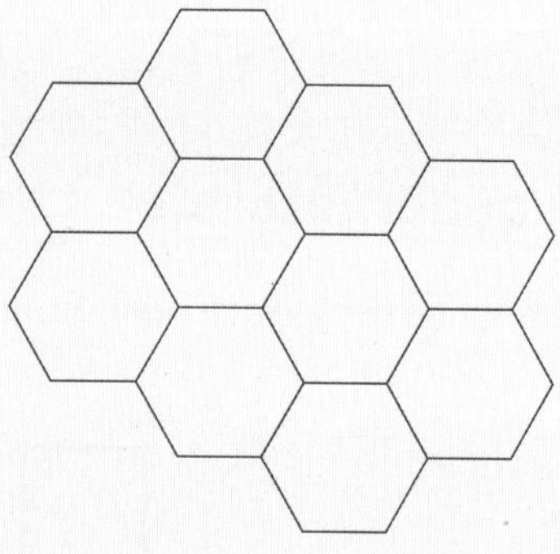

Exercise 4c

1 On 1 cm squared paper, draw two different tessellations using a rectangle.

2 Repeat question 1 using the parallelogram in Exercise 4b.

3 Repeat question 1 using the rhombus in Exercise 4b.

4 Draw any triangle. Trace it several times and then cut out your triangles. Make some tessellations using your triangles.

5 Will all triangles tessellate? Try repeating question **4** with different triangles.

6 Regular hexagons, squares and regular triangles can be combined to make interesting patterns. Some examples are given below:

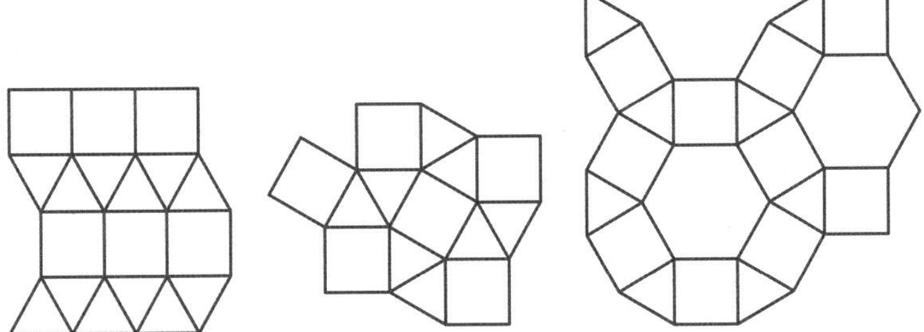

Copy these patterns and extend them. (If you make templates to help you, make each shape of side 2 cm.)

7 Make some patterns of your own using the shapes in question **6**.

Investigation

The diagram shows a circle with 2 evenly spaced dots and a line segment joining the dots.

The diagram has 2 regions.

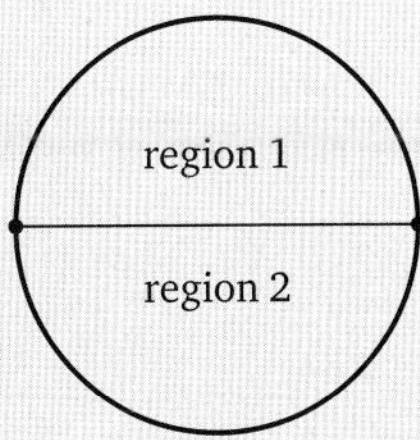

These diagrams show circles with 3 evenly spaced dots, 4 evenly spaced dots and 5 evenly spaced dots respectively. Lines are drawn between the dots.

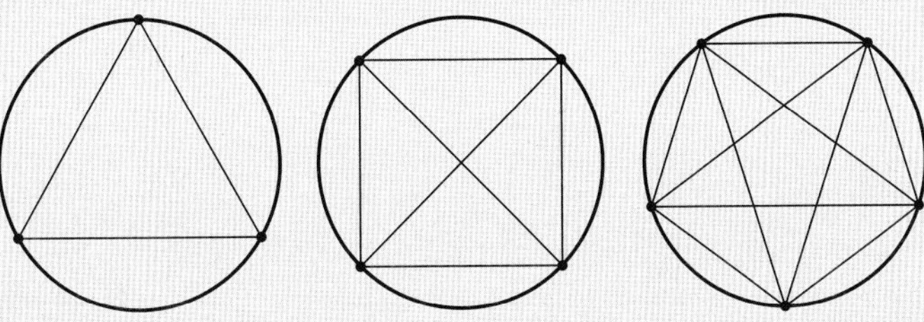

1 Copy and complete this table.

Number of dots	2	3	4	5			
Number of regions	2	4					

2 Trace this circle and its dots. Draw lines joining all the dots and count the regions. Add these numbers to your table.

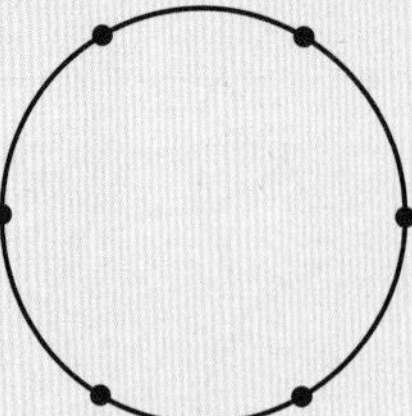

3 Can you see a pattern connecting the number of dots and the number of regions? You can try adding further circles with more dots, but make sure that the dots are evenly spaced.

4 Explain why it is important that the dots are evenly spaced.

Solidc

The solids we investigate in this chapter have plane faces, edges and vertices (singular vertex). The edge is where the faces meet and the vertex is where the edges meet.

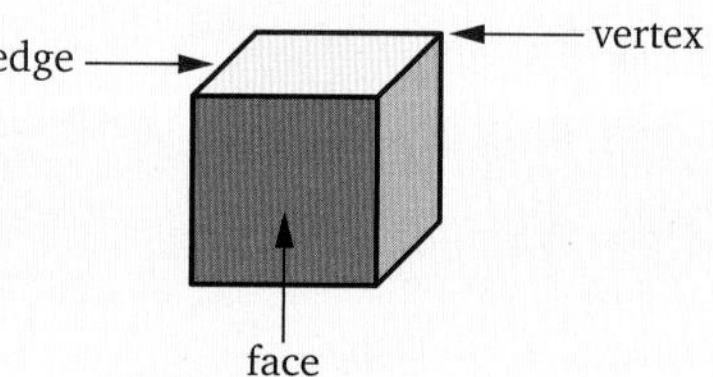

This drawing of a cube shows the hidden edges as broken lines. It shows that a cube has

6 faces
12 edges
8 vertices.

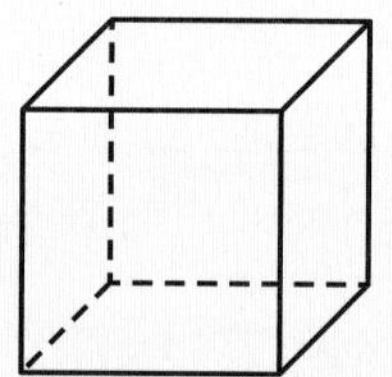

Nets

A *net* is a flat drawing that can be cut out and folded to make a solid shape. You can make a cube from a net.

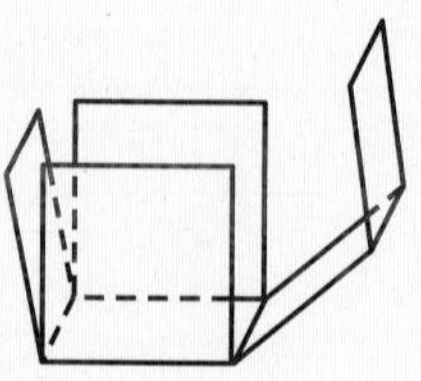

Exercise 4d

1 Below is the net of a cube of edge 4 cm.

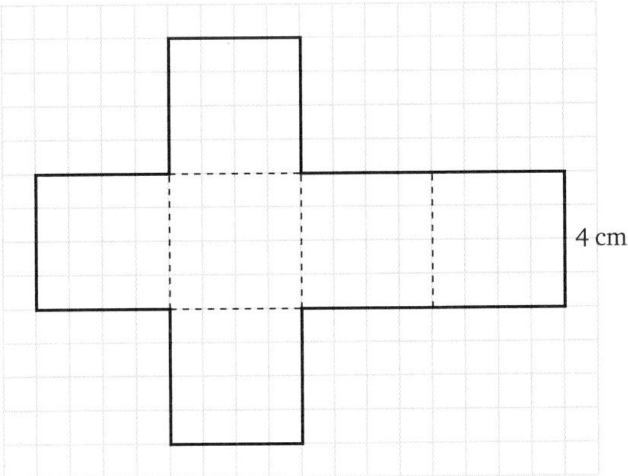

Draw the net on 1 cm squared paper and cut it out. Fold it along the broken lines. Fix it together with sticky tape.

If you mark the faces with the numbers 1 to 6, you can make a dice.

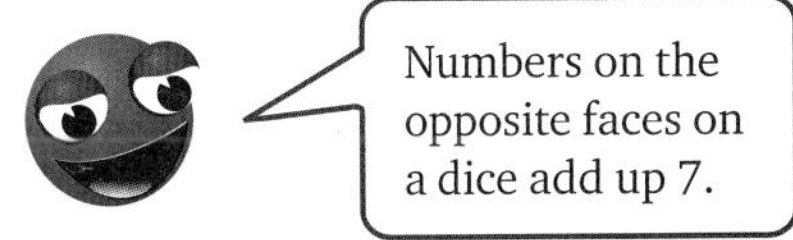

2 Draw this net full-size on 1 cm squared paper.

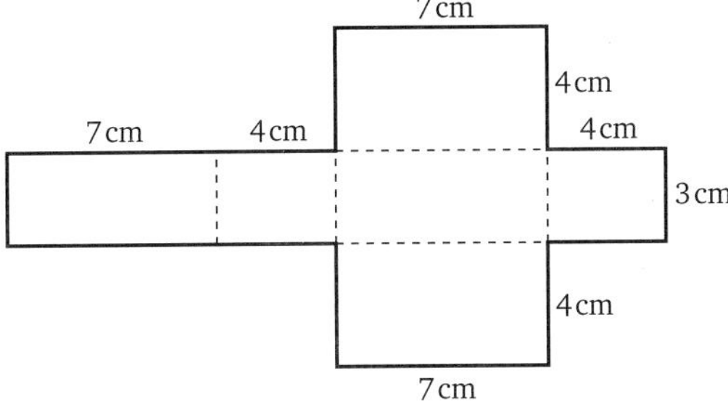

Cut the net out and fold along the dotted lines. Stick the edges together. This solid is called a cuboid.

a **i** How many faces are rectangles measuring 7 cm by 4 cm?

ii How many faces are rectangles measuring 7 cm by 3 cm?

iii What are the measurements of the remaining faces?

b Draw another arrangement of the rectangles to give a different net which will fold up to make the same cuboid.

3 This cuboid is 4 cm long, 2 cm wide and 1 cm high.

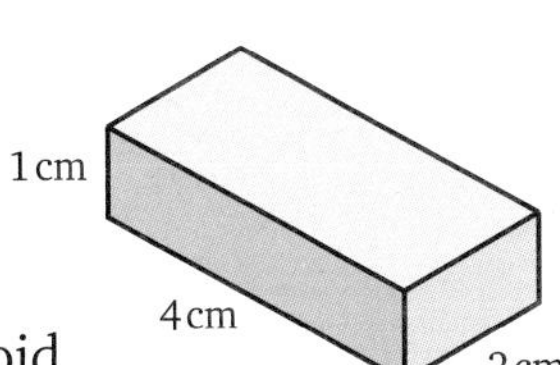

a How many faces does this cuboid have?

b Sketch the faces, showing their measurements.

c On 1 cm squared paper, draw a net that will make this cuboid.

4 This net makes a solid called a square-based pyramid.

Copy this net onto 2 cm squared paper.

Cut out your net and fold the triangles up.

Stick the edges together with sticky tape.

a How many faces does this pyramid have?

b How many edges does this pyramid have?

c How many vertices does this pyramid have?

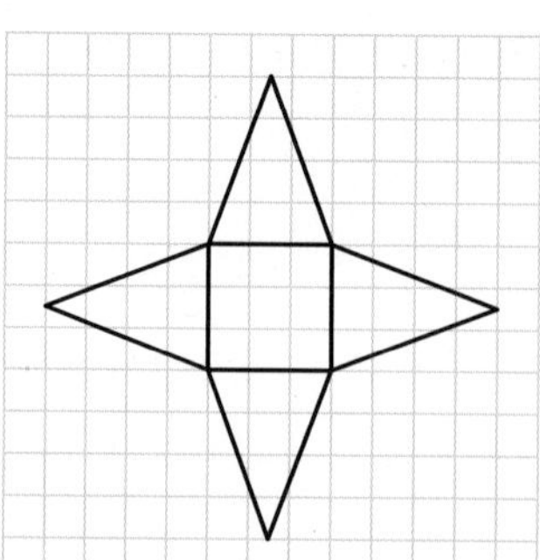

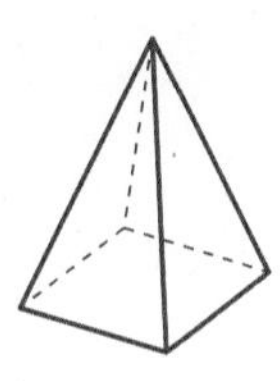

5 This net makes a solid called a prism with a triangular cross-section.

Copy this net onto 2 cm squared paper.

Cut your net out and fold it up to make the prism.

a How many faces does this prism have?

b How many edges does this prism have?

c How many vertices does this prism have?

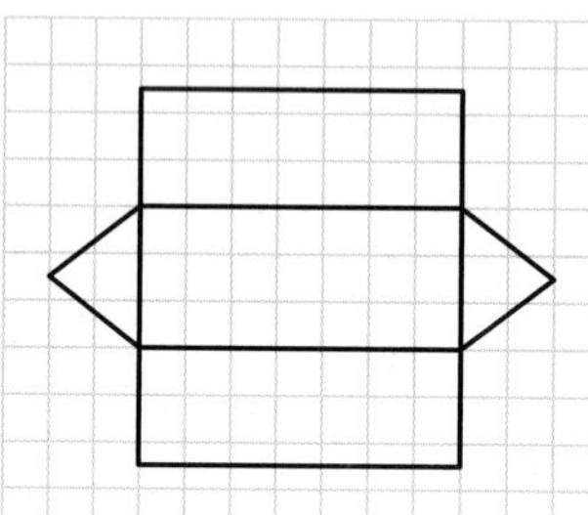

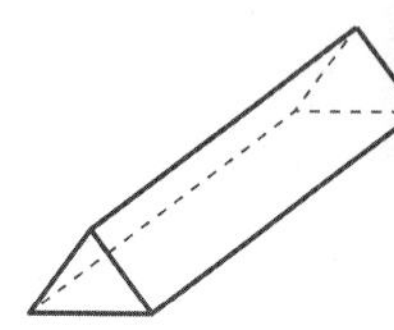

Exercise 4e

Select the letter that gives the correct answer.

1 This shape is a

A rhombus **B** rectangle **C** trapezium **D** parallelogram

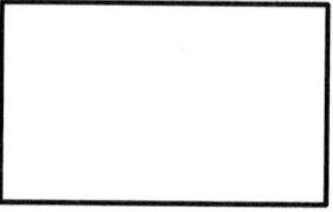

2 This shape is a

A kite **B** square **C** rectangle **D** parallelogram

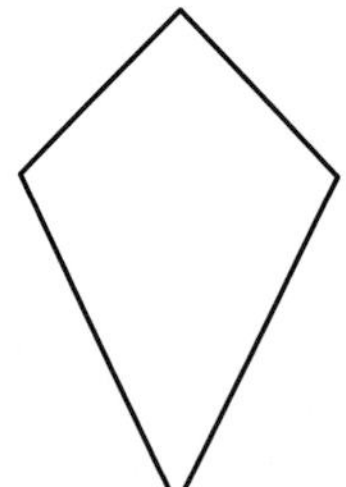

3 The number of faces a cube has is

A 4 **B** 5 **C** 6 **D** 8

4 The number of faces this prism has is

A 4 **B** 5 **C** 6 **D** 8

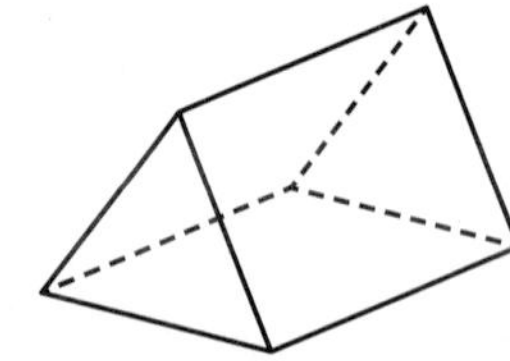

5 The number of edges on a cube is

A 6 **B** 8 **C** 10 **D** 12

6 Which of these shapes will not tessellate?

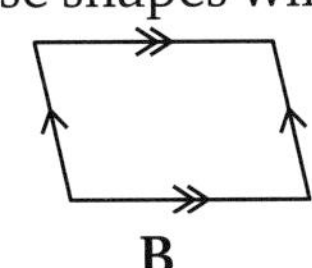

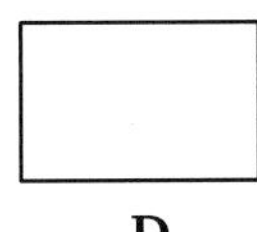

A **B** **C** **D**

Did you know?

In a platonic solid, every face is the same size of regular polygon.

A simple platonic solid is a cube.

Another platonic solid is called a dodecahedron; all its faces are regular pentagons.

A solid you will probably recognise is made from 20 hexagons and 12 pentagons. What is it?

In this chapter you have seen that...

✔ the special quadrilaterals each have a name and can be identified by the properties of their sides

✔ some polygons will tessellate

✔ solids with plane faces can be made from a net.

5 Fractions: addition and subtraction

At the end of this chapter you should be able to...

1 express one quantity as a fraction of another

2 write a fraction equivalent to a given fraction

3 order a set of fractions according to magnitude

4 add and subtract fractions

5 solve problems using addition and subtraction of fractions.

Did you know?

The system of writing one number above the other, as in $\frac{1}{2}$, is attributed to a Hindu mathematician, Brahmagupta. The bar between the two numbers as in $\frac{1}{2}$ was first used by the Arabs, about CE 1150.

You need to know...

✔ how to add and subtract whole numbers

✔ how to divide by a whole number

✔ what LCM means and how to find it.

Key words

cancel, common denominator, common factor, denominator, equivalent fraction, fraction, improper fraction, lowest common multiple, mixed number, numerator, proper fraction, rational number, simplify a fraction, the symbols < and >

The meaning of fractions

Think of cutting a cake right through the middle into two equal pieces. Each piece is one half of the cake. One half is a *fraction*, written as $\frac{1}{2}$.

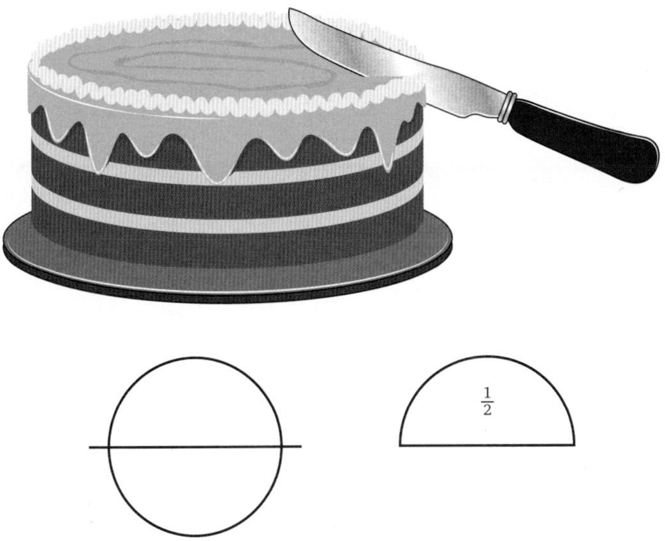

If we cut the cake into four equal pieces, each piece is one quarter, written $\frac{1}{4}$, of the cake. When one piece is taken away there are three pieces left, so the fraction that is left is three quarters, or $\frac{3}{4}$.

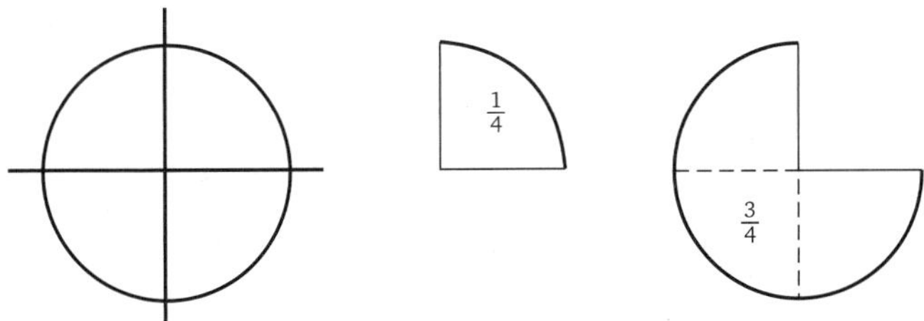

When the cake is divided into five equal slices, one slice is $\frac{1}{5}$, two slices is $\frac{2}{5}$, three slices is $\frac{3}{5}$ and four slices is $\frac{4}{5}$ of the cake.

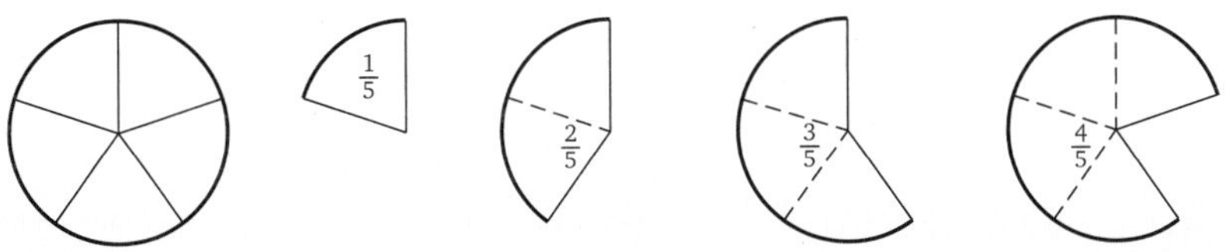

Notice that the top number in each fraction (called the *numerator*) tells you *how many* slices and the bottom number (called the *denominator*) tells you about the total number of slices to make a whole cake.

Fractions where the numerator and denominator are whole numbers are called *rational numbers*.

Exercise 5a

Write the fraction that is shaded in each of these sketches:

1

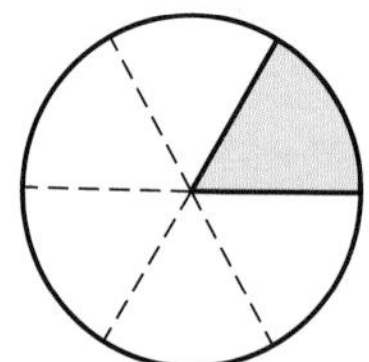

3

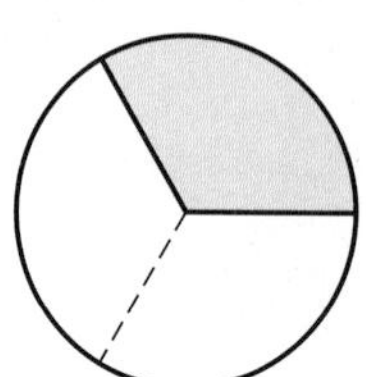

5

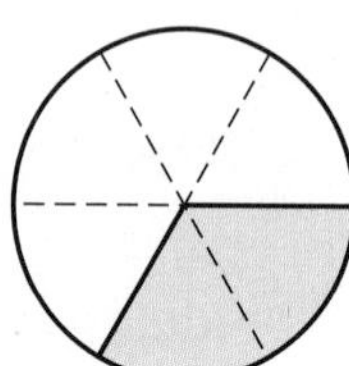

2

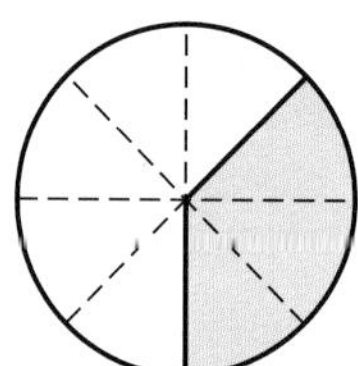

4

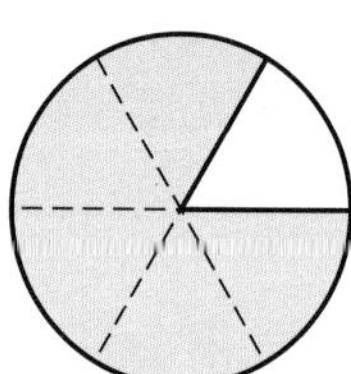

6

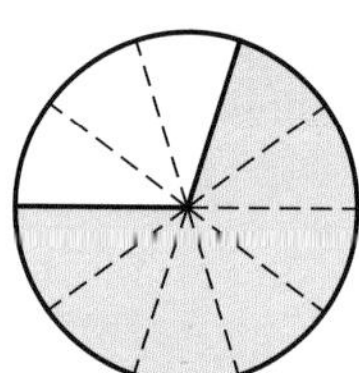

It is not only cakes that can be divided into fractions. Anything at all that can be split up into equal parts can be divided into fractions.

Write the fraction that is shaded in each of the following diagrams:

7

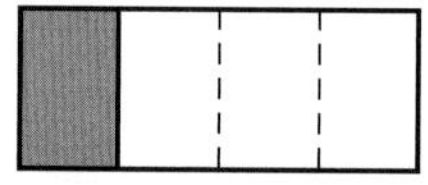

8

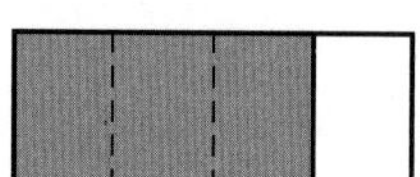

9

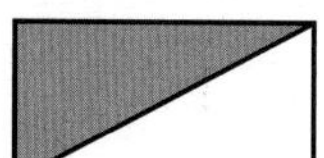

10

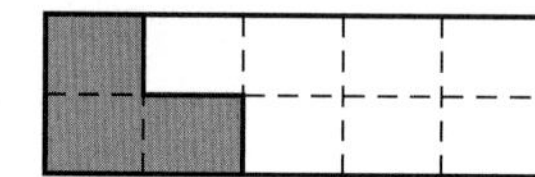

11

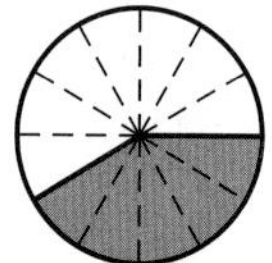

12

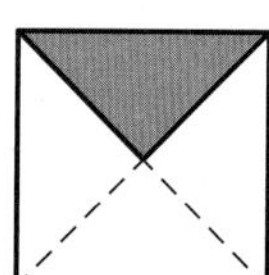

13

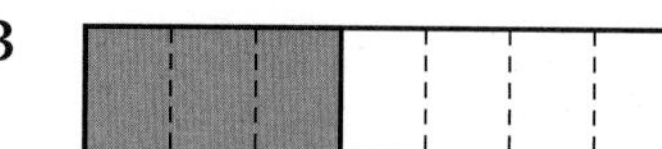

14

15

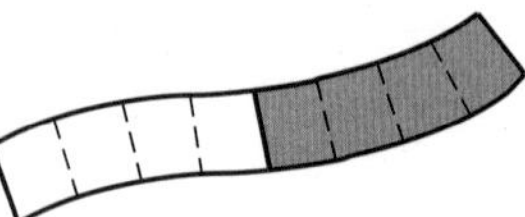

16

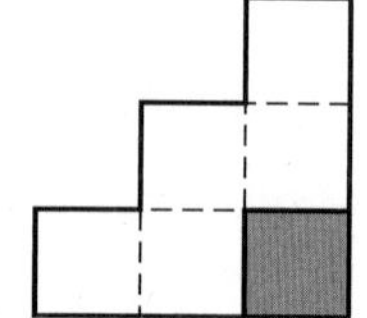

One quantity as a fraction of another

Quite a lot of things are divided into equal parts. For instance a week is divided into seven days, so each day is $\frac{1}{7}$ of a week. One dollar is divided into one hundred cents, so each cent is $\frac{1}{100}$ of a dollar.

Exercise 5b

In June there were 23 sunny days. What fraction of June was sunny?

There are 30 days in June, so you need to find 23 as a fraction of 30.

$$23 \text{ sunny days} = \frac{23}{30} \text{ of June}$$

1 One hour is divided into 60 minutes. What fraction of an hour is

- **a** one minute
- **b** nine minutes
- **c** thirty minutes
- **d** forty-five minutes?

2 You go to school on five days each week. What fraction of a week is this?

3 In the month of January, it rained on eleven days. What fraction of all the days in January did it rain?

Write 10 minutes as a fraction of 1 hour.

(We must always use the same unit for both quantities. Here we will use minutes, so we want to write 10 minutes as a fraction of 60 minutes.)

$$10 \text{ minutes} = \frac{10}{60} \text{ of 1 hour}$$

In questions **4** to **13** write the first quantity as a fraction of the second quantity:

4 51 days; 1 year (not a leap year)

5 35 c; $1

6 90 c; $5

7 35 seconds; 3 minutes

8 3 days; the month of January

9 17 days; the months of June and July together

10 5 days; 3 weeks

11 $1.50; $5

12 45 minutes; 2 hours

13 37 seconds; 1 hour

14 A boy gets 80 c pocket money. If he spends 45 c, what fraction of his pocket money is left?

15 In a class of thirty-two children, ten take French, eight take music and twenty-five take geography. What fraction of the children in the class take

a French **b** music **c** geography?

16 A girl's journey to school costs \$1.00 on one bus and \$1.50 on another bus. What fraction of the total cost arises from each bus?

17 In an orchard there are twenty apple trees, eighteen plum trees, fourteen cherry trees and ten pear trees. What fraction of all the trees are

a apple trees **b** pear trees **c** *not* cherry trees?

18 In a Youth Club with 37 members, 12 members are more than 15 years old and 8 members are under 14 years old. What fraction of the members are

a over 15 **b** under 14 **c** 14 and over?

19 During an Easter holiday of fourteen days there were three rainy days, two cloudy days and all the other days were sunny. What fraction of the holiday was

a sunny **b** rainy?

Equivalent fractions

In the first sketch below, a cake is cut into four equal pieces.
One slice is $\frac{1}{4}$ of the cake.

In the second sketch the cake is cut into eight pieces.
Two slices is $\frac{2}{8}$ of the cake.

In the third sketch the cake is cut into sixteen equal slices.
Four slices is $\frac{4}{16}$ of the cake.

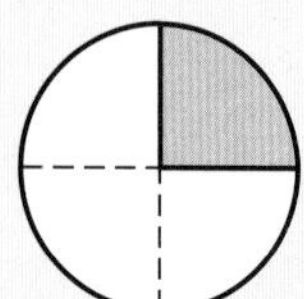

$\frac{1}{4}$

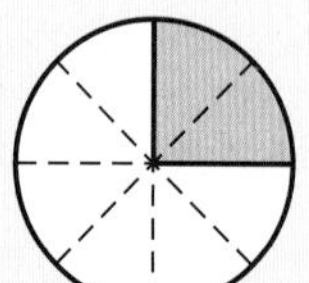

$\frac{2}{8}$

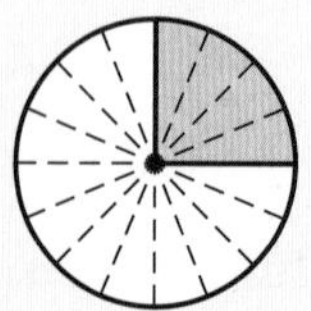

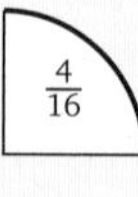

But the same amount of cake has been taken each time.

Therefore $\quad \frac{1}{4} = \frac{2}{8} = \frac{4}{16}$

and we say that $\frac{1}{4}, \frac{2}{8}$ and $\frac{4}{16}$ are *equivalent fractions*.

Now $\quad \frac{1}{4} = \frac{1\times 2}{4\times 2} = \frac{2}{8} \quad$ and $\quad \frac{1}{4} = \frac{1\times 4}{4\times 4} = \frac{4}{16}$

So all we have to do to find equivalent fractions is to multiply the numerator and the denominator by the same number. For instance

$$\frac{1}{4} = \frac{1\times 3}{4\times 3} = \frac{3}{12}$$

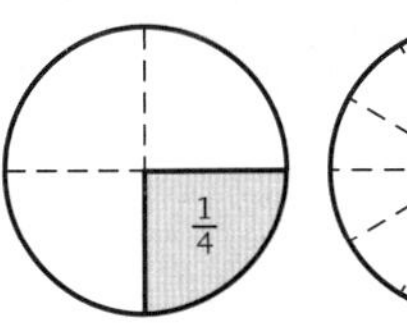

and $\quad \frac{1}{4} = \frac{1\times 5}{4\times 5} = \frac{5}{20}$

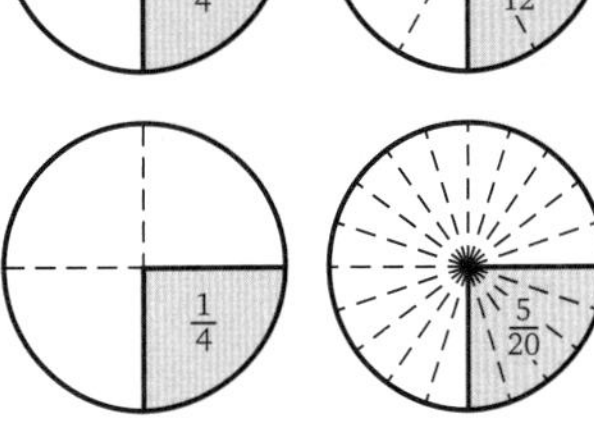

Any fraction can be treated in this way.

Exercise 5c

In questions **1** to **6** draw cake diagrams to show that:

1 $\frac{1}{3} = \frac{2}{6}$ **3** $\frac{1}{5} = \frac{2}{10}$ **5** $\frac{2}{3} = \frac{6}{9}$

2 $\frac{1}{2} = \frac{3}{6}$ **4** $\frac{3}{4} = \frac{9}{12}$ **6** $\frac{2}{3} = \frac{8}{12}$

Fill in the missing numbers to make equivalent fractions:

a $\frac{1}{5} = \frac{3}{\ }$ **b** $\frac{1}{5} = \frac{\ }{20}$

a If $\frac{1}{5} = \frac{3}{\ }$ the numerator has been multiplied by 3 so we need to multiply the denominator by 3.

$$\frac{1}{5} = \frac{1\times 3}{5\times 3} = \frac{3}{15}$$

b If $\frac{1}{5} = \frac{\ }{20}$ the denominator has been multiplied by 4 so you need to multiply the numerator by 4.

$$\frac{1}{5} = \frac{1\times 4}{5\times 4} = \frac{4}{20}$$

In questions **7** to **33** fill in the missing numbers to make equivalent fractions:

7 $\frac{1}{3}=\frac{2}{}$

8 $\frac{2}{5}=\frac{}{10}$

9 $\frac{3}{7}=\frac{9}{}$

10 $\frac{9}{10}=\frac{}{40}$

11 $\frac{1}{6}=\frac{3}{}$

12 $\frac{1}{3}=\frac{}{12}$

13 $\frac{2}{5}=\frac{6}{}$

14 $\frac{3}{7}=\frac{}{28}$

15 $\frac{9}{10}=\frac{90}{}$

16 $\frac{1}{6}=\frac{}{36}$

17 $\frac{4}{5}=\frac{}{20}$

18 $\frac{2}{3}=\frac{12}{}$

19 $\frac{2}{9}=\frac{4}{}$

20 $\frac{3}{8}=\frac{}{80}$

21 $\frac{5}{11}=\frac{}{22}$

22 $\frac{4}{5}=\frac{8}{}$

23 $\frac{1}{10}=\frac{10}{}$

24 $\frac{2}{9}=\frac{}{36}$

25 $\frac{3}{8}=\frac{}{800}$

26 $\frac{5}{11}=\frac{50}{}$

27 $\frac{4}{5}=\frac{}{50}$

28 $\frac{1}{10}=\frac{100}{}$

29 $\frac{2}{9}=\frac{20}{}$

30 $\frac{3}{8}=\frac{3000}{}$

31 $\frac{5}{11}=\frac{}{121}$

32 $\frac{4}{5}=\frac{400}{}$

33 $\frac{1}{10}=\frac{1000}{}$

Write $\frac{2}{3}$ as an equivalent fraction with denominator 24.

You need to write $\frac{2}{3}$ as $\frac{?}{24}$; 3×8 is 24 so you need to multiply the top and bottom of $\frac{2}{3}$ by 8.

$$\frac{2}{3}=\frac{2\times 8}{3\times 8}=\frac{16}{24}$$

34 Write each of the following fractions as an equivalent fraction with denominator 24:

a $\frac{1}{2}$ **b** $\frac{1}{3}$ **c** $\frac{1}{6}$ **d** $\frac{3}{4}$ **e** $\frac{5}{12}$ **f** $\frac{3}{8}$

35 Write each of the following fractions in equivalent form with denominator 45:

a $\frac{2}{15}$ **b** $\frac{4}{9}$ **c** $\frac{3}{5}$ **d** $\frac{1}{3}$ **e** $\frac{14}{15}$ **f** $\frac{1}{5}$

36 Find an equivalent fraction with denominator 36 for each of the following fractions:

a $\frac{3}{4}$ **b** $\frac{5}{9}$ **c** $\frac{1}{6}$ **d** $\frac{5}{18}$ **e** $\frac{7}{12}$ **f** $\frac{2}{3}$

37 Change each of the following fractions into an equivalent fraction with numerator 12:

a $\frac{1}{6}$ b $\frac{3}{4}$ c $\frac{6}{7}$ d $\frac{4}{5}$ e $\frac{2}{3}$ f $\frac{1}{2}$

38 Some of the following equivalent fractions are correct but two of them are wrong. Find the wrong ones and correct them by altering the numerator:

a $\frac{2}{5}=\frac{6}{15}$ b $\frac{2}{3}=\frac{4}{9}$ c $\frac{3}{7}=\frac{6}{14}$ d $\frac{4}{9}=\frac{12}{27}$ e $\frac{7}{10}=\frac{77}{100}$

Investigation

Using the numbers 1, 2, 4 and 8 write down all the fractions you can think of that are equal to or smaller than 1. Use a single number for the numerator and a single number for the denominator. You can use a number more than once in the same fraction.

1 **a** How many fractions can you find?

b Which fractions are equivalent fractions?

c What fraction does not have an equivalent fraction in the list you have written down?

2 Add 16 to the list of numbers 1, 2, 4, 8 and repeat part **1**.

3 Two-digit numbers, such as 14 and 82, can be made from the digits 1, 2, 4 and 8. Use such numbers to repeat part **1**.

Comparing the sizes of fractions

A fraction whose numerator is 1 is called a *unit fraction*. For example $\frac{1}{2}$, $\frac{1}{3}$, and $\frac{1}{10}$ are unit fractions.

We can compare the sizes of unit fractions using cake diagrams.

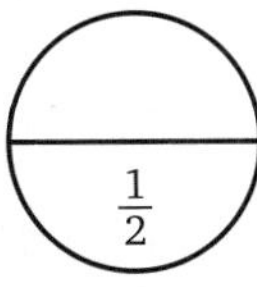

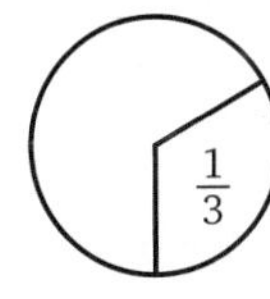

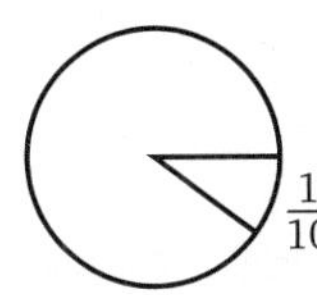

Suppose that we want to see which is bigger, $\frac{5}{7}$ or $\frac{2}{3}$. Before we can compare these two fractions we must change them into the *same kind* of fraction. That means we must find equivalent fractions that have the same denominator. This denominator must be a number that both 7 and 3 divide into, which is the lowest common multiple of 7 and 3. So our new denominator is 21. Now

$$\frac{5}{7}=\frac{15}{21} \quad \text{and} \quad \frac{2}{3}=\frac{14}{21}$$

We can see that $\frac{15}{21}$ is bigger than $\frac{14}{21}$, i.e. $\frac{5}{7}$ is bigger than $\frac{2}{3}$.

We often use the symbol > instead of writing the words 'is bigger than'. Using this symbol we could write $\frac{15}{21} > \frac{14}{21}$, so $\frac{5}{7} > \frac{2}{3}$.

Similarly we use < instead of writing 'is less than'.

Exercise 5d

Using an analogue clock face helps to judge the size of the slice.

1 Sketch cake diagrams to illustrate the size of these unit fractions.

a $\frac{1}{4}$ **b** $\frac{1}{5}$ **c** $\frac{1}{12}$ **d** $\frac{1}{15}$

Which is the bigger fraction, $\frac{3}{5}$ or $\frac{7}{11}$?

You need to change $\frac{3}{5}$ and $\frac{7}{11}$ into equivalent fractions with the same denominator, so you need to find the LCM of 5 and 11.

$\frac{3}{5} = \frac{33}{55}$ and $\frac{7}{11} = \frac{35}{55}$ (55 divides by 5 and by 11)

$\frac{35}{55} > \frac{33}{55}$ so $\frac{7}{11}$ is the bigger fraction.

In the questions **2** to **25**, find which is the bigger fraction:

2 $\frac{1}{2}$ or $\frac{1}{3}$

3 $\frac{3}{4}$ or $\frac{5}{6}$

4 $\frac{2}{3}$ or $\frac{4}{5}$

5 $\frac{2}{9}$ or $\frac{1}{7}$

6 $\frac{2}{7}$ or $\frac{3}{8}$

7 $\frac{2}{3}$ or $\frac{3}{4}$

8 $\frac{2}{5}$ or $\frac{3}{7}$

9 $\frac{5}{6}$ or $\frac{3}{5}$

10 $\frac{3}{8}$ or $\frac{1}{5}$

11 $\frac{4}{5}$ or $\frac{6}{7}$

12 $\frac{3}{5}$ or $\frac{4}{7}$

13 $\frac{3}{4}$ or $\frac{2}{3}$

14 $\frac{1}{4}$ or $\frac{3}{11}$

15 $\frac{5}{7}$ or $\frac{3}{5}$

16 $\frac{3}{8}$ or $\frac{5}{11}$

17 $\frac{3}{10}$ or $\frac{4}{11}$

18 $\frac{1}{4}$ or $\frac{2}{7}$

19 $\frac{5}{8}$ or $\frac{4}{7}$

20 $\frac{2}{9}$ or $\frac{3}{11}$

21 $\frac{5}{7}$ or $\frac{7}{9}$

22 $\frac{9}{11}$ or $\frac{7}{9}$

23 $\frac{2}{5}$ or $\frac{1}{3}$

24 $\frac{4}{7}$ or $\frac{3}{5}$

25 $\frac{5}{8}$ or $\frac{6}{11}$

In questions **26** to **37**, put either > or < between the fractions:

26 $\frac{1}{4}$ $\frac{2}{7}$

27 $\frac{2}{3}$ $\frac{5}{8}$

28 $\frac{3}{7}$ $\frac{1}{2}$

29 $\frac{5}{8}$ $\frac{7}{10}$

30 $\frac{3}{10}$ $\frac{1}{4}$

31 $\frac{1}{3}$ $\frac{2}{5}$

32 $\frac{3}{5}$ $\frac{2}{3}$

33 $\frac{2}{9}$ $\frac{1}{5}$

You need to change $\frac{1}{4}$ and $\frac{2}{7}$ into equivalent fractions with the same denominator. Then you can see if $\frac{1}{4}$ is bigger or smaller than $\frac{2}{7}$.

34 $\frac{4}{9}$ $\frac{5}{11}$

35 $\frac{2}{11}$ $\frac{1}{7}$

36 $\frac{8}{11}$ $\frac{3}{4}$

37 $\frac{7}{8}$ $\frac{7}{9}$

Arrange these fractions in ascending order: $\frac{3}{4}, \frac{7}{10}, \frac{1}{2}, \frac{4}{5}$

$$\frac{3}{4} = \frac{15}{20}$$

$$\frac{7}{10} = \frac{14}{20}$$

$$\frac{1}{2} = \frac{10}{20} \quad \text{(20 divides by 4, 10, 2 and 5)}$$

$$\frac{4}{5} = \frac{16}{20}$$

So the ascending order is $\frac{1}{2}, \frac{7}{10}, \frac{3}{4}, \frac{4}{5}$.

Arrange the following fractions in ascending order:

38 $\frac{2}{3}, \frac{1}{2}, \frac{3}{5}, \frac{7}{30}$

39 $\frac{13}{20}, \frac{3}{4}, \frac{4}{10}, \frac{5}{8}$

40 $\frac{1}{3}, \frac{5}{6}, \frac{1}{2}, \frac{7}{12}$

41 $\frac{2}{5}, \frac{3}{8}, \frac{17}{20}, \frac{1}{2}, \frac{7}{10}$

42 $\frac{5}{7}, \frac{11}{14}, \frac{3}{4}, \frac{17}{28}, \frac{1}{2}$

43 $\frac{7}{10}, \frac{2}{5}, \frac{3}{5}, \frac{14}{25}, \frac{1}{2}$

You need to change all four fractions into equivalent fractions with the same denominator. Then you can see which is the smallest, which is the next smallest, and so on.

Arrange the following fractions in descending order:

44 $\frac{5}{6}, \frac{1}{2}, \frac{7}{9}, \frac{11}{18}, \frac{2}{3}$

45 $\frac{13}{20}, \frac{3}{5}, \frac{1}{2}, \frac{3}{4}, \frac{7}{10}$

46 $\frac{7}{12}, \frac{1}{6}, \frac{2}{3}, \frac{17}{24}, \frac{3}{4}$

47 $\frac{7}{10}, \frac{11}{15}, \frac{2}{3}, \frac{23}{30}, \frac{4}{5}$

48 $\frac{7}{16}, \frac{1}{2}, \frac{5}{8}, \frac{19}{32}, \frac{3}{4}$

49 $\frac{4}{5}, \frac{7}{12}, \frac{5}{6}, \frac{1}{2}, \frac{3}{4}$

Simplifying fractions

Think of the way you find equivalent fractions. For example

$$\frac{2}{5} = \frac{2 \times 7}{5 \times 7} = \frac{14}{35}$$

Looking at this the other way round we see that

$$\frac{14}{35} = \frac{\not{7} \times 2}{\not{7} \times 5} = \frac{2}{5}$$

In the middle step, 7 is a factor of both the numerator and the denominator and it is called a *common factor*. To get the final value of $\frac{2}{5}$ we have 'crossed out' the common factor and this is called *cancelling*. What we have really done is to divide the top and the bottom by 7 and this *simplifies* the fraction.

When all the simplifying is finished we say that the fraction is in its *lowest terms*.

Any fraction whose numerator and denominator have a common factor (perhaps more than one) can be simplified in this way. Suppose, for example, that we want to simplify $\frac{24}{27}$. As 3 is a factor of 24 and of 27, we say

$$\frac{24}{27} = \frac{3\times 8}{3\times 9} = \frac{8}{9}$$

A quicker way to write this down is to divide the numerator and the denominator mentally by the common factor, crossing them out and writing the new numbers beside them (it is a good idea to write the new numbers smaller so that you can see that you have simplified the fraction), i.e.

$$\frac{\cancel{24}^{8}}{\cancel{27}_{9}} = \frac{8}{9}$$

Exercise 5e

Simplify $\frac{66}{176}$ by cancelling the common factors.

$$\frac{\cancel{66}^{\cancel{33}^{3}}}{\cancel{176}_{\cancel{88}_{8}}} = \frac{3}{8}$$

(We divided top and bottom by 2 and then by 11.)

Simplify the following fractions:

When you cancel, check that you have cancelled ALL possible common factors. For example, if you cancel $\frac{6}{12}$ by 2, you are left with $\frac{3}{6}$; this has a common factor of 3 so will simplify further.

1 $\frac{2}{6}$

2 $\frac{30}{50}$

3 $\frac{3}{9}$

4 $\frac{6}{12}$

5 $\frac{9}{27}$

6 $\frac{4}{8}$

7 $\frac{5}{15}$

8 $\frac{12}{18}$

9 $\frac{10}{20}$

10 $\frac{8}{32}$

11 $\frac{8}{28}$

12 $\frac{27}{90}$

13 $\frac{14}{70}$

14 $\frac{24}{60}$

15 $\frac{16}{56}$

16 $\frac{10}{30}$

17 $\frac{36}{72}$

18 $\frac{15}{75}$

19 $\frac{60}{100}$

20 $\frac{36}{90}$

21 $\frac{70}{126}$

22 $\frac{49}{77}$

23 $\frac{99}{132}$

24 $\frac{33}{121}$

25 $\frac{80}{100}$

26 $\frac{48}{84}$

27 $\frac{54}{162}$

28 $\frac{54}{66}$

29 $\frac{27}{36}$

30 $\frac{800}{1000}$

Adding fractions

Suppose there is a bowl of oranges and apples. First you take three oranges and then two more oranges. You then have five oranges; we can add the 3 and the 2 together because they are the same kind of fruit. But three oranges and two apples cannot be added together because they are different kinds of fruit.

For fractions it is the denominator that tells us the kind of fraction, so we can add fractions together if they have the same denominator but not while their denominators are different. For example:

$\frac{2}{5}+\frac{1}{5}=\frac{3}{5}$ (Here we are adding fifths. We add two-fifths and one-fifth to get three-fifths.)

$\frac{3}{10}+\frac{4}{10}=\frac{7}{10}$ (Here we are adding tenths. We add three-tenths and four-tenths to get seven-tenths.)

Exercise 5f

$\frac{9}{22}+\frac{5}{22}$

$\frac{9}{22}+\frac{5}{22}=\frac{9+5}{22}$

$=\frac{14^{7}}{22_{11}}$ When you have added the numerators, always check to see if the fraction will simplify.

$=\frac{7}{11}$

Add the fractions given in questions **1** to **24**, simplifying the answers where you can:

1 $\frac{1}{4}+\frac{2}{4}$

2 $\frac{1}{8}+\frac{3}{8}$

3 $\frac{3}{11}+\frac{2}{11}$

4 $\frac{3}{13}+\frac{7}{13}$

5 $\frac{11}{23}+\frac{8}{23}$

6 $\frac{1}{7}+\frac{2}{7}$

7 $\frac{2}{5}+\frac{1}{5}$

8 $\frac{3}{10}+\frac{1}{10}$

9 $\frac{2}{21}+\frac{9}{21}$

10 $\frac{7}{30}+\frac{8}{30}$

11 $\frac{6}{13}+\frac{5}{13}$

12 $\frac{1}{10}+\frac{7}{10}$

13 $\frac{2}{7}+\frac{4}{7}$

14 $\frac{4}{17}+\frac{5}{17}$

15 $\frac{3}{14}+\frac{4}{14}$

16 $\frac{8}{30}+\frac{19}{30}$

17 $\frac{5}{16}+\frac{7}{16}$

18 $\frac{8}{19}+\frac{3}{19}$

19 $\frac{3}{20}+\frac{7}{20}$

20 $\frac{21}{100}+\frac{19}{100}$

21 $\frac{4}{11}+\frac{2}{11}$

22 $\frac{14}{23}+\frac{1}{23}$

23 $\frac{11}{18}+\frac{5}{18}$

24 $\frac{7}{15}+\frac{3}{15}$

We can add more than two fractions in the same way.

Add the fractions given in questions **25** to **34**:

25 $\frac{2}{15}+\frac{4}{15}+\frac{6}{15}$

26 $\frac{8}{100}+\frac{21}{100}+\frac{11}{100}$

27 $\frac{3}{31}+\frac{2}{31}+\frac{7}{31}+\frac{11}{31}$

28 $\frac{1}{14}+\frac{3}{14}+\frac{5}{14}+\frac{2}{14}$

29 $\frac{2}{51}+\frac{4}{51}+\frac{6}{51}+\frac{8}{51}+\frac{7}{51}$

30 $\frac{3}{19}+\frac{2}{19}+\frac{7}{19}$

31 $\frac{7}{60}+\frac{8}{60}+\frac{11}{60}$

32 $\frac{4}{45}+\frac{11}{45}+\frac{8}{45}+\frac{2}{45}$

33 $\frac{3}{100}+\frac{14}{100}+\frac{31}{100}+\frac{2}{100}$

34 $\frac{3}{99}+\frac{11}{99}+\frac{4}{99}+\frac{7}{99}$

Fractions with different denominators

To add fractions with different denominators we must first change the fractions into equivalent fractions with the same denominator. This new denominator must be a number that both original denominators divide into. For instance, if we want to add $\frac{2}{5}+\frac{1}{2}$ we choose 10 (the LCM of 5 and 2) for our new denominator because 10 can be divided by both 5 and 2:

$$\frac{2}{5}=\frac{4}{10}$$

$$\frac{1}{2}=\frac{5}{10}$$

So $$\frac{2}{5}+\frac{1}{2}=\frac{4}{10}+\frac{5}{10}=\frac{9}{10}$$

Exercise 5g

Find $\frac{2}{5}+\frac{1}{3}$

You need to change $\frac{2}{5}$ and $\frac{1}{3}$ into equivalent fractions with the same denominator.

5 and 3 both divide into 15 so choose 15 as the new denominator.

$$\frac{2}{5}+\frac{1}{3}=\frac{6}{15}+\frac{5}{15}=\frac{11}{15}$$

Find:

1 $\frac{2}{3}+\frac{1}{5}$

2 $\frac{1}{5}+\frac{3}{8}$

3 $\frac{1}{5}+\frac{1}{6}$

4 $\frac{2}{5}+\frac{3}{7}$

5 $\frac{3}{10}+\frac{2}{3}$

6 $\frac{4}{7}+\frac{1}{8}$

7 $\frac{3}{7}+\frac{1}{6}$

8 $\frac{2}{3}+\frac{2}{7}$

9 $\frac{1}{6}+\frac{2}{7}$

10 $\frac{5}{6}+\frac{1}{7}$

11 $\frac{3}{11}+\frac{5}{9}$

12 $\frac{2}{9}+\frac{3}{10}$

The new denominator, which is called the *common denominator*, is not always as big as you might first think. For instance, if we want to add $\frac{3}{4}$ and $\frac{1}{12}$, the common denominator is 12 because it divides by both 4 and 12.

Find $\frac{3}{4}+\frac{1}{12}$

$$\begin{aligned}\frac{3}{4}+\frac{1}{12} &= \frac{9}{12}+\frac{1}{12}\\ &= \frac{10}{12}\\ &= \frac{5}{6}\end{aligned}$$

Find:

13 $\frac{2}{5}+\frac{3}{10}$ **15** $\frac{3}{7}+\frac{8}{21}$ **17** $\frac{1}{4}+\frac{7}{10}$ **19** $\frac{2}{3}+\frac{2}{9}$ **21** $\frac{1}{20}+\frac{3}{5}$ **23** $\frac{2}{5}+\frac{7}{15}$

14 $\frac{3}{8}+\frac{7}{16}$ **16** $\frac{3}{10}+\frac{3}{100}$ **18** $\frac{1}{4}+\frac{3}{8}$ **20** $\frac{4}{9}+\frac{5}{18}$ **22** $\frac{4}{11}+\frac{5}{22}$ **24** $\frac{7}{12}+\frac{1}{6}$

More than two fractions can be added in this way. The common denominator must be divisible by *all* of the original denominators.

Find $\frac{1}{8}+\frac{1}{2}+\frac{1}{3}$

(8, 2 and 3 all divide into 24)

$$\begin{aligned}\frac{1}{8}+\frac{1}{2}+\frac{1}{3} &= \frac{3}{24}+\frac{12}{24}+\frac{8}{24}\\ &= \frac{3+12+8}{24}\\ &= \frac{23}{24}\end{aligned}$$

Find:

25 $\frac{1}{5}+\frac{1}{4}+\frac{1}{2}$ 28 $\frac{5}{12}+\frac{1}{6}+\frac{1}{3}$ **31** $\frac{1}{2}+\frac{3}{8}+\frac{1}{10}$ **34** $\frac{2}{9}+\frac{2}{3}+\frac{1}{18}$

26 $\frac{1}{8}+\frac{1}{4}+\frac{1}{3}$ **29** $\frac{1}{7}+\frac{3}{14}+\frac{1}{2}$ **32** $\frac{1}{3}+\frac{2}{9}+\frac{1}{6}$ **35** $\frac{2}{15}+\frac{1}{10}+\frac{2}{5}$

27 $\frac{3}{10}+\frac{2}{5}+\frac{1}{4}$ **30** $\frac{1}{3}+\frac{1}{6}+\frac{1}{2}$ **33** $\frac{7}{20}+\frac{3}{10}+\frac{1}{5}$ **36** $\frac{1}{4}+\frac{1}{12}+\frac{1}{3}$

Subtracting fractions

Exactly the same method is used for subtracting fractions as for adding them. To work out the value of $\frac{7}{8}-\frac{3}{8}$ we notice that the denominators are the same, so

$$\frac{7}{8}-\frac{3}{8}=\frac{7-3}{8}$$

$$=\frac{\cancel{4}^{1}}{\cancel{8}_{2}}$$

$$=\frac{1}{2}$$

Exercise 5h

Find $\frac{7}{9}-\frac{1}{4}$

(The denominators are not the same so we use equivalent fractions with the LCM of the two denominators, 36.)

$$\frac{7}{9}-\frac{1}{4}=\frac{28}{36}-\frac{9}{36}$$

$$=\frac{28-9}{36}$$

$$=\frac{19}{36} \quad \text{(This will not simplify.)}$$

Find:

1 $\frac{8}{9}-\frac{2}{9}$

2 $\frac{7}{10}-\frac{2}{10}$

3 $\frac{6}{17}-\frac{1}{17}$

4 $\frac{3}{4}-\frac{1}{5}$

5 $\frac{9}{10}-\frac{1}{2}$

6 $\frac{5}{7}-\frac{2}{7}$

7 $\frac{8}{13}-\frac{3}{13}$

8 $\frac{19}{20}-\frac{7}{20}$

9 $\frac{2}{3}-\frac{3}{7}$

10 $\frac{4}{7}-\frac{1}{3}$

11 $\frac{11}{15}-\frac{4}{15}$

12 $\frac{13}{18}-\frac{7}{18}$

13 $\frac{8}{11}-\frac{2}{5}$

14 $\frac{7}{9}-\frac{2}{3}$

15 $\frac{8}{13}-\frac{1}{2}$

16 $\frac{11}{12}-\frac{5}{6}$

17 $\frac{19}{100}-\frac{1}{10}$

18 $\frac{5}{8}-\frac{2}{7}$

19 $\frac{15}{16}-\frac{3}{4}$

20 $\frac{7}{15}-\frac{1}{5}$

21 $\frac{3}{4}-\frac{5}{8}$

22 $\frac{7}{12}-\frac{1}{3}$

23 $\frac{13}{18}-\frac{5}{9}$

24 $\frac{13}{15}-\frac{3}{5}$

Adding and subtracting fractions

Fractions can be added and subtracted in one problem in a similar way.
For example:

$$\frac{7}{9}+\frac{1}{18}-\frac{1}{6}=\frac{14}{18}+\frac{1}{18}-\frac{3}{18}$$
$$=\frac{14+1-3}{18}$$
$$=\frac{15-3}{18}$$
$$=\frac{\cancel{12}^{2}}{\cancel{18}_{3}}$$ This will simplify by cancelling by 6.
$$=\frac{2}{3}$$

It is not always possible to work from left to right in order because we have to subtract too much too soon. In this case we can do the adding first. Remember that it is the operation (i.e. add or subtract) *in front* of a number that tells you what to do with that number.

Exercise 5i

Find $\frac{1}{8}-\frac{3}{4}+\frac{11}{16}$

$$\frac{1}{8}-\frac{3}{4}+\frac{11}{16}=\frac{2}{16}-\frac{12}{16}+\frac{11}{16}=\frac{2}{16}+\frac{11}{16}-\frac{12}{16}$$
$$=\frac{2+11-12}{16}=\frac{13-12}{16}$$
$$=\frac{1}{16}$$

Find:

1 $\frac{3}{4}+\frac{1}{2}-\frac{7}{8}$

2 $\frac{6}{7}-\frac{9}{14}+\frac{1}{2}$

3 $\frac{3}{8}+\frac{7}{16}-\frac{3}{4}$

4 $\frac{11}{12}+\frac{1}{6}-\frac{2}{3}$

5 $\frac{3}{5}+\frac{3}{25}-\frac{27}{50}$

6 $\frac{2}{3}+\frac{1}{6}-\frac{5}{12}$

7 $\frac{4}{5}-\frac{7}{10}+\frac{1}{2}$

8 $\frac{7}{9}-\frac{2}{3}+\frac{5}{6}$

9 $\frac{7}{10}-\frac{41}{100}+\frac{1}{20}$

10 $\frac{5}{8}-\frac{21}{40}+\frac{2}{5}$

Remember that the operation (+ or –) in front of a number tells you what to do with that number only.

11 $\frac{7}{12}-\frac{1}{6}+\frac{1}{3}$

12 $\frac{2}{3}-\frac{7}{18}+\frac{2}{9}$

13 $\frac{2}{9}-\frac{1}{3}+\frac{1}{6}$

14 $\frac{1}{6}-\frac{2}{3}+\frac{7}{12}$

15 $\frac{2}{5}-\frac{1}{2}+\frac{3}{10}$

16 $\frac{1}{8}-\frac{13}{16}+\frac{3}{4}$

17 $\frac{1}{6}-\frac{5}{18}+\frac{1}{3}$

18 $\frac{1}{5}-\frac{7}{10}+\frac{17}{20}$

19 $\frac{1}{4}-\frac{5}{8}+\frac{1}{2}$

20 $\frac{2}{3}-\frac{5}{6}+\frac{1}{2}$

21 $\frac{3}{10}-\frac{61}{100}+\frac{1}{2}$

22 $\frac{1}{8}-\frac{7}{24}+\frac{5}{12}$

23 $\frac{1}{3}-\frac{5}{18}+\frac{2}{9}$

24 $\frac{3}{10}+\frac{2}{15}-\frac{2}{5}$

Remember that you can do the addition before you do the subtraction. For example, to find $\frac{4-6+3}{18}$, you can add 4 and 3 before taking 6 away.

Problems

Exercise 5j

In a class of school children, $\frac{1}{3}$ of the children come to school by bus, $\frac{1}{4}$ come to school on bicycles and the rest walk to school. What fraction of the children ride to school? What fraction do not use a bus?

Riding to school means coming by bus or on a bicycle.

$$\text{The fraction who ride to school on bicycle or bus} = \frac{1}{3}+\frac{1}{4} = \frac{4+3}{12} = \frac{7}{12}$$

Therefore $\frac{7}{12}$ of the children ride to school.

The complete class of children is a whole unit, i.e. 1.

The fraction of children who do not use a bus is found by taking the bus users from the complete class, i.e.

$$\frac{1}{1}-\frac{1}{3}=\frac{3-1}{3}=\frac{2}{3}$$

Remember to read the questions carefully. Read it several times if necessary to make sure that you understand what you are being asked to find.

1 A girl spends $\frac{1}{5}$ of her pocket money on sweets and $\frac{2}{3}$ on clothes. What fraction has she spent? What fraction has she left?

2 A group of friends went to a hamburger bar. $\frac{2}{5}$ of them bought a hamburger, $\frac{1}{3}$ of them just bought chips. The rest bought cola. What fraction of the group bought food? What fraction bought a drink?

3 At a calypso final, $\frac{2}{3}$ of the groups were all boys, $\frac{1}{4}$ of the groups included one girl and the rest included more than one girl. What fraction of the groups

a were not all boys

b included more than one girl?

4 At a Youth Club, $\frac{1}{2}$ of the meetings are for playing table tennis only, $\frac{1}{8}$ of the meetings are discussions only and the rest are disco sessions only. What fraction of the meetings are

a disco sessions only

b not for discussions?

5 At a school, $\frac{1}{8}$ of the time is spent in mathematics classes, $\frac{3}{20}$ of the time in English classes and $\frac{1}{20}$ on games. What fraction of the time is spent on

a English and maths together

b all lessons except games

c maths and games?

Mixed numbers and improper fractions

Most of the fractions we have met so far have been less than a whole unit. These are called *proper* fractions. But we often have more than a whole unit. Suppose, for instance, that we have one and a half bars of chocolate:

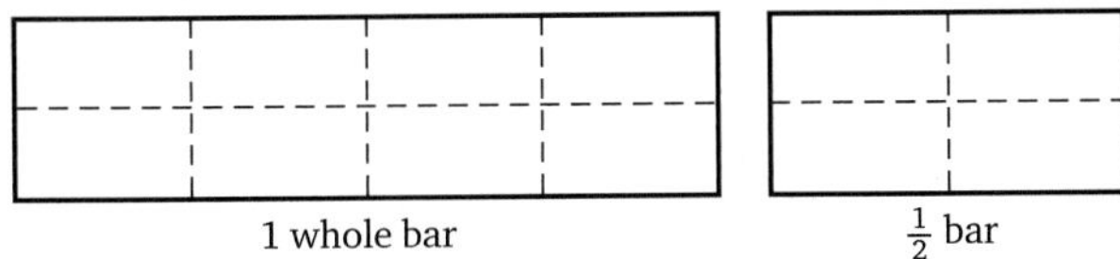

We have $1\frac{1}{2}$ bars, and $1\frac{1}{2}$ is called a *mixed number*.

Another way of describing the amount of chocolate is to say that we have three half bars.

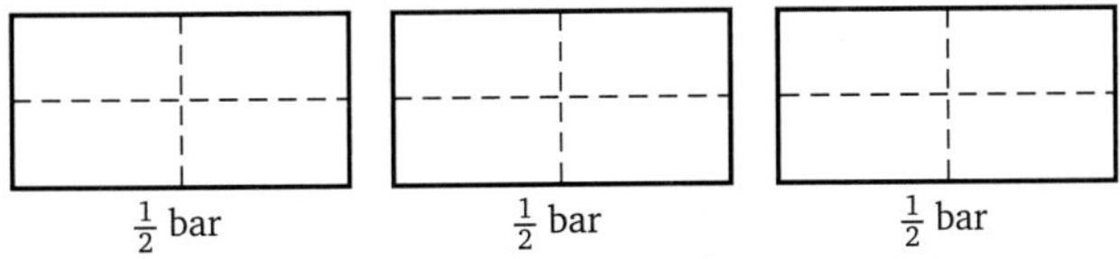

We have $\frac{3}{2}$ bars and $\frac{3}{2}$ is called an *improper* fraction because the numerator is bigger than the denominator.

But the amount of chocolate in the two examples is the same, so

$$\frac{3}{2} = 1\frac{1}{2}$$

Improper fractions can be changed into mixed numbers by finding out how many whole units there are. We know that three thirds $\left(\frac{3}{3}\right)$ is one whole, therefore

$$\frac{8}{3} = \frac{3}{3} + \frac{3}{3} + \frac{2}{3} \text{ (gives two wholes and two thirds)}$$
$$= 2\frac{2}{3}$$

Exercise 5k

In questions **1** to **20** change the improper fractions into mixed numbers:

Find the number of 4s in 9: this gives the units. The remainder is the numbers of quarters.

1 $\frac{9}{4}$

2 $\frac{19}{4}$

3 $\frac{37}{6}$

4 $\frac{53}{10}$

5 $\frac{88}{9}$

6 $\frac{7}{2}$

7 $\frac{27}{4}$

8 $\frac{41}{8}$

9 $\frac{127}{5}$

10 $\frac{114}{11}$

11 $\frac{109}{8}$

12 $\frac{83}{7}$

13 $\frac{121}{9}$

14 $\frac{91}{6}$

15 $\frac{87}{11}$

16 $\frac{77}{6}$

17 $\frac{41}{3}$

18 $\frac{67}{5}$

19 $\frac{73}{3}$

20 $\frac{49}{10}$

Puzzle

An old lady went to market with a basket of eggs. To the first customer she sold half of what she had plus half an egg. The second customer bought half of what remained plus half an egg and the third customer bought half of what now remained and half an egg. That left the lady with thirty-six eggs. There were no broken eggs at any time. How many eggs did she have in her basket at the start?

We can also change mixed numbers into improper fractions. For instance, in $2\frac{4}{5}$ we have two whole units and $\frac{4}{5}$. In each whole unit there are five fifths, so in $2\frac{4}{5}$ we have ten fifths and four fifths, i.e.

$$2\frac{4}{5} = \frac{10}{5} + \frac{4}{5} = \frac{14}{5}$$

Exercise 5I

Change $3\frac{1}{7}$ into an improper fraction.

$$\begin{aligned} 3\frac{1}{7} &= 3 + \frac{1}{7} \\ &= \frac{21}{7} + \frac{1}{7} \\ &= \frac{22}{7} \end{aligned}$$

In $3\frac{1}{7}$ we have 3 whole units and $\frac{1}{7}$. There are seven sevenths in 1 whole, 14 sevenths in 2 wholes and 21 sevenths in 3 wholes. So in $3\frac{1}{7}$ we have 21 sevenths plus one seventh. Altogether, we have 22 sevenths.

In questions **1** to **20** change the mixed numbers into improper fractions:

1	$4\frac{1}{3}$	**5**	$8\frac{1}{7}$	**9**	$3\frac{2}{3}$	**13**	$3\frac{4}{5}$	**17**	$1\frac{9}{10}$
2	$8\frac{1}{4}$	**6**	$6\frac{3}{5}$	**10**	$5\frac{1}{2}$	**14**	$4\frac{7}{9}$	**18**	$6\frac{2}{3}$
3	$1\frac{7}{10}$	**7**	$2\frac{6}{7}$	**11**	$7\frac{2}{5}$	**15**	$8\frac{3}{4}$	**19**	$7\frac{3}{8}$
4	$10\frac{8}{9}$	**8**	$4\frac{1}{6}$	**12**	$2\frac{4}{9}$	**16**	$10\frac{3}{7}$	**20**	$10\frac{1}{10}$

The meaning of 13 ÷ 5

$13 \div 5$ means ‘how many fives are there in 13?’.

There are 2 fives in 13 with 3 left over, so $15 \div 5 = 2$, remainder 3.

Note that the remainder, 3, is $\frac{3}{5}$ of 5. Thus we can say that there are $2\frac{3}{5}$ fives in 13

i.e. $\quad 13 \div 5 = 2\frac{3}{5}$

But $\quad \frac{13}{5} = 2\frac{3}{5}$ $\quad$ Therefore $\quad 13 \div 5$ and $\frac{13}{5}$ mean the same thing.

Exercise 5m

Find 27 ÷ 8

$$27 \div 8 = \frac{27}{8}$$

There are 3 eighths in 27 with 3 left over: so there are 3 units and 3 eighths.

$$= 3\frac{3}{8}$$

Calculate the following divisions, giving your answers as mixed numbers:

1	$36 \div 7$	**4**	$20 \div 8$	**7**	$41 \div 3$	**10**	$107 \div 10$
2	$59 \div 6$	**5**	$82 \div 5$	**8**	$64 \div 9$	**11**	$37 \div 5$
3	$52 \div 11$	**6**	$29 \div 4$	**9**	$98 \div 12$	**12**	$52 \div 8$

Adding mixed numbers

If we want to find the value of $2\frac{1}{3}+3\frac{1}{4}$ we add the whole numbers and then the fractions, i.e.

$$\begin{aligned} 2\frac{1}{3}+3\frac{1}{4} &= 2+3+\frac{1}{3}+\frac{1}{4} \\ &= 5+\frac{4+3}{12} \\ &= 5+\frac{7}{12} \\ &= 5\frac{7}{12} \end{aligned}$$

Sometimes there is an extra step in the calculation. For example

$$\begin{aligned} 3\frac{1}{2}+2\frac{3}{8}+5\frac{1}{4} &= 3+2+5+\frac{1}{2}+\frac{3}{8}+\frac{1}{4} \\ &= 10+\frac{4+3+2}{8} \\ &= 10+\frac{9}{8} \end{aligned}$$

But $\frac{9}{8}$ is an improper fraction, so we change it into a mixed number, i.e.

$$\begin{aligned} 3\frac{1}{2}+2\frac{3}{8}+5\frac{1}{4} &= 10+\frac{8+1}{8} \\ &= 10+1+\frac{1}{8} \\ &= 11\frac{1}{8} \end{aligned}$$

Exercise 5n

Find:

1 $2\frac{1}{4}+3\frac{1}{2}$

2 $1\frac{1}{2}+2\frac{1}{3}$

3 $4\frac{1}{5}+1\frac{3}{8}$

4 $5\frac{1}{9}+4\frac{1}{3}$

5 $3\frac{1}{4}+2\frac{5}{9}$

6 $1\frac{1}{3}+2\frac{5}{6}$

7 $3\frac{1}{4}+1\frac{1}{5}$

8 $2\frac{1}{7}+1\frac{1}{14}$

9 $6\frac{3}{10}+1\frac{2}{5}$

10 $8\frac{1}{7}+5\frac{2}{3}$

11 $7\frac{3}{8}+3\frac{7}{16}$

12 $1\frac{3}{4}+4\frac{7}{12}$

13 $3\frac{5}{7}+7\frac{1}{2}$

14 $6\frac{1}{2}+1\frac{9}{16}$

15 $8\frac{7}{8}+3\frac{3}{16}$

16 $2\frac{7}{10}+9\frac{1}{5}$

17 $5\frac{7}{10}+2\frac{3}{5}$

18 $9\frac{2}{3}+8\frac{5}{6}$

19 $2\frac{4}{5}+7\frac{3}{10}$

20 $6\frac{3}{10}+4\frac{4}{5}$

21 $1\frac{1}{4}+3\frac{2}{3}+6\frac{7}{12}$

22 $5\frac{1}{7}+4\frac{1}{2}+7\frac{11}{14}$

23 $3\frac{3}{4}+5\frac{1}{8}+8\frac{5}{16}$

24 $10\frac{2}{3}+3\frac{1}{6}+7\frac{2}{9}$

25 $4\frac{4}{5}+9\frac{4}{15}+1\frac{1}{3}$

26 $4\frac{3}{5}+8\frac{7}{10}+2\frac{1}{2}$

27 $3\frac{7}{10}+9\frac{21}{100}+1\frac{3}{5}$

28 $4\frac{1}{4}+7\frac{1}{8}+6\frac{1}{32}$

29 $1\frac{5}{7}+11\frac{1}{2}+9\frac{1}{14}$

30 $10\frac{7}{9}+6\frac{1}{3}+5\frac{7}{18}$

Remember that $2\frac{1}{4}$ means $2+\frac{1}{4}$ and that $3\frac{1}{2}$ means $3+\frac{1}{2}$. Add the units first, then add the fractions. Always check the fraction in your answer: if it is improper change it to a mixed number, then add the units.

Subtracting mixed numbers

If we want to find the value of $5\frac{3}{4}-2\frac{2}{5}$ we can use the same method as for adding:

$$\begin{aligned}5\frac{3}{4}-2\frac{2}{5} &= 5-2+\frac{3}{4}-\frac{2}{5}\\ &= 3+\frac{15-8}{20}\\ &= 3+\frac{7}{20}\\ &= 3\frac{7}{20}\end{aligned}$$

But when we find the value of $6\frac{1}{4}-2\frac{4}{5}$ we get

$$6\frac{1}{4}-2\frac{4}{5}=6-2+\frac{1}{4}-\frac{4}{5}$$
$$=4+\frac{1}{4}-\frac{4}{5}$$

This time it is not so easy to deal with the fractions because $\frac{4}{5}$ is bigger than $\frac{1}{4}$. So we take one of the whole units and change it into a fraction, giving

$$3+1+\frac{1}{4}-\frac{4}{5}$$
$$=3+\frac{20+5-16}{20}$$
$$=3+\frac{9}{20}$$
$$=3\frac{9}{20}$$

Exercise 5p

Find:

1 $2\frac{3}{4}-1\frac{1}{8}$

2 $3\frac{2}{3}-1\frac{4}{5}$

3 $1\frac{5}{6}-\frac{2}{3}$

4 $3\frac{1}{4}-2\frac{1}{2}$

5 $7\frac{3}{4}-2\frac{1}{3}$

6 $3\frac{5}{6}-2\frac{1}{3}$

7 $2\frac{6}{7}-1\frac{1}{2}$

8 $4\frac{1}{2}-2\frac{1}{5}$

9 $4\frac{4}{5}-3\frac{1}{10}$

10 $6\frac{5}{7}-3\frac{2}{5}$

11 $3\frac{1}{3}-1\frac{1}{5}$

12 $5\frac{3}{4}-2\frac{1}{2}$

13 $8\frac{4}{5}-5\frac{1}{2}$

14 $5\frac{7}{9}-3\frac{5}{7}$

15 $4\frac{5}{8}-1\frac{1}{3}$

16 $6\frac{3}{4}-3\frac{6}{7}$

17 $7\frac{1}{2}-5\frac{3}{4}$

18 $4\frac{3}{5}-1\frac{1}{4}$

19 $7\frac{6}{7}-4\frac{3}{5}$

20 $8\frac{8}{11}-2\frac{2}{3}$

21 $8\frac{6}{7}-5\frac{3}{4}$

22 $3\frac{1}{2}-1\frac{7}{8}$

23 $2\frac{1}{2}-1\frac{3}{4}$

24 $5\frac{4}{7}-3\frac{4}{5}$

25 $3\frac{1}{4}-1\frac{7}{8}$

26 $5\frac{3}{5}-2\frac{9}{10}$

You will need to change one of the units into a fraction.

27 $9\frac{7}{10}-6\frac{1}{5}$

28 $6\frac{3}{10}-3\frac{4}{5}$

29 $8\frac{2}{3}-7\frac{8}{9}$

30 $4\frac{1}{6}-2\frac{2}{3}$

31 $6\frac{2}{3}-3\frac{5}{6}$

32 $7\frac{3}{4}-4\frac{7}{8}$

33 $9\frac{7}{10}-5\frac{4}{5}$

34 $2\frac{5}{12}-1\frac{3}{4}$

35 $4\frac{7}{9}-3\frac{11}{18}$

36 $5\frac{1}{3}-2\frac{4}{7}$

Puzzle

Fred is an old man. He lived one-eighth of his life as a boy, one-twelfth as a youth, one-half as a man and has spent 28 years in his old age. How old is Fred now?

Mixed exercises

Exercise 5q

1 Calculate:

a $\frac{2}{3}+\frac{4}{7}$

b $\frac{5}{6}-\frac{3}{8}$

c $\frac{3}{8}+\frac{1}{9}$

d $1\frac{1}{2}+\frac{2}{3}$

e $2\frac{1}{4}-1\frac{1}{3}$

2 Simplify:

a $\frac{54}{24}$

b $3\frac{15}{75}$

3 Write the first quantity as a fraction of the second quantity:

a 3 days; 1 week

b 17 children; 30 children

4 Write the following fractions in ascending size order:

a $\frac{1}{2}, \frac{7}{10}, \frac{3}{5}, \frac{13}{20}$

b $\frac{3}{4}, \frac{7}{12}, \frac{5}{6}, \frac{2}{3}$

c $\frac{3}{5}, \frac{7}{10}, \frac{17}{20}, \frac{71}{100}$

5 Write either $>$ or $<$ between the following pairs of fractions, to make true statements:

a $\frac{5}{12} \quad \frac{7}{16}$

b $\frac{3}{8} \quad \frac{7}{24}$

c $\frac{13}{22} \quad \frac{19}{33}$

6 A cricket club consists of 7 members who are good batsmen only, 5 who are good bowlers only, 4 all-rounders and some non-players. If there are 22 people in the club, what fraction of them are

a non-players

b good batsmen only?

Exercise 5r

Select the letter that gives the correct answer.

1 $\frac{2}{3}+\frac{4}{7}=$

A $1\frac{1}{7}$ B $1\frac{2}{7}$ C $1\frac{5}{21}$ D $1\frac{3}{7}$

2 $2\frac{1}{4}-1\frac{1}{3}=$

A $\frac{3}{4}$ B $\frac{5}{6}$ C $\frac{11}{12}$ D $\frac{13}{12}$

3 Six days as a fraction of one week is

A $\frac{1}{5}$ B $\frac{1}{7}$ C $\frac{5}{7}$ D $\frac{6}{7}$

4 The fraction $\frac{54}{24}$ simplifies to

A $1\frac{3}{4}$ B $2\frac{1}{4}$ C $2\frac{1}{2}$ D $2\frac{3}{4}$

5 Which of the fractions $\frac{1}{2}, \frac{7}{10}, \frac{3}{5}, \frac{13}{20}$ is the largest?

A $\frac{1}{2}$ B $\frac{3}{5}$ C $\frac{7}{10}$ D $\frac{13}{20}$

6 $5\frac{1}{4}-2\frac{3}{5}=$

A $2\frac{13}{20}$ B $2\frac{9}{10}$ C $2\frac{19}{20}$ D $3\frac{1}{20}$

Exercise 5s

1 Calculate:

a $\frac{6}{7}+\frac{1}{5}-\frac{3}{4}$ c $\frac{1}{2}+\frac{7}{8}-1\frac{1}{4}$ e $4\frac{1}{5}-5\frac{1}{2}+1\frac{3}{10}$

b $\frac{3}{5}+\frac{4}{9}-\frac{2}{3}$ d $2\frac{1}{4}-1\frac{1}{3}+2\frac{1}{6}$ f $6\frac{1}{3}-2\frac{4}{5}+1\frac{7}{15}$

2 Simplify:

a $1\frac{18}{48}$ b $2\frac{18}{45}$ c $\frac{10}{32}$

3 Write either > or < between the following pairs of fractions:

a $\frac{5}{8}$ $\frac{7}{11}$ b $\frac{4}{5}$ $\frac{5}{6}$

4 Arrange the following fractions in ascending size order:

a $\frac{3}{4}, \frac{3}{5}, \frac{1}{2}, \frac{5}{6}$ b $\frac{1}{2}, \frac{5}{6}, \frac{5}{9}, \frac{2}{3}$

5 Write the first quantity as a fraction of the second quantity:

a 7 minutes; 1 hour

b 1200 people; 3600 people

c 76 c; $1.58

6 In a bag of potatoes there are 6 large good ones, 11 small good ones and 2 rotten ones. What fraction of the potatoes in the bag are

a good ones　　b not large good ones?

Exercise 5t

1 Calculate:

a $\frac{4}{5}+\frac{2}{3}-\frac{3}{10}$　　c $1\frac{1}{3}+\frac{5}{6}-2\frac{1}{12}$　　e $2\frac{1}{3}-3\frac{1}{4}+1\frac{5}{6}$

b $\frac{7}{8}+\frac{3}{5}-\frac{17}{20}$　　d $3\frac{1}{5}-2\frac{1}{4}+1\frac{1}{2}$　　f $6\frac{3}{4}-4\frac{2}{3}+1\frac{7}{12}$

2 Simplify:

a $4\frac{12}{32}$　　b $\frac{30}{240}$　　c $\frac{108}{42}$

3 Write the first quantity as a fraction of the second quantity:

a 5 hours; 24 hours

b 6 seconds; 1 minute

c 5 months; 1 year

4 Write either > or < between the following pairs of fractions:

a $\frac{7}{10}\quad\frac{5}{9}$　　b $\frac{2}{3}\quad\frac{5}{7}$

5 Arrange the following fractions in ascending size order:

a $\frac{5}{11}, \frac{1}{2}, \frac{13}{22}, \frac{23}{44}$　　b $\frac{2}{3}, \frac{5}{9}, \frac{3}{4}, \frac{7}{12}$

6 A vase of flowers contains 5 pink ones, 3 red ones and 7 white ones. What fraction of the flowers in the vase are

a red　　b not white　　c pink?

Did you know?

Did you know that the almanac writer Benjamin Banneker (1731–1806) was the son of a freed slave? He taught himself mathematics and chemistry. It is said that he became a long time correspondent of Thomas Jefferson.

In this chapter you have seen that...

- ✔ you can find a fraction equivalent to a given fraction by multiplying the numerator and denominator by the same number
- ✔ you can simplify fractions by dividing the numerator and denominator by their common factors
- ✔ you can add and subtract fractions by changing them to equivalent fractions with the same denominator
- ✔ you can find one quantity as a fraction of another by first making sure that they are in the same units, then by placing the first quantity over the second
- ✔ $15 \div 4$ and $\frac{15}{4}$ mean the same thing
- ✔ you can compare the size of fractions by changing them to equivalent fractions with the same denominator and then comparing their numerators
- ✔ as with whole numbers, the order in which you add and subtract fractions does not matter, but it is often convenient to do the addition first.

6 Fractions: multiplication and division

At the end of this chapter you should be able to...

1 solve word problems involving fractional operations

2 perform operations involving multiplication and division of fractions including mixed numbers.

Did you know?

This is a technique for simplifying fractions.

Find the difference between the numerator and the denominator, and then divide each by the difference.

For example: simplify $\frac{112}{119}$.

Difference between numerator and denominator = 119 − 112 = 7.

$$112 \div 7 = 16 \qquad 119 \div 7 = 17$$

$$\therefore \quad \frac{112}{119} = \frac{16}{17}$$

If this does not work, divide by factors of the difference.

For example: simplify $\frac{117}{135}$.

Difference between numerator and denominator = 135 − 117 = 18.

18 is not a common factor.

Try the largest factor of 18, i.e. 9.

$$135 \div 9 = 15 \qquad 117 \div 9 = 13$$

$$\therefore \quad \frac{117}{135} = \frac{13}{15}$$

You need to know...

✔ how to add and subtract fractions

✔ how to simplify a fraction

✔ how to express a mixed number as an improper fraction and how to express an improper fraction as a mixed number

✔ how to convert a fraction into an equivalent fraction with a different denominator.

Key words

cancel, common factor, denominator, expression, improper fraction, mixed number, mixed operation, numerator, product

Multiplying fractions

When fractions are multiplied the result is given by multiplying together the numbers in the numerator and also multiplying together the numbers in the denominator.

For example

$$\frac{1}{2} \times \frac{1}{3} = \frac{1 \times 1}{2 \times 3}$$
$$= \frac{1}{6}$$

If we look at a cake diagram we can see that $\frac{1}{2}$ of $\frac{1}{3}$ of the cake is $\frac{1}{6}$ of the cake.

So $\frac{1}{2}$ of $\frac{1}{3} = \frac{1}{6}$

and $\frac{1}{2} \times \frac{1}{3} = \frac{1}{6}$

We see that 'of' means 'multiplied by'.

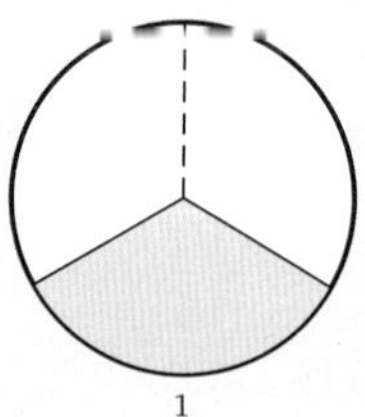
$\frac{1}{3}$

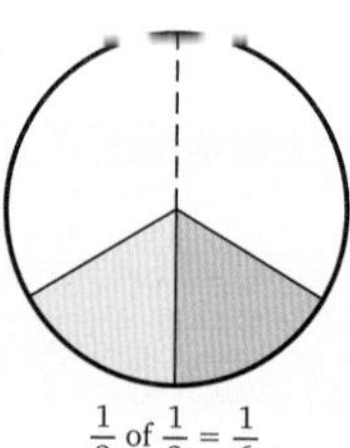
$\frac{1}{2}$ of $\frac{1}{3} = \frac{1}{6}$

Exercise 6a

Draw diagrams to show that:

1 $\frac{1}{2} \times \frac{1}{4} = \frac{1}{8}$

2 $\frac{1}{3} \times \frac{1}{2} = \frac{1}{6}$

3 $\frac{1}{2} \times \frac{3}{4} = \frac{3}{8}$

4 $\frac{2}{3} \times \frac{1}{3} = \frac{2}{9}$

5 $\frac{1}{3} \times \frac{2}{5} = \frac{2}{15}$

6 $\frac{1}{4} \times \frac{1}{3} = \frac{1}{12}$

Simplifying

Sometimes we can simplify a product by *cancelling* the common factors.

For example

$$\frac{2}{3} \times \frac{3}{4} = \frac{2 \times 3}{3 \times 4} = \frac{\cancel{2}^{1}}{\cancel{3}_{1}} \times \frac{\cancel{3}^{1}}{\cancel{4}_{2}} = \frac{1 \times 1}{1 \times 2}$$
$$= \frac{1}{2}$$

You can see that 3 is a common factor of the top and the bottom, so can be cancelled. Similarly 2 is a common factor of the top number (2) and the bottom number (4), so we can also cancel the 2.

The diagram shows that

$\frac{2}{3}$ of $\frac{3}{4} = \frac{1}{2}$

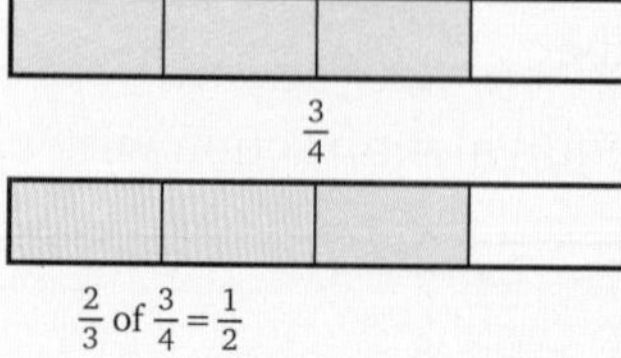

Exercise 6b

Find $\frac{4}{25}\times\frac{15}{16}$

$\frac{\not{4}^{1}}{_{5}\not{25}}\times\frac{\not{15}^{3}}{\not{16}_{4}}$ Cancel 5, which is a common factor of 15 and 25, and 4, which is a common factor of 4 and 16.

$=\frac{1\times3}{5\times4}=\frac{3}{20}$

Find:

1 $\frac{3}{4}\times\frac{1}{2}$

2 $\frac{2}{3}\times\frac{5}{7}$

3 $\frac{2}{5}\times\frac{1}{3}$

4 $\frac{1}{2}\times\frac{7}{8}$

5 $\frac{3}{4}\times\frac{4}{7}$

6 $\frac{4}{9}\times\frac{1}{7}$

7 $\frac{3}{7}\times\frac{2}{5}$

8 $\frac{2}{5}\times\frac{3}{5}$

9 $\frac{5}{6}\times\frac{1}{4}$

10 $\frac{2}{3}\times\frac{7}{9}$

11 $\frac{3}{4}\times\frac{1}{5}$

12 $\frac{1}{7}\times\frac{3}{5}$

13 $\frac{7}{8}\times\frac{4}{21}$

14 $\frac{3}{4}\times\frac{16}{21}$

15 $\frac{21}{22}\times\frac{11}{27}$

16 $\frac{8}{9}\times\frac{33}{44}$

17 $\frac{7}{9}\times\frac{3}{21}$

18 $\frac{3}{4}\times\frac{5}{7}$

19 $\frac{4}{5}\times\frac{15}{16}$

20 $\frac{10}{11}\times\frac{33}{35}$

21 $\frac{4}{15}\times\frac{25}{64}$

22 $\frac{2}{3}\times\frac{33}{40}$

23 $\frac{3}{7}\times\frac{28}{33}$

24 $\frac{48}{55}\times\frac{5}{12}$

Find:

25 $\frac{3}{7}\times\frac{5}{9}\times\frac{14}{15}$

26 $\frac{11}{21}\times\frac{30}{31}\times\frac{7}{55}$

27 $\frac{15}{16}\times\frac{8}{9}\times\frac{4}{5}$

28 $\frac{5}{6}\times\frac{8}{25}\times\frac{3}{4}$

29 $\frac{3}{10}\times\frac{5}{9}\times\frac{6}{7}$

30 $\frac{5}{7}\times\frac{3}{8}\times\frac{21}{30}$

31 $\frac{1}{2}\times\frac{7}{12}\times\frac{18}{35}$

32 $\frac{7}{11}\times\frac{8}{9}\times\frac{33}{28}$

33 $\frac{6}{5}\times\frac{4}{3}\times\frac{10}{4}$

34 $\frac{9}{8}\times\frac{1}{3}\times\frac{4}{27}$

35 $\frac{7}{16}\times\frac{9}{11}\times\frac{8}{21}$

36 $\frac{5}{14}\times\frac{21}{25}\times\frac{5}{9}$

Express as $\frac{3\times5\times14}{7\times9\times15}$ then look for common factors in the numerator and denominator.

Puzzle

What is one-half of two-thirds of three-quarters of four-fifths of five-sixths of six-sevenths of seven-eighths of eight-ninths of nine-tenths of 500?

Multiplying mixed numbers

Suppose that we want to find the value of $2\frac{1}{3}\times\frac{5}{21}\times1\frac{1}{5}$.

We cannot multiply mixed numbers together unless we change them into improper fractions first. So we change $2\frac{1}{3}$ into $\frac{7}{3}$ and we change $1\frac{1}{5}$ into $\frac{6}{5}$.

Then we can use the same method as before, e.g. $2\frac{1}{3}\times\frac{5}{21}\times1\frac{1}{5}=\frac{7\times5\times6}{3\times21\times5}$.

Now look for common factors to cancel.

Exercise 6c

Find $2\frac{1}{3}\times\frac{5}{21}\times1\frac{1}{5}$

$$2\frac{1}{3}\times\frac{5}{21}\times1\frac{1}{5}=\frac{7}{3}\times\frac{5}{21}\times\frac{6}{5}$$

$$=\frac{\cancel{7}^{1}\times\cancel{5}^{1}\times\cancel{6}^{2}}{\cancel{3}_{1}\times\cancel{21}_{3}\times\cancel{5}_{1}}$$

$$=\frac{2}{3}$$

Find:

1 $1\frac{1}{2}\times\frac{2}{5}$

2 $2\frac{1}{2}\times\frac{4}{5}$

3 $3\frac{1}{4}\times\frac{3}{13}$

4 $4\frac{2}{3}\times2\frac{2}{5}$

5 $2\frac{1}{5}\times\frac{5}{22}$

6 $1\frac{1}{4}\times\frac{2}{5}$

7 $2\frac{1}{3}\times\frac{3}{8}$

8 $\frac{10}{11}\times2\frac{1}{5}$

9 $3\frac{1}{2}\times4\frac{2}{3}$

10 $4\frac{1}{4}\times\frac{4}{21}$

11 $5\frac{1}{4}\times2\frac{2}{3}$

12 $3\frac{5}{7}\times1\frac{1}{13}$

13 $8\frac{1}{3}\times3\frac{3}{5}$

14 $2\frac{1}{10}\times7\frac{6}{7}$

15 $6\frac{3}{10}\times1\frac{4}{21}$

16 $4\frac{2}{7}\times2\frac{1}{10}$

17 $6\frac{1}{4}\times1\frac{3}{5}$

18 $5\frac{1}{2}\times1\frac{9}{11}$

19 $8\frac{3}{4}\times2\frac{2}{7}$

20 $16\frac{1}{2}\times3\frac{7}{11}$

21 $6\frac{2}{5}\times1\frac{7}{8}\times\frac{7}{12}$

22 $2\frac{4}{7}\times4\frac{2}{3}\times1\frac{1}{4}$

Remember to look for common factors to cancel.

23 $3\frac{2}{3}\times1\frac{1}{5}\times1\frac{3}{22}$

24 $1\frac{1}{18}\times1\frac{4}{5}\times3\frac{1}{3}$

25 $4\frac{4}{5}\times1\frac{5}{8}\times3\frac{3}{4}$

26 $7\frac{1}{2}\times1\frac{1}{3}\times\frac{9}{10}$

27 $3\frac{1}{5}\times2\frac{1}{2}\times1\frac{3}{4}$

28 $4\frac{1}{2}\times1\frac{1}{7}\times2\frac{1}{3}$

29 $2\frac{1}{3}\times\frac{6}{11}\times2\frac{5}{14}$

30 $3\frac{9}{10}\times1\frac{2}{3}\times1\frac{3}{13}$

Whole numbers as fractions

A whole number can be written as a fraction with a denominator of 1.

For instance $6=\frac{6}{1}$.

Doing this makes it easier to multiply a whole number by a fraction or a mixed number.

Exercise 6d

Find $6\times7\frac{1}{3}$

$$6\times7\frac{1}{3}=\frac{6}{1}\times\frac{22}{3}$$

$$=\frac{\overset{2}{\cancel{6}}\times22}{1\times\cancel{3}_1} \quad \text{(cancel by 3)}$$

$$=\frac{2\times22}{1\times1}=44$$

Find:

1 $5\times4\frac{3}{5}$

2 $2\frac{1}{7}\times14$

3 $3\frac{1}{8}\times4$

4 $4\frac{1}{6}\times9$

5 $18\times6\frac{1}{9}$

6 $4\times3\frac{3}{8}$

7 $3\frac{3}{5}\times10$

8 $2\frac{5}{6}\times3$

9 $5\frac{5}{7}\times21$

10 $3\times6\frac{1}{9}$

11 $1\frac{3}{4}\times8$

12 $28\times1\frac{4}{7}$

Fractions of quantities

Exercise 6e

Find three-fifths of 95 metres.

Remember that 'of' means 'multiply', so to find $\frac{3}{5}$ of 95 you have to multiply $\frac{3}{5}$ by 95.

This is the same as multiplying by $\frac{95}{1}$.

$$\frac{3}{5}\times\frac{95}{1}=\frac{3\times\overset{19}{\cancel{95}}}{\underset{1}{\cancel{5}}\times1}$$

$$=\frac{3\times19}{1\times1} \quad \text{(cancelling by 5)}$$

$$=57$$

$\frac{3}{5}$ of 95 metres is 57 metres.

Find three-quarters of $1.

You need to convert $1 into cents first.

$1 = 100 cents

$$\frac{3}{\cancel{4}_1} \times \frac{\cancel{100}^{25}}{1} = 75$$

$\frac{3}{4}$ of $1 is 75 cents.

Find:

1 $\frac{1}{3}$ of 18

2 $\frac{1}{5}$ of 30

3 $\frac{1}{7}$ of 21

4 $\frac{2}{3}$ of 24

5 $\frac{5}{7}$ of 14

<u>6</u> $\frac{1}{4}$ of 24

<u>7</u> $\frac{1}{6}$ of 30

<u>8</u> $\frac{1}{8}$ of 64

<u>9</u> $\frac{5}{6}$ of 36

<u>10</u> $\frac{3}{8}$ of 40

11 $\frac{3}{5}$ of 20 metres

12 $\frac{5}{9}$ of 45 dollars

13 $\frac{9}{10}$ of 50 litres

14 $\frac{3}{8}$ of 88 miles

15 $\frac{7}{16}$ of 48 gallons

<u>16</u> $\frac{4}{9}$ of 18 metres

<u>17</u> $\frac{5}{8}$ of 16 dollars

<u>18</u> $\frac{4}{9}$ of 63 litres

<u>19</u> $\frac{3}{7}$ of 35 miles

<u>20</u> $\frac{8}{11}$ of 121 gallons

21 $\frac{1}{4}$ of $2

22 $\frac{2}{9}$ of 36 cents

23 $\frac{3}{10}$ of $1

24 $\frac{2}{7}$ of 42 cents

25 $\frac{4}{5}$ of 1 year (365 days)

<u>26</u> $\frac{3}{8}$ of 1 day (24 hours)

<u>27</u> $\frac{1}{7}$ of 1 week

<u>28</u> $\frac{1}{3}$ of $9

<u>29</u> $\frac{3}{5}$ of $1

<u>30</u> $\frac{7}{8}$ of 1 day (24 hours)

Dividing by fractions

When we divide 6 by 3 we are finding how many threes there are in 6 and we say $6 \div 3 = 2$.

In the same way, when we divide 10 by $\frac{1}{2}$ we are finding how many halves there are in 10; we know that in 1 whole number there are 2 halves,

i.e. $\frac{1}{1} \div \frac{1}{2} = 2$ (1 divided by one-half equals 2)

But $\frac{1}{1} \times \frac{2}{1} = 2$ (1 times 2 equals 2)

So $\frac{1}{1} \div \frac{1}{2} = \frac{1}{1} \times \frac{2}{1}$ (therefore 1 divided by one-half gives the same result as 1 times 2)

Also, in 2 wholes there are 4 halves:

i.e. $\frac{2}{1} \div \frac{1}{2} = 4$ (2 divided by one-half equals 4)

and $\frac{2}{1} \times \frac{2}{1} = 4$ (2 times 2 equals 4)

So $\frac{2}{1} \div \frac{1}{2} = \frac{2}{1} \times \frac{2}{1} = 4$ (therefore 2 divided by one-half gives the same result as 2 times 2)

Continuing in this way, we see that in 10 wholes there are 20 halves,

i.e. $\frac{10}{1} \div \frac{1}{2} = 20$ (10 divided by one-half equals 20)

and $\frac{10}{1} \times \frac{2}{1} = 20$ (10 times 2 equals 20)

So $\frac{10}{1} \div \frac{1}{2} = \frac{10}{1} \times \frac{2}{1} = 20$ (therefore 10 divided by one-half gives the same result as 10 times 2)

From the above examples, we divided by a fraction by 'turning the fraction upside down' (inverting it) and then multiplying.

This rule holds for division by fractions.

To divide by a fraction we turn that fraction upside down and multiply.

Exercise 6f

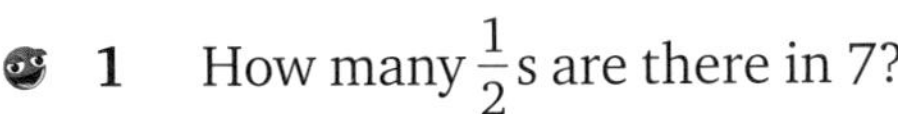

1 How many $\frac{1}{2}$s are there in 7?

2 How many $\frac{1}{4}$s are there in 5?

3 How many times does $\frac{1}{7}$ go into 3?

4 How many $\frac{3}{5}$s are there in 9?

5 How many times does $\frac{2}{3}$ go into 8?

Find:

6 $8 \div \frac{4}{5}$

7 $18 \div \frac{6}{7}$

8 $40 \div \frac{8}{9}$

9 $72 \div \frac{8}{11}$

<u>10</u> $28 \div \frac{14}{15}$

<u>11</u> $15 \div \frac{5}{6}$

<u>12</u> $14 \div \frac{7}{8}$

<u>13</u> $35 \div \frac{5}{7}$

14 $44 \div \frac{4}{9}$ **15** $27 \div \frac{9}{13}$ **16** $36 \div \frac{4}{7}$ **17** $34 \div \frac{17}{19}$

18 $\frac{21}{32} \div \frac{7}{8}$ **19** $\frac{9}{25} \div \frac{3}{10}$ **20** $\frac{3}{56} \div \frac{9}{14}$ **21** $\frac{21}{22} \div \frac{7}{11}$

22 $\frac{8}{75} \div \frac{4}{15}$ **23** $\frac{35}{42} \div \frac{5}{6}$ **24** $\frac{28}{27} \div \frac{4}{9}$ **25** $\frac{22}{45} \div \frac{11}{15}$

26 $\frac{15}{26} \div \frac{5}{13}$ **27** $\frac{49}{50} \div \frac{7}{10}$ **28** $\frac{8}{21} \div \frac{4}{7}$ **29** $\frac{9}{26} \div \frac{12}{13}$

Dividing by whole numbers and mixed numbers

If we want to divide 3 by 5 we can say

$$3 \div 5 = \frac{3}{1} \div \frac{5}{1} \quad \text{(3 divided by 5)}$$

$$= \frac{3}{1} \times \frac{1}{5} \quad \text{(3 times one-fifth)}$$

$$= \frac{3}{5} \quad \text{(three-fifths)}$$

So $3 \div 5$ is the same as $\frac{3}{5}$. Similarly $7 \div 11$ is $\frac{7}{11}$.

Division with mixed numbers can be done as long as all the mixed numbers are first changed into improper fractions. For example if we want to divide $2\frac{1}{2}$ by $1\frac{1}{4}$ we first change $2\frac{1}{2}$ into $\frac{5}{2}$ and $1\frac{1}{4}$ into $\frac{5}{4}$. Then we can use the same method as before.

Exercise 6g

Find the value of $2\frac{1}{2} \div 1\frac{1}{4}$.

$2\frac{1}{2} \div 1\frac{1}{4} = \frac{5}{2} \div \frac{5}{4}$ (Express each mixed number as an improper fraction.)

$= \frac{5}{2} \times \frac{4}{5}$ (To divide by a fraction turn it upside down and multiply.)

$= \frac{20}{10} = 2$

Give the answer to:

1 $5\frac{4}{9} \div \frac{14}{27}$

2 $3\frac{1}{8} \div 3\frac{3}{4}$

3 $7\frac{1}{5} \div 1\frac{7}{20}$

4 Divide $8\frac{1}{4}$ by $1\frac{3}{8}$

5 Divide $6\frac{2}{3}$ by $2\frac{4}{9}$

6 $4\frac{2}{7} \div \frac{9}{14}$

7 $5\frac{5}{8} \div 6\frac{1}{4}$

8 $6\frac{4}{9} \div 1\frac{1}{3}$

9 Divide $5\frac{1}{4}$ by $2\frac{11}{12}$

10 Divide $7\frac{1}{7}$ by $1\frac{11}{14}$

11 $10\frac{2}{3} \div 1\frac{7}{9}$

12 $8\frac{4}{5} \div 3\frac{3}{10}$

13 Divide $11\frac{1}{4}$ by $\frac{15}{16}$

14 Divide $9\frac{1}{7}$ by $1\frac{11}{21}$

15 $31\frac{1}{2} \div 5\frac{5}{8}$

16 $9\frac{3}{4} \div 1\frac{5}{8}$

17 $12\frac{1}{2} \div 8\frac{3}{4}$

18 Divide $10\frac{5}{6}$ by $3\frac{1}{4}$

19 Divide $8\frac{2}{3}$ by $5\frac{7}{9}$

20 $22\frac{2}{3} \div 1\frac{8}{9}$

Investigation

Investigate what happens to a number when you multiply it by a fraction which is less than 1.

Does it matter whether the number itself is more or less than 1?

Mixed multiplication and division

Suppose we want to find the value of an *expression* like $2\frac{1}{4} \times \frac{3}{14} \div 1\frac{2}{7}$.
Two things need to be done:

Step 1 If there are any mixed numbers, change them into improper fractions.

Step 2 Turn the fraction *after* the ÷ sign upside down and change ÷ into ×.

Then

$$2\frac{1}{4} \times \frac{3}{14} \div 1\frac{2}{7} = \frac{9}{4} \times \frac{3}{14} \div \frac{9}{7}$$ (mixed numbers changed to improper fractions)

$$= \frac{\overset{1}{\cancel{9}}}{4} \times \frac{3}{\underset{2}{\cancel{14}}} \times \frac{\overset{1}{\cancel{7}}}{\underset{1}{\cancel{9}}}$$ ($\frac{9}{7}$ turned upside down and ÷ changed to ×)

$$= \frac{3}{8}$$

Exercise 6h

Find:

1 $\frac{5}{8} \times 1\frac{1}{2} \div \frac{15}{16}$

2 $2\frac{3}{4} \times \frac{5}{6} \div \frac{11}{12}$

3 $\frac{2}{3} \times 1\frac{1}{5} \div \frac{12}{25}$

4 $\frac{4}{7} \times \frac{8}{9} \div \frac{16}{21}$

5 $\frac{2}{5} \times \frac{9}{10} \div \frac{27}{40}$

6 $\frac{3}{4} \times 2\frac{1}{3} \div \frac{21}{32}$

7 $3\frac{2}{5} \times \frac{4}{5} \div \frac{8}{15}$

8 $\frac{3}{7} \times 2\frac{1}{2} \div \frac{10}{21}$

9 $\frac{3}{5} \times \frac{9}{11} \div \frac{18}{55}$

10 $\frac{1}{4} \times \frac{11}{12} \div \frac{22}{27}$

11 $\frac{3}{7} \times \frac{2}{5} \div \frac{8}{21}$

12 $\frac{14}{25} \times \frac{5}{9} \div \frac{7}{18}$

Mixed operations

When brackets are placed round a pair of fractions it means that we have to work out what is *inside* the brackets before doing anything else.

For example
$$\left(\frac{1}{2}+\frac{1}{4}\right)\times\frac{5}{7}=\left(\frac{2+1}{4}\right)\times\frac{5}{7}$$
$$=\frac{3}{4}\times\frac{5}{7}$$
$$=\frac{15}{28}$$

If we meet an expression in which +, −, × and ÷ occur, we need to know the order in which to do the calculations. We use the same rule for fractions as we used for whole numbers, that is

Brackets first, then Multiply and Divide, then Add and Subtract.

You may remember this order from the sentence

Bless My Dear Aunt Sally.

Exercise 6i

Find $\frac{2}{5}-\frac{1}{2}\times\frac{3}{5}+\frac{1}{10}$

$$\frac{2}{5}-\frac{1}{2}\times\frac{3}{5}+\frac{1}{10}=\frac{2}{5}-\frac{3}{10}+\frac{1}{10}$$ (do the multiplication first)

$$=\frac{4-3+1}{10}$$ (use the LCM to find the common denominator, then add and subtract)

$$=\frac{\cancel{2}^{1}}{\cancel{10}_{5}}$$ (simplify)

$$=\frac{1}{5}$$

Calculate:

1. $\frac{1}{2}+\frac{1}{4}\times\frac{2}{5}$
2. $\frac{2}{3}\times\frac{1}{2}+\frac{1}{4}$
3. $\frac{4}{5}-\frac{3}{10}\div\frac{1}{2}$
4. $\frac{2}{7}\div\frac{2}{3}-\frac{3}{14}$
5. $\frac{4}{5}+\frac{3}{10}\times\frac{2}{9}$
6. $\frac{1}{3}-\frac{1}{2}\times\frac{1}{4}$
7. $\frac{3}{4}\div\frac{1}{2}+\frac{1}{8}$
8. $\frac{1}{7}+\frac{5}{8}\div\frac{3}{4}$
9. $\frac{5}{6}\times\frac{3}{10}-\frac{3}{16}$
10. $\frac{3}{7}-\frac{1}{4}\times\frac{8}{21}$
11. $\left(\frac{4}{9}-\frac{1}{3}\right)\times\frac{6}{7}$
12. $\frac{3}{5}\times\left(\frac{2}{3}+\frac{1}{2}\right)$
13. $\frac{7}{8}\div\left(\frac{3}{4}+\frac{2}{3}\right)$
14. $\left(\frac{3}{10}+\frac{2}{5}\right)\div\frac{7}{15}$
15. $\left(\frac{5}{11}-\frac{1}{3}\right)\times\frac{3}{8}$
16. $\frac{3}{8}\div\left(\frac{2}{3}+\frac{1}{4}\right)$

Work out the value inside the brackets first.

17 $\left(\frac{4}{7}+\frac{1}{3}\right)\div 3\frac{4}{5}$

18 $\frac{5}{9}\times\left(\frac{2}{3}-\frac{1}{6}\right)$

19 $\left(\frac{6}{11}-\frac{1}{2}\right)\div\frac{3}{4}$

20 $\frac{9}{10}\div\left(\frac{1}{6}+\frac{2}{3}\right)$

21 $\frac{1}{6}\times\left(\frac{2}{3}-\frac{1}{2}\right)\div\frac{7}{12}$

22 $\frac{7}{10}\div\left(\frac{2}{5}+\frac{4}{15}\times\frac{3}{5}\right)$

23 $\left(2\frac{1}{4}+\frac{3}{8}\right)\times\frac{2}{3}-1\frac{1}{2}$

24 $1\frac{3}{11}-\frac{6}{7}\times1\frac{5}{9}+\frac{13}{33}$

25 $\frac{5}{8}\times\left(\frac{4}{9}-\frac{1}{6}\right)\div1\frac{9}{16}$

26 $\frac{2}{9}+\left(\frac{6}{7}\div\frac{3}{4}\right)\times3\frac{1}{2}$

27 $1\frac{1}{10}\times\frac{23}{24}\div\left(\frac{3}{5}+\frac{1}{6}\right)$

28 $2\frac{2}{5}-\frac{7}{10}\times\left(\frac{4}{7}-\frac{1}{3}\right)$

29 $\frac{5}{9}\div\left(1\frac{1}{3}+\frac{4}{9}\right)+\frac{3}{8}$

30 $1\frac{2}{9}+\left(\frac{5}{6}-\frac{3}{4}\div4\frac{1}{2}\right)$

State whether each of the following statements is true or false:

31 $\frac{1}{2}\times\frac{2}{3}+\frac{1}{3}=\frac{1}{3}+\frac{1}{3}$

32 $\frac{1}{3}\times\frac{3}{4}+\frac{1}{4}=\frac{1}{3}\times1$

33 $\frac{1}{4}\div\frac{3}{4}+\frac{1}{2}=\frac{1}{3}+\frac{1}{2}$

34 $\frac{1}{3}+\frac{2}{3}\times\frac{1}{4}=\frac{1}{3}+\frac{1}{6}$

35 $\frac{1}{2}+\frac{1}{4}\div\frac{1}{2}=\frac{3}{4}\times\frac{2}{1}$

36 $\frac{3}{4}-\frac{1}{2}\times\frac{2}{3}=\frac{1}{4}\times\frac{2}{3}$

37 $\frac{2}{3}-\frac{1}{4}+\frac{1}{2}=\frac{2}{3}+\frac{1}{2}-\frac{1}{4}$

38 $\frac{3}{5}\times\frac{2}{3}+\frac{1}{2}=\frac{3}{5}+\frac{1}{2}\times\frac{2}{3}$

39 $\frac{4}{7}-\frac{1}{4}\div\frac{1}{3}=\left(\frac{4}{7}-\frac{1}{4}\right)\div\frac{1}{3}$

40 $\frac{3}{8}\div\frac{1}{4}-\frac{1}{4}=\frac{3}{8}\times\frac{4}{1}-\frac{1}{4}$

Exercise 6j

In this exercise you will find +, −, × and ÷. Read the question carefully and then decide which method to use. Find:

1 $1\frac{1}{2}+3\frac{1}{4}$

2 $2\frac{3}{8}-1\frac{1}{4}$

3 $1\frac{1}{5}\times\frac{5}{8}$

4 $3\frac{1}{2}\div\frac{7}{8}$

5 $\frac{4}{7}+1\frac{1}{2}$

6 $4\frac{1}{4}\times\frac{2}{9}$

7 $3\frac{2}{3}\div\frac{1}{6}$

8 $2\frac{1}{5}-1\frac{1}{3}$

9 $5\frac{1}{2}\times\frac{6}{11}$

10 $1\frac{3}{8}+2\frac{1}{2}$

11 $5\frac{1}{2}+\frac{3}{4}$

12 $4\frac{1}{3}\times\frac{6}{13}$

13 $3\frac{4}{5}-2\frac{1}{10}$

14 $3\frac{1}{7}\div1\frac{3}{8}$

15 $4\frac{1}{5}\times\frac{4}{7}$

16 $2\frac{5}{6}\div3\frac{1}{3}$

17 $1\frac{4}{7}+2\frac{1}{2}$

18 $2\frac{3}{4}+1\frac{7}{8}$

19 $2\frac{3}{8}+1\frac{7}{16}$

20 $5\frac{1}{4}\div1\frac{1}{6}$

21 $1\frac{1}{4}+\frac{2}{3}-\frac{5}{6}$

22 $2\frac{1}{2}-\frac{2}{3}-1\frac{1}{4}$

23 $3\frac{1}{2}+1\frac{1}{4}-\frac{5}{8}$

24 $2\frac{1}{3}+1\frac{1}{2}-\frac{3}{4}$

25 $4\frac{1}{8}-5\frac{3}{4}+2\frac{1}{2}$

26 $4\frac{1}{2}-5\frac{1}{4}+2\frac{1}{8}$

27 $3\frac{4}{5}+\frac{3}{10}-1\frac{1}{20}$

28 $5\frac{1}{2}-1\frac{3}{4}-2\frac{1}{4}$

29 $3\frac{1}{7}+2\frac{1}{2}-\frac{3}{14}$

30 $5\frac{1}{2}-\frac{3}{4}-4\frac{1}{4}$

31 $1\frac{1}{2}+2\frac{2}{3}\times\frac{3}{4}$

32 $2\frac{1}{3}\times1\frac{1}{2}-2\frac{1}{2}$

33 $4\frac{1}{3}\div2\frac{1}{6}+\frac{1}{4}$

34 $2\frac{2}{5}-\frac{6}{7}\div\frac{5}{14}$

35 $1\frac{1}{8}\times\frac{4}{9}\div2\frac{1}{2}$

36 $2\frac{3}{8}-1\frac{1}{5}\times1\frac{2}{3}$

37 $1\frac{3}{4}\div4\frac{2}{3}-\frac{5}{16}$

38 $2\frac{1}{7}\times3\frac{1}{4}\div1\frac{5}{8}$

39 $1\frac{1}{2}+2\frac{5}{7}-1\frac{5}{14}$

40 $\frac{3}{5}\times1\frac{1}{4}\div\frac{3}{8}$

Problems

Exercise 6k

If Jane can iron a shirt in $4\frac{3}{4}$ minutes, how long will it take her to iron 10 shirts?

You know the time to iron 1 shirt. It will take 10 times as long to iron 10 shirts.

Time to iron 1 shirt $= 4\frac{3}{4}$ minutes

Time to iron 10 shirts $= 4\frac{3}{4}\times10$ minutes

$= \frac{19}{\cancel{4}_2}\times\frac{\cancel{10}^5}{1}$ minutes

$= \frac{95}{2}$ minutes

$= 47\frac{1}{2}$ minutes

A piece of string of length $22\frac{1}{2}$ cm is to be cut into small pieces each $\frac{3}{4}$ cm long. How many pieces can be obtained?

Number of small pieces = length of string ÷ length of one short piece

You want to find the number of $\frac{3}{4}$ cm pieces in $22\frac{1}{2}$ cm so you need to find $22\frac{1}{2}\div\frac{3}{4}$.

Number of small pieces $= 22\frac{1}{2}\div\frac{3}{4}$

(Express $22\frac{1}{2}$ as an improper fraction and multiply by $\frac{3}{4}$ turned upside down.)

$= \frac{{}^{15}\cancel{45}\times\cancel{4}^{2}}{{}_{1}\cancel{2}\times\cancel{3}_{1}} = 30$

Thus 30 pieces can be obtained.

1 A bag of flour weighs $1\frac{1}{2}$ kilograms. What is the weight of 20 bags?

2 A cook adds $3\frac{1}{2}$ cups of water to a stew. If the cup holds $\frac{1}{10}$ of a litre how many litres of water were added?

3 My journey to school starts with a walk of $\frac{1}{2}$ km to the bus stop, then a bus ride of $2\frac{1}{5}$ km followed by a walk of $\frac{3}{10}$ km. How long is my journey to school?

4 It takes $3\frac{1}{4}$ minutes for a cub scout to clean a pair of shoes. If he cleans 18 pairs of shoes to raise money for charity, how long does he spend on the job?

5 A burger bar chef cooks some beefburgers and piles them one on top of the other. If each burger is $9\frac{1}{2}$ mm thick and the pile is 209 mm high, how many did he cook?

6 If you read 30 pages of a book in $\frac{3}{4}$ of an hour, how many minutes does it take to read each page?

Mixed exercises

Exercise 6I

Select the letter that gives the correct answer.

1 $\frac{3}{14}\times\frac{8}{9}=$

A $\frac{1}{7}$ B $\frac{2}{21}$ C $\frac{4}{21}$ D $\frac{7}{21}$

2 $\frac{5}{9}$ of $\frac{3}{4}$

A $\frac{5}{6}$ B $\frac{11}{12}$ C $\frac{5}{12}$ D $\frac{3}{12}$

3 $\frac{8}{5}\times\frac{3}{4}\times\frac{10}{6}=$

A $\frac{2}{3}$ B $\frac{3}{4}$ C $1\frac{1}{3}$ D 2

4 $3\frac{1}{8}\div3\frac{3}{4}=$

A $\frac{5}{9}$ B $\frac{2}{3}$ C $\frac{5}{6}$ D $\frac{6}{7}$

5 $\frac{9}{10}\div\frac{4}{5}\times\frac{40}{27}=$

A $\frac{4}{15}$ B $\frac{8}{15}$ C $1\frac{1}{15}$ D $1\frac{2}{3}$

6 $1\frac{3}{4}+3\frac{1}{4}\div1\frac{5}{8}=$

A $\frac{13}{42}$ B $3\frac{1}{13}$ C $3\frac{1}{2}$ D 13

Exercise 6m

1 Find:

a $4\frac{1}{2} \times 3\frac{1}{3}$

b $3\frac{2}{5} \div \frac{3}{10}$

2 Find:

a $\frac{8}{9} + \frac{21}{27}$

b $2\frac{1}{3} + \frac{4}{9} + 1\frac{5}{6}$

3 Put > or < between the following pairs of numbers:

a $\frac{4}{7} \quad \frac{5}{8}$

b $\frac{11}{9} \quad 1\frac{3}{10}$

4 Calculate:

a $5\frac{1}{4} - 1\frac{2}{3} \div \frac{2}{5}$

b $3\frac{3}{8} \times \left(8\frac{1}{2} - 5\frac{5}{6}\right)$

5 Arrange in ascending order: $\frac{7}{15}, \frac{1}{3}, \frac{2}{5}$

6 What is $1\frac{1}{2}$ subtracted from $\frac{2}{3}$ of $5\frac{1}{4}$?

7 Find:

a $4\frac{1}{2} \times 3\frac{2}{3} - 10\frac{1}{4}$

b $3\frac{1}{2} \div \left(2\frac{1}{8} - \frac{3}{4}\right)$

8 What is $1\frac{2}{3}$ of 1 minute 15 seconds (in seconds)?

9 Fill in the missing numbers:

a $\frac{4}{5} = \frac{}{30}$

b $\frac{2}{7} = \frac{6}{}$

10 Express as mixed numbers:

a $\frac{25}{8}$

b $\frac{49}{9}$

c $\frac{37}{6}$

11 A car travels $5\frac{1}{4}$ km north, then $2\frac{1}{2}$ km west and finally $4\frac{3}{8}$ km north. What is the total distance travelled (in kilometres)? What fraction of the journey was travelled in a northerly direction?

12 A man can paint a door in 1 hour 15 minutes. How many similar doors can he paint in $7\frac{1}{2}$ hours?

Exercise 6n

1 Find:

a $1\frac{5}{6}+\frac{5}{18}+\frac{7}{12}$ b $1\frac{2}{3}-2\frac{1}{5}+\frac{8}{15}$

2 Find:

a $1\frac{5}{6}\div 7\frac{1}{3}$ b $2\frac{1}{4}\times\frac{16}{45}$

3 What is $\frac{5}{6}$ of the number of days in June?

4 Arrange in descending order: $\frac{17}{20}$, $\frac{3}{4}$, $\frac{7}{10}$

5 Calculate:

a $4\frac{1}{2}\times 3\frac{2}{3}-10\frac{1}{4}$ b $3\frac{1}{4}+5\frac{1}{2}\div\frac{3}{8}$

6 Which is smaller, $\frac{8}{11}$ or $\frac{7}{9}$?

7 Find $3\frac{9}{10}\div\left(3\frac{3}{5}-1\frac{1}{2}\right)$.

8 What is $\frac{4}{7}$ of $4\frac{2}{3}$ divided by $1\frac{1}{9}$?

9 Express as mixed numbers:

a $\frac{22}{3}$ b $\frac{46}{5}$ c $\frac{106}{10}$

10 Which of the following statements are true?

a $3\frac{1}{2}\div 1=3\frac{1}{2}\times 1$ b $\frac{1}{2}\times\left(\frac{1}{4}+\frac{1}{8}\right)=\text{half of }\frac{3}{8}$ c $\frac{1}{2}+\frac{1}{2}\div 2=\frac{3}{4}$

11 It takes $1\frac{3}{4}$ minutes to wrap a parcel and a half a minute to address it. How long does it take to wrap and address 8 similar parcels?

12 My bag contains 2 books each of weight $\frac{3}{7}$ kg and 3 folders each of weight $\frac{5}{21}$ kg. What is the total weight in my bag? What fraction of the total weight is books?

? Puzzle

Gary spent one-third of his money at the Sports Club and two-thirds of the remainder at the supermarket. He had $12 left. How much did he have to start with?

Did you know?

Hypatia (CE 370–415) was the daughter of Theon, a professor of mathematics at the University of Alexandria. It is said that her father was determined to produce 'a perfect human being'. She was immersed in an atmosphere of learning, questioning and exploration, and her reputation soon eclipsed her father's. She studied medicine as well as mathematics.

In this chapter you have seen that...

- ✔ 'of' means 'multiplied by'
- ✔ you can multiply and divide whole numbers by fractions, by writing the whole number over 1
- ✔ to multiply fractions by fractions you multiply the numerators together and you multiply the denominators together
- ✔ to divide by a fraction you turn the fraction upside down and multiply
- ✔ you can multiply and divide with mixed numbers by turning the mixed numbers into improper fractions.

7 Geometry 1

At the end of this chapter you should be able to...

1 express the amount of 'turn' of a clock hand as a fraction of a revolution
2 express a change in direction as a fraction of a revolution
3 identify an angle as a change in direction
4 describe a right angle as a quarter of a revolution
5 define acute, obtuse and reflex angles in terms of right angles
6 identify acute, obtuse and reflex angles
7 define a degree as a fraction of a revolution
8 use a protractor to measure angles
9 draw angles of given size using a protractor
10 state the properties of vertically opposite angles, angles on a straight line, supplementary angles, angles at a point and complementary angles
11 calculate the size of angles using the properties above.

Did you know?

The word 'geometry' means land measurement. Historians state that the term originated in Egypt where the River Nile, in its floods, overflowed its banks and changed the boundaries of neighbouring farms. 'Geo' is the Greek word for 'earth'. What other common words start with 'geo'?

You need to know...

✔ what an analogue clock face looks like
✔ the four main compass directions
✔ how to add and subtract whole numbers
✔ how to find a fraction of a quantity.

Key words

acute angle, angles at a point, angles on a straight line, anticlockwise, clockwise, complementary angles, degree, obtuse angle, protractor, reflex angle, revolution, right angle, supplementary angles, vertex, vertically opposite angles

Fractions of a revolution

When the seconds hand of a clock starts at 12 and moves round until it stops at 12 again it has gone through one complete turn.

One complete turn is called a *revolution*.

When the seconds hand starts at 12 and stops at 3 it has turned through $\frac{1}{4}$ of a revolution.

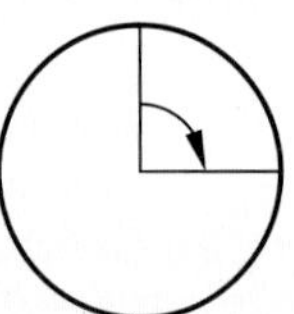

Exercise 7a

What fraction of a revolution does the seconds hand of a clock turn through when:

1. it starts at 12 and stops at 9
2. it starts at 12 and stops at 6
3. it starts at 6 and stops at 9
4. it starts at 3 and stops at 9
5. it starts at 9 and stops at 12

Draw a clock face with the initial and final positions of the hand, like the diagram above. Draw a curved arrow going clockwise from the start position to the end position of the hand.

6. it starts at 1 and stops at 7
7. it starts at 5 and stops at 11
8. it starts at 10 and stops at 4
9. it starts at 8 and stops at 8
10. it starts at 8 and stops at 11
11. it starts at 10 and stops at 2
12. it starts at 12 and stops at 4
13. it starts at 8 and stops at 5
14. it starts at 5 and stops at 2
15. it starts at 9 and stops at 5?

Where does the seconds hand stop if:

16 it starts at 12 and turns through $\frac{1}{2}$ a turn

17 it starts at 12 and turns through $\frac{3}{4}$ of a turn

18 it starts at 6 and turns through $\frac{1}{4}$ of a turn

19 it starts at 9 and turns through $\frac{1}{2}$ a turn

20 it starts at 6 and turns through a complete turn

21 it starts at 9 and turns through $\frac{3}{4}$ of a turn

22 it starts at 12 and turns through $\frac{1}{3}$ of a turn

23 it starts at 12 and turns through $\frac{2}{3}$ of a turn

24 it starts at 9 and turns through a complete turn

25 it starts at 6 and turns through $\frac{1}{2}$ a turn?

Compass directions

The four main compass directions are north, south, east and west.

If you stand facing north and turn clockwise through $\frac{1}{2}$ a revolution you are then facing south.

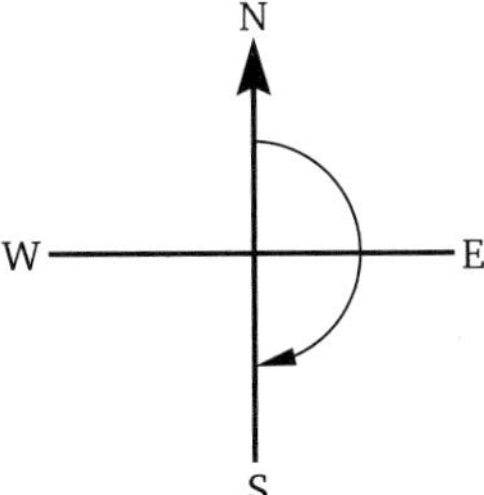

Exercise 7b

1 If you stand facing west and turn anticlockwise through $\frac{3}{4}$ of a revolution, in which direction are you facing?

2 If you stand facing south and turn clockwise through $\frac{1}{4}$ of a revolution, in which direction are you facing?

Draw the compass directions like the diagram above. Then draw the turning arrow from the start to the end position to show the turn.

3 If you stand facing north and turn, in either direction, through a complete revolution, in which direction are you facing?

4 If you stand facing west and turn through $\frac{1}{2}$ a revolution, in which direction are you facing? Does it matter if you turn clockwise or anticlockwise?

5 If you stand facing south and turn through $1\frac{1}{2}$ revolutions, in which direction are you facing?

6 If you stand facing west and turn clockwise to face south what part of a revolution have you turned through?

7 If you stand facing north and turn clockwise to face west how much of a revolution have you turned through?

8 If you stand facing east and turn to face west what part of a revolution have you turned through?

Angles

When the hand of a clock moves from one position to another it has turned through an angle.

Right angles

A quarter of a revolution is called a *right angle*.

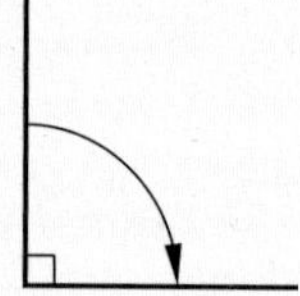

Half a revolution is two right angles.

The lines enclosing a right angle are perpendicular.

The lines that enclose the angle are called the arms of the angle.

The point where the lines meet is called the vertex.

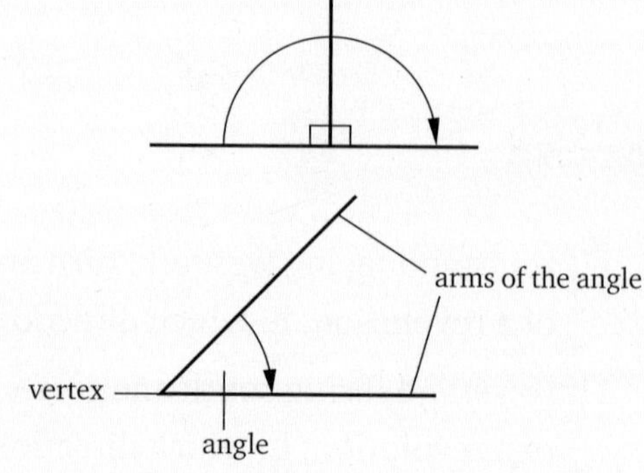

Exercise 7c

How many right angles does the seconds hand of a clock turn through when it starts at 3 and stops at 12?

Draw the start and end position of the hand with a curved arrow from the start to the end position.

Now you can see that it turns through three right angles.

How many right angles does the seconds hand of a clock turn through when:

1 it starts at 6 and stops at 9

2 it starts at 3 and stops at 9

3 it starts at 12 and stops at 9

4 it starts at 3 and stops at 6

5 it starts at 12 and stops at 12

6 it starts at 8 and stops at 2

7 it starts at 9 and stops at 6

8 it starts at 7 and stops at 7?

How many right angles do you turn through if you:

9 face north and turn clockwise to face south

10 face west and turn clockwise to face north

11 face south and turn clockwise to face west

12 face north and turn anticlockwise to face east

13 face north and turn to face north again?

Acute, obtuse and reflex angles

Any angle that is smaller than a right angle is called an *acute angle*.

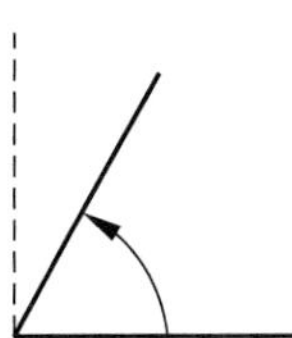

Any angle that is greater than one right angle and less than two right angles is called an *obtuse angle*.

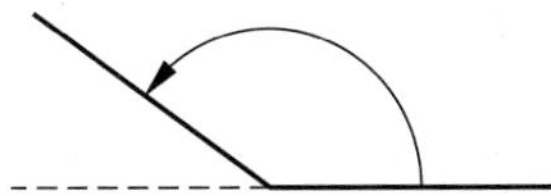

Any angle that is greater than two right angles is called a *reflex angle*.

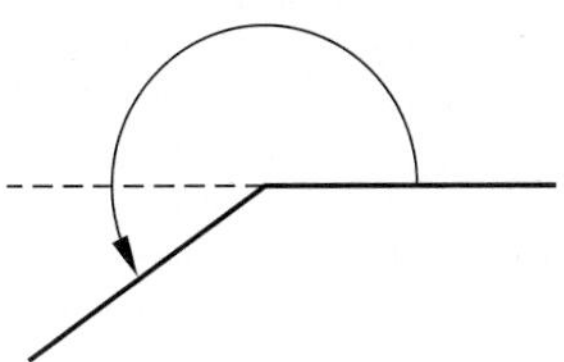

Exercise 7d

What type of angle is each of the following?

1 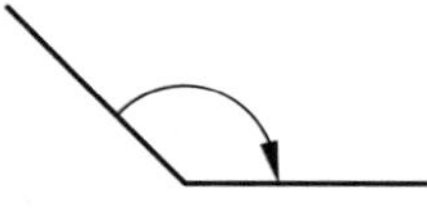

2 

3 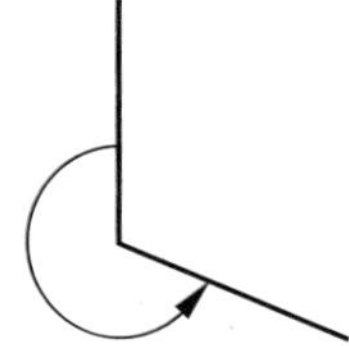

4 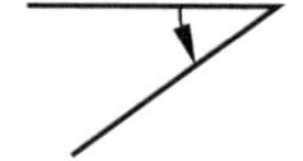

5 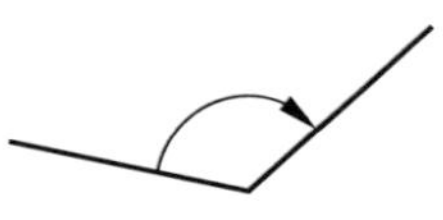

6 

7 

8 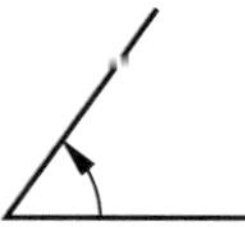

9 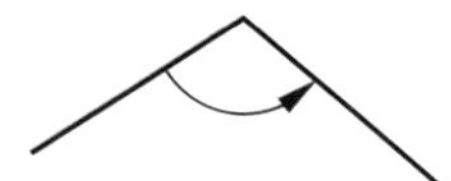

10 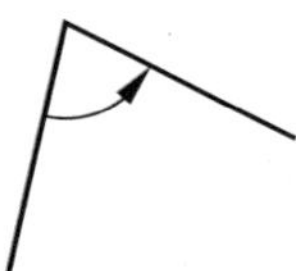

11 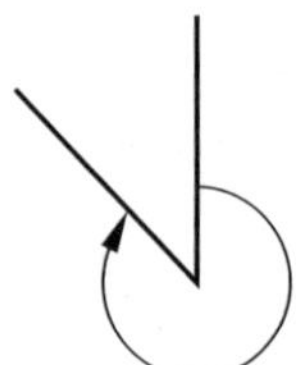

12 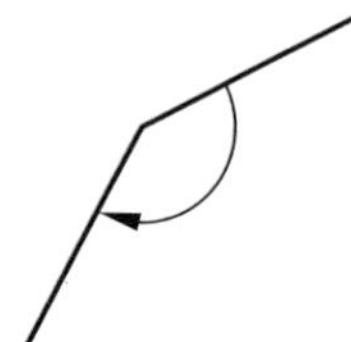

13 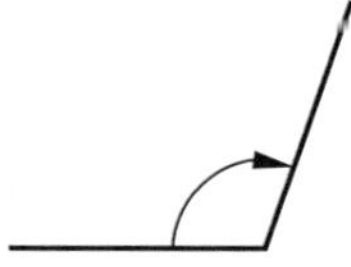

14 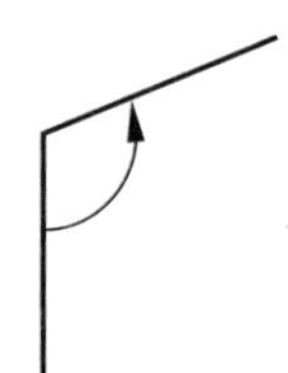

15 

Degrees

One complete revolution is divided into 360 parts. Each part is called a *degree*. 360 degrees is written 360°.

360 seems a strange number of parts to have in a revolution but it is a good number because so many whole numbers divide into it exactly. This means that there are many fractions of a revolution that can be expressed as an exact number of degrees.

Exercise 7e

1 How many degrees are there in half a revolution?

2 How many degrees are there in one right angle?

3 How many degrees are there in three right angles?

How many degrees has the seconds hand of a clock turned through when it moves from 6 to 9?

Drawing the clock face as before shows that it has turned through 90°, i.e. 1 right angle.

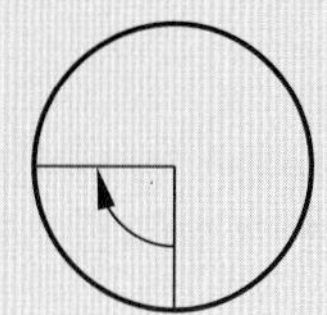

How many degrees has the seconds hand of a clock turned through when it moves from:

4	12 to 6	7	9 to 3	10	7 to 11	<u>13</u>	4 to 10
5	3 to 6	8	9 to 6	11	1 to 10	<u>14</u>	5 to 8
6	6 to 3	9	2 to 5	<u>12</u>	8 to 5	<u>15</u>	6 to 12?

How many degrees has the seconds hand of a clock turned through when it moves from 6 to 8?

Drawing the clock face shows that the hand moves through 2 out of 3 equal divisions of 90°, i.e. it moves through $\frac{2}{3}$ of 90° and $\frac{2}{3}$ of $90° = \frac{2}{3} \times \frac{90°}{1} = 60°$.

Another way of looking at it is to say that the hand moves through 2 out of 12 equal divisions of a revolution, i.e. $\frac{2}{12}$ of 360°.

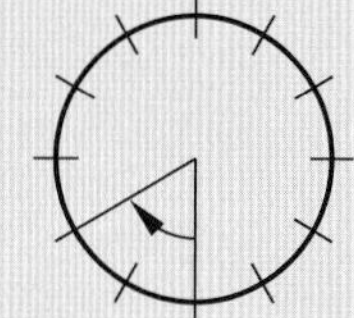

How many degrees has the seconds hand of a clock turned through when it moves from:

16	8 to 9	26	3 to 10
17	10 to halfway between 11 and 12	27	2 to 8
18	6 to 10	28	10 to 8
19	1 to 3	29	12 to 11
20	3 to halfway between 4 and 5	30	9 to 2
<u>21</u>	4 to 5	<u>31</u>	8 to 3
<u>22</u>	7 to 11	<u>32</u>	7 to 5
<u>23</u>	5 to 6	<u>33</u>	10 to 5
<u>24</u>	7 to 9	<u>34</u>	11 to 4
<u>25</u>	11 to 3	<u>35</u>	2 to 9?

Investigation

The Babylonians chose to divide one complete revolution into 360 degrees. We still use this division. Why do you think that this division has not been decimalised?

You may find that the answer is clear if you list all the numbers between 1 and 20 that divide exactly into 360 and that divide exactly into 100.

Using a protractor to measure angles

A protractor looks like this:

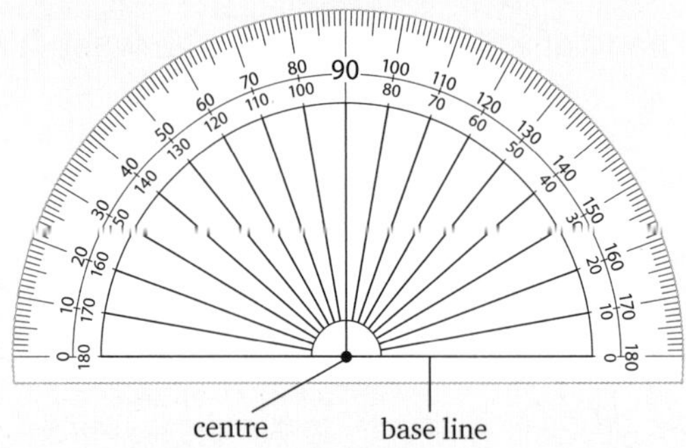

It has a straight line at or near the straight edge. This line is called the *base line*.

The *centre* of the base line is marked.

The protractor has two scales, an inside one and an outside one.

To measure the size of this angle, first decide whether it is acute or obtuse.

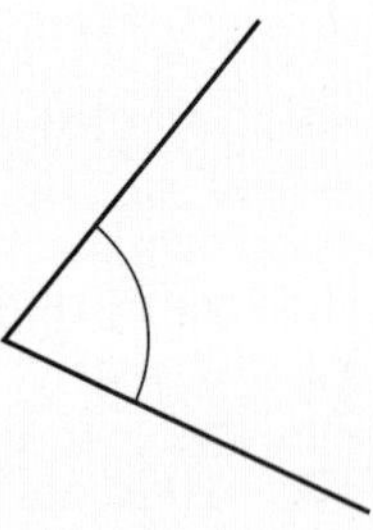

This is an acute angle because it is *less* than 90°.

Next place the protractor on the angle as shown.

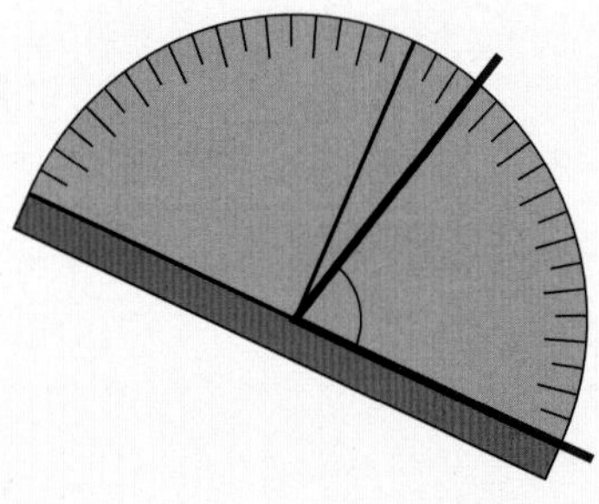

One arm of the angle is on the base line.

The vertex (point) of the angle is at the centre of the base line.

Choose the scale that starts at 0° on the arm of the base line. Read off the number where the other arm cuts this scale.

Check with your estimate to make sure that you have chosen the right scale.

Exercise 7f

Measure the following angles (if necessary, turn the page to a convenient position):

1

2

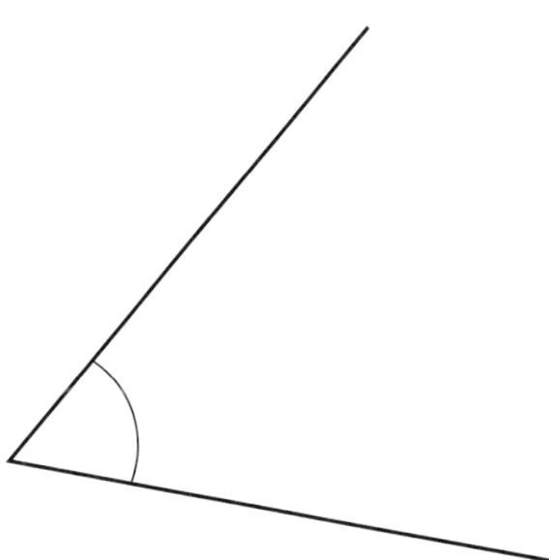

3

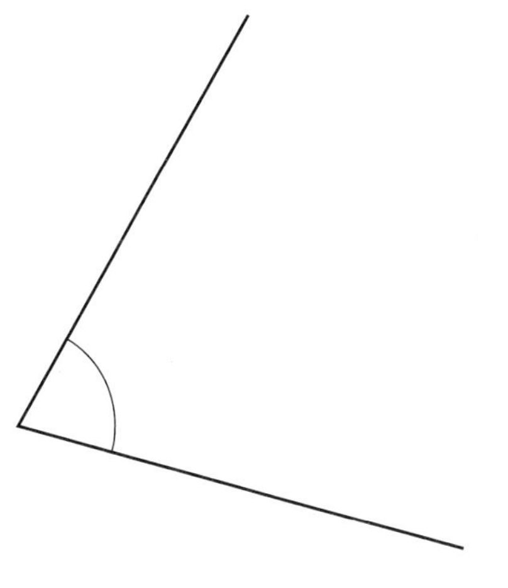

4

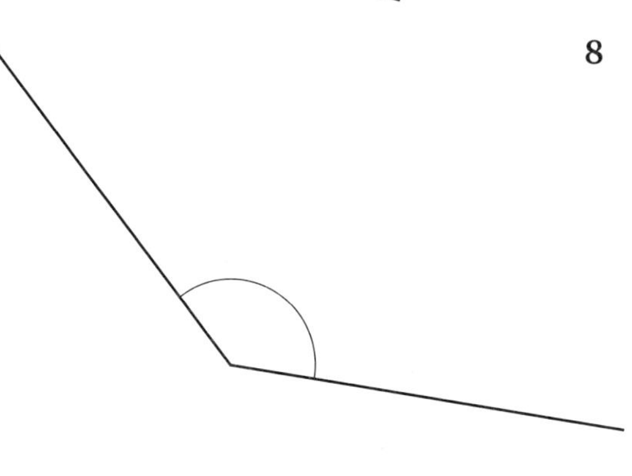

5

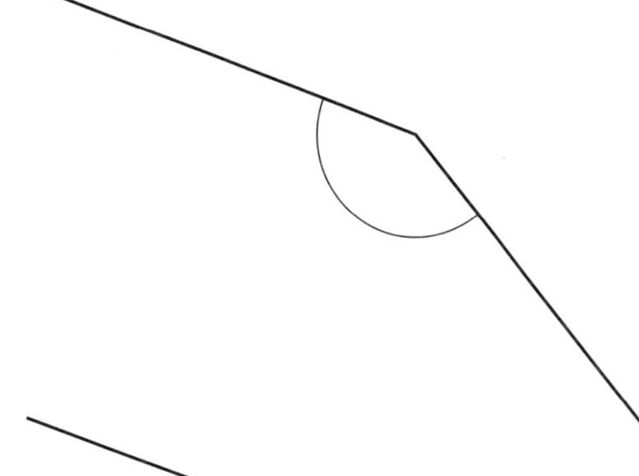

6

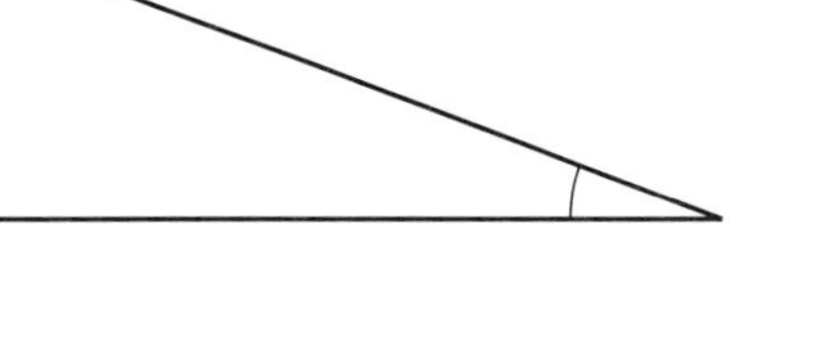

7

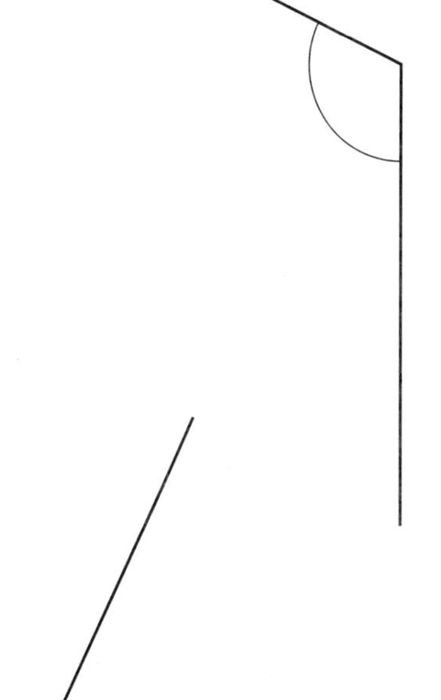

8

9

10

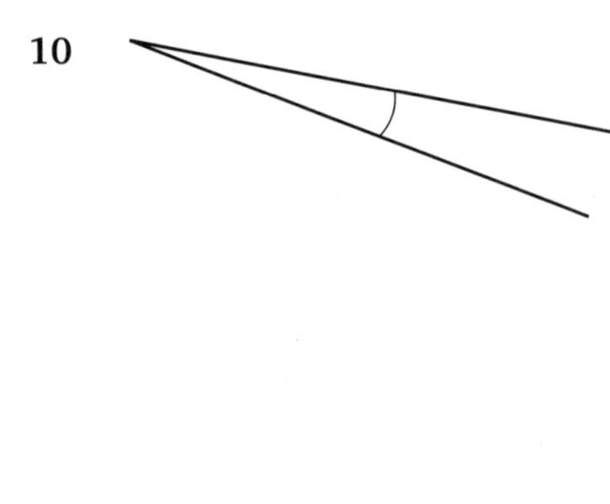

Find the size of the angle p.

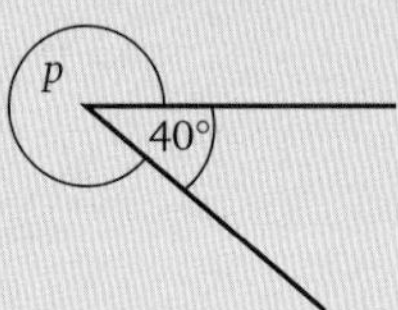

Angle p and 40° make 360°.

So angle p is 360° – 40° = 320°.

In questions **11** to **15** write down the size of the angle marked with a letter:

11

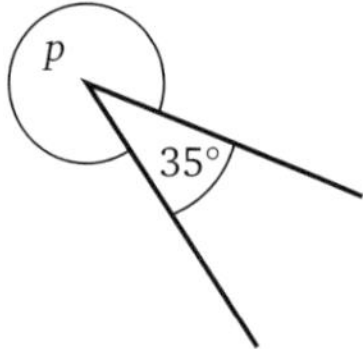

12

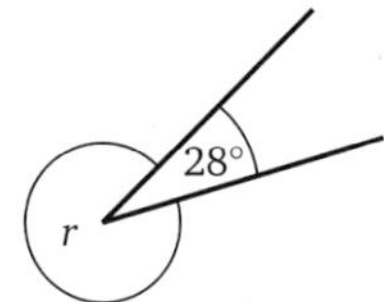

13

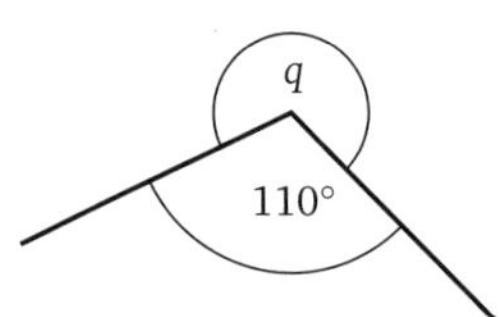

14

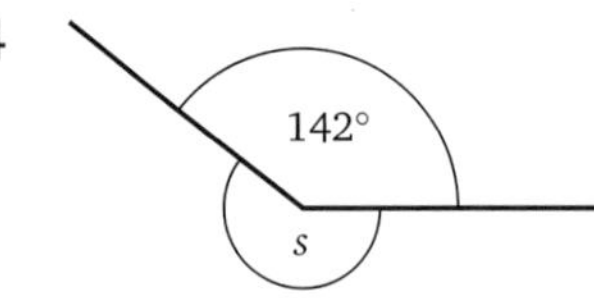

15

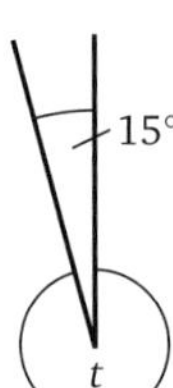

Find the following angle:

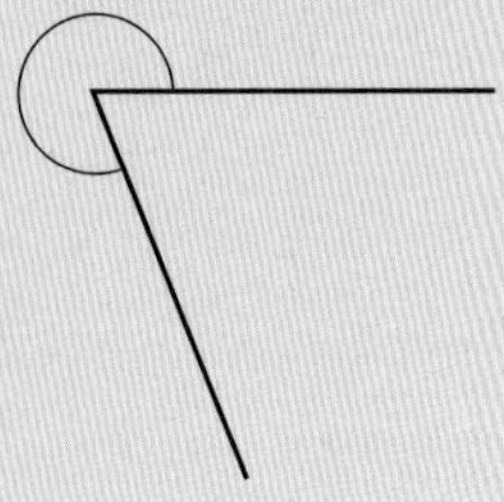

This is a reflex angle and it is bigger than three right angles, i.e. it is greater than 270°.

To find this angle, we need to measure the smaller angle, marked p.

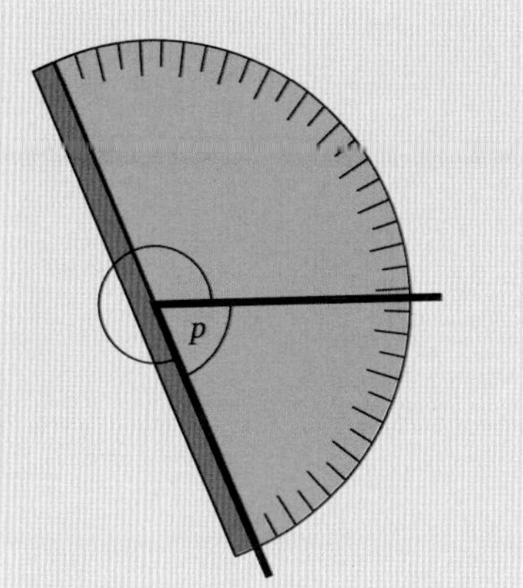

Angle p is 68° so the reflex angle is $360° - 68° = 292°$.

Find the following angles:

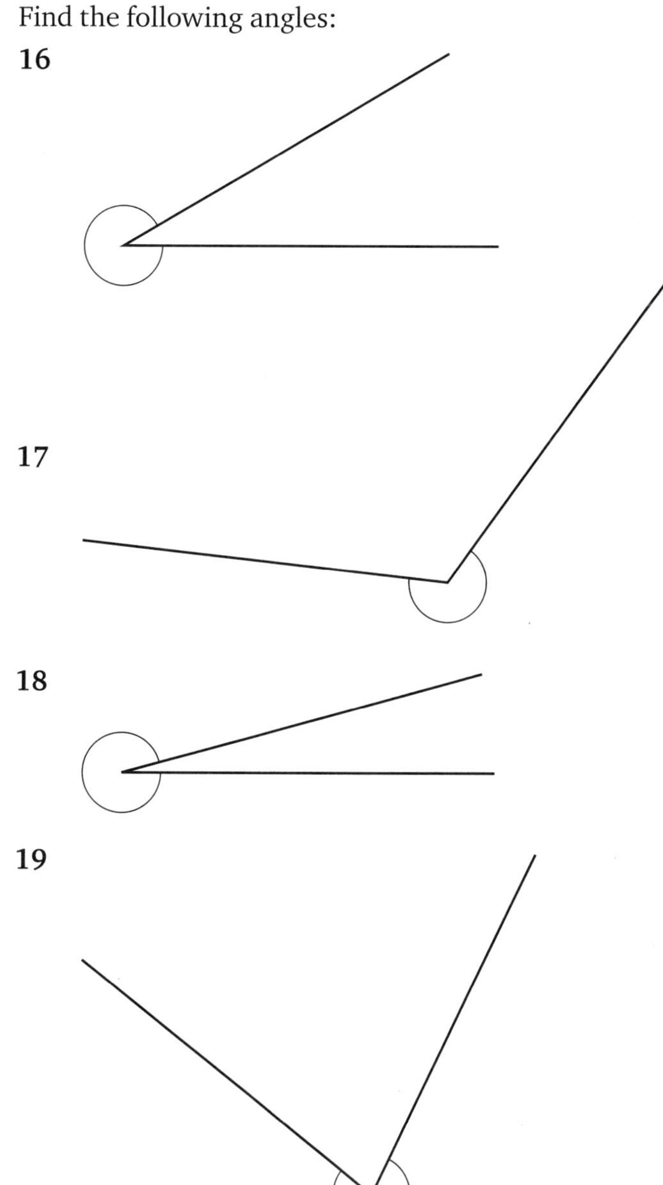

16

17

18

19

20

21

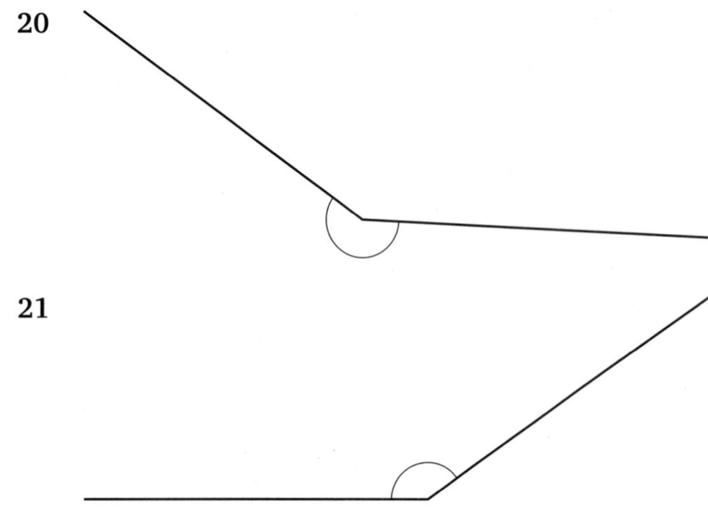

22 Draw a reflex angle. Now find its size. Change books with your neighbour and each check the other's measurement.

Mixed questions

Exercise 7g

Use a clock diagram to draw the angle that the *minute* hand of a clock turns through in the following times. In each question write down the size of the angle in degrees:

1	5 minutes	**3**	15 minutes	**5**	25 minutes
2	10 minutes	**4**	20 minutes	**6**	30 minutes

The seconds hand of a clock starts at 12. Which number is it pointing to when it has turned through an angle of:

7	90°	**11**	150°	**15**	420°	**19**	540°
8	60°	**12**	270°	**16**	180°	**20**	240°
9	120°	**13**	30°	**17**	450°	**21**	390°
10	360°	**14**	300°	**18**	210°	**22**	720°?

Draw a sketch to show which direction you will be facing in if you start by facing north and turn clockwise through 60°.

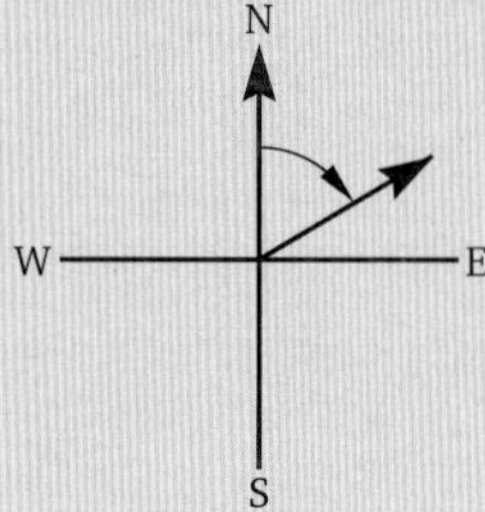

Suppose you start by facing north. Draw a sketch to show roughly the direction in which you are facing if you turn clockwise through these angles:

23	45°	**27**	200°	**31**	270°
24	70°	**28**	300°	**32**	10°
25	120°	**29**	20°	**33**	80°
26	50°	**30**	100°	**34**	250°

Start by drawing the four compass directions like the diagram in the worked example.

Estimate the size, in degrees, of each of the following angles:

35

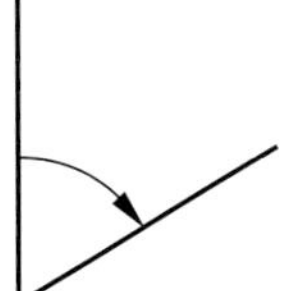

36

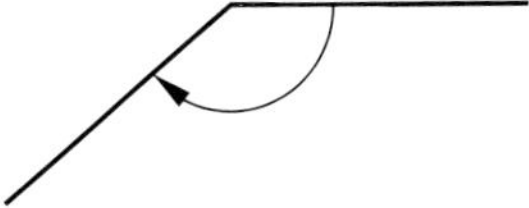

37

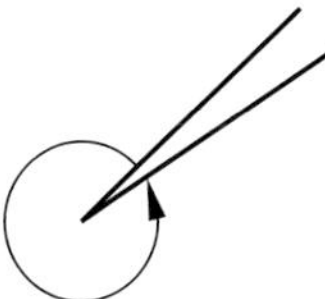

38

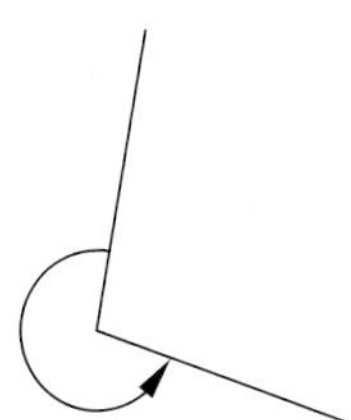

39

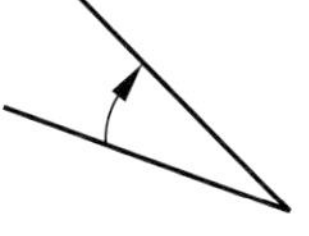

40

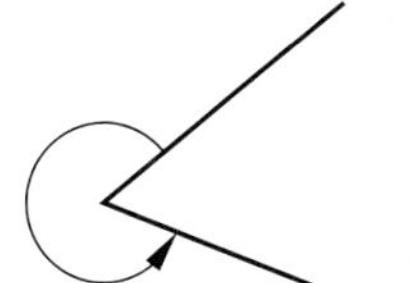

41

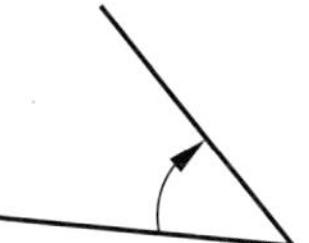

42

43

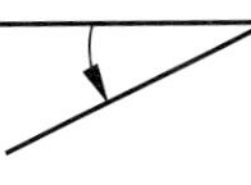

44

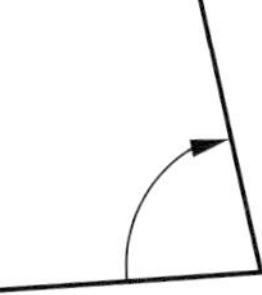

45

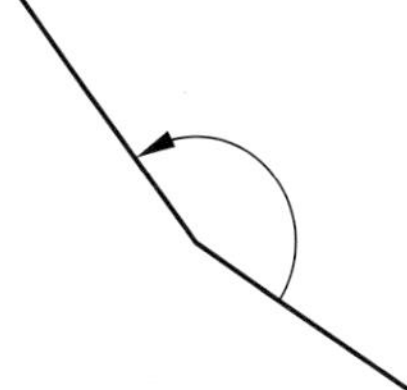

46

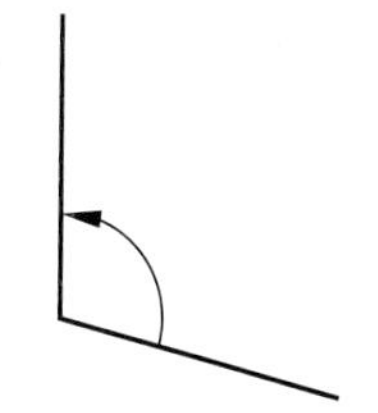

Draw the following angles as well as you can by estimating, i.e. without using a protractor. Use a clock face if it helps. Then measure your angles with a protractor. Extend your lines in order to use the protractor.

47	45°	**50**	30°	**53**	150°	**56**	20°	**59**	330°
48	90°	**51**	60°	**54**	200°	**57**	5°	**60**	95°
49	120°	52	10°	**55**	290°	**58**	170°	**61**	250°

Puzzle

This is an exercise for two people. You need a good map and a protractor.

Toss a coin to see who takes the first turn.

One player finds two places on the map. This player shows the other player the position of one place on the map and gives the direction of the second place from the first by estimating the angle that must be turned through clockwise from north. If the second player finds this place within 10 seconds, he has won and it is his turn. Otherwise the first player has won and gets another turn. Play as many times at you wish.

The winner is the player with the most successes.

Any disputes about the direction given are solved by measuring the actual angle with a protractor. Directions within 10° are acceptable. If 10 seconds is not long enough, increase the time allowed to 15 seconds.

Drawing angles using a protractor

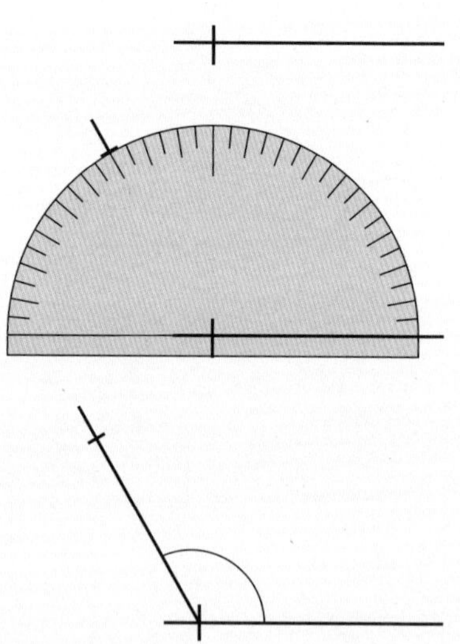

To draw an angle of 120° start by drawing one arm and mark the vertex.

Place your protractor as shown in the diagram. Make sure that the vertex is at the centre of the base line.

Choose the scale that starts at 0° on your drawn line and mark the paper next to the 120° mark on the scale.

Remove the protractor and join your mark to the vertex.

Now look at your angle: does it look the right size?

Exercise 7h

Use your protractor to draw the following angles accurately:

1 25°	**4** 160°	**7** 110°	**<u>10</u>** 125°	**<u>13</u>** 105°
2 37°	**5** 83°	**8** 49°	**<u>11</u>** 175°	**<u>14</u>** 136°
3 55°	**6** 15°	**9** 65°	**<u>12</u>** 72°	**<u>15</u>** 85°

Change books with your neighbour and measure each other's angles as a check on accuracy.

Exercise 7i

In questions **1** and **2** first measure the angle marked r. Then estimate the size of the angle marked s. Check your estimate by measuring angle s.

1

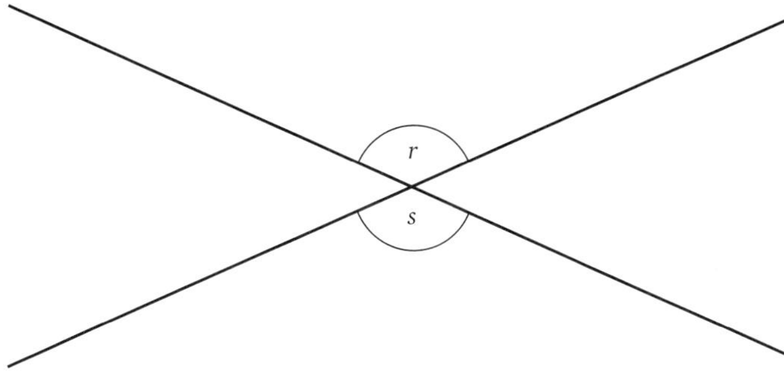

2

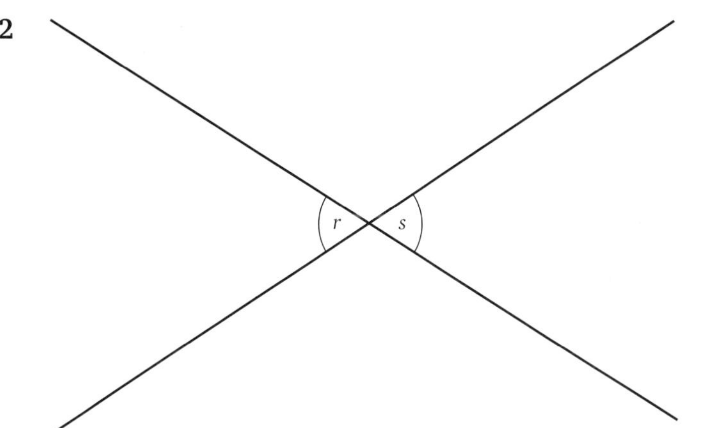

3 Draw some more similar diagrams and repeat questions **1** and **2**.

In questions **4** to **9**, write down the size of the angle marked t, without measuring it:

4

5

6

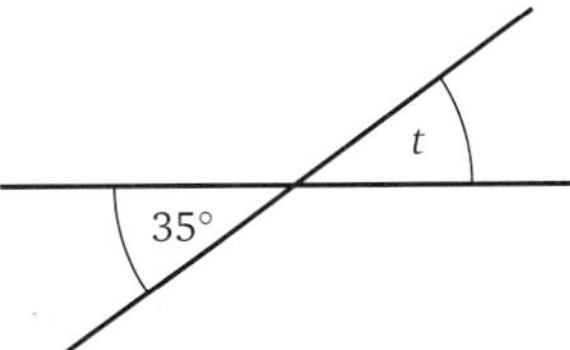

7

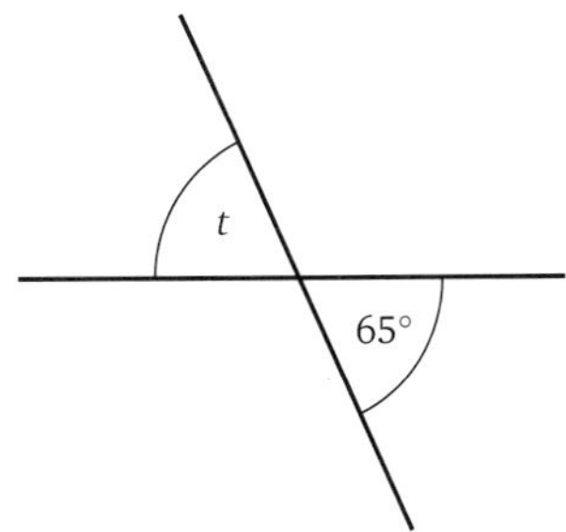

8

140°

t

9

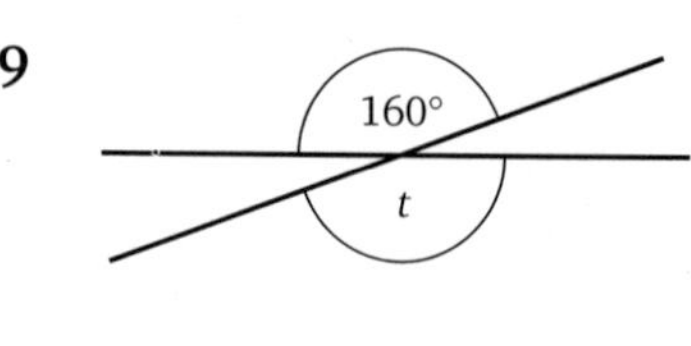

Vertically opposite angles

When two straight lines cross, four angles are formed.

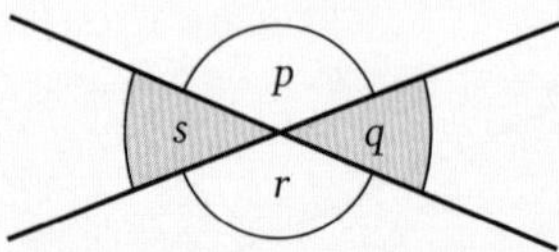

The two angles that are opposite each other are called *vertically opposite angles*. After working through the last exercise you should now be convinced that

vertically opposite angles are equal

i.e. $p = r$ and $s = q$.

Angles on a straight line

The seconds hand of a clock starts at 9 and stops at 11 and then starts again and finally stops at 3.

Altogether the seconds hand has turned through half a revolution, so $p + q = 180°$.

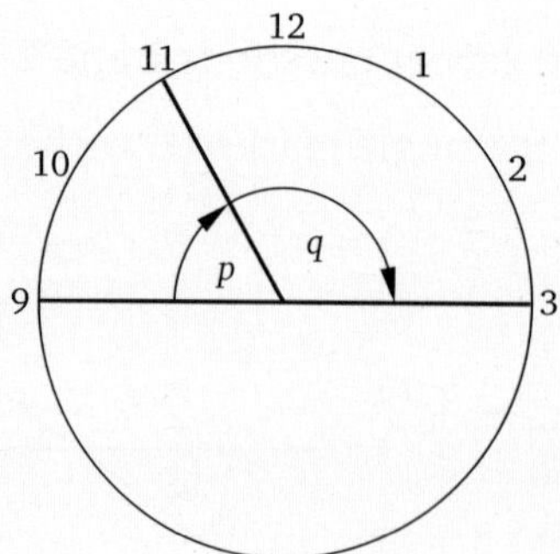

Exercise 7j

1 Draw a diagram showing the two angles that you turn through if you start by facing north and then turn clockwise through 60°, stop for a moment and then continue turning until you are facing south. What is the sum of these two angles?

2 Draw a clock diagram to show the two angles turned through by the seconds hand if it is started at 2, stopped at 6, started again and finally stopped at 8. What is the sum of these two angles?

3 Draw an angle of 180°, without using your protractor.

Complementary angles

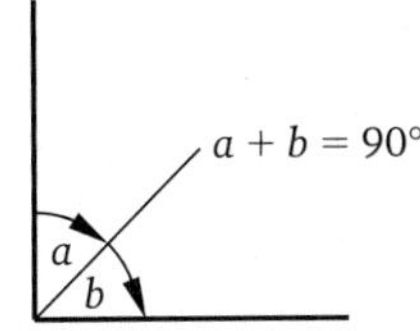

Angles in a right angle add up to 90°.

The angles a and b are adjacent. They share an arm.

Two angles that add up to 90° are called *complementary angles*.

Any two angles that add to 90° are complementary. They do not have to be adjacent angles.

Supplementary angles

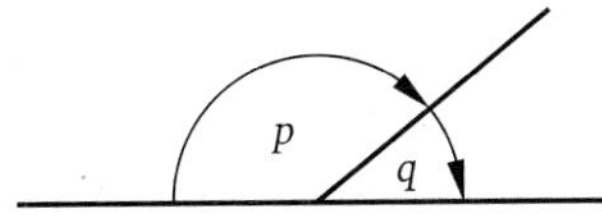

Angles on a straight line add up to 180°.

An angle of 180° is called a straight line.

Two angles that add up to 180° are called *supplementary angles*.

Any two angles that add to 180° are supplementary. They do not have to be adjacent angles.

Exercise 7k

Calculate the size of angle d.

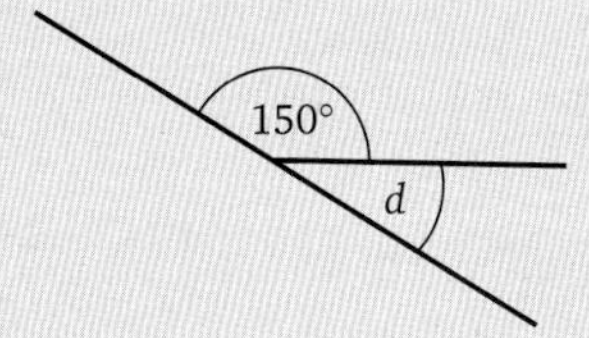

Angles d and 150° together make a straight line.

So $d + 150° = 180°$

$\therefore \quad d = 30°$

($\therefore$ means 'therefore' or 'it follows that')

In questions **1** to **12** calculate the size of the angle marked with a letter.
Give a reason for your answer.

1

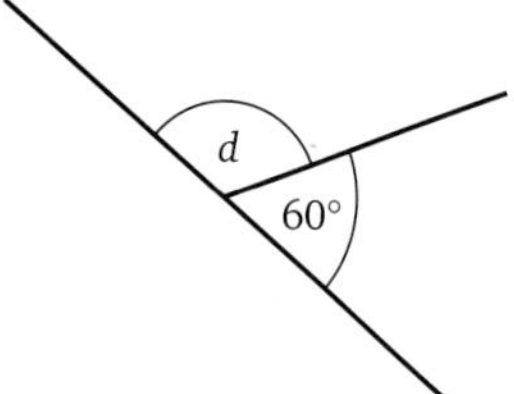

2

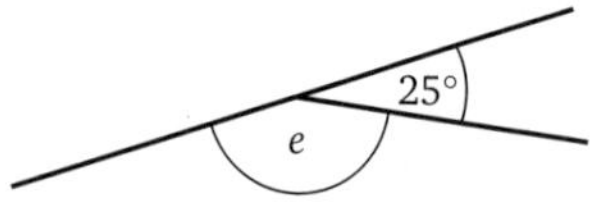

3

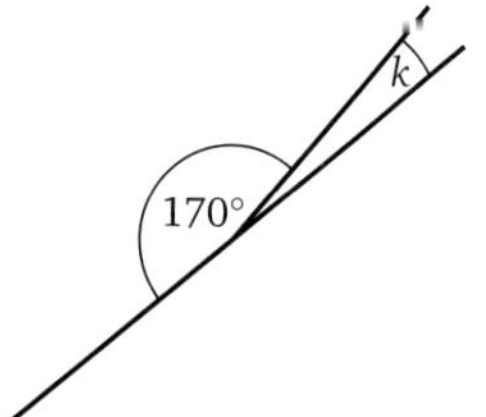

4

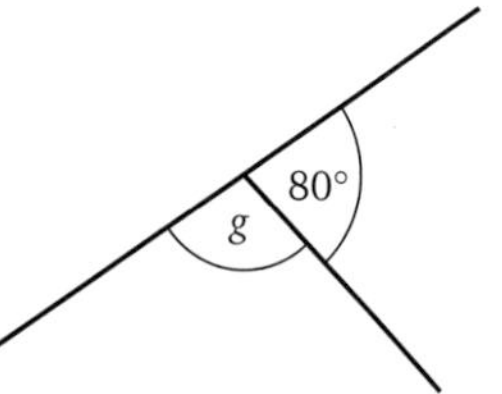

5

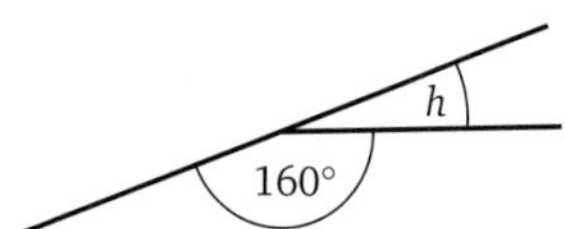

6

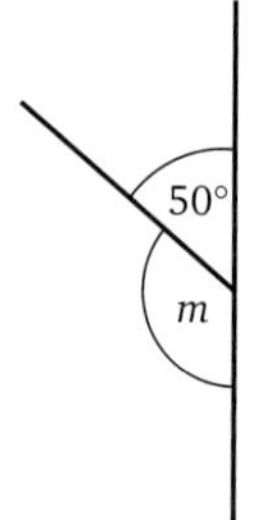

7

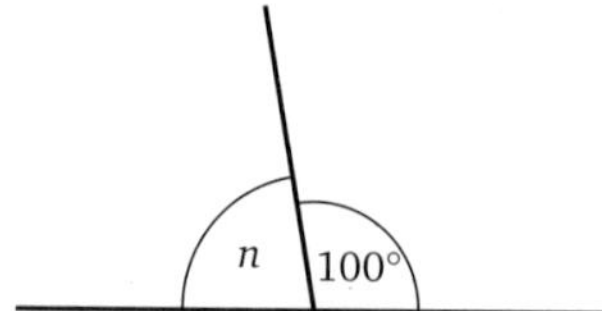

8

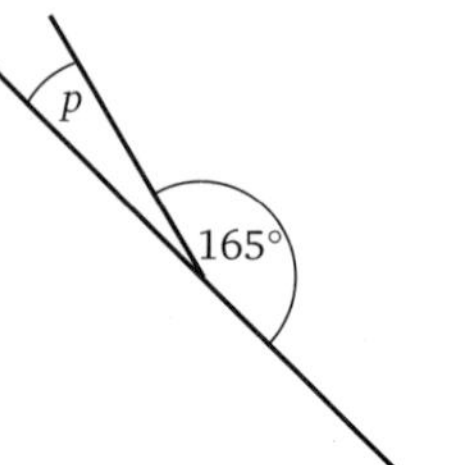

9

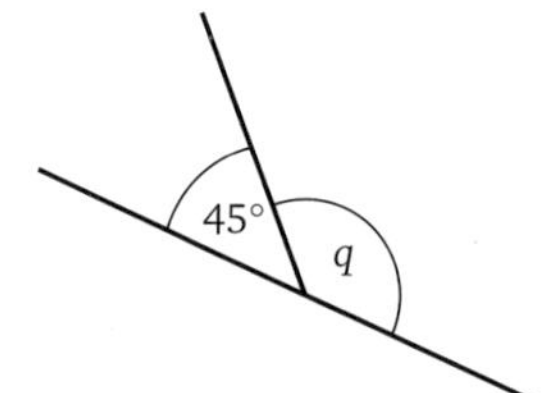

10

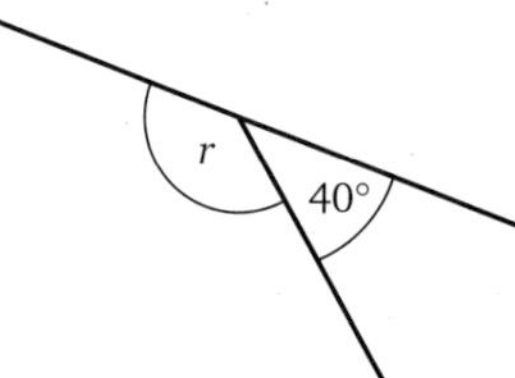

11

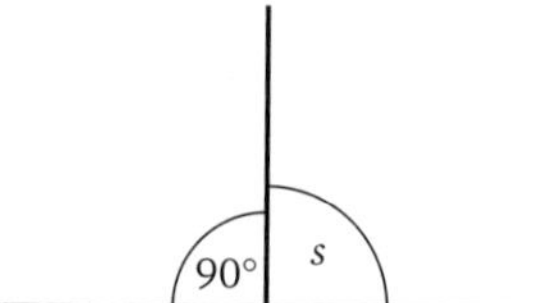

12

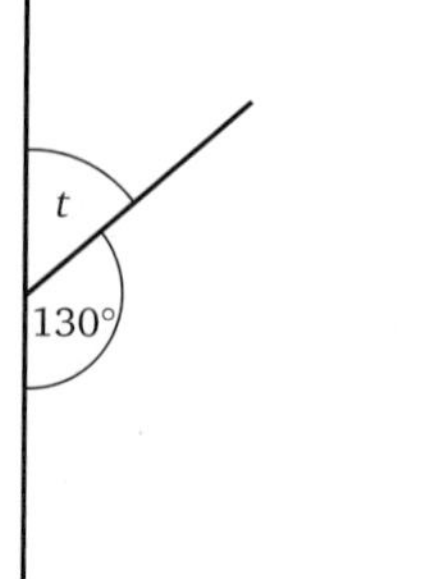

In questions **13** to **18** write down the pairs of angles that are supplementary:

13

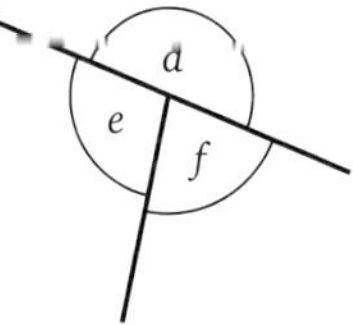

16

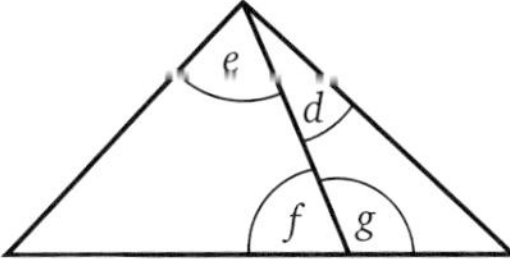

14

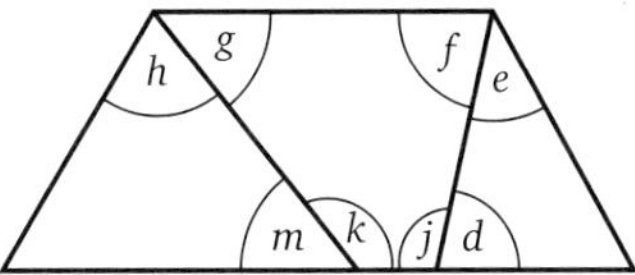

17

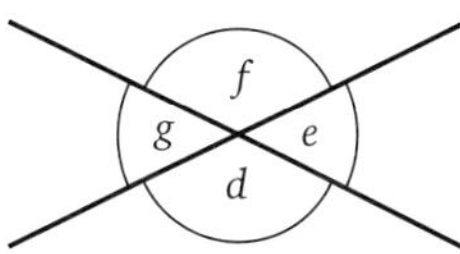

15

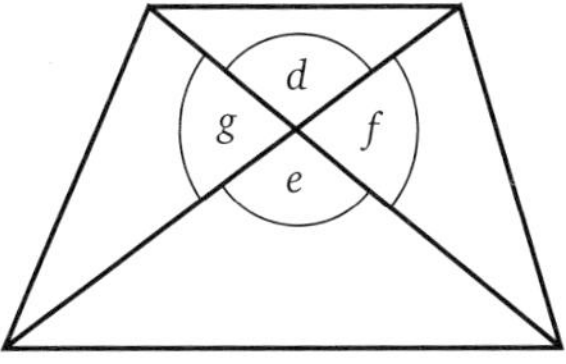

18

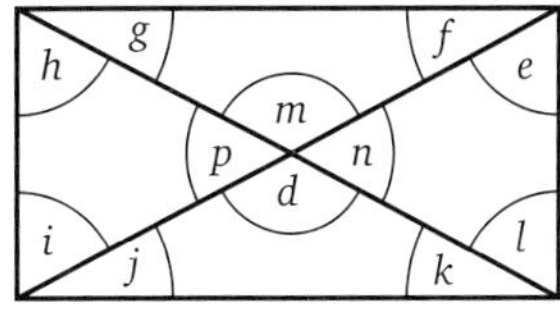

Calculate the sizes of angles d, e and f.

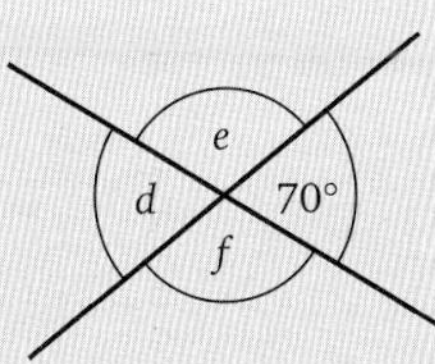

d and 70° are equal (they are vertically opposite)

$\therefore \quad d = 70°$

e and 70° add up 180° (they are angles on a straight line)

$\therefore \quad e = 110°$

f and e are equal (they are vertically opposite)

$\therefore \quad f = 110°$

In questions **19** to **26** calculate the size of the angles marked with a letter.
Give a reason for your answer.

19

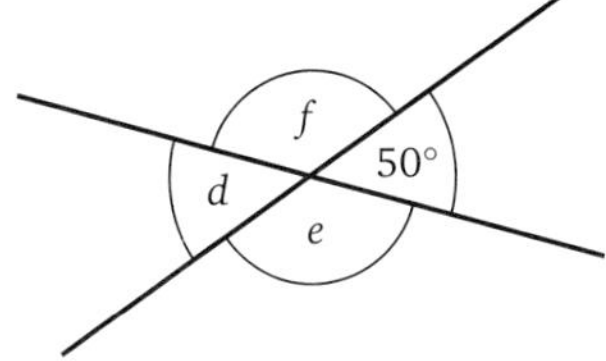

20

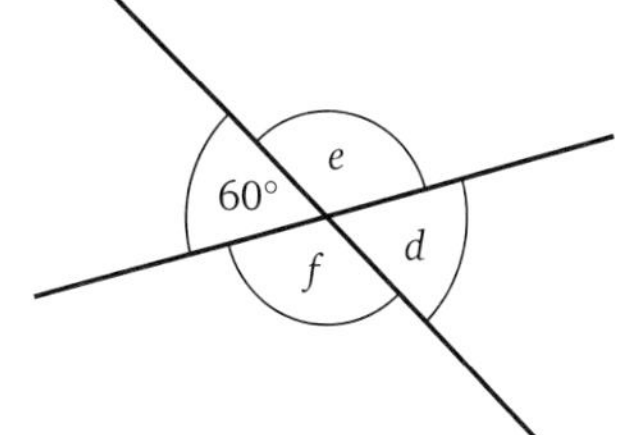

21

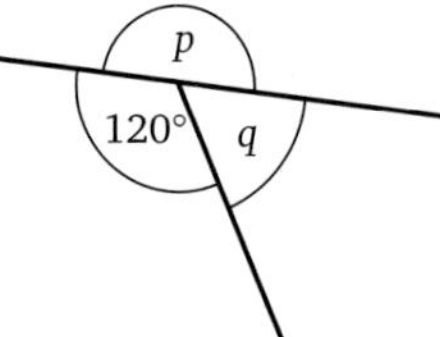

22

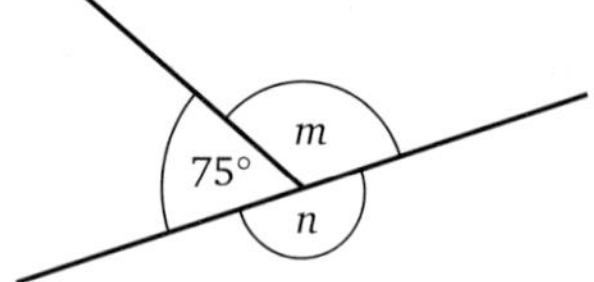

23

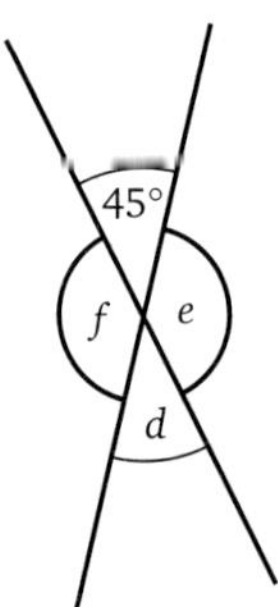

24

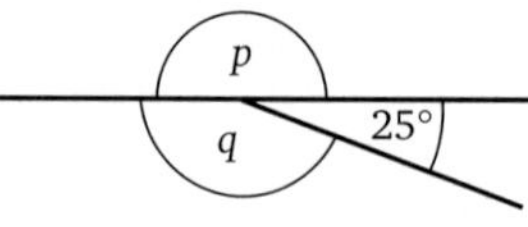

25

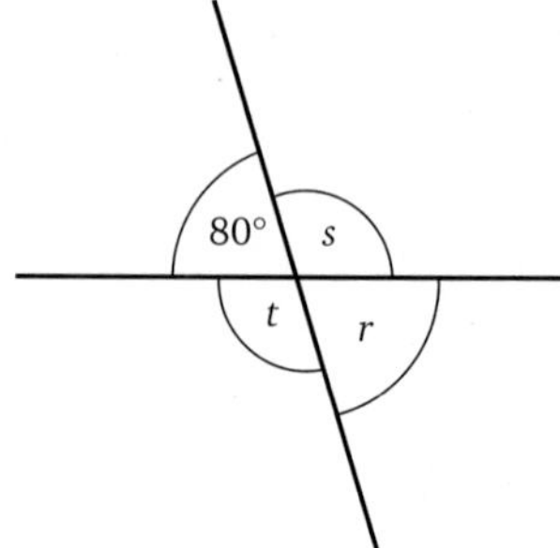

26

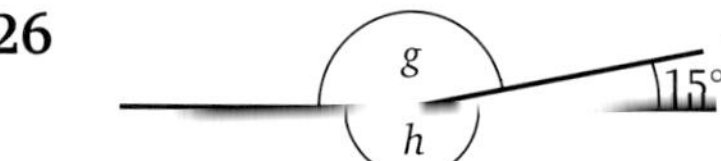

Angles at a point

When several angles make a complete revolution they are called *angles at a point*.

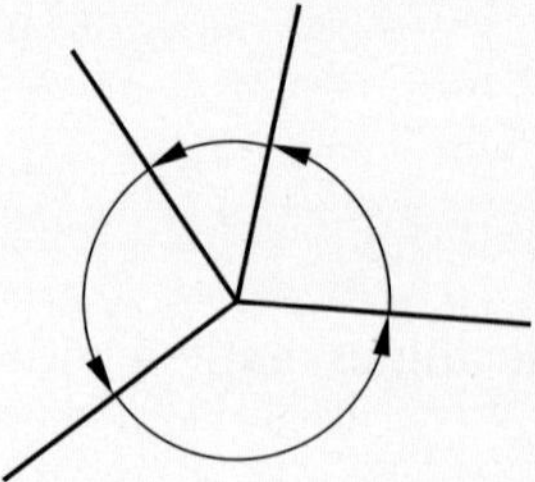

Angles at a point add up to 360°.

Exercise 7I

Find the size of angle d. Give a reason for your answer.

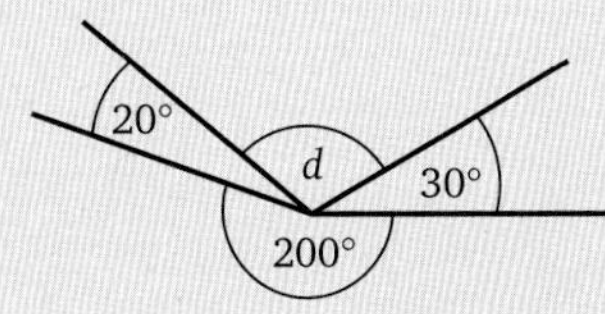

The four angles at the point add up to 360°.

The three given angles add up to 250°.

$\therefore \quad d = 360° - 250°$

$d = 110°$

$$\begin{array}{r} 30 \\ 200 \\ +20 \\ \hline 250 \\ \hline \end{array}$$

In questions **1** to **10** find the size of the angle marked with a letter.
Give a reason for your answer.

1

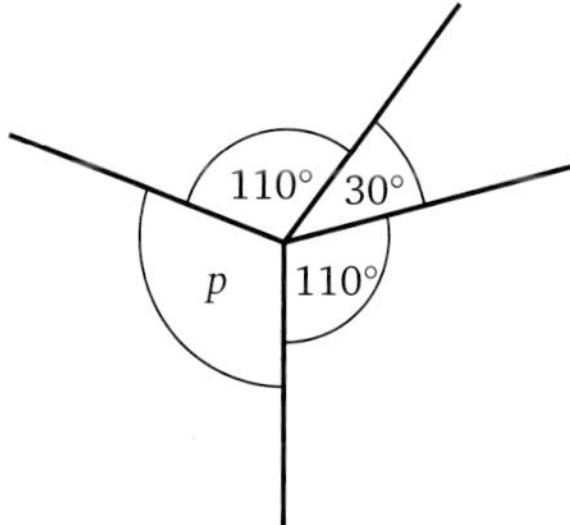

5

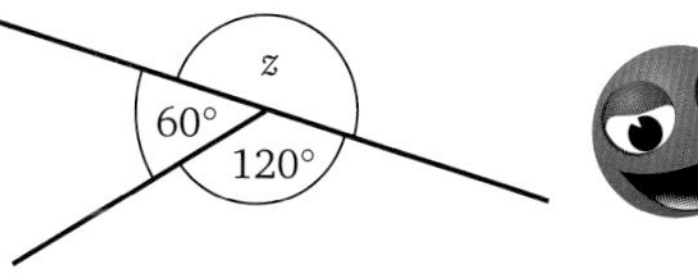

Remember that, however many angles there are at a point, their sum is 360°.

2

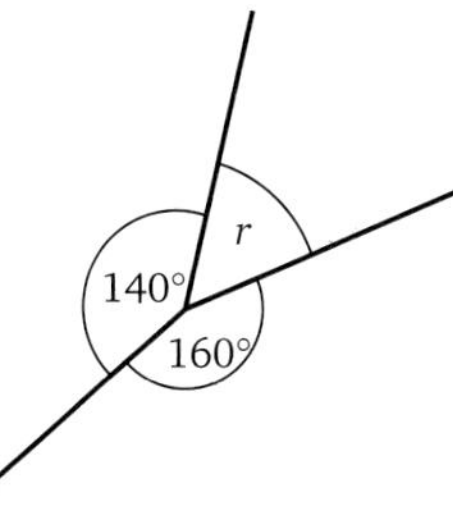

6

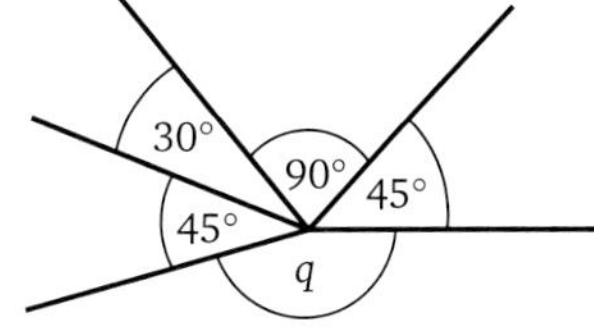

9

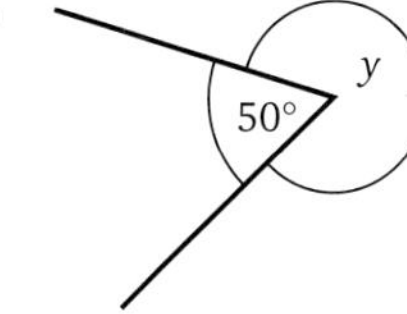

3

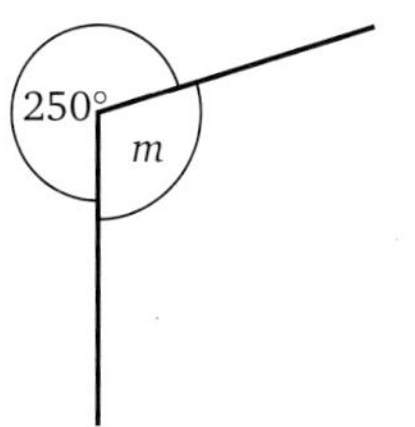

7

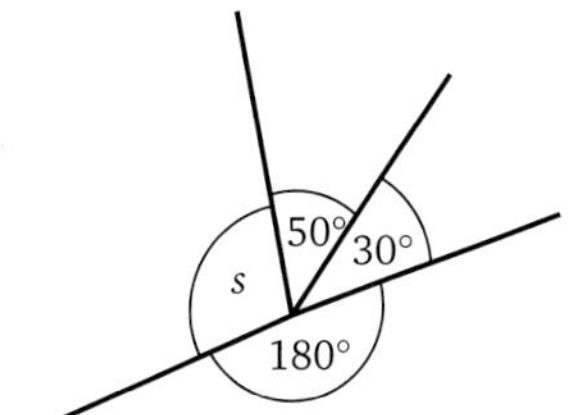

10

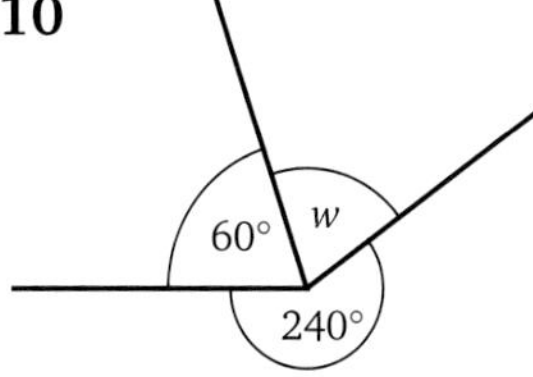

4

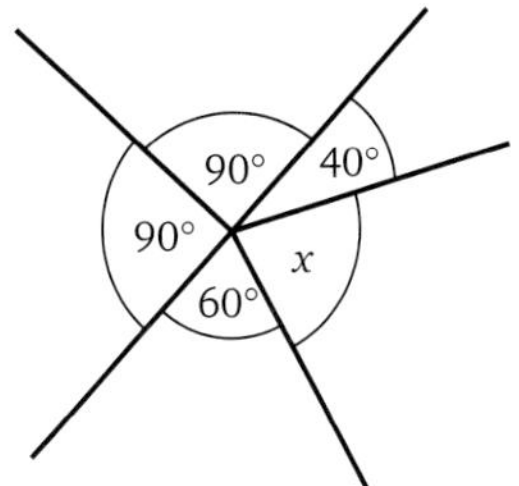

8

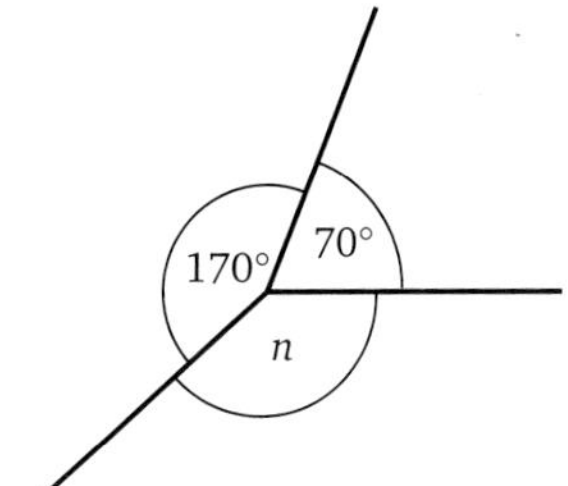

Problems

Exercise 7m

1 Find each of the equal angles marked s.

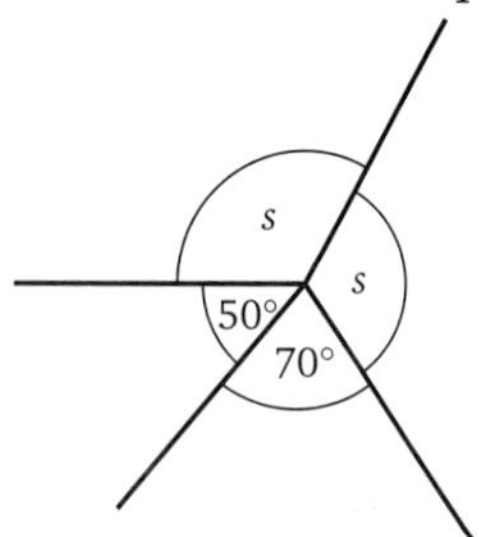

Do not always expect to see immediately how to find the angles asked for. Copy the diagram. On your copy, mark the sizes of any angles that you know or can work out. This may prompt you where to go next.

2 The angle marked f is twice the angle marked g. Find angles f and g.

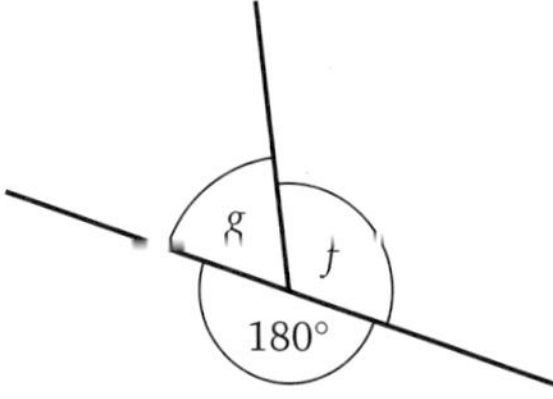

3 Find each of the equal angles marked d.

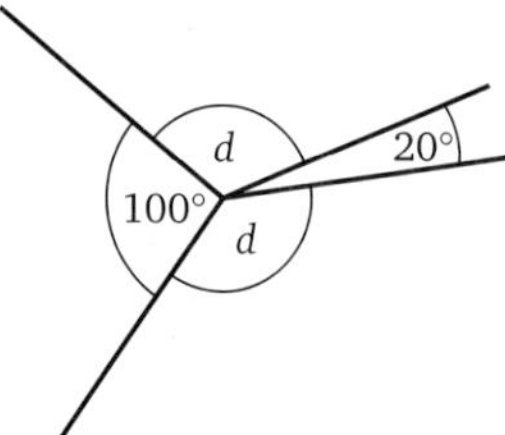

4 Each of the equal angles marked p is 25°. Find the reflex angle q.

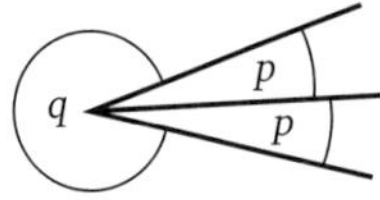

5 Each of the equal angles marked d is 30°. Angle d and angle e are supplementary. Find angles e and f. (An angle marked with a square is a right angle.)

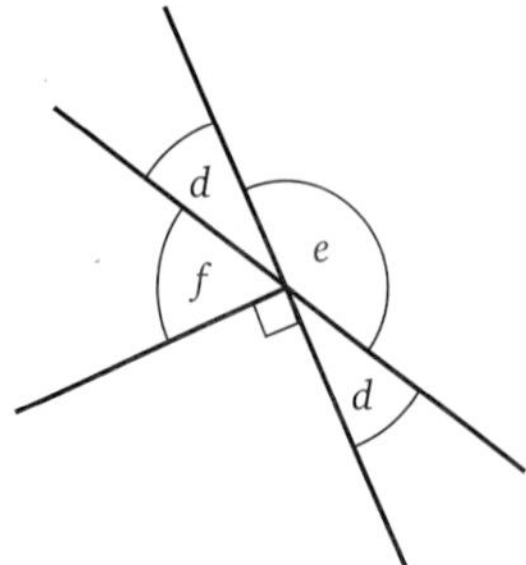

6 Angle s is twice angle t. Find angle r.

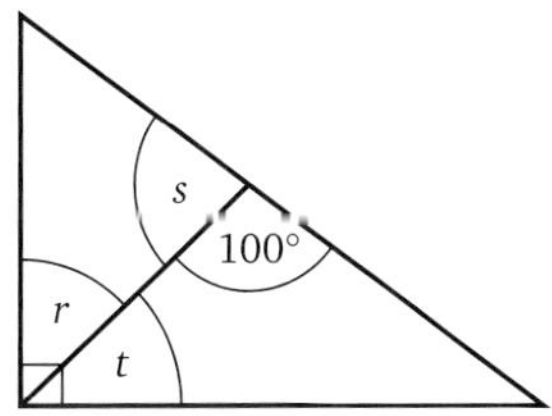

7 The angle marked d is 70°. Find angle e.

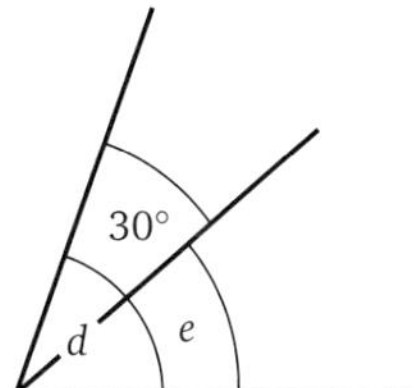

8 Find the angles marked p, q, r and s.

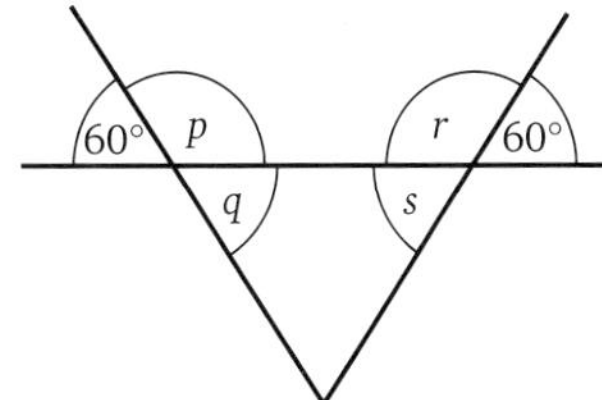

Investigation

1 How do you find the angle turned through by the hour hand of a clock in a given time?

Start by finding the angle turned through in 12 hours, then the angle for any other complete number of hours.

Next find the angle turned through for any fraction of an hour and, lastly, through a number of minutes.

2 Extend your investigation to the minute hand and the seconds hand.

3 How do you find the angle between the hands of a clock at any time? Start with times that give you the angles that are easiest to find. Remember that at 4.30 the minute hand will point to the 6 and the hour hand will be exactly halfway between 4 and 5.

4 Find out how many times there are in a day when the angle between the hour hand and the minute hand has a particular value, say 90°, 180°, or 120°.

5 What happens if the clock loses 10 minutes each hour? How many degrees would the minute hand turn through in 1 hour, or 15 minutes, or any other time?

6 What happens if the clock gains 5 minutes every hour?

Mixed exercises

Exercise 7n

Select the letter that gives the correct answer.

1 The angle that the minute hand of a clock turns through as it moves from 1 to 9 is

A 210° B 240° C 255° D 260°

2 Estimate the size of this angle.

A 20°
B 45°
C 60°
D 90°

3 The angle marked p is

A an acute angle
B a right angle
C an obtuse angle
D a reflex angle

4 The size of the angle marked s is

A 110°
B 130°
C 140°
D 150°

5 The size of each the angles marked e is

A 125° B 130° C 135° D 140°

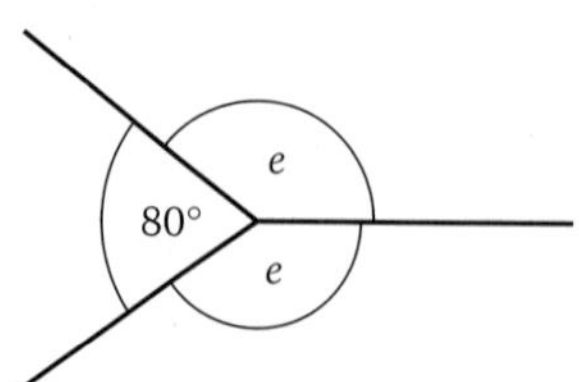

6 If you start facing east and turn clockwise through an angle of 270° the direction you are now facing is

A north B south C west D none of these

Exercise 7p

1 What angle does the minute hand of a clock turn through when it moves from 10 to 6?

2 If you start facing north and turn clockwise through an angle of 270°, in which direction are you then facing?

3 Use your protractor to find the angle marked q.

4 Write down the sizes of the angles marked f and g. Give a reason for your answer.

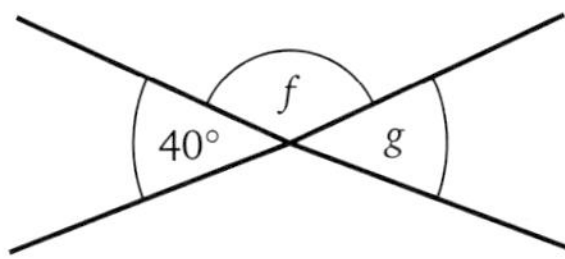

5 Write down the size of the angle marked h. Give a reason for your answer.

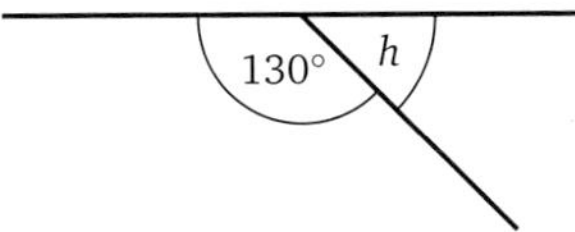

6 Angles p and q are supplementary. Angle p is five times the size of angle q. What is the size of angle q?

7 Angles x and y are complementary. If x is 20° more than y, what is the size of angle y?

Did you know?

Euclid was a mathematician in Ancient Greece. He collected the known geometry of the day in one of his books, *The Elements*. In doing so, he added ideas of his own.

In this chapter you have seen that...

- ✔ a revolution can be divided into four right angles
- ✔ a revolution can be divided into 360°
- ✔ an acute angle is smaller than 90°
- ✔ an obtuse angle is larger than 90° but smaller than 180°
- ✔ a reflex angle is larger than 180°
- ✔ angles at a point add to give 360°
- ✔ vertically opposite angles are formed when two lines cross and they are equal
- ✔ angles on a straight line add up to 180°
- ✔ two angles that add up to 180° are called supplementary angles
- ✔ two angles that add up to 90° are called complementary angles.

REVIEW TEST 1: CHAPTERS 1–7

In questions **1** to **12**, choose the letter for the correct answer.

1 To the nearest ten, 187 =

A 100 B 180 C 190 D 200

2 Given $X = \{2, 4, 6, 8\}$, $Y = \{4, 8, 12, 16\}$, then $X \cap Y =$

A {4, 8} B {2, 4, 6, 8, 12, 16}

C {2, 6} D {2, 6, 12, 16}

3 $2\frac{1}{3} \times 1\frac{2}{7} =$

A $\frac{1}{21}$ B $1\frac{1}{21}$ C $2\frac{2}{21}$ D $\frac{3}{1}$

4 The HCF of 12, 15 and 30 is

A 3 B 6 C 60 D 180

5 The prime factors of 12 are

A 2 and 3 B 3 and 4 C 2 and 6 D 1 and 12

6 $2 \times 1\frac{3}{4} =$

A $2\frac{3}{8}$ B $2\frac{3}{4}$ C $3\frac{1}{2}$ D $3\frac{3}{4}$

7 $A = \{\text{square numbers less than 10}\}$ and $B = \{\text{prime numbers less than 10}\}$.

$A \cap B =$

A {1, 9} B {9} C {2} D { }

8 At seven o'clock, the obtuse angle between the minute and hour hands of a clock measures

A 90° B 120° C 150° D 210°

9 Which of the following statements are true?

i Vertically opposite angles are complementary.

ii Angles at a point add up to 360 degrees.

iii An angle of 90 degrees is called a right angle.

A i and ii only B i and iii only C ii and iii only D i, ii and iii

10 An angle measuring 340° is

A acute B right C reflex D obtuse

Use the diagram below to answer questions **11** and **12**.

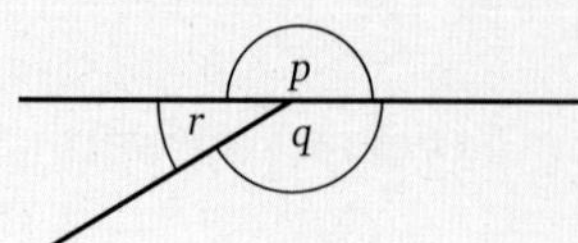

11 Angles q and r are

A both acute

B supplementary

C complementary

D vertically opposite

12 Given that $r = 50°$, $q =$

A $50°$ B $130°$ C $180°$ D $310°$

13 **a** Simplify $\frac{7}{12} \div \frac{21}{4}$ **b** Express 140 in prime factors.

14 In the diagram below calculate the sizes of the angles marked x, y and z.

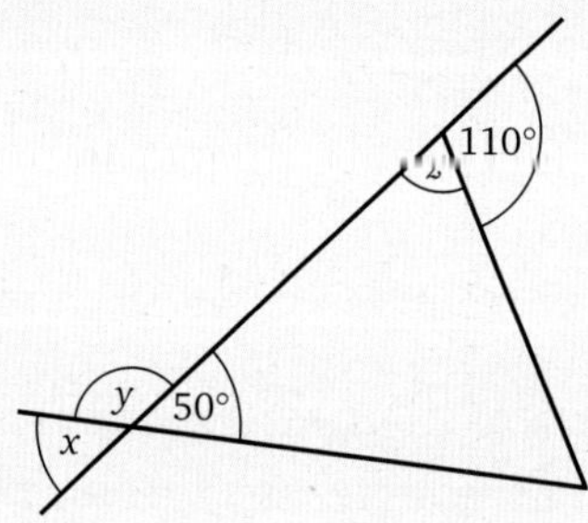

15 **a** Find the greatest common factor of 60 and 72.

b Given that $12\,740 = 2 \times 2 \times 5 \times 7 \times 7 \times 13$,

Does 13 divide 12 740? Why?

Does 9 divide 12 740? Why?

16 **a** An engine uses $\frac{3}{16}$ litres of oil in 1 hour. How many litres of oil will it use in 3 hours 10 minutes at this rate?

b If $\frac{7}{8}$ of a fence can be built in $3\frac{1}{2}$ hours, what fraction of the fence would be built in 1 hour working at the same rate?

17 **a** Given $P = \{\text{factors of } 36\}$, $Q = \{\text{factors of } 42\}$, list the members of

i $P \cap Q$ **ii** $P \cup Q$.

b Show in a Venn diagram $A = \{2, 3, 4, 6, 12\}$, $B = \{2, 4, 8\}$.

18 **a** Which of the following numbers are square numbers?

2, 6, 8, 9, 16, 18, 34, 36, 61, 73, 140, 169

b Which of the following numbers are *not* rectangular numbers?

5, 6, 11, 14, 15, 72, 91, 325, 403

Give a reason for your answer.

8 Introduction to decimals

At the end of this chapter you should be able to...

1 write a given number in expanded form – under the headings hundreds, tens, units, etc.

2 write a decimal number as a fraction and vice versa

3 add and subtract decimal numbers

4 multiply and divide decimal numbers by 10, 100, 1000, . . .

5 solve problems using operations on decimal numbers.

Did you know?

Theano, wife of Pythagoras, and two of her daughters were members of Pythagoras' mathematical school that included women who supported each other.

She wrote a biography of her husband, and it is believed that she and her daughters were responsible for attaching his name to a theorem which was well known at least 2000 years before his time.

You need to know...

✔ how to add and subtract whole numbers

✔ how to do short and long division

✔ how to multiply whole numbers.

Key words

decimal, fraction, triangle, quadrilateral, rectangle, regular pentagon

The meaning of decimals

Consider the number 426. The position of the digits indicates what each digit represents. We can write:

hundreds	tens	units
4	2	6

Each quantity in the heading is $\frac{1}{10}$ of the quantity to its left: ten is $\frac{1}{10}$ of a hundred, a unit is $\frac{1}{10}$ of ten. Moving further to the right we can have further headings: tenths of a unit, hundredths of a unit and so on (a hundredth of a unit is $\frac{1}{10}$ of a tenth of a unit). For example:

tens	units		tenths	hundredths
1	6	.	0	2

To mark where the units come we put a point after the units position. 16.02 is 1 ten, 6 units and 2 hundredths or $16\frac{2}{100}$.

units		tenths	hundredths	thousandths
0	.	0	0	4

0.004 is 4 thousandths or $\frac{4}{1000}$. In this case, 0 is written before the point to help make it clear where the point comes.

Exercise 8a

Write the following numbers in headed columns:

	tens	units		tenths	hundredths
34.62 =	3	4	.	6	2

	units		tenths	hundredths	thousandths	ten-thousandths
0.0207 =	0	.	0	2	0	7

1 2.6 **4** 0.09 **7** 1.046 **10** 0.604

2 32.1 **5** 101.3 **8** 12.001 **11** 15.045

3 6.03 **6** 0.00007 **9** 6.34 **12** 0.0092

Changing decimals to fractions

Exercise 8b

Write the following decimals as fractions in their lowest terms (using mixed numbers where necessary):

	units		tenths		
0.6 =	0	.	6	$= \frac{6}{10}$	Now cancel.
				$= \frac{3}{5}$	

	tens	units		tenths	hundredths		
12.04 =	1	2	.	0	4	$= 12\frac{4}{100}$	Now cancel the fraction.
						$= 12\frac{1}{25}$	

1	0.2	**4**	0.0007	**7**	0.7	**10**	1.7
2	0.06	**5**	0.001	**8**	2.01	**11**	15.5
3	1.3	**6**	6.4	**9**	1.8	**12**	8.06

You can go straight from the decimal to one fraction.

0.302

	units		tenths	hundredths	thousandths	
0.302 =	0	.	3	0	2	$= \frac{3}{10} + \frac{2}{1000}$

Now write these with a common denominator. $= \frac{300}{1000} + \frac{2}{1000}$

Now cancel. $= \frac{302}{1000}$

$= \frac{151}{500}$

You can miss out the first two steps and go straight to one fraction.

Write as fractions:

13	0.73	**16**	0.0029	**19**	0.071	**22**	0.63
14	0.081	**17**	0.000 67	**20**	0.3001	**23**	0.031
15	0.207	**18**	0.17	**21**	0.0207	**24**	0.47

Write as fractions in their lowest terms:

25	0.25	**28**	0.0305	**31**	0.35	**34**	0.125
26	0.072	**29**	0.15	**32**	0.0016	**35**	0.48
27	0.38	**30**	0.025	**33**	0.044	**36**	0.625

Changing fractions to decimals

Exercise 8c

Write the following numbers as decimals:

$3\frac{3}{100}$

		units		tenths	hundredths	
$3\frac{3}{100}$	=	3	.	0	3	= 3.03

1	$\frac{7}{100}$	**4**	$\frac{2}{1000}$	**7**	$\frac{4}{100}$	**10**	$\frac{6}{10000}$
2	$\frac{9}{10}$	**5**	$\frac{4}{10}$	**8**	$7\frac{8}{10}$	**11**	$4\frac{5}{1000}$
3	$1\frac{1}{10}$	**6**	$2\frac{6}{100}$	**9**	$7\frac{8}{100}$	**12**	$\frac{29}{10000}$

Addition of decimals

To add decimals you can write them in columns. It is important to keep the decimal points in line.

		tens	units		tenths	
$4.2 + 13.1 = 17.3$			4	.	2	2 tenths + 1 tenth = 3 tenths
	+	1	3	.	1	
		1	7	.	3	
$5.3 + 6.8 = 12.1$			5	.	3	3 tenths + 8 tenths = 11 tenths
	+		6	.	8	= 1 unit and 1 tenth
		1	2	.	1	
		/	/			

The headings above the digits need not be written as long as we know what they are and the decimal points are in line (including the invisible point after a whole number, e.g. 4 = 4.0).

Exercise 8d

Find 3 + 1.6 + 0.032 + 2.0066

Write the numbers in a column, keeping the decimal points in line.

$$\begin{array}{r} 3 \\ 1.6 \\ 0.032 \\ +\,2.0066 \\ \hline 6.6386 \\ \hline \end{array}$$

3 + 1.6 + 0.032 + 2.0066 = 6.6386

Find:

1 7.2 + 3.6

2 6.21 + 1.34

3 0.013 + 0.026

4 3.87 + 0.11

5 4.6 + 1.23

<u>6</u> 13.14 + 0.9

<u>7</u> 4 + 3.6

<u>8</u> 9.24 + 3

<u>9</u> 3.6 + 0.08

<u>10</u> 7.2 + 0.32 + 1.6

11 0.0043 + 0.263

12 0.002 + 2.1

13 0.000 52 + 0.001 24

14 0.068 + 0.003 + 0.06

15 4.62 + 0.078

<u>16</u> 0.32 + 0.032 + 0.0032

<u>17</u> 4.6 + 0.0005

<u>18</u> 16.8 + 3.9

<u>19</u> 1.62 + 2.078 + 3.1

<u>20</u> 7.34 + 6 + 14.034

21 Add 0.68 to 1.7.

22 Find the sum of 3.28 and 14.021.

23 To 7.9 add 4 and 3.72.

24 Evaluate 7.9 + 0.62 + 5.

25 Find the sum of 8.6, 5 and 3.21.

Remember that 4 is the same as 4.0.

Puzzle

4.33	0.59	2.36	5.608	3.182	0.57	0.649
6.25	1.89	5.81	3.218	1.14	2.98	3.902
3.72	0.9	3.7	5.989	6.27	6.804	0.098
0.13	5.91	3.241	0.68	1.291	2.99	4.2

1 Pair off as many numbers as possible so that all your number pairs add up to a number between 5 and 7. When your time is up your score is the sum of all the remaining numbers. The lower the score the better. (You will probably find it helpful to copy the list and cross out each pair of numbers that satisfies the condition.)

You have a time limit of two minutes for this exercise.

2 Repeat the exercise to try to reduce your score.

3 What is the lowest score possible?

4 Try to write down twelve numbers written as three rows with four numbers in each row so that the rules given in part **1** apply and the lowest possible score is 0. If you think you've succeeded, try it on a friend.

5 Using the same list of decimals pair them off so that the difference between the pairs lies between 0 and 1.

Subtraction of decimals

Exercise 8e

Subtraction also may be done by writing the numbers in columns, making sure that the decimal points are in line.

Find 24.2 – 13.7

$$\begin{array}{r} 24.2 \\ -\ 13.7 \\ \hline 10.5 \\ \hline \end{array}$$

24.2 – 13.7 = 10.5

Find:

1	6.8 – 4.3	**4**	0.62 – 0.21	**7**	3.273 – 1.032	**10**	7.32 – 0.67
2	9.6 – 1.8	**5**	0.0342 – 0.0021	**8**	0.262 – 0.071	**11**	54.07 – 12.62
3	32.7 – 14.2	**6**	17.23 – 0.36	**9**	102.6 – 31.2	**12**	7.063 – 0.124

It may be necessary to add zeros so that there is the same number of digits after the point in both cases.

Find 4.623 – 1.7   Fill 'empty' places with zeros.

$$\begin{array}{r} 4.623 \\ -\ 1.700 \\ \hline 2.923 \\ \hline \end{array}$$

4.623 – 1.7 = 2.923

Find 4.63 – 1.0342   Fill 'empty' places with zeros.

$$\begin{array}{r} 4.6300 \\ -\ 1.0342 \\ \hline 3.5958 \\ \hline \end{array}$$

4.63 – 1.0342 = 3.5958

Find:

13 3.26 – 0.2

14 3.2 – 0.26

15 14.23 – 11.1

16 6.8 – 4.14

17 11 – 8.6

18 7.98 – 0.098

19 7.098 – 0.98

20 3.2 – 0.428

21 11.2 – 0.0026

22 0.000 32 – 0.000 123

23 0.0073 – 0.0006

24 0.0073 – 0.006

25 0.006 – 0.000 73

26 0.06 – 0.000 73

27 6 – 0.73

28 6 – 0.073

29 7.3 – 0.06

30 730 – 0.6

31 0.73 – 0.000 06

32 0.73 – 0.6

33 Take 19.2 from 76.8.

34 Subtract 1.9 from 10.2.

35 From 0.168 subtract 0.019.

36 Evaluate 7.62 – 0.81.

11 is the same as 11.0.

Exercise 8f

Find the value of:

1 8.62 + 1.7

2 8.62 – 1.7

3 3.8 – 0.82

4 0.08 + 0.32 + 6.2

5 5 – 0.6

6 100 + 0.28

7 100 – 0.28

8 0.26 + 0.026

9 0.26 – 0.026

10 78.42 – 0.8

11 38.2 + 1.68

12 38.2 – 1.68

13 0.84 + 2 + 200

14 16 + 1.6 + 0.16

15 1.4 – 0.81

16 0.02 – 0.013

17 0.062 + 0.32

18 6.83 – 0.19

19 17.2 + 20 + 1.62

20 9.2 + 13.21 – 14.6

The distance all round this triangle is 6.5 cm.

What is the length of the third side?

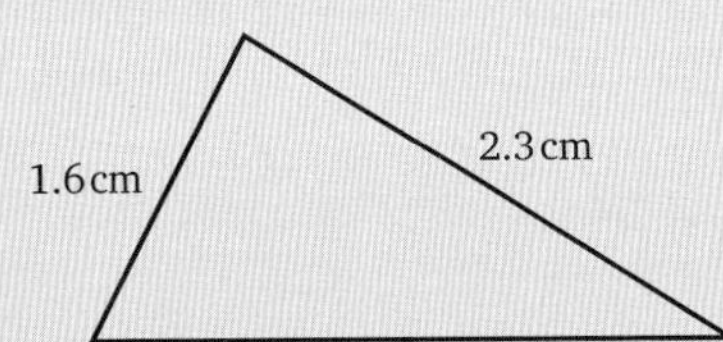

As the distance round the three sides is 6.5 cm, you can find the third side by adding the lengths of the two sides that you know, then take the result from 6.5 cm.

1.6 cm + 2.3 cm = 3.9 cm

$$\begin{array}{r} 1.6 \\ +\ 2.3 \\ \hline 3.9 \end{array}$$

The length of the third side is 6.5 cm – 3.9 cm = 2.6 cm

$$\begin{array}{r} 6.5 \\ -\ 3.9 \\ \hline 2.6 \end{array}$$

21 A tape is to be placed round this rectangle. Find the length of tape required.

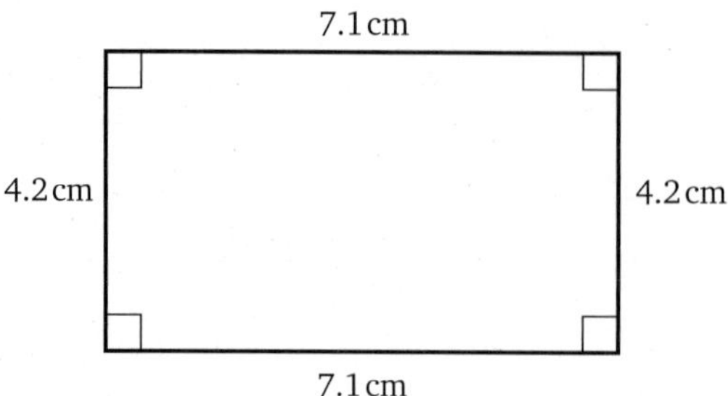

22 A piece of webbing is 7.6 m long. If 2.3 m is cut off, how much is left?

23 Find the total bill for three articles costing \$5, \$6.52 and \$13.25.

24 The bill for two books came to \$28.48. One book cost \$7.44. What was the cost of the other one?

25 Add 2.32 and 0.68 and subtract the result from 4.

26 The diagram shows the measurements of the sides of a field. Find the length of fencing required to enclose the field.

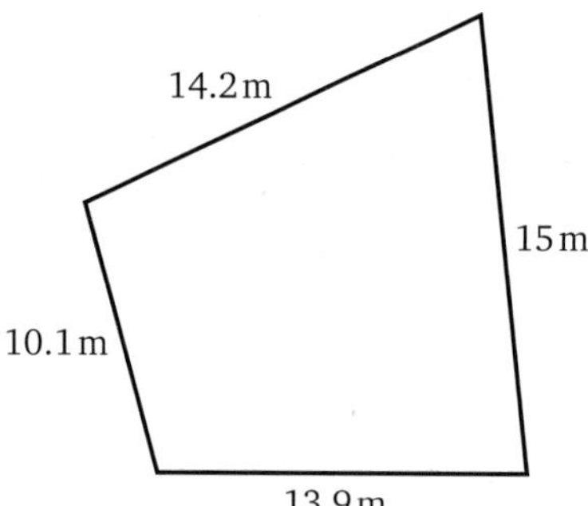

27 The bill for three meals was \$30. The first meal cost \$7.15 and the second \$13.60. What was the cost of the third?

28 The total distance round the sides of this quadrilateral is 19 cm. What is the length of the fourth side?

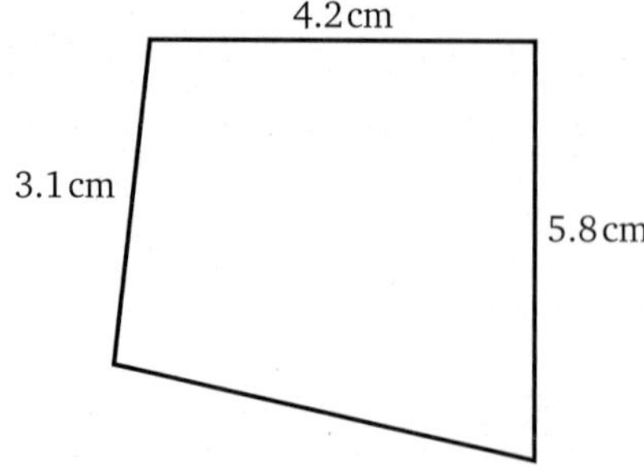

Puzzle

If the sum of the numbers in all the rows, columns and diagonals of a square is the same the square is called a magic square.

For example in this magic square the total in every row, column and diagonal is 21.

9	8	4
2	7	12
10	6	5

1 Fill in the blanks in this magic square if the total is always 18.9.

		8.1
5.4	6.3	7.2
	10.8	

2 This magic square contains two wrong numbers. Find these wrong numbers and correct them.

6.3	5.5	2.8
1.4	4.9	8.5
7.0	4.2	3.5

3 Insert decimal points so that this is a magic square.

15	10	30	60
40	50	16	90
14	11	20	70
10	80	13	12

Multiplication by 10, 100, 1000, ...

Consider $32 \times 10 = 320$. Writing 32 and 320 in headed columns gives

hundreds	tens	units
	3	2
3	2	0

Multiplying by 10 has made the number of units become the number of tens, and the number of tens has become the number of hundreds, so that all the digits have moved one place to the left.

Consider 0.2×10. When multiplied by 10, tenths become units $\left(\frac{1}{10} \times 10 = 1\right)$, so

units		tenths				units
0	.	2	$\times$	10	=	2

Again the digit has moved one place to the left.

Multiplying by 100 means multiplying by 10 and then by 10 again, so the digits move 2 places to the left.

	tens	units		tenths	hundredths	thousandths		
		0	.	4	2	6	×	100
=	4	2	.	6				

Notice that the digits move to the left while the point stays put but without headings it looks as though the digits stay put and the point moves to the right.

When necessary we fill in an empty space with a zero.

units		tenths				hundreds	tens	units
4	.	2	×	100	=	4	2	0

Exercise 8g

Find the value of:

a 368×100 $\quad 368 \times 100 = 36\,800$

b 3.68×10 $\quad 3.68 \times 10 = 36.8$

c 3.68×1000 $\quad 3.68 \times 1000 = 3680$

Find the value of:

1 72×1000

2 8.24×10

3 0.0024×100

4 46×10

5 32.78×100

6 $0.043 \times 10\,000$

7 0.0602×100

8 3.206×10

9 72.81×1000

10 $0.000\,0063 \times 10$

11 $0.007\,03 \times 100$

12 $0.0374 \times 10\,000$

Division by 10, 100, 1000, ...

When we divide by 10, hundreds become tens and tens become units.

hundreds	tens	units		tens	units
6	4	0	÷ 10 =	6	4

The digits move one place to the right and the number becomes smaller but it looks as though the decimal point moves to the left so

$$2.72 \div 10 = 0.272$$

To divide by 100 the point is moved two places to the left.
To divide by 1000 the point is moved three places to the left.

Exercise 8h

Find the value of:

a $3.2 \div 10$

b $320 \div 10\,000$

a $3.2 \div 10 = 0.32$

b The units become ten-thousandths, the tens become thousandths, and so on.

$320 \div 10\,000 = 0.0320 = 0.032$

The final zero can be omitted because it doesn't affect the value of anything.

Find the value of:

1 $277.2 \div 100$

2 $76.26 \div 10$

3 $0.000\,24 \div 10$

4 $1.4 \div 100$

5 $27 \div 10$

6 $6.8 \div 100$

7 $0.26 \div 10$

8 $15.8 \div 1000$

9 $426 \div 10\,000$

10 $13.4 \div 10$

11 $3.74 \div 1000$

12 $0.92 \div 100$

Mixed multiplication and division

Exercise 8i

Find:

1 $1.6 \div 10$

2 1.6×10

3 0.078×100

4 $0.078 \div 100$

5 14.2×100

6 0.068×100

7 $1.63 \div 100$

8 $2 \div 1000$

9 $140 \div 1000$

10 $7.8 \times 10\,000$

11 $24 \div 100$

12 0.063×1000

13 0.32×10

14 $7.9 \div 100$

15 $0.000\,78 \times 100$

16 $2.4 \div 10$

17 11.1×1000

18 $0.038 \div 100$

19 $0.38 \div 100$

20 $3.8 \times 100\,000$

21 $0.024 \div 100$

22 $0.3 \div 100\,000$

23 0.0041×1000

24 0.1004×100

25 Share 42 m of string equally amongst 10 people.

26 Find the total cost of 100 articles at $1.52 each.

27 Evaluate $13.8 \div 100$ and 13.8×100.

28 Multiply 1.6 by 100 and then divide the result by 1000.

29 Add 16.2 and 1.26 and divide the result by 100.

30 Take 9.6 from 13.4 and divide the result by 1000.

Mixed exercises

Exercise 8j

Select the letter that gives the correct answer.

1 0.02 as a fraction in its lowest terms is

A $\frac{1}{500}$ B $\frac{1}{50}$ C $\frac{1}{5}$ D none of these

2 $\frac{91}{1000}$ as a decimal is

A 0.0091 B 0.091 C 0.91 D 0.09

3 The sum of 4.27, 31 and 1.6 is

A 35.87 B 35.9 C 36.87 D 36.9

4 When 1.82 is subtracted from 4.2 the result is

A 2.16 B 2.28 C 2.38 D 6.02

5 $0.0301 \times 100 =$

A 3 B 3.01 C 3.1 D 30.1

6 The distance around this quadrilateral in centimetres is

A 15.84 B 19.68 C 20.52 D 20.72

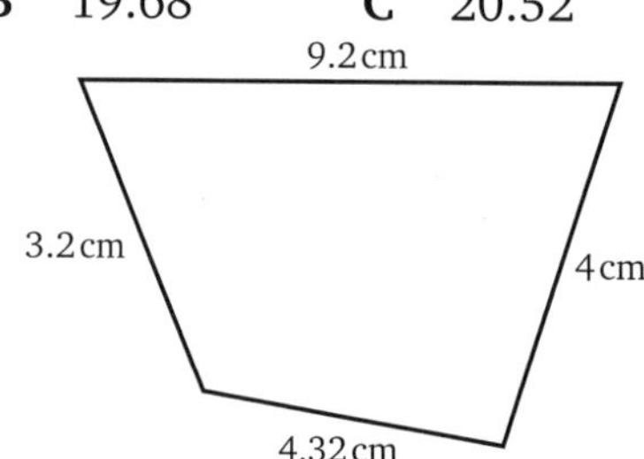

Exercise 8k

1 Give 0.3 as a fraction.

2 Express $\frac{14}{100}$ as a decimal.

3 Find the sum of 16.2, 4.12 and 7.

4 Find the value of $0.062 \div 100$.

5 Find the total bill for three books costing $4.26, $5 and $1.32.

6 Subtract 14.8 from 16.3.

7 Give 0.008 as a fraction in its lowest terms.

8 Add 14.2, 6, 0.38 and 7.21 together.

9 Subtract 14.96 from 100.

10 Divide 8.6 by 1000.

11 Find 8.2 – 1.92.

12 Add 4.2 and 0.28 and subtract 1.5 from the result.

13 Multiply 0.028 by 10 000.

14 I go into a shop with $19.44 and buy two articles, one costing $7.39 and the other $9.53. How much do I have left?

Did you know?

Pythagoras was a member of a closely knit brotherhood. He was founder of the famous Pythagorean school, which was devoted to the study of philosophy, mathematics and natural science.

These Pythagoreans believed that natural numbers were the building blocks of everything, and attached special significance to certain natural numbers.

Some examples are:

One – the number of reason

Two – the first female number, represented diversity of opinion

Three – the first male number, represented harmony

Four – suggested the squaring of accounts

Five – the union of the first male and female numbers, represented marriage.

In this chapter you have seen that...

✔ the decimal point divides the units from the tenths

✔ you can add and subtract decimals by writing them in columns, making sure that the decimal points are in line

✔ you can multiply decimals by 10, 100, . . . by moving the digits to the left

✔ you can divide decimals by 10, 100, . . . by moving the digits to the right

✔ a decimal can be changed to a fraction by writing the numbers after the point as tenths, hundredths, . . . and simplifying.

9 Multiplication and division of decimals

At the end of this chapter you should be able to...

1 multiply two decimal numbers
2 write a given fraction as a recurring decimal
3 write a number correct to a given number of decimal places
4 multiply and divide decimal numbers by whole numbers
5 divide by a decimal number
6 change a fractional number to a decimal number
7 order a set of numbers by size.

Did you know?

Srinivasa Ramanujan was known as a 'mathematician's mathematician'. He came from India to England in 1914 to study mathematics with Godfrey H. Hardy. He developed a notebook of over 6000 theorems. He died in 1920 at the age of 33.

You need to know...

✔ how to multiply fractions together
✔ place value in decimals
✔ how to multiply or divide by 10, 100, . . .
✔ how to divide by a whole number.

Key words

denominator, equilateral triangle, numerator, product, recurring decimal

Long method of multiplication

Exercise 9a

From Chapter 6 you know how to multiply fractions. Convert each decimal to a fraction, then multiply the fractions.

Calculate the following products:

1 0.3×0.02
2 0.1×0.1
3 0.003×6
4 3×0.02
5 0.001×0.3
6 0.4×0.0001
7 4×0.06
8 0.4×0.0012
9 0.08×0.01
10 0.0003×0.002
11 0.9×0.02
12 0.004×2

$0.3 \times 0.02 = \frac{3}{10} \times \frac{2}{100} = \frac{6}{1000} = 0.006$

Short method of multiplication

In the examples above, if we add together the number of digits (including zeros) after the decimal points in the original two numbers, we get the number of digits after the point in the answer.

The number of digits after the point is called the number of decimal places. In the first example in Exercise 9a, 0.3 has one decimal place, 0.02 has two decimal places and the answer, 0.006, has three decimal places, which is the sum of one and two.

We can use this fact to work out 0.3×0.02 without using fractions. Multiply 3 by 2 ignoring the decimal points; count up the number of decimal places after the decimal points and then put the point in the correct position in the answer, writing in zeros where necessary, i.e. $0.3 \times 0.02 = 0.006$.

Any zeros that come after the point must be included when counting the decimal places.

Exercise 9b

Find 0.08×0.4

(First ignore the decimal points; just multiply the numbers together, i.e. $8 \times 4 = 32$. Now count the number of decimal places in each of the two numbers you are multiplying together. Adding them gives the number of places in the answer, counting back from the right-hand digit. Sometimes you have to put a zero in too, because there aren't enough decimal places.)

0.08	×	0.4	=	0.032	$8 \times 4 = 32$
(2 places)		(1 place)		(3 places)	

Find 6×0.002

6	×	0.002	=	0.012	$6 \times 2 = 12$
(0 places)		(3 places)		(3 places)	

Calculate the following products:

1 0.6×0.3

2 0.04×0.06

3 0.009×2

4 0.07×0.008

<u>**5**</u> 0.12×0.09

<u>**6**</u> 0.07×0.0003

<u>**7**</u> 0.5×0.07

<u>**8**</u> 8×0.6

<u>**9**</u> 0.08×0.08

<u>**10**</u> 3×0.0006

<u>**11**</u> 0.7×0.06

<u>**12**</u> 9×0.08

13 0.07×12

14 4×0.009

<u>**15**</u> 0.9×9

<u>**16**</u> 0.0008×11

<u>**17**</u> 7×0.011

<u>**18**</u> 0.04×7

Zeros appearing in the multiplication in the middle or at the right-hand end must also be considered when counting the places.

0.252×0.4

0.252	×	0.4	=	0.1008
(3 places)		(1 place)		(4 places)

$$\begin{array}{r} 252 \\ \times \quad 4 \\ \hline 1008 \\ \hline \end{array}$$

2.5×6

2.5	×	6	=	15.0
(1 place)		(0 places)		(1 place)

$$\begin{array}{r} 25 \\ \times \quad 6 \\ \hline 150 \\ \hline \end{array}$$

300×0.2

300	×	0.2	=	60.0	$300 \times 2 = 600$
(0 places)		(1 place)		(1 place)	

Calculate the following products:

19 0.751×0.2
20 3.2×0.5
21 0.35×4
22 1.52×0.0006
23 400×0.6
24 31.5×2
25 5.6×0.02
26 0.008×256
27 320×0.07
28 0.4×0.0055
29 0.5×0.06
30 0.04×0.352
31 1.6×0.4
32 1.6×0.5
33 160×0.004
34 0.16×0.005
35 4×1.6
36 5×0.016
37 0.00004×0.00016
38 16000×0.05
39 0.16×4
40 0.0016×5
41 0.072×0.6
42 310×0.04

Multiplication

Exercise 9c

Find 0.26×1.3

0.26	$\times$	1.3	=	0.338
(2 places)		(1 place)		(3 places)

$$\begin{array}{r} 26 \\ \times 13 \\ \hline 78 \\ 260 \\ \hline 338 \end{array}$$

Calculate the following products:

1 4.2×1.6
2 52×0.24
3 0.68×0.14
4 48.2×26
5 310×1.4
6 1.68×0.27
7 13.2×2.5
8 0.0082×0.034
9 17.8×420
10 3.2×37
11 39×0.23
12 0.264×750
13 14.4×4.5
14 1.36×0.082
15 0.081×0.032
16 1.6×1.6
17 0.16×16
18 0.0016×1600
19 0.28×0.28
20 0.34×0.31
21 14×0.123
22 1.9×9.1
23 8.2×2.8
24 0.047×0.66

Division by whole numbers

We can see that

units		tenths		units		tenths
0	.	6	$\div 2 =$	0	.	3

because 6 tenths $\div$ 2 = 3 tenths. So we may divide by a whole number using the same layout as we do with whole numbers as long as we keep the digits in the correct columns and the points are in line.

Each number in a division calculation has its own name. The number we are dividing into is called the dividend, the number we are dividing by is called the divisor and the result is called the quotient.

$$0.6 \div 2 = 0.3$$

dividend divisor quotient

i.e. dividend ÷ divisor = quotient

Exercise 9d

Find the value of:

1 $0.4 \div 2$

2 $3.2 \div 2$

3 $0.63 \div 3$

4 $7.8 \div 3$

5 $0.9 \div 9$

6 $0.95 \div 5$

7 $0.672 \div 3$

8 $26.6 \div 7$

9 $42.6 \div 2$

10 $7.53 \div 3$

11 $6.56 \div 4$

12 $0.75 \div 5$

It may sometimes be necessary to fill spaces with zeros.

$0.000\,36 \div 3$

$0.000\,36 \div 3 = 0.000\,12$

$$3\overline{)0.00036}$$
$$0.000\,12$$

$0.45 \div 5$

$0.45 \div 5 = 0.09$

$$5\overline{)0.45}$$
$$0.09$$

$6.12 \div 3$

$6.12 \div 3 = 2.04$

$$3\overline{)6.12}$$
$$2.04$$

13 $0.057 \div 3$

14 $0.000\,65 \div 5$

15 $0.008\,72 \div 4$

16 $0.168 \div 4$

<u>17</u> $0.012 \div 6$

<u>18</u> $0.000\,36 \div 6$

<u>19</u> $1.62 \div 2$

<u>20</u> $4.24 \div 4$

<u>21</u> $1.232 \div 4$

<u>22</u> $0.6552 \div 6$

<u>23</u> $0.0285 \div 5$

<u>24</u> $0.1359 \div 3$

25 $0.0076 \div 4$

26 $0.81 \div 9$

27 $0.5215 \div 5$

28 $0.000\,075 \div 5$

<u>29</u> $6.3 \div 7$

<u>30</u> $0.0636 \div 6$

<u>31</u> $0.038 \div 2$

<u>32</u> $4.62 \div 6$

<u>33</u> $14.749 \div 7$

<u>34</u> $1.86 \div 3$

<u>35</u> $0.222 \div 6$

<u>36</u> $6.24 \div 8$

It may be necessary to add zeros at the end of a number in order to finish the division.

2.9 ÷ 8

2.9 ÷ 8 = 0.3625

$8\overline{)2.9000}$

0.3625

Find the value of:

37 6 ÷ 5

38 7.4 ÷ 4

39 0.83 ÷ 2

40 0.9 ÷ 6

41 3.6 ÷ 5

42 0.0002 ÷ 5

43 7.1 ÷ 8

44 7 ÷ 4

45 9.1 ÷ 2

46 0.00031 ÷ 2

47 9.4 ÷ 4

48 0.062 ÷ 5

49 0.5 ÷ 4

50 0.31 ÷ 8

51 2.6 ÷ 5

52 7.62 ÷ 4

53 13 ÷ 5

54 0.3 ÷ 6

55 0.01 ÷ 4

56 3.014 ÷ 5

57 6.83 ÷ 8

58 14.7 ÷ 6

59 2.3 ÷ 4

60 0.446 ÷ 8

If we divide 7.8 m of tape equally amongst 5 people, how long a piece will they each have?

We need to divide 7.8 m into 5 equal lengths, so we need to find 7.8 ÷ 5.

Length of each piece = 7.8 ÷ 5 m

= 1.56 m

$5\overline{)7.80}$

1.56

61 The total distance round the sides of a square is 14.6 cm. What is the length of a side?

62 Divide 32.6 m into 8 equal parts.

63 Share 14.3 kg equally between 2 people.

64 The total distance round the sides of a regular pentagon (a five-sided figure with all the sides equal) is 16 cm. What is the length of one side?

65 Share $36 equally amongst 8 people.

Long division

We can also use long division. The decimal point is used only in the original number and the answer, and not in the lines of working below these.

Exercise 9e

Find $2.56 \div 16$

$2.56 \div 16 = 0.16$

$$\begin{array}{r} 0.16 \\ 16\overline{)2.56} \\ \underline{1\,6} \\ 96 \\ \underline{96} \end{array}$$

$4.2 \div 25$

$4.2 \div 25 = 0.168$

$$\begin{array}{r} 0.168 \\ 25\overline{)4.200} \\ \underline{2\,5} \\ 1\,70 \\ \underline{1\,50} \\ 200 \\ \underline{200} \end{array}$$

Find the value of:

1	$26.4 \div 24$	**<u>7</u>**	$0.0615 \div 15$	**13**	$35.52 \div 111$	**<u>19</u>**	$20.79 \div 99$
2	$2.1 \div 14$	**<u>8</u>**	$0.864 \div 24$	**14**	$7.28 \div 28$	**<u>20</u>**	$0.01426 \div 20$
3	$1.56 \div 13$	**<u>9</u>**	$8.48 \div 16$	**15**	$1.296 \div 54$	**<u>21</u>**	$23.4 \div 45$
4	$9.45 \div 21$	**<u>10</u>**	$5.2 \div 20$	**16**	$0.00805 \div 35$	**<u>22</u>**	$71.76 \div 23$
<u>5</u>	$11.22 \div 22$	**<u>11</u>**	$7.84 \div 14$	**<u>17</u>**	$54.4 \div 17$	**<u>23</u>**	$39.48 \div 47$
<u>6</u>	$80 \div 25$	**<u>12</u>**	$25.2 \div 36$	**<u>18</u>**	$21.93 \div 51$	**<u>24</u>**	$0.2556 \div 45$

Changing fractions to decimals (exact values)

We may think of $\frac{3}{4}$ as $3 \div 4$ and hence write it as a decimal.

Exercise 9f

Express $\frac{3}{4}$ as a decimal.

$\frac{3}{4} = 3 \div 4 = 0.75$

$$\begin{array}{r} 4\overline{)3.{}^{3}0{}^{2}0} \\ 0.75 \end{array}$$

Express the following fractions as decimals:

1 $\frac{1}{4}$

2 $\frac{3}{8}$

3 $\frac{3}{5}$

4 $\frac{5}{16}$

5 $\frac{1}{25}$

6 $2\frac{4}{5}$

7 $\frac{5}{8}$

8 $\frac{7}{16}$

9 $\frac{3}{25}$

10 $\frac{1}{32}$

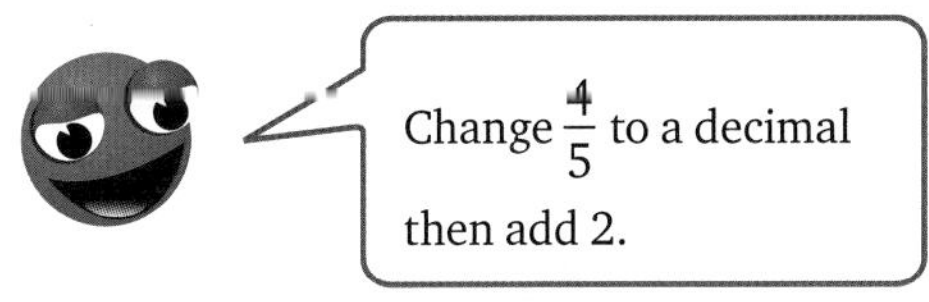

Standard decimals and fractions

It is worthwhile knowing a few equivalent fractions and decimals. For example

$\frac{1}{2} = 0.5$ $\frac{1}{4} = 0.25$ $\frac{3}{4} = 0.75$ $\frac{1}{8} = 0.125$

Exercise 9g

Write the following decimals as fractions in their lowest terms, without any working if possible:

(Notice that $\frac{2}{5} = \frac{4}{10} = 0.4$)

1 0.2

2 0.3

3 0.8

4 0.75

5 0.6

6 0.7

7 0.9

8 0.05

Write the following fractions as decimals:

9 $\frac{9}{10}$

10 $\frac{1}{4}$

11 $\frac{4}{5}$

12 $\frac{3}{8}$

13 $\frac{3}{100}$

14 $\frac{3}{4}$

15 $\frac{5}{8}$

16 $\frac{7}{100}$

Investigation

If we divide 2 by 5 we get an exact answer, namely 0.4.

However, if we divide 2 by 3 the answer is 0.666 666 6… going on forever, i.e. $2 \div 3$ does not give an exact decimal. We say that 6 recurs. Some of the numbers we get when we divide one whole number by another are interesting and are worth investigating.

(You should not use a calculator for this work before you have used pencil and paper methods.)

1 Find $0.4 \div 7$. Continue working until you have at least 12 non-zero digits in your answer. Use a calculator to check the first 8 non-zero digits of your answer. What do you notice about the pattern of digits in your answer?

2 Now try $0.2 \div 7$. Do you get the same digits in the same order? How does this answer differ from the answer you got in part **1**?

3 Can you find any other decimals which, when divided by 7, give the same pattern of digits, but start in a different place in the pattern?

4 Now try any numbers larger than 1 that 7 does not divide into exactly. For example $1.5 \div 7$ and $2.2 \div 7$.

5 Is it true to say that every decimal, when divided by 7, gives either an exact answer, or a recurring answer that involves the same cycle of digits?

6 Repeat parts **1** to **5** but divide by 9 instead of 7.

7 What happens if you divide by the other odd prime numbers less than 10?

8 What happens if you divide by the even numbers less than 10?

Problems

Exercise 9h

Find the cost of 6 books at \$2.35 each.

The total cost is equal to the cost of 1 book multiplied by the number of books.

$\therefore$ Cost = \$2.35 × 6
= \$14.10

$$\begin{array}{r} 235 \\ \times \quad 6 \\ \hline 1410 \\ \hline \end{array}$$

1 Find the cost of 10 articles at \$32.50 each.

2 The total distance round the sides of a square is 17.6 cm. Find the length of one side of the square.

Read the question slowly to make sure you understand what you are being asked to do. Read it several times if necessary.

3 Divide 26.6 kg into 7 equal parts.

4 Find the total distance round the sides of a square of side 4.2 cm.

5 Find the cost of 62 notebooks at 68 c each, first in cents and then in dollars.

6 Multiply 3.2 by 0.6 and divide the result by 8.

7 If 68.25 m of ribbon is divided into 21 equal pieces, how long is each piece?

8 The length of a side of a regular twelve-sided polygon (a shape with 12 equal sides) is 4.2 m.
Find the total distance round the sides of the polygon.

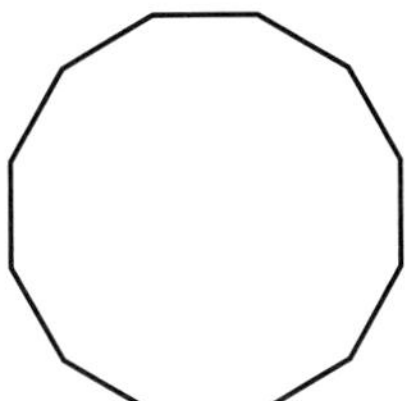

Puzzle

6.21	0.822	0.095	0.673	3.92	6.753	7.138	0.77
34.08	1.37	4.316	3.645	0.547	6.44	1.273	0.75

This is a number game. The aim is to pair off as many numbers as possible so that all the number pairs multiply together to give an answer between 3 and 5.

The time limit is 1 minute.

Choose a pair of numbers, multiply them together on your calculator and cross them off the list if their product is between 3 and 5. Any numbers not used are added together to give your score.

Repeat in an effort to get a lower score!

Recurring decimals

Consider the calculation

$$3 \div 4 = 0.75 \qquad \begin{array}{r} 4\overline{)3.00} \\ 0.75 \end{array}$$

By adding two zeros after the point we are able to finish the division and give an exact answer. Now consider

$$2 \div 3 = 0.666\ldots \qquad \begin{array}{r} 3\overline{)2.0000\ldots} \\ 0.6666\ldots \end{array}$$

We can see that we will continue to obtain 6s for ever, also written as ..., and we say that the 6 *recurs*.

Consider

$31 \div 11 = 2.8181\ldots$

$$11\overline{)31.0000}$$
$$2.8181$$

Here 81 recurs.

Sometimes it is one digit which is repeated and sometimes it is a group of digits. If one digit or a group continues to *recur* we have a *recurring decimal*.

Exercise 9i

Calculate $0.2 \div 7$

$0.2 \div 7 = 0.028\,571\,428\,571\,4\ldots$

$$7\overline{)0.200\,000\,000\,000\,000\ldots}$$
$$0.028\,571\,428\,571\,428\ldots$$

Calculate:

1. $1.4 \div 6$
2. $0.03 \div 11$
3. $4 \div 7$
4. $0.43 \div 3$
5. $0.03 \div 7$
6. $1.1 \div 9$

Express $\frac{4}{3}$ as a decimal.

$\frac{4}{3} = 4 \div 3 = 1.333\ldots$

$$3\overline{)4.00}$$
$$1.33$$

Express the following fractions as decimals:

7. $\frac{4}{9}$
8. $\frac{2}{3}$
9. $\frac{2}{11}$
10. $\frac{5}{7}$
11. $\frac{7}{9}$
12. $\frac{8}{7}$

Dot notation

To save writing so many digits we use a dot notation for recurring decimals.

For example

$\frac{1}{6} = 1 \div 6 = 0.1666$

$= 0.1\dot{6}$

$$6\overline{)1.000}$$
$$0.166$$

and $0.2 \div 7 = 0.0\dot{2}8\,571\,\dot{4}$

$$7\overline{)0.2}$$
$$0.028\,571\,428\,571\,428$$

The dots are placed over the single recurring number or over the first and last digits of the recurring group.

Exercise 9j

Write the answers to questions **1** to **12** in Exercise 9i using the dot notation.

Correcting to a given number of decimal places

Often we need to know only the first few digits of a decimal. For instance, if we measure a length with an ordinary ruler we usually need an answer to the nearest $\frac{1}{10}$ cm and are not interested, or cannot see, how many $\frac{1}{100}$ cm are involved.

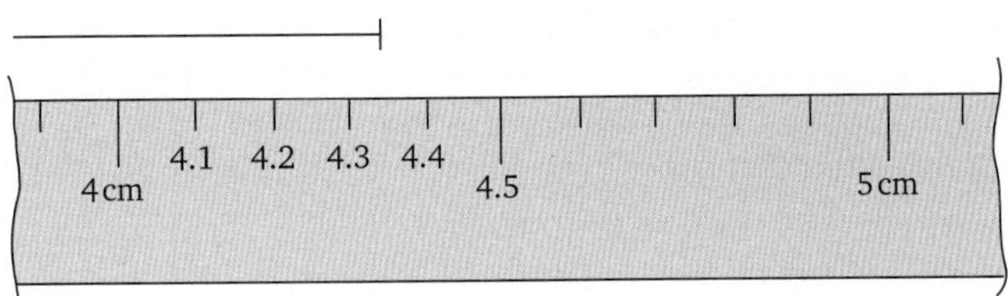

Look at this enlarged view of the end of a line which is being measured. We can see that with a more accurate measure we might be able to give the length as 4.34 cm. However on the given ruler we would probably measure it as 4.3 cm because we can see that the end of the line is nearer 4.3 than 4.4. We cannot give the exact length of the line but we can say that it is 4.3 cm long to the nearest $\frac{1}{10}$ cm. We write this as 4.3 cm correct to 1 decimal place.

Consider the numbers 0.62, 0.622, 0.625, 0.627 and 0.63. To compare them we write 0.62 as 0.620 and 0.63 as 0.630 so that each number has 3 digits after the point. When we write them in order in a column:

0.620

0.622

0.625

0.627

0.630

we can see that 0.622 is nearer to 0.620 than to 0.630 while 0.627 is nearer to 0.630 so we write

$0.62 \vdots 2 = 0.62$ (correct to 2 decimal places)

$0.62 \vdots 7 = 0.63$ (correct to 2 decimal places)

It is not so obvious what to do with 0.625 as it is halfway between 0.62 and 0.63. To save arguments, if the digit after the cut-off line is 5 or more we add 1 to the digit before the cut-off line, i.e. we round the number *up*, so we write

$0.62 \vdots 5 = 0.63$ (correct to 2 decimal places)

Exercise 9k

Give 10.9315 correct to

a the nearest whole number **b** 1 decimal place **c** 3 decimal places.

a 10.¦9315 = 11 (correct to the nearest whole number)

b 10.9¦315 = 10.9 (correct to 1 decimal place)

c 10.931¦5 = 10.932 (correct to 3 decimal places)

Give 4.699 and 0.007 correct to 2 decimal places.

4.69¦9 = 4.70 (correct to 2 decimal places)

0.00¦7 = 0.01 (correct to 2 decimal places)

Give the following numbers correct to 2 decimal places:

1	0.328	**6**	0.6947
2	0.322	**7**	0.8351
3	1.2671	**8**	3.927
4	2.345	**9**	0.0084
5	0.0416	**10**	3.9999

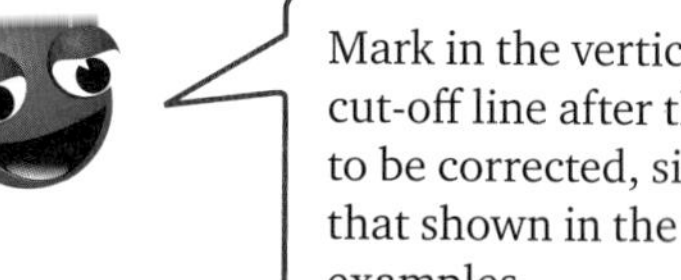

Give the following numbers correct to the nearest whole number:

11	13.9	**13**	26.5	**15**	4.45	**17**	109.7	**19**	74.09
12	6.34	**14**	2.78	**16**	6.783	**18**	6.145	**20**	3.9999

Give the following numbers correct to 3 decimal places:

21	0.3627	**26**	0.0843
22	0.026 234	**27**	0.084 47
23	0.007 14	**28**	0.3251
24	0.0695	**29**	0.032 51
25	0.000 98	**30**	3.9999

Don't forget the cut-off line.

Give the following numbers correct to the number of decimal places indicated in the brackets:

31	1.784	(1)	**36**	1.639	(2)
32	42.64	(1)	**37**	1.639	(1)
33	1.0092	(2)	**38**	1.689	(nearest whole number)
34	0.009 42	(4)	**39**	3.4984	(2)
35	0.7345	(3)	**40**	3.4984	(1)

If we are asked to give an answer correct to a certain number of decimal places, we work out one more decimal place than is asked for. Then we can find the size of the last digit required.

Exercise 9I

Find $4.28 \div 6$ giving your answer correct to 2 decimal places.

$4.28 \div 6 = 0.71|3\ldots$

$= 0.71$ (correct to 2 decimal places)

$6\overline{)4.280}$
$0.713\ldots$

Calculate $302 \div 14$ correct to 1 decimal place.

$302 \div 14 = 21.5|7\ldots$

$= 21.6$ (correct to 1 decimal place)

```
      21.57...
14)302.00
   28
    22
    14
     8 0
     7 0
     1 00
       98
```

Calculate, giving your answers correct to 2 decimal places:

Remember to work to one more decimal place than asked for.

1	$0.496 \div 3$	6	$2.35 \div 15$		
2	$6.49 \div 7$	7	$0.68 \div 16$		
3	$3.12 \div 9$	8	$0.99 \div 21$		
4	$12.2 \div 6$	9	$5.68 \div 24$	11	$1.73 \div 8$
5	$25.68 \div 9$	10	$3.85 \div 101$	12	$48.4 \div 51$

Calculate, giving your answers correct to 1 decimal place:

13	$32.9 \div 8$	16	$9.76 \div 11$	19	$45 \div 21$	22	$8.4 \div 13$
14	$402 \div 7$	17	$124 \div 17$	20	$15.1 \div 16$	23	$26 \div 15$
15	$15.3 \div 6$	18	$16.2 \div 14$	21	$213 \div 22$	24	$519 \div 19$

Find, giving your answers correct to 3 decimal places:

25	$0.023 \div 4$	28	$0.23 \div 11$	31	$0.654 \div 23$	34	$0.321 \div 17$
26	$0.123 \div 7$	29	$0.45 \div 12$	32	$0.98 \div 32$	35	$1.26 \div 32$
27	$1.25 \div 3$	30	$0.012 \div 13$	33	$0.2584 \div 16$	36	$0.88 \div 24$

Changing fractions to decimals

Exercise 9m

Give $\frac{4}{25}$ as a decimal.

$\frac{4}{25} = 4 \div 25 = 0.16$

(This is an exact answer.)

$$\begin{array}{r} 0.16 \\ 25\overline{)4.00} \\ 2\,5 \\ \hline 1\,50 \end{array}$$

Give $\frac{4}{7}$ as a decimal correct to 3 decimal places.

$\frac{4}{7} = 4 \div 7 = 0.5714$

$= 0.571$ (correct to 3 decimal places)

(This is an approximate answer.)

$$\begin{array}{r} 7\underline{)4.0000} \\ 0.5714 \end{array}$$

Give the following fractions as exact decimals:

1 $\frac{5}{8}$

2 $\frac{3}{40}$

3 $\frac{3}{16}$

4 $\frac{3}{5}$

5 $\frac{9}{25}$

6 $\frac{7}{50}$

7 $\frac{1}{16}$

8 $\frac{11}{8}$

9 $\frac{13}{25}$

10 $\frac{3}{80}$

Remember, you change a fraction to a decimal by dividing the bottom into the top.

Give the following fractions as decimals correct to 3 decimal places:

11 $\frac{3}{7}$

12 $\frac{4}{9}$

13 $\frac{1}{6}$

14 $\frac{2}{3}$

15 $\frac{9}{11}$

16 $\frac{6}{7}$

17 $\frac{8}{7}$

18 $\frac{1}{9}$

19 $\frac{1}{3}$

20 $\frac{4}{11}$

21 $\frac{3}{14}$

22 $\frac{4}{17}$

23 $\frac{6}{13}$

24 $\frac{4}{21}$

25 $\frac{3}{19}$

26 $\frac{3}{17}$

27 $\frac{4}{15}$

28 $\frac{7}{18}$

29 $\frac{3}{22}$

30 $\frac{4}{33}$

This is a game for two or more players.

1 Get someone who is not playing to call out a fraction.

2 Each player now estimates the decimal equivalent of the fraction to two decimal places and keeps a record in a table like the one shown below.

3 The player or players with the nearest estimate scores 1 point.

4 The game ends after an agreed number of fractions – say 6 or 10. The person with the highest score wins.

Use a score sheet like this.

Fraction	Estimated decimal value	Actual decimal value (to 3 d.p.)	Difference between estimated value and actual value	Score
$\frac{7}{12}$	0.6	0.583	0.017	

Division by decimals

$0.012 \div 0.06$ can be written as $\frac{0.012}{0.06}$. We know how to divide by a whole number so we need to find an equivalent fraction with denominator 6 instead of 0.06. Now $0.06 \times 100 = 6$. Therefore we multiply the numerator and denominator by 100.

$$\frac{0.012}{0.06} = \frac{0.012 \times 100}{0.06 \times 100} = \frac{1.2}{6}$$
$$= 0.2$$

To divide by a decimal, the denominator must be made into a whole number but the numerator need not be. We can write, for short,

$$0.012 \div 0.06 = \frac{0.01{\vdots}2}{0.06{\vdots}} = \frac{1.2}{6} \quad \text{(keeping the points in line)}$$

The dashed line indicates where we want the point to be so as to make the denominator a whole number.

Exercise 9n

Find 0.024 ÷ 0.6

$0.024 \div 0.6 = \frac{0.0|24}{0.6|} = \frac{0.24}{6}$

$= 0.04$

(See that the decimal points are lined up one beneath the other. Draw a line through the fraction where you want the decimal point to be.)

$6\overline{)0.24}$
0.04

Find 64 ÷ 0.08

$64 \div 0.08 = \frac{64.00|}{0.08|} = \frac{6400}{8}$ (Multiplying the top and bottom by 100 makes the bottom a whole number.)

$= 800$

$8\overline{)6400}$
800

Find the exact answers to the following questions:

1 0.04 ÷ 0.2
2 0.0006 ÷ 0.03
3 4 ÷ 0.5
4 0.8 ÷ 0.04
5 90 ÷ 0.02
6 0.48 ÷ 0.04
7 0.032 ÷ 0.2
8 3.6 ÷ 0.6
9 3.6 ÷ 0.06
10 3 ÷ 0.6
11 6.5 ÷ 0.5
12 8.4 ÷ 0.07
13 72 ÷ 0.09
14 1.08 ÷ 0.003
15 0.0012 ÷ 0.1
16 0.009 ÷ 0.9
17 0.9 ÷ 0.009
18 0.92 ÷ 0.4
19 16.8 ÷ 0.8
20 0.001 32 ÷ 0.11
21 0.000 068 4 ÷ 0.04
22 20.8 ÷ 0.0004
23 0.0012 ÷ 0.3
24 4.8 ÷ 0.08
25 1.76 ÷ 2.2
26 144 ÷ 0.16
27 0.496 ÷ 1.6
28 0.0288 ÷ 0.18
<u>29</u> 34.3 ÷ 1.4
<u>30</u> 10.24 ÷ 3.2
<u>31</u> 0.0204 ÷ 0.017
<u>32</u> 102.5 ÷ 2.5
<u>33</u> 9.8 ÷ 1.4
<u>34</u> 0.168 ÷ 0.14
<u>35</u> 1.35 ÷ 0.15
<u>36</u> 0.192 ÷ 2.4

Use long division.

Exercise 9p

Find the value of 16.9 ÷ 0.3 giving your answer correct to 1 decimal place.

$16.9 \div 0.3 = \frac{16.9|}{0.3|} = \frac{169}{3}$

$= 56.3|3\ldots$

$= 56.3$ (correct to 1 decimal place)

$3\overline{)169.00}$
56.33...

Calculate, giving your answers correct to 2 decimal places:

1	3.8 ÷ 0.6	**6**	1.25 ÷ 0.03
2	0.59 ÷ 0.07	**7**	0.0024 ÷ 0.09
3	15 ÷ 0.9	**8**	0.65 ÷ 0.7
4	5.633 ÷ 0.2	**9**	0.0072 ÷ 0.007
5	0.796 ÷ 1.1	**10**	5 ÷ 7

Work to 3 decimal places, then correct to 2.

Calculate, giving your answers correct to the number of decimal places indicated in the brackets:

Remember to work to one more decimal place than you need in your answer. For an answer correct to 1 decimal place you must work to 2 decimal places.

11	0.123 ÷ 6	(2)
12	2.3 ÷ 0.8	(1)
13	90 ÷ 11	(1)
14	0.0078 ÷ 0.09	(3)
15	12 ÷ 9	(4)
16	0.23 ÷ 0.007	(1)
17	16.2 ÷ 0.8	(1)
18	0.21 ÷ 6.5	(3)
19	85 ÷ 0.3	(3)
20	1.37 ÷ 0.8	(1)
21	56.9 ÷ 1.6	(nearest whole number)
22	0.89 ÷ 0.23	(1)
23	0.75 ÷ 4.5	(3)
24	0.023 ÷ 0.021	(1)
25	3.2 ÷ 1.4	(1)
26	0.045 ÷ 0.012	(nearest whole number)
27	12.3 ÷ 17	(2)
28	0.0054 ÷ 0.021	(4)
29	0.012 ÷ 0.021	(2)
30	0.52 ÷ 0.21	(1)

Mixed multiplication and division

Exercise 9q

Calculate, giving your answers exactly:

1 0.48×0.3
2 $0.48 \div 0.3$
3 2.56×0.02
4 $2.56 \div 0.02$
5 3.6×0.8
6 9.6×0.6
7 0.0042×0.03
8 $0.0042 \div 0.03$
9 16.8×0.4
10 $1.68 \div 0.4$
11 20.4×0.6
12 $5.04 \div 0.06$

Find $\frac{0.12 \times 3}{0.006}$

$\frac{0.12 \times 3}{0.006} = \frac{0.36}{0.006}$ (Multiply 0.12 by 3 first.) $12 \times 3 = 36$

$= \frac{360}{6}$ (Multiply top and bottom by 1000.)

$= 60$

Find the value of:

13 $\frac{0.2 \times 0.6}{0.4}$
14 $\frac{1.2 \times 0.04}{0.3}$
15 $\frac{4.8 \times 0.2}{0.6 \times 0.4}$
16 $\frac{3.2}{4 \times 0.2}$
17 $\frac{3}{0.6 \times 0.5}$
18 $\frac{4.4 \times 0.3}{11}$
19 $\frac{2.5 \times 0.7}{3.5 \times 4}$
20 $\frac{5.6 \times 0.8}{6.4}$
21 $\frac{0.9 \times 4}{0.5 \times 0.6}$

Relative sizes

To compare the sizes of numbers they need to be in the same form, either as fractions with the same denominators, or as decimals.

Exercise 9r

Express 0.82, $\frac{4}{5}$, $\frac{9}{11}$ as decimals where necessary and write them in order of size with the smallest first.

$\frac{4}{5} = 0.8$

$\frac{9}{11} = 0.8181\ldots$ $\quad 11\overline{)9.000}$ gives 0.8181

In order of size: $\frac{4}{5}, \frac{9}{11}, 0.82$

Express the following sets of numbers as decimals or as fractions and write them in order of size with the smallest first:

1 $\frac{1}{4}$, 0.2

2 $\frac{2}{5}$, $\frac{4}{9}$

3 $\frac{1}{2}$, $\frac{4}{9}$

4 $\frac{1}{3}$, 0.3, $\frac{3}{11}$

5 $\frac{8}{9}$, 0.9, $\frac{7}{8}$

6 $\frac{3}{4}$, $\frac{17}{20}$

7 $\frac{3}{8}$, $\frac{9}{25}$, 0.35

8 $\frac{3}{5}$, $\frac{4}{7}$, 0.59

9 $\frac{3}{7}$, $\frac{5}{11}$, $\frac{6}{13}$

10 $0.\dot{7}$, $\frac{8}{11}$

11 $0.\dot{3}$, $\frac{5}{12}$

12 $\frac{1}{2}$, 0.45, $\frac{9}{19}$

Mixed exercises

Exercise 9s

Select the letter that gives the correct answer.

1 When 0.68 is multiplied by 1000 the result is

A 6.8 B 68 C 680 D 6800

2 $\frac{7}{8}$ expressed as a decimal is

A 0.0875 B 0.75 C 0.875 D 0.88

3 The decimal 2.999 correct to 2 decimal places is

A 2.99 B 3.00 C 3.01 D 3.10

4 $3.2 \times 1.4 =$

A 3.48 B 3.58 C 4.38 D 4.48

5 $16.1 - 4.28 =$

A 11.73 B 11.82 C 12.73 D 12.82

6 Which is the largest of the numbers 6.4, $6\frac{2}{3}$, 6.6, 6.5?

A $6\frac{2}{3}$ B 6.4 C 6.5 D 6.6

Exercise 9t

1 Express 0.06 as a fraction in its lowest terms.

2 Divide 6.24 by **a** 100 **b** 12.

3 Add 3.2 and 0.9 and subtract the result from 5.8.

4 The total distance round the sides of an equilateral triangle (a triangle with three equal sides) is 19.2 cm. Find the length of one side.

5 Divide 0.0432 by 0.9.

6 Express $\frac{6}{25}$ as a decimal.

7 Find the cost of 24 articles at \$2.32 each.

8 Give 7.7815 correct to

a the nearest whole number **b** 1 decimal place **c** 3 decimal places.

Exercise 9u

1 Give $\frac{5}{7}$ as a recurring decimal.

2 Divide each number by 100: **a** 6.4 **b** 0.064.

3 Multiply 14.8 by 1.1.

4 Express 0.62 as a fraction in its lowest terms.

5 Add 6.7, 0.67, 0.067 and 0.0067 together.

6 Divide 16.4 by 8.

7 Which is bigger, 0.7 or $\frac{7}{9}$?

8 How many pieces of ribbon of length 0.3 m can be cut from a piece 7.5 m long?

Exercise 9v

1 Express $\frac{4}{25}$ as a decimal.

2 Find $6.43 \div 0.7$ correct to 3 decimal places.

3 Find 0.06×0.06.

4 Express 0.0095 as a fraction in its lowest terms.

5 Find $13.8 + 2.43 - 1.6$.

6 Find the cost of 3.5 m of ribbon at 58 c per metre.

7 Find $\frac{0.6 \times 0.3}{0.09}$.

8 Write $0.\dot{6}$ in another way as a decimal. Why is it not easy to find $0.7 - 0.\dot{6}$?

Did you know?

Could you give the answer to 95^2 or 85^2 quickly without using your calculator?

Let us investigate. Start with smaller numbers.

$1 \times 2 = 2$ and $15^2 = 225$

$2 \times 3 = 6$ and $25^2 = 625$

$3 \times 4 = 12$ and $35^2 = 1225$

What do you notice? Can you now write the answer to 65^2?

Here it is: $6 \times 7 = 42$, therefore $65^2 = 4225$.

Try using this pattern to find 85^2 and 95^2. When you have studied more algebra, your teacher will explain to you that it works because $(10x + 5)^2 = x(x + 1)100 + 25$.

In this chapter you have seen that...

- ✔ you must take great care with the position of the decimal point when you multiply decimals: the sum of the decimal places in the numbers that are multiplied together gives the number of decimal places in the answer
- ✔ you must also be careful with division: to divide by a decimal, multiply the top and the bottom by the same number so that the denominator becomes a whole number
- ✔ some answers are not exact so must be given correct to a given number of places. Remember to work to one more place than you need in the answer
- ✔ fractions can be changed into decimals by dividing the bottom number into the top number. When some fractions are changed into decimals, you get a repeating pattern of digits. These are called recurring decimals
- ✔ you should learn that $\frac{1}{2} = 0.5$, $\frac{1}{4} = 0.25$, $\frac{3}{4} = 0.75$, $\frac{1}{8} = 0.125$
- ✔ sizes of numbers can be compared by converting them into decimals.

10 Statistics

At the end of this chapter you should be able to...

1 organise statistical data in a frequency table
2 draw bar charts, pie charts and pictographs to illustrate statistical data
3 interpret information from pictographs
4 calculate the arithmetic mean of a set of numbers
5 find the missing number from a set, given the mean and the remaining numbers
6 find the mode of a given set of numbers
7 find the median of a given set of numbers.

Did you know?

Florence Nightingale gathered statistics during the Crimean War (1853–1856) and put them to good use. When she arrived at Scutari in Crimea she found that 42% of the soldiers admitted to the hospital died, mainly from disease, not war wounds. With a team of nurses she reduced this number to 2%. She went on to set up the first professional nursing service.

You need to know...

✔ how to work with whole numbers and with decimals.

Key words

arithmetic average, bar chart, data, frequency, frequency column, frequency table, horizontal, mean, median, mode, pictograph, tally

Frequency tables

The branch of mathematics called statistics is used for dealing with large collections of information in the form of numbers. The number of items of information can run into thousands as, for instance, when the incomes of everyone in Trinidad and Tobago are being considered, but to learn the methods we start with smaller collections.

If we collect the heights in centimetres of 72 children in the first year we are faced with a disorganised set of numbers:

147	146	151	137	149	159	142	150	151
138	139	155	151	152	145	139	135	153
139	151	145	162	152	138	142	140	155
146	165	155	149	162	145	152	148	152
132	152	142	152	152	143	145	157	152
148	145	154	145	149	155	137	144	140
139	145	151	152	152	140	160	155	151
136	151	149	151	156	142	134	156	160

To make sense of these numbers we must put them in order. One way of doing this is to form a *frequency table*. We do not always wish to write down every number so we group them, as shown in the next table. Work down the columns, making a *tally* mark, |, in the tally column opposite the appropriate group. (Do *not* go through the columns looking for numbers that fit into the first group and the second group and so on.) Count up the tally marks and write the total in the *frequency column*. Check by adding up the numbers in the frequency column.

(Arrange the tally marks in fives either by leaving a gap between blocks, or by crossing four tally marks with the fifth, as is done in this table.)

Height in cm (correct to nearest cm)	Tally	Frequency
131–135	|||	3
136–140	~~||||~~ ~~||||~~ ||	12
141–145	~~||||~~ ~~||||~~ |||	13
146–150	~~||||~~ ~~||||~~	10
151–155	~~||||~~ ~~||||~~ ~~||||~~ ~~||||~~ ~~||||~~	25
156–160	~~||||~~		6
161–165	|||	3
	Total	72

We can see now that there are a few children with small or large heights and that the greatest number have heights in the 151–155 cm range.

Exercise 10a

Draw up frequency tables like the one on the previous page, using the groups suggested.

1 The following numbers are the heights in centimetres of the same children as those on page 179, when they had reached the third year:

154	166	153	166	149	154	153	160	165
164	156	166	156	166	161	155	164	164
156	159	161	150	163	163	154	157	159
150	146	157	168	167	154	166	150	157
154	162	164	152	154	153	163	157	163
161	168	150	152	163	164	157	159	160
164	158	158	165	167	170	156	164	164
152	155	163	164	157	166	161	148	168

Use groups 146–150 cm, 151–155 cm, 156–160 cm, 161–165 cm, 166–170 cm

2 The following numbers are the masses in kilograms (to the nearest kg) of the same 72 children in the third form:

41	50	54	52	65	54	48	50	43
48	58	46	43	50	48	47	44	48
43	44	47	45	57	54	42	52	49
47	40	53	41	41	49	44	59	43
35	51	44	44	49	45	62	46	51
55	54	54	41	43	70	40	44	59
45	43	45	37	51	39	55	53	45
61	44	57	39	51	44	48	44	51

Use groups 35–39 kg, 40–44 kg, 45–49 kg, 50–54 kg, 55–59 kg, 60–64 kg, 65–69 kg, 70–74 kg.

<u>3</u> The following are the marks of 82 pupils in a mathematics examination:

78	41	56	66	76	65	50	37	45	40
87	38	49	82	41	79	66	95	19	38
31	75	54	49	65	53	69	63	67	91
62	34	79	84	71	85	42	59	74	56
56	50	53	68	61	54	25	64	84	80
48	64	72	53	44	55	35	63	36	81
70	73	47	63	42	57	51	63	52	45
38	62	64	47	62	48	28	60	61	58
57	39								

Use groups 11–20, 21–30, 31–40, and so on.

Bar charts

When information (or *data*) is collected, it can be illustrated in various ways and one of the most common is the *bar chart*.

This data is from a group of people who were asked to select their favourite colour from a card showing six colours. The following results were recorded.

Colour	Rose pink	Sky blue	Golden yellow	Violet	Lime green	Tomato red
Number of people (frequency)	6	8	8	2	1	10

We can illustrate this data using bars where the height of each bar represents the frequency of each category.

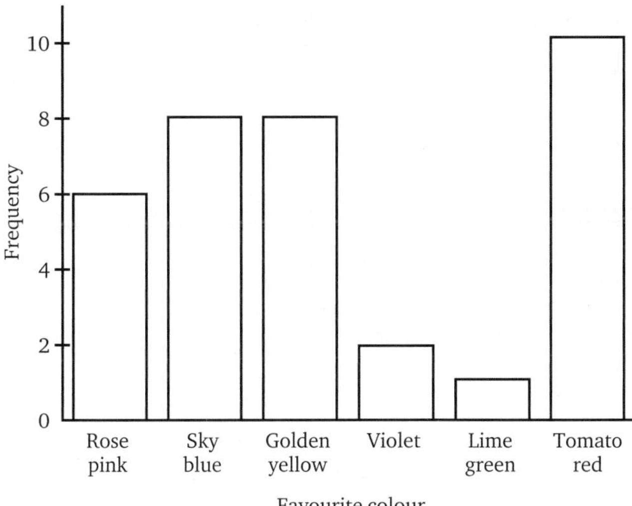

The bars must all be the same width but they do not have to touch. The spaces between the bars must all be the same.

Notice that the groups are arranged along the base line and the frequencies are marked on the vertical axis.

Exercise 10b

In questions **1** to **3** draw bar charts to show the information given in the frequency tables. Mark the frequency on the vertical axis and label the bars below the horizontal axis.

1 Types of vehicles moving along a busy road during one hour:

Vehicle	Cars	Vans	Lorries	Motorcycles	Bicycles
Frequency	62	11	15	10	2

2 Thirty pupils were asked to state their favourite subject chosen from their school timetable:

Subject	English	Mathematics	French	PE	History	Geography
Frequency	5	7	4	3	7	4

3 Use the information from the frequency table in Exercise **10a** (page 180), question **3**.

4 The number of tourist arrivals by country, to a certain Caribbean island, in the first six months of 2018 (to the nearest thousand) were:

Country	USA	Canada	UK	Caricom	Other
No. of tourists	80 000	46 000	18 000	31 000	15 000

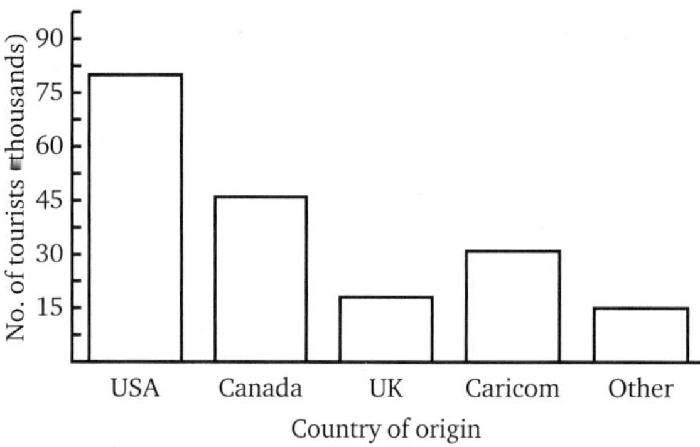

In an attempt to save space, in the bar chart shown above the scale for the number of tourists was started at 15 000 instead of at 0.

a Redraw the bar chart with the scale for the number of tourists going from 0 to 90 000 (suggested scale 1 cm to 15 000).

b Compare the two bar charts. The impression given by one of them is misleading. Why?

Bar charts can be used to represent information other than frequencies and can appear in different forms. The bars are usually vertical but occasionally they are horizontal.

Exercise 10c

1 The average price per tonne of sugar earned by a Caribbean country in the ten-year period 2009–2018:

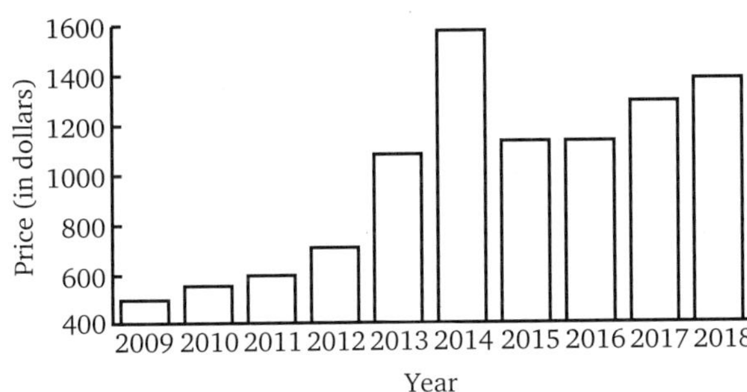

a In which year was the price lowest? Highest?

b In which year was the price increase from the previous year the greatest?

c In which year was the price of sugar above $1400 per tonne?

d In which two years did the price remain the same?

2 The tourist arrivals (in thousands) to destinations A and B for the period 2009–2018:

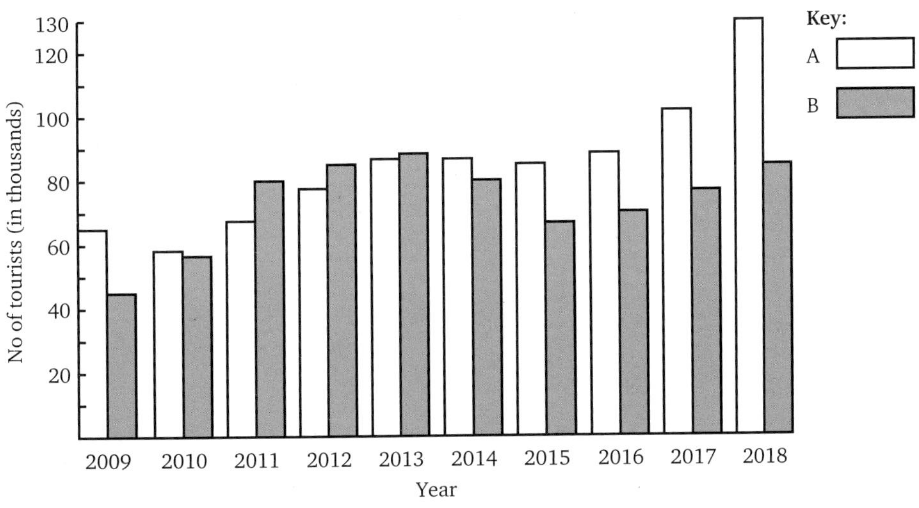

a Did more tourists visit B or A during the period 2009–2018?

b In which year did destination B have fewest tourists?

c In which years did B have better tourist seasons than A?

3 Cost of defence, health, education and housing over a three-year period:

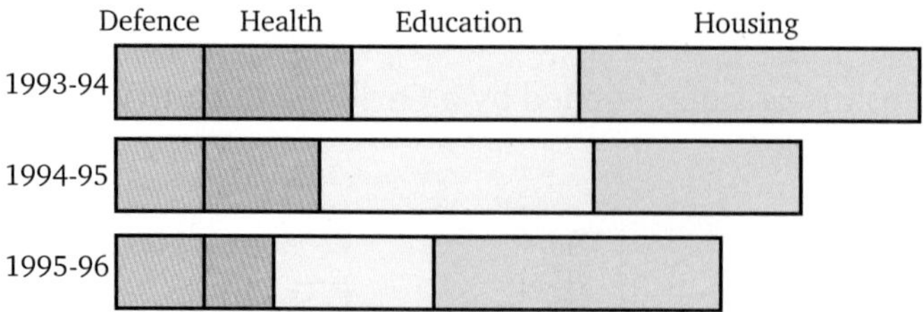

No numbers are given, but we can get a good idea about the relative costs.

a In which year was the most money spent?

b On what was the least money spent?

c In which year did education cost most?

d In which year did health cost least?

e In which year was the least money spent?

Puzzle

A rough guide to the distance to keep behind another car on the road:

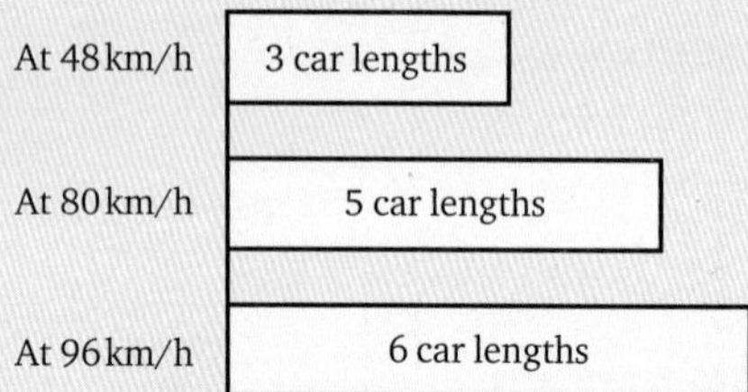

Can you puzzle out what rule has been used to decide on the distances?

Why is the guide only 'rough'? What other factors should be taken into account?

Exercise 10d

1 a Draw a bar chart to show the number of full lorries leaving a quarry each day for one seven-day period.

Day	Monday	Tuesday	Wednesday	Thursday	Friday	Saturday	Sunday
Number of lorries	30	50	25	27	40	10	0

b During which day were the most full lorries leaving the quarry?

c Give a reason why no lorries left on Sunday.

d The quarry produced material by blasting the rock. When do you think blasting took place? Give a reason.

2 **a** Draw a bar chart to show the birth rates per 1000 population in ten Caribbean countries in 1996.

Country	Antigua	Barbados	Dominica	Grenada	Guadeloupe	Jamaica	St Kitts	Trinidad	St Vincent
Birth rate per 1000	24	21	39	30	28	34	25	27	36

b Which country has the highest birth rate?

c Which country has the lowest birth rate?

Pictographs

To attract attention, *pictographs* are often used on posters and in newspapers and magazines. The best pictographs give the numerical information as well; the worst give the wrong impression.

Exercise 10e

1 Road deaths in the past 4 years at an accident black spot:

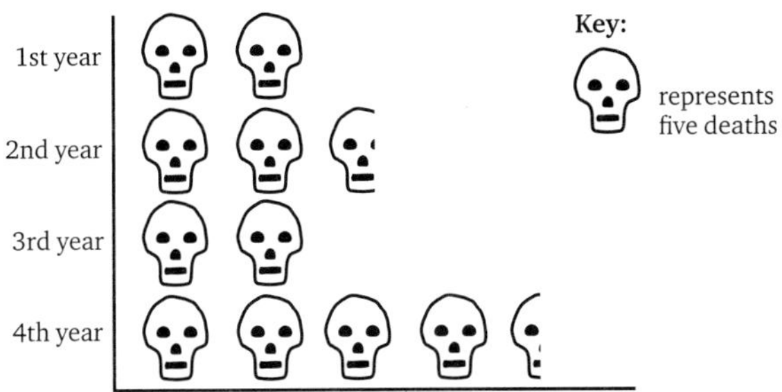

a Give an estimate of the number of deaths in each year.

b What message is the poster trying to convey?

c How effective do you think it is?

2 The most popular subject among first year pupils:

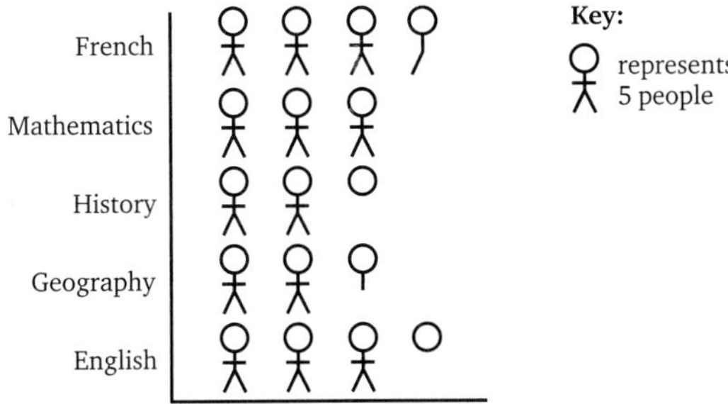

a Which is the most popular subject?

b How many pupils chose each subject and how many were asked altogether?

c Is this a good way of presenting the information?

3 Bar chart in an advertisement showing the consumption of Fizz lemonade:

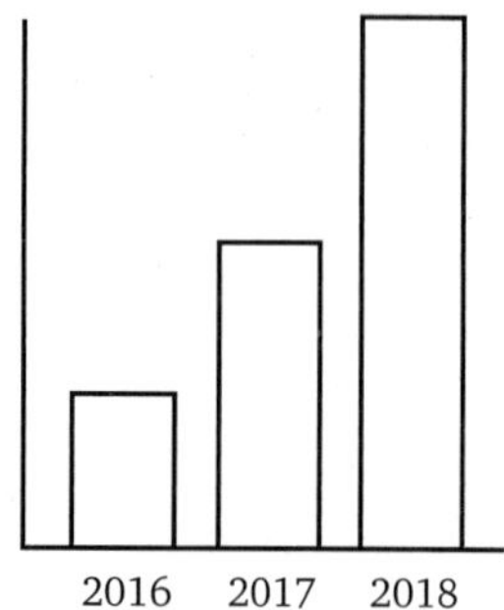

a What does this show about the consumption of lemonade?

It was decided to change from a bar chart to a pictograph for the next advertisement:

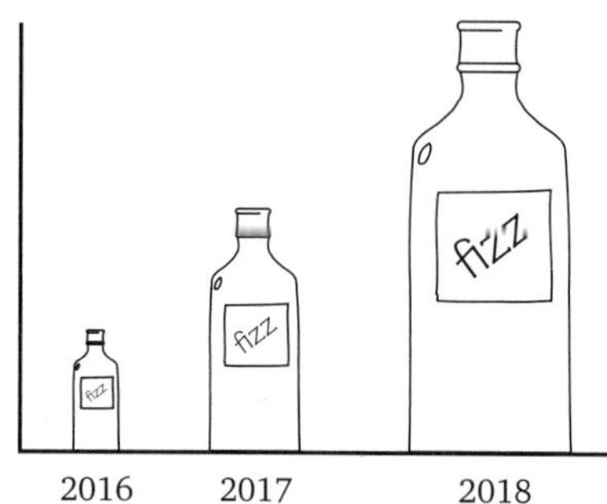

b This looks impressive but it could be misleading. Why?

Drawing pictographs

Make sure when using drawings that each drawing takes up the same amount of space and is simple and clear.

Exercise 10f

1 Eighty-five people were asked how they travelled to work and the following information was recorded:

Transport	Car	Bus	Walk	Bicycle
Number of people	30	40	10	5

Draw a pictograph using one drawing to 5 people.

2 Thirty pupils in a class were asked what they were writing with. The following information was recorded:

Writing implement	Black pen	Blue pen	Pencil
Frequency	12	9	9

Draw a pictograph using one drawing to 3 pens.

3 Some children were asked what pets they owned:

Pet	Dog	Cat	Bird	Small animal	Fish
Frequency	9	7	6	10	2

Use one drawing to one pet. Make the symbols simple.

The symbol for fish could be 

Did you know?

You may become a statistic by census, sampling or record. These are only three of the ways.

Census

A census is a direct counting of a nation, state or school. From time to time the government of your island takes a census, recording the number and age of persons in the region and other information.

See if you can find the National Census Report for your island from the CARICOM 2000 Round of Population and Housing Census.

Sampling

A sample is a subset of a population. Conducting a census may be expensive or time-consuming if the population is large. In this case a sample will be used to get an indication of the situation for the population.

At election time predictions are made using samples.

Records

Brian Lara holds the record for the highest score in a test match. What is the score? Who was the last person to hold this record before Brian Lara?

Some records are obtained by chance while others are attained after long practice.

Averages

We are frequently looking for ways of representing a set of numbers in a simple form. Can we choose a single number that will adequately represent a set of numbers?

We try to do this by using averages.

Three different types of average are used, each with its own individual advantages and disadvantages. They are the *arithmetic average* or *mean*, the *mode* and the *median*.

The arithmetic average or mean

Consider a group of five children. When they are asked to produce the money they are carrying the amounts collected are 55 c, \$1.40, 95 c, 60 c and 75 c respectively. If the total of this money (\$4.25) is shared equally amongst the five children, each will receive 85 c. This is called the arithmetic average or mean of the five amounts.

> The arithmetic average or mean of a set of numbers is the sum of the numbers divided by the number of numbers in the set.

For example, the average or mean of 12, 15, 25, 42 and 16 is

$$\frac{12+15+25+42+16}{5}=\frac{110}{5}=22$$

One commonplace use of the arithmetic average is to compare the marks of pupils in a group or form. The pupils are given positions according to their average mark over the full range of subjects they study. An advantage is that we can compare the results of pupils who study 7 subjects with those who study 11 subjects. A disadvantage is that one very poor mark may pull the mean down significantly.

The mean may also be rather artificial, for example, giving $5\frac{1}{3}$ c to each of a group of people, or having a mean shoe size of 5.1, or a mean family size of 2.24 children.

Exercise 10g

Find the arithmetic average or mean of the following sets of numbers:

1 3, 6, 9, 14

2 2, 4, 9, 13

3 12, 13, 14, 15, 16, 17, 18

4 23, 25, 27, 29, 31, 33, 35

5 19, 6, 13, 10, 32

6 34, 14, 39, 20, 16, 45

7 1.2, 2.4, 3.6, 4.8

8 18.2, 20.7, 32.5, 50, 78.6

9 6.3, 4.5, 6.8, 5.2, 7.3, 7.1

10 3.1, 0.4, 7.2, 0.7, 6.1

11 38.2, 17.6, 63.5, 80.7

12 0.76, 0.09, 0.35, 0.54, 1.36

Nikolai's examination percentages in 8 subjects were 83, 47, 62, 49, 55, 72, 58 and 62. What was his mean mark?

Mean mark for 8 subjects

$$= \frac{\text{sum of the marks in the 8 subjects}}{\text{number of subjects}}$$

$$= \frac{83+47+62+49+55+72+58+62}{8}$$

$$= \frac{488}{8}$$

$$= 61$$

13 In the Christmas terminal examinations Lisa scored a total of 504 in 8 subjects. Find her mean mark.

14 A darts player scored 2304 in 24 visits to the board. What was his average number of points per visit?

15 A bowler took 110 wickets for 1815 runs. Calculate his average number of runs per wicket.

16 Kemuel's examination percentages in 7 subjects were 64, 43, 86, 74, 55, 53 and 66. What was his mean mark?

17 In six consecutive English examinations, Joy's percentage marks were 83, 76, 85, 73, 64 and 63. Find her mean mark.

<u>18</u> A football team scored 54 goals in 40 league games. Find the average number of goals per game.

<u>19</u> The first Hockey XI scored 14 goals in their first 16 matches. What was the average number of goals per match?

20 In a dancing competition the recorded scores for the winners were 5.8, 5.9, 6.0, 5.8, 5.8, 5.8, 5.6 and 5.7. Find their mean score.

21 The recorded rainfall each day at a holiday resort during the first week of my holiday was 3 mm, 0, 4.5 mm, 0, 0, 5 mm and 1.5 mm. Find the mean daily rainfall for the week.

22 The masses of the members of a rowing eight were 82 kg, 85 kg, 86 kg, 86 kg, 84 kg, 88 kg, 92 kg and 85 kg. Find the average mass of the 'eight'. If the cox weighed 41 kg, what was the average mass of the crew?

On average my car travels 28.5 miles on each gallon of petrol. How far will it travel on 30 gallons?

If the car travels 28.5 miles on 1 gallon of petrol it will travel 30×28.5 miles, i.e. 855 miles, on 30 gallons.

23 My father's car travels on average 33.4 miles on each gallon of petrol. How far will it travel on 55 gallons?

24 Olga's car travels on average 12.6 km on each litre of petrol. How far will it travel on 205 litres?

25 The average daily rainfall in Puddletown during April was 2.4 mm. How much rain fell during the month?

26 The daily average number of hours of sunshine during my 14-day holiday in Florida was 9.4. For how many hours did the sun shine while I was on holiday?

Elaine's average mark after 7 subjects is 56 and after 8 subjects it has risen to 58. How many does she score in her eighth subject?

We can find the total scored in 7 subjects and the total scored in 8 subjects. Then the score in the 8th subject is the difference between these two totals.

Total scored in 7 subjects is, $56 \times 7 = 392$

Total scored in 8 subjects is, $58 \times 8 = 464$

Score in her eighth subject

= total for 8 subjects – total for 7 subjects

$= 464 - 392$

$= 72$

Therefore Elaine scores 72 in her eighth subject.

27 Zachary's batting average after 11 completed innings was 62. After 12 completed innings it had increased to 68. How many runs did he score in his twelfth innings?

28 Richard was collecting money for charity. The average amount collected from the first 15 houses at which he called was 30 c, while the average amount collected after 16 houses was 35 c. How much did he collect from the sixteenth house?

29 After six examination results Tom's average mark was 57. His next result increased his average to 62. What was his seventh mark?

30 Anne's average mark after 8 results was 54. This dropped to 49 when she received her ninth result, which was for French. What was her French mark?

31 During a certain week the number of lunches served in a school canteen were: Monday 213, Tuesday 243, Wednesday 237 and Thursday 239. Find the average number of meals served daily over the four days. If the daily average for the week (Monday–Friday) was 225, how many meals were served on Friday?

32 A paperboy's sales during a certain week were: Monday 84, Tuesday 112, Wednesday 108, Thursday 95 and Friday 131. Find his average daily sales. When he included his sales on Saturday his daily average increased to 128. How many papers did he sell on Saturday?

33 The number of hours of sunshine in Barbados for successive days during a certain week were 11.1, 11.9, 11.2, 12.0, 11.7, 12.9 and 11.8. Find the daily average. The following week the daily average was 11 hours. How many more hours of sunshine were there the first week than the second?

34 Tissha's marks in the end of term examinations were 46, 80, 59, 83, 54, 67, 79, 82 and 62. Find her average mark. It was found that there had been an error in her mathematics mark. It should have been 74, not 83. What difference did this make to her average?

35 The heights of the 11 girls in a hockey team are 162 cm, 152 cm, 166 cm, 149 cm, 153 cm, 165 cm, 169 cm, 145 cm, 155 cm, 159 cm and 163 cm. Find the average height of the team. If the girl who was 145 cm tall were replaced by a girl 156 cm tall, what difference would this make to the average height of the team?

36 During the last five years the distances I travelled in my car, in miles, were 10 426, 12 634, 11 926, 14 651 and 13 973. How many miles did I travel in the whole period? What was my yearly average? How many miles should I travel this year to reduce the average annual mileage over the six years to 11 984?

37 The average mass of the 18 boys in a class is 63.2 kg. When two new boys join the class the average mass increases to 63.7 kg. What is the combined mass of the two new boys?

38 The average height of the 12 boys in a class is 163 cm and the average height of the 18 girls is 159 cm. Find the average height of the class.

> You can find the total height of the boys and the total height of the girls. From this you can find the total height of all 30 pupils. Then you can work out the average height.

39 The average mass of the 15 girls in a class is 54.4 kg while the average mass of the 10 boys is 57.4 kg. Find the average mass of the class.

40 In a school the average size of the 14 lower school forms is 30, the average size of the 16 middle school forms is 25 and the average size of the 20 upper school forms is 24. Find the average size of form for the whole school.

41 Northshire has an area of 400 000 hectares and last year the annual rainfall was 274 cm, while Southshire has an area of 150 000 hectares and last year the annual rainfall was 314 cm. What was the annual rainfall last year for the combined area of the two counties? Give your answer to the nearest cm.

42 After 10 three-day matches and 8 one-day matches, the average *daily* attendances for a cricket season were 2160 for three-day matches and 4497 for one-day matches. Calculate the average *daily* attendance for the 18 matches.

? Puzzle

How is it possible for a student, whose average examination mark is 53, to increase that average by scoring 35 in the next examination?

Mode

The mode of a set of numbers is the number that occurs most frequently, e.g. the mode of the numbers 6, 4, 6, 8, 10, 6, 3, 8 and 4 is 6, since 6 is the only number occurring more than twice.

It would obviously be of use for a company with a chain of shoe shops to know that the mode or modal size for men's shoes in one part of the country is 8, whereas in another part of the country it is 7. Such information would influence the number of pairs of shoes of each size kept in stock.

If all the numbers in a set of numbers are different, there cannot be a mode, for no number occurs more frequently than all the others. On the other hand, if two numbers are equally the most popular, there will be two modes.

Earlier in the chapter we used bar charts to show such things as the types of vehicles moving along a busy road and the favourite colour of a group of people. Bar charts may also be used to determine the mode of the group.

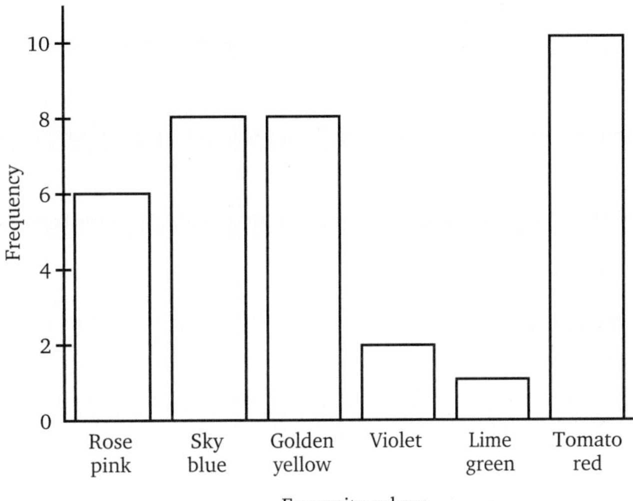

Here is the bar chart from page 181. It shows the colour selected by 35 people when asked to choose their favourite colour from a card showing six colours.

This chart shows that the most popular colour, or the modal colour, is tomato red.

Exercise 10h

Find the mode of each of the following sets of numbers:

1 10, 8, 12, 14, 12, 10, 12, 8, 10, 12, 4

2 3, 9, 7, 9, 5, 4, 8, 2, 4, 3, 5, 9

3 1.2, 1.8, 1.9, 1.2, 1.8, 1.7, 1.4, 1.3, 1.8

4 58, 56, 59, 62, 56, 63, 54, 53

5 5.9, 5.6, 5.8, 5.7, 5.9, 5.9, 5.8, 5.7

6 26.2, 26.8, 26.4, 26.7, 26.5, 26.4, 26.6, 26.5, 26.4

7 The table shows the number of goals scored by a football club last season.

Numbers of goals	0	1	2	3	4	5	6
Frequency	12	16	7	4	2	0	1

Draw a bar chart to show these results and find the modal score.

8 Given below are the marks out of 10 obtained by 30 girls in a history test.

8, 6, 5, 7, 8, 9, 10, 10, 3, 7, 3, 5, 4, 8, 7, 8, 10, 9, 8, 7, 10, 9, 9, 7, 5, 4, 8, 1, 9, 8

Draw a bar chart to show this information and find the mode.

9 The heights of 10 girls, correct to the nearest centimetre, are:

155, 148, 153, 154, 155, 149, 162, 154, 156, 155

What is their modal height?

10 The number of letters in the words of a sentence were:

2, 4, 3, 5, 2, 3, 8, 2, 5, 7, 9, 3, 6, 3, 7, 3, 4, 9, 2, 3, 8, 3, 5, 2, 10, 3, 4, 6, 2, 3, 4

How many words were there in the sentence? What is the modal number of letters per word?

11 The shoe sizes of pupils in a class are:

4, 4, 7, 6, 5, 5, 6, 6, 6, 4, 5, 8, 6, 7, 4, 7, 9, 6,
5, 7, 6, 7, 8, 6, 4, 4, 4, 5, 5, 7, 7, 7, 5, 8, 6, 5

How many pupils are there in the class?

What is the modal shoe size?

Median

The median value of a set of numbers is the value of the middle number when they have been placed in ascending (or descending) order of magnitude.

Imagine nine children arranged in order of their height.

The height of the fifth or middle child is 154 cm,

i.e. the median height is 154 cm.

Similarly 24 is the median of 12, 18, 24, 37 and 46. Two numbers are smaller than 24 and two are larger.

To find the median of 16, 49, 53, 8, 32, 19 and 62, rearrange the numbers in ascending order:

8, 16, 19, 32, 49, 53, 62

then we can see that the middle number of these is 32,

i.e. the median is 32.

If there is an even number of numbers, the median is found by finding the average or mean of the two middle values after they have been placed in ascending or descending order.

To find the median of 24, 32, 36, 29, 31, 34, 35, 39, rearrange in ascending order:

24, 29, 31, <u>32</u>, <u>34</u>, 35, 36, 39

Then the median is $\frac{32+34}{2} = \frac{66}{2}$

i.e. the median is 33.

Exercise 10i

Find the median of each of the following sets of numbers:

1 1, 2, 3, 5, 7, 11, 13

2 26, 33, 39, 42, 64, 87, 90

3 13, 24, 19, 13, 6, 36, 17

4 4, 18, 32, 16, 9, 7, 29

5 1.2, 3.4, 3.2, 6.5, 9.8, 0.4, 1.8

6 5, 7, 11, 13, 17, 19

7 34, 46, 88, 92, 104, 116, 118, 144

8 34, 42, 16, 83, 97, 24, 18, 38

9 1.92, 1.84, 1.89, 1.86, 1.96, 1.98, 1.73, 1.88

10 15.2, 6.3, 14.8, 9.5, 16.3, 24.9

Investigation

Investigate whether or not it is possible to write down a set of seven different whole numbers such that their mean, mode and median are all the same.

Collecting data

If you toss three coins, you will get either zero heads, one head, two heads or three heads.

Suppose you want to repeat this several times and want to record the number of heads each time. If you write down the number of heads each time, you will end up with a disorganised list. You can avoid this by making a table like the one below.

Number of heads	Tally
0	
1	
2	
3	

Each time you toss the coins you can put a tally mark next to the number of heads.

You can then add a column to record the frequencies.

When the data you want to collect contains a lot of different numbers, you can group them before you start. For example, if you are recording the heights of students in your class, you could use groups 100–119 cm, 120–129 cm, 130–139 cm, and so on.

If you are collecting data about more than one category, such as the money that a group of boys and girls get each week, you will need to ask people. If you want to see if there are differences between the amounts that boys get and the amounts that girls get you can use two tally columns, one for boys and one for girls.

You also need to think about the kind of data you want to collect. If, for example, you are asking people for their favourite colour, you will probably get a large variety of names for colours. In this case, decide before you start the colours you will ask them to choose from

Investigation

Collect the information; where it is necessary, decide on the groups it can be divided into and record the information in a frequency table as on page 179. Write a short report on any problems you had collecting the information.

Suggestions for class projects

1 Heights of children in the class.

2 Masses of children in the class.

3 Handspan. Stretch your hand out as wide as it will go on a piece of paper and mark the positions of the end of the thumb and of the little finger. Measure the distance between these points to the nearest centimetre.

4 Times of journeys to school in minutes.

5 Times of arrival at school.

For projects **6** to **12**, illustrate your information. Decide whether a bar chart or a pictograph would be more suitable for representing the data.

6 Find out the size of the family of each student in your class. Find out the numbers of boys and girls in each family. Compare the fraction of boys over girls to the National data for this fraction.

7 Pets owned.

8 Pets you would *like* to own, but decide on categories first before collecting the information.

9 Birthday months.

10 Number of houses in the street where a pupil lives. Decide what to record if houses are isolated or the pupil lives in an apartment block.

11 Colours of cars seen passing during, say, 20 minutes.

12 Number of people in cars travelling at a given time of day, say on the way to school.

Suggestions for individual projects

For projects **13** to **18**, also find, where possible, the mode, mean and median.

Add to your report which one of these is best at representing the data. Also add anything else you notice about the data.

13 Throw one dice 120 times and record the scores.

14 Throw two dice 120 times and record the combined score each time.

15 Choose a page of a book of plain text and record the occurrence of the different letters of the alphabet.

16 Choose a page of text in a different language and repeat number 15. Compare the two sets of results.

17 Choose pages of text from a book and record the lengths of, say, 60 sentences.

18 Choose a page of text and record the number of letters used in each word. Decide beforehand what to do about words with hyphens.

Mixed exercises

Exercise 10j

Select the letter that gives the correct answer.

Use the following data to answer questions **1** to **3**.

In successive rounds a golfer recorded the following scores:

73, 72, 85, 67, 72, 75, 74

1 The mean score is

A 71 **B** 74 **C** 75 **D** 76

2 The mode for this set of data is

A 72 **B** 73 **C** 74 **D** 75

3 The median score is

A 71 B 72 C 73 D 74

Use the following data to answer questions **4** to **6**.

This frequency table shows the marks out of 6 scored by a group of students in a test.

Mark	0	1	2	3	4	5	6
Frequency	2	2	4	6	7	12	8

4 The mean mark scored by the group is

A 3.8 B 3.9 C 4 D 4.5

5 The modal mark is

A 2 B 3 C 4 D 5

6 The median mark is

A 2 B 3 C 4 D 5

Exercise 10k

In questions **1** to **5** find **a** the mean **b** the mode and **c** the median, of each set of numbers:

1 21, 16, 25, 21, 19, 32, 27

2 67, 71, 69, 82, 70, 66, 81, 66, 67

3 43, 46, 47, 45, 45, 42, 47, 49, 43, 43

4 84, 93, 13, 16, 28, 13, 32, 63, 45

5 30, 27, 32, 27, 28, 27, 26, 27

6 In seven rounds of golf, a golfer returns scores of: 72, 87, 73, 72, 86, 72 and 77. Find the mean, mode and median of these scores.

7 The heights (correct to the nearest centimetre) of a group of girls are: 159, 155, 153, 154, 157, 162, 152, 160, 161, 157.
Find:

a their mean height **b** their modal height **c** their median height.

8 The marks, out of 100, in a geography test for the members of a class were: 64, 50, 35, 85, 52, 47, 72, 31, 74, 49, 36, 44, 54, 48, 32, 52, 53, 48, 71, 52, 56, 49, 81, 45, 52, 80, 46.
Find:

a the mean mark **b** the modal mark **c** the median mark.

9 Find the mean, mode and median of the following golf scores:
85, 76, 91, 83, 88, 84, 84, 82, 77, 79, 80, 83, 86, 84.

10 The table shows how many pupils in a form were absent for various numbers of sessions during a certain school week.

Number of sessions absent	0	1	2	3	4	5	6	7	8	9	10
Frequency	20	2	4	0	2	0	1	2	0	0	1

Find:

a the mode **b** the median **c** the mean.

11 The table shows the number of children per family in the families of the pupils in a class.

Number of children	1	2	3	4	5	6	7
Frequency	1	3	9	5	5	2	1

Find:

a the mode **b** the median **c** the mean.

? Puzzle

Find the missing number in this set.

6	10	5	3
7	6	7	8
8	9	8	

In this chapter you have seen that...

✔ large quantities of information can be made sense of by grouping the data and putting it into a frequency table. The frequency of a group is the number of items in that group

✔ frequency tables can be represented by bar charts or pictographs

✔ the heights of the bars in a bar chart correspond to the frequencies of the groups

✔ the arithmetic average or mean of a set of numbers is their sum divided by the number of them

✔ the mode is the number that occurs most often

✔ the median is the middle number when they have been placed in ascending or descending order.

11 Directed numbers

At the end of this chapter you should be able to...

1 use positive or negative numbers to describe displacements on one side or the other of a given point on a line

2 apply positive and negative numbers, where appropriate, in a physical situation

3 perform operations of addition, subtraction, multiplication or division on positive and negative numbers.

Did you know?

David Blackwell is, to mathematicians, the most famous, perhaps the greatest, African American mathematician. A biannual prize has been inaugurated in his honour: the Blackwell–Tapia Prize. The first recipient was Dr Arlie O. Petters. Dr Petters emigrated from Belize to the United States in 1979 and became a US citizen in 1990.

You need to know...

✔ how to add, subtract, multiply and divide simple numbers mentally.

Key words

directed number, integer, negative, number line, positive

Positive and negative numbers

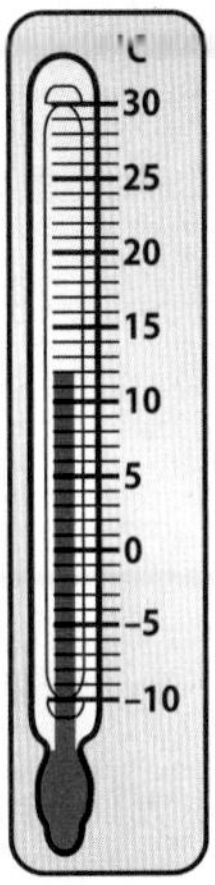

There are many quantities that can be measured above or below a natural zero.

For example, we are used to temperatures above and below 0 °C (Celsius) which is the freezing point of water.

A temperature of 5 °C below freezing point is writen as –5 °C.

Most people would call –5 °C 'minus 5 °C' but we will call it 'negative 5 °C' and there are good reasons for doing so because in mathematics 'minus' means 'take away'.

A temperature of 5 °C above freezing point is called 'positive 5 °C' and can be written as +5 °C.

Most people would just call it 5 °C and write it without the positive symbol.

A number without any symbol in front of it is a positive number,

i.e.	2 means +2
and	+3 can be written as 3

Positive and negative numbers are collectively known as *directed numbers*.

Directed numbers can be used to describe any quantity that can be measured above or below a natural zero. For example, a distance of 50 m above sea level and a distance of 50 m below sea level could be written as + 50 m and – 50 m respectively.

They can also be used to describe time before and after a particular event. For example, 5 seconds before the start of a race and 5 seconds after the start of a race could be written as –5 s and +5 s respectively.

Directed numbers can also be used to describe quantities that involve one of two possible directions. For example, if a car is travelling north at 70 km/h and another car is travelling south at 70 km/h they can be described as going at +70 km/h and –70 km/h respectively.

Exercise 11a

Draw a Celsius thermometer and mark a scale on it from –10 ° to +10 °. Use your drawing to write the following temperatures as positive or negative numbers:

1 10 ° above freezing point

2 7 ° below freezing point

3 3 ° below zero

4 5 ° above zero

5 8 ° below zero

6 freezing point

Write in words, the meaning of the following temperatures:

7 −2 °C

8 +3 °C

9 4 °C

10 −10 °C

11 +8 °C

12 0 °C

Which temperature is higher?

13 +8° or +10°

14 12° or 3°

15 −2° or +4°

16 −3° or −5°

17 −8° or 2°

18 −2° or −5°

19 1° or −1°

20 +3° or −5°

21 −7° or −10°

22 −2° or −9°

23 The contour lines on the map below show distances above sea level as positive numbers and distances below sea level as negative numbers.

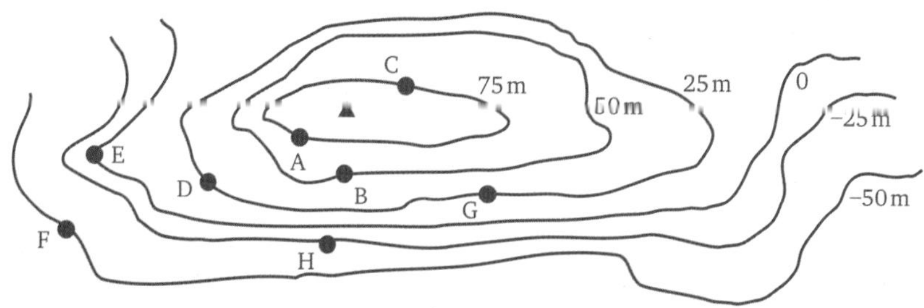

Write down in words the position relative to sea level of the points A, B, C, D, E, F, G and H.

In questions **24** to **34** use positive or negative numbers to describe the quantities.

A ball thrown up a distance of 5 m.

Up is above the start point so a positive number describes this.

+5 m

24 5 seconds before blast off of a rocket.

25 5 seconds after blast off of a rocket.

26 50 c in your purse.

27 50 c owed.

28 1 minute before the train leaves the station.

29 A win of $50 on a lottery.

30 A debt of $5.

31 Walking forwards five paces.

32 Walking backwards five paces.

33 The top of a hill which is 200 m above sea level.

34 A ball thrown down a distance of 5 m.

35 At midnight the temperature was –2 °C. One hour later it was 1° colder. What was the temperature then?

36 At midday the temperature was 18 °C. Two hours later it was 3° warmer. What was the temperature then?

37 A rock climber started at +200 m and came a distance of 50 m down the rock face. How far above sea level was he then?

38 At midnight the temperature was –5 °C. One hour later it was 2° warmer. What was the temperature then?

39 At the end of the week my financial state could be described as –25 c. I was later given 50 c. How could I then describe my financial state?

40 Positive numbers are used to describe a number of paces forwards and negative numbers are used to describe a number of paces backwards. Describe where you are in relation to your starting point if you walk +10 paces followed by –4 paces.

The number line

If we draw a straight line and mark a point on it as zero, then we can describe the whole numbers as equally spaced points to the right of zero as 1, 2, 3, 4, 5, … These are called positive numbers.

Numbers to the left of zero are called negative numbers and can be described as equally spaced points to the left of zero.

This line is called a *number line*.

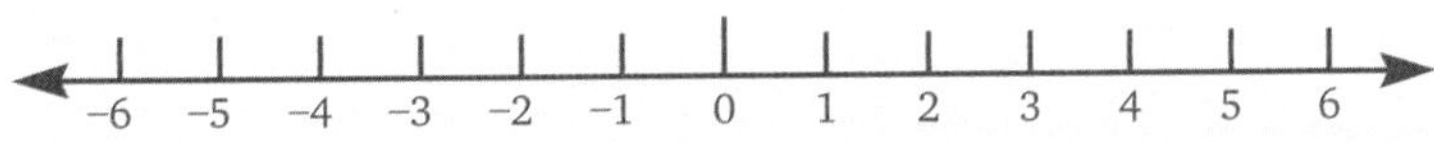

On this number line,		5 is to the *right* of 3
and we say that		5 is *greater* than 3
	or	5 > 3 (> means 'is greater than')
Also		–2 is to the *right* of –4
and we say that		–2 is *greater* than –4
	or	–2 > –4

So 'greater' means 'higher up the scale'.

(A temperature of –2 °C is higher than a temperature of –4 °C.)

Now		2 is to the *left* of 6
and we say that		2 is *less* than 6
	or	$2 < 6$ ($<$ means 'is smaller than')
Also		-3 is to the *left* of -1
and we say that		-3 is *less* than -1
	or	$-3 < -1$

So 'less than' means 'lower down the scale'.

Note that the numbers … −6, −5, −4, −3, −2, −1, 0, 1, 2, 3, 4, 5, 6, … are called *integers*.

Exercise 11b

Draw a number line.

In questions **1** to **12** write either > or < between the two numbers:

1	3 2	**4**	−3 −1	**7**	3 −2	**10**	−7 3
2	5 1	**5**	1 −2	**8**	5 −10	**11**	−1 0
3	−1 −4	**6**	−4 1	**9**	−3 −9	**12**	1 −1

In questions **13** to **24** write down the next two numbers in the sequence:

13	4, 6, 8	**16**	−4, −2, 0	**19**	5, 1, −3	**22**	−10, −8, −6
14	−4, −6, −8	**17**	9, 6, 3	**20**	2, 4, 8	**23**	−1, −2, −4
15	4, 2, 0	**18**	−4, −1, 2	**21**	36, 6, 1	**24**	1, 0, −1

Addition and subtraction of positive numbers

If you were asked to work out 5 − 7 you would probably say that it cannot be done. But if you were asked to work out where you would be if you walked 5 steps forwards and then 7 steps backwards, you would say that you were 2 steps behind your starting point.

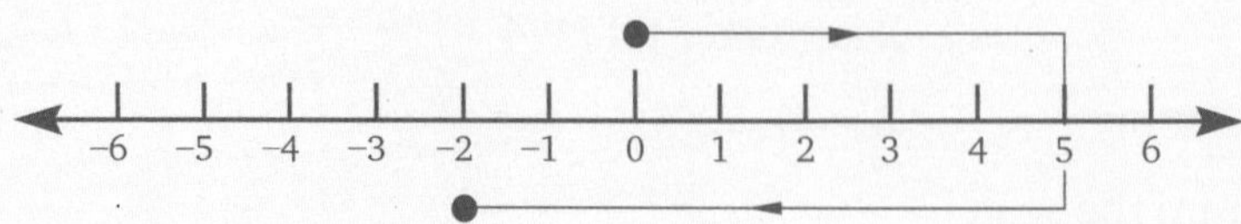

On the number line, $5 - 7$ means

start at 0 and go 5 places to the right

and then go 7 places to the left

So $5 - 7 = -2$

i.e. 'minus' a positive number means move to the left

and 'plus' a positive number means move to the right.

In this way $3 + 2 - 8 + 1$ can be shown on the number line as follows:

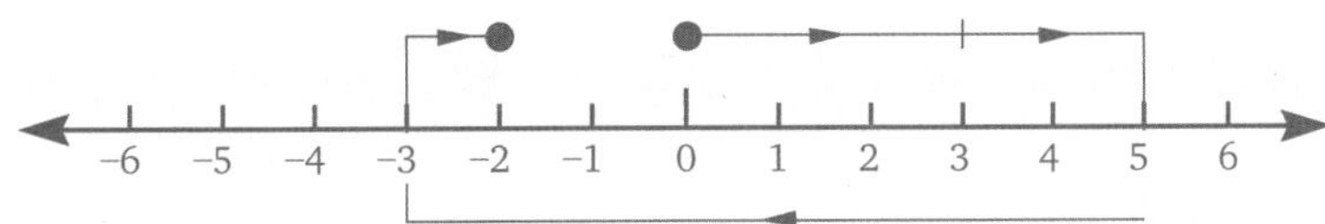

Therefore $3 + 2 - 8 + 1 = -2$.

Exercise 11c

Find, using a number line if it helps:

1 $3 - 6$ **3** $4 - 6$ **5** $4 - 2$ **7** $-2 + 3$ **9** $-5 - 7$

2 $5 - 2$ **4** $5 - 7$ **6** $5 + 2$ **8** $-3 + 5$ **10** $-3 + 2$

$(+4) - (+3)$

$(+4) - (+3) = 4 - 3$ $\quad(+4 = 4 \text{ and } +3 = 3)$

$= 1$

Remember that +3 is the same as 3.

11 $(+3) + (+2)$

12 $(+2) - (+4)$

13 $(+5) - (+7)$

14 $(-3) + (+2)$

15 $(-1) + (+5)$

16 $5 - 2 + 3$

17 $7 - 9 + 4$

18 $5 - 11 + 3$

19 $10 - 4 - 9$

20 $3 + 6 - 10$

21 $-4 + 2 + 5$

22 $-3 + 1 - 4$

23 $5 - 6 - 9$

<u>24</u> $-3 - 4 + 2$

<u>25</u> $-2 - 3 + 9$

<u>26</u> $(+3) + (+4) - (+1)$

<u>27</u> $(+2) - (+5) + (+6)$

<u>28</u> $(+9) - (+7) - (+2)$

<u>29</u> $(-3) + (+5) - (+5)$

<u>30</u> $(-8) - (+4) + (+7)$

Addition and subtraction of negative numbers

Most of you will have some money of your own, from pocket money and other sources. Many of you will have borrowed money at some time.

At any one time you have a *balance* of money, i.e. the total sum that you own or owe!

If you own \$3 and you borrow \$4, your balance is a debt of \$1. We can write this as

$$(+3) + (-4) = (-1)$$

or as $\quad 3 + (-4) = -1$

But $\quad 3 - 4 = -1$

$\therefore \quad +(-4) \text{ means } -4$

If you owe \$2 and then take away that debt, your balance is zero. We can write this as

$$(-2) - (-2) = 0$$

You can pay off the debt on your balance only if someone gives you \$2.
So subtracting a negative number is equivalent to adding a positive number, i.e. $-(-2)$ is equivalent to $+2$.

$$-(-2) \text{ means } +2$$

Exercise 11d

Find:

1. $3 + (-1)$
2. $5 + (-8)$
3. $4 - (-3)$
4. $-1 - (-4)$
5. $-2 + (-7)$
6. $-2 - (-5)$
7. $4 + (-7)$
8. $-3 - (-9)$
9. $-4 + (-10)$
10. $2 - (-8)$
11. <u>11</u> $-7 + (-7)$
12. <u>12</u> $-3 - (-3)$
13. <u>13</u> $+4 + (-4)$
14. <u>14</u> $+2 - (-4)$
15. <u>15</u> $-3 + (-3)$

$+(-1) = -1$

$-(-3) = +3$

$2 + (-1) - (-4)$

$+(-1) = -1$ and $-(-4) = +4$

$2 + (-1) - (-4) = 2 - 1 + 4$

$= 5$

16 $5 + (-1) - (-3)$

17 $(-1) + (-1) + (-1)$

18 $4 - (-2) + (-4)$

19 $-2 - (-2) + (-4)$

20 $6 - (-7) + (-8)$

21 $9 + (-5) - (-9)$

22 8 – (–7) + (–[illegible])

23 $10 + (-9) + (-7)$

24 $12 + (-8) - (-4)$

25 $9 + (-12) - (-4)$

Addition and subtraction of directed numbers

We can now use the following rules:

$+(+a) = +a$ and $-(+a) = -a$

$+(-a) = -a$ and $-(-a) = +a$

Exercise 11e

Find:

1 $3 + (-2)$

2 $-3 - (+2)$

3 $6 - (-3)$

4 $4 + (+4)$

5 $-5 - (-7)$

6 $9 - (+2)$

7 $7 + (-3)$

8 $8 + (+2)$

9 $10 - (-5)$

10 $-2 - (-4)$

11 $12 + (-7)$

12 $-4 - (+8)$

13 $3 - (-2)$

14 $-5 + (-4)$

15 $8 + (-7)$

16 $4 - (-5)$

17 $7 + (-3) - (+5)$

18 $2 - (-4) + (-6)$

19 $5 + (-2) - (+1)$

20 $8 - (-3) + (+5)$

21 $7 + (-4) - (-2)$

22 $3 - (+2) + (-5)$

23 $-9 + (-2) - (-3)$

24 $8 + (+9) - (-2)$

25 $7 + (-9) - (+2)$

26 $4 + (-1) - (+7)$

27 $-3 + (+5) - (-2)$

28 $-4 + (+8) + (-7)$

29 $-9 - (+4) - (-10)$

30 $-2 - (+8) + (-9)$

$-8 - (4 - 7)$

$$-8 - (4 - 7) = -8 - (-3) \quad \text{(brackets first)}$$
$$= -8 + 3$$
$$= -5$$

31 $3 - (4 - 3)$

32 $5 + (7 - 9)$

33 $4 + (8 - 12)$

34 $-3 - (7 - 10)$

35 $6 + (8 - 15)$

36 $(3 - 5) + 2$

37 $5 - (6 - 10)$

38 $(4 - 9) - 2$

39 $(7 + 4) - 15$

40 $8 + (3 - 8)$

41 $(3 - 8) - (9 - 4)$

42 $(3 - 1) + (5 - 10)$

43 $(7 - 12) - (6 - 9)$

44 $(4 - 8) - (10 - 15)$

45 Add (+7) to (–5).

46 Subtract 7 from –5.

47 Subtract (–2) from 1

48 Find the value of '8 take away –10'.

49 Add –5 to +3

50 Find the sum of –3 and +4.

51 Find the sum of –8 and +10.

52 Subtract positive 8 from negative 7.

53 Find the sum of –3 and –3 and –3.

54 Find the value of twice negative 3.

55 Find the value of four times –2.

? Puzzle

An early Greek mathematician set up a secret society in the sixth century BCE. Members swore never to give away any mathematical secrets. One member was killed because he told one of the secrets to a friend who was not a member. The first letters to complete each of the statements below taken in order will spell his name.

The distance around a plane figure is called its ________.

There are 365 days in a ________.

A plane figure with three sides is a ________.

2 is ________ of 4.

The ________ of a triangle add up to 180 degrees.

> means 'is ________ than'.

An angle whose size is between 90° and 180° is ________.

2 is to the ______ of –1 on a number line.

To find the ________ of a rectangle we multiply the length by the width.

–8 is the ________ of –6 and –2.

Multiplication of directed numbers

From previous work we know that

a $(+3) \times (+2) = +6$

This is just the multiplication of positive numbers,

i.e. $(+3) \times (+2) = 3 \times 2 = 6$

b $(-3) \times (+2) = -6$

Here we could write $(-3) \times (+2) = -3(2)$.

This is equivalent to subtracting 3 twos, i.e. subtracting 6.

c $(+4) \times (-3) = -12$

This means four lots of -3,

i.e. $(-3) + (-3) + (-3) + (-3) = -12$

d $(-2) \times (-3) = +6$

This can be thought of as taking away two lots of -3,

i.e. $-2(-3) = -(-6)$

We have already seen that taking away a negative number is equivalent to adding a positive number, so $(-2) \times (-3) = +6$.

To summarise:

- when two positive numbers are multiplied, the answer is positive
- when two negative numbers are multiplied, the answer is positive
- when a positive number and a negative number are multiplied the answer is negative.

Exercise 11f

Calculate: **a** $(+2) \times (+4)$ **b** 2×4.

a $(+2) \times (+4) = 8$

b $2 \times 4 = 8$

This shows that $(+2) \times (+4)$ means the same as 2×4.

Calculate: **a** $(-3) \times (+4)$ **b** -3×4.

a $(-3) \times (+4) = -12$

b $-3 \times 4 = -12$

This shows that $(-3) \times (+4)$ means the same as -3×4.

Because order does not matter when two quantities are multiplied together, $(+4) \times (-3)$ gives the same answer of -12.

So -3 and $+4$ can be multiplied together in two different ways, but they mean the same thing.

Calculate:

1	$(-3) \times (+5)$	**<u>11</u>**	$(-3) \times (-9)$	**<u>21</u>**	$3(-2)$
2	$(+4) \times (-2)$	**<u>12</u>**	$(-2) \times (+8)$	**<u>22</u>**	5×3
3	$(-7) \times (-2)$	**13**	$7 \times (-5)$	**<u>23</u>**	$6 \times (-3)$
4	$(+4) \times (+1)$	**14**	$-6(-4)$	**<u>24</u>**	$-5(-4)$
5	$(+6) \times (-7)$	**15**	-3×5	**25**	$6 \times (-4)$
6	$(-4) \times (-3)$	**16**	$5 \times (-9)$	**26**	$-3(+8)$
7	$(-6) \times (+3)$	**17**	$-6(4)$	**27**	$(+5) \times (+9)$
8	$(-8) \times (-2)$	**18**	$-2(-4)$	**28**	-4×5
<u>9</u>	$(+5) \times (-1)$	**19**	$-(-3)$	**<u>29</u>**	$7(-4)$
<u>10</u>	$(-6) \times (-3)$	**20**	$4 \times (-2)$	**<u>30</u>**	$(-4) \times (-9)$

Division of directed numbers

The rules for multiplying directed numbers also show us what happens when we divide with directed numbers. We also use the fact that because $2 \times 3 = 6$ it follows that $6 \div 3 = 2$.

a In the same way, $(-3) \times 4 = -12$, so $(-12) \div 4 = -3$.

Notice that the order *does* matter in division, e.g.

$$(-12) \div 4 = -3$$

but $4 \div (-12) = -\frac{4}{12}$ which simplifies to $-\frac{1}{3}$.

b Also $(-4) \times (-2) = 8$ so it follows that $8 \div (-2) = -4$

c Now $3 \times (-2) = -6$ so again it follows that $(-6) \div (-2) = 3$

a and **b** show that:

> When a negative number is divided by a positive number and when a positive number is divided by a negative number the answer is negative.

c shows that:

> When a negative number is divided by a negative number the answer is positive.

Exercise 11g

Calculate: **a** $-8 \div 4$ **b** $8 \div (-4)$

a $-8 \div 4 = -2$

b $8 \div (-4) = -2$

These examples show that the answer is negative when a division involves one positive number and one negative number.

Calculate: **a** $8 \div 4$ **b** $(-8) \div (-4)$

a $8 \div 4 = 2$

b $(-8) \div (-4) = 2$

These examples show that the answer is positive when a division involves two numbers with the same sign.

Calculate:

1	$-12 \div 6$	**6**	$(-28) \div (-7)$	**11**	$15 \div (-12)$	**16**	$\frac{-8}{4}$
2	$25 \div 5$	**7**	$36 \div (-12)$	**12**	$-5 \div 3$	**17**	$\frac{12}{-6}$
3	$16 \div (-4)$	**8**	$(-2) \div (-2)$	**13**	$-36 \div (-10)$	**18**	$\frac{27}{-3}$
4	$(-24) \div (-12)$	**9**	$-18 \div 6$	**14**	$1 \div (-1)$	**19**	$\frac{-27}{-9}$
5	$3 \div (-3)$	**10**	$20 \div (-4)$	**15**	$44 \div (-10)$	**20**	$\frac{45}{-40}$

Calculate: **a** $-2 + 6 \div (-3)$ **b** $-3 \div 6 \times (-9)$ **c** $5 \times (2 - 5) \div 3$

a $-2 + 6 \div (-3) = -2 + (-2)$

$= -4$

Remember that multiplication and division is done before addition and subtraction.

b $-3 \div 6 \times (-9) = (-3) \times (-9) \div 6$

$= 27 \div 6 = \frac{27}{6} = \frac{9}{2} = 4\frac{1}{2}$

Remember that multiplication and division can be done in any order.

c $5 \times (2 - 5) \div 3 = 5 \times (-3) \div 3$

$= 5 \times (-1) = -5$

Remember that numbers in brackets are calculated first.

Calculate:

21 $16 \div 4(3-5)$

22 $24-3\times(-4)$

23 $3\times(4-7)$

24 $5\div(8-7)$

25 $6+8(-2)$

26 $2+6\div(-3)$

27 $12-2(1+5)$

28 $7-3(2-4)$

29 $7\times2-(6+4)$

30 $(-8)\div2(12+4)$

31 $3(2-6)+4\,(12-10)$

32 $2(6-3)\div2(4-6)$

33 $3-7\div2(5-3)$

34 $(-3)(2-5)\times4(7-6)$

35 $5(7+8)\div6\times(-2)$

Did you know?

If the sum of two numbers is 24 and the difference is 6, then one of the numbers is $\frac{(24+6)}{2}=15$

or

If the sum of two numbers is 28 and the difference is 12, then one of them is $\frac{(28+12)}{2}=20.$

What are the other numbers that make each sum? Can you find the numbers for other sums and differences?

Investigation

Try this on a group of pupils or friends.

- Think of a number between 1 and 10.
- Add 4.
- Multiply the result by 5.
- Double your answer.
- Divide the result by 10.
- Take away the number you first thought of.
- Write down your answer.

However many times you try this, the answer is always 4.

Investigate what happens when you use numbers other than numbers between 1 and 10. Try, for example, larger whole numbers, decimals, negative whole numbers, fractions.

Is the answer always 4?

Mixed exercises

Exercise 11h

Select the letter that gives the correct answer.

1 $-4+3+7=$

A -6 B 0 C 4 D 6

2 $(-4)-(-5)+3=$

A 2 B 3 C 4 D 5

3 $(-8)-(+7)+20=$

A -5 B 5 C 13 D 18

4 When 5 is subtracted from -3 the result is

A -8 B -5 C 2 D 8

5 $(-4)\times(5)$ equals

A -40 B -20 C 16 D 20

6 $(-24)\div(-3)=$

A -8 B -6 C 6 D 8

Exercise 11i

Find:

1 $4\div(-2)$

2 $(-5)\times(-10)$

3 $(-5)\div(-10)$

4 $(-6)\div 6$

5 $3-4\div(-2)$

6 $(-2-7)\div 3\times 6$

7 $2\times 4-3(6-4)$

8 $2\times 4\div 3(6-4)$

9 $4(6-3)\div 2(4-6)$

10 $3(5+1)\times(-2)(3-2)$

11 $(-1)(5-6)\div 2(4-3)$

12 $3\times 2+4\times 6-2\div(-4)$

Did you know?

Astragalia is the name given to the large number of bones claimed to have been discovered by archaeologists at prehistoric sites.

It is said that these bones were used as dice in ancient games.

In this chapter you have seen that...

✔ directed numbers is the collective name for positive and negative numbers

✔ directed numbers can be used to describe quantities that can be measured above or below a natural zero

✔ the rules for addition and subtraction are:

$+(+a)$ and $-(-a)$ both give $+a$ and

$+(-a)$ and $-(+a)$ both give $-a$

You can remember these as

SAME SIGNS GIVE POSITIVE, DIFFERENT SIGNS GIVE NEGATIVE

✔ $5 \times (-3)$, $(+5) \times (-3)$,

$(-3) \times 5$, $(-3) \times (+5)$

ALL MEAN THE SAME

✔ the rules for multiplication and division are:

- when a negative number is divided by a positive number and when a positive number is divided by a negative number the answer is negative
- when a negative number is divided by a negative number the answer is positive.

12 Algebra 1

At the end of this chapter you should be able to...

1 use letters to represent numbers in mathematical statements

2 use index notation to write down products

3 multiply or divide algebraic fractions

4 simplify simple expressions in one or more variables

5 substitute numbers into expressions.

Did you know?

Arabic numerals became known in the West through a book by the Arabian mathematician Muhammad ibn Musa al-Khwarizmi, written in the year 820 CE under the title al-Jabr wa'l-Muqabala. It is said that the word 'algebra' came from the title of this book.

You need to know...

✔ how to work with simple numbers

✔ how to work with fractions.

Key words

algebraic fraction, coefficient, expression, index (plural indices), like terms, unlike terms, variable

The idea of algebra

Algebra uses letters for numbers so that some facts can be discovered when the numbers involved are not known. For example think of a bag of sweets. Different people will think of varying numbers of sweets in the bag. If we use the letter n, we can say that there are n sweets in the bag. Letters used in this way are called *variables*.

Expressions

'I think of a number and take away 3.'

If we use the letter x for the number, we can write the sentence as $x - 3$.

$x - 3$ is called an *expression*.

Exercise 12a

Form an expression from the sentence 'I think of a number and add 4'.

Let the number be x. Then adding 4 to x can be written as

$$x + 4$$

Form expressions from the following sentences.

1 Think of a number and subtract 3.

2 Think of a number and add 1.

3 Think of a number and subtract 6.

4 The number 5 is subtracted from another number.

Think of a number and multiply it by 3.

Let the number be x.

The expression is $3 \times x$.

5 A number is doubled.

6 A number is multipled by 4.

7 7 is multiplied by an unknown number.

8 6 times an unknown number.

$4 \times n$ Any letter can be used to describe an unknown number.

$4 \times n$ means 4 times an unknown number.

Write sentences to show the meaning of the following expressions.

9 $3 \times n$	**11** $n - 5$	**13** $8 \times n$	**15** $12 + n$
10 $x + 9$	**12** $x + 8$	**14** $7 - x$	**16** $x \div 6$

Simplifying expressions

Expressions like $4 \times n$ are abbreviated to $4n$.

This means that, for example, $5x$ means $5 \times x$.

The known number multiplied by an unknown is called the *coefficient* of the unknown.

So 4 is the coefficient of n and 5 is the coefficient of x.

Like terms

Consider $3x + 5x - 4x + 2x$.

This is an expression and can be simplified to $6x$.

$3x$, $5x$, $4x$ and $2x$ are all *terms* in this expression. Each term contains x. They are of the same type and are called *like terms*.

Exercise 12b

Simplify $4h - 6h + 7h - h$

You can do the addition before the subtraction, i.e. $4h + 7h - 6h - h$

$$4h - 6h + 7h - h = 4h$$

Simplify:

1 $3x + x + 4x + 2x$	**5** $9y - 3y + 2y$
2 $3x - x + 4x - 2x$	**6** $2 - 3 + 9 - 1$
3 $8x - 6x$	**7** $5 - 3 - 1$
4 $6 - 1 + 4 - 7$	**8** $3x - 2x - x$

Remember that the sign in front of a number applies to that number only.

Unlike terms

$3x + 2x - 7$ can be simplified to $5x - 7$, and $5x - 2y + 4x + 3y$ can be simplified to $9x + y$.

Terms containing x are different from terms without an x. They are called *unlike terms* and cannot be collected. Similarly $9x$ and $5y$ are unlike terms; therefore $9x - 5y$ cannot be simplified.

Exercise 12c

Simplify $3x - 4 + 7 - 2x + 4x$

You can rearrange this to have the like terms together, i.e.

$3x - 2x + 4x + 7 - 4$

$$3x - 4 + 7 - 2x + 4x = 5x + 3$$

Simplify $2x + 4y - x + 5y$

$$2x + 4y - x + 5y = 2x - x + 4y + 5y = x + 9y$$

Simplify:

1 $2x + 4 + 3 + 5x$

2 $2x - 4 + 3x + 9$

3 $5x - 2 + 3 - x$

4 $4a + 5c + 6a$

5 $6x + 5y + 2x - 3y$

6 $6x + 5y + 2x + 3y$

7 $6x + 5y - 2x - 3y$

8 $6x + 5y - 2x + 3y$

9 $4x + 1 + 3x + 2 + x$

10 $6x + 9 + 2x - 1$

11 $7x - 3 + 9 - 4x$

12 $9x + 3y + 10x$

13 $6x + 5y + 2x + 3y + 2x$

14 $6x + 5y - 2x - 3y + 7x + y$

15 $30x + 2 - 15x - 6 + 4$

16 $2z + 3x + 4y + 6z + x - 3y$

17 $4x + 3y - 4 + 6x - 2y + 7 - x$

18 $7x + 3 - 9 - 9x + 2x + 6 + 11$

There are three sets of like terms here: x's, y's and z's.

Brackets

Sometimes brackets are used to hold two quantities together. For instance, if we wish to multiply the sum of x and 3 by 4 we write $4(x + 3)$. The multiplication sign is invisible just as it is in $5x$, which means $5 \times x$.

$4(x + 3)$ means 'four times everything in the brackets'

so we have $4 \times x$ and 4×3, and we write $4(x + 3) = 4x + 12$.

Exercise 12d

Multiply out the brackets:

1 $2(x+1)$
2 $3(3x+2)$
3 $5(x+6)$
4 $4(3x+3)$
5 $2(4+5x)$
6 $2(6+5a)$
7 $5(a+b)$
8 $4(4x+3)$
9 $3(6+4x)$
10 $5(x+1)$
11 $7(2+x)$
12 $8(3+2x)$

Multiply each term in the bracket by 2.

To simplify an expression containing brackets we first multiply out the brackets and then collect like terms.

Exercise 12e

Simplify $2+(3x+7)$

First deal with the brackets, then collect like terms.

$$2+(3x+7) \qquad \text{(This means } 2+1(3x+7)\text{)}$$
$$=2+3x+7$$
$$=3x+9$$

Simplify the following expressions:

1 $2x+4(x+1)$
2 $3+5(2x+3)$
3 $3(x+1)+4$
4 $7+2(2x+5)$
5 $2(x+4)+3(x+5)$
6 $3x+(2x+5)$
7 $4+(3x+1)$
8 $3x+2(3x+4)$

Multiply out both brackets, then collect like terms.

Investigation

Meg wanted to find out Malcolm's age without asking him directly what it was.

The following conversation took place.

Meg: Think of your age but don't tell me what it is
Malcolm: Right.
Meg: Multiply it by 5, add 4 and take away your age.
Malcolm: Yes.
Meg: Divide the result by 4 and tell me your answer.
Malcolm: 15

Meg: That means you are 14.

Malcolm: Correct. How do you know that?

However many times Meg tried this on her friends and relations she found their age by taking 1 away from the number they gave.

Does it always work?

Can you use simple algebra to prove that it always gives the correct answer?

Indices

We have already seen that the shorthand way of writing $2 \times 2 \times 2 \times 2$ is 2^4.
In the same way we can write $a \times a \times a \times a$ as a^4. The 4 is called the *index*.

Exercise 12f

Write the following expressions in index form:

1 $z \times z \times z$

2 $a \times a$

3 $b \times b \times b \times b \times b$

4 $y \times y \times y \times y \times y$

5 $s \times s \times s$

6 $z \times z \times z \times z \times z \times z$

There are three z's multiplied together so the index is 3.

Give the meanings of the following expressions:

7 a^3

8 x^4

9 b^2

10 a^5

<u>11</u> x^6

<u>12</u> z^4

a^3 means three a's multiplied together.

Simplify $2 \times x \times y \times x \times 3$

(Write the numbers first, then the letters in alphabetical order.)

$$2 \times x \times y \times x \times 3 = 2 \times 3 \times x \times x \times y \qquad (2 \times 3 \text{ is } 6 \text{ and } x \times x \text{ is } x^2)$$

$$= 6x^2y$$

Simplify the following expressions:

13 $2 \times a$

14 $4 \times x \times x$

15 $3 \times a \times 4$

16 $a \times a \times b$

17 $3 \times z \times x \times 5 \times z$

18 $5 \times a \times b \times b \times a$

Write each expression in full without using indices:

19 $3z^2$

20 $2abc$

21 $4zy^2$

22 $6a^2b$

<u>23</u> $2x^3$

<u>24</u> $3a^4b^2$

Simplify the following expressions:

25 $3x \times 2z$

26 $x \times 6x^2$

27 $4a^2 \times 3$

28 $3a \times 2a \times a$

29 $a \times b \times c \times 2a$

30 $4x \times 3y \times 2x$

31 $z \times z \times z \times z$

32 $2z \times 3z$

33 $4x^2 \times 6$

34 $2 \times 4 \times x \times 2$

35 $4s^2 \times s$

36 $x^2 \times x^4$

37 $y \times z \times y \times z$

38 $2x \times 5z \times y$

39 $a \times a \times a \times a \times a \times a \times a$

40 $4x^2 \times 2x^2$

41 $x \times y \times z \times a$

42 $s^4 \times s^3$

> $3x \times 2z = 3 \times x \times 2 \times z$
> You can change the order to $3 \times 2 \times x \times z$.
> What is a simpler way of writing $x \times z$?

Multiplication and division of algebraic fractions

Algebraic fractions can be multiplied and simplified in the same way as arithmetic fractions.

To multiply fractions together, multiply the numerators together and multiply the denominators together.

Exercise 12g

Simplify the following fractions:

a $\frac{24}{5} \times \frac{10}{9}$

b $\frac{2z}{3} \times \frac{6}{z^2}$

a $\frac{24}{5} \times \frac{10}{9} = \frac{{}^{8}\not{24} \times \not{10}^{2}}{{}_{1}\not{5} \times \not{9}_{3}}$ (Cancel common factors)

$= \frac{16}{3}$

$= 5\frac{1}{3}$

b $\frac{2z}{3} \times \frac{6}{z^2} = \frac{2 \times {}^{1}\not{z} \times \not{6}^{2}}{{}_{1}\not{3} \times {}_{1}\not{z} \times z}$ (z^2 means $z \times z$)

$= \frac{4}{z}$ (z and 3 are common factors)

Simplify the following fractions:

1 $\frac{5}{6} \times \frac{12}{5}$

2 $\frac{11}{9} \times \frac{18}{5}$

3 $\frac{2}{3} \times \frac{15}{16}$

4 $\frac{z}{3} \times \frac{z}{2}$

5 $\frac{a}{4} \times \frac{6b}{5}$

6 $\frac{2c}{5} \times \frac{10}{3c}$

7 $\frac{p}{3} \times \frac{9}{p}$

8 $\frac{y}{6} \times \frac{y}{4}$

9 $\frac{3c}{5} \times \frac{c}{6}$

10 $\frac{4z}{3} \times \frac{9}{2z}$

11 $\frac{5x}{2} \times \frac{x}{10}$

12 $\frac{7}{y} \times \frac{2y}{14}$

Division of algebraic fractions follows the same rules as for arithmetic fractions. To divide by a fraction, turn it upside down and multiply.

Simplify the following fractions:

a $\frac{4}{5} \div \frac{8}{15}$

b $\frac{4y}{3z} \div \frac{16y^2}{9}$

a $\frac{4}{5} \div \frac{8}{15} = \frac{4}{5} \times \frac{15}{8}$ To divide by a fraction, turn it upside down and multiply.

$= \frac{{}^{1}\cancel{4} \times \cancel{15}^{3}}{{}_{1}\cancel{5} \times \cancel{8}_{2}}$ Cancel

$= \frac{3}{2}$

$= 1\frac{1}{2}$

b $\frac{4y}{3z} \div \frac{16y^2}{9} = \frac{{}^{1}\cancel{4} \times {}^{1}\cancel{y} \times \cancel{9}^{3}}{{}_{1}\cancel{3} \times z \times {}_{4}\cancel{16} \times \cancel{y}_{1} \times y}$ Cancel

$= \frac{3}{4yz}$

Simplify the following fractions:

13 $\frac{1}{3} \div \frac{5}{6}$

14 $\frac{7}{9} \div \frac{2}{3}$

15 $\frac{3}{4} \div \frac{7}{12}$

16 $\frac{z}{2} \div \frac{z}{4}$

17 $\frac{2y}{3} \div \frac{y}{6}$

18 $\frac{6}{5y} \div \frac{3}{y}$

19 $\frac{4c}{3} \div \frac{8y}{9}$

20 $\frac{6z}{25} \div \frac{4z^2}{5}$

21 $\frac{r}{4} \times \frac{r}{6}$

22 $\frac{4y}{3} \times \frac{15z}{8y}$

23 $\frac{3b}{7} \div \frac{9ab}{14}$

24 $\frac{ab}{bc} \times \frac{c}{a}$

25 $\frac{4}{x} \div \frac{16}{x^2}$

26 $\frac{3s}{2} \div \frac{6s}{7}$

27 $\frac{16a}{9} \div \frac{4ab}{15}$

28 $\frac{yz}{xy} \times \frac{vx}{zv}$

29 $\frac{3a^2}{4y} \times \frac{2y^2}{6a}$

30 $\frac{3}{x} \div \frac{6}{y}$

31 $\frac{10a}{7} \times \frac{14}{5ab}$

32 $\frac{3x}{2} \div \frac{9y}{4}$

Substituting numbers into expressions

We can find a value for an expression when we substitute numbers for the variables in an expression. (Substituting numbers for variables means giving the variables numerical values.) For example, when $x = 6$, we replace x with 6

so the value of $2x - 4$ is $2 \times 6 - 4$

$$= 12 - 4 = 8$$

Exercise 12h

1 Find the value of $x - 7$ when	**a**	$x = 12$	**b**	$x = 4$	**c**	$x = -2$
2 Find the value of $16 - x$ when	**a**	$x = 9$	**b**	$x = 16$	**c**	$x = 20$
3 Find the value of $16 + x$ when	**a**	$x = 4$	**b**	$x = -6$	**c**	$x = -20$
4 Find the value of $5 - x$ when	**a**	$x = 4$	**b**	$x = 6$	**c**	$x = -2$
5 Find the value of $3x + 4$ when	**a**	$x = 2$	**b**	$x = 3$	**c**	$x = -1$
6 Find the value of $6 - 2x$ when	**a**	$x = 2$	**b**	$x = 3$	**c**	$x = -2$
7 Find the value of $6 + y$ when	**a**	$y = 4$	**b**	$y = -5$	**c**	$y = -10$
8 Find the value of $3n - 4$ when	**a**	$n = 3$	**b**	$n = 1$	**c**	$n = -1$
9 Find the value of $2n^2$ when	**a**	$n = 2$	**b**	$n = 5$	**c**	$n = -2$
10 Find the value of y^3 when	**a**	$y = 2$	**b**	$y = 3$	**c**	$y = -2$

$2n^2 = 2 \times n \times n$

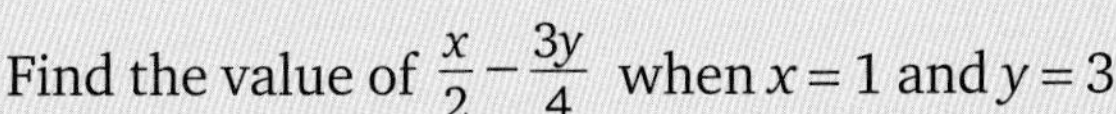

Find the value of $\frac{x}{2} - \frac{3y}{4}$ when $x = 1$ and $y = 3$

Replacing x with 1 and y with 3 gives

$$\frac{1}{2} - \frac{3 \times 3}{4} = \frac{1}{2} - \frac{9}{4}$$

$$= \frac{2 - 9}{4}$$

$$= \frac{-7}{4} = -1\frac{3}{4}$$

11 Find the value of $\frac{3x}{2} - \frac{3}{4}$ when $x = 1$.

12 Find the value of $3xy$ when $x = 4$ and $y = 2$.

13 Find the value of $\frac{3x}{2} - \frac{y}{4}$ when $x = 3$ and $y = 5$.

14 Find the value of $n(2n-1)$ when $n = 10$.

15 Find the value of $\frac{n}{2}(n-1)$ when $n=6$.

16 Find the value of $p(q-9)$ when $p=10$ and $q=12$.

17 Find the value of $\frac{n^2}{4}$ when $n=8$.

18 Find the value of $\frac{5x}{4}-\frac{y}{3}$ when $x=2$ and $y=11$

19 Find the value of $\frac{PRT}{100}$ when $P=50$, $R=10$ and $T=4$.

20 Find the value of b^2-4ac when $a=6$, $b=5$ and $c=2$.

Mixed exercises

Exercise 12i

Select the letter that gives the correct answer.

1 $3x-2y+7x+3y$ simplifies to

A $4x+y$ B $8x+y$ C $10x-y$ D $10x+y$

2 $3(7x+1)$ simplifies to

A $7x+3$ B $14x+3$ C $21x+1$ D $21x+3$

3 What does $4a^3$ mean?

A $4\times a\times a$ B $4\times a\times a\times a$ C $4\times a\times a\times a\times a$ D $64\times a\times a\times a$

4 Simplify $2x\times 4x\times 7x$

A $8x^3$ B $14x^3$ C $28x^3$ D $56x^3$

5 Simplify $\frac{2x}{3y}\times\frac{9y}{2x}$

A 2 B $2x$ C 3 D $3y$

6 The value of $5xy+24$ when $x=3$ and $y=-2$ is

A -30 B -12 C -6 D 0

Exercise 12j

1 Simplify $4(x+3)+1$

2 Simplify $3a\times 5b\times 4c$

3 Simplify $\frac{2x}{3y}\times\frac{6y}{4x}$

4 Find the value of $3xy-6$ when $x=3$ and $y=-2$.

5 Simplify $a^3\times a^3$.

Exercise 12k

1 Simplify $3+2(x+2)$
2 Simplify $3(x-1)+4(2x+3)+5(x+1)$
3 What does x^5 mean?
4 Form an expression from the sentence 'I think of a number, multiply it by 3 and subtract 10.'
5 Find the value of $n^2(n-1)$ when $n=3$.

Exercise 12l

1 Peter had 14 marbles and lost x of them. John had 8 marbles and won y marbles. The two boys put all their marbles into one bag. Write an expression for the number of marbles in the bag.
2 Find the value of $\frac{1}{x}+\frac{1}{y}$ when $x=4$ and $y=3$.
3 Simplify $\frac{4x}{11}\div\frac{5x}{22}$.
4 Find the value of $3(2-x)+4(3-y)$ when $x=1$ and $y=-2$.
5 Simplify $2x\times 4x\times 3y$.

Investigation

Each student must bring a calendar page for the month of his or her birth and choose any four by four grid of sixteen days, not including blank squares. Outline this grid and find

1 the sum of the four centre numbers
2 the sum of the four numbers on each diagonal.

What do you notice?

Compare your results with those of other members of the class.

Do calendars from the same month give the same or different sums when using different four by four squares?

What happens if other months are used that begin on a different day?

In this chapter you have seen that...

- ✔ an expression is a collection of terms without an 'is equal to' sign
- ✔ like terms are groups of numbers or groups of terms with the same letter
- ✔ you can add and subtract like terms to simplify them but you cannot add and subtract unlike terms
- ✔ you can simplify algebraic expressions involving brackets by multiplying out the brackets
- ✔ index form with letters means the same as with numbers
- ✔ you can multiply and divide simple algebraic fractions with more than one letter (variable) using the same rules as for number fractions
- ✔ you can substitute numbers for variables to find a value of an expression.

13 Geometry 2

At the end of this chapter you should be able to...

1 use geometrical instruments to draw lines and angles

2 use geometrical instruments to measure line segments and angles

3 name the sides and angles of a given triangle

4 draw rough copies of given triangles

5 state the sum of the angles of a triangle

6 calculate the third angle of a triangle given the other two angles

7 construct triangles given:

   a one side and two angles

   b two sides and the included angle

   c three sides

8 classify triangles as isosceles or equiateral

9 identify equal sides (angles) of an isosceles triangle, given the angles (sides)

10 calculate angles of isosceles triangles from necessary data

11 use geometrical instruments to copy given patterns.

Did you know?

The area between two concentric circles (circles having the same centre) is called an annulus.

You need to know...

✔ how to add and subtract whole numbers

✔ that vertically opposite angles are equal

✔ that angles on a straight line add up to 180°.

Key words

construction, equilateral triangle, isosceles triangle, line of symmetry, pair of compasses, parallelogram, protractor, quadrilateral, radius, rectangle, rhombus, square, tetrahedron, trapezium, triangle, vertex (vertices), vertically opposite

Constructions

When a new object, for example a new car, is designed there are many jobs that have to be done before it can be made. One of these jobs is to make accurate drawings of the parts.

To draw accurately you need

a *sharp* pencil
a ruler
a pair of compasses
a protractor.

Using a pair of compasses

Using a pair of compasses is not easy: it needs practice. Draw several circles. Make some of them small and some large. You should not be able to see the place at which you start and finish. Holding the compasses at the tip only will give the most accurate results.

Now try drawing the daisy pattern opposite.

Draw a circle of radius 5 cm. Keeping the radius the same, put the point of the compasses at A and draw an arc to cut the circle in two places, one of which is B. Move the point to B and repeat. Carry on moving the point of your compasses round the circle until the pattern is complete.

Repeat the daisy pattern but this time draw complete circles instead of arcs.

There are some more patterns using compasses in the Activity on page 229.

Drawing straight lines of a given length

To draw a straight line that is 5 cm long, start by using your ruler to draw a line that is *longer* than 5 cm.

Then mark a point on this line near one end as shown. Label it A.

Next use your compasses to measure 5 cm on your ruler.

Then put the point of the compasses on the line at A and draw an arc to cut the line as shown.

The length of line between A and B should be 5 cm. Measure it with your ruler.

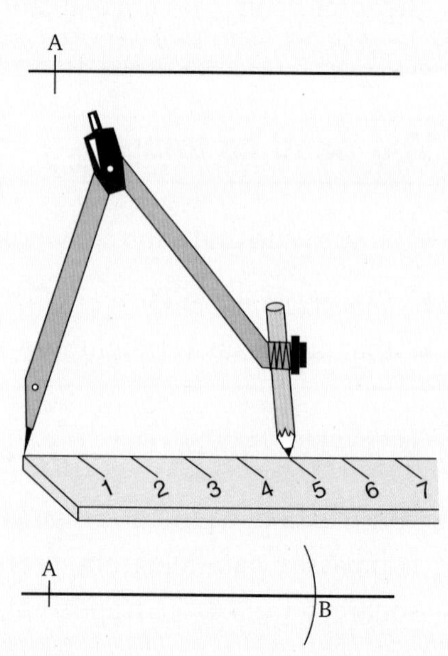

Exercise 13a

Draw, as accurately as you can, straight lines of the following lengths:

1 6 cm
2 2 cm
3 12 cm
4 9 cm
5 8.5 cm
6 3.5 cm
7 4.5 cm
8 6.8 cm

Activity

The patterns below are made using a pair of compasses. Try copying them. Some instructions are given which should help.

1

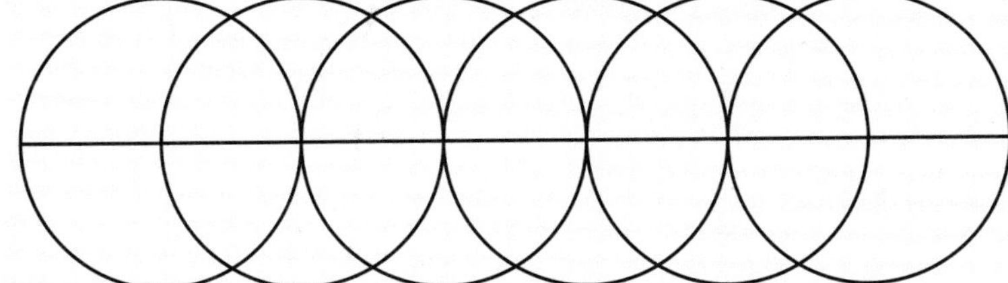

Draw a straight line. Open your compasses to a radius of 3 cm and draw a circle with its centre on the line. Move the point of the compasses 3 cm along the line and draw another circle. Repeat as often as you can.

2 Draw a square of side 4 cm. Open your compasses to a radius of 4 cm and with the point on one corner of the square draw an arc across the square. Repeat on the other three corners.

Try the same pattern, but leave out the sides of the square; just mark the corners. A block of four of these looks good.

3 Draw a square of side 8 cm. Mark the midpoint of each side. Open your compasses to a radius of 4 cm, and with the point on the middle of one side of the square, draw an arc. Repeat at the other three midpoints.

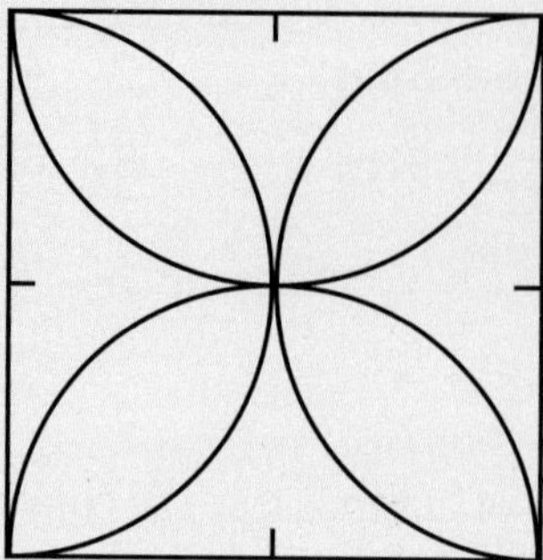

Triangles

A triangle has three sides and three angles.

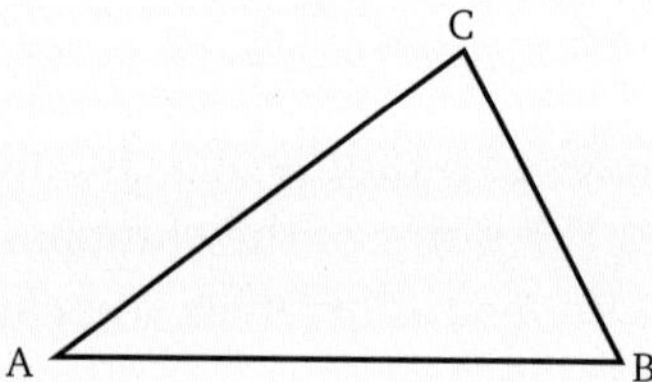

The corners of the triangle are called *vertices*. (One corner is called a *vertex*.) So that we can refer to one particular side, or to one particular angle, we label the vertices using capital letters. In the diagram above we use the letters A, B and C so we can now talk about 'the triangle ABC' or '△ABC'.

The side between A and B is called 'the side AB' or AB.

The side between A and C is called 'the side AC' or AC.

The side between B and C is called 'the side BC' or BC.

The angle at the corner A is called 'angle A' or $\hat{A}$ for short.

Exercise 13b

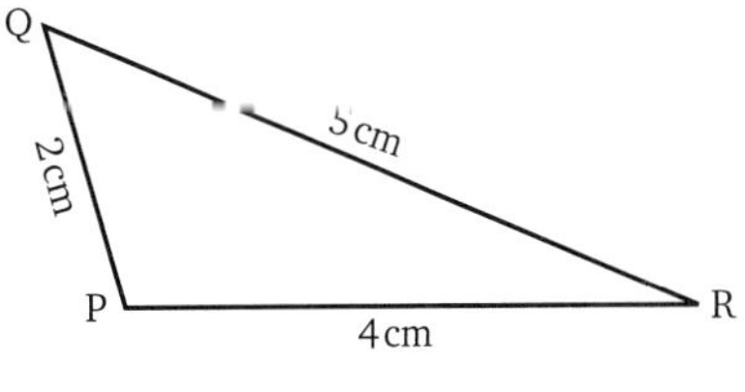

1 Write down the name of the side which is 4 cm long.

Write down the name of the side which is 2 cm long.

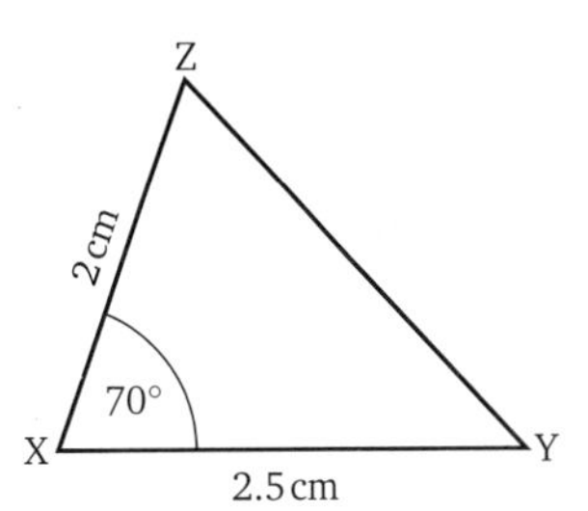

2 Write down the name of

a the side which is 2.5 cm long

b the side which is 2 cm long

c the angle which is 70°.

In the following questions, draw a rough copy of the triangle and mark the given measurements on your drawing:

3 In $\triangle ABC$, $AB = 4$ cm, $\hat{B} = 60°$, $\hat{C} = 50°$.

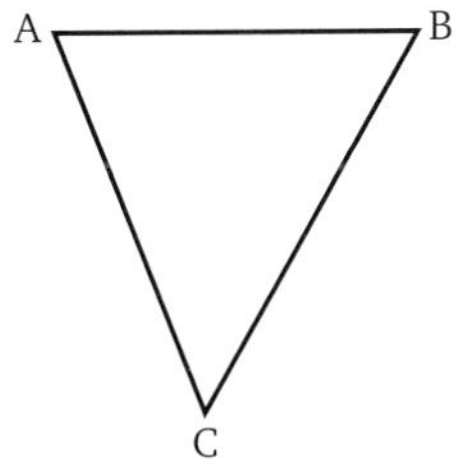

4 In $\triangle DEF$, $\hat{E} = 90°$, $\hat{F} = 70°$, $EF = 3$ cm.

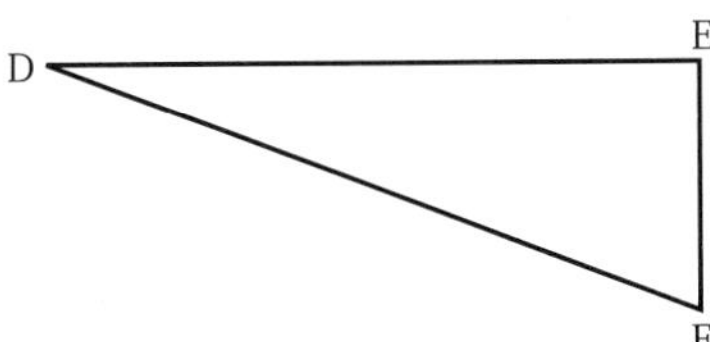

5 In $\triangle LMN$, $\hat{L} = 100°$, $\hat{N} = 30°$, $NL = 2.5$ cm.

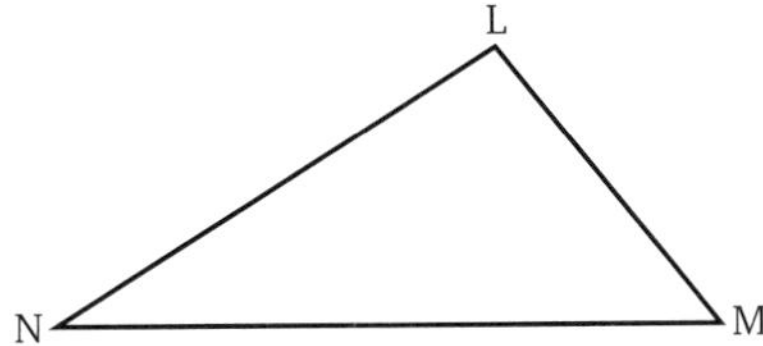

6 In $\triangle FGH$, $FG = 3.5$ cm, $GH = 3$ cm, $\hat{H} = 35°$.

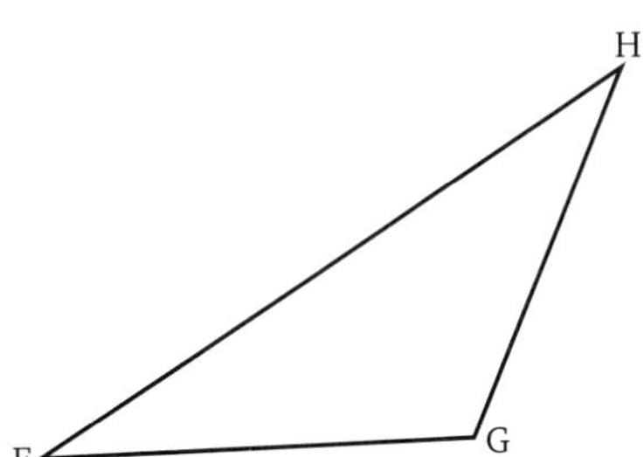

Make a rough drawing of the following triangles. Label each one and mark the measurements given:

7 $\triangle ABC$ in which AB = 10, cm, BC = 8 cm and $\hat{B} = 60°$

8 $\triangle PQR$ in which $\hat{P} = 90°$, $\hat{Q} = 30°$ and PQ = 6 cm

9 $\triangle DEF$ in which DE = 8 cm, $\hat{D} = 50°$ and DF = 6 cm

10 $\triangle XYZ$ in which XY = 10 cm, $\hat{X} = 30°$ and $\hat{Y} = 80°$

Investigation

Five different-shaped triangles can be drawn on a 2 × 2 grid.

Two of them are shown. Sketch the other three.

Remember that 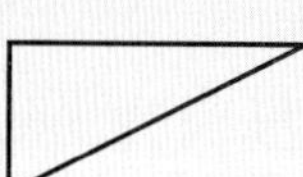 is the same as

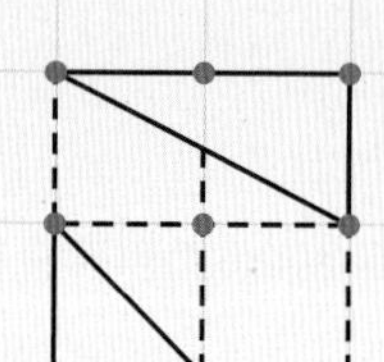

Investigate the number of different triangles that can be drawn on a 3 × 3 grid.

Extend your investigation to a 4 × 4 grid and then a 5 × 5 grid.

Can you find a connection between the number of different triangles that can be drawn and the length of the side of the grid?

Angles of a triangle

Activity

Draw a large triangle of any shape. Use a straight edge to draw the sides. Measure each angle in this triangle, turning your page to a convenient position when necessary. Add up the sizes of the three angles.

Draw another triangle of a different shape. Again measure each angle and then add up their sizes.

Now try this: on a piece of paper draw a triangle of any shape and cut it out. Next tear off each corner and place the three corners together.

They should look like this:

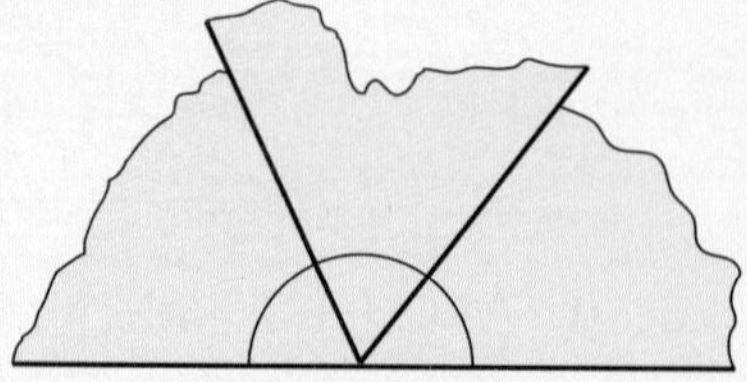

The three angles of a triangle add up to 180°.

Can you tell why this is so? Hint: the sum of the angles on a straight line is 180°.

Exercise 13c

Find the size of angle A (an angle marked with a square is a right angle):

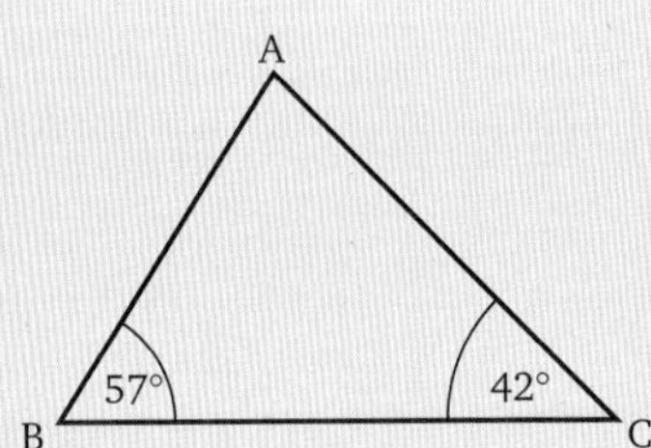

$\hat{A} + 57° + 42° = 180°$ (angles of $\triangle$ add up to 180°)

$\therefore \quad \hat{A} = 180° - 99°$

$= 81°$

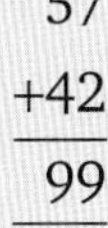

1

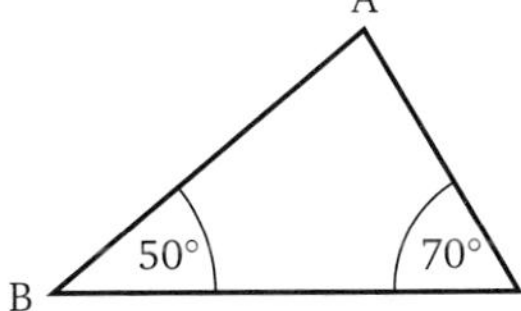

2

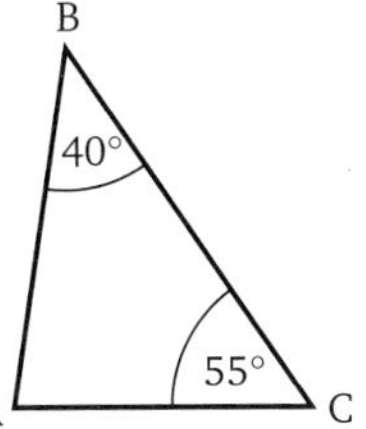

3

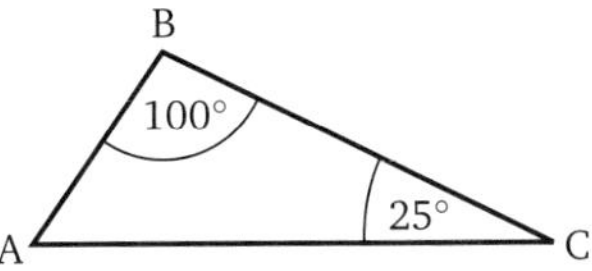

4

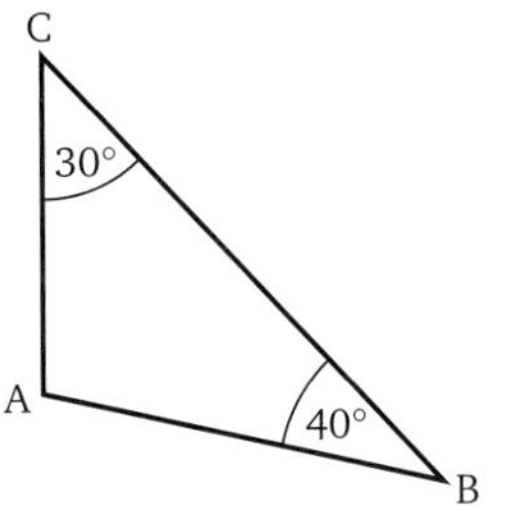

5

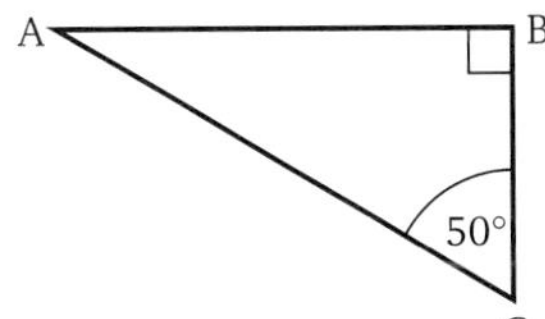

6

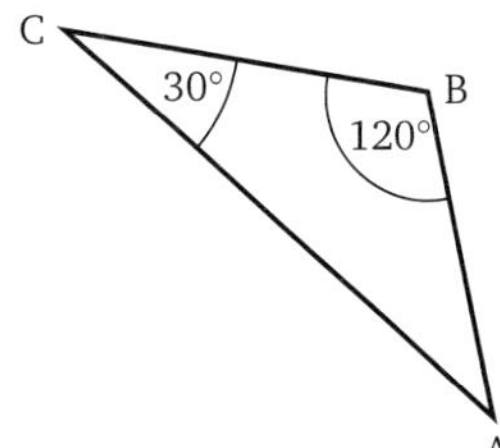

7

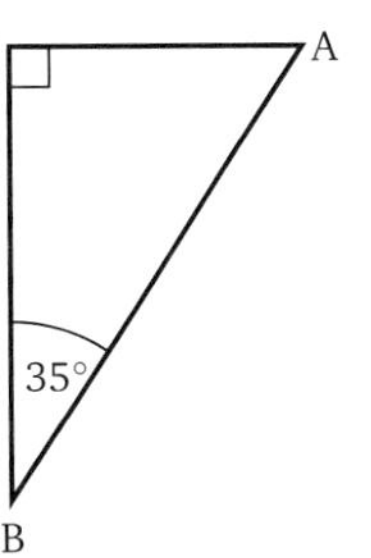

8

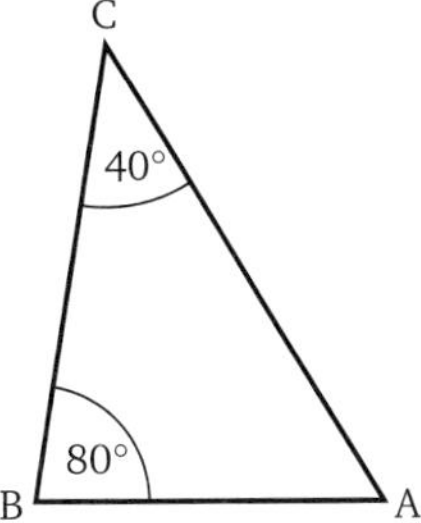

9

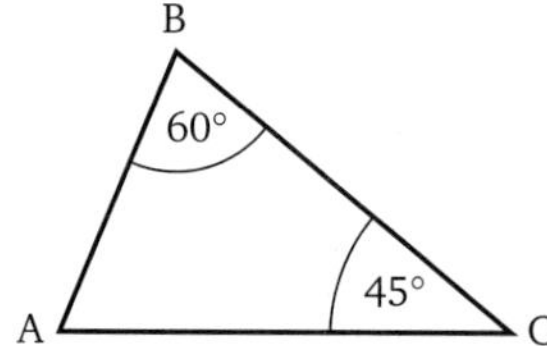

10

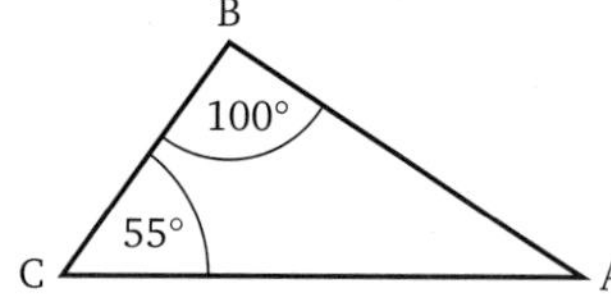

11

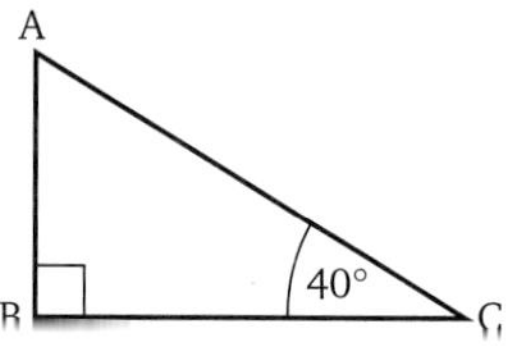

12

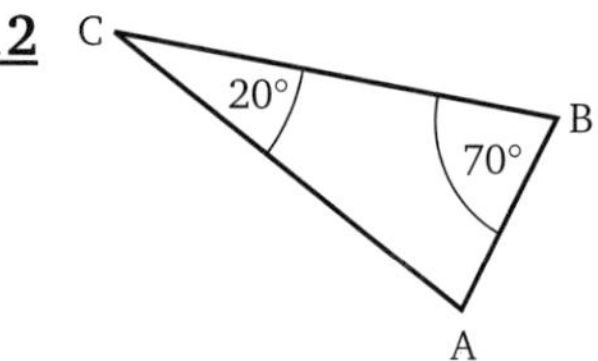

13

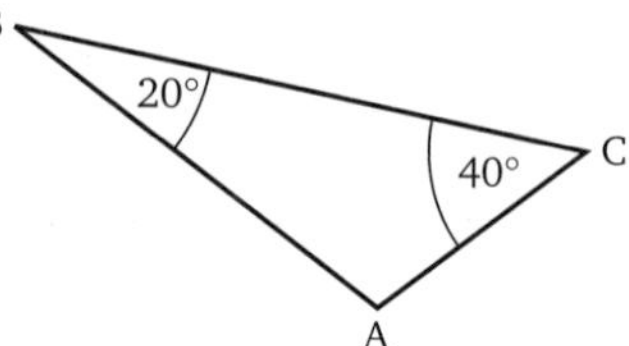

14

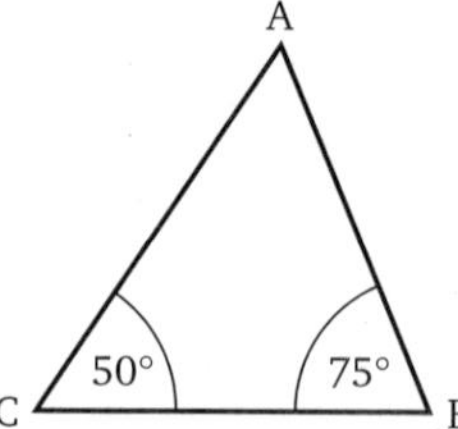

15

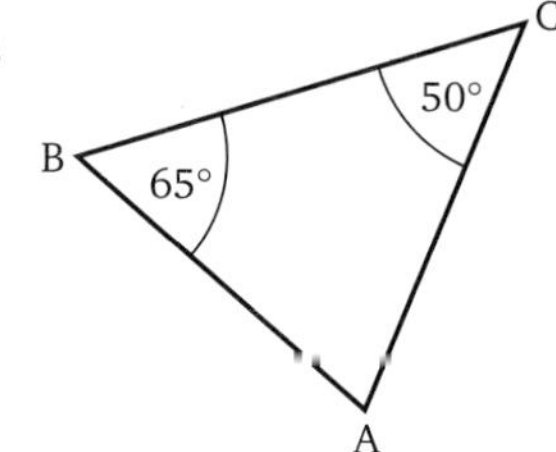

Problems

Reminder: Vertically opposite angles are equal.
Angles on a straight line add up to 180°.

You will need these facts in the next exercise.

Exercise 13d

1 Find angles d and f.

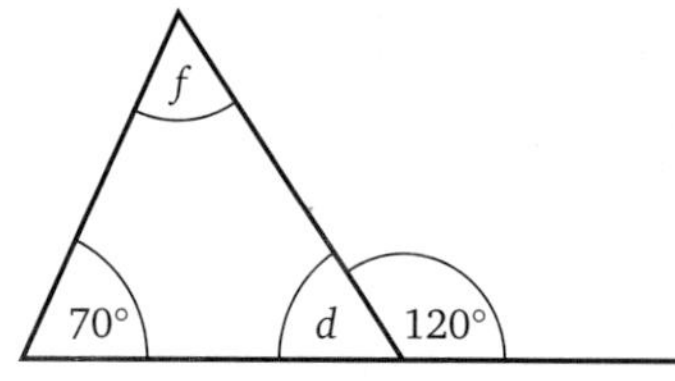

In each question make a rough copy of the diagram and mark the sizes of the angles that you are asked to find. You do not need to find them in alphabetical order. You can also mark in any other angles that you know. This may help you find the angles asked for.

2 Find angles s and t.

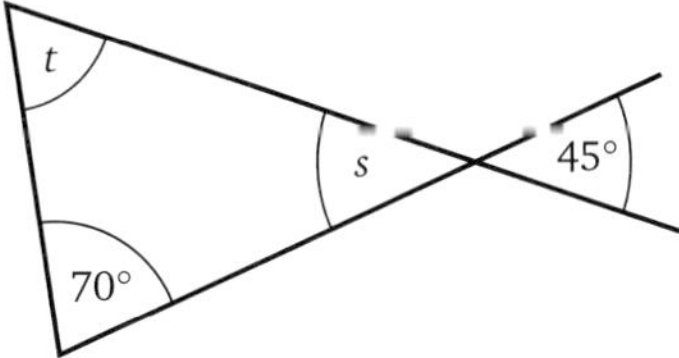

3 Find each of the equal angles x.

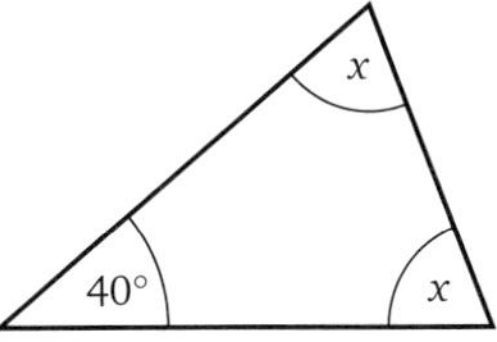

4 Find angles p and q

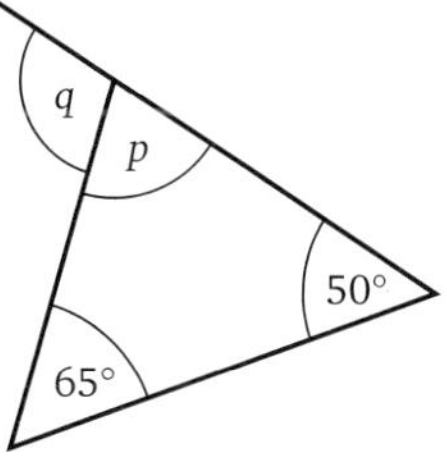

5 Find angles s and t.

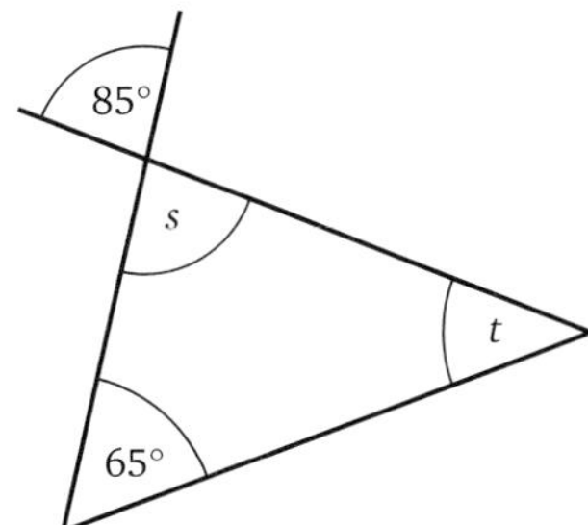

6 Find each of the equal angles g.

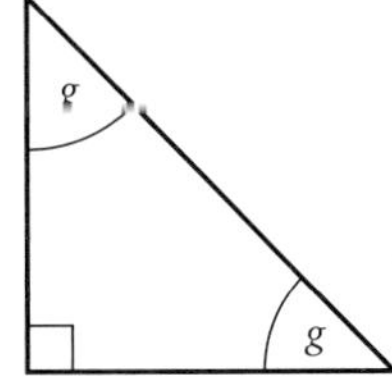

7 Find each of the equal angles x.

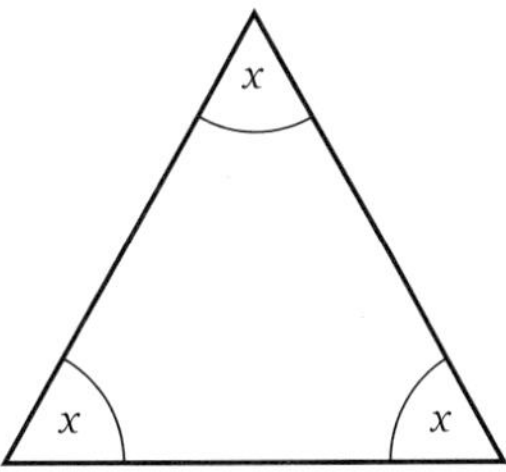

8 Angle h is twice angle j.
Find angles h and j

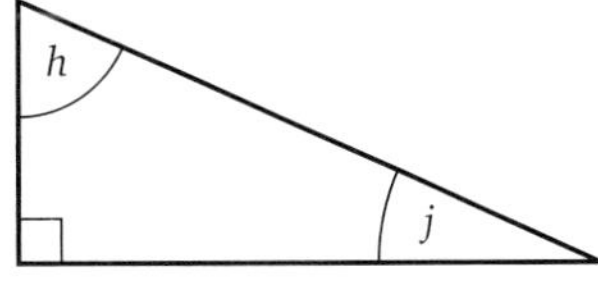

9 Find each of the equal angles q, and angle p.

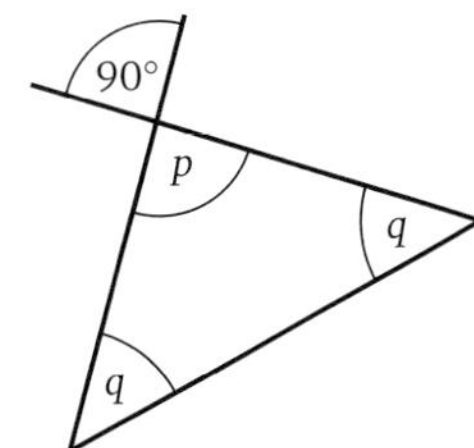

Constructing triangles given one side and two angles

If we are given enough information about a triangle we can make an accurate drawing of that triangle. The mathematical word for 'make an accurate drawing of' is 'construct'.

For example: construct $\triangle ABC$ in which $AB = 7\text{ cm}$, $\hat{A} = 30°$ and $\hat{B} = 40°$.

First make a rough sketch of $\triangle ABC$ and put all the given measurements in your sketch.

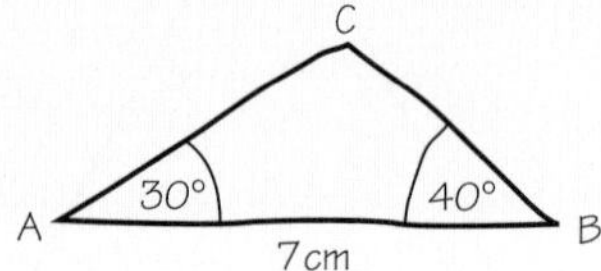

Next draw the line AB making it 7 cm long. Label the ends.

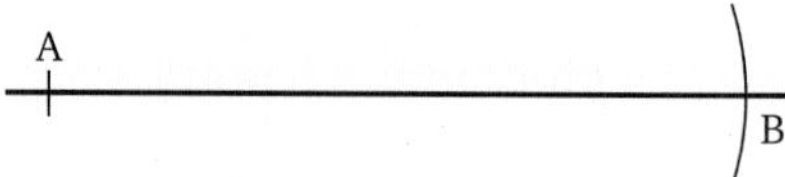

Then use your protractor to make an angle of 30° at A.

Next make an angle of 40° at B. If necessary extend the arms of the angles until they cross; this is the point C.

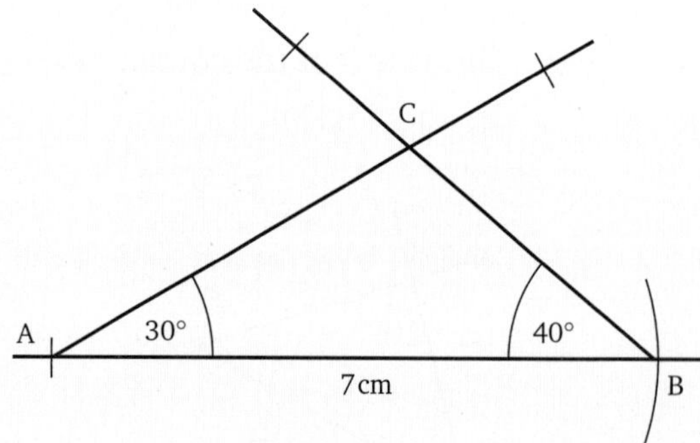

We can calculate $\hat{C}$ because $\hat{A} + \hat{B} + \hat{C} = 180°$ so $\hat{C} = 110°$. Now as a check we can measure $\hat{C}$ in our construction.

You can also use the following fact to check your construction.

In any triangle, the longest side is opposite the largest angle.

Exercise 13e

Construct the following triangles; calculate the third angle in each triangle and then measure this angle to check the accuracy of your construction.

1 $\triangle ABC$ in which $AB = 8$ cm, $\hat{A} = 50°$, $\hat{B} = 20°$

2 $\triangle PQR$ in which $QR = 5$ cm, $\hat{Q} = 30°$, $\hat{R} = 90°$

3 $\triangle DEF$ in which $EF = 6$ cm, $\hat{E} = 50°$, $\hat{F} = 60°$

4 $\triangle XYZ$ in which $YZ = 5.5$ cm, $\hat{Y} = 100°$, $\hat{Z} = 40°$

5 $\triangle UVW$ in which $\hat{V} = 35°$, $VW = 5.5$ cm, $\hat{W} = 75°$

<u>6</u> $\triangle FGH$ in which $\hat{F} = 55°$, $\hat{G} = 70°$, $FG = 4.5$ cm

<u>7</u> $\triangle KLM$ in which $KM = 10$ cm, $\hat{K} = 45°$, $\hat{M} = 45°$

<u>8</u> $\triangle BCD$ in which $\hat{B} = 100°$, $BC = 8.5$ cm, $\hat{C} = 45°$

<u>9</u> $\triangle GHI$ in which $GI = 7$ cm, $\hat{G} = 25°$, $\hat{I} = 45°$

<u>10</u> $\triangle JKL$ in which $\hat{J} = 50°$, $JL = 6.5$ cm, $\hat{L} = 35°$

Start by drawing a rough sketch of the triangle and then put all the given measurements on your sketch. Make sure your pencil is *sharp*.

Constructing triangles given two sides and the angle between the two sides

To construct $\triangle PQR$ in which $PQ = 4.5$ cm, $PR = 5.5$ cm and $\hat{P} = 35°$, first draw a rough sketch of $\triangle PQR$ and put in all the measurements that you are given.

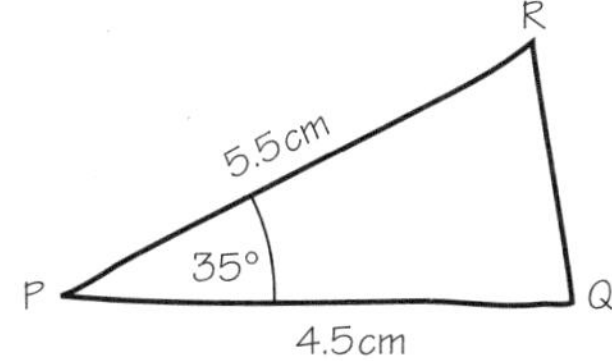

Draw one of the sides whose length you know; we will draw PQ.

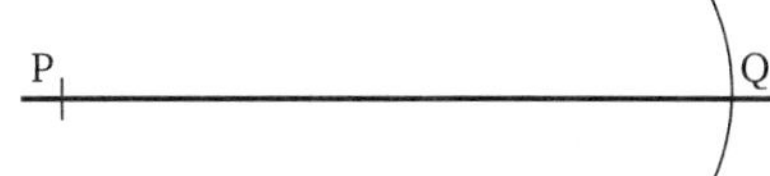

Now using your protractor make an angle of 35° at P. Make the arm of the angle quite long.

Next use your compasses to measure the length of PR on your ruler.

Then with the point of your compasses at P, draw an arc to cut the arm of the angle. This is the point R.

Now join R and Q.

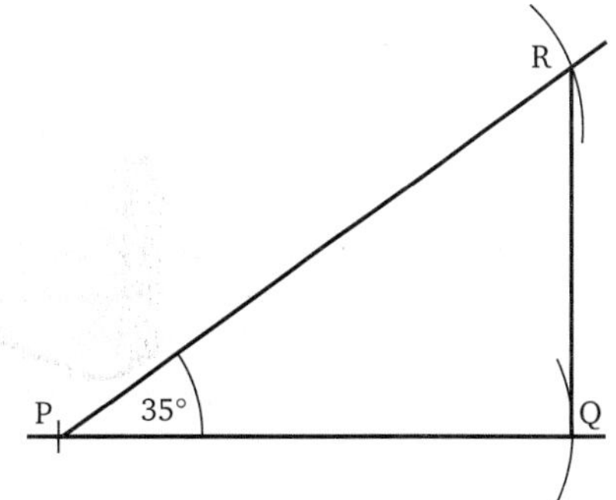

Exercise 13f

Construct each of the following triangles and measure the third side and the other two angles:

1. △ABC in which AB = 5.5 cm, BC = 6.5 cm, $\hat{B} = 40°$

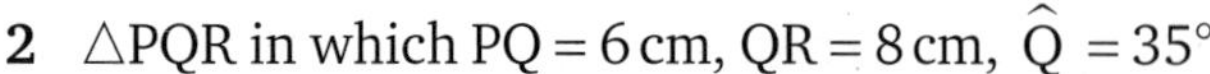

2. △PQR in which PQ = 6 cm, QR = 8 cm, $\hat{Q} = 35°$
3. △XYZ in which XZ = 4.5 cm, YZ = 6.5 cm, $\hat{Z} = 70°$
4. △DEF in which DE = 6 cm, $\hat{E} = 50°$, EF = 11 cm
5. △HJK in which HK = 4.2 cm, $\hat{H} = 45°$, HJ = 5.3 cm
6. △ABC in which AC = 6.3 cm, $\hat{C} = 48°$, CB = 5.1 cm
7. △XYZ in which $\hat{Y} = 65°$, XY = 3.8 cm, YZ = 4.2 cm
8. △PQR in which $\hat{R} = 52°$, RQ = 5.8 cm, PR = 7 cm
9. △LMN in which $\hat{N} = 73°$, LN = 4.1 cm, MN = 6.3 cm
10. △ABC in which AC = 5.2 cm, BA = 7.3 cm, $\hat{A} = 56°$

Remember to start with a rough sketch with all the given measurements on it. Make sure that your pencil is *sharp*.

Constructing triangles given the lengths of three sides

To construct, △XYZ, in which, XY = 5.5 cm, XZ = 3.5 cm, YZ = 6.5 cm, first draw a rough sketch of the triangle and put in all the given measurements.

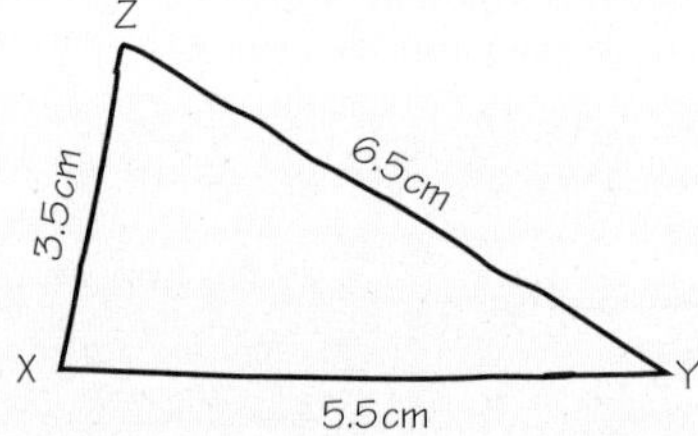

Next draw one side; we will draw XY.

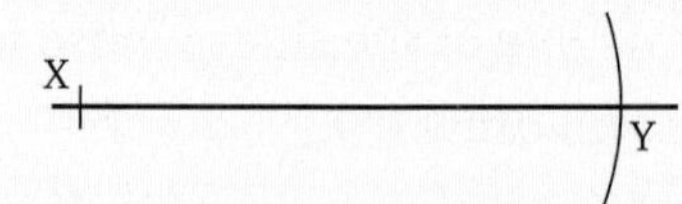

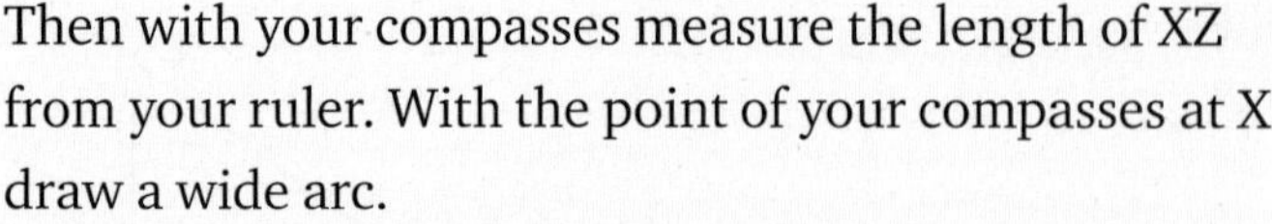

Then with your compasses measure the length of XZ from your ruler. With the point of your compasses at X draw a wide arc.

Next use your compasses to measure the length of YZ from your ruler. Then with your compasses point at Y draw another large arc to cut the first arc. Where the two arcs cross is the point Z. Join ZX and ZY.

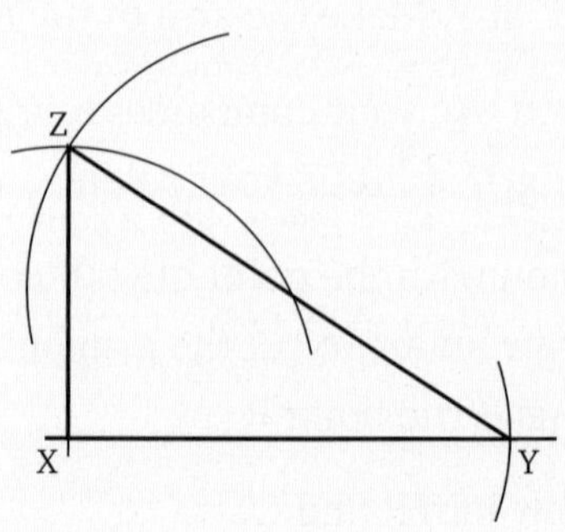

Exercise 13g

Construct the following triangles:

1 $\triangle ABC$ in which AB = 7 cm, BC = 8 cm, AC = 12 cm
2 $\triangle PQR$ in which PQ = 4.5 cm, PR = 6 cm, QR = 8 cm
3 $\triangle XYZ$ in which XZ = 10.4 cm, XY = 6 cm, YZ = 9.6 cm
4 $\triangle DEF$ in which DE = 8 cm, DF = 10 cm, EF = 6 cm
5 $\triangle ABC$ in which AB = 7.3 cm, BC = 6.1 cm, AC = 4.7 cm
6 $\triangle DEF$ in which DE = 10.4 cm, EF = 7.4 cm, DF = 8.2 cm
7 $\triangle PQR$ in which PQ = 8.8 cm, QR = 6.6 cm, PR = 11 cm
8 $\triangle LMN$ in which LN = 7 cm, NM = 5.3 cm, LM = 6.1 cm
9 $\triangle XYZ$ in which XY = 12 cm, YZ = 5 cm, XZ = 13 cm
10 $\triangle ABC$ in which AB = 5.5 cm, BC = 6 cm, AC = 6.5 cm

Exercise 13h

Construct the following triangles. Remember to draw a rough diagram of the triangle first and then decide which method you need to use:

1 $\triangle ABC$ in which AB = 7 cm, $\hat{A} = 30°$, $\hat{B} = 50°$
2 $\triangle PQR$ in which PQ = 5 cm, QR = 4 cm, RP = 7 cm
3 $\triangle BCD$ in which $\hat{B} = 60°$, BC = 5 cm, BD = 4 cm
4 $\triangle WXY$ in which WX = 5 cm, XY = 6 cm, $\hat{X} = 90°$
5 $\triangle KLM$ in which KL = 6.4 cm, LM = 8.2 cm, KM = 12.6 cm
6 $\triangle ABC$ in which $\hat{A} = 45°$, AC = 8 cm, $\hat{C} = 110°$
7 $\triangle DEF$ in which $\hat{E} = 125°$, DE = 4.5 cm, FE = 5.5 cm
8 $\triangle PQR$ in which $\hat{P} = 72°$, $\hat{R} = 53°$, PR = 5.1 cm
9 $\triangle XYZ$ in which XY = 4 cm, YZ = 6 cm, XZ = 9 cm
10 $\triangle CDE$ in which CD = DE = 6 cm, $\hat{D} = 60°$
What type of triangle is $\triangle CDE$?
11 Try to construct a triangle ABC in which $\hat{A} = 30°$, AB = 5 cm, BC = 3 cm.
12 Construct two triangles which fit the following measurements: $\triangle PQR$ in which $\hat{P} = 60°$, PQ = 6 cm, QR = 5.5 cm.

Puzzle

You can cut a triangle into 4 smaller triangles using just three cuts.

Here is one way of doing it.

Can you find other ways?

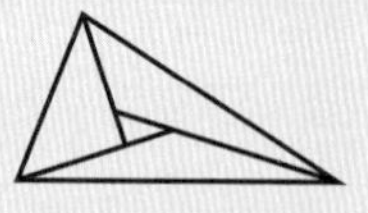

Quadrilaterals

A quadrilateral is bounded by four straight sides. These shapes are examples of quadrilaterals:

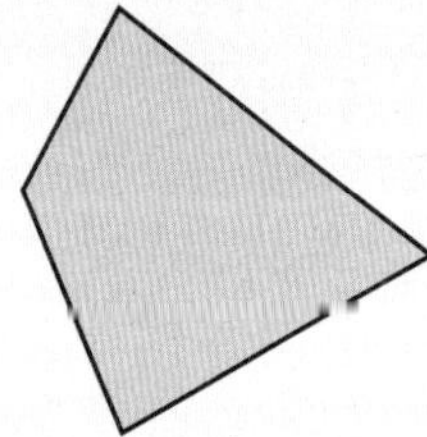

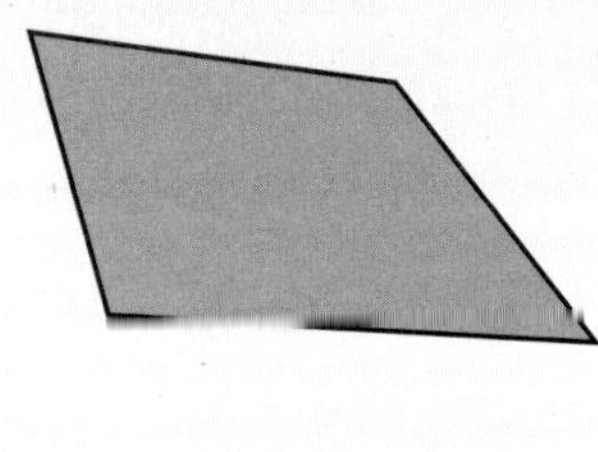

The following diagrams are also quadrilaterals, but each one is a 'special' quadrilateral with its own name:

square

rectangle

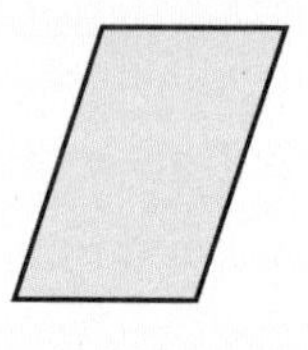

parallelogram

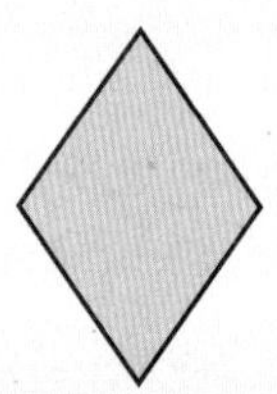

rhombus

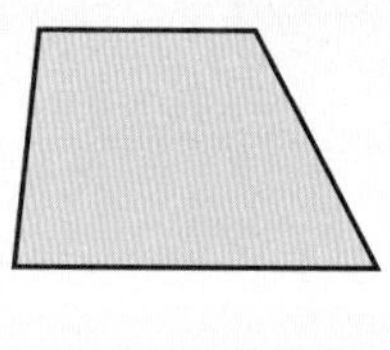

trapezium

In a square	all four sides are the same length both pairs of opposite sides are parallel all four angles are right angles
In a rectangle	the opposite sides are the same length both pairs of opposite sides are parallel all four angles are right angles
In a rhombus	all four sides are the same length both pairs of opposite sides are parallel the opposite angles are equal
In a parallelogram	the opposite sides are the same length both pairs of opposite sides are parallel the opposite angles are equal
In a trapezium	just one pair of opposite sides are parallel.

Draw yourself a large quadrilateral, but do not make it one of the special cases.
Measure each angle and then add up the sizes of the four angles.

Do this again with another three quadrilaterals.

Now try this: on a piece of paper draw a quadrilateral.
Tear off each corner and place the vertices together.
It should look like this:

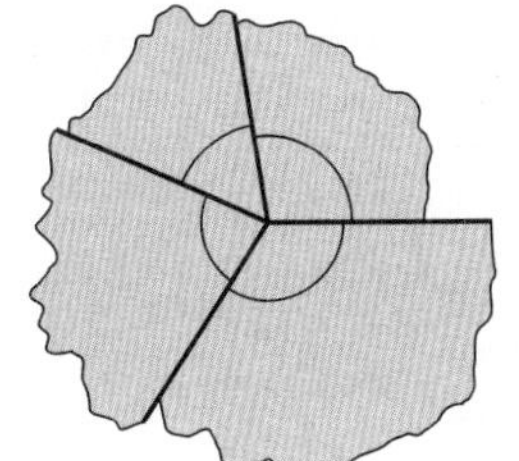

The sum of the four angles of a quadrilateral is 360°.

This is true of any quadrilateral whatever its shape or size.

Can you tell why? Hint: draw one of its diagonals.

Exercise 13i

In questions **1** to **10** find the size of the angle marked d:

Make a rough copy of the following diagrams and mark on your diagram the sizes of the required angles. You can also write in the sizes of any other angles that you can: this may help you find the angles you need.

1 130°, d

2 100°, 70°, 110°, $d°$

3 d, 120°, 70°, 60°

4 100°, 120°, d

5 d, 120°, 120°, 60°

6 140°, d

7 d

8 110°, 80°, 110°, d

9 60°, 80°, 100°, d

10 d

11 Find each of the equal angles *d*

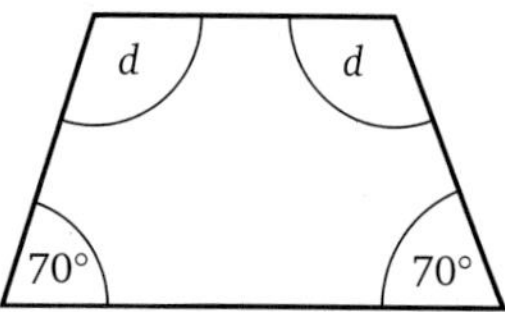

12 Find each of the equal angles *d*.

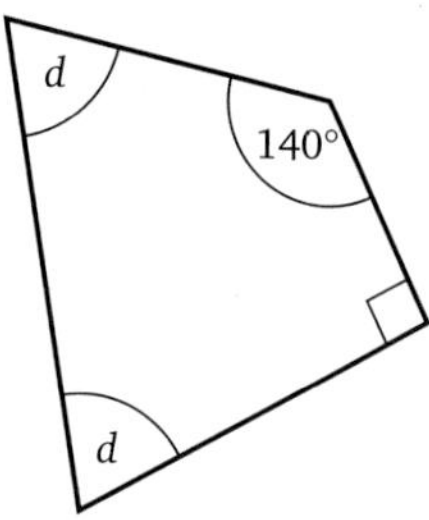

13 Angle *e* is twice angle *d*.
Find angles *d* and *e*.

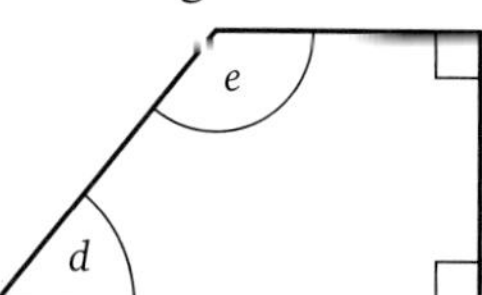

14 Find angles *d* and *e*.

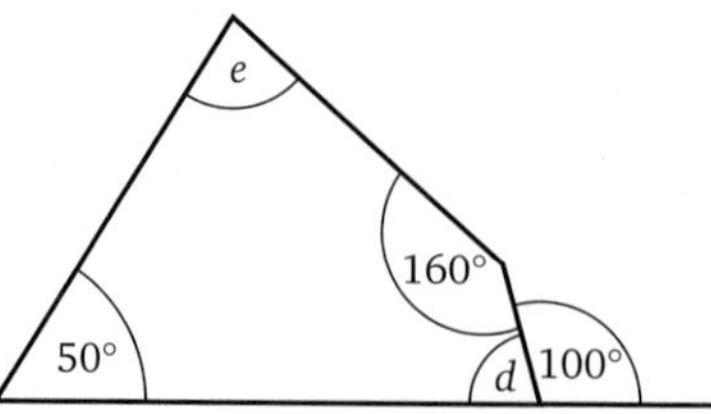

15 Find *d* and each of the equal angles *e*.

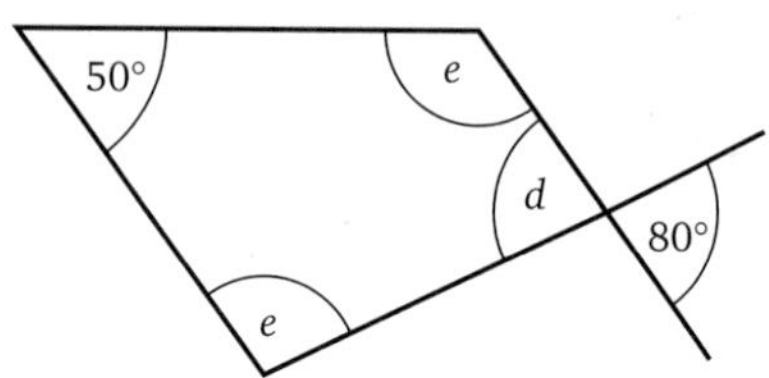

16 Angles *d* and *e* are supplementary.
Find *d* and each of the equal angles *e*.

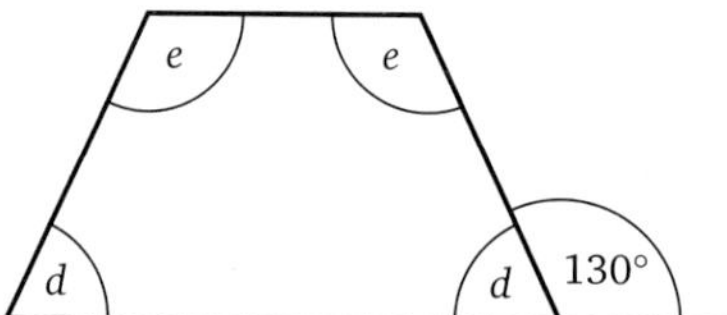

Drawing quadrilaterals

You can make accurate drawings of quadrilaterals using what you know about their angles and properties together with what you know about drawing triangles.

Exercise 13j

Make an accurate drawing of this parallelogram.

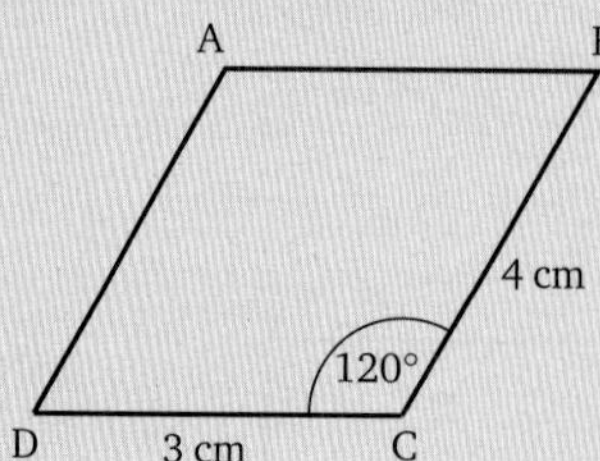

ABCD is a parallelogram, therefore AB = 3 cm and AD = 4 cm.

Start by drawing the line DC, making it 3 cm long.

Next draw an angle of 120° at C and mark B, 4 cm from C.

With the point of the compasses on B and a radius of 3 cm, draw an arc.

Then with the point of the compasses on D and a radius of 4 cm, draw an arc to cross the first arc.

The point where the arcs cross is A.

Finally draw a line through A and B and a line through A and D to form the other two sides of the parallelogram.

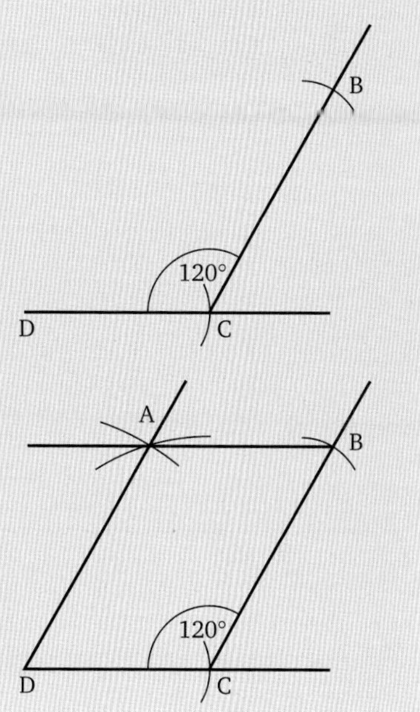

Make accurate drawings of these quadrilaterals.

1 The square ABCD

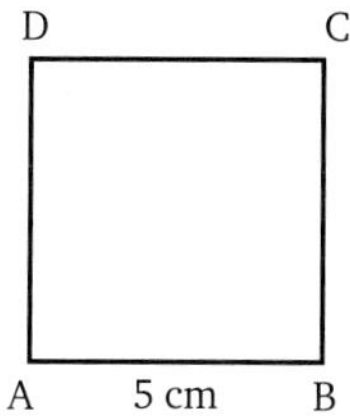

4 The parallelogram ABCD

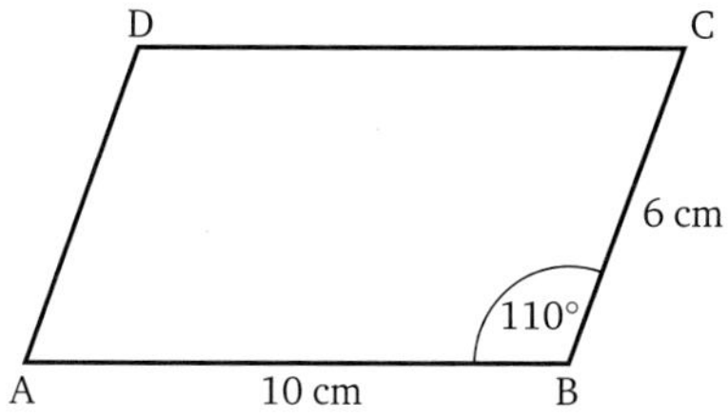

Divide ABCD into two triangles by joining AC.

2 The rhombus ABCD

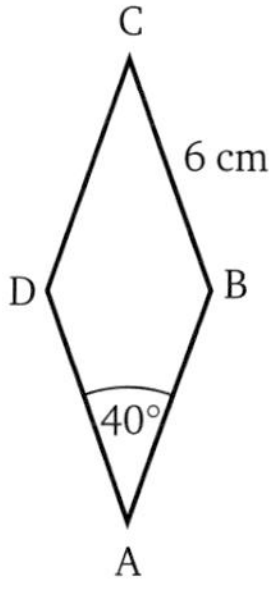

5 The quadrilateral PQRS

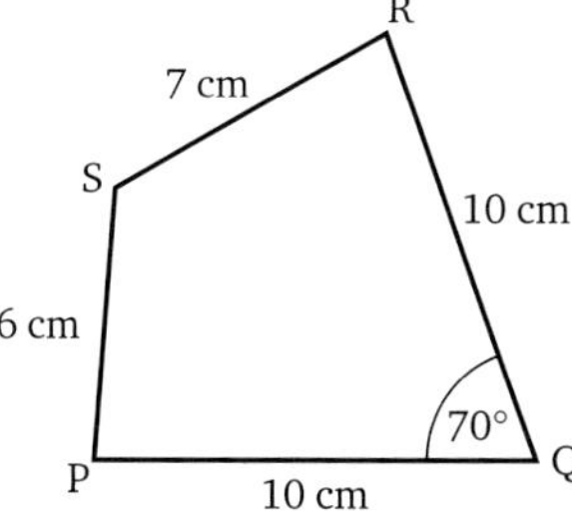

3 The rectangle ABCD

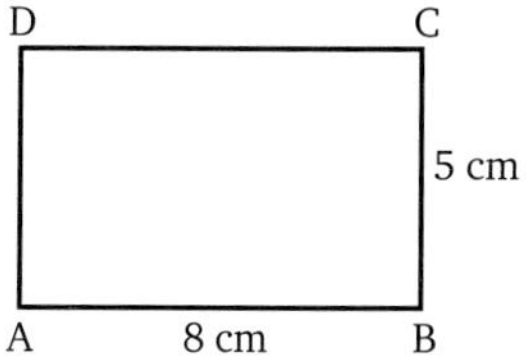

6 The trapezium PQRS

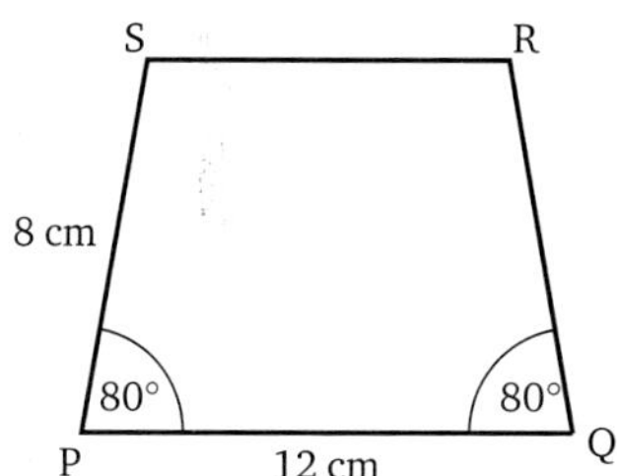

Puzzle

Eight square serviettes are placed flat but overlapping on a table and give the outlines shown in the diagram. In which order must they be removed if the top one is always next.

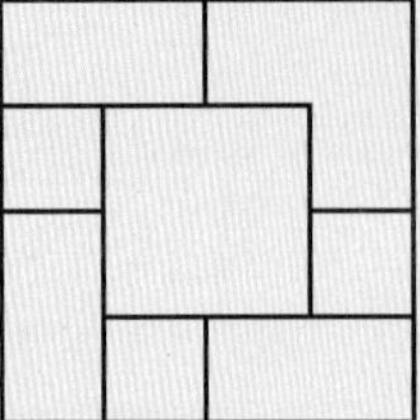

Some special triangles: equilateral and isosceles

A triangle in which all three sides are the same length is called an *equilateral triangle*.

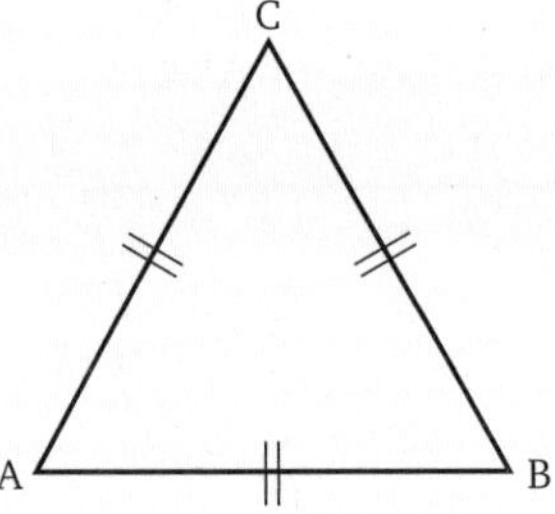

Activity

Construct an equilateral triangle in which the sides are each of length 6 cm. Label the vertices A, B and C.

On a separate piece of paper construct a triangle of the same size and cut it out. Label the angles A, B and C inside the triangle.

Place it on your first triangle. Now turn it round and it should still fit exactly. What do you think this means about the three angles? Measure each angle in the triangle.

> In an equilateral triangle all three sides are the same length and each of the three angles is 60°.

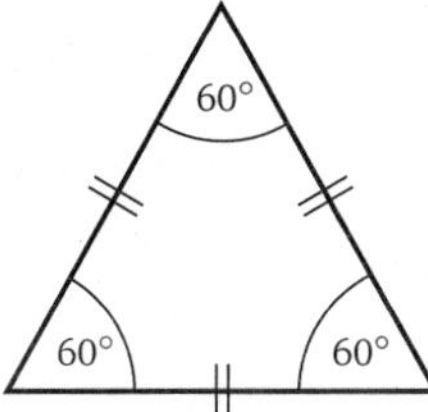

A triangle in which two sides are equal is called an *isosceles triangle*.

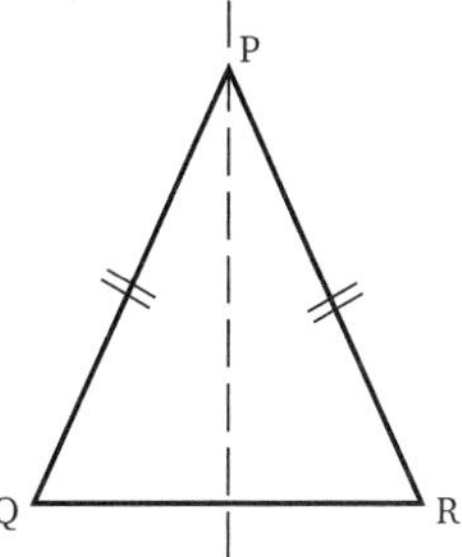

Activity

On a piece of paper construct an isosceles triangle PQR in which PQ = 8 cm, PR = 8 cm and P = 80°. Cut it out and fold the triangle through P so that the corners at Q and R meet. You should find that $\hat{Q} = \hat{R}$. (The fold line is a line of symmetry.)

> In an isosceles triangle two sides are equal and the two angles opposite the equal sides are equal.

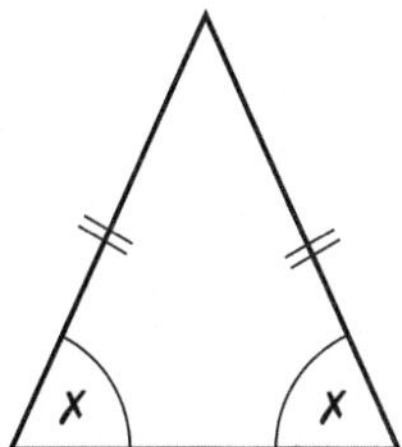

Exercise 13k

In questions **1** to **10** make a rough sketch of the triangle and mark angles that are equal:

1

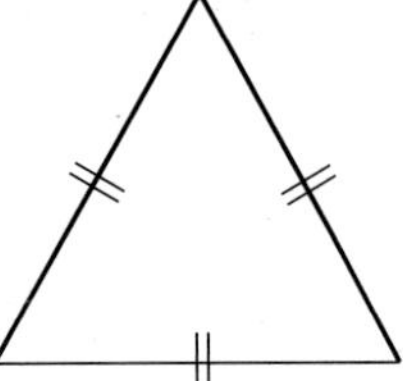

6

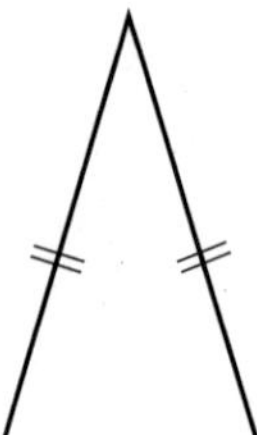

2

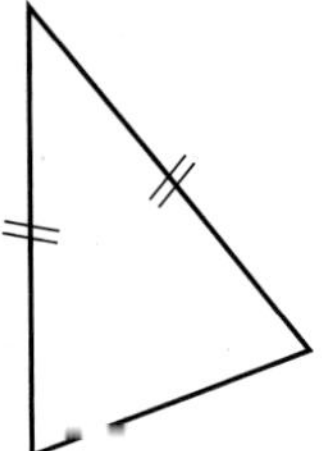

7

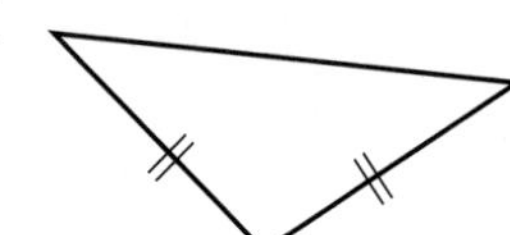

3

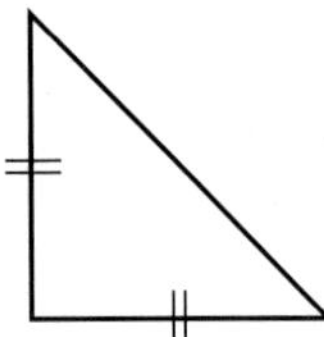

8

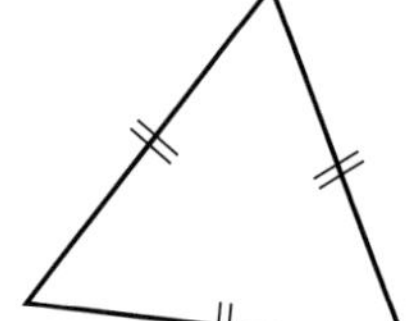

4

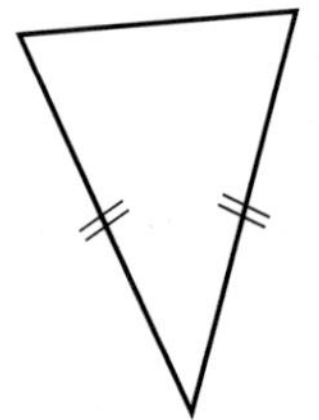

9

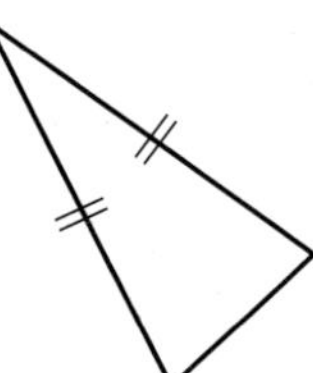

5

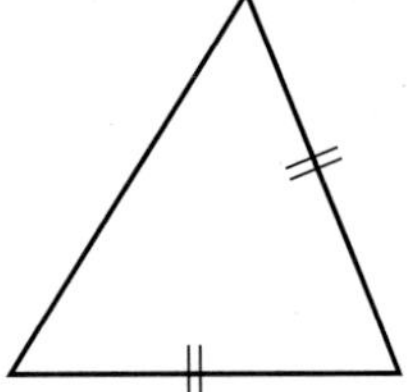

10

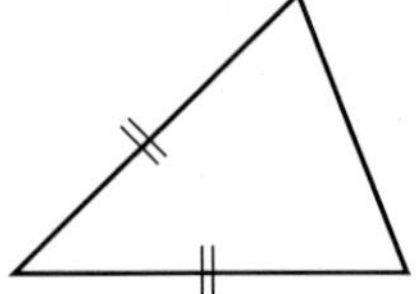

In questions **11** to **22** find angle d:

11

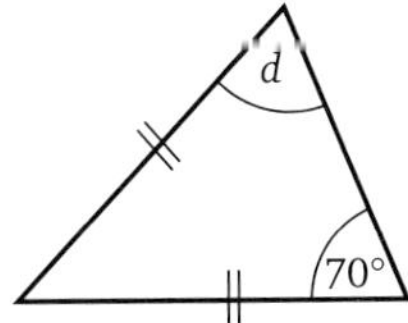

12

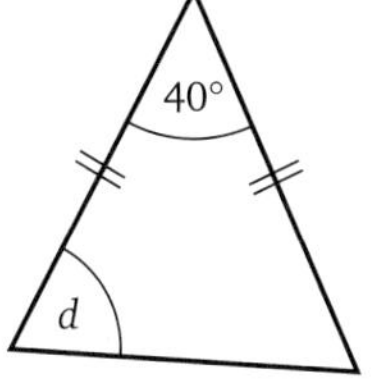

13

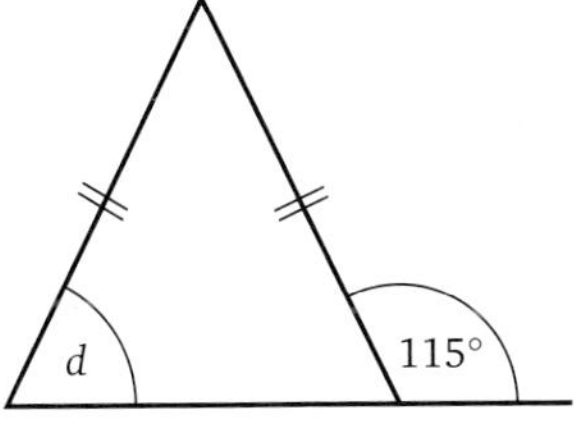

14

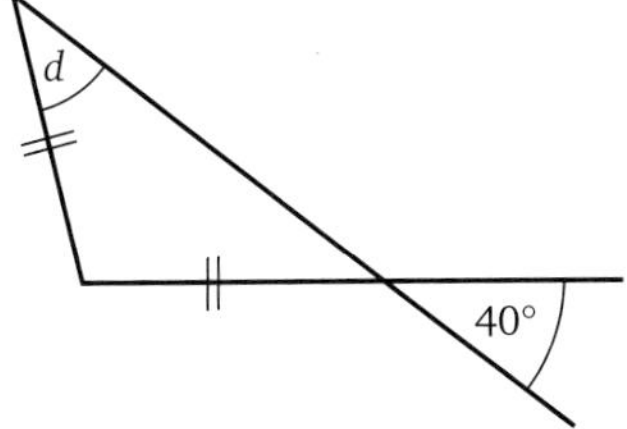

15

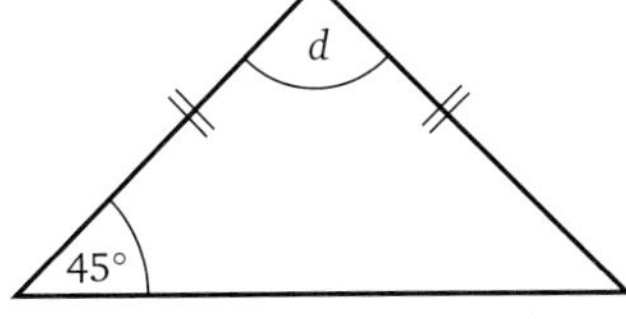

16

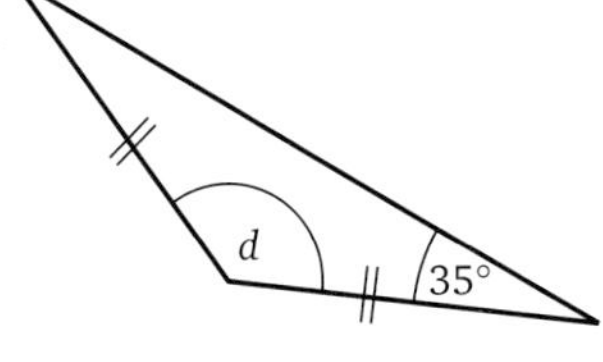

17

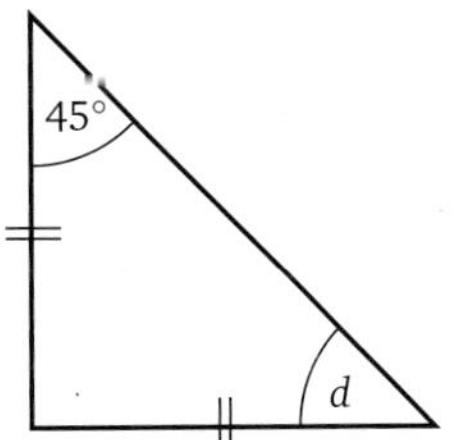

18

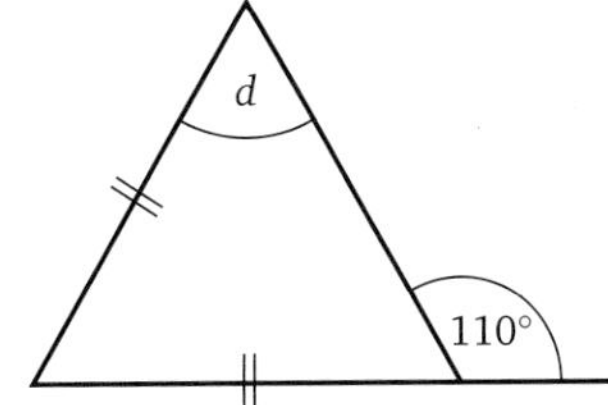

19

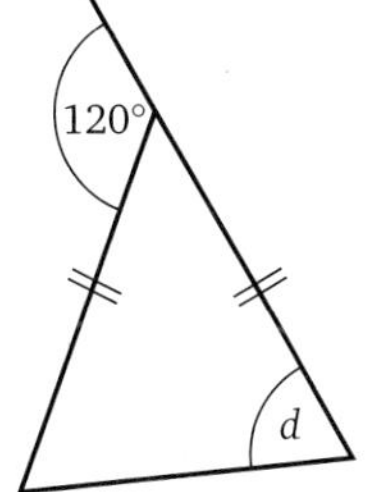

20

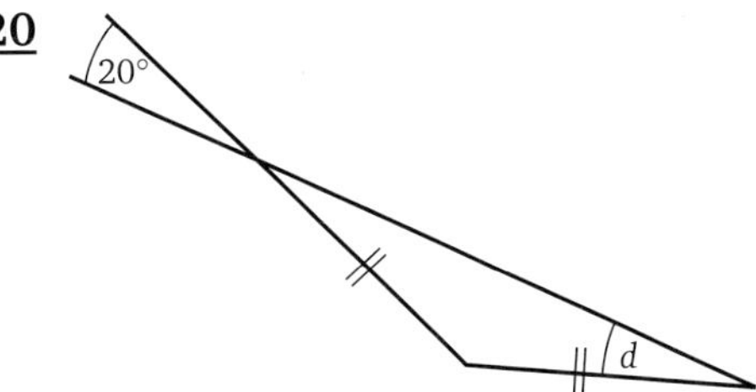

21

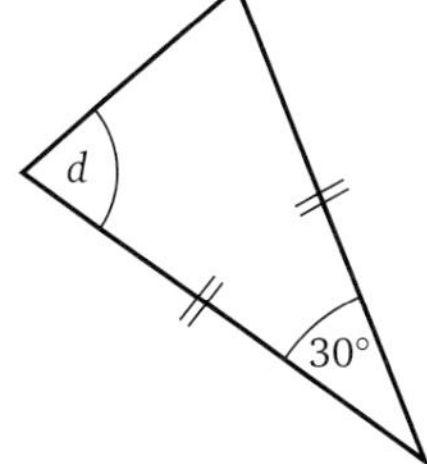

22

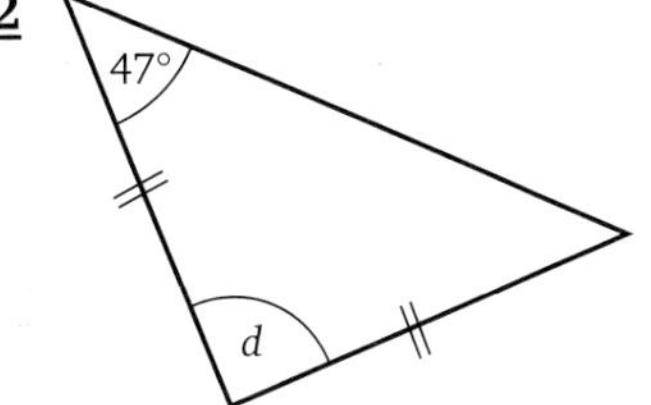

In questions **23** to **26** make a rough sketch of the triangles and mark the equal sides:

23

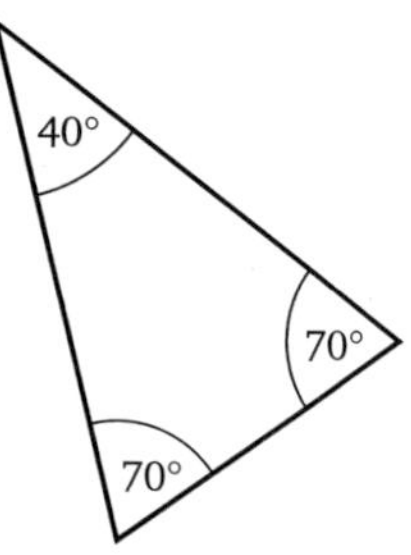

25

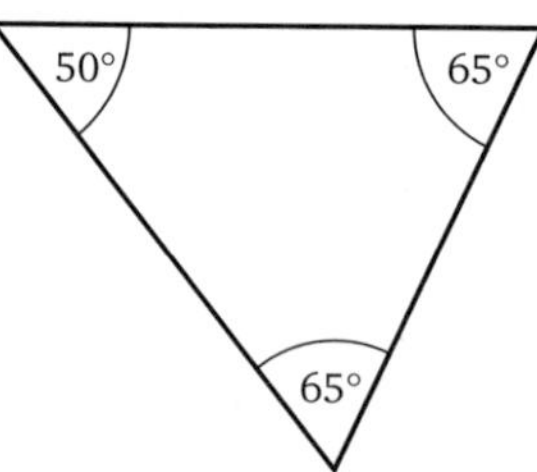

24

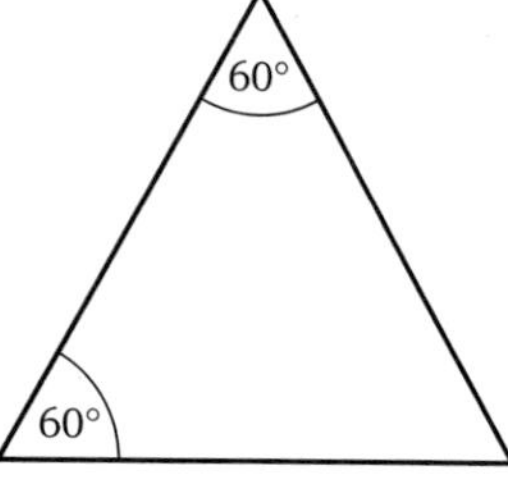

26

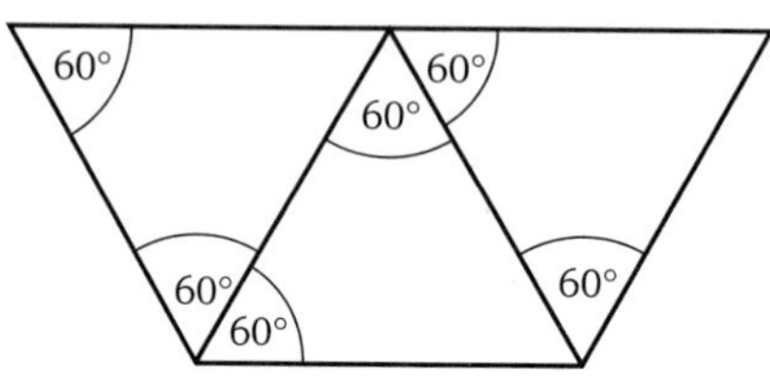

In questions **27** to **32** find angles *d* and *e*:

27

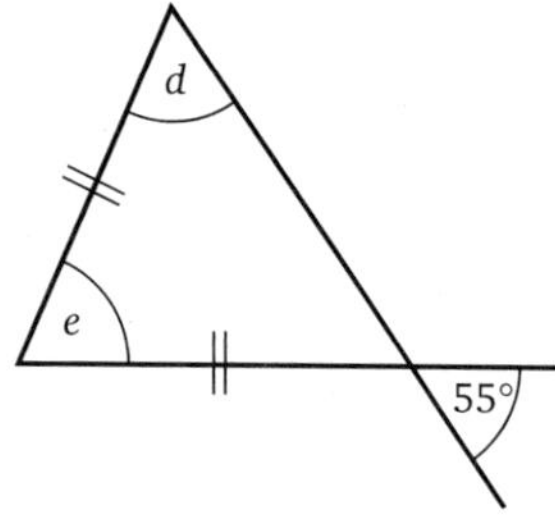

There are two equal sides in an isosceles triangle. The third side is the base.

28

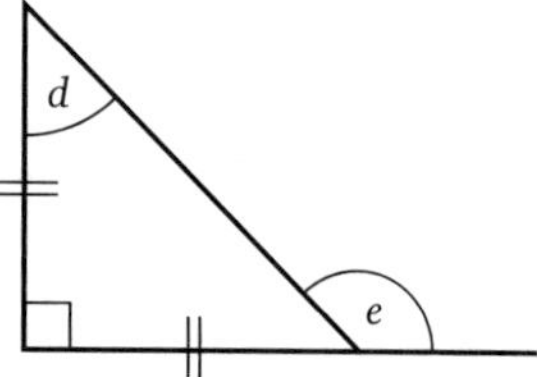

31

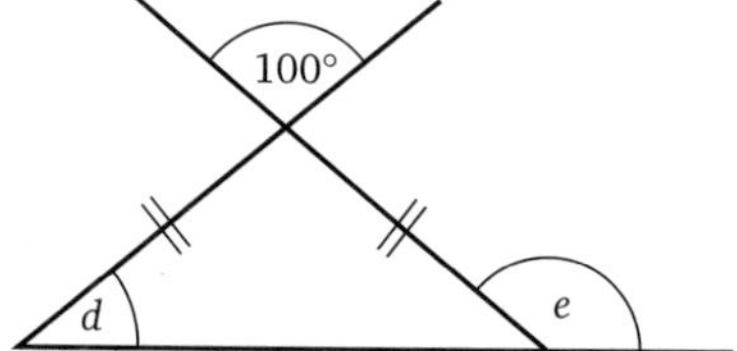

29

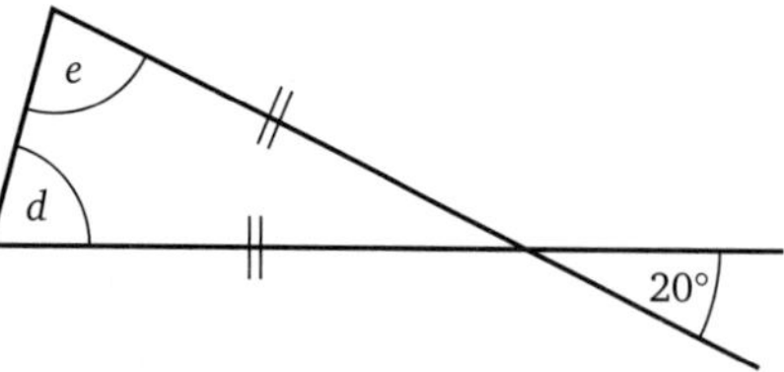

32

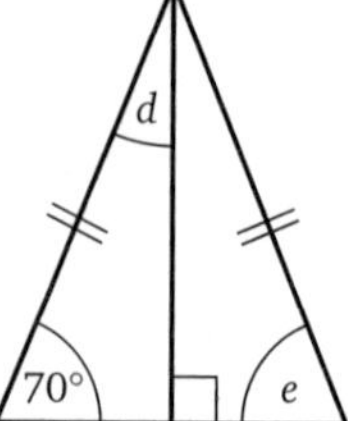

30

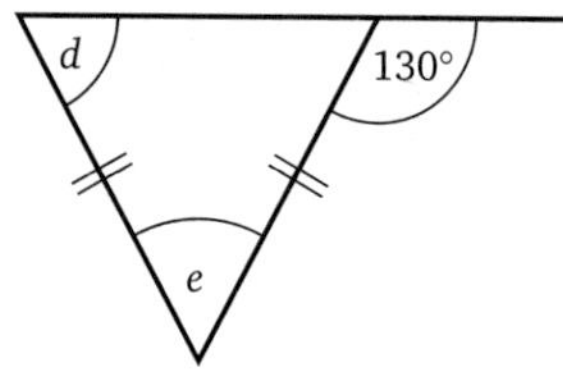

Activity

On a piece of paper construct an equilateral triangle of side 4 cm.

Construct an equilateral triangle, again of side 4 cm, on each of the three sides of the first triangle.

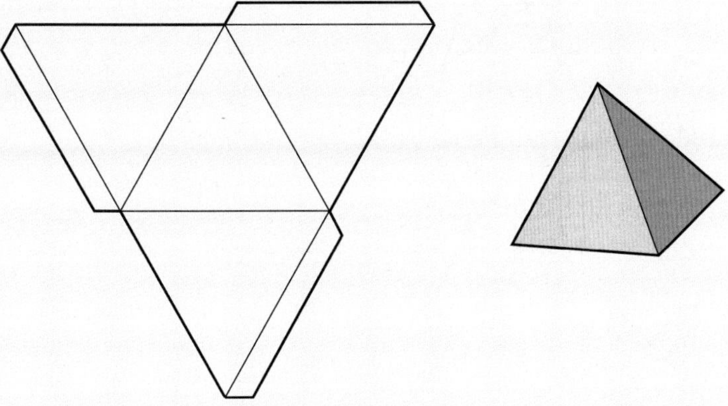

Cut out the complete diagram. Fold the outer triangles up so that the corners meet. Stick the edges together using the tabs. You have made a tetrahedron. (These make good Christmas tree decorations if made out of foil-covered paper.)

Mixed exercises

Exercise 13I

Select the letter that gives the correct answer.

1 The size of the angle marked x is

A 45° **B** 65° **C** 68° **D** 75°

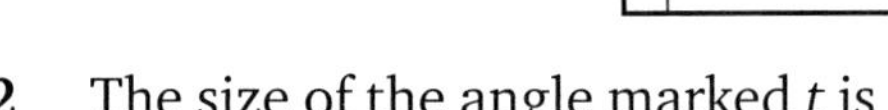

2 The size of the angle marked t is

A 20° **B** 40° **C** 60° **D** 70°

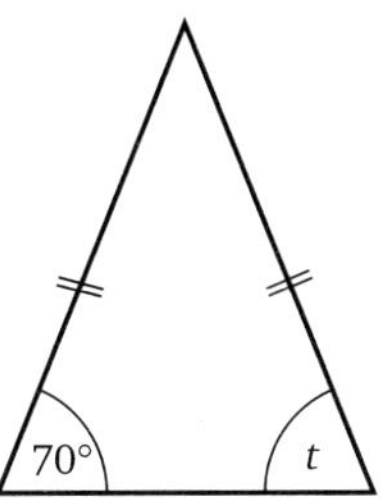

3 The size of the angle marked y is

A 40° **B** 70° **C** 80° **D** 100°

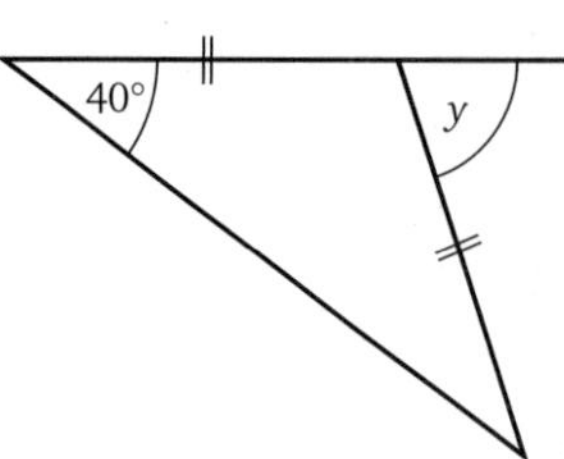

4 The size of the third angle in this triangle is

A 40° **B** 77° **C** 80° **D** 90°

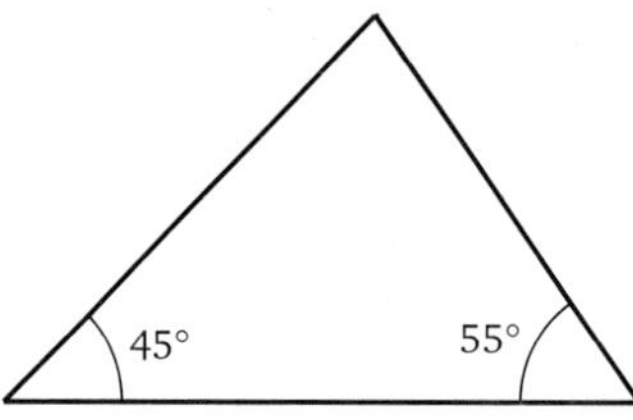

5 The size of the obtuse angle in this triangle is

A 98° **B** 106° **C** 108° **D** 118°

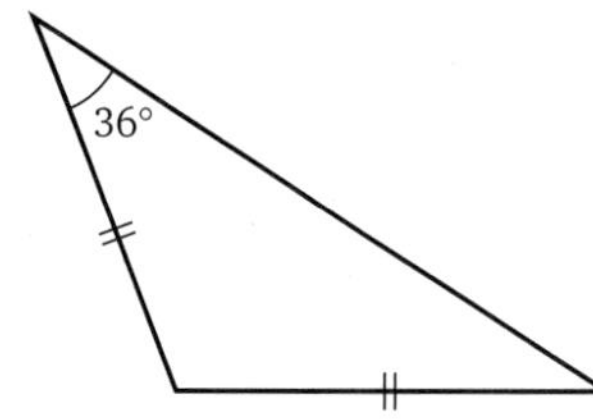

6 The value of the angle marked a in this diagram is

A 40° **B** 44° **C** 46° **D** 54°

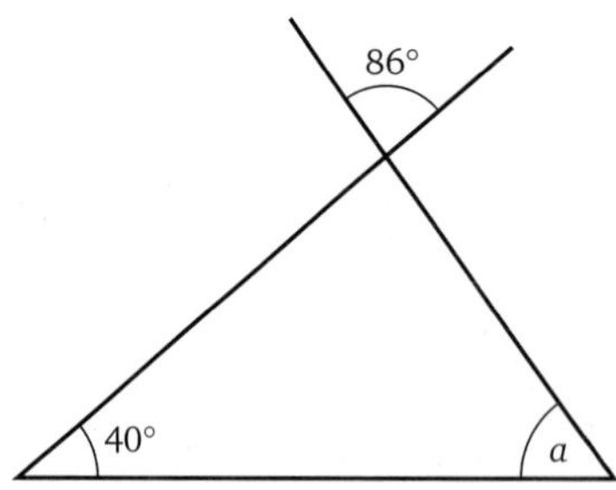

Exercise 13m

1 Find the size of the angles marked p and q.

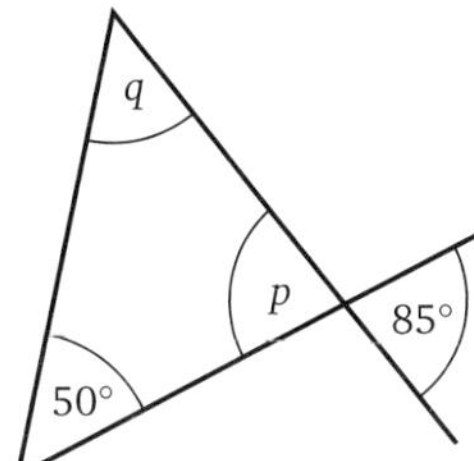

2 Find the size of the angles marked x and y.

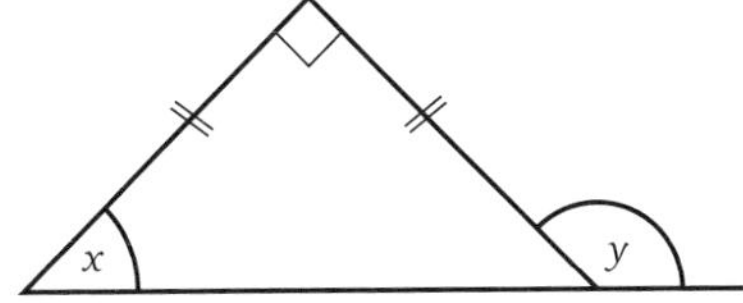

3 Find the size of the angles marked u and v.

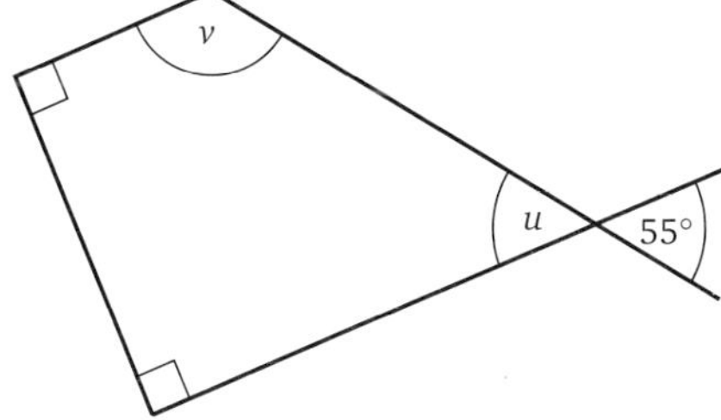

4 Construct △ABC in which $\hat{A} = 50°$, $\hat{B} = 60°$, and BC = 5 cm. Be careful: this question needs some calculation before you can construct △ABC.

5 Construct the isosceles triangle ABC in which AB = BC = 6 cm and one of the base angles is 70°.

Exercise 13n

1 All three sides of the large triangle are equal. Find angles r and s.

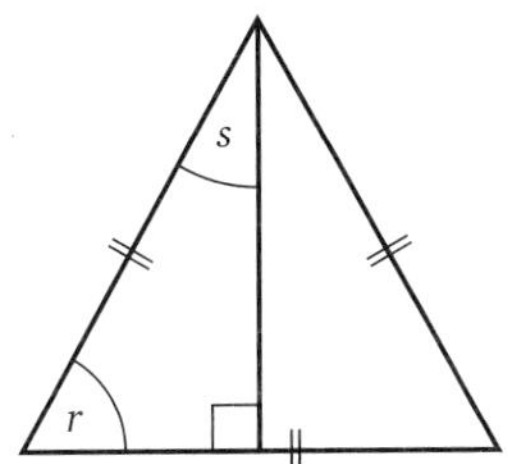

2 Find angles x, y and z.

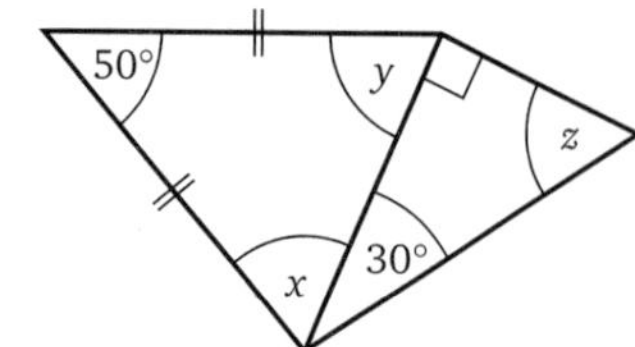

3 Find angles f and g.

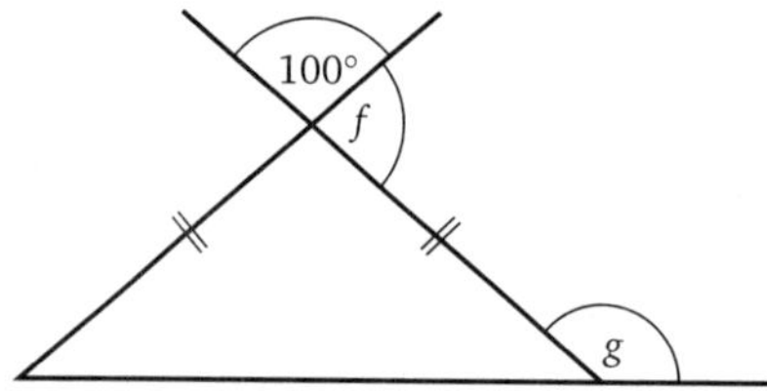

4 Construct an isosceles triangle in which the equal sides are of length 5 cm and one of the base angles is 45°.

5 Construct a quadrilateral ABCD in which AB = 5 cm, $\hat{A} = 70°$, AD = 3 cm, BC = 5 cm, DC = 5 cm. Measure all four angles in the quadrilateral and find their sum.

Puzzle

Find a way of cutting up an equilateral triangle into four pieces so that the pieces fit together to form a square.

In this chapter you have seen that...

✔ the three angles of a triangle add up to 180°

✔ you can make an accurate copy of a triangle if you know

one side and two angles

or two sides and the angle between them

or all three sides

✔ the four angles of a quadrilateral add up to 360°

✔ an equilateral triangle has three equal sides and each of its angles is 60°

✔ an isosceles triangle has two equal sides and that the two angles at the base of these sides are equal.

REVIEW TEST 2: CHAPTERS 8–13

In questions **1** to **13** choose the letter for the correct answer.

1 Written as a fraction 1.4 =

A $1\frac{4}{7}$ B $1\frac{4}{9}$ C $1\frac{4}{10}$ D $1\frac{4}{11}$

2 Written as a decimal, $\frac{9}{10} + \frac{7}{1000} =$

A 0.097 B 0.907 C 0.97 D 9.07

3 $0.3 \times 0.02 =$

A 0.006 B 0.060 C 0.600 D 6.000

4 $0.8 \div 0.4 =$

A 0.02 B 0.2 C 0.32 D 2

5 Each of the equal angles of an isosceles triangle measures 40°. How many degrees does the other angle measure?

A 40 B 80 C 100 D 140

6 Three angle of a quadrilateral measure 50°, 70° and 80°. What is the measure of the other angle in degrees?

A 120 B 130 C 150 D 160

Use the figure below to answer questions **7**, **8** and **9**.

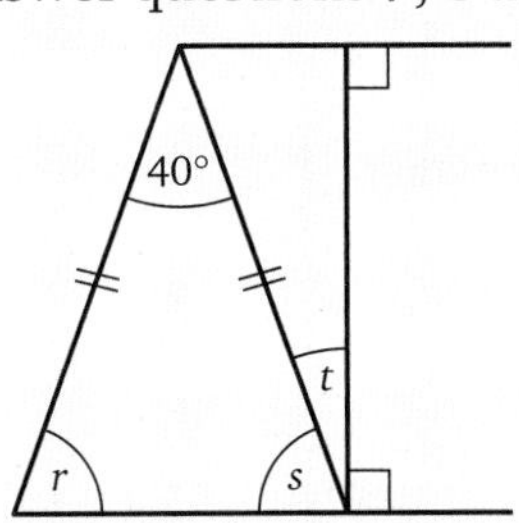

7 The measure of the angle r in degrees is

A 40 B 50 C 60 D 70

8 The measure of the angle s in degrees is

A 40 B 50 C 60 D 70

9 The measure of the angle t in degrees is

A 20 B 50 C 60 D 90

10 $\frac{6x}{7} \div \frac{x}{14} =$

A 12 B $12x$ C 3 D $3x$

11 The median of the numbers 2, 4, 6, 7 is

A 4.5 B 4.75 C 5.0 D 6.0

12 The value of $-9 + 3 - (-4)$ is

A -16 B -10 C -2 D 2

13 When simplified, $8 - 3(x - 2) =$

A $5x - 10$ B $14 - 3x$ C $6 - 3x$ D $5x - 2$

14 A calendar is 0.375 cm thick when new. Each month is printed on a sheet 0.031 25 cm thick.
What thickness remains when the calendar shows the month of April?

15 Find the value of $2x - 3y$ when $x = 6$ and $y = -7$.

16 a If n is an even integer what is the next even number above n?

b If you are m years old, what must be your father's present age if he is 6 years more than three times your age?

c Simplify $\frac{14}{3x} \div \frac{42}{x}$

17 Complete the following table showing the marks in an examination awarded to a class of students.

Marks	Tally	Frequency
41–45	|	
46–50	|||	
51–55	~~||||~~ ~~||||~~ |	11
56–60	~~||||~~ ||||	
61–65	||||	4
66–70	|||	

Draw a bar chart showing the information.

18 The marks out of 20 in a maths test were
5, 7, 4, 15, 17, 12, 15, 13, 19, 20, 15, 18, 4, 10, 11, 9, 17, 15, 8, 12, 14.
Find a the mean mark b the modal mark c the median mark.

19 Construct the triangle PQR in which PQ = 6.5 cm, PR = 5.4 cm, and the angle QPR = 55°. Measure the angles PQR and PRQ.

14 Introducing percentages

At the end of this chapter you should be able to...

1 express given percentages as fractions and vice versa
2 express percentages as decimals
3 solve problems involving percentages
4 express one quantity as a percentage of another
5 calculate a percentage of a given quantity.

Did you know?

It is thought that every prime number can be expressed as the sum of not more than four square numbers.

For example, $5 = 2^2 + 1^2$ and $19 = 4^2 + 1^2 + 1^2 + 1^2$

Try to express some prime numbers as the sum of four or fewer square numbers.

You need to know...

- ✔ how to simplify fractions
- ✔ how to change a mixed number to an improper fraction
- ✔ how to multiply by a fraction
- ✔ how to find one quantity as a fraction of another quantity
- ✔ the meaning of decimals
- ✔ how to multiply and divide fractions and decimals by 100
- ✔ the units of length, area, mass and capacity
- ✔ how to change units.

Key words

decimal, fraction, hundred, percentage

Expressing percentages as fractions

'Per cent' means per hundred, i.e. if 60 per cent of the workers in a factory are women it means that 60 out of every 100 workers are women. If there are 700 workers in the factory, $60 \times 7 = 420$ are women, while if there are 1200 workers, $60 \times 12 = 720$ are women.

In mathematics we are always looking for shorter ways of writing statements and especially for symbols to stand for words. The symbol that means 'per cent' is %, i.e. 60 per cent and 60% have exactly the same meaning.

60 per cent means 60 per hundred and this can be written as the fraction $\frac{60}{100}\left(\text{or } \frac{3}{5}\right)$

i.e. 60% of a quantity is exactly the same as $\frac{60}{100}\left(\text{or } \frac{3}{5}\right)$ of that quantity.

If there are 800 cars in a car park and 60% of them are British, then $\frac{60}{100}$ of the cars are British.

i.e. the number of British cars is $\frac{60}{100} \times 800 = 480$

Exercise 14a

Express **a** 40% **b** $22\frac{1}{2}\%$ as fractions in their lowest terms.

a $40\% = \frac{40}{100} = \frac{2}{5}$

b $22\frac{1}{2}\% = \frac{45}{2}\% = \frac{45}{2 \times 100} = \frac{9}{40}$

Express as fractions in their lowest terms:

1. 20%
2. 45%
3. 25%
4. 72%
5. $33\frac{1}{3}\%$
6. $12\frac{1}{2}\%$
7. $2\frac{1}{2}\%$
8. 50%
9. 65%
10. 56%
11. 37%
12. $66\frac{2}{3}\%$
13. $62\frac{1}{2}\%$
14. 125%
15. 70%
16. 75%
17. 48%
18. 69%
19. $37\frac{1}{2}\%$
20. $5\frac{1}{3}\%$
21. $17\frac{1}{2}\%$
22. 95%
23. 15%
24. 8%
25. 82%
26. $87\frac{1}{2}\%$
27. $6\frac{1}{4}\%$
28. 150%

Express **a** 54% **b** $6\frac{1}{2}\%$ **c** $27\frac{1}{3}\%$ as decimals.

a $54\% = \frac{54}{100} = 0.54$

b $6\frac{1}{2}\% = \frac{6.5}{100} = 0.065$

c $27\frac{1}{3}\% = \frac{82}{3}\% = \frac{82}{3 \times 100} = 0.273$ to 3 decimal places

Express the following percentages as decimals, giving your answers correct to 3 d.p. where necessary:

29 47%

30 12%

31 $5\frac{1}{2}\%$

32 145%

33 $58\frac{1}{3}\%$

34 58%

35 30%

36 $62\frac{1}{4}\%$

37 350%

38 $48\frac{2}{3}\%$

39 92%

40 65%

41 120%

42 231%

43 $85\frac{2}{3}\%$

44 8%

45 3%

46 180%

47 $5\frac{1}{3}\%$

48 $54\frac{1}{7}\%$

Expressing fractions and decimals as percentages

If $\frac{4}{5}$ of the pupils in a school have been away for a holiday, it means that 80 in every 100 have been on holiday,

i.e. $\frac{4}{5}$ is the same as 80%.

A fraction may be converted into a percentage by multiplying that fraction by 100%. This does not alter its value, since 100% is the whole.

A decimal may be converted into a percentage by multiplying it by 100%.

Exercise 14b

Express $\frac{7}{20}$ as a percentage.

$$\frac{7}{20} = \frac{7}{\cancel{20}_1} \times \cancel{100}^5\% = 35\%$$

Express the following fractions as percentages, giving your answers correct to 1 decimal place where necessary:

1 $\frac{1}{2}$	**5** $\frac{21}{40}$	**9** $\frac{3}{8}$	**13** $\frac{7}{5}$	**17** $\frac{7}{20}$
2 $\frac{7}{10}$	**6** $\frac{1}{4}$	**10** $\frac{23}{60}$	**14** $\frac{5}{8}$	**18** $\frac{31}{25}$
3 $\frac{13}{20}$	**7** $\frac{3}{20}$	**11** $\frac{3}{4}$	**15** $\frac{8}{3}$	**19** $\frac{7}{8}$
4 $\frac{1}{3}$	**8** $\frac{4}{25}$	**12** $\frac{9}{20}$	**16** $\frac{3}{5}$	**20** $\frac{8}{5}$

Express **a** 0.7 **b** 1.24 as percentages.

a $0.7 = 0.7 \times 100\% = 70\%$ **b** $1.24 = 1.24 \times 100\% = 124\%$

Express the following decimals as percentages:

21 0.5	**25** 0.625	**29** 2.64	**33** 1.25	**37** 0.16
22 0.22	**26** 0.9	**30** 0.845	**34** 3.41	**38** 1.39
23 0.83	**27** 0.04	**31** 0.25	**35** 0.075	**39** 6.35
24 1.72	**28** 0.55	**32** 0.74	**36** 0.36	**40** 0.1825

Exercise 14c

1 Express as fractions in their lowest terms:

a 30% **b** 85% **c** $42\frac{1}{2}\%$ **d** $5\frac{1}{4}\%$

2 Express as decimals:

a 44% **b** 68% **c** 170% **d** $16\frac{1}{2}\%$

3 Express as percentages:

a $\frac{2}{5}$ **b** $\frac{17}{20}$ **c** $\frac{1}{8}$ **d** $\frac{17}{15}$

4 Express as percentages:

a 0.2 **b** 0.62 **c** 0.845 **d** 1.78

Copy and complete the following table:

	Fraction	Percentage	Decimal
	$\frac{3}{4}$	75%	0.75
5	$\frac{4}{5}$		
6		60%	
7			0.7
8	$\frac{11}{20}$		
9		44%	
10			0.32

Problems

Suppose that in the town of Doxton 25 families in every 100 own a car. We can deduce from this that 75 in every 100 families do not. Since every family either owns a car or does not own a car, if we are given one percentage we can deduce the other.

Exercise 14d

If 56% of homes have a landline, what percentage do not?

All homes (i.e. 100% of homes) either have, or do not have, a landline.

If 56% have a landline, then (100 – 56)% do not,

i.e. 44% do not.

1 If 48% of the pupils in a school are girls, what percentage are boys?

2 If 87% of households have a computer, what percentage do not?

3 In the fourth year, 64% of the pupils do not study chemistry.
What percentage study chemistry?

4 In a box of oranges, 8% are bad. What percentage are good?

5 Twelve per cent of the persons taking a driver's test fail to pass first time. What percentage pass first time?

6 A hockey team won 62% of their matches and drew 26% of them. What percentage did they lose?

7 A rugby team drew 12% of their matches and lost 45% of them. What percentage did they win?

8 Deductions from a youth's wage were: income tax 18%, other deductions 14%. What percentage did he keep?

9 In an election, 40% of the electorate voted for Mrs Long, 32% for Mr Singhe and the remainder voted for Miss Berry. What percentage voted for Miss Berry if there were only three candidates and 8% of the electorate failed to vote?

10 In a school, 36% of the pupils study French and 38% study German. If 12% study both languages, what percentage do not study either?

11 85% of the first year pupils in a school study craft and 72% study photography. If 60% study both subjects, what percentage study neither?

12 A concert is attended by 1200 people. If 42% are adult females and 37% are adult males, how many children attended?

13 The attendance at an athletics meeting is 14 000. If 68% are men and boys and 22% are women, how many are girls?

14 In a book, 98% of the pages contain text, diagrams or both. If 88% of the pages contain text and 32% contain diagrams, what percentage contain

a neither text nor diagrams

b only diagrams

c only text

d both text and diagrams?

Puzzle

Alice's Adventures in Wonderland was created by Lewis Carroll, whose real name was Charles Lutwidge Dodgson. Dodgson was a mathematician who thought up many puzzles. This is one, with the title of 'Casualties':

If 70% have lost an eye, 75% an ear, 80% an arm, 85% a leg, what percentage, at least, must have lost all four?

Expressing one quantity as a percentage of another

If we wish to find 4 as a percentage of 20, we know that 4 is $\frac{4}{20}$ of 20

and $\quad \frac{4}{20} = \frac{4}{20} \times 100\%$

i.e. 4 as a percentage of 20 is

$$\frac{4}{20} \times 100\% = 20\%$$

To express one quantity as a percentage of another, we divide the first quantity by the second and multiply this fraction by 100%.

Exercise 14e

Express 20 cm as a percentage of 300 cm.

The first quantity as a percentage of the second quantity is

$$\frac{20}{300} \times 100\% = \frac{20}{3}\% = 6\frac{2}{3}\%$$

Express the first quantity as a percentage of the second:

Make sure that both quantities are measured in the same unit.

1 3, 12

2 30 cm, 50 cm

3 3 m, 9 m

4 4 in, 12 in

5 15, 20

6 24 cm, 40 cm

7 60 cm, 4 m

8 10 ft, 40 ft

9 20 m^2, 80 m^2

10 75 cm^2, 200 cm^2

11 25 cm^2, 125 cm^2

12 4 litres, 10 litres

13 3 pints, 5 pints

14 5, 50

15 2 cm, 10 cm

16 600 m, 2 km

17 $3\frac{1}{2}$ yd, 7 yd

18 40, 20

19 35 m, 56 m

20 50 cm, 5 m

21 8 in, 12 in

22 200 mm^2, 800 mm^2

23 198 mm^2, 275 mm^2

24 50 m^2, 15 m^2

25 3.6 t, 5 t

26 33.6 g, 80 g

Finding a percentage of a quantity

To find a percentage of a quantity, change the percentage to a fraction and multiply by the quantity.

Exercise 14f

Find the value of **a** 12% of 450 **b** $7\frac{1}{3}\%$ of 3.75 m

a 12% of $450 = \frac{12}{100} \times 450 = 54$ (the term 'of' means to multiply by)

b $7\frac{1}{3}\%$ of $3.75\text{ m} = 7\frac{1}{3}\%$ of $375\text{ cm} = \frac{22}{3}\%$ of 375 cm

$$= \frac{22}{3 \times 100} \times 375\text{ cm}$$

$$= 27.5\text{ cm}$$

Find the value of:

1 40% of 120

2 12% of 800 g

3 74% of 75 cm

4 44% of 650 km

5 8% of \$2

6 77% of 4 kg

7 70% of 360

8 86% of 1150 g

9 55% of 8.6 m

10 96% of 215 cm^2

11 63% of 4 m

12 96% of 15 m^2

13 45% of 740

14 33% of 600 kg

15 6% of 24 m

16 15% of \$10

17 17% of 2 km

18 32% of 5 litres

19 30% of \$250

20 66% of 300 m

21 $33\frac{1}{3}\%$ of 270 g

22 $5\frac{1}{4}\%$ of 56 mm

23 $37\frac{1}{2}\%$ of 48 cm

24 $22\frac{1}{2}\%$ of 40 m^2

25 $66\frac{2}{3}\%$ of 480 m^2

26 $32\frac{1}{7}\%$ of 140 km

27 $62\frac{1}{2}\%$ of 8 km

28 $74\frac{1}{2}\%$ of 200 cm^2

29 $33\frac{1}{3}\%$ of 42 c

30 $82\frac{1}{5}\%$ of \$65

31 12% of \$4

32 $7\frac{1}{2}\%$ of 80 g

33 $2\frac{1}{3}\%$ of 90 m

34 $16\frac{2}{3}\%$ of \$60

35 $3\frac{1}{8}\%$ of 64 kg

36 $87\frac{1}{2}\%$ of 16 mm

Investigation

Banks offer many different accounts. Get an up-to-date leaflet from one bank that gives details of all its different accounts and the rate of interest offered on each.

Write a short report on which account you would use, and why, if

1 you are saving to buy a pair of trainers
2 a relative has given you \$1000 and you want to keep it safe until you leave school.

Problems

Exercise 14g

In the second year, 287 of the 350 pupils study geography. What percentage study geography?

Express 287 as a fraction of 350, then multiply by 100%.

$$\text{Percentage studying geography} = \frac{287}{350} \times 100\%$$
$$= 82\%$$

Read the question carefully to make sure that you understand what you are being asked to find. Read it several times if necessary.

1 There are 60 boys in the third year, 24 of whom study chemistry. What percentage of third year boys study chemistry?

2 In a history test, Victoria scored 28 out of a possible 40. What was her percentage mark?

3 Out of 20 drivers tested in one day for a driver's licence, 4 of them failed. What percentage failed?

4 There are 60 photographs in a book, 12 of which are coloured. What is the percentage of coloured photographs?

5 Forty-two of the 60 choristers in a choir wear spectacles. What percentage do not?

6 Each week a boy saves \$3 of the \$12 he earns. What percentage does he spend?

7 A secretary takes 56 letters to the post office for posting. 14 are registered and the remainder are ordinary mail. What percentage go by ordinary mail?

8 Monique obtained 80 marks out of a possible 120 in her end of term maths examination. What was her percentage mark?

9 Sherry's gross wage is \$120 per week, but her 'take home' pay is only \$78.
What percentage is this of her gross wage?

10 If 8% of a crowd of 24 500 at a football match were females, how many females attended?

If 54% of the 1800 pupils in a school are boys, how many girls are there in the school?

Method 1 First find the number of boys in the school: this is 54% of 1800.

$$\text{Number of boys} = \frac{54}{100} \times 1800 = 972$$

Now you can find the number of girls:

$$\text{Number of girls} = 1800 - 972 = 828$$

Method 2 As 54% of the pupils are boys, 100% − 54%, i.e. 46% of the pupils are girls.
So the number of girls is 46% of 1800 $= \frac{46}{100} \times 1800 = 828$

11 In a garage, 16 of the 30 cars which are for sale are second hand. What percentage of the cars are

a new **b** second hand?

12 There are 80 houses in my street and 65% of them have an internet connection. How many houses

a have the internet **b** do not have the internet?

13 In my class there are 30 pupils and 40% of them have a bicycle. How many pupils

a have a bicycle **b** do not have a bicycle?

14 Yesterday, of the 350 international flights leaving Miami International Airport, 2% were bound for Kingston. How many of these flights

a flew to Kingston **b** did not fly to Kingston?

15 In a particular year, 64% of the 16 000 Jewish immigrants into Israel came from Eastern Europe. How many of the immigrants did not come from Eastern Europe?

16 There are 120 shops in the High Street, 35% of which sell food. How many High Street shops do not sell food?

17 Last year the amount I paid in rates on my house was \$520. This year my rates will increase by 12%. Find the increase.

18 A mathematics book has 320 pages, 40% of which are on algebra, 25% on geometry and the remainder on arithmetic. How many pages of arithmetic are there?

Mixed exercises

Exercise 14h

Select the letter that gives the correct answer.

1 Expressed as a percentage $2\frac{3}{4}$ is

A 27.5% B 75% C 95% D 275%

2 15 metres expressed as a percentage of 35 metres correct to 2 decimal places is

A 42.80% B 42.86% C 43.80% D 44.85%

3 Expressed as a percentage of $4, 25 cents is

A 0.625% B 6.25% C 6.30% D 62.5%

4 55% of 240 cm is

A 115 cm B 120 cm C 132 cm D 142 cm

5 48% expressed as a vulgar fraction in its lowest term is

A $\frac{5}{12}$ B $\frac{1}{2}$ C $\frac{12}{25}$ D $\frac{24}{50}$

6 $\frac{3}{8}$ as a percentage is

A 37% B 37.5% C 38% D 40%

Exercise 14i

1 Express 36%

a as a fraction in its lowest terms

b as a decimal.

2 Express as a percentage, giving your answer correct to 1 d.p. if necessary:

a $\frac{5}{8}$ b $1\frac{1}{3}$ c 2.5

3 Express 250 g as a percentage of 2000 kg.

4 Find 85% of 340 m^2.

5 The cost of insuring a car in Barbados is about 8% of its value.
Find the cost of insuring a car valued at $18 000.

Exercise 14j

1 Find the first quantity as a percentage of the second quantity:

  a 10 m, 80 m b \$0.75, \$2 c 150 cm, 300 cm

2 Express as a percentage, giving your answer correct to 1 d.p. where necessary:

  a $\frac{2}{7}$ b 0.279 c $1\frac{2}{9}$

3 Express $12\frac{1}{2}\%$ as

  a a fraction in its lowest terms

  b a decimal.

4 Find 36% of \$2.50.

5 There are 450 children in a primary school, 12% of whom do not speak English at home. Find the number of children for whom English is not their home language.

? Puzzle

If 5 September falls on a Friday, on which day of the week will Christmas Day fall?

Did you know?

You can use this calculator method to find the number of gifts received in the song *The Twelve Days of Christmas*.

1 The number of gifts received on the *n*th day is calculated by

[AC] [1] [+] [2] [+] [3] [+] … [+] [*n*] [=]

2 The total number of gifts is found by

[AC] [1] [M+] [+] [2] [M+] [+] [3] … [M+] [+] [1] [2] [M+] [MR]

In this chapter you have seen that...

- ✔ a percentage can be expressed as a fraction by putting it over 100 and simplifying, e.g. $70\% = \frac{70}{100} = \frac{7}{10}$
- ✔ a percentage can be expressed as a decimal by dividing it by 100, e.g. $65\% = 65 \div 100 = 0.65$
- ✔ a fraction, or a decimal, can be expressed as a percentage by multiplying it by 100, e.g. $\frac{2}{5} = \frac{2}{5} \times 100\% = 40\%$ and $0.8 = 0.8 \times 100\% = 80\%$
- ✔ to express one quantity as a percentage of another, first express the quantity as a fraction of the second and multiply by 100, e.g. 4 as a percentage of 20 is $\frac{4}{20} \times 100\% = 20\%$
- ✔ to find a percentage of a quantity, multiply the percentage by the quantity and divide by 100, e.g. 20% of 80 cm $= \frac{20}{100} \times 80\,\text{cm} = 16\,\text{cm}$.

15 Units of measurement

At the end of this chapter you should be able to...

1 use suitable metric units of measure for length and mass

2 change from small to large metric units of measure and vice versa

3 add and subtract metric quantities

4 change from a.m. and p.m. time to 24-hour clock times and vice versa

6 express quantities in given imperial units of measure

7 make rough equivalence between imperial and metric units

8 convert between temperatures measured in degrees Celsius and degrees Fahrenheit.

Did you know?

The story of zero – the number that we use so often.

The word zero came from Italian. It was not always as important as it is today.

We were using numbers for thousands of years before zero (0) was introduced to us.

Zero is special:

- If we add or subtract 0 from a number, the result is the original number.
- If we multiply a number by 0, the result is zero.
- If we raise a number other than 0 to the power 0, the result is 1.
- If we divide 0 by a number other than 0, the result is 0.

We cannot define a number divided by 0.

You need to know...

✔ how to multiply and divide by 10, 100 and 1000

✔ how to multiply by any number

✔ the basic number facts including your tables

✔ how to deal with simple decimals.

Key words

approximation, centimetre, degrees Celsius, degrees Fahrenheit, foot, gram, hundredweight, inch, kilogram, kilometre, mass, metre, mile, millimetre, ounce, perimeter, pound, ton, tonne, yard

The need for standard units

Tyrone needs a new shutter for his window. He describes the size by saying it is as wide as his table and as high as the length of his walking stick. These measurements are no use for ordering the shutter. Measurements have to be in units that everyone understands.

There are two standard sets of units. Metric units are used in most countries but imperial units are used in the USA and a few other countries.

Whenever we want to measure a length, or weigh an object, we find the length or mass in standard units. We might for instance give the length of a line in millimetres or the mass of a bag of apples in pounds. The millimetre belongs to a set of units called the metric system. The pound is one of the imperial units.

The metric system was developed in France in 1790 so that units in the system would be related to each other by a factor of ten.

The basic unit of capacity is the litre. The litre has the volume of a cube of side 10 centimetres.

Units of length

The basic unit of length is the *metre* (m). To get an idea of how long a metre is, remember that a standard bed is about 2 m long. However, a metre is not a useful unit for measuring either very large things or very small things so we need larger units and smaller units.

We get the larger unit by multiplying the metre by 1000. We get the smaller units by dividing the metre into 100 parts or 1000 parts.

1000 metres is called 1 kilometre (km)

(It takes about 15 minutes to walk a distance of 1 km.)

$\frac{1}{100}$ of a metre is called 1 centimetre (cm)

$\frac{1}{1000}$ of a metre is called 1 millimetre (mm)

(You can see centimetres and millimetres on your ruler.)

Some uses of metric units of length

Millimetres (mm) for lengths of nails and screws, widths of film, tapes and ribbons.

Centimetres (cm) for body sizes, i.e. height, chest, etc., widths of wallpaper, belts and ties.

Metres (m) for sizes of rooms, swimming pools, garden beds, hoses, ladders, etc.

Kilometres (km) for road signs, maps, distances between places.

Exercise 15a

1 Which metric unit would you use to measure

- **a** the length of your classroom
- **b** the length of your pencil
- **c** the length of a soccer pitch
- **d** the distance from Castries to Roseau
- **e** the length of a page in this book
- **f** the thickness of your exercise book?

2 Use your ruler to draw a line of length

a	10 cm	**d**	50 mm	**g**	15 mm	**j**	16 mm
b	3 cm	**e**	20 mm	**h**	12 cm	**k**	5 cm
c	15 cm	**f**	4 cm	**i**	25 mm	**l**	75 mm

3 Estimate the length, in centimetres, of the following lines:

a ______________________

b ___________

c ____________________________

d _____

e ____

Now use your ruler to measure each line.

4 Estimate the length, in millimetres, of the following lines:

a ___________

b _____

c __

d ________

e ____________

Now use your ruler to measure each line.

5 Use a straight edge (not a ruler with a scale) to draw a line that is approximately

a 10 cm long **b** 5 cm long **c** 15 cm long **d** 20 mm long

Now measure each line to see how good your approximation was.

6 Estimate the width of your classroom in metres.

7 Estimate the length of your classroom in metres.

8 Measure the length and width of your exercise book in centimetres. Draw a rough sketch of your book with the measurements on it. Find the perimeter (the distance all round) of your book.

9 Each side of a square is 10 cm long. Draw a rough sketch of the square with the measurements on it. Calculate the perimeter of the square.

10 A sheet is 200 cm wide and 250 cm long. What is the perimeter of the sheet?

Activity

This shows a woman near a tree.

The woman is 170 cm tall.

1 Estimate the height of the tree.

2 Use a person or an object (e.g. a door) whose height you know to estimate the height and width of the main building in your school.

3 Explain how you could estimate the length and height of a bridge.

Changing from large units to smaller units

The metric units of length are the kilometre, the metre, the centimetre and the millimetre where

$1\,\text{km} = 1000\,\text{m}$ $\quad$ $1\,\text{m} = 100\,\text{cm}$

$1\,\text{m} = 1000\,\text{mm}$ $\quad$ $1\,\text{cm} = 10\,\text{mm}$

Exercise 15b

Express 3 km in metres.

1 km is 1000 m, so 3 km is 3 times 1000 m

$$3\,\text{km} = 3 \times 1000\,\text{m}$$
$$= 3000\,\text{m}$$

Express 3.5 m in centimetres.

1 m is 100 cm, so 3.5 m is 3.5 times 100 cm

$$3.5\,\text{m} = 3.5 \times 100\,\text{cm}$$
$$= 350\,\text{cm}$$

Express the given quantity in terms of the unit in brackets:

1	2 m	(cm)	9	3 m	(mm)	17	1.9 m	(mm)
2	5 km	(m)	10	2 km	(mm)	18	3.5 km	(m)
3	3 cm	(mm)	11	5 m	(cm)	19	2.7 m	(cm)
4	4 m	(cm)	12	7 m	(mm)	20	1.9 km	(cm)
5	12 km	(m)	13	1.5 m	(cm)	21	3.8 cm	(mm)
6	15 cm	(mm)	14	2.3 cm	(mm)	22	9.2 m	(mm)
7	6 m	(mm)	15	1.6 km	(m)	23	2.3 km	(m)
8	1 km	(cm)	16	3.7 m	(mm)	24	8.4 m	(cm)

Units of mass

The most familiar units used for weighing are the *kilogram* (kg) and the *gram* (g). We shall use the term 'mass', not 'weight'.

Most groceries that are sold in tins or packets have masses given in grams. For example the mass of the most common packet of butter is 250 g. One eating apple weighs roughly 100 g, so the gram is a small unit of mass. Kilograms are used to give the mass of sugar or flour: the mass of the most common bag of sugar is 1 kg and the most common bag of flour weighs 1.5 kg.

For weighing large loads (timber or steel for example) a larger unit of mass is needed, and we use the *tonne* (t). For weighing very small quantities (for example the mass of a particular drug in one pill) we use the *milligram* (mg).

The relationships between these masses are

$$1\,\text{t} = 1000\,\text{kg}$$
$$1\,\text{kg} = 1000\,\text{g}$$
$$1\,\text{g} = 1000\,\text{mg}$$

Exercise 15c

Express 2 t in grams.

First change tonnes to kg, then change kg to grams.

1 t is 1000 kg and 1 kg is 1000 g

$$
\begin{aligned}
2\,\text{t} &= 2 \times 1000\,\text{kg} \\
&= 2000\,\text{kg} \\
&= 2000 \times 1000\,\text{g} \\
&= 2\,000\,000\,\text{g}
\end{aligned}
$$

Express each quantity in terms of the unit given in brackets:

1	12 t	(kg)	**9**	4 kg	(g)	**17**	5.2 kg	(mg)
2	3 kg	(g)	**10**	2 kg	(mg)	**18**	0.6 g	(mg)
3	5 g	(mg)	**11**	3 t	(kg)	**19**	11.3 t	(kg)
4	1 t	(g)	**12**	4 g	(mg)	**20**	2.5 kg	(g)
5	1 kg	(mg)	**13**	1.5 kg	(g)	**21**	7.3 g	(mg)
6	13 kg	(g)	**14**	2.7 t	(kg)	**22**	0.3 kg	(mg)
7	6 g	(mg)	**15**	1.8 g	(mg)	**23**	0.5 t	(kg)
8	2 t	(g)	**16**	0.7 t	(kg)	**24**	0.8 g	(mg)

Mixed units

When you use your ruler to measure a line, you will probably find that the line is not an exact number of centimetres. For example the width of this page is 19 cm and 5 mm. We can say that the width of this page is 19 cm 5 mm or we could give the width in millimetres alone.

Now $\quad 19\,\text{cm} = 19 \times 10\,\text{mm}$

$\qquad = 190\,\text{mm}$

So $\quad 19\,\text{cm}\ 5\,\text{mm} = 195\,\text{mm}$

Exercise 15d

Express each quantity in terms of the unit given in brackets:

4 kg 50 g (g)
Change 4 kg to grams, then add 50 g

$$4\,\text{kg} = 4 \times 1000\,\text{g}$$
$$= 4000\,\text{g}$$

Therefore $4\,\text{kg}\ 50\,\text{g} = 4050\,\text{g}$

1 1 m 36 cm (cm)
2 3 cm 5 mm (mm)
3 1 km 50 m (m)
4 4 cm 8 mm (mm)
5 2 m 7 cm (cm)
6 3 km 20 m (m)
7 5 m 2 cm (cm)
8 5 km 500 m (m)
9 20 cm 2 mm (mm)
10 8 m 9 mm (mm)
11 3 kg 500 g (g)
12 2 kg 8 g (g)
13 5 g 500 mg (mg)
14 2 t 800 kg (kg)
15 3 t 250 kg (kg)
16 1 kg 20 g (g)
17 1 g 250 mg (mg)
18 3 kg 550 g (g)
19 2 t 50 kg (kg)
20 1 kg 10 g (g)

Changing from small units to larger units

Exercise 15e

Express 400 cm in metres.

100 cm = 1 m, so 1 cm = 1 ÷ 100 m

So $400\,\text{cm} = 400 \div 100\,\text{m}$
$= 4\,\text{m}$

In questions **1** to **20**, express the given quantity in terms of the unit given in brackets:

1 300 mm (cm)
2 6000 m (km)
3 150 cm (m)
4 250 mm (cm)

5	1600 m	(km)	**13**	1500 mg	(g)
6	72 m	(km)	**14**	5020 g	(kg)
7	12 cm	(m)	**15**	3800 kg	(t)
8	88 mm	(cm)	**16**	86 kg	(t)
9	1250 mm	(m)	**17**	560 g	(kg)
10	2850 m	(km)	**18**	28 mg	(g)
11	1500 kg	(t)	**19**	190 kg	(t)
12	3680 g	(kg)	**20**	86 g	(kg)

Express 5 m 36 cm in metres.

First change 36 cm to metres, then add 5.

$$36\text{ cm} = 36 \div 100\text{ m}$$
$$= 0.36\text{ m}$$

So $5\text{ m }36\text{ cm} = 5.36\text{ m}$

In questions **21** to **40** express the given quantity in terms of the unit given in brackets:

21	3 m 45 cm	(m)	**31**	5 kg 142 g	(kg)
22	8 cm 4 mm	(cm)	**32**	48 g 171 mg	(g)
23	11 km 2 m	(km)	**33**	9 kg 8 g	(kg)
24	2 km 42 m	(km)	**34**	9 g 88 mg	(g)
25	4 cm 4 mm	(cm)	**35**	12 kg 19 g	(kg)
26	5 m 3 cm	(m)	**36**	4g 111 mg	(g)
27	7 km 5 m	(km)	**37**	1 t 56 kg	(t)
28	4 m 5 mm	(m)	**38**	5 g 3 mg	(g)
29	1 km 10 cm	(km)	**39**	250 g 500 mg	(kg)
30	8 cm 5 mm	(km)	**40**	850 kg 550 g	(t)

Exercise 15f

Find 1 kg + 158 g in **a** grams **b** kilograms.

a
$$1\text{ kg} = 1000\text{ g}$$
$$\therefore\ 1\text{ kg} + 158\text{ g} = 1158\text{ g}$$
($\therefore$ means 'therefore' or 'it follows that')

b
$$158\text{ g} = 158 \div 1000\text{ kg}$$
$$= 0.158\text{ kg}$$
$$\therefore\ 1\text{ kg} + 158\text{ g} = 1.158\text{ kg}$$

Find the sum of 5 m, 4 cm and 97 mm in **a** metres **b** centimetres.

a

$$4\text{ cm} = 4 \div 100\text{ m} = 0.04\text{ m}$$

$$97\text{ mm} = 97 \div 1000\text{ m} = 0.097\text{ m}$$

$$\therefore \quad 5\text{ m} + 4\text{ cm} + 97\text{ mm} = (5 + 0.04 + 0.097)\text{ m}$$

$$= 5.137\text{m}$$

b

$$5\text{ m} = 5 \times 100\text{ cm} = 500\text{ cm}$$

$$97\text{ mm} = 97 \div 10\text{ cm} = 9.7\text{ cm}$$

$$\therefore \quad 5\text{ m} + 4\text{ cm} + 97\text{ mm} = (500 + 4 + 9.7)\text{ cm}$$

$$= 513.7\text{ cm}$$

Alternatively, use your answer from **a**: $5.137\text{ m} = 5.137 \times 100\text{ cm}$

$$= 513.7\text{ cm}$$

Quantities must be expressed in the same units before they are added or subtracted.

Find, giving your answer in metres:

1 5 m + 86 cm

2 92 cm + 115 mm

3 3 km + 136 cm

4 51 m + 3 km

5 36 cm + 87 mm + 520 cm

6 120 mm + 53 cm + 4 m

If you are changing to a smaller unit, e.g. from metres to centimetres, *multiply*. If you are changing to a larger unit, e.g. from grams to kilograms, *divide*.

Find, giving your answer in millimetres:

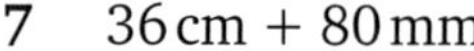

7 36 cm + 80 mm

8 5 cm + 5 mm

9 1 m + 82 cm

10 2 m + 45 cm + 6 mm

11 3 cm + 5 m + 2.9 cm

12 34 cm + 18 mm + 1 m

Find, giving your answer in grams:

13 3 kg + 250 g

14 5 kg + 115 g

15 5.8 kg + 9.3 kg

16 1 kg + 0.8 kg + 750 g

17 116 g + 0.93 kg + 680 mg

18 248 g + 0.06 kg + 730 mg

Find, expressing your answer in kilograms:

19 2 t + 580 kg

20 1.8 t + 562 kg

21 390 g + 1.83 kg

22 1.6 t + 3.9 kg + 2500 g

23 1.03 t + 9.6 kg + 0.05 t

24 5.4 t + 272 kg + 0.3 t

Find, expressing your answer in the unit given in brackets:

25 8 m − 52 cm (cm)

26 52 mm + 87 cm (m)

27 1.3 kg − 150 g (g)

28 1.3 m − 564 mm (cm)

29 2.05 t + 592 kg (kg)

30 20 g − 150 mg (mg)

31 36 kg − 580 g (g)

32 1.5 t − 590 kg (kg)

33 3.9 m + 582 mm (cm)

34 0.3 m − 29.5 cm (mm)

Investigation

1 This is a map of an island. Explain how you could estimate the length of its coastline.

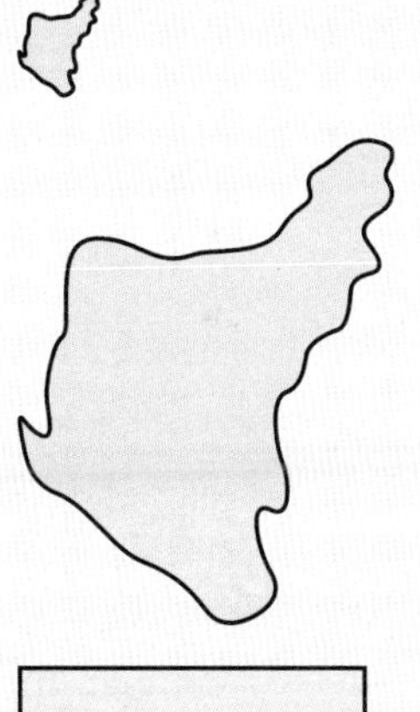

2 This is the same island, drawn to a larger scale. Would you get the same answer for the length of its coastline from this drawing?

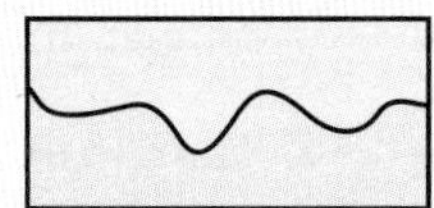

3 This shows the coastline of part of the island drawn to a much larger scale. If you used a map of the whole island drawn with this scale, how would your estimate of the length of the coastline compare with your first estimate?

4 Do you think it is possible to measure the length of the coastline exactly?

(Think of a bit of coastline you know and imagine measuring a short length of it.)

5 Now suppose that you want to measure the length of the table you are sitting at.

You could measure it with a ruler.

You could measure it with a tape measure marked in centimetres and millimetres.

You could measure it with a precision instrument that will read lengths to tenths of a millimetre, or even hundredths of a millimetre.

You could measure the length in several different places.

Write down, with reasons, whether it is possible to find the length exactly.

Do you think it is possible to give any measurement exactly?

Multiplying metric units

Exercise 15g

Calculate, expressing your answer in the unit given in brackets:

$3 \times 2\,\text{g}\ 741\,\text{mg}$ (g)

First express the mass in grams.

$$2\,\text{g}\ 741\,\text{mg} = 2.741\,\text{g}$$

$$\therefore \quad 3 \times 2\,\text{g}\ 741\,\text{mg} = 3 \times 2.741\,\text{g}$$

$$= 8.223\,\text{g}$$

$$\begin{array}{r} 2741 \\ \times \quad 3 \\ \hline 8223 \\ \hline \end{array}$$

1. $4 \times 3\,\text{kg}\ 385\,\text{g}$ (g)
2. $9 \times 5\,\text{m}\ 88\,\text{mm}$ (mm)
3. $3 \times 4\,\text{kg}\ 521\,\text{g}$ (kg)
4. $5 \times 2\,\text{m}\ 51\,\text{cm}$ (m)
5. $10 \times 3\,\text{t}\ 200\,\text{kg}$ (t)
6. $2 \times 5\,\text{cm}\ 3\,\text{mm}$ (cm)
7. $6 \times 2\,\text{g}\ 561\,\text{mg}$ (mg)
8. $8 \times 3\,\text{km}\ 56\,\text{m}$ (km)
9. $3 \times 7\,\text{t}\ 590\,\text{kg}$ (t)
10. $7 \times 2\,\text{km}\ 320\,\text{m}$ (m)

First change the measurement to the unit required.

Puzzle

If a box of bananas weighs 7 kilograms and half of its own mass, how much does a box and a half of bananas weigh?

Problems

Exercise 15h

Find, in kilograms, the total mass of a bag of flour of mass 1.5 kg, a jar of jam of mass 450 g and a packet of rice of mass 500 g.

The total mass means the sum of the three masses.

First change each mass to kg, then add them.

$$\text{The mass of the jar of jam} = 450 \div 1000\,\text{kg} = 0.45\,\text{kg}$$

$$\text{The mass of the packet of rice} = 500 \div 1000\,\text{kg} = 0.5\,\text{kg}$$

$$\text{The total mass} = (1.5 + 0.45 + 0.5)\,\text{kg} = 2.45\,\text{kg}$$

1 Find the sum, in metres, of 5 m, 52 cm, 420 cm.

2 Find the sum, in grams, of 1 kg, 260 g, 580 g.

3 Subtract 52 kg from 0.8 t, giving your answer in kilograms.

4 Find the difference, in grams, between 5 g and 890 mg.

5 Find the total length, in millimetres, of a piece of wood 82 cm long and another piece of wood 260 mm long.

6 Find the total mass, in kilograms, of 500 g of butter, 2 kg of potatoes, 1.5 kg of flour.

7 One can of baked beans has a mass of 220 g. What is the mass, in kilograms, of ten of these cans?

8 One fence post is 150 cm long. What length of wood, in metres, is needed to make ten such fence posts?

9 Find the perimeter of a square if each side is of length 8.3 cm. Give your answer in centimetres.

10 A wooden vegetable crate and its contents have a mass of 6.5 kg. If the crate has a mass of 1.2 kg what is the mass of its contents?

Read each question carefully to make sure that you understand what you are asked to find. Read it several times if necessary.

Imperial units of length

Some imperial units are still used. For instance, in some places distances on road signs are still given in miles. One *mile* is roughly equivalent to $1\frac{1}{2}$ km. A better approximation is

5 miles is about 8 kilometres

Yards, *feet* and *inches* are other imperial units of length that are still used. In this system units are not always divided into ten parts to give smaller units so we have to learn 'tables'.

12 inches (in) = 1 foot (ft)

3 feet = 1 yard (yd)

1760 yards = 1 mile

Exercise 15i

Express 2 ft 5 in in inches.

First convert the number of feet into inches then add the number of inches.

$$2 \text{ ft} = 2 \times 12 \text{ in}$$
$$= 24 \text{ in}$$
$$\therefore \quad 2 \text{ ft } 5 \text{ in} = 24 + 5 \text{ in}$$
$$= 29 \text{ in}$$

Express the given quantity in the unit in brackets:

1 5 ft 8 in (in)

2 4 yd 2 ft (ft)

3 1 mile 49 yd (yd)

4 2 ft 11 in (in)

5 8 ft 4 in (in)

6 2 miles 800 yd (yd)

7 5 yd 2 ft (ft)

8 10 ft 3 in (in)

9 9 yd 1 ft (ft)

10 9 ft 10 in (in)

Express 52 inches in feet and inches.

There are 12 inches in 1 foot so we need to find how many complete 12's there are in 52.
A number of inches may be left over.

$$52 \text{ in} = 52 \div 12$$
$$= 4 \text{ ft } 4 \text{ in}$$

$$12\overline{)52} \quad 4 \text{ r } 4$$

11 36 in (ft)

12 29 in (ft and in)

13 86 in (ft and in)

14 9 ft (yd)

15 13 ft (yd and ft)

16 2000 yd (miles and yd)

17 75 in (ft and in)

18 100 ft (yd and ft)

19 120 in (ft and in)

20 30 000 yd (miles and yd)

Imperial units of mass

The imperial units of mass that are still used are *pounds* and *ounces*. Other units of mass that you may still see are *hundredweights* and *tons* (not to be confused with tonnes).

16 ounces (oz) = 1 pound (lb)

112 pounds = 1 hundredweight (cwt)

20 hundredweight = 1 ton

Exercise 15j

Express the given quantity in terms of the units given in brackets:

1	2 lb 6 oz	(oz)	**6**	24 oz	(lb and oz)
2	1 lb 12 oz	(oz)	**7**	18 oz	(lb and oz)
3	4 lb 3 oz	(oz)	**8**	36 oz	(lb and oz)
4	3 tons 4 cwt	(cwt)	**9**	30 cwt	(tons and cwt)
5	1 cwt 50 lb	(lb)	**10**	120 lb	(cwt and lb)

Rough equivalence between metric and imperial units

If you shop in a supermarket you will find that nearly all goods are sold in grams or kilograms. However, some shops still sell goods in pounds and ounces. It is often useful to be able to convert, roughly, pounds into kilograms or grams into pounds. For a rough conversion it is good enough to say that

1 kg is about 2 lb

although one kilogram is slightly more than two pounds.

One metre is slightly longer than one yard but for a rough conversion it is good enough to say that

1 m is about 1 yd

Remember that the symbol ≈ means 'is approximately equal to' so

$1\text{ kg} \approx 2\text{ lb}$

$1\text{ m} \approx 1\text{ yd or } 3\text{ ft}$

Exercise 15k

Write 5 kg roughly in terms of the unit in brackets: 5 kg (lb)

1 kg ≈ 2 lb, so 5 kg is approximately 5 times 2 lb

$$5\,\text{kg} \approx 5 \times 2\,\text{lb}$$

$$\therefore \quad 5\,\text{kg} \approx 10\,\text{lb}$$

Write 10 ft roughly in terms of the unit in brackets: 10 ft (m)

3 ft ≈ 1 m, so you need to find the number of 3's in 10

$$10\,\text{ft} \approx 10 \div 3\text{m}$$

$$\therefore \quad 10\,\text{ft} \approx 3.3\,\text{m (to 1 d.p.)}$$

In questions **1** to **10**, write the first unit roughly in terms of the unit in brackets:

1 3 kg (lb)

2 2 m (ft)

3 4 lb (kg)

4 9 ft (m)

5 1.5 kg (lb)

6 5 m (ft)

7 3.5 kg (lb)

8 8 ft (m)

9 250 g (oz)

10 500 g (lb)

In questions **11** to **16** use the approximation 5 miles ≈ 8 km to convert the given number of miles into an approximate number of kilometres:

11 10 miles

12 20 miles

13 15 miles

14 100 miles

15 75 miles

16 40 miles

17 I buy a 5 lb bag of potatoes and two 1.5 kg bags of flour. What mass, roughly, in pounds do I have to carry?

18 A window is 6 ft high. Roughly, what is its height in metres?

19 I have a picture which measures 2 ft by 1 ft. Wood for framing it is sold by the metre. Roughly, what length of framing, in metres, should I buy?

20 In the supermarket I buy a 4 kg packet of sugar and a 5 lb bag of potatoes. Which is heavier?

21 In one catalogue a table cloth is described as measuring 4 ft by 8 ft. In another catalogue a different table cloth is described as measuring 1 m by 2 m. Which one is bigger?

22 The distance between Antigua and St Kitts is about 50 miles. The distance between Dominica and Martinique is about 140 kilometres. What is the difference, in miles, between the distances the two pairs of islands are apart?

23 A recipe requires 250 grams of flour. Roughly, how many ounces is this?

Converting from inches to centimetres and from centimetres to inches is often useful. For most purposes it is good enough to say that 1 inch $\approx 2\frac{1}{2}$ cm.

24 An instruction in an old knitting pattern says knit 6 inches. Maria has a tape measure marked only in centimetres. How many centimetres should she knit?

25 The instructions for repotting a plant say that it should go into a 10 cm pot. The flower pots that Tom has in his shed are marked 3 in, 4 in and 5 in. Which one should he use?

26 Mr Smith wishes to extend his gas pipe lines which were installed several years ago in 1 in and $\frac{1}{2}$ in diameter copper tubing. The only new piping he can buy has diameters of 10 mm, 15 mm, 20 mm or 25 mm. Use the approximation 1 in $\approx$ 2.5 cm to determine which piping he should buy that would be nearest to

a the 1 in pipes

b the $\frac{1}{2}$ in pipes.

27 A carpenter wishes to replace a 6 in floorboard. The only sizes available are metric and have widths of 12 cm, 15 cm, 18 cm and 20 cm. Use the approximation 1 in $\approx$ 2.5 cm to determine which one he should buy.

28 A shop sells material at \$10.50 per metre while the same material is sold in the local market at \$9 per yard. Using 4 in $\approx$ 10 cm find which is cheaper.

Investigation

1 Some imperial units have specialised uses, for example, furlongs are used to measure distances in horse racing courses and fathoms are used to measure the depth of water.

a Use reference materials to find out the relationships between these units and the more common imperial units of length.

b Find out as much as you can about other imperial units of distance and mass.

c Nautical miles are used to measure distances at sea. Find out what you can about nautical miles, including the rough equivalence of 1 nautical mile in miles and in kilometres.

2 A group of young secondary school pupils were asked to write down their heights and masses on sheets of paper which were gathered in.

This is a list of *exactly* what was written down.

a This group of children used a mixture of units. Some of the entries are unbelievable.

Which are they?

Give some of the reasons for these unbelievable entries.

Height	Mass
141 cm	35 kg
1.38 cm	4 stone
1.8 m	6.26 stone
4 feet 5 inches	4 kg
52 feet	6 stone
5 foot 4	8 stone
1 metre 53	$7\frac{1}{2}$ stone
1 metre 41 cm	28.0 kg
141 cm	5 stone 4 pounds
4 feet 7 inches	32 kg

b Find out how your group know their heights and masses; each of you write down your own height and mass on a piece of paper. Use whatever unit you know them in, and do not write your name on it.

Collect in the pieces of paper and write out a list like the one above.

c What official forms do you know about that ask for height?

What unit is required?

d Write down your own height and mass in both metric and imperial units.

Time

Time is measured in millennia (1 millennium = 1000 years), centuries, decades, years, months, weeks, days, hours, minutes and seconds.

There are 12 months in a year but the number of days in a month varies.

There are 365 days in a year, except for leap years when there are 366.

Remember:
Thirty days hath September, April, June and November. All the rest have thirty-one except for February clear, which has twenty-eight and twenty-nine in each leap year.

The relationships between weeks, days, hours, minutes and seconds are fixed:

$$1 \text{ week} = 7 \text{ days}$$
$$1 \text{ day} = 24 \text{ hours}$$
$$1 \text{ hour} = 60 \text{ minutes}$$
$$1 \text{ minute} = 60 \text{ seconds}$$

When you change units of time, remember that you multiply when you change to a smaller unit, and you divide when you change to a larger unit.

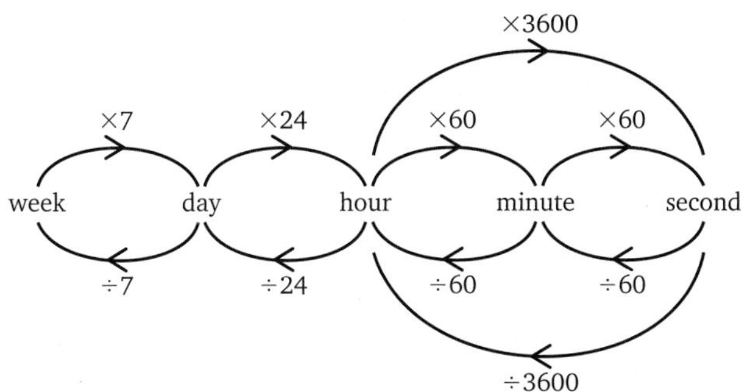

There are two ways of measuring the time of day: the 24-hour clock and the 12-hour clock.

The 24-hour clock uses the full 24 hours in a day, measuring from midnight through to the next midnight.

The time is given as a four-figure number, for example, 1346 hr and 0730 hr. The first two figures give the hours and the second two figures give the minutes. So 1346 hr means 13 hours and 46 minutes after midnight and 0730 hr means 7 hours and 30 minutes after midnight.

Sometimes there is a space or a colon between the hours and the minutes, for example 13 46 or 13:46.

The 12-hour clock uses the 12 hours from midnight to midday as a.m. times.

and the 12 hours from midday to midnight as p.m. times.

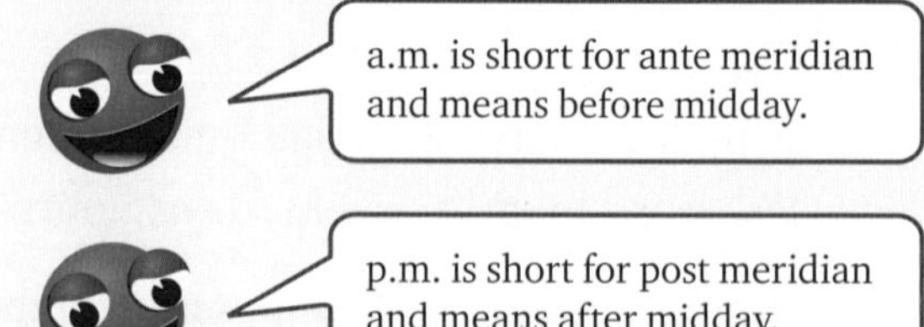

The time is written as a number of hours and a number of minutes followed by a.m. or p.m.
The hours and the minutes are usually separated by a stop, for example 6.30 a.m. means 6 hours and 30 minutes after midnight and 10.05 p.m. means 10 hours and 5 minutes after midday.

In the 24-hour clock, it is clear that 0000 hr means midnight and 1200 hr means midday.

But in the 12-hour clock, you need to write 'midnight' or 'midday' because 12.00 could mean either.

Noon is another word for midday.

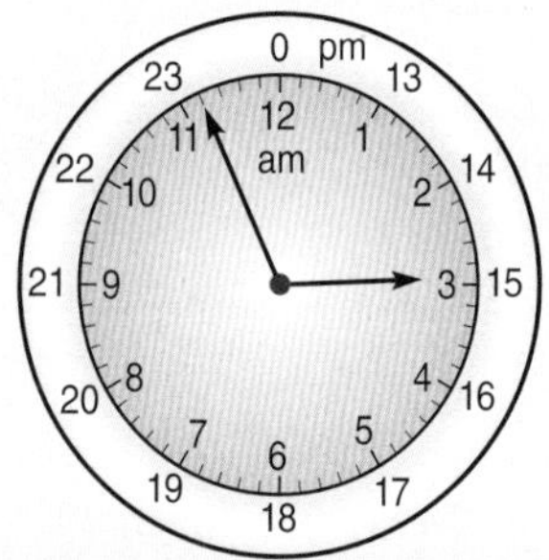

The time on this clock can be read as 2.56 pm or 1456 hr.

Exercise 15I

1 Look at this calendar.

Mon.	Tue.	Wed.	Thur.	Fri.	Sat.	Sun.
		1	2	3	4	5
6	7	8	9	10	11	12
13	14	15	16	17	18	19
20	21	22	23	24	25	26
27	28	29	30			

a Which month is this – August, September or October?

b Today is the 9th of the month. What day of the week is it?

c Today is the 24th of the month. What was the date a week ago today?

d The day after tomorrow is the third Wednesday of the month. What is the date today?

2 Elspeth goes on holiday on 8 June.
She returns on 21 June.
How many nights is she away?

3 David starts work on 1 September.
He gets paid on the twentieth of each month.
How many times does he get paid before Christmas?

4 The dates of birth of three people are:

Julie 14–3–93 Dennis 14–1–92 Johanne 14–8–93

a Who is the eldest?
b Who is the youngest?
c In which year will the youngest be 30?

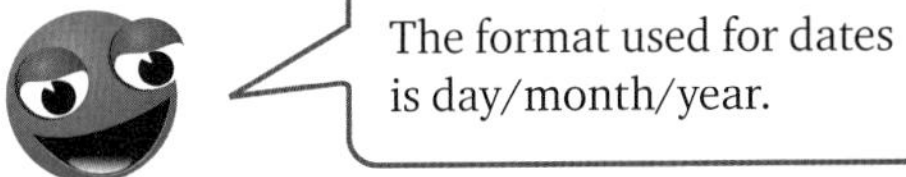

5 The president of the local cricket club is elected every year at the Annual General Meeting.
This is a list of the presidents since the club was formed.

1928–42	S. Green
1942–48	P. Cave
1948–57	D. S. Short
1957–74	P. Baldrick
1974–82	H. Anthony
1982–96	D. S Short
1996–99	W. May
1999–07	C. D. Bowen
2007–	O. D. Williams

a For how many years was P. Baldrick president?
b Who was president for the greatest number of years without a break?
c Assuming that O. D. Williams continues as president, which year will he be elected to begin his 15th year?

6 Write
a 190 minutes in hours and minutes
b 450 hours in days and hours.

7 Write
a 5 minutes and 8 seconds in seconds.
b $3\frac{1}{2}$ hours in minutes.

8 Find

a 20 minutes as a fraction of an hour

b 36 seconds as a fraction of an hour.

9 These clock faces show the time at the beginning and end of a history lesson.

a What time did the lesson start?

b What time did the lesson end?

c How long was the lesson?

Lesson begins   Lesson ends

10 My ferry is due at 5.34 pm.

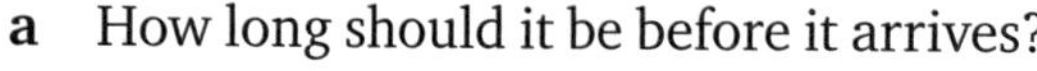

a How long should it be before it arrives?

b Write 5.34 pm in 24-hour time.

11 Find the number of hours and minutes between

a 9.30 a.m. and 11.15 a.m. the same day

b 8.30 a.m. and 5.10 p.m. the same day

c 10.20 p.m. and 12.30 a.m. the next day.

12 The time needed to cook a chicken is 40 minutes per kilogram plus 20 minutes. How long should it take to cook a $3\frac{1}{2}$ kg chicken?

13 Susan's bus is due at 2005 hr.

a How many minutes should she have to wait?

b Write 2005 hr as an a.m. or p.m. time.

14 Find the period of time between

a 0320 hours and 0950 hours on the same day.

b 0535 hours and 1404 hours on the same day.

c 2100 hours and 0500 hours next day.

d 0000 hours and 0303 hours next day.

15 A plane leaves Kingston for Port of Spain.

The flight should take 2 hours 10 minutes.

The plane leaves Kingston on time at 1450 hours and is 15 minutes late arriving in Port of Spain. When does the plane arrive in Port of Spain?

16 The bus service from Westwick to Plimpton runs twice a day. This is the timetable.

Westwick		0945	1420
Red Farm Hill		1004	1439
Astleton	arr	1056	1531
	dep	1116	1545
Morgan's Hollow		1129	1559
Plimpton		1207	1637

a How long does each bus take to go from Westwick to Plimpton?

b Which two bus stops do you think are closest together?

Give a reason for your answer.

Temperature

There are two commonly used units for measuring temperature.
One is degrees Celsius.

The freezing point of water is zero degrees Celsius. This is written 0 °C.
The boiling point of water is 100 degrees Celsius. This is written 100 °C.

The other unit is degrees Fahrenheit.
The freezing point of water is 32 degrees Fahrenheit. This is written 32 °F.
The boiling point of water is 212 °F.

Some thermometers have both scales on them.

Exercise 15m

1 **a** What is the temperature shown on this thermometer?

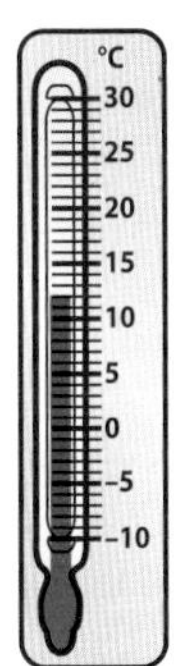

b What is the temperature shown on this thermometer?

c Which thermometer shows the higher temperature?

Give a reason for your answer.

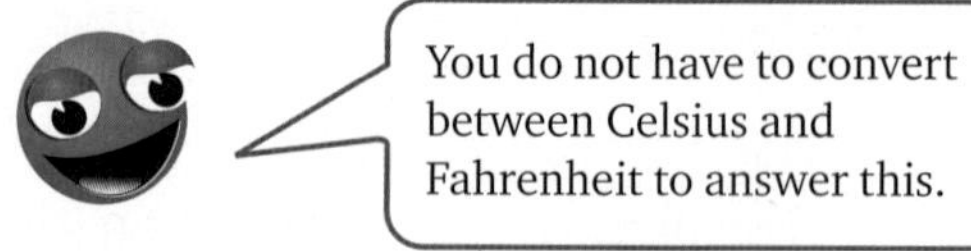

2 This thermometer is marked in degrees Fahrenheit and in degrees Celsius.

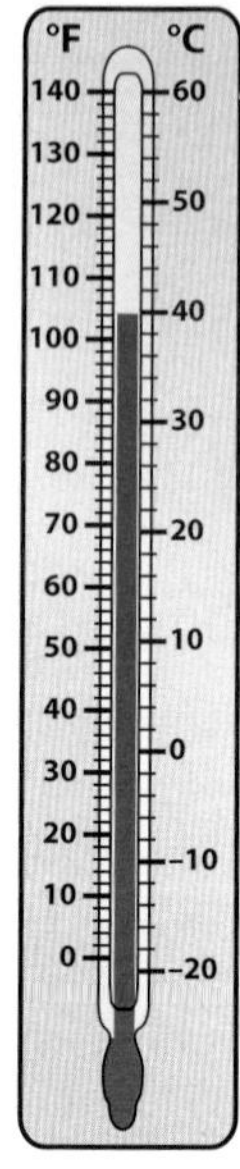

a What Fahrenheit temperature does the thermometer show?

b What Celsius temperature does the thermometer show?

The temperature goes down by 20 °C.

c What is the new Celsius reading?

d What is the new Fahrenheit reading?

3 Use the thermometer in question **2** to convert

a 10 °C to degrees Fahrenheit

b 5 °C to degrees Fahrenheit

c 80 °F to degrees Celsius

d 35 °F to degrees Celsius

4 In August 2003, the temperature in London reached a record high of 101 °F.

Use these instructions to convert 101 °F to degrees Celsius.

1 Subtract 32 °.

2 Divide your answer by 9.

3 Multiply your answer by 5.

Check your answer on the thermometer in question **2**.

5 The temperature in December in Scotland can go as low as −8 °C.

Use the thermometer in question **2** to convert −8 °C to degrees Fahrenheit.

6 Use these instructions to convert −8 °C to degrees Fahrenheit.

1 Multiply −8 by 9.

2 Divide your answer by 5.

3 Add 32 to your answer.

How does your result compare with your answer to question **5**?

Mixed exercises

Exercise 15n

Select the letter that gives the correct answer.

1 Expressed in metres, 3.75 kilometres is

A 37.5 m B 375 m C 3750 m D 37 500 m

2 Expressed in centimetres, 0.54 kilometres is

A 54 cm B 540 cm C 5400 cm D 54 000 cm

3 Expressed in kilometres, 24 700 millimetres is

A 0.0247 km B 0.247 km C 2.47 km D 24.7 km

4 In kilograms, 2.75 tonnes is equal to

A 27.5 kg B 275 kg C 2750 kg D 2800 kg

5 Expressed in miles, 40 kilometres is about

A 10 miles B 25 miles C 40 miles D 64 miles

6 The number of minutes in $2\frac{1}{4}$ hours is

A 125 B 135 C 140 D 145

Exercise 15p

Express the given quantity in terms of the unit in brackets:

1 236 cm (m)

2 0.02 m (mm)

3 5 kg (g)

4 500 mg (g)

5 4 km 250 m (km)

6 3.6 t (kg)

7 2 kg 350 g (kg)

8 2 g (mg)

9 Give 2 kg as an approximate number of pounds.

10 Use 1 inch ≈ 2.5 cm to give a rough conversion of 12 inches to cm.

Exercise 15q

Express the given quantity in terms of the unit in brackets:

1	5.78 t	(kg)	**5**	1 t 560 kg	(t)
2	£3.54	(p)	**6**	780 days	(years and days)
3	350 kg	(t)	**7**	$1\frac{1}{2}$ hours	(minutes)
4	0.155 mm	(cm)	**8**	2 km 50 m	(km)

9 A road sign in the UK says road works in 600 yards. Approximately how many metres is this?

10 Use 1 mile ≈ 1.6 km to convert 50 miles to an approximate number of kilometres.

Did you know?

Why are there 112 pounds in a hundredweight?

Years ago, when a farmer had to pay tithes (a tithe is a tenth part), he had to pay the church one tenth of what he produced. One tenth of 112 is 11.2. Take this from 112 and you're left with 100.8. Rounded down to the nearest whole number this is 100. So, to have 100 pounds of wheat to sell a farmer needed to bring 112 pounds from the field. This is why there are 112 pounds in a hundredweight.

In this chapter you have seen that...

✔ the metric units of length in common use are the kilometre, the metre, the centimetre and the millimetre, where

$$1\,\text{cm} = 10\,\text{mm}$$
$$1\,\text{m} = 100\,\text{cm}$$
$$1\,\text{km} = 1000\,\text{m}$$

✔ the metric units of mass in common use are the tonne, the kilogram, the gram and the milligram, where

$$1\,\text{g} = 1000\,\text{mg}$$
$$1\,\text{kg} = 1000\,\text{g}$$
$$1\,\text{t} = 1000\,\text{kg}$$

✔ common imperial units of length are inches (in), feet (ft), yards (yd), and miles and the relationships between them are

$$12\,\text{in} = 1\,\text{ft}$$
$$3\,\text{ft} = 1\,\text{yd}$$
$$1760\,\text{yd} = 1\text{ mile}$$

✔ common imperial units of mass are ounces (oz), pounds (lb), hundredweights (cwt) and tons and the relationships between them are

$$16\,\text{oz} = 1\,\text{lb}$$
$$112\,\text{lb} = 1\,\text{cwt}$$
$$20\,\text{cwt} = 1\text{ ton}$$

✔ the time of day can be measured as a.m. or p.m. times or as 24-hour time

✔ to change to a smaller unit, e.g. km to m, multiply

✔ to change to a larger unit, e.g. mm to cm, divide

✔ you can roughly convert between metric and imperial units using

$$1\,\text{kg} \approx 2\,\text{lb}$$
$$1\,\text{m} \approx 1\text{ yd}$$
$$5\text{ miles} \approx 8\,\text{km}$$

✔ degrees Celsius and degrees Fahrenheit are two different scales for measuring temperature. The freezing point of water is 0 °C and 32 °F. The boiling point of water is 100 °C and 212 °F.

16 Symmetry, reflections and translations

At the end of this chapter you should be able to...

1 identify lines of symmetry in given shapes

2 identify shapes which have rotational symmetry

3 draw lines of symmetry in given shapes

4 identify:

- **a** isosceles triangles
- **b** equilateral triangles
- **c** rhombuses
- **d** congruent shapes.

5 understand the meaning of reflection

6 understand the meaning of translation.

Did you know?

To most people symmetrical objects are a pleasure to look at. These shapes are all around us, whether they are man-made things like a plane or a suspension bridge, or shapes that occur in nature such as a snowflake or an open flower.

You need to know...

✔ how to use a ruler to draw straight lines

✔ how to use tracing paper.

Key words

congruent, equilateral, image, isosceles, line symmetry, line of symmetry, mirror line, object, parallel, reflection, rhombus, rotate, symmetry, triangle, translation

Line symmetry

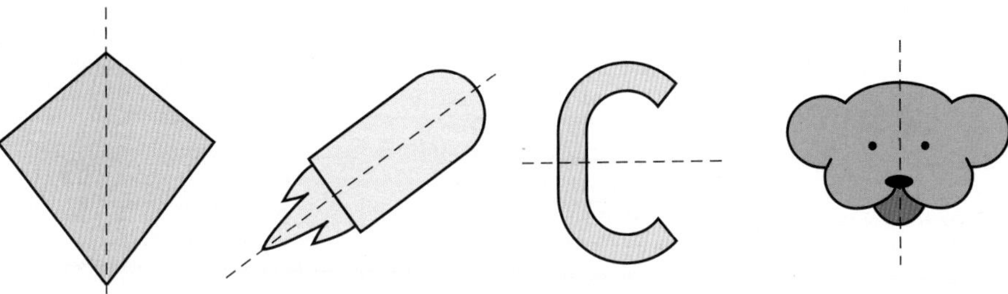

The four shapes above are *symmetrical*. If they were folded along the broken line, one half of the drawing would fit exactly over the other half.

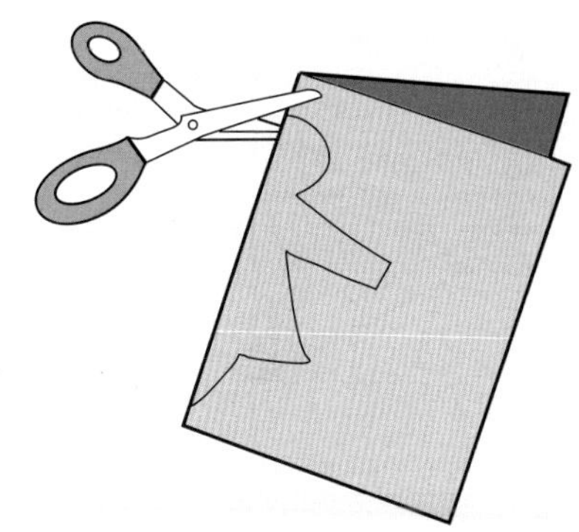

Fold a piece of paper in half and cut a shape from the folded edge. When unfolded, the resulting shape is symmetrical. The fold line is the *line of symmetry*.

Exercise 16a

Some of the shapes below have one line of symmetry and some have none.
State which of the drawings **1** to **6** have a line of symmetry.

1

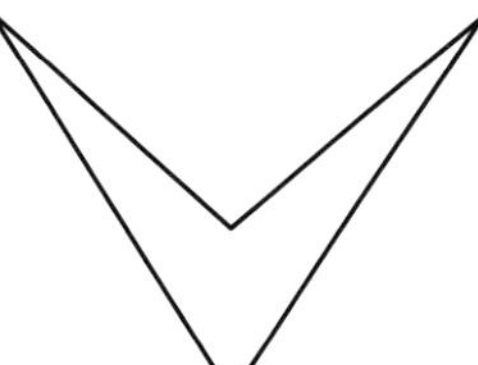

3

5

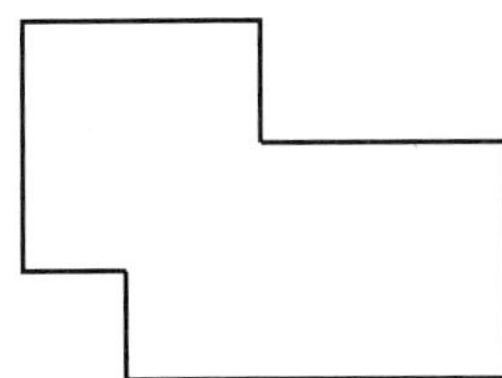

2

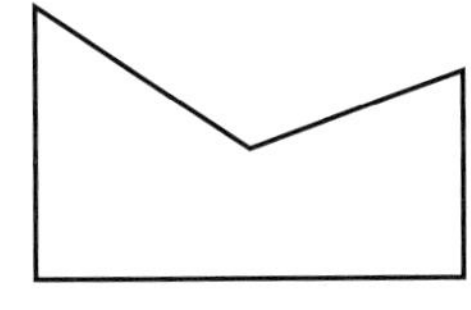

4

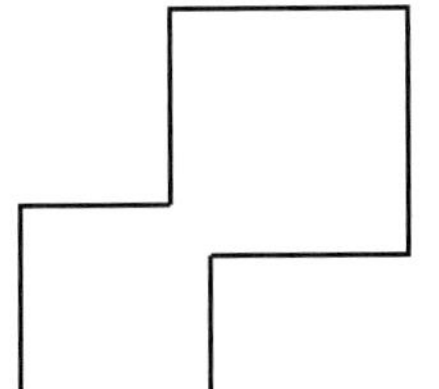

6

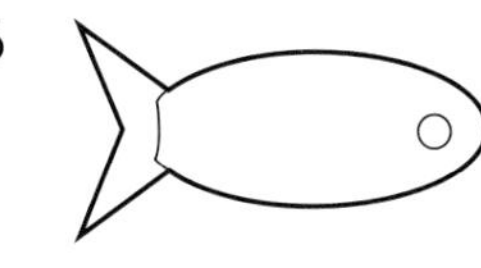

Copy the following drawings on square grid paper and complete them so that the broken line is the line of symmetry:

7

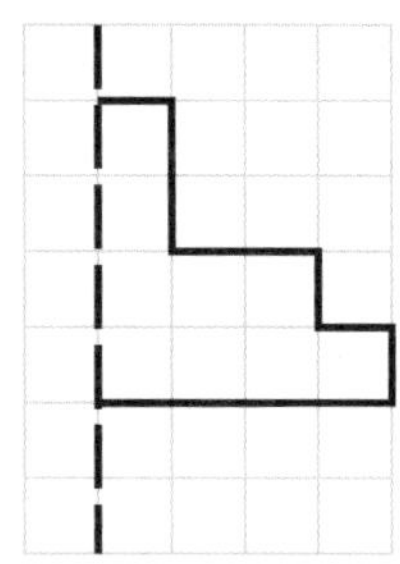

9

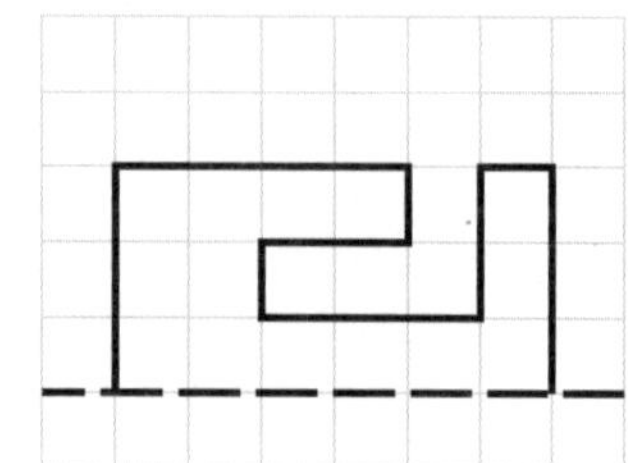

11

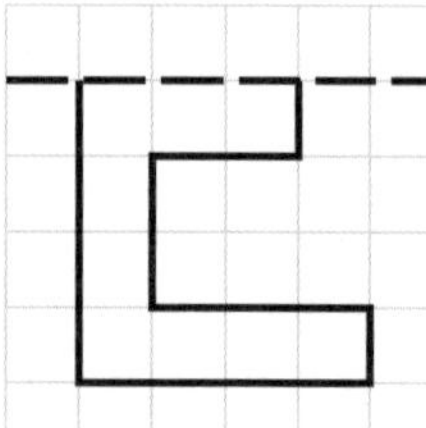

8

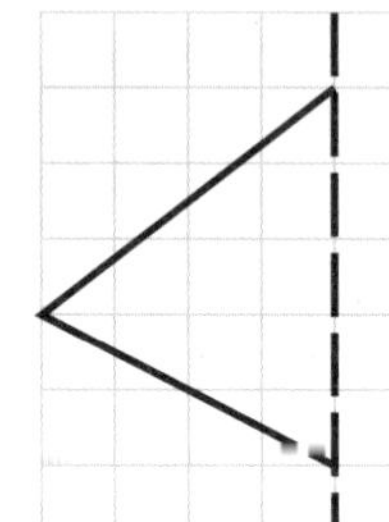

10

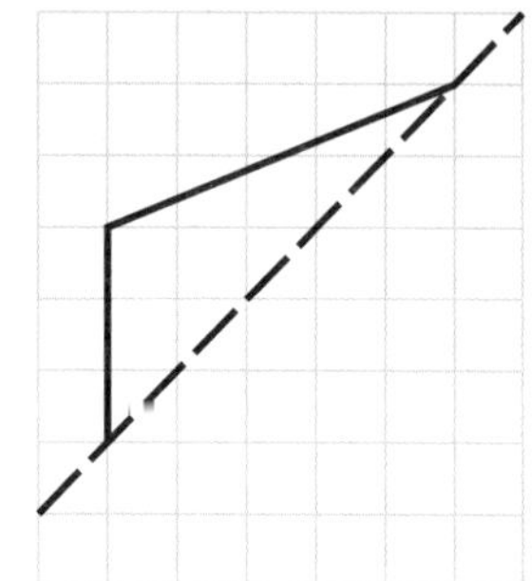

12

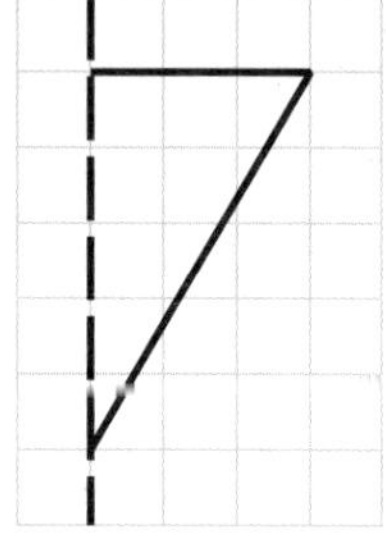

Congruency

This shape has a line of symmetry.

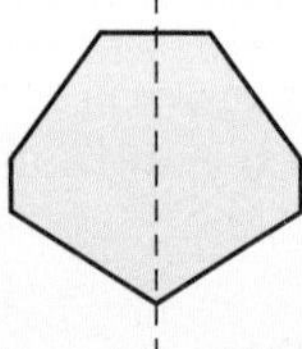

If we cut the shape along the line of symmetry, we get two identical shapes.

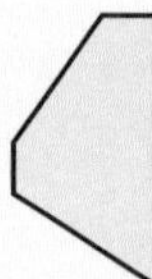

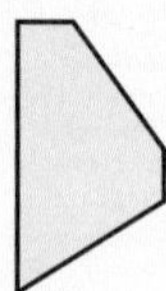

If we turn one over and rotate it, it is still identical to the other shape.

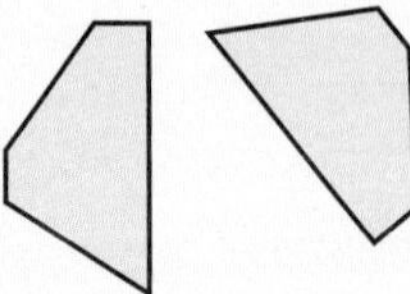

When two shapes are exactly the same shape and size, they are called *congruent* shapes.

Investigation

1 Which of these shapes are congruent?

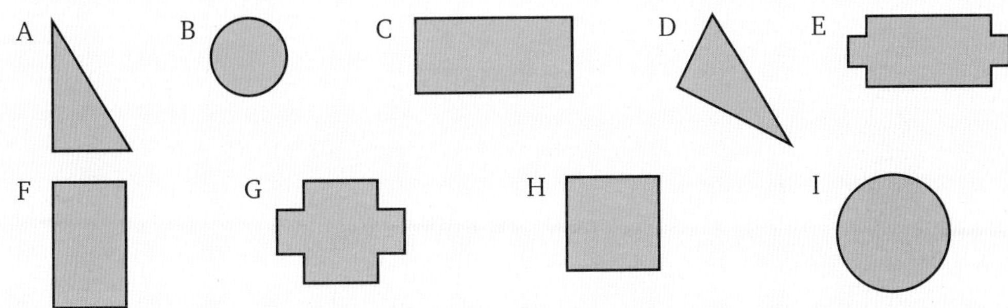

2 Draw a clock face without hands, like the one below.

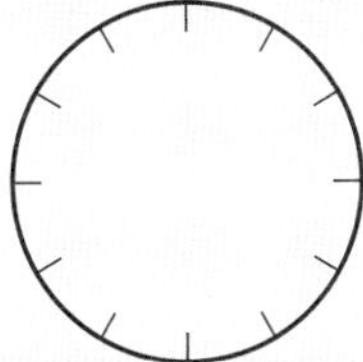

Although there are no figures on the clock face assume that the 12 is at the top, that is, in its normal position.

a How many lines of symmetry does this face have?

b How many lines of symmetry would it have if the position of the 12 was marked with a double line?

c Repeat parts **a** and **b** if the figures 1 to 12 are added to the face.

d The time on this clock face is 6 o'clock.

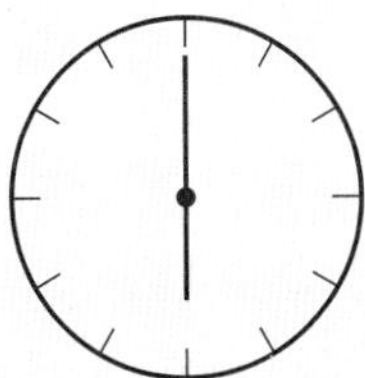

What we see is symmetrical about a vertical line drawn through the centre of the clock.

Can you find any other time when the position of the hands is symmetrical about this vertical line through the centre?

Would your answer be the same if the hour hand and minute hand were the same length?

Illustrate your answers with sketches.

e The sketch shows that the time is 2.25.

Make a copy and mark the position of the hour hand and the position of the minute hand when they are reflected in the broken line.

(It is probably better to do this in a different colour.)

Do the reflected hands give an acceptable time?

If so, what time is it?

f

Actual time	'Reflected' time
1.55	
2.50	
3.45	
4.40	
5.35	
6.30	
7.25	
8.20	
9.15	
10.10	
11.05	

Copy the table above and for each time shown

i draw this clock face and mark in the time

ii mark (in a different colour) the position of the hands if they are reflected in the broken line

iii complete the corresponding 'reflected' time in the table.

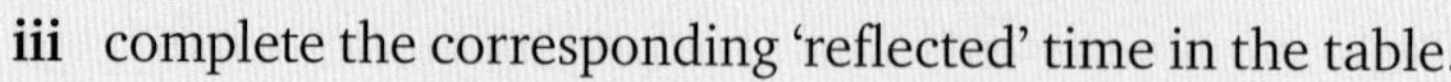

Can you see a connection between the actual times and the 'reflected' times?

g Copy this clock face and draw a horizontal broken line through the centre.

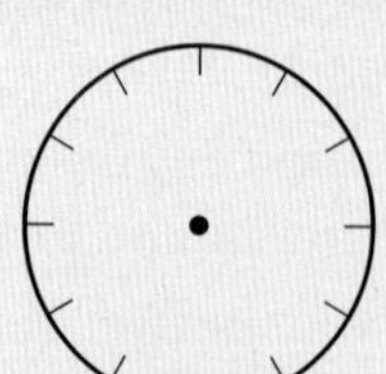

Mark the time 1.10.

Draw the position of the hands if they are reflected in the broken line.

Is the 'reflected' time an acceptable time?

Justify your answer.

Two lines of symmetry

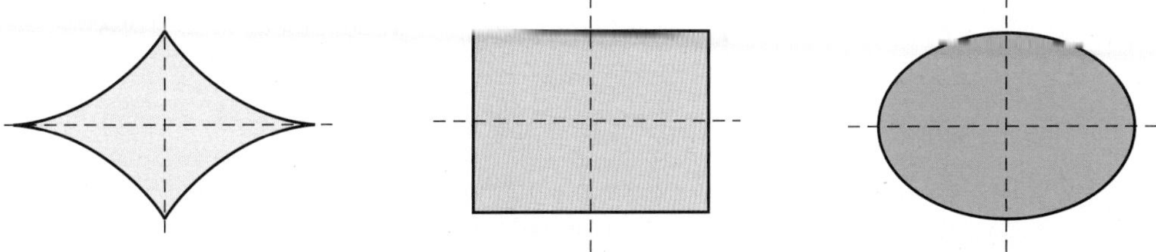

In these shapes there are two lines along which it is possible to fold the paper so that one half fits exactly over the other half.

Fold a piece of paper twice, cut a shape as shown and unfold it. The resulting shape has two lines of symmetry.

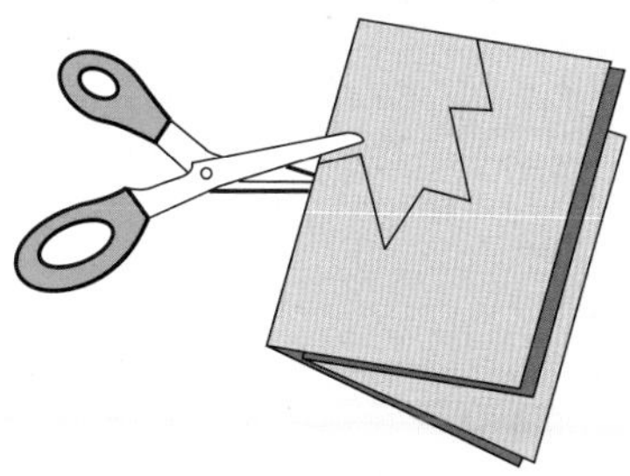

Exercise 16b

How many lines of symmetry are there in each of the following shapes?

1 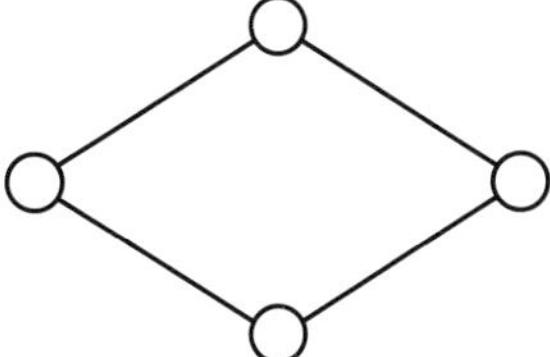

4 

2 

5 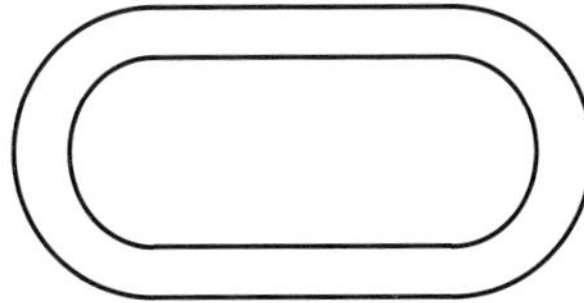

3 

6 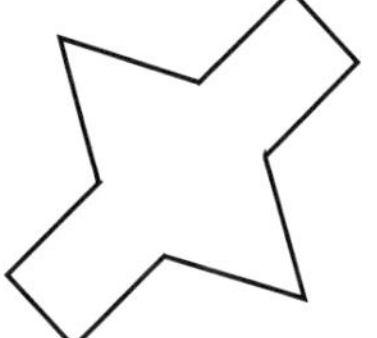

Copy the following drawings on square grid paper and complete them so that the two broken lines are the two lines of symmetry.

7

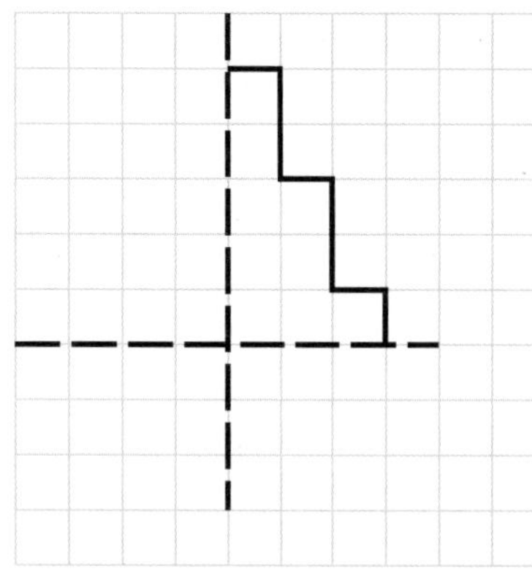

10

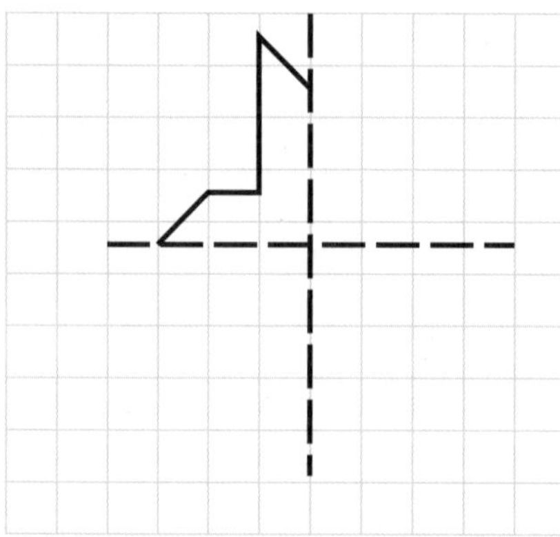

8

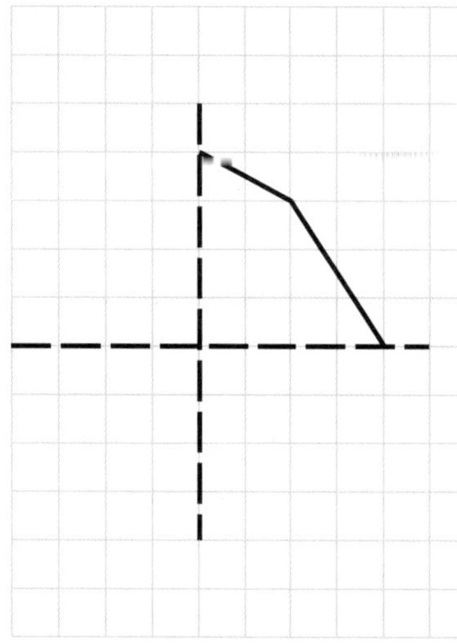

11

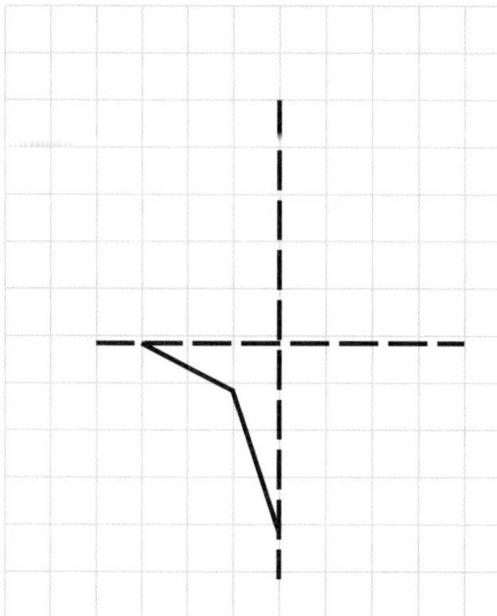

9

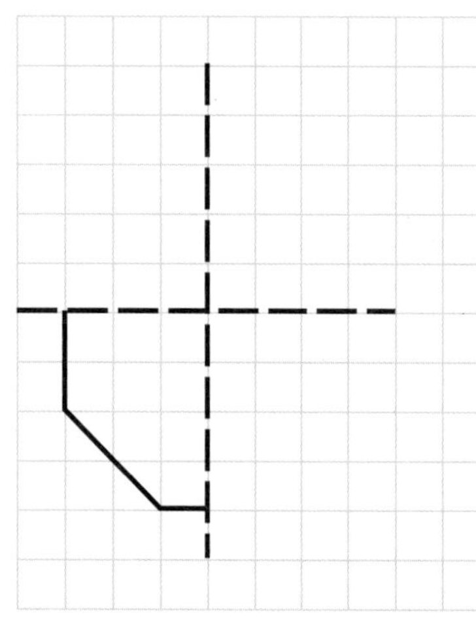

12

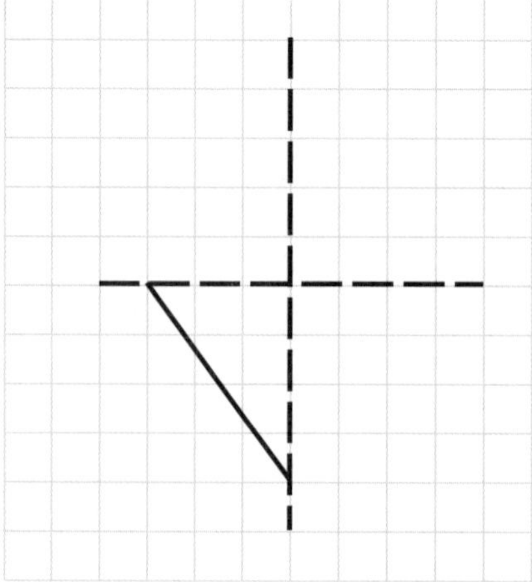

Three or more lines of symmetry

It is possible to have more than two lines of symmetry.

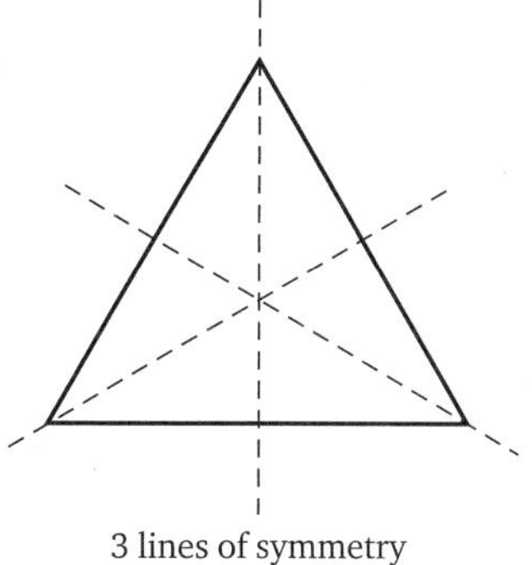

3 lines of symmetry

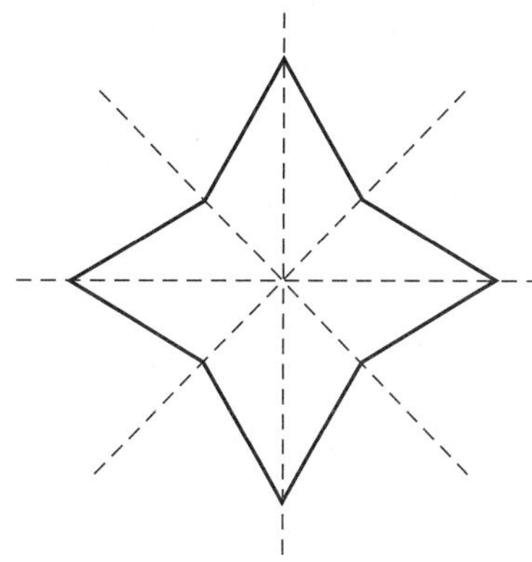

4 lines of symmetry

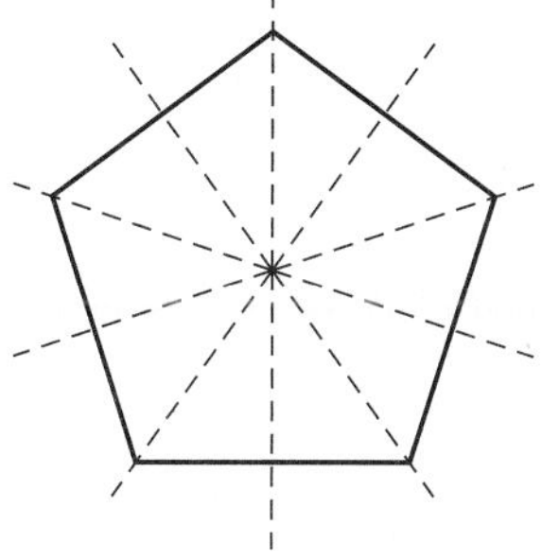

5 lines of symmetry

Exercise 16c

How many lines of symmetry are there for each of the following shapes?

1

2

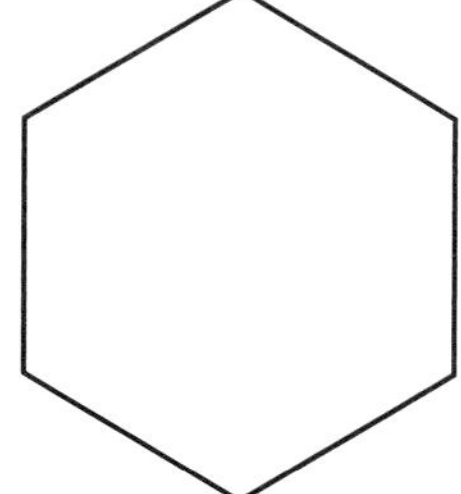

3

4

5

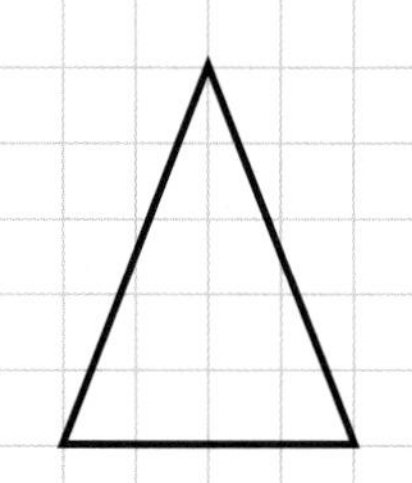

Copy the triangle on square grid paper and mark in the line of symmetry.

A triangle with a line of symmetry is called an *isosceles triangle.*

6

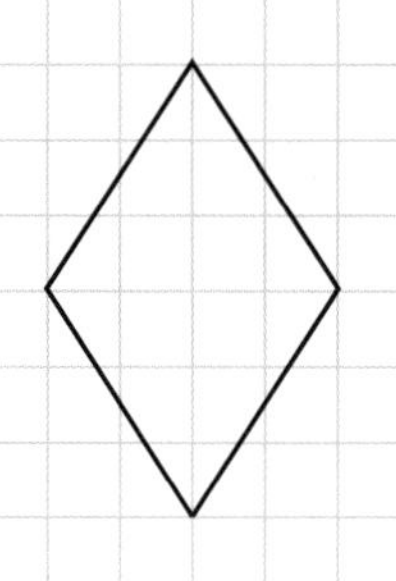

Copy the quadrilateral on square grid paper and mark in the two lines of symmetry.

This quadrilateral (which has four equal sides) is called a *rhombus*.

7 Trace the triangle. Draw in its lines of symmetry.

Measure its three sides.

This triangle is called an *equilateral triangle*.

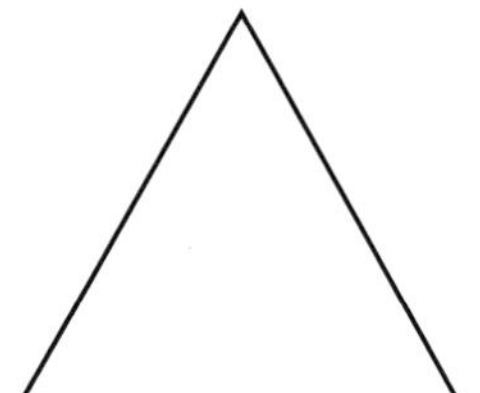

Activity

Fold a square piece of paper twice then fold it a third time along the broken line. Cut a shape, simple or complicated, and unfold the paper. How many lines of symmetry does it have?

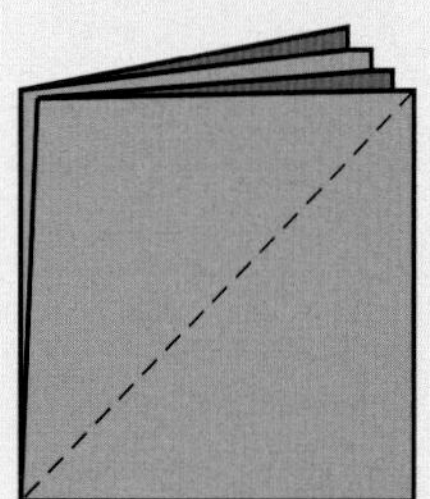

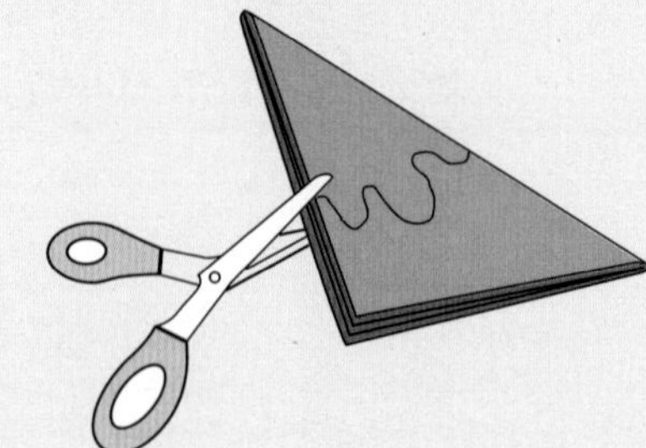

Investigation

Two squares can be put together to give just one shape that has at least one line of symmetry.

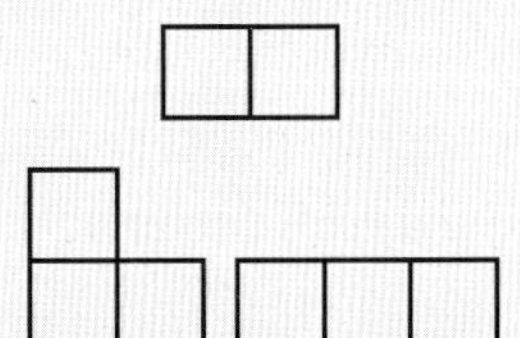

There are two ways in which three squares can be arranged to give shapes that have at least one line of symmetry.

Investigate how many different shapes can be made that have at least one line of symmetry, when 4, 5, 6, … squares are used to make a shape.

Is there any connection between the number of squares used and the number of different shapes that satisfy the given condition?

Reflections

Consider a piece of paper, with a drawing on it, lying on a table. Stand a mirror upright on the paper and the reflection can be seen as in the picture.

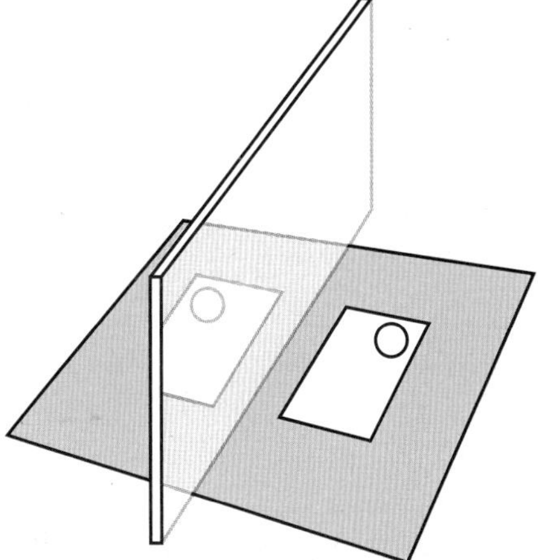

If we did not know about such things as mirrors, we might imagine that there were two pieces of paper lying on the table like this:

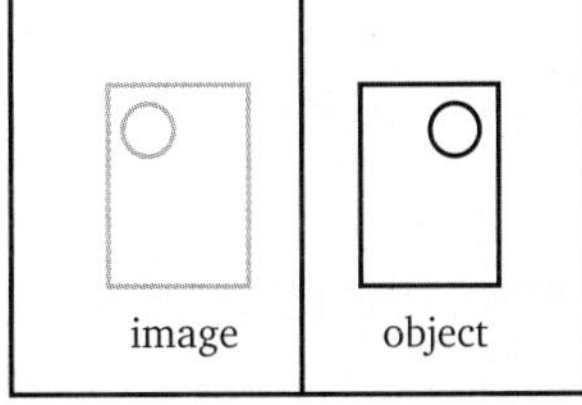

The *object* and the *image* together form a symmetrical shape and the *mirror line* is the line of symmetry.

Exercise 16d

In this exercise it may be helpful to use a small rectangular mirror, or you can use tracing paper to trace the object and turn the tracing paper over, to find the shape of the image.

Copy the objects and mirror lines (indicated by dotted lines) on to square grid paper and draw the image of each object.

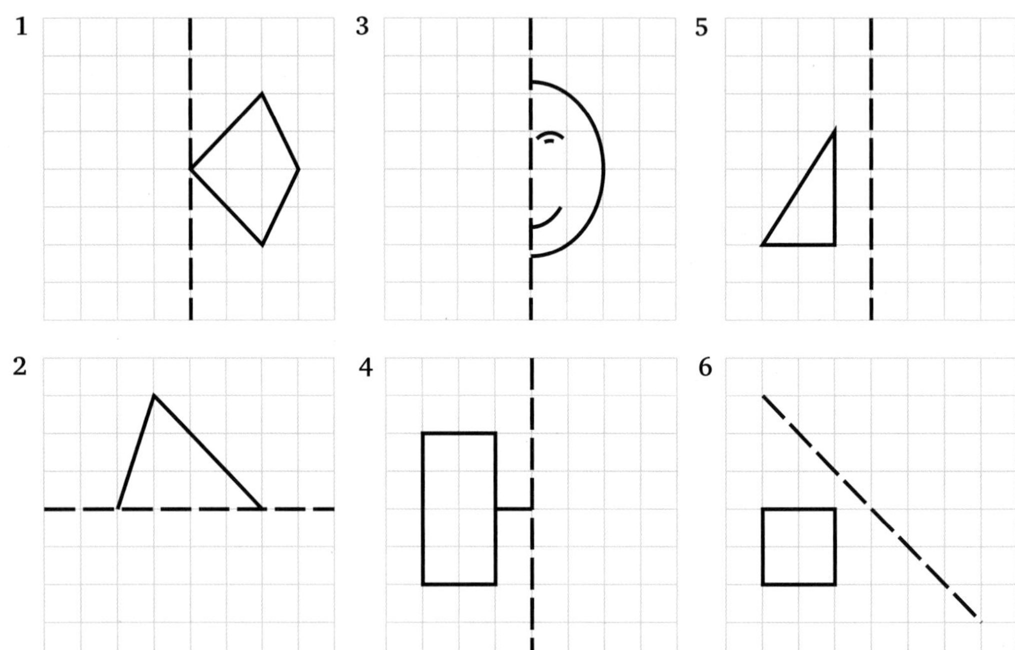

Copy triangle ABC and the mirror line on to square grid paper. Draw the image. Label the corresponding vertices (corners) of the image A′, B′, C′.

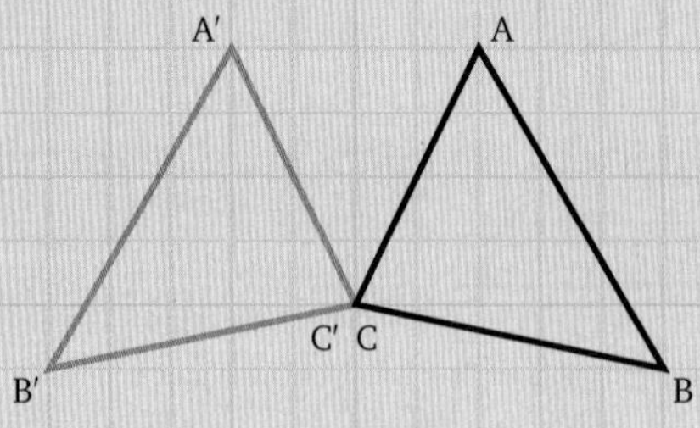

(In this case C and C′ are the same point.)

In each of the following questions, copy the object and the mirror line on to square grid paper. Draw the image. Label the vertices of the object A, B, C, etc. and label the corresponding vertices of the image A′, B′, C′, etc.

7

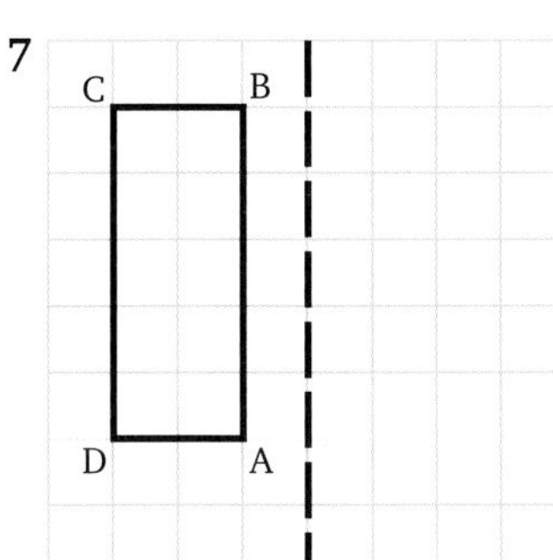

8

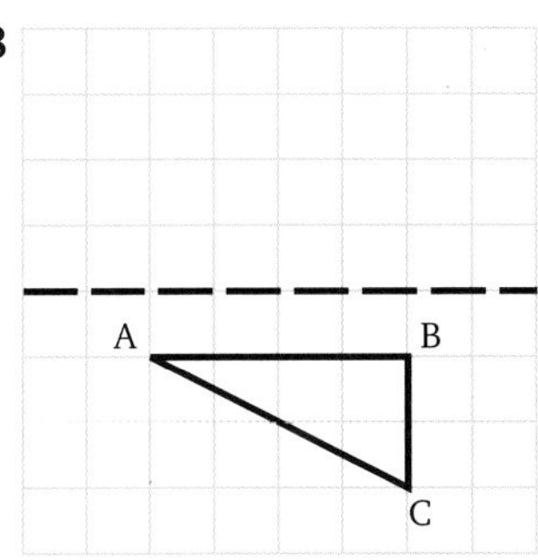

9

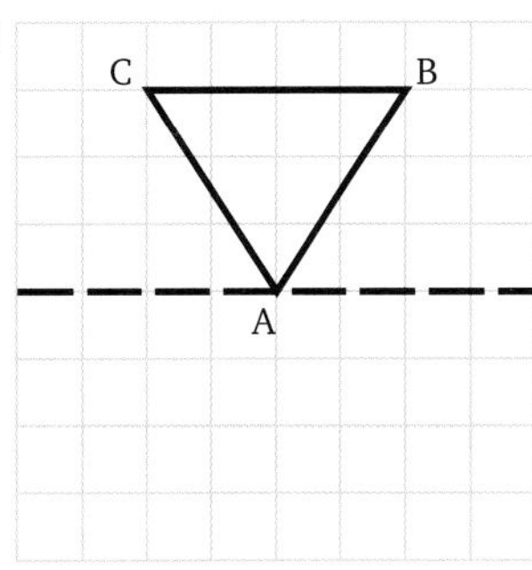

In mathematical reflection, though not in real life, the object can cross the mirror line.

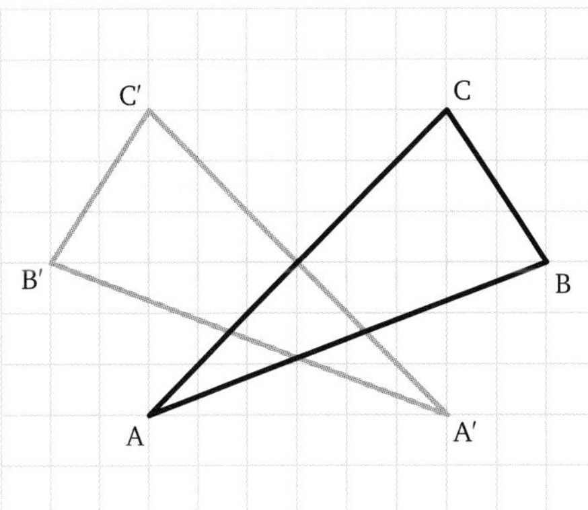

10

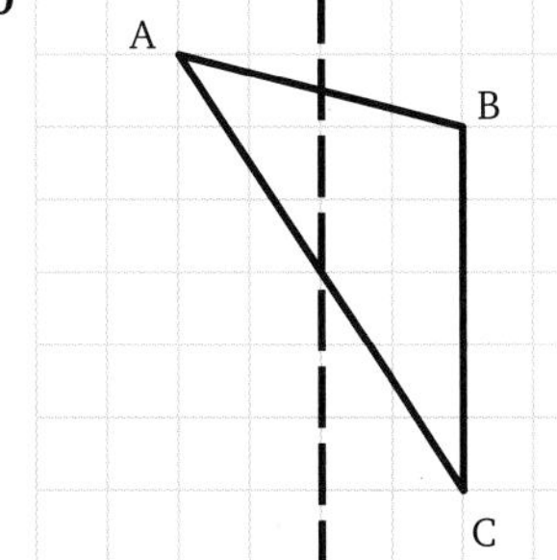

12

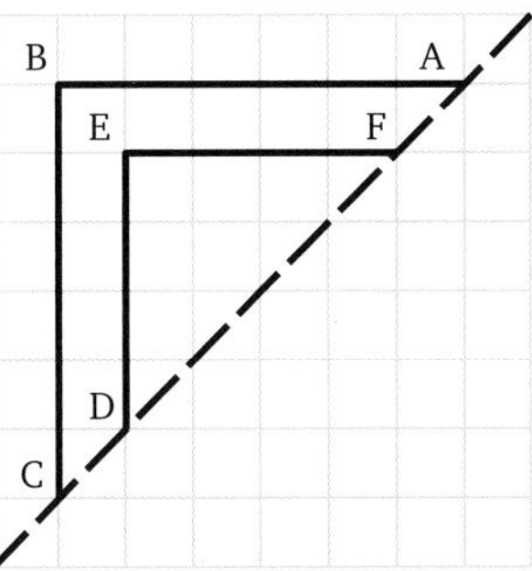

14

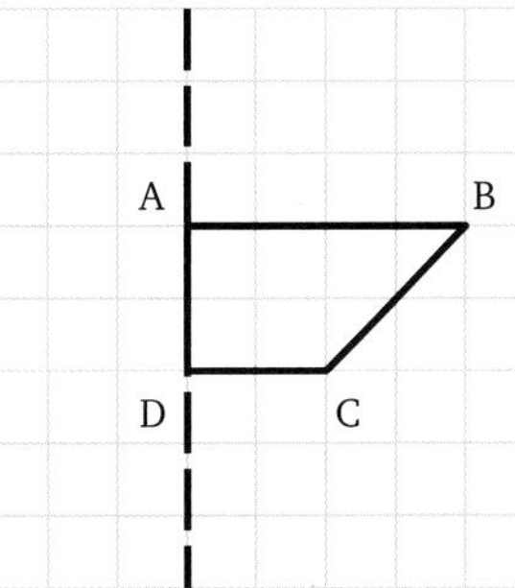

11

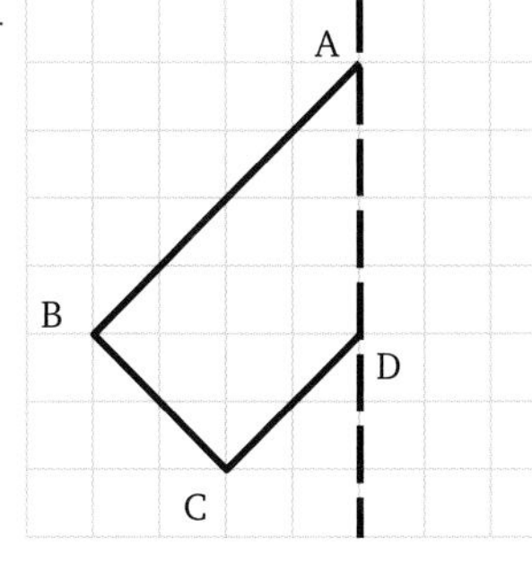

13

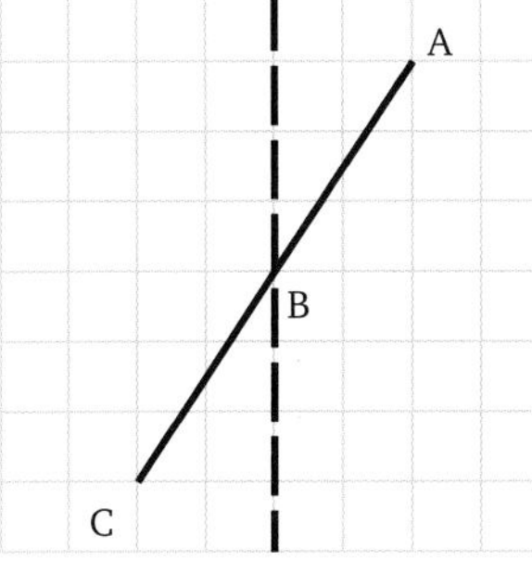

15

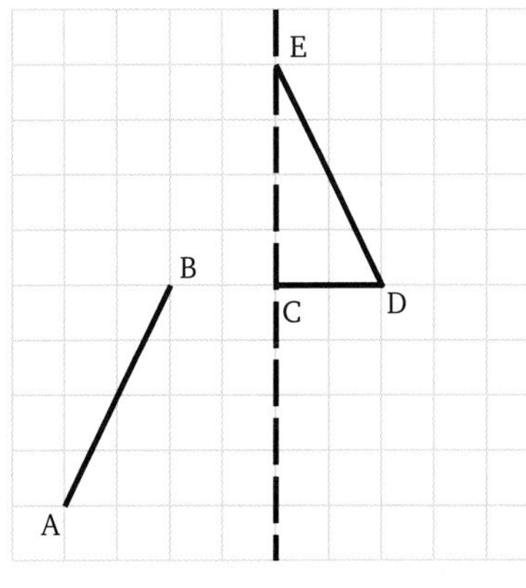

16

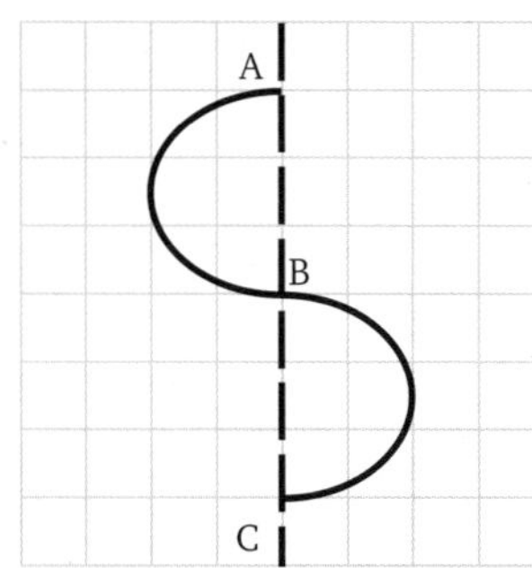

17

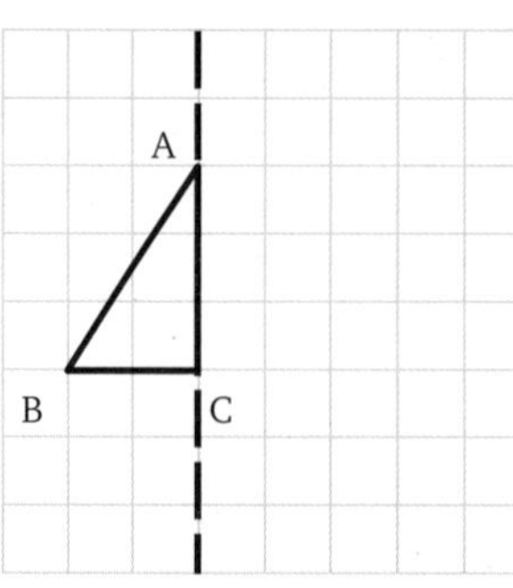

18

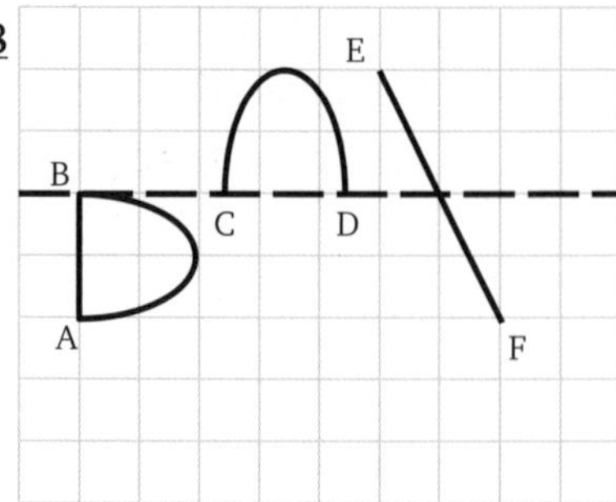

19 Which points in questions **7** to **18** are labelled twice? What is special about their positions?

20 In the diagram for question **10**, join A and A′.

a Measure the distances of A and A′ from the mirror line. What do you notice?

b At what angle does the line AA′ cut the mirror line?

21 Repeat question **20** on other suitable diagrams, in each case joining each object point to its image point. What conclusions do you draw?

Translations

Consider the movements in the diagram:

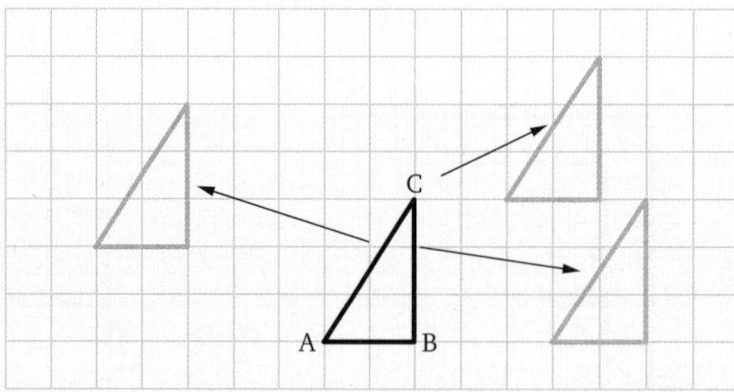

All these movements are of the same type. The side AB remains parallel to the horizontal grid lines and the triangle continues to face in the same direction. This type of movement is called a *translation*.

Although not a reflection we still use the words *object* and *image*.

Exercise 16e

1 In the following diagram, which images of $\triangle ABC$ are given by translations?

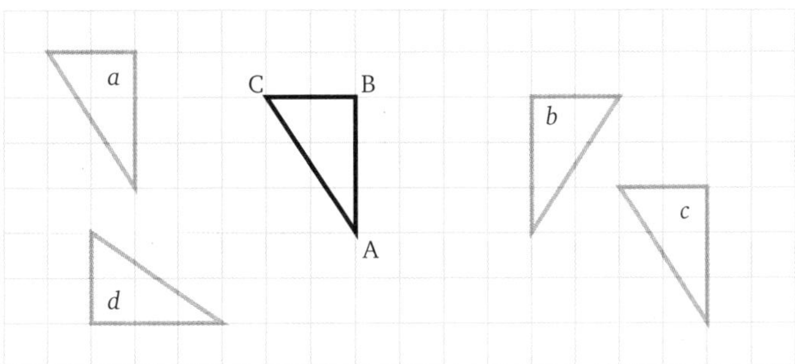

2 In the following diagram, which images of $\triangle ABC$ are given by a translation, which by a reflection and which by neither?

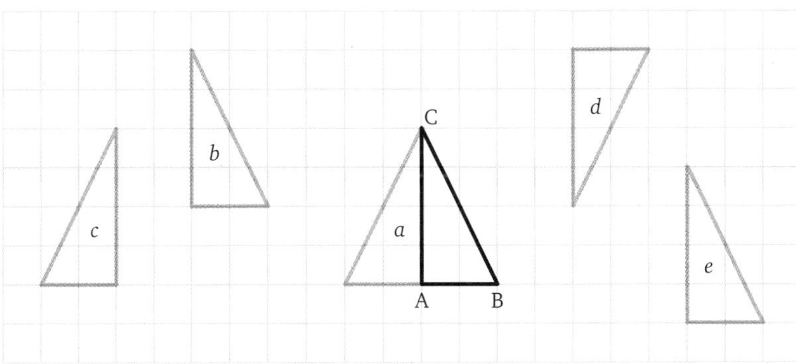

Draw sketches to illustrate the following translations:

3 An object is translated 6 cm to the left.

4 An object is translated 4 cm to the right.

5 An object is translated 3 m due north.

6 An object is translated 5 km south-east.

7

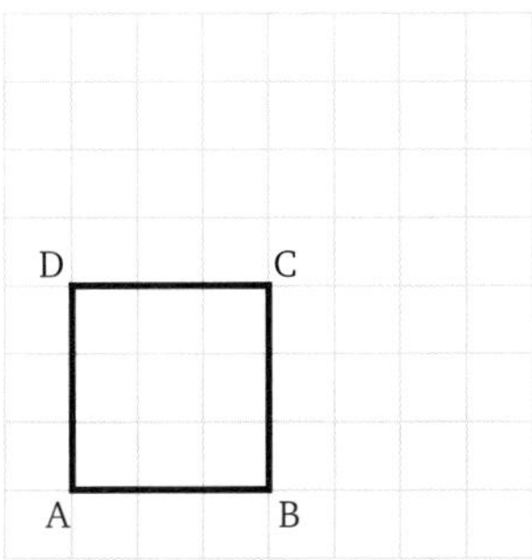

a Square ABCD is translated parallel to AB a distance equal to AB. Sketch the diagram and draw the image of ABCD.

b Square ABCD is translated parallel to AC a distance equal to AC. Sketch the diagram and draw the image of ABCD.

Mixed exercise

Exercise 16f

Select the letter that gives the correct answer.

1 How many lines of symmetry does this equilateral triangle have?

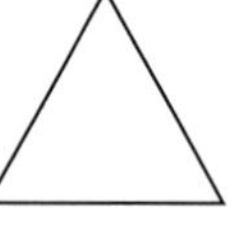

A 0 **B** 1 **C** 2 **D** 3

2 How many lines of symmetry does this square have?

A 1 **B** 2 **C** 3 **D** 4

3 How many lines of symmetry does this regular pentagon have?

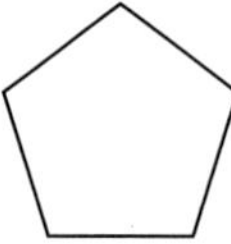

A 1 **B** 4 **C** 5 **D** 6

4

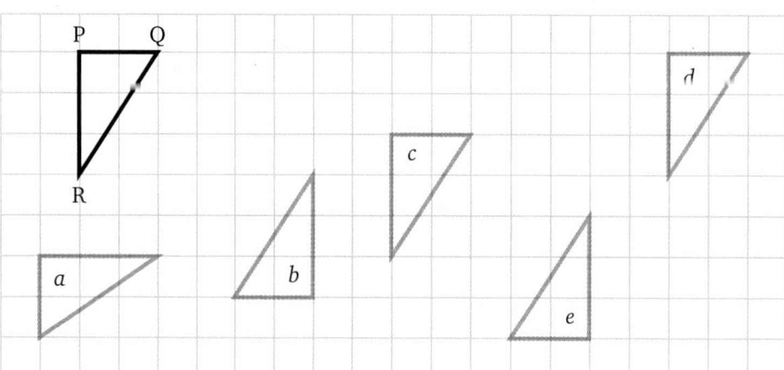

Which images of triangle PQR are given by a translation?

A *a* and *b* **B** *a* and *c* **C** *b* and *e* **D** *c* and *d*

5 Which letter shows a translation of the square PQRS 4 squares to the right and 4 squares down?

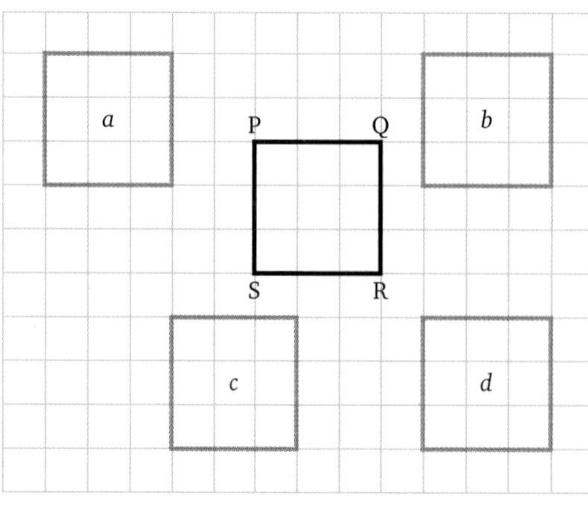

A *a* **B** *b* **C** *c* **D** *d*

6 Which triangles are a reflection of triangle PQR?

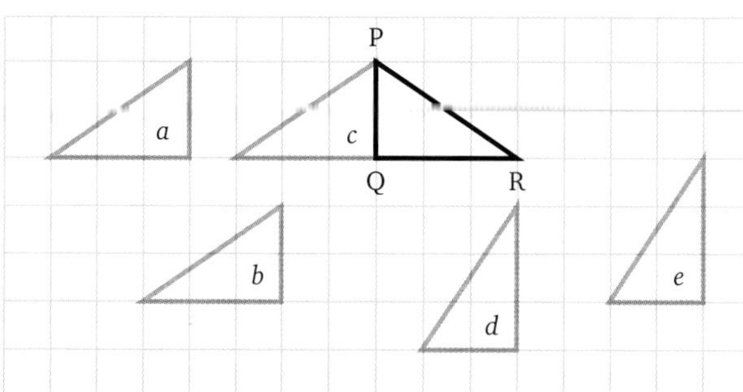

A *a* and *b* **B** *a* and *c* **C** *b* and *d* **D** *d* and *e*

7 Which letter indicates a square that is not the result of a reflection of square PQRS in a mirror line?

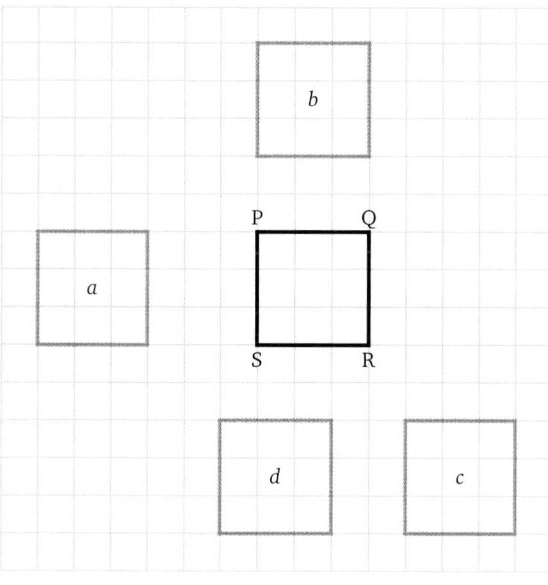

A *a* **B** *b* **C** *c* **D** *d*

Did you know?

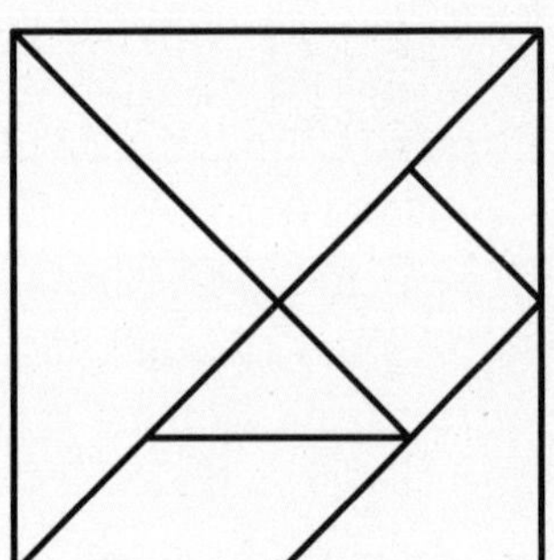

What is a tangram?

A tangram is a puzzle composed of seven parts called tans. The tans are formed by cutting a square and its interior into five triangles, a square and a parallelogram.

Measure all angles of the tans. What do you find?

Find the areas of a large triangle and a small triangle. What is the relationship?

Can you find other relationships?

Tangram play began in China and was introduced into the western world during the 1800s. John Q. Adams and Edgar A. Poe are said to have enjoyed tangrams.

The object of the puzzle is to put the seven tans together to form outlines of all sorts. Use all the pieces, and do not overlap the tans.

It is said that tangrams contain serious as well as playful mathematics.

In this chapter you have seen that...

- ✔ congruent shapes are exactly the same shape and size
- ✔ many shapes have more than one line of symmetry
- ✔ when an object is reflected in a mirror line, the object and the image are symmetrical about the mirror line
- ✔ a translation moves an object without turning it or reflecting it.

17 Area and perimeter

At the end of this chapter you should be able to...

1. identify area as a measure of the amount of surface enclosed by the given shape
2. find an approximate area of a shape by counting the number of equal squares enclosed by the shape
3. identify a unit square as a square with side of unit length
4. use the unit square as the unit of measure for area
5. calculate the area of a square given the length of its side
6. calculate the area of a rectangle given its length and width
7. calculate the area of a compound rectilinear plane figure
8. identify the distance around a given shape as its perimeter
9. calculate the perimeter of a figure given the necessary measurements of its sides
10. calculate the number of squares, of given size, required to cover a given rectangle
11. convert from one metric unit of area to another.

Did you know?

The original definition of a metre was the length of a platinum–iridium bar kept in controlled conditions in Paris, but in 1960 it was redefined as the length of the path travelled by light in a vacuum in an interval of $\frac{1}{299\,792\,458}$ of a second.

You need to know...

- ✔ how to multiply and divide by 10, 100, 1000, ...
- ✔ the multiplication tables up to 10×10
- ✔ how to multiply fractions.

Key words

area, perimeter, rectangle, square, square centimetre, square kilometre, square metre, square millimetre

Counting squares

The *area* of a shape or figure is the amount of surface enclosed within the lines which bound it. Below, six letters have been drawn on squared paper.

We can see by counting squares, that the area of the letter E is 15 squares.

Exercise 17a

What is the area of:

1 the letter T **2** the letter H?

What is the approximate area of the letter A?

Sometimes the squares do not fit exactly on the area we are finding. When this is so we count a square if more than half of it is within the area we are finding, but exclude it if more than half of it is outside.

By counting squares in this way the approximate area of the letter A is 13 squares.

What is the approximate area of:

3 the letter P **4** the letter O?

The next set of diagrams shows the outlines of three leaves.

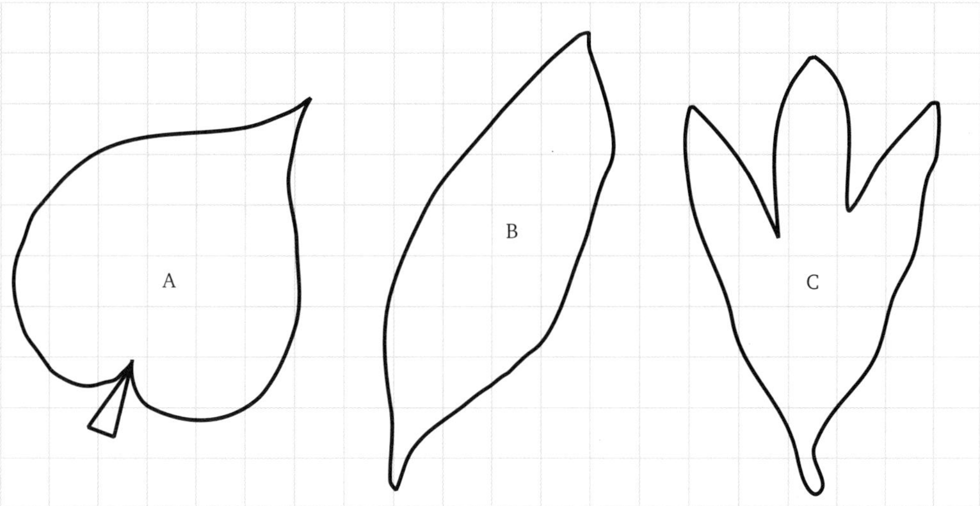

By counting squares find the approximate area of:

5 the leaf marked A

6 the leaf marked B

7 the leaf marked C.

8 Which leaf has

a the largest area

b the smallest area?

In each of the following questions find the area of the given figure by counting squares:

The following method may be used to find the area:

1 Count the number of complete squares.

2 Count the number of incomplete squares and divide this number by 2.

3 Add the results obtained in steps **1** and **2** above.

The answer is the required area.

9

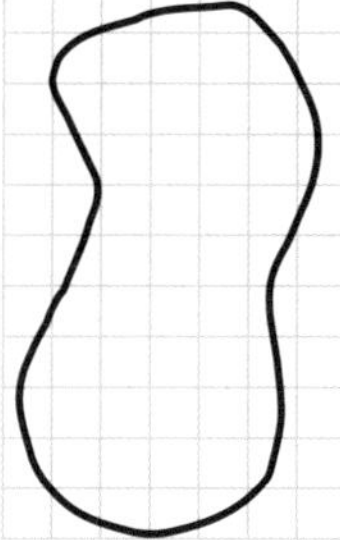

10

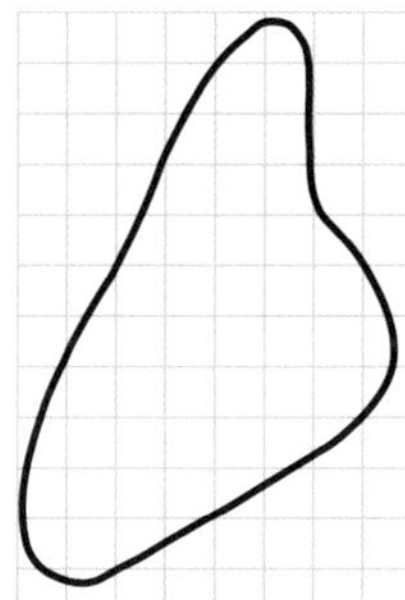

11

12

13

14

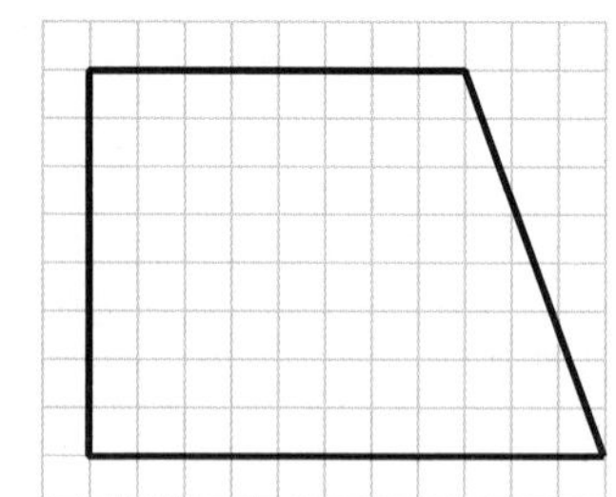

15

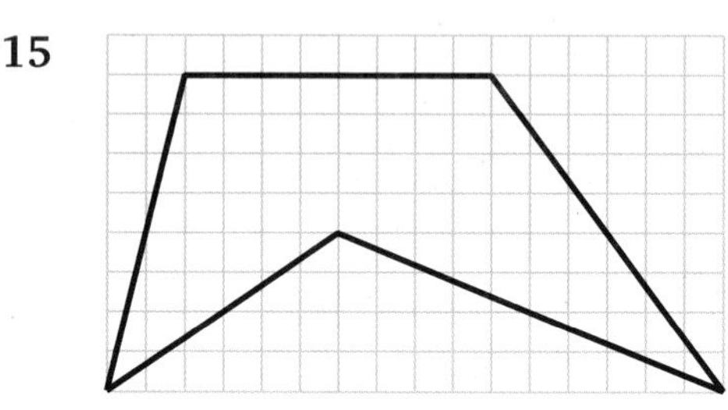

16

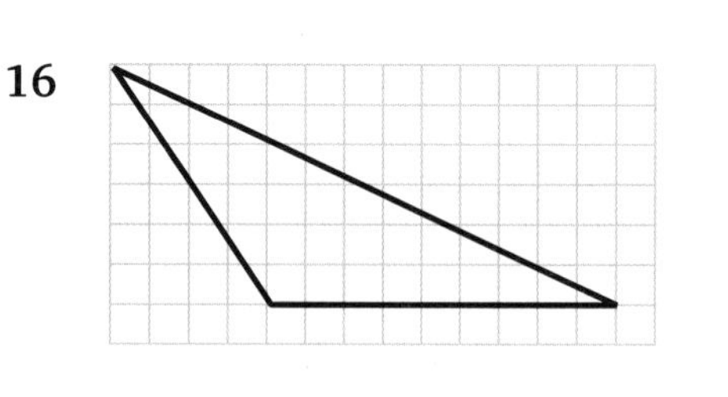

Puzzle

A man has a square swimming pool in his garden with a concrete post at the outside on each corner as shown.

He wants to double the area of his pool and still keep it square, so that none of the posts have to be moved and are still outside the pool.

How can he do this?

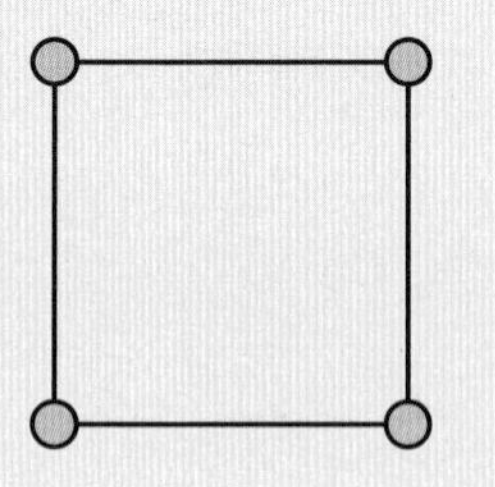

Units of area

There is nothing special about the size of square we have used. If other people are going to understand what we are talking about when we say that the area of a certain shape is 12 squares, we must have a square or unit of area which everybody understands and which is always the same.

A metre is a standard length and a square with sides 1 m long is said to have an area of one *square metre*. We write one square metre as $1\,m^2$. Other agreed lengths such as millimetres, centimetres and kilometres, are also in use. The unit of area used depends on what we are measuring.

We could measure the area of a small coin in *square millimetres* (mm^2), the area of the page of a book in *square centimetres* (cm^2), the area of a roof in square metres (m^2) and the area of an island in *square kilometres* (km^2).

Area of a square

The square is the simplest figure of which to find the area. If we have a square whose side is 4 cm long it is easy to see that we must have 16 squares, each of side 1 cm, to cover the given square,

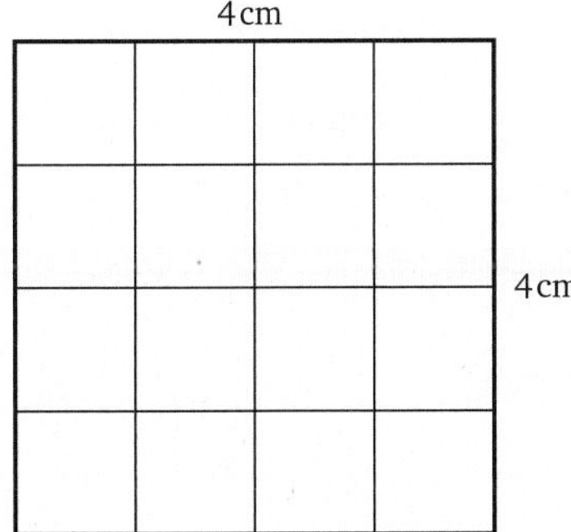

i.e. the area of a square of side 4 cm is 16 cm^2.

Area of a rectangle

If we have a rectangle measuring 6 cm by 4 cm we require 4 rows each containing 6 squares of side 1 cm to cover this rectangle,

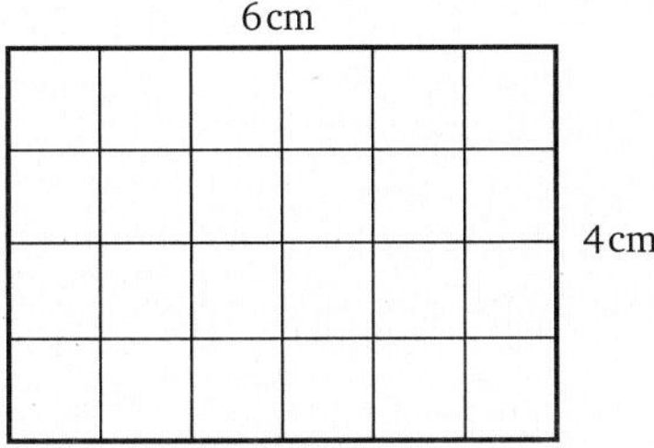

i.e. the area of the rectangle $= 6 \times 4\ cm^2$

$= 24\ cm^2$

A similar result can then be found for a rectangle of any size; for example a rectangle of length 4 cm and breadth $2\frac{1}{2}$ cm has an area of $4 \times 2\frac{1}{2}\ cm^2$.

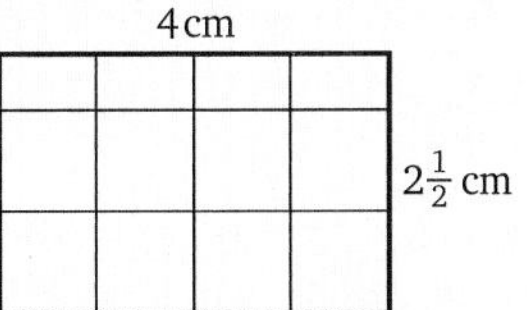

In general, for any rectangle

$$\text{area} = \text{length} \times \text{breadth}$$

Exercise 17b

Find the area of each of the following shapes, clearly stating the units involved:

1 A square of side 2 cm

2 A square of side 8 cm

3 A square of side 10 cm

4 A square of side 5 cm

5 A square of side 1.5 cm

6 A square of side 2.5 cm

7 A square of side 0.7 m

8 A square of side 1.2 cm

9 A square of side $\frac{1}{2}$ km

10 A square of side $\frac{3}{4}$ m

11 A rectangle measuring 5 cm by 6 cm

12 A rectangle measuring 6 cm by 8 cm

13 A rectangle measuring 3 m by 9 m

14 A rectangle measuring 14 cm by 20 cm

15 A rectangle measuring 1.8 mm by 2.2 mm

16 A rectangle measuring 35 km by 42 km

17 A rectangle measuring 1.5 m by 1.9 m

18 A rectangle measuring 4.8 cm by 6.3 cm

19 A rectangle measuring 95 cm by 240 cm

20 A rectangle measuring 150 mm by 240 mm

Compound figures

Exercise 17c

You can often find the area of a figure by dividing it into two or more rectangles.

Find the area of the following figure.

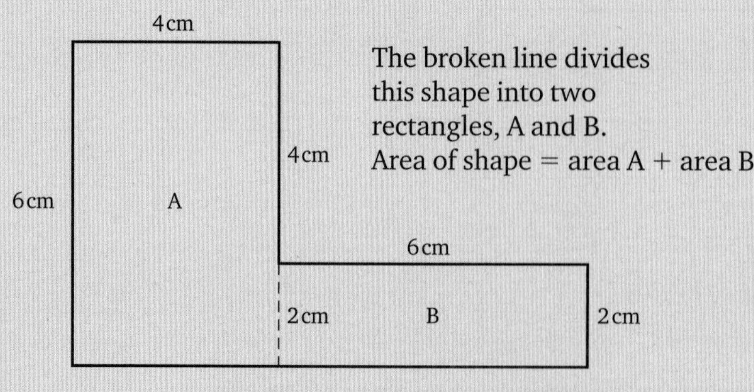

Area of A $= 6 \times 4\,\text{cm}^2 = 24\,\text{cm}^2$

Area of B $= 6 \times 2\,\text{cm}^2 = 12\,\text{cm}^2$

Therefore area of whole figure $= 24\,\text{cm}^2 + 12\,\text{cm}^2 = 36\,\text{cm}^2$.

Find the areas of the following figures by dividing them into rectangles.

1

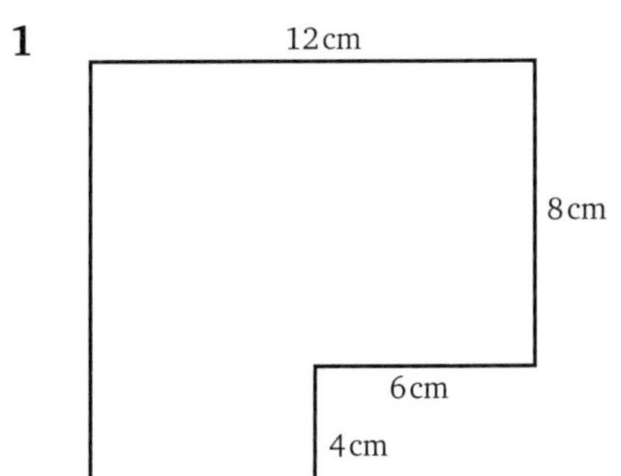

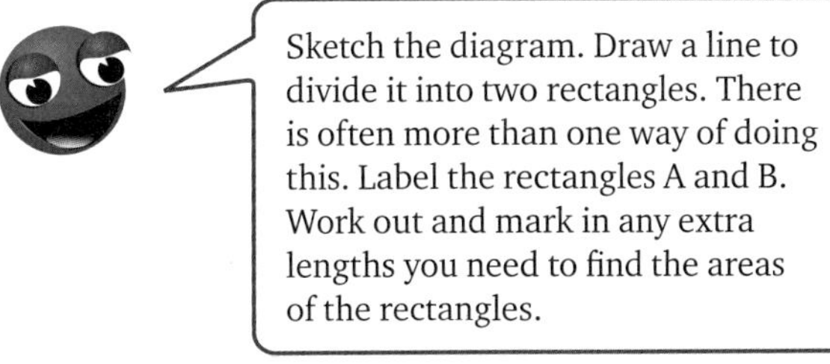

2

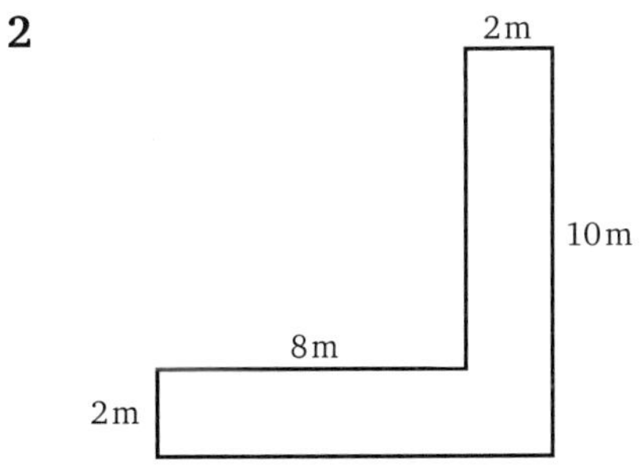

3

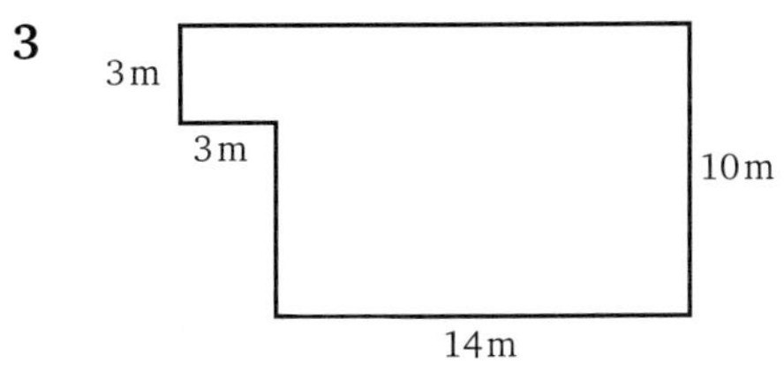

4

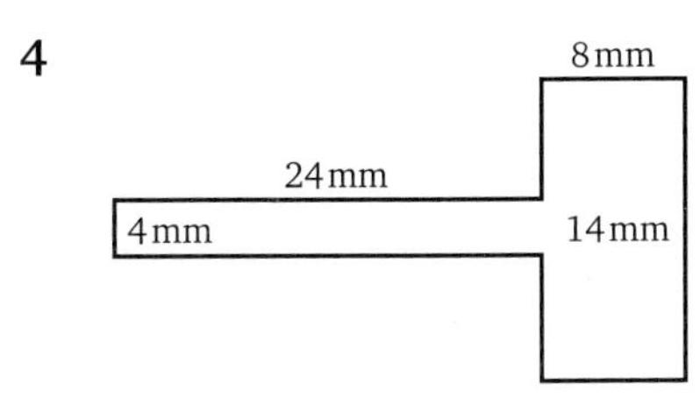

5

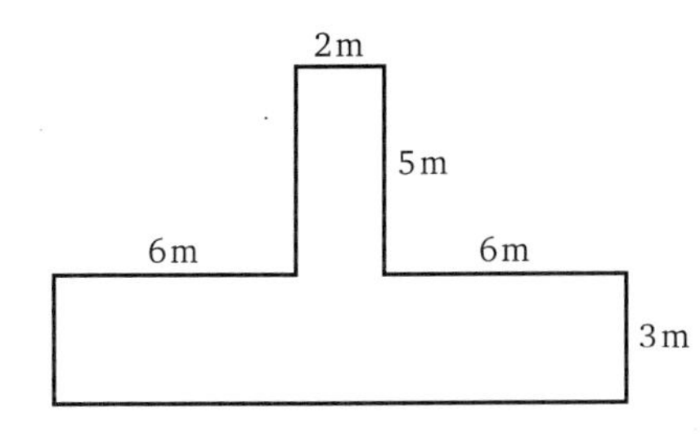

6

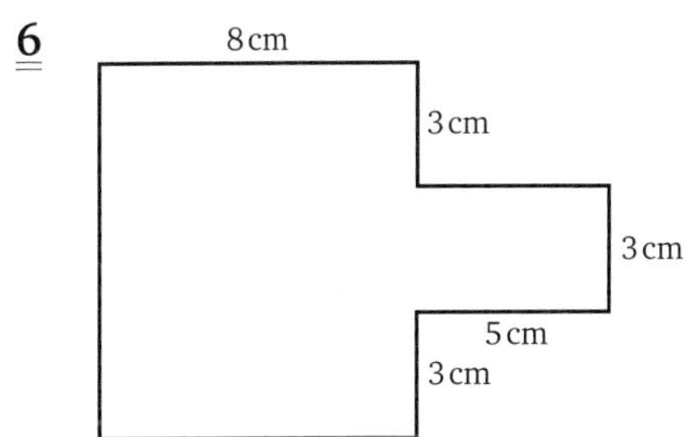

7

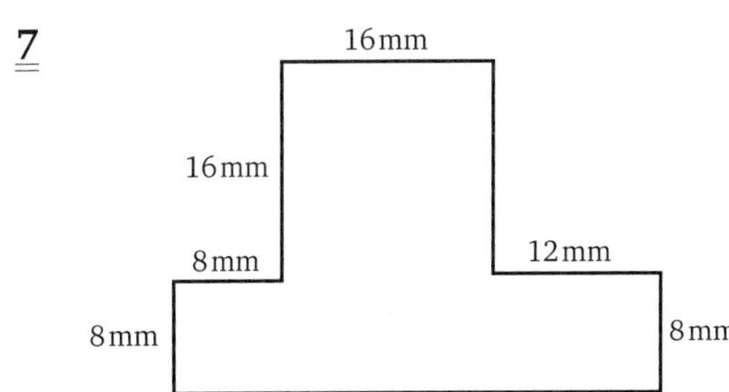

8

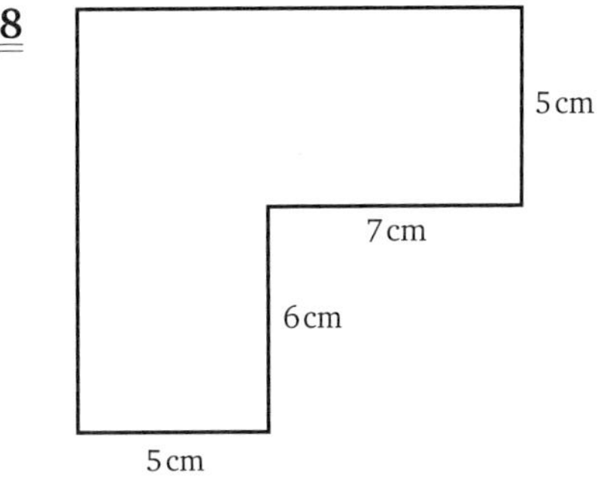

9

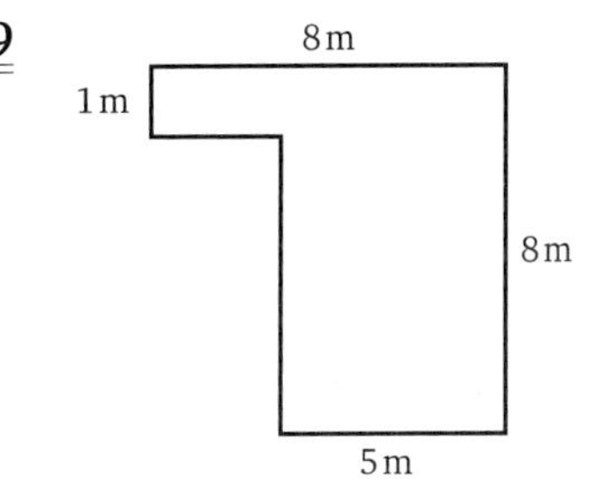

10

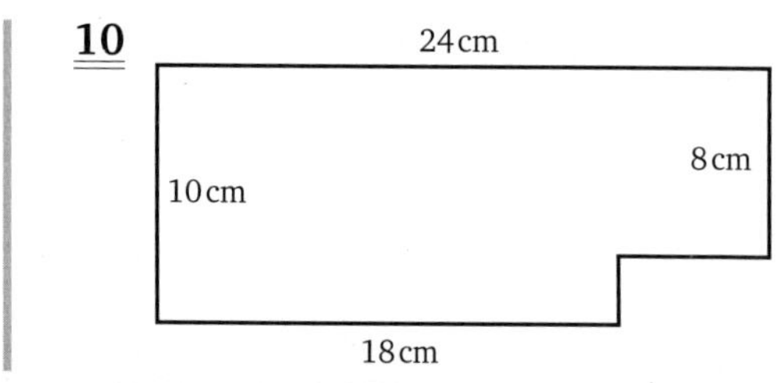

Puzzle

A farmer has a square field. He has already planted a quarter of the field with sugar cane as shown in the diagram. He now wants to divide the remainder of the field into four equal plots all the same size and shape. How will he do it?

Perimeter

The *perimeter* is the distance around a shape. The distance is found by measuring the total lengths of all its sides.

The perimeter of the square on page 315 is

$$4\text{ cm} + 4\text{ cm} + 4\text{ cm} + 4\text{ cm} = 16\text{ cm}$$

Exercise 17d

Find the perimeter of each shape given in Exercise **17b**, clearly indicating units.

If we are given a rectangle whose perimeter is 22 cm and told that the length of the rectangle is 6 cm it is possible to find its breadth and its area.

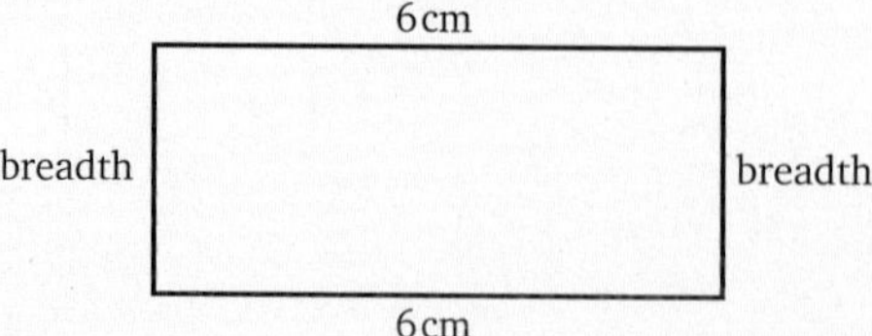

The two lengths add up to 12 cm so the two breadths add up to (22 – 12) cm = 10 cm.

Therefore the breadth is 5 cm.

The area of this rectangle $= 6 \times 5\text{ cm}^2$
$= 30\text{ cm}^2$

Exercise 17e

The following table gives some of the measurements for various rectangles.
Fill in the values that are missing:

	Length	Breadth	Perimeter	Area
1	4 cm		12 cm	
2	5 cm		14 cm	
3		3 m	16 m	
4		6 mm	30 mm	
5	6 cm			30 cm²
6	12 m			120 m²
7		4 km		36 km²
8		7 mm		63 mm²
9		5 cm	60 cm	
10	21 cm			1680 cm²

Problems

Exercise 17f

Find for the following figure

a the perimeter **b** the area.

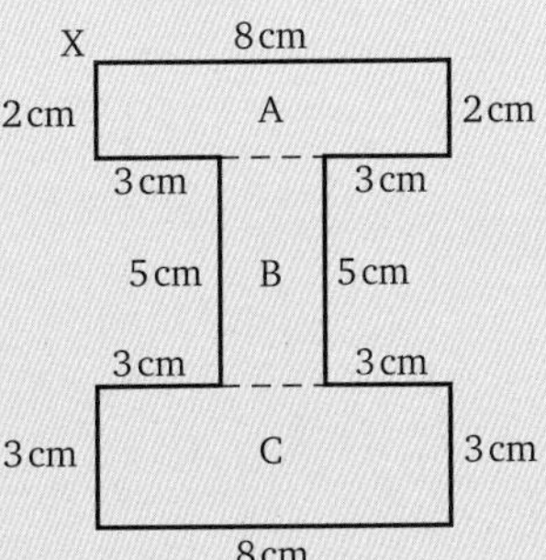

a Starting at X, the distance all round the figure and back to X is

$8 + 2 + 3 + 5 + 3 + 3 + 8 + 3 + 3 + 5 + 3 + 2$ cm $= 48$ cm.

Therefore the perimeter is 48 cm.

b Divide the figure into three rectangles A, B and C.

Then the area of A $= 8 \times 2\,\text{cm}^2 = 16\,\text{cm}^2$

the area of B $= 5 \times 2\,\text{cm}^2 = 10\,\text{cm}^2$

and the area of C $= 8 \times 3\,\text{cm}^2 = 24\,\text{cm}^2$

Therefore the total area $= (16 + 10 + 24)\,\text{cm}^2 = 50\,\text{cm}^2$.

Find for each of the following figures

a the perimeter **b** the area.

1

6cm
6cm
4cm
4cm

2

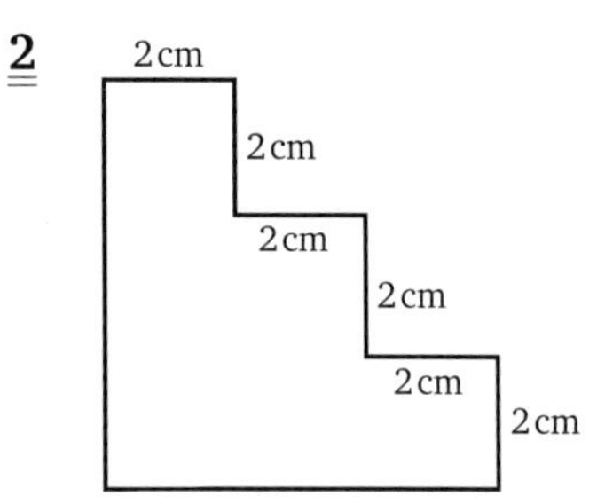

3

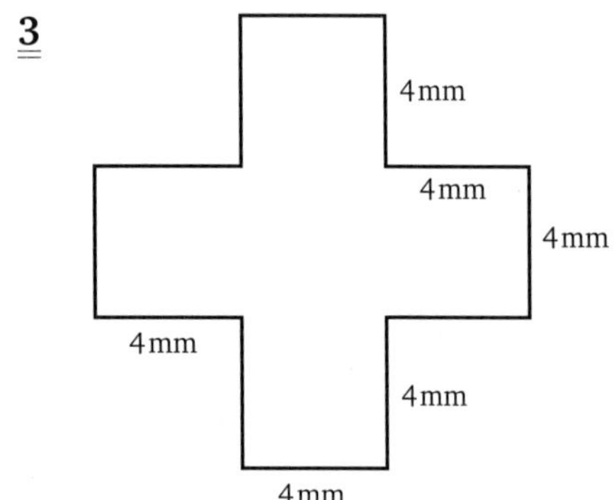

4

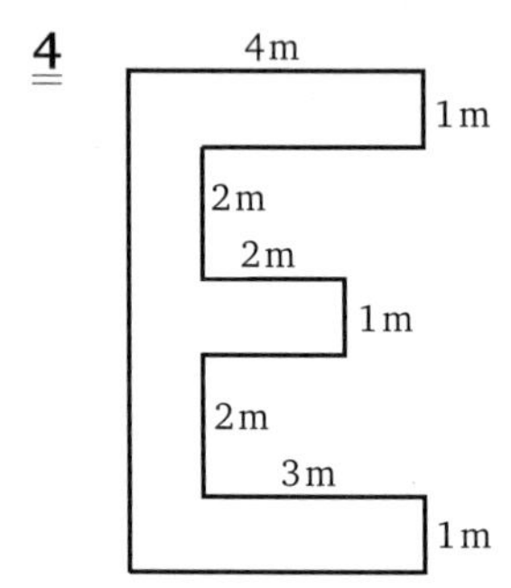

5

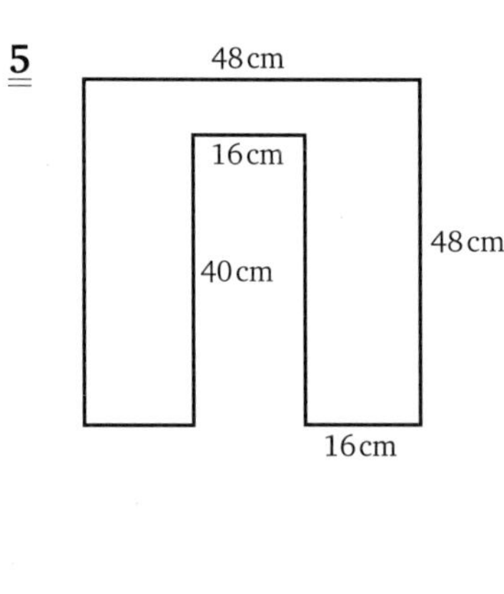

Find the areas of the following figures in square centimetres.
The measurements are all in centimetres.

6 10, 6, 6, 4

8 3, 15, 3, 14

You can divide this into two rectangles.

7 12, 4, 4, 12

9

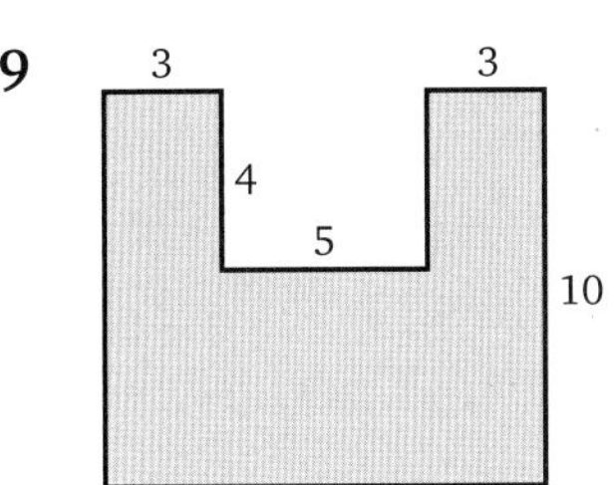

In each of the following figures find the area that is shaded:

10

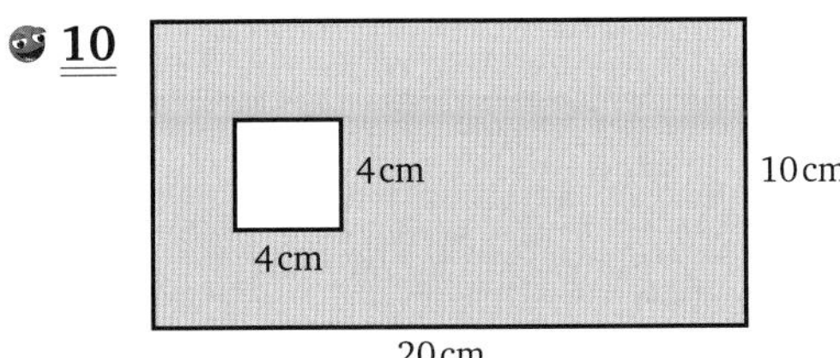

You can subtract the area of the centre 'hole' from the area of the larger rectangle.

11

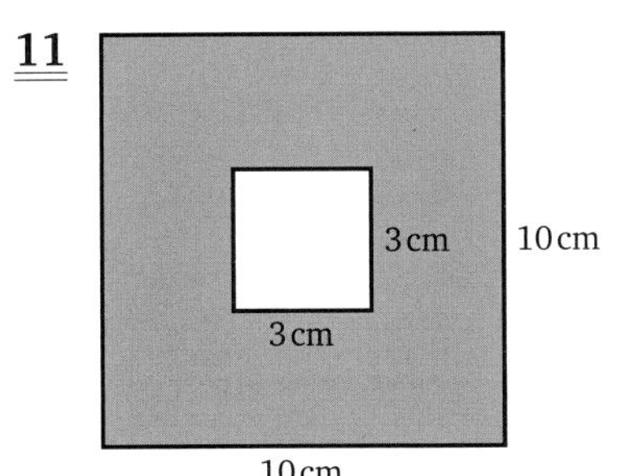

13

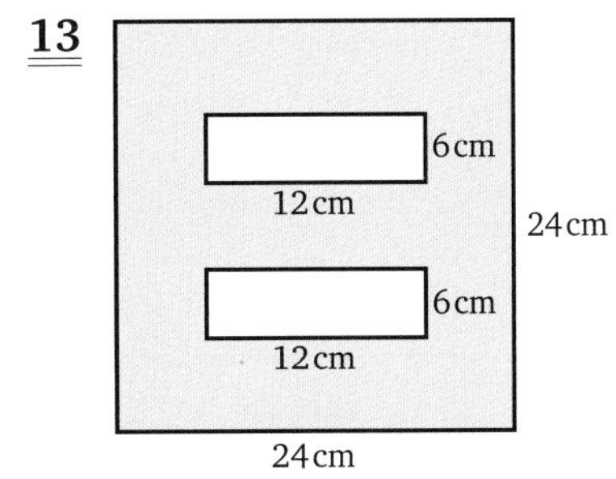

12

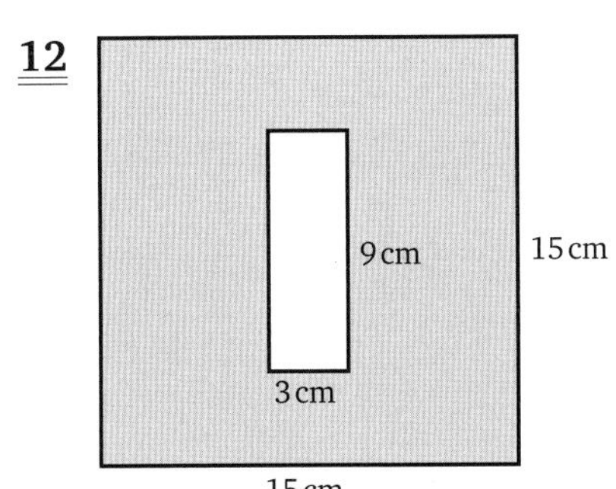

14

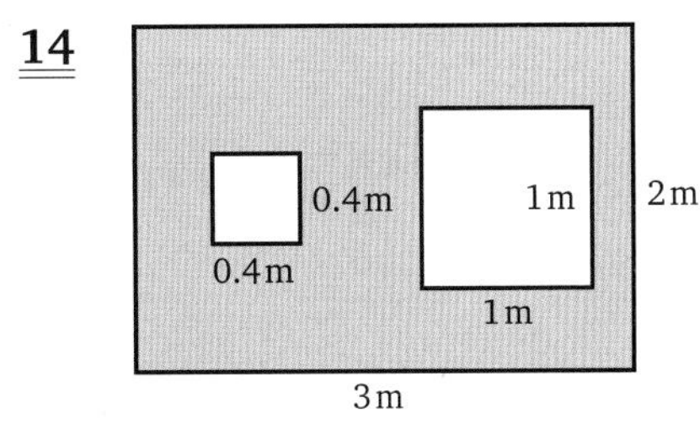

Investigation

This shape is made with 1 cm squares.

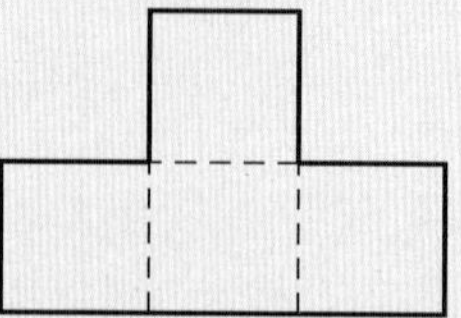

1 This shape has a perimeter of 10 cm. What is its area?

2 Find other shapes made from 1 cm squares that also have a perimeter of 10 cm.

Which one has the largest area?

3 Find other shapes that have the same area as the shape above.

Which shape has the shortest perimeter?

4 Investigate different shapes with a perimeter of 16 cm.

Find the shape with the largest possible area.

5 Investigate different shapes with an area of 6 cm^2.

Which shape has the shortest perimeter?

6 For a given area, what shape has the shortest perimeter?

7 A rectangle has the same number of square centimetres of area as it has centimetres of perimeter.

Find possible whole number values for the length and breadth of this rectangle. (There are two different rectangles with this property.)

Exercise 17g

Draw a square of side 6 cm. How many squares of side 2 cm are required to cover it?

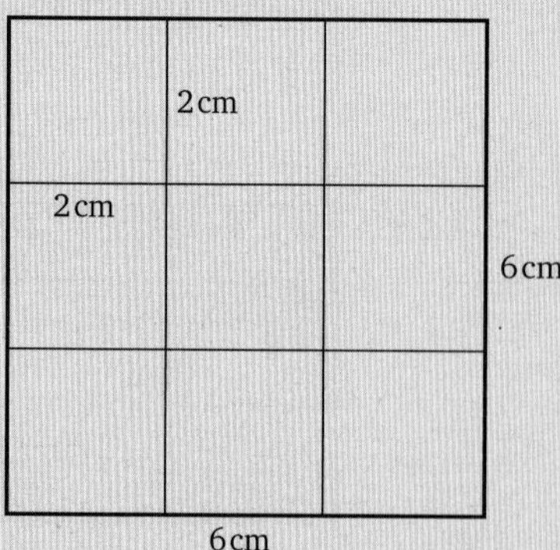

Three 2 cm squares will fit along each edge.

We see that 9 squares of side 2 cm are required to cover the larger square whose side is 6 cm.

1. Draw a square of side 4 cm. How many squares of side 2 cm are required to cover it?
2. Draw a square of side 9 cm. How many squares of side 3 cm are required to cover it?
3. Draw a rectangle measuring 6 cm by 4 cm. How many squares of side 2 cm are required to cover it?
4. Draw a rectangle measuring 9 cm by 6 cm. How many squares of side 3 cm are required to cover it?
5. How many squares of side 5 cm are required to cover a rectangle measuring 45 cm by 25 cm?
6. How many squares of side 4 cm are required to cover a rectangle measuring 1 m by 80 cm?

Changing units of area

A square of side 1 cm may be divided into 100 equal squares of side 1 mm,

$$1\text{ cm} \times 1\text{ cm} = 10\text{ mm} \times 10\text{ mm}$$

i.e. $1\text{ cm}^2 = 100\text{ mm}^2$

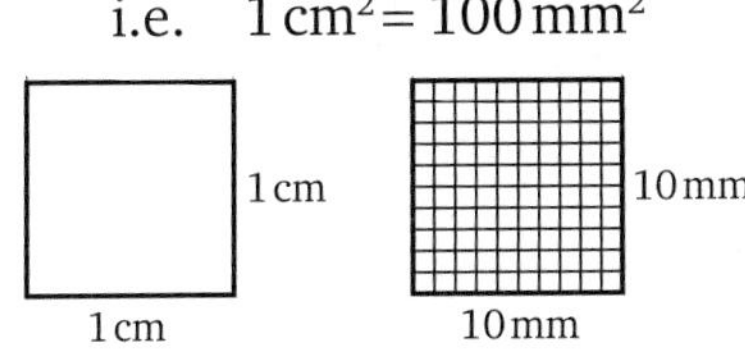

Similarly since $1\text{ m} = 100\text{ cm}$

$$1\text{ m} \times 1\text{ m} = 100\text{ cm} \times 100\text{ cm}$$

i.e. $1\text{ m}^2 = 10\,000\text{ cm}^2$

and as $1\text{ km} = 1000\text{ m}$

$$1\text{ km} \times 1\text{ km} = 1000\text{ m} \times 1000\text{ m}$$

i.e. $1\text{ km}^2 = 1\,000\,000\text{ m}^2$

When we convert from a unit of area which is large to a unit of area which is smaller we must remember that the number of units will be bigger,

e.g. $2\text{ km}^2 = 2 \times 1000\text{ m} \times 1000\text{ m} = 2 \times 1\,000\,000\text{ m}^2$

$= 2\,000\,000\text{ m}^2$

and $12\text{ m}^2 = 12 \times 10\,000\text{ cm}^2$

$= 120\,000\text{ cm}^2$

while if we convert from a unit of area which is small into one which is larger the number of units will be smaller,

e.g. $500\,\text{mm}^2 = \frac{500}{100}\,\text{cm}^2 = 5\,\text{cm}^2$

Exercise 17h

Express $5\,\text{m}^2$ in **a** cm^2 **b** mm^2.

a Since $1\,\text{m}^2 = 100\,\text{cm} \times 100\,\text{cm}$

$5\,\text{m}^2 = 5 \times 100\,\text{cm} \times 100\,\text{cm} = 50\,000\,\text{cm}^2$

b Since $1\,\text{cm}^2 = 100\,\text{mm}^2$

$50\,000\,\text{cm}^2 = 50\,000 \times 100\,\text{mm}^2 = 5\,000\,000\,\text{mm}^2$

Therefore $5\,\text{m}^2 = 50\,000\,\text{cm}^2 = 5\,000\,000\,\text{mm}^2$.

1 Express in cm^2:

a $3\,\text{m}^2$ **b** $12\,\text{m}^2$ **c** $7.5\,\text{m}^2$ **d** $82\,\text{m}^2$ **e** $8\frac{1}{2}\,\text{m}^2$

2 Express in mm^2:

a $14\,\text{cm}^2$ **b** $3\,\text{cm}^2$ **c** $7.5\,\text{cm}^2$ **d** $26\,\text{cm}^2$ **e** $32\frac{1}{2}\,\text{cm}^2$

3 Express $0.056\,\text{m}^2$ in

a cm^2 **b** mm^2

Express $354\,000\,000\,\text{mm}^2$ in **a** cm^2 **b** m^2.

a Since $100\,\text{mm}^2 = 1\,\text{cm}^2$

$354000000\,\text{mm}^2 = \frac{354000000}{100}\,\text{cm}^2 = 3\,540\,000\,\text{cm}^2$

b Since $100 \times 100\,\text{cm}^2 = 1\,\text{m}^2$

$3540000\,\text{cm}^2 = \frac{3540000}{100 \times 100}\,\text{m}^2 = 354\,\text{m}^2$

Therefore $354\,000\,000\,\text{mm}^2 = 3\,540\,000\,\text{cm}^2 = 354\,\text{m}^2$.

4 Express in cm^2:

a $400\,\text{mm}^2$ **b** $2500\,\text{mm}^2$ **c** $50\,\text{mm}^2$ **d** $25\,\text{mm}^2$ **e** $734\,\text{mm}^2$

5 Express in m^2:

a $5500\,\text{cm}^2$ **b** $140\,000\,\text{cm}^2$ **c** $760\,\text{cm}^2$ **d** $18\,600\,\text{cm}^2$ **e** $29\,700\,000\,\text{cm}^2$

6 Express in km^2:

a $7\,500\,000\,\text{m}^2$ **b** $430\,000\,\text{m}^2$ **c** $50\,000\,\text{m}^2$ **d** $245\,000\,\text{m}^2$ **e** $176\,000\,000\,\text{m}^2$

Sometimes questions ask us to find the area of a rectangle in different square units from those in which the length and breadth are given. When this is so, we must change the units of the measurements we are given so that they 'match' the square units required in the answer.

Exercise 17i

Find the area of a rectangle measuring 50 cm by 35 cm.
Give your answer in m^2.

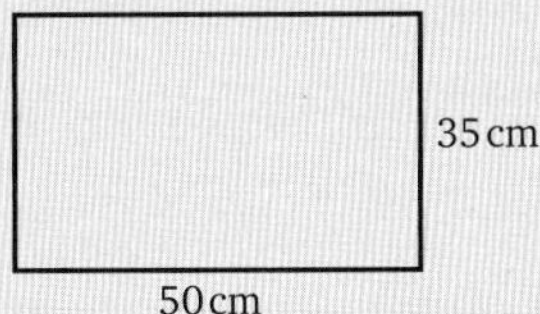

(Since the answer is to be given in m^2 we express both the length and breadth in m.)

Breadth of rectangle = 35 cm = 0.35 m

Length of rectangle = 50 cm = 0.5 m

Therefore area of rectangle = $0.35 \times 0.5 = 0.175\ m^2$

Find the area of each of the following rectangles, giving your answer in the unit in brackets:

	Length	Breadth			Length	Breadth	
1	10 m	0.5 m	(cm^2)	**6**	3 m	$\frac{1}{2}$ m	(cm^2)
2	6 cm	3 cm	(mm^2)	**7**	$2\frac{1}{2}$ m	$1\frac{1}{2}$ m	(cm^2)
3	50 m	0.35 m	(cm^2)	**8**	1.5 cm	1.2 cm	(mm^2)
4	1.4 m	1 m	(cm^2)	**9**	0.4 km	0.3 km	(m^2)
5	400 cm	200 cm	(m^2)	**10**	0.45 km	0.05 km	(m^2)

Mixed problems

Exercise 17j

In questions **1** to **4** find

a the area of the playing surface

b the perimeter of the playing surface.

1 A soccer field measuring 110 m by 75 m.

2 A rugby pitch measuring 100 m by 70 m.

3 A playing field measuring 120 m by 70 m.

4 A tennis court measuring 26 m by 12 m.

5 A roll of wallpaper is 10 m long and 50 cm wide. Find its area in square metres.

6 A school hall measuring 20 m by 15 m is to be covered with square floor tiles of side 50 cm.
How many tiles are required?

7 A rectangular carpet measures 4 m by 3 m. Find its area. How much would it cost to clean at 75 c per square metre?

8 The top of my desk is 150 cm long and 60 cm wide. Find its area.

9 How many square linen serviettes, of side 50 cm, may be cut from a roll of linen 25 m long and 1 m wide?

10 How many square concrete paving slabs, each of side $\frac{3}{4}$ m, are required to pave a rectangular yard measuring 9 m by 6 m?

Exercise 17k

Select the letter that gives the correct answer.

1 The area of a square of side 12 cm is

A 48 cm² B 72 cm² C 144 cm² D 288 cm²

2 The area of a rectangle measuring 4 cm by 8 cm is

A 16 cm² B 32 cm² C 64 cm² D 84 cm²

3 The area of a rectangle measuring 8 cm by 8 mm is

A 6.4 cm² B 32 cm² C 64 cm² D 128 cm²

4 The area of this shape is

A 208 cm²
B 256 cm²
C 264 cm²
D 312 cm²

26 cm
8 cm
12 cm
14 cm

5 The perimeter of the shape given in question **4** is

A 64 cm B 68 cm C 74 cm D 76 cm

6 The area of a rectangle is 168 cm². If it is 14 cm long its breadth is

A 10 cm B 12 cm C 14 cm D 16 cm

Did you know?

Why study mathematics?

Mathematics is found in:

- Your home

  Mathematics is used in home building.

  Frames are strengthened by triangle-bracing.

  Geometric shapes are used to beautify houses.

- Your diet

  A good diet contains proper amounts of basic food nutrients. Grams and percentages of daily amounts of nutrients are written on the packaging of foods.

  Persons on special diets use metric scales to measure their intake.

- Your career

  The career you choose may require mathematics. Some are Accountants, Architects, Bank workers, Dieticians, Draftsmen, Engineers, Electricians, Carpenters, Surveyors and others.

- Your sports

  We use mathematics to calculate batting and other averages.

  To find the chance of a victory we use probability.

These are but a few uses of mathematics.

In this chapter you have seen that...

✔ you can find the area of an irregular shape by putting it on a grid and counting squares

✔ the unit of area used has to be a standard size square. Those in common use are

- square millimetres (mm^2)
- square centimetres (cm^2)
- square metres (m^2)
- square kilometres (km^2)

The relationships between them are

- $1\,cm^2 = 100\,mm^2$
- $1\,m^2 = 10\,000\,cm^2$
- $1\,km^2 = 1\,000\,000\,m^2$

✔ the area of a square is found by multiplying the length of a side by itself

✔ the area of a rectangle is found by multiplying its length by its breadth

✔ compound shapes can often be divided into two or more rectangles

✔ the perimeter of a figure is the total length of all its sides

✔ when you convert to a smaller unit of area you multiply, and when you convert to a larger unit of area you divide.

18 Areas of parallelograms and triangles

At the end of this chapter you should be able to...

1 calculate the area of a rectangle, given its length and width
2 calculate the length or width of a rectangle, given its width or length and area
3 calculate the area of given figure by dividing it into rectangular shapes
4 calculate the area of a parallelogram given the length of a side and its height
5 calculate the area of a triangle, given its base and height
6 calculate the base or height of a triangle given its area and height or base
7 calculate the area of a compound shape by subdividing it into parallelograms and triangles.

Did you know?

The area of Trinidad is 4828 square kilometres.

You need to know...

✔ the units of length and of area and the relationships between them
✔ how to work with fractions and decimals
✔ the basic properties of a square, rectangle, triangle, parallelogram, rhombus, quadrilateral and pentagon.

Key words

base, diagonal, kite, line of symmetry, parallelogram, pentagon, perpendicular height, quadrilateral, rectangle, rhombus, square, triangle

Area of a rectangle

Reminder: We can find the area of a rectangle by multiplying its length by its width (or breadth).

$$\text{Area} = \text{length} \times \text{width}$$

or $$A = l \times b$$

The units we use for the two measurements must be the same.

Exercise 18a

Find the areas of the rectangles in questions **1** to **10**.
When finding areas, draw a diagram even if the question is simple.

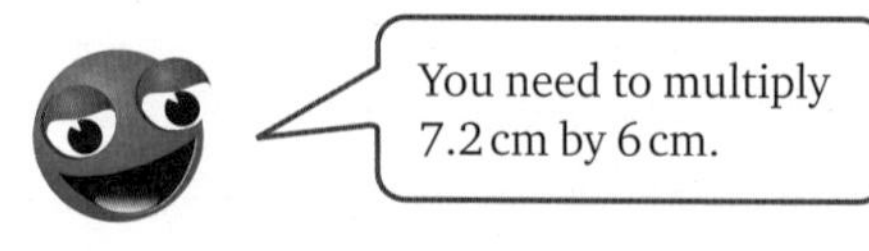

1

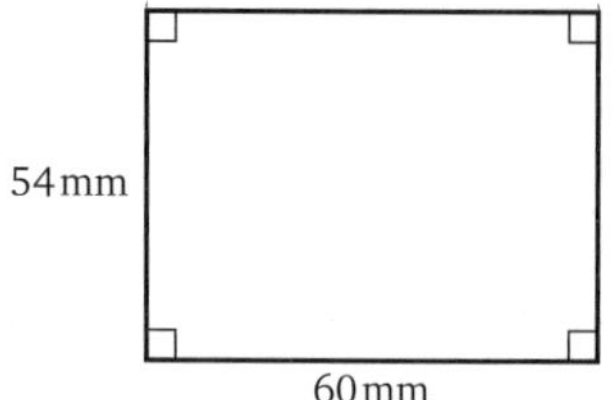

2

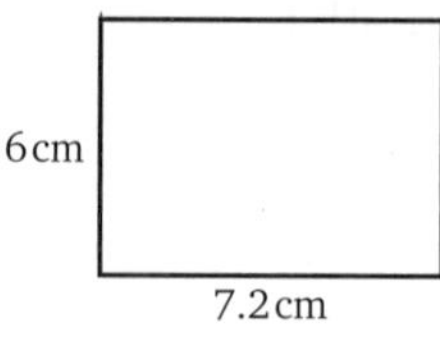

3 Rectangle, measuring 3.04 m by 1.5 m

4 Rectangle, measuring $1\frac{1}{2}$ m by $\frac{3}{4}$ m

5 Rectangle, measuring $3\frac{1}{4}$ cm by $1\frac{1}{3}$ cm

Find the area of a rectangle, measuring 54 mm by 60 mm, in square centimetres.

The area is required in square centimetres so the length and the width both need to be in centimetres.

To change millimetres to centimetres, we divide by 10.

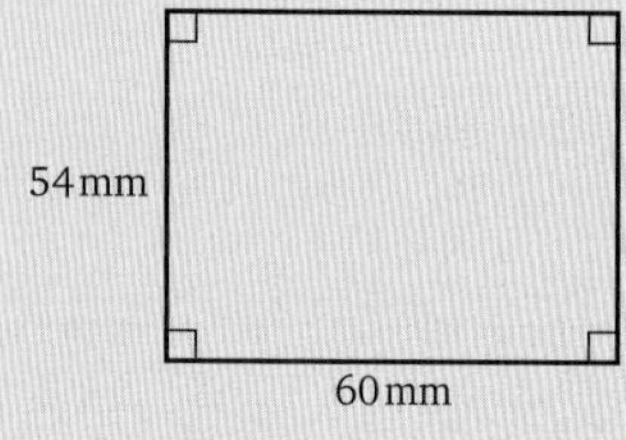

Length = 60 mm = 6.0 cm

Width = 54 mm = 5.4 cm

Area = length × width

$= 6 \times 5.4\ \text{cm}^2$

$= 32.4\ \text{cm}^2$

6 Rectangle, length 7.2 cm, width 3 cm. Find the area in cm^2.

7 Rectangle, length 0.2 m, width 0.16 m. Find the area in cm^2.

8 Rectangle, measuring 600 mm by 92 mm. Find the area in cm^2.

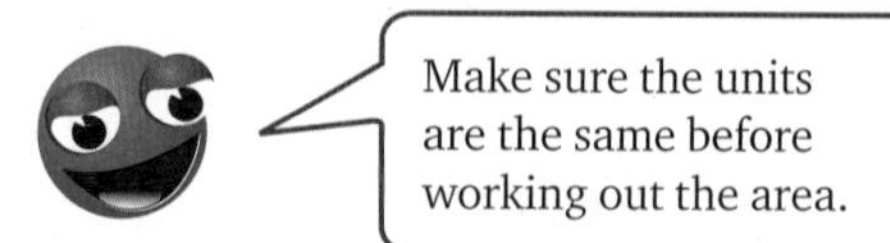

9 Rectangle, measuring 420 mm by 160 mm. Find the area in cm^2.

10 Rectangle, measuring 41 mm by 70 mm. Find the area in mm^2.

Lance has three square vegetable plots. Their total area is $1977\,\text{m}^2$. Two are identical and the third is a bit smaller. What is the area of each plot?

Finding a length when the area is given

Exercise 18b

Find the length of a rectangle of area $20\,\text{cm}^2$ and width 2.5 cm.

$20\,\text{cm}^2$ 2.5 cm

$$\text{Area} = \text{length} \times \text{width}, \quad \text{or} \quad A = l \times b,$$

then

$$\text{length} = \frac{\text{area}}{\text{width}} \quad \text{or} \quad l = \frac{A}{b}$$

$$\text{length} = \frac{20}{2.5}\text{ cm}$$

$$= \frac{200}{25}\text{ cm}$$

$$= 8\text{ cm}$$

Find the missing measurements for the following rectangles:

	Area	Length	Width
1	$2.4\,\text{cm}^2$	6 cm	
2	$20\,\text{cm}^2$	4 cm	
3	$36\,\text{m}^2$		3.6 m
4	$108\,\text{mm}^2$	27 mm	
5	$3\,\text{cm}^2$		0.6 cm
6	$6\,\text{m}^2$	4 m	
7	$20\,\text{cm}^2$		16 cm
8	$7.2\,\text{m}^2$		2.4 m
9	$4.2\,\text{m}^2$		0.6 m
10	$14.4\,\text{cm}^2$	2.4 cm	

Area of a parallelogram

Knowing how to find the area of a rectangle helps us to deal with parallelograms.

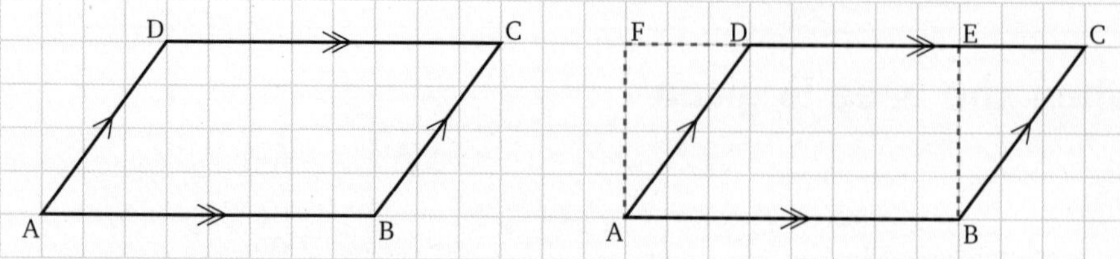

Copy the first diagram on to squared paper. Draw the line BE and remove △BEC from the right-hand side. Draw an equal triangle, FDA, at the left-hand side to replace △BEC. Then you can see that the area of the parallelogram ABCD is equal to the area of rectangle ABEF.

$$\text{Area of parallelogram} = AB \times BE$$
$$= \text{base} \times \text{perpendicular height}$$

When we use the word *height* we mean the *perpendicular height* BE, not the slant height BC, so we can say

$$\text{Area of parallelogram} = \text{base} \times \text{height}$$

Exercise 18c

Find the area of a parallelogram of base 7 cm, height 5 cm and slant height 6 cm.

The height of a parallelogram means the perpendicular height, which is the perpendicular distance between a pair of parallel sides.

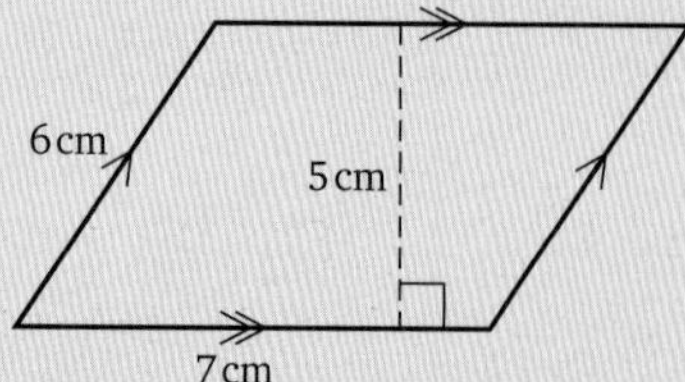

$$\text{Area} = \text{base} \times \text{height}$$
$$= 7 \times 5\ \text{cm}^2$$
$$= 35\ \text{cm}^2$$

(Notice that we do not use the length of the 6 cm side to find the area of the parallelogram.)

Find the areas of the following parallelograms:

1

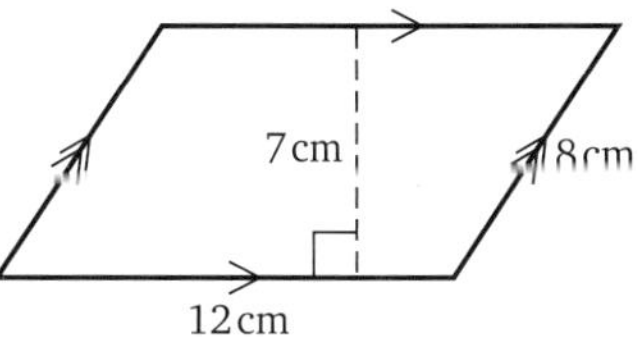

2

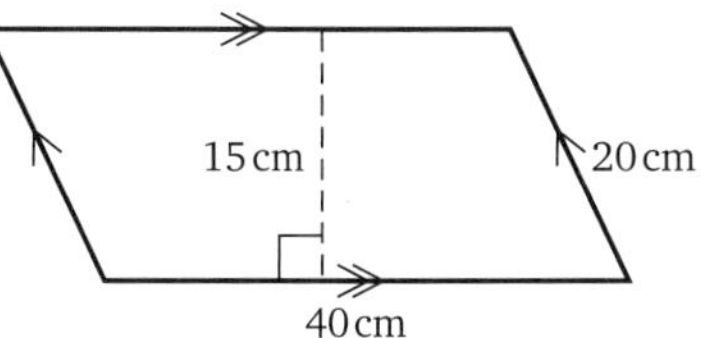

3

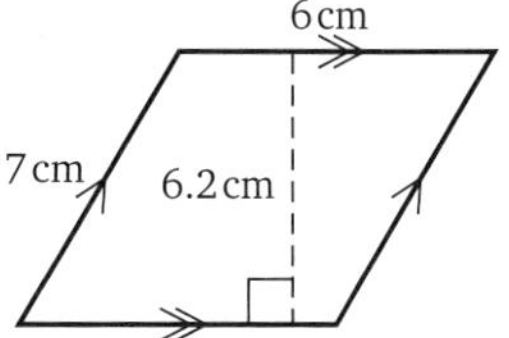

4

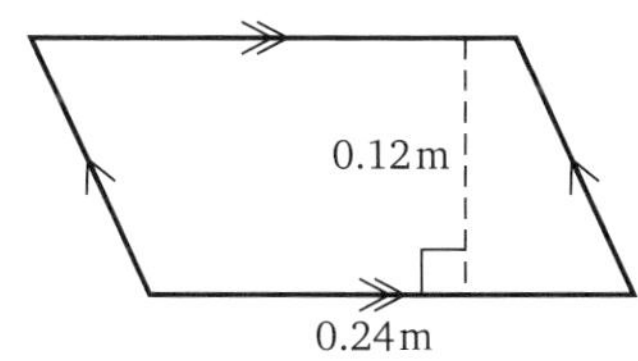

5

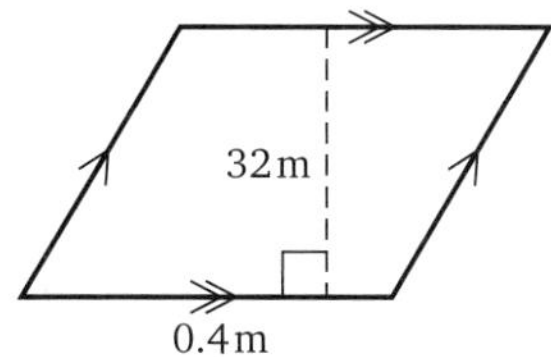

6

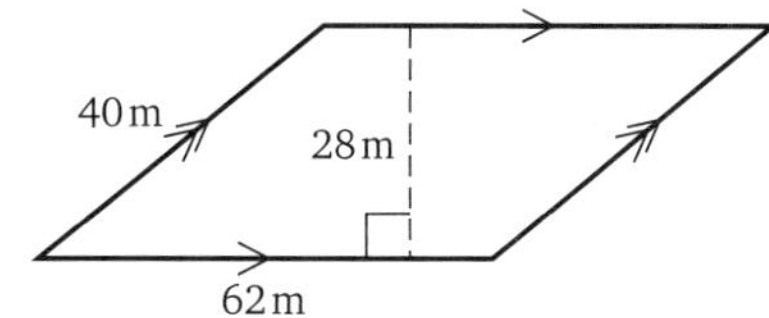

7

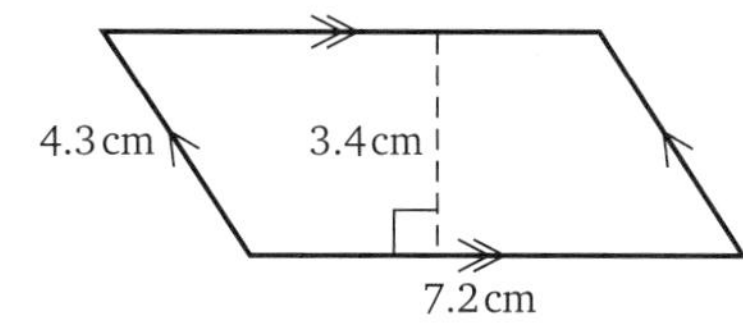

8

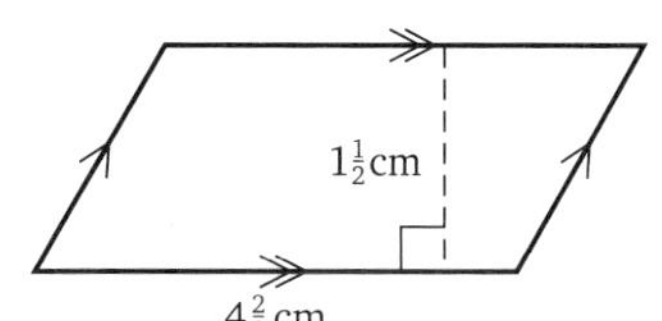

Find the area of the parallelogram.

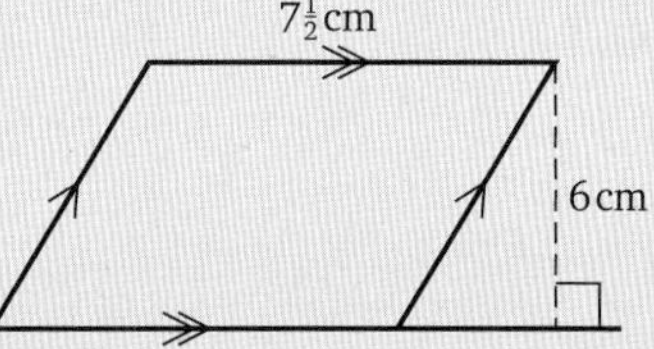

(Notice that it does not matter if the height is measured inside or outside of the parallelogram.)

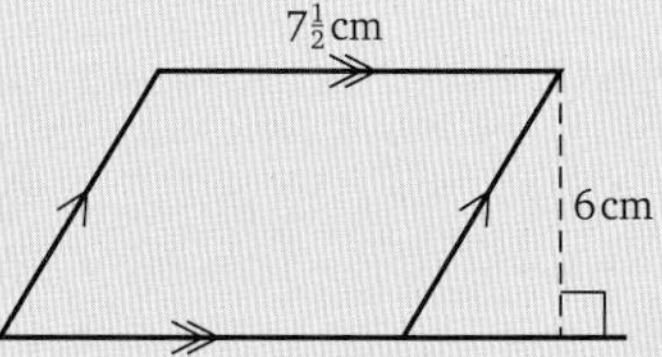

Area = base × height

$= 7\frac{1}{2} \times 6 \text{ cm}^2$

$= \frac{15}{2_1} \times 6^3 \text{ cm}^2$

$= 45 \text{ cm}^2$

Find the areas of these parallelograms.

9

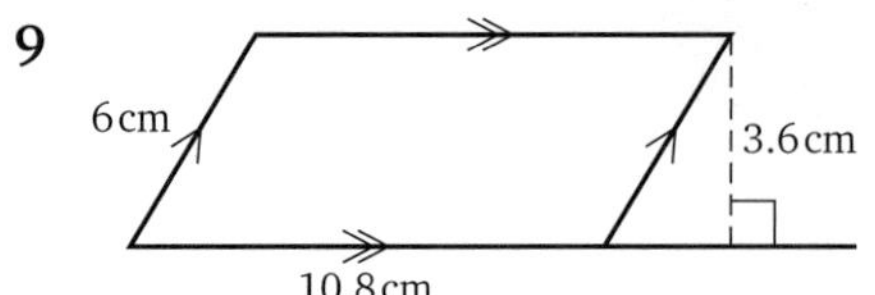

11

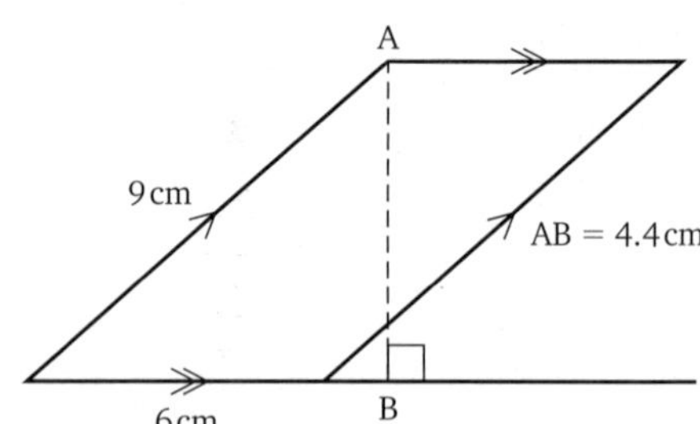

10

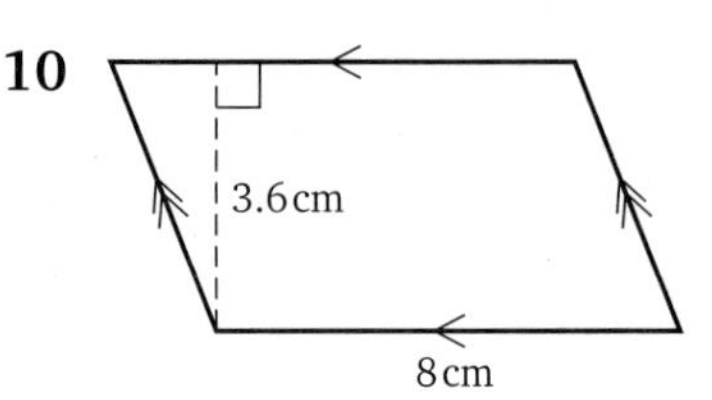

12

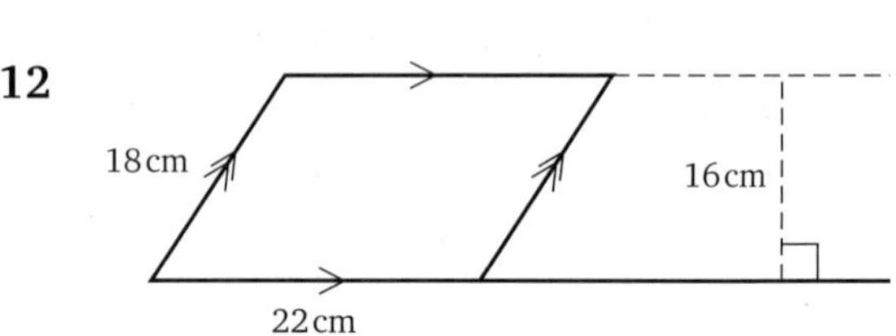

In questions **13** to **18**, turn the page round if necessary so that you can see which is the base and which the height.

13

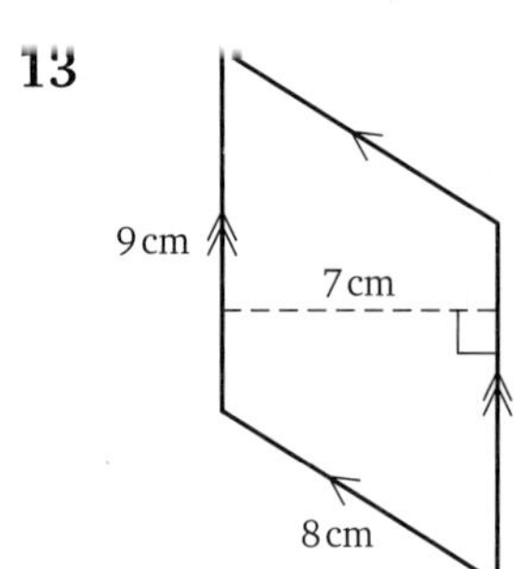

16

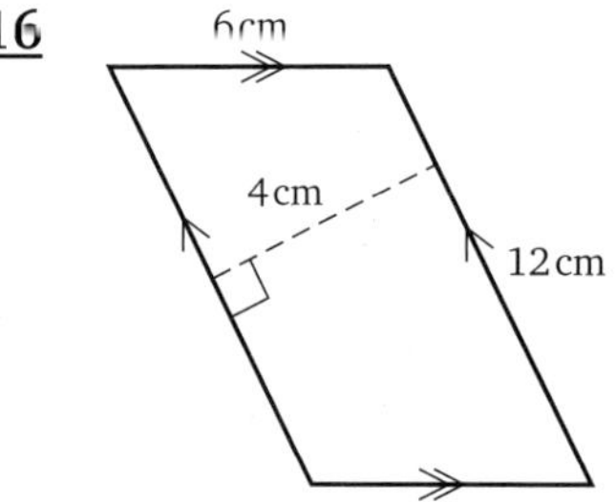

14

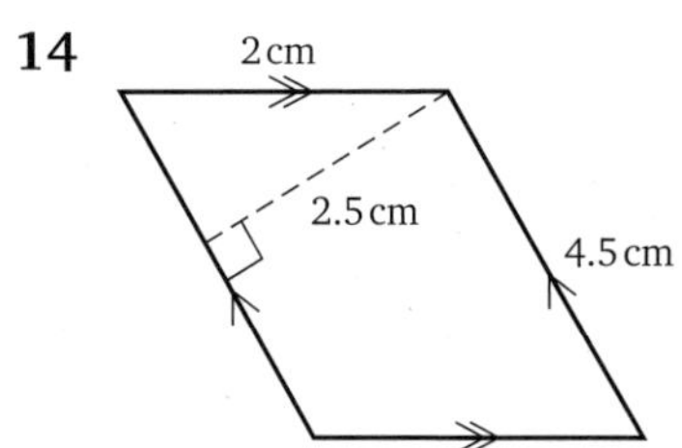

17

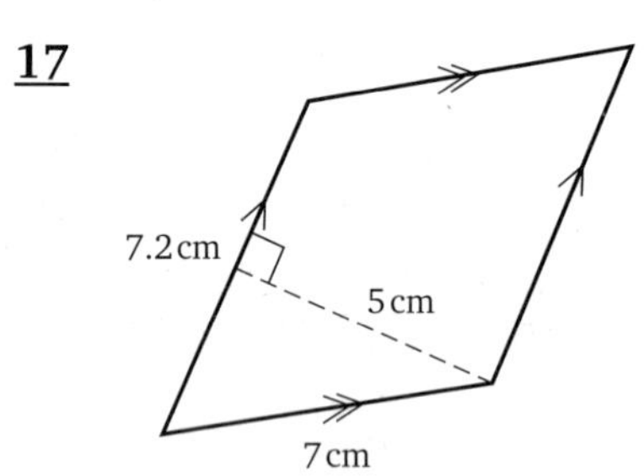

15

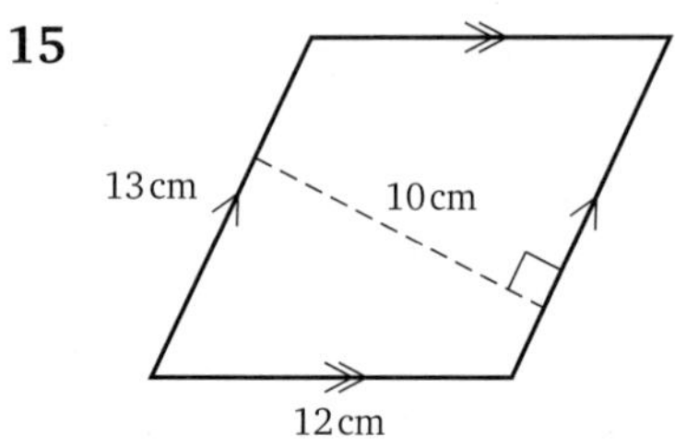

18

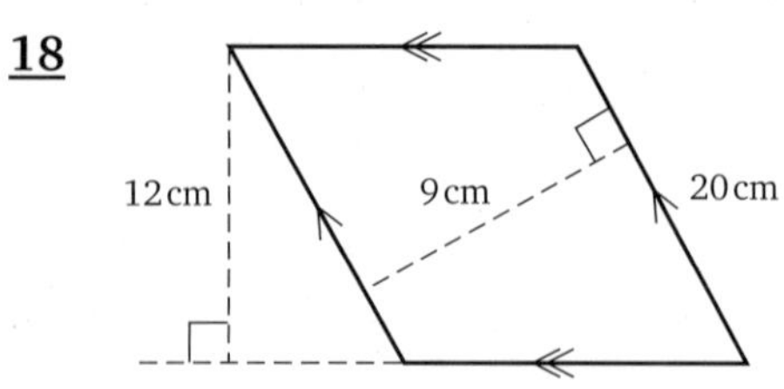

19 In questions **15** to **18** which of the given measurements did you not use?

Divide this trapezium into four pieces all of which are exactly the same shape and size.

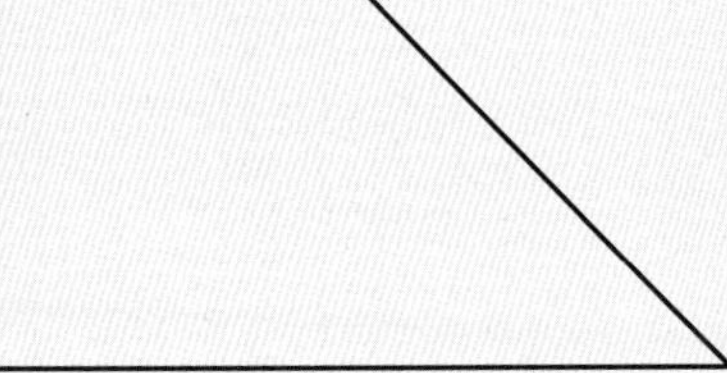

Area of a triangle

There are two ways of finding how to calculate the area of a triangle.

First, if we think of a triangle as half a parallelogram we get

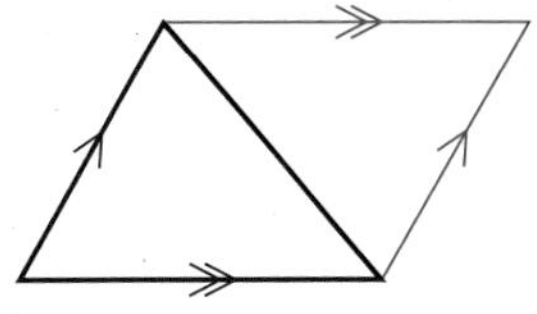

$$\text{Area of triangle} = \frac{1}{2} \times \text{area of parallelogram}$$

$$= \frac{1}{2}\,(\text{base} \times \text{height})$$

Second, if we enclose the triangle in a rectangle we see again that the area of the triangle is half the area of the rectangle.

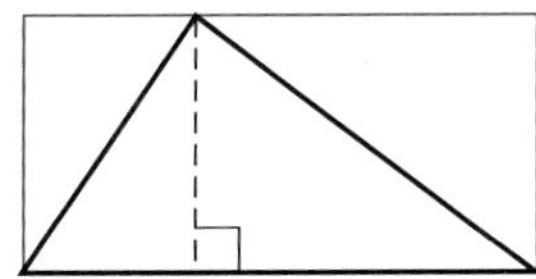

These diagrams can be drawn on squared paper and then cut out to show how the pieces fit.

Height of a triangle

As with the parallelogram, when we talk about the height of a triangle we mean its perpendicular height and not its slant height.

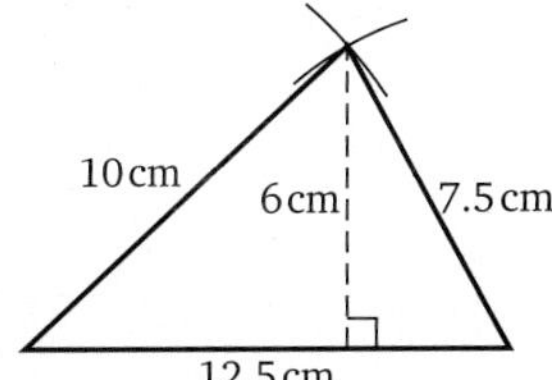

If we draw the given triangle accurately on squared paper, we can see that the height of the triangle is not 10 cm or 7.5 cm but 6 cm. (We can also see that the foot of the perpendicular is *not* the midpoint of the base.)

Finding areas of triangles

Exercise 18d

Find the area of a triangle with base 7 cm and height 6 cm.

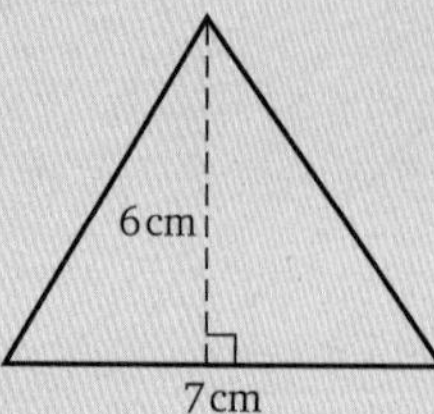

$$\text{Area} = \frac{1}{2}(\text{base} \times \text{height})$$
$$= \frac{1}{2} \times 7 \times 6 \text{ cm}^2$$
$$= 21 \text{ cm}^2$$

Find the areas of the following triangles.

1

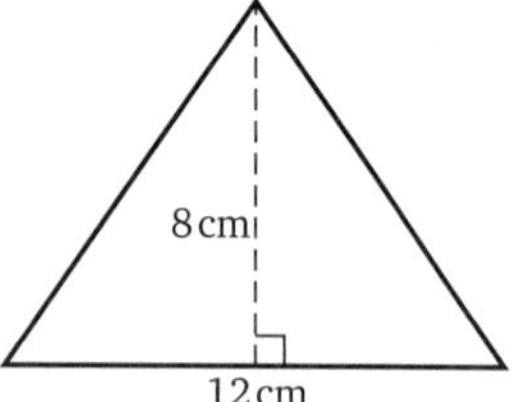

2

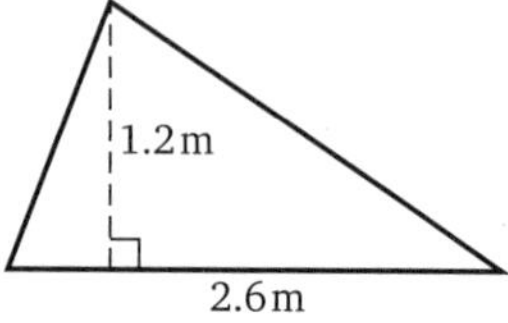

3

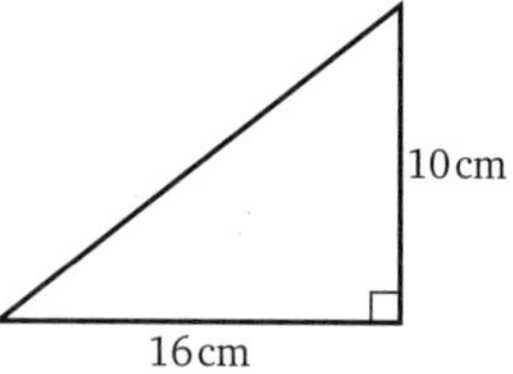

4

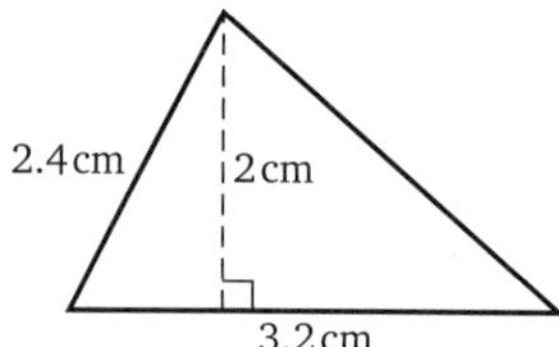

5

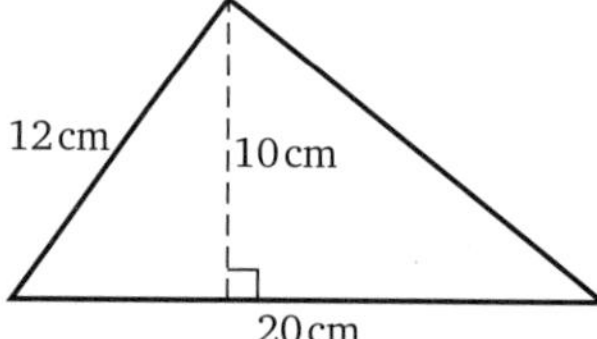

6

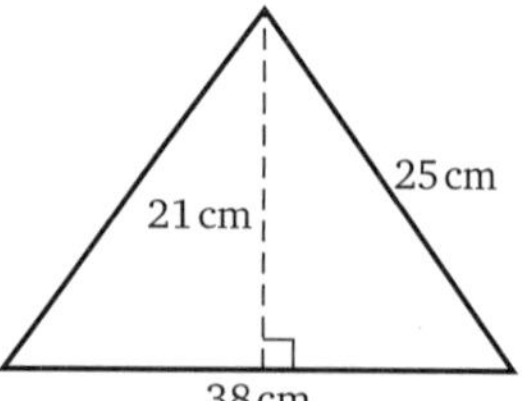

7 In questions **4**, **5** and **6**, one of the given measurements is redundant. Which one is it?

Remember that you want the perpendicular height, which is the perpendicular distance from the base to the opposite vertex.

8

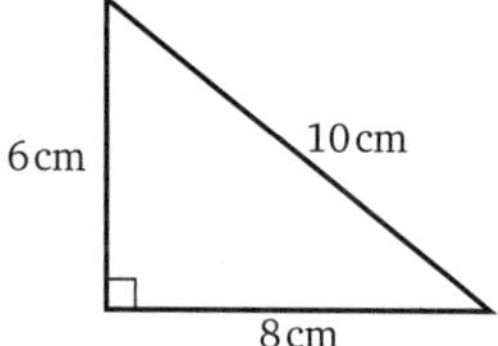

9

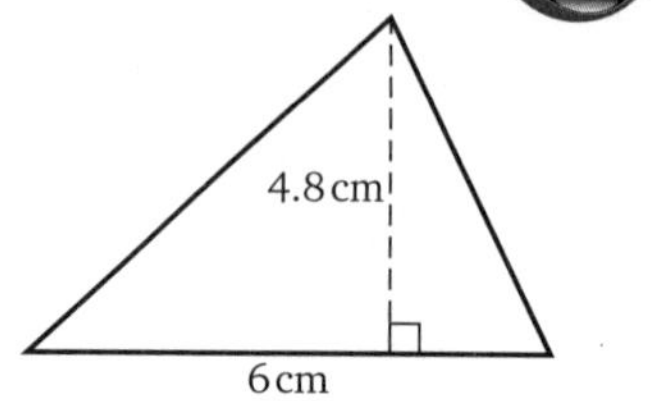

10

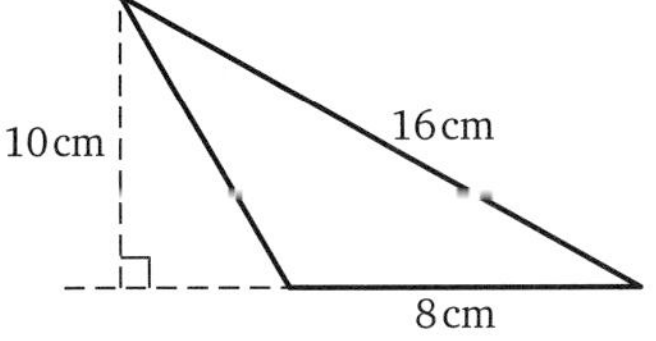

11

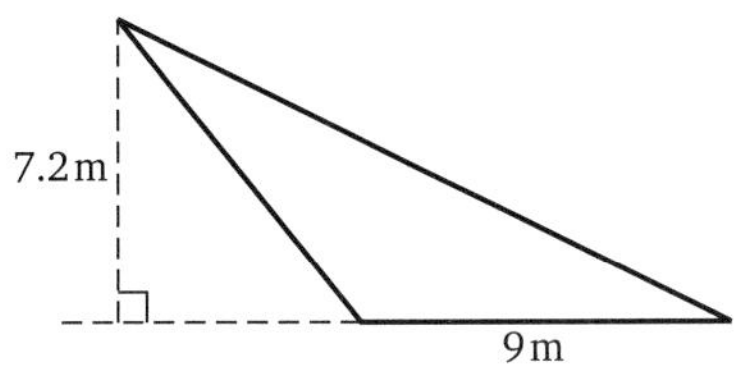

12

13

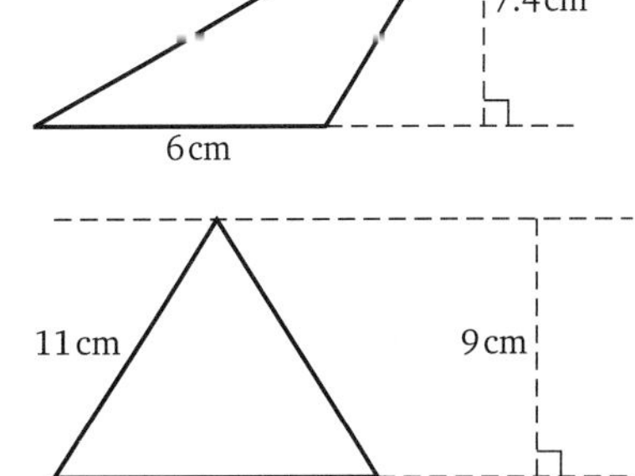

Find the area of the triangle.

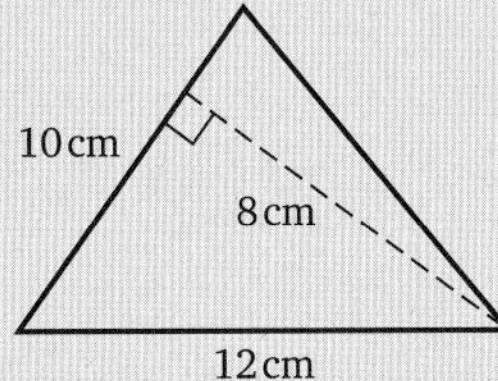

Look at this diagram from the direction of the arrow.

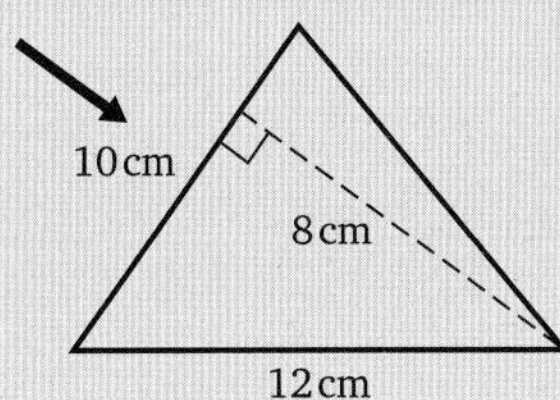

$$\text{Area} = \frac{1}{2}(\text{base} \times \text{height})$$

$$= \frac{1}{\not{2}_1} \times 10 \times \not{8}^{4}\ \text{cm}^2$$

$$= 40\ \text{cm}^2$$

If necessary turn the page round and look at the triangle from a different direction.

14

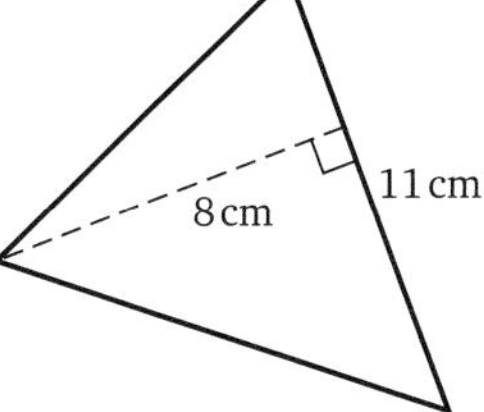

15

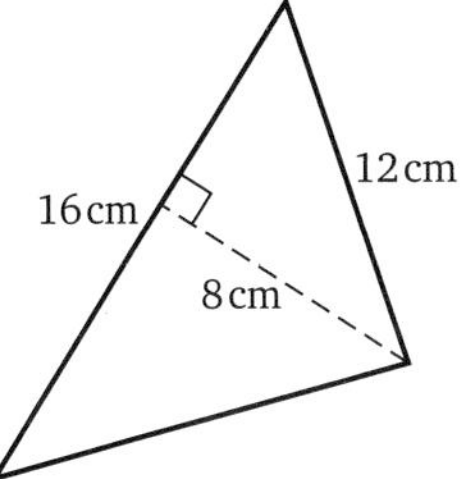

16

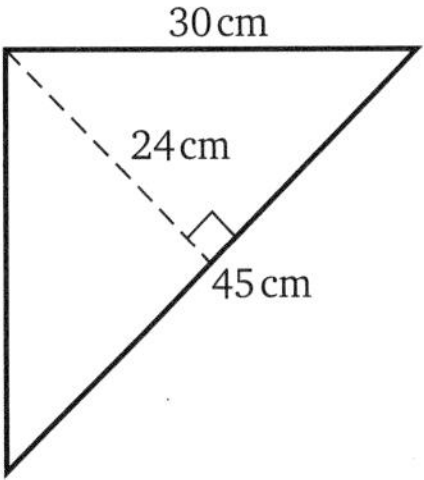

17

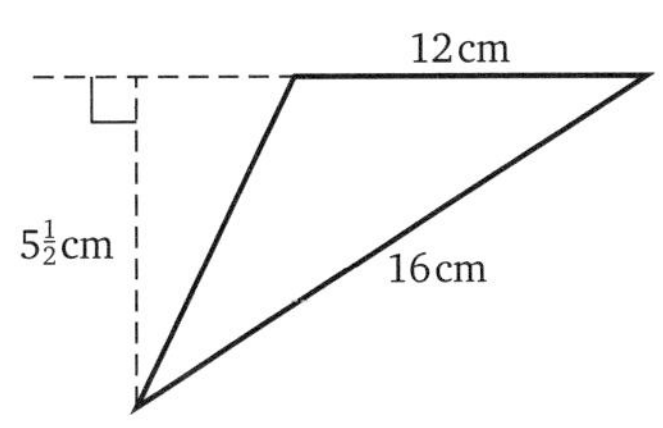

18

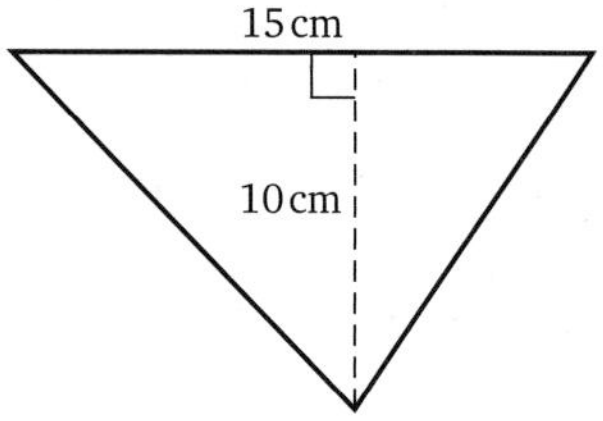

15 cm
10 cm

19

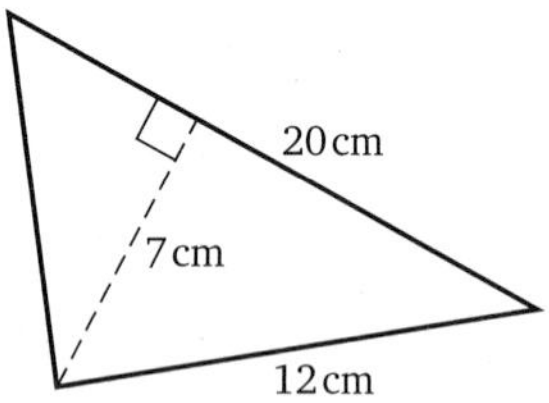

20 cm
7 cm
12 cm

20

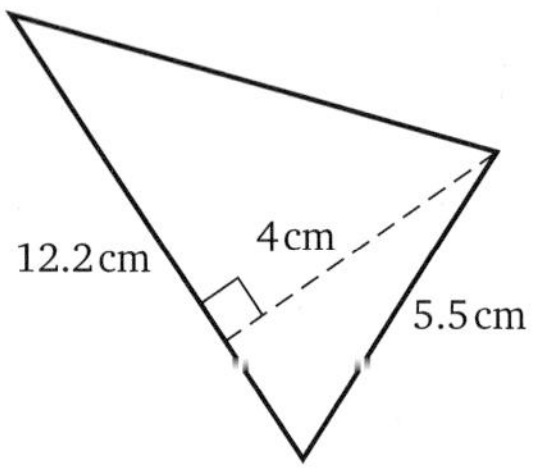

12.2 cm
4 cm
5.5 cm

21

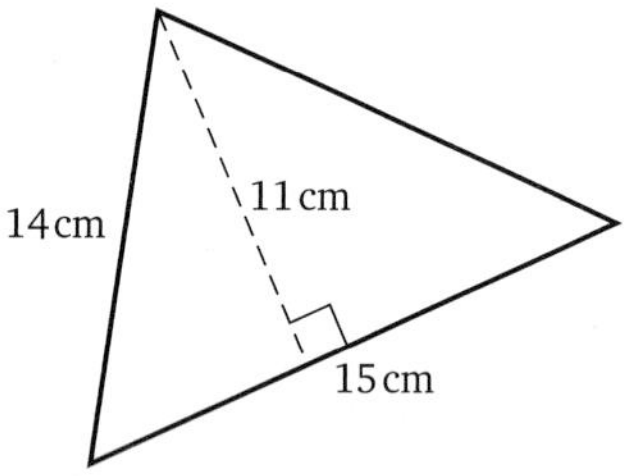

14 cm
11 cm
15 cm

22

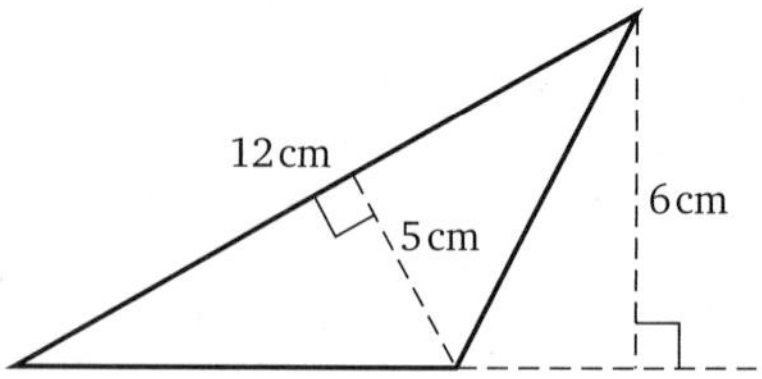

12 cm
5 cm
6 cm

23

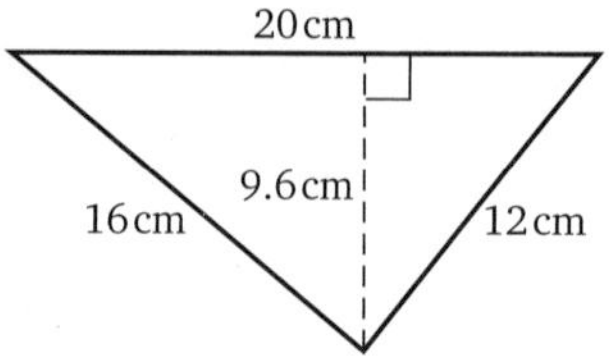

20 cm
9.6 cm
16 cm
12 cm

24

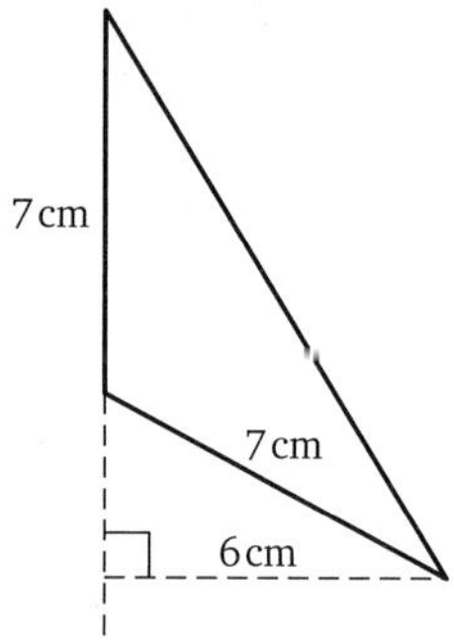

7 cm
7 cm
6 cm

25

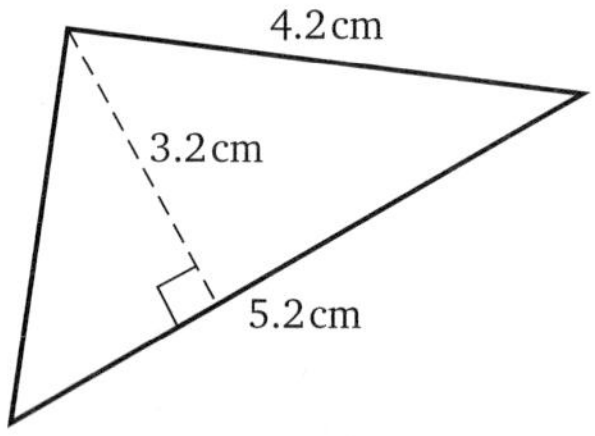

4.2 cm
3.2 cm
5.2 cm

Finding missing measurements

Exercise 18e

The area of a triangle is $20\,\text{cm}^2$. The height is 8 cm. Find the length of the base.

Let the base be b cm long.

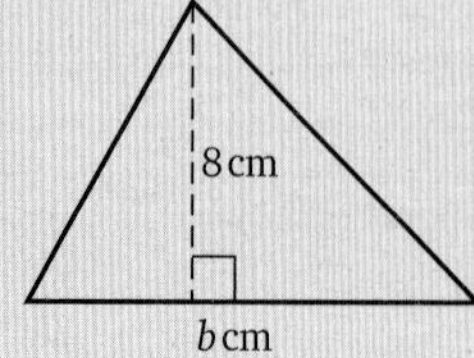

Using the formula for the area of a triangle, we substitute the values we know and b for the base.

$$\text{Area} = \frac{1}{2}(\text{base} \times \text{height})$$

$$20 = \frac{1}{2} \times b \times 8$$

Now we can see that

$$20 = 4b$$

$$b = 5$$

The base is 5 cm long.

Find the missing measurements of the following triangles.

	Area	Base	Height
1	24 cm^2	6 cm	
2	30 cm^2		10 cm
3	48 cm^2		16 cm
4	10 cm^2	10 mm	
5	36 cm^2	24 cm	
<u>6</u>	108 cm^2		6 cm

	Area	Base	Height
<u>7</u>	96 cm^2		64 cm
<u>8</u>	4 cm^2		3 cm
<u>9</u>	2 cm^2	10 cm	
<u>10</u>	1.2 cm^2	0.4 cm	
<u>11</u>	72 cm^2		18 cm
<u>12</u>	1.28 cm^2	0.64 cm	

Investigation

These triangles are drawn on a grid of dots 1 cm apart.

1 Copy and complete this table for each triangle.

Number of dots on edge	Number of dots inside	Area (cm^2)

2 Find a relationship between the number of dots on the edge, the number of dots inside and the area of each shape. Does this relationship hold for any triangle drawn on the grid?

3 Investigate the relationship between the number of dots on the edge, the number of dots inside and the areas of rectangles and parallelograms.

Compound shapes

Exercise 18f

ABCE is a square of side 8 cm. The total height of the shape is 12 cm. Find the area of ABCDE.

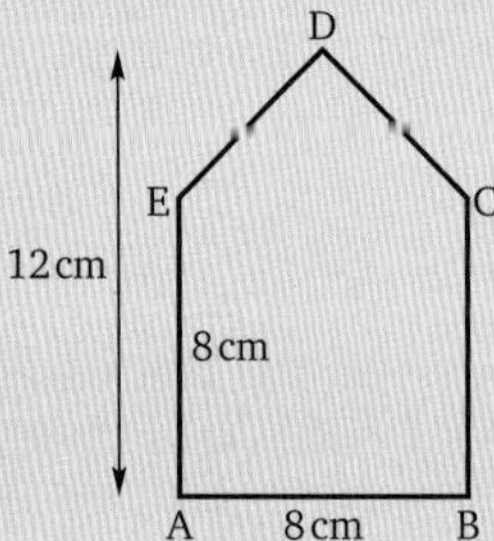

We can divide this shape into a square and a triangle. From the measurements given we see that the height of the triangle is 4 cm and the length of the base is 8 cm

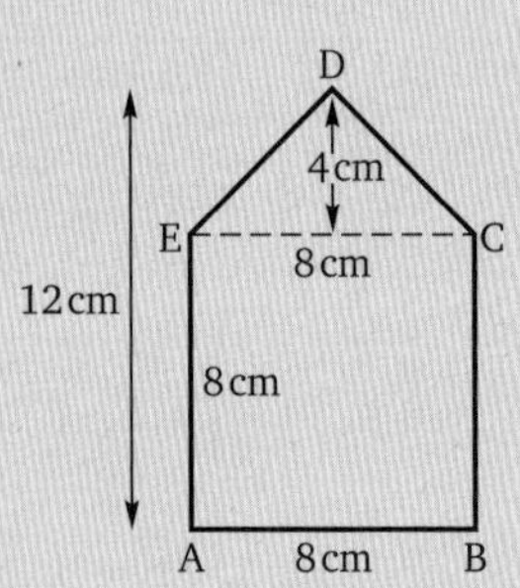

$$\text{Area of } \triangle\text{ECD} = \frac{1}{2}(\text{base} \times \text{height})$$

$$= \frac{1}{2} \times 8 \times 4\,\text{cm}^2$$

$$= 16\,\text{cm}^2$$

$$\text{Area of ABCE} = 8 \times 8\,\text{cm}^2$$

$$= 64\,\text{cm}^2$$

$$\text{Total area} = 80\,\text{cm}^2$$

Find the areas of the following shapes.

1

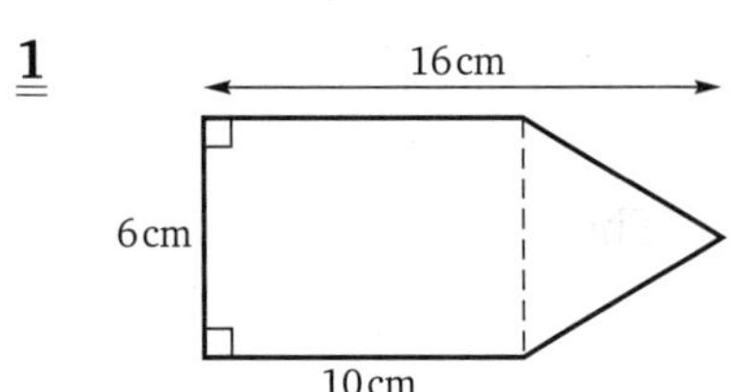

Remember to draw a diagram for each question and mark in all the measurements.

2

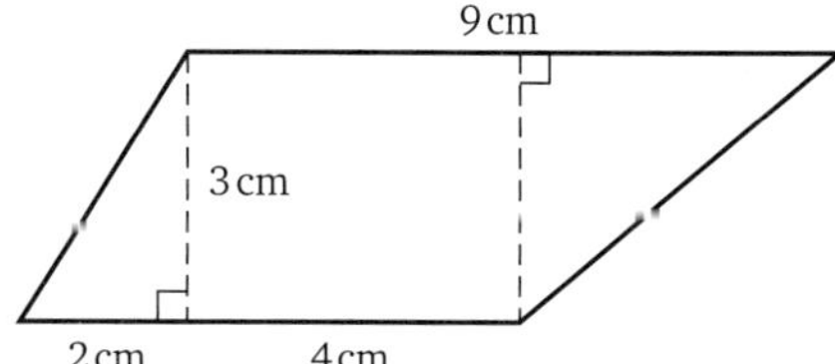

6

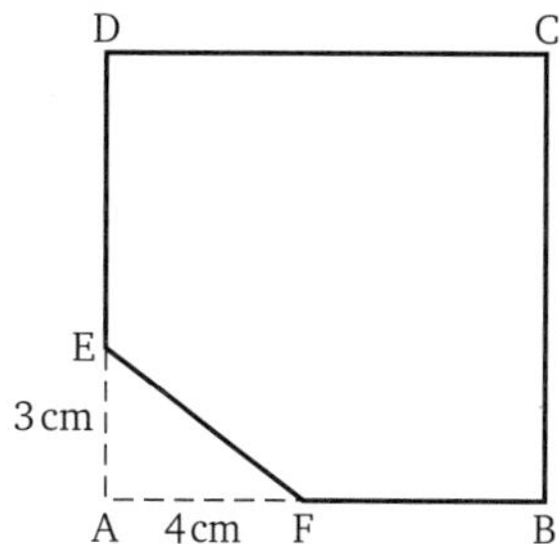

A square ABCD, of side 9 cm, has a triangle EAF cut off it.

3

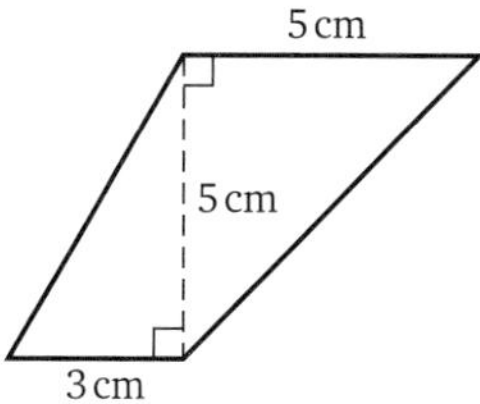

7

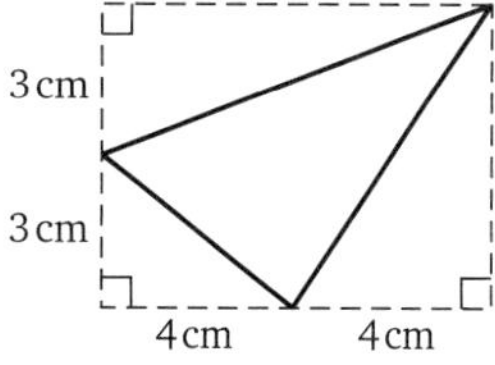

4

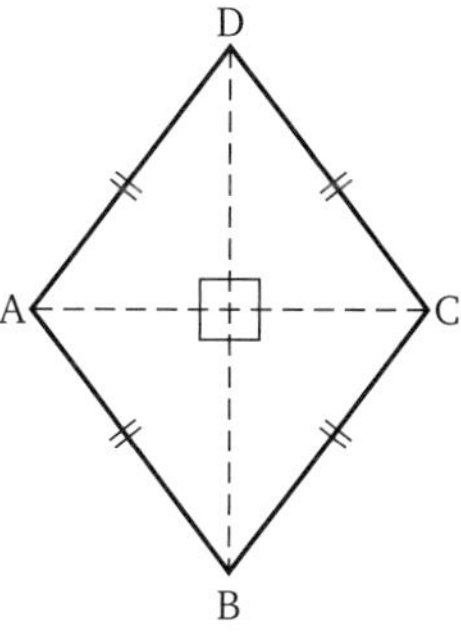

ABCD is a rhombus.

AC = 9 cm

BD = 12 cm

8

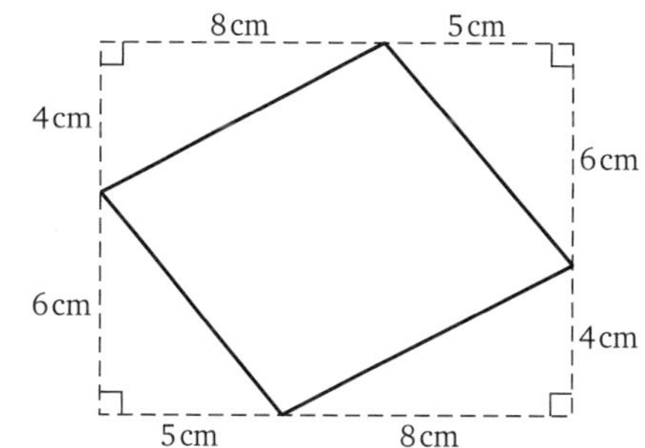

5

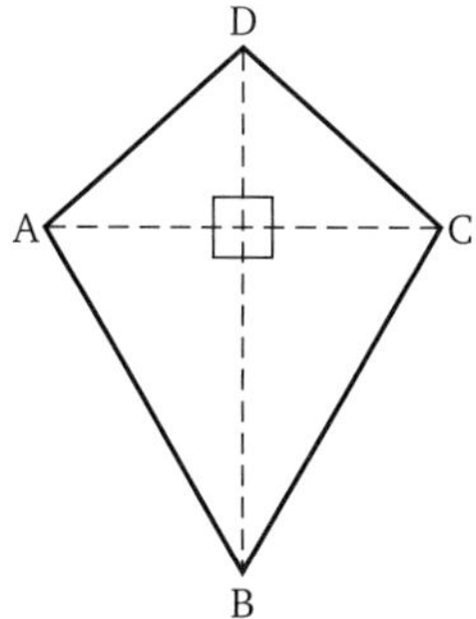

ABCD is a kite

(A *kite* has two pairs of adjacent sides that are equal in length. BD is the line of symmetry.
The diagonals cut at right angles.)

AC = 10 cm BD = 12 cm

9 ABCD is a rhombus whose diagonals measure 7 cm and 11 cm.

10 ABCD is a kite whose diagonals measure 12 cm and 8 cm. (There are several possible kites you can draw with these measurements but their areas are all the same. See question **5** for the properties of a kite.)

Mixed exercises

Exercise 18g

Find the areas of the following figures:

1

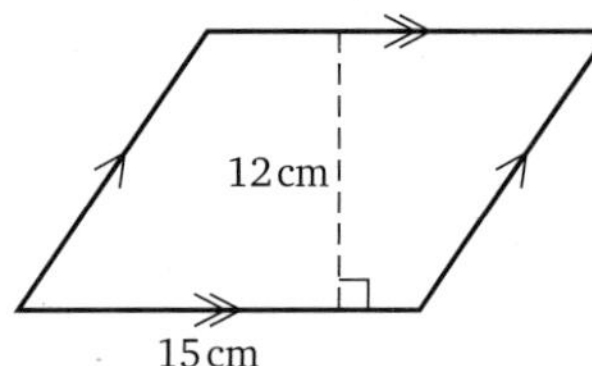

2

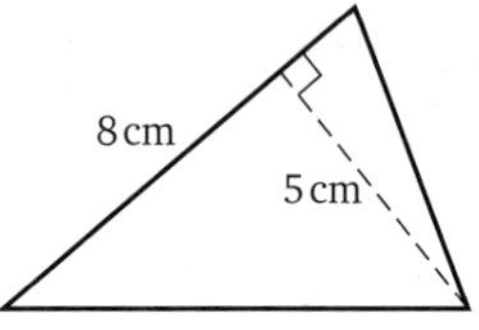

3

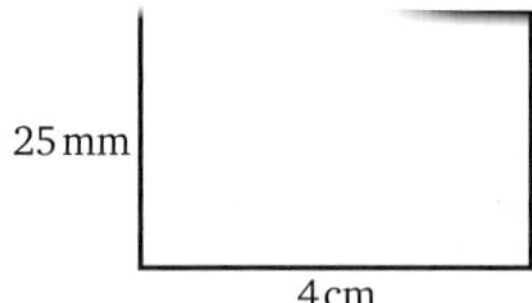

4

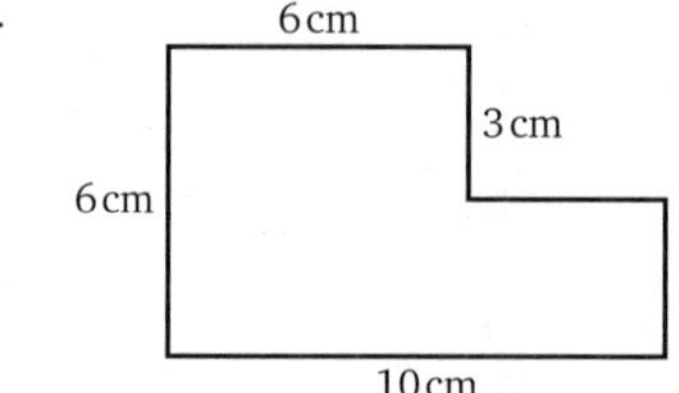

5 The area of a rectangle is $84\,\text{cm}^2$ and its width is 6 cm. Find its length.

6 The area of the parallelogram below is $52\,\text{cm}^2$. Find the distance, d cm, between the parallel lines.

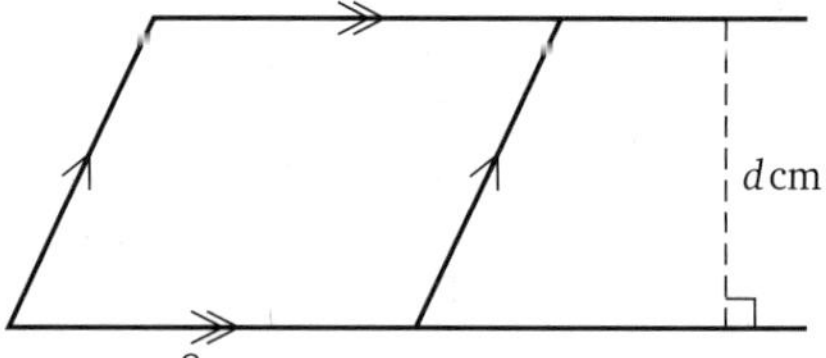

Exercise 18h

Select the letter that gives the correct answer.

1 The area of this triangle is

A $6\,\text{cm}^2$

B $7\frac{1}{2}\,\text{cm}^2$

C $10\,\text{cm}^2$

D $12\,\text{cm}^2$

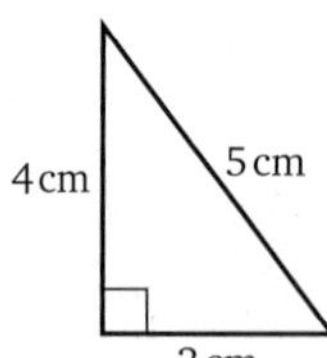

2 The area of this parallelogram is

A $24\,\text{cm}^2$

B $36\,\text{cm}^2$

C $48\,\text{cm}^2$

D $60\,\text{cm}^2$

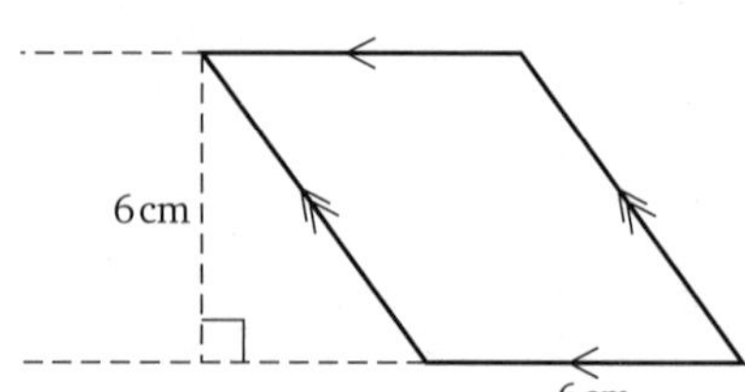

3 The area of this rectangle is

A 10 cm²

B 100 cm²

C 1000 cm²

D 10 000 cm²

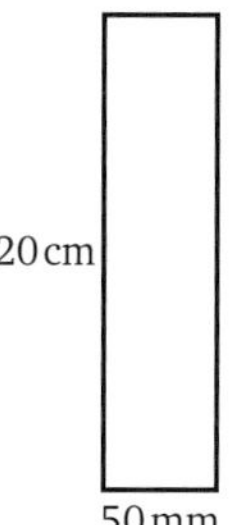

4 The area of this shape is

A 26 cm²

B 36 cm²

C 46 cm²

D 66 cm²

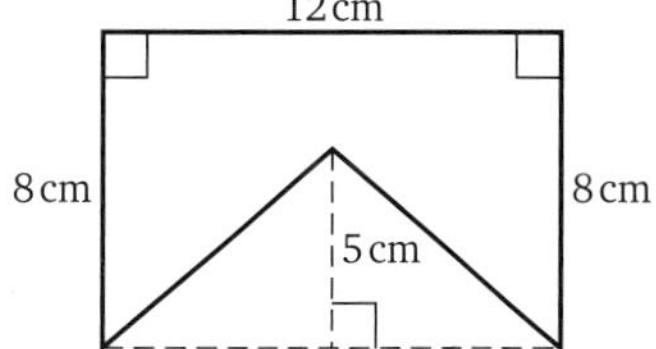

5 The area of this shape is

A 30 cm²

B 40 cm²

C 50 cm²

D 60 cm²

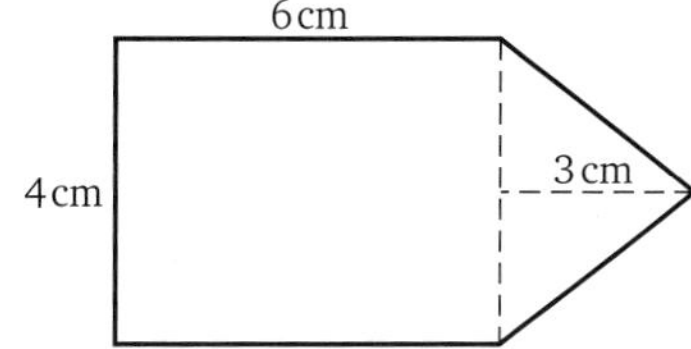

6 The area of a triangle is 24 cm². The height of the triangle is 8 cm. The length of its base is

A 6 cm **B** 8 cm **C** 9 cm **D** 12 cm

Activity

Design a patchwork mat measuring approximately 40 cm by 40 cm. Base your design on a mixture of triangles, parallelograms, squares and rectangles.

Include an estimate of the area of each colour, or texture, that you want to use.

Here are a few ideas. You can find other ideas in books.

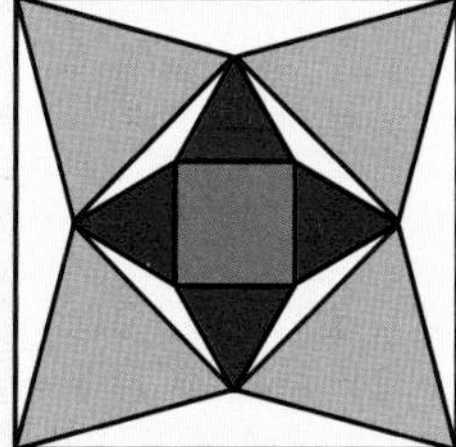

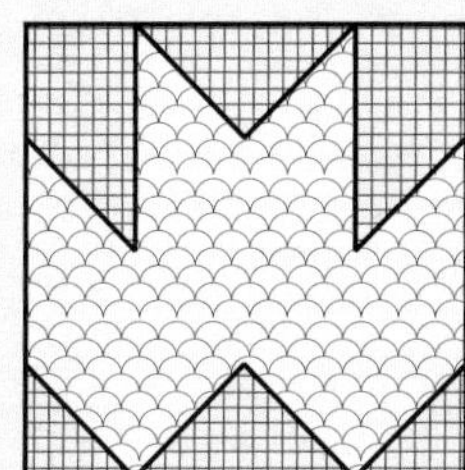

In this chapter you have seen that...

- ✔ when you multiply lengths to find an area, both lengths must be in the same unit
- ✔ the height of a parallelogram or a triangle is the perpendicular height, which is the length of a line perpendicular to the base
- ✔ in some parallelograms and triangles, the line showing the height lies outside the shape
- ✔ the area of a parallelogram is found by multiplying the base by the height
- ✔ the area of a triangle is found by multiplying half the base by the height
- ✔ compound shapes can sometimes be separated into two or more basic shapes
- ✔ a kite is a quadrilateral with two pairs of adjacent sides equal in length. The diagonals are perpendicular.

19 Algebra 2

At the end of this chapter you should be able to...

1 solve simple equations

2 construct and solve simple equations to solve problems

3 form and solve equations containing brackets.

Did you know?

In his treatises, René Descartes signed his name in Latin – Renatus Cartesius. It is from this that the name Cartesian originated.

When you plot points on a graph, you will use Cartesian coordinates.

You need to know...

✔ how to distinguish between like and unlike terms

✔ how to collect like terms

✔ how to work with directed numbers.

Key words

equation, expression, like terms, perimeter, solve, unlike terms

The idea of equations

'I think of a number, and take away 3; the result is 7.'

We can see the number must be 10.

Using a letter to stand for the unknown number we can write the first sentence as an *equation*:

$$x - 3 = 7$$

Then if $\quad x = 10$

$$10 - 3 = 7$$

so $\quad x = 10 \quad$ fits the equation.

Exercise 19a

Form equations to illustrate the following statements and find the unknown numbers:

I think of a number, add 4 and the result is 10.

Let the number be x.

Then add 4 to x. This gives $x+4$ which we know is 10, i.e. $x+4$ and 10 are the same so they are equal. This gives the equation.

The equation is $x+4=10$.

The number is 6.

1 I think of a number, subtract 3 and get 4.

2 I think of a number, add 1 and the result is 3.

3 If a number is added to 3 we get 9.

4 If 5 is subtracted from a number we get 2.

I think of a number, multiply it by 3 and the result is 12.

Let the number be x.

Multiplying by 3 gives $3 \times x$ which can be shortened to $3x$.

We know that $3x$ gives 12.

So the equation is $3x=12$.

The number is 4.

5 I think of a number, double it and get 8.

6 If a number is multiplied by 7 the result is 14.

7 When we multiply a number by 3 we get 15.

8 Six times an unknown number gives 24.

$4x=20$

$4x=20$ means 4 times an unknown number gives 20, or, I think of a number, multiply it by 4 and the result is 20.

Write sentences to show the meaning of the following equations:

9 $3x=18$

10 $x+6=7$

11 $x-2=9$

12 $5x=20$

13 $5+x=7$

14 $x-4=1$

15 $4x=8$

16 $x+1=4$

In three years' time I shall be three times as old as I was three years ago.

How old am I?

Solving equations

Some equations need an organised approach, not guesswork.

Imagine a balance:

On this side there is a bag containing an unknown number of marbles, say x marbles, and 4 loose marbles.

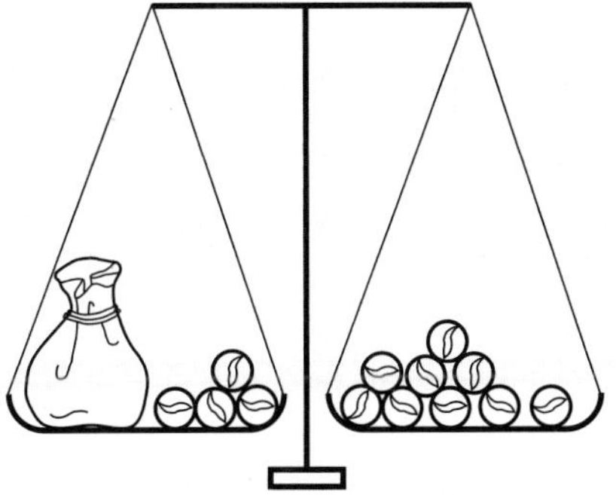

On this side, there are 9 separate marbles, balancing the marbles on the other side.

$$x + 4 = 9$$

Take 4 loose marbles from each side, so that the two sides still balance.

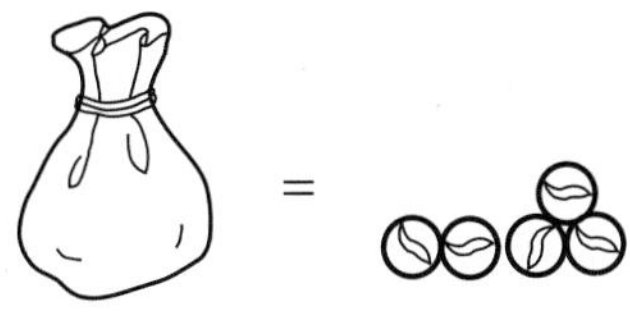

$$x = 5$$

We write: $x + 4 = 9$

Take 4 from both sides $x = 5$

When we have found the value of x we have *solved the equation*.

As a second example suppose that:

On this side there is a bag that originally held x marbles but now has 2 missing.

On this side, there are 5 loose marbles.

$$x-2=5$$

We can make the bag complete by putting back 2 marbles but, to keep the balance, we must add 2 marbles to the right-hand side also.

So we write $\quad x-2=5$

Add 2 to both sides $\quad x=7$

Whatever you do to one side of an equation you must also do to the other side.

Exercise 19b

Solve the following equations:

$y+4=6$

$y+4=6$

Take 4 from both sides $\quad y=2$

1 $x+7=15$

2 $x+9=18$

3 $10+y=12$

4 $2+c=9$

5 $a+3=7$

6 $x+4=9$

7 $a+5=11$

8 $9+a=15$

<u>**9**</u> $a+1=6$

<u>**10**</u> $a+8=15$

<u>**11**</u> $7+c=10$

<u>**12**</u> $c+2=3$

You can 'see' the solution of these equations without doing any working: use this to check your answers.

$x-6=2$

$x-6=2$

Add 6 to both sides $\quad x=8$

13 $x-6=4$

14 $a-2=1$

15 $y-3=5$

16 $x-4=6$

17 $c-8=1$

18 $x-5=7$

19 $s-4=1$

20 $x-9=3$

<u>**21**</u> $a-4=8$

<u>**22**</u> $x-3=0$

<u>**23**</u> $c-1=1$

<u>**24**</u> $y-7=2$

Exercise 19c

Sometimes the letter term is on the right-hand side instead of the left.

$3 = x - 4$

	$3 = x - 4$	
Add 4 to both sides	$7 = x$	($7 = x$ is the same as $x = 7$)
	$x = 7$	

Solve the following equations:

1 $4 = x + 2$

2 $6 = x - 3$

3 $7 = a + 4$

4 $6 = x - 7$

5 $1 = c - 2$

6 $5 = s + 2$

7 $x + 3 = 10$

8 $c + 4 = 4$

9 $3 = b + 2$

10 $6 + c = 10$

11 $7 = x + 3$

12 $x + 1 = 9$

13 $x + 3 = 15$

14 $y - 6 = 4$

15 $x - 7 = 4$

16 $6 = x - 4$

17 $x - 4 = 2$

18 $x - 9 = 2$

19 $x - 1 = 4$

20 $10 = a - 1$

21 $c - 7 = 9$

22 $x - 4 = 8$

23 $y - 1 = 9$

24 $x - 3 = 6$

25 $c - 7 = 10$

26 $4 = b - 1$

27 $x - 4 = 12$

28 $y - 9 = 14$

29 $2 = z - 2$

30 $x + 1 = 8$

31 $x - 1 = 8$

32 $x - 8 = 1$

33 $c + 5 = 9$

34 $d - 3 = 1$

35 $1 = c - 3$

36 $z + 3 = 5$

Multiples of x

Imagine that on this side of the scales there are 3 bags each containing an equal unknown number of marbles, say x in each.

On this side there are 12 loose marbles.

$$3 \times x = 12$$
$$3x = 12$$

We can keep the balance if we divide the contents of each scale pan by 3.

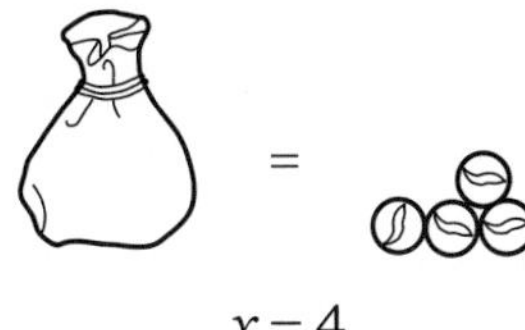

$$x = 4$$

Exercise 19d

Solve $6x = 12$

$$6x = 12$$

Divide both sides by 6 $\quad x = 2$

Solve $3x = 7$

$$3x = 7$$

Divide both sides by 3 $\quad x = \frac{7}{3}$

$$x = 2\frac{1}{3}$$

Solve the following equations:

1	$5x = 10$	**7**	$3a = 1$	**13**	$6x = 36$	**19**	$3x = 27$
2	$3x = 9$	**8**	$6z = 18$	**14**	$6x = 6$	**20**	$8x = 16$
3	$2x = 5$	**9**	$5p = 7$	**15**	$6x = 1$	**21**	$4y = 3$
4	$7x = 21$	**10**	$2x = 40$	**16**	$5z = 10$	**22**	$5x = 6$
5	$4b = 16$	**11**	$7y = 14$	**17**	$5z = 9$	**23**	$2z = 10$
6	$4c = 9$	**12**	$6a = 3$	**18**	$2y = 7$	**24**	$7x = 1$

Mixed operations

Exercise 19e

Solve the following equations:

1	$x + 4 = 8$	**<u>10</u>**	$x - 2 = 11$	**<u>19</u>**	$x + 3 = 5$
2	$x - 4 = 8$	**<u>11</u>**	$12 = x + 4$	**<u>20</u>**	$3x = 5$
3	$4x = 8$	**<u>12</u>**	$x - 12 = 4$	**<u>21</u>**	$z - 5 = 6$
4	$5 + y = 6$	**13**	$8 = c + 2$	**22**	$c + 5 = 5$
5	$5y = 6$	**14**	$3x = 10$	**23**	$5a = 25$
6	$4x = 12$	**15**	$20 = 4x$	**24**	$a + 5 = 25$
7	$4 + x = 12$	**16**	$7y = 2$	**25**	$a - 5 = 25$
8	$x - 4 = 12$	**17**	$3x = 8$	**<u>26</u>**	$a - 25 = 5$
<u>9</u>	$2x = 11$	**<u>18</u>**	$3 = a - 4$	**<u>27</u>**	$25a = 5$

Two operations

Exercise 19f

Solve $7 = 3x - 5$

The aim is to get the letter term on its own	$7 = 3x - 5$
Add 5 to both sides (to isolate the x term)	$12 = 3x$
Divide both sides by 3	$4 = x$
i.e.	$x = 4$

Solve $2x + 3 = 5$

	$2x + 3 = 5$
Take 3 from both sides (to get $2x$ on its own)	$2x = 2$
Divide both sides by 2	$x = 1$

(It is possible to check whether your answer is correct. We can put $x = 1$ in the left-hand side of the equation and see if we get the same value on the right-hand side.)

Check: If $x = 1$, left-hand side $= 2 \times 1 + 3 = 5$

Right-hand side $= 5$, so $x = 1$ fits the equation.

Solve the following equations:

1 $6f + 2 = 26$

2 $4x + 7 = 19$

3 $17 = 7x + 3$

4 $4d - 5 = 19$

5 $7x + 1 = 22$

6 $3a + 12 = 12$

7 $10 = 10x - 50$

8 $6 = 2h - 4$

9 $3p - 4 = 4$

10 $3x + 4 = 25$

11 $2x + 15 = 25$

12 $13 = 3e + 4$

13 $5z - 9 = 16$

14 $20 = 12x - 4$

15 $9g + 1 = 28$

16 $9 = 8x - 15$

17 $8 = 8 + 3z$

18 $5x - 4 = 5$

19 $15 = 1 + 7c$

20 $9x - 4 = 14$

21 $3x - 2 = 3$

22 $7 = 2z + 6$

23 $5 = 7x - 23$

24 $2x + 6 = 6$

25 $19x - 16 = 22$

26 $3x + 1 = 11$

27 $16 = 7x - 1$

28 $10x - 6 = 24$

29 $5x - 7 = 4$

30 $8 = 3x + 7$

Add 50 to both sides.

31 $9 = 6a - 27$

32 $4z + 3 = 4$

33 $2x + 4 = 14$

34 $3 = 7x - 3$

Problems

Exercise 19g

I think of a number, double it and add 3. The result is 15.

What is the number?

Let the number be x. Double it is $2x$, then add 3 gives $2x+3$.

The result is 15 so the equation is $\quad 2x+3=15$

Take 3 from both sides $\quad 2x=12$

Divide both sides by 2 $\quad x=6$

The number is 6.

The side of a square is x cm. Its perimeter is 20 cm.

Find x.

Draw a diagram.

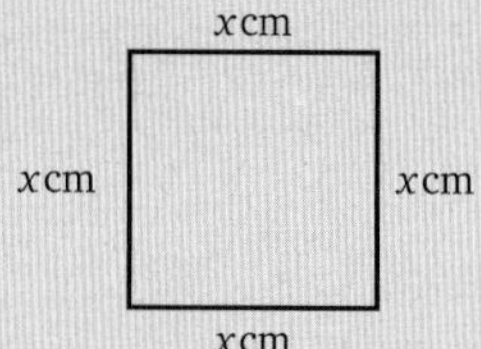

Now you can see that the perimeter is $(x+x+x+x)$ cm which is $4x$ cm.

You also know that the perimeter is 20 cm.

so the equation is $\quad 4x=20$

Divide both sides by 4 $\quad x=5$

Check: $5+5+5+5=10+5+5=15+5=20$.

Form equations and solve the problems:

1 I think of a number, multiply it by 4 and subtract 8. The result is 20. What is the number?

2 I think of a number, multiply it by 6 and subtract 12. The result is 30. What is the number?

3 I think of a number, multiply it by 3 and add 6. The result is 21. What is the number?

4 When 8 is added to an unknown number the result is 10. What is the number?

5 I think of a number, multiply it by 3 and add the result to 7. The total is 28. What is the number?

6 The sides of a rectangle are x cm and 3 cm. Its perimeter is 24 cm. Find x.

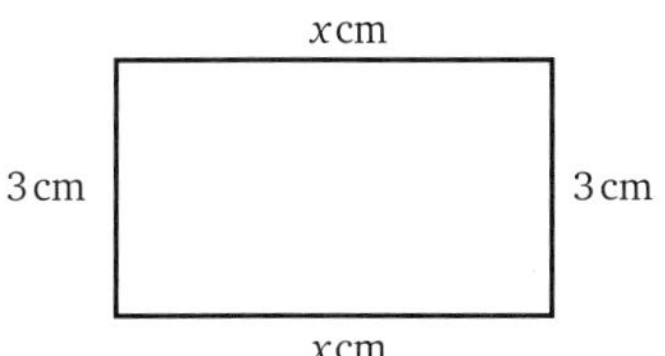

7 The lengths of the three sides of a triangle are x cm, x cm and 6 cm. Its perimeter is 20 cm. Find x.

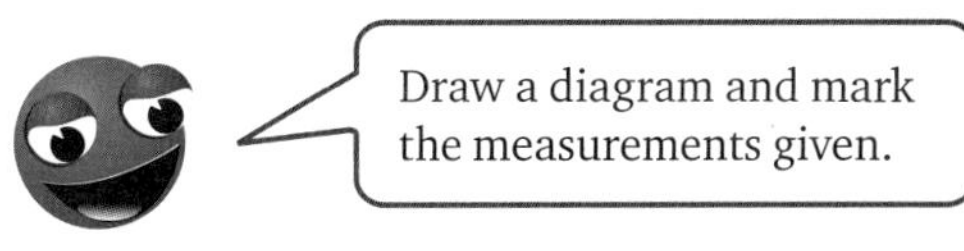

8 Cassie and Amelia each have x sweets and Leela has 10 sweets. Amongst them they have 24 sweets. What is x?

9 Three boys had x sweets each. Amongst them they gave 9 sweets to a fourth boy and then found that they had 18 sweets left altogether. Find x.

10 I have two pieces of ribbon each x cm long and a third piece 9 cm long. Altogether there are 31 cm of ribbon. What is the length of each of the first two pieces?

Brackets

Remember that $3(x-2)$ means 'three times everything in the bracket',

so
$$\begin{aligned} 3(x-2) &= 3 \times x + 3 \times (-2) \\ &= 3x - 6 \end{aligned}$$

Exercise 19h

Multiply out the following brackets:

1	$5(x+3)$	**3**	$7(x-2)$	**5**	$2(3x-7)$
2	$3(x+4)$	**4**	$4(2x+3)$	**6**	$6(2x-1)$

Simplify the following expressions:

7	$7-2(3-x)$	**10**	$3x+2(x+1)$
8	$5+(x-2)$	**11**	$3(x-2)+2(x+5)$
9	$5-4(3-2x)$	**12**	$7x-(3-x)$

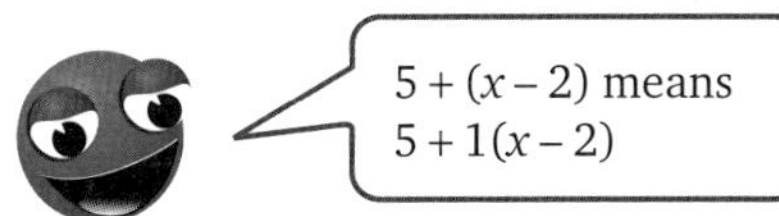

Equations containing brackets

If we wish to solve equations containing brackets we first multiply out the brackets and then collect like terms.

Exercise 19i

Solve $4 + 2(x + 1) = 22$.

Remember whatever you do to one side of an equation you must do to the other.

$4 + 2(x + 1) = 22$ First multiply out the brackets

$4 + 2x + 2 = 22$

$2x + 6 = 22$ You want the x term on its own.

Take 6 from both sides $2x = 16$

Divide both sides by 2 $x = 8$

Check: If $x = 8$, left-hand side $= 4 + 2(8 + 1)$

$= 4 + 2 \times 9$

$= 22$

Right-hand side $= 22$, so $x = 8$ is the solution.

Solve the following equations:

1 $6 + 3(x + 4) = 24$

2 $3x + 2 = 2(2x + 1)$

3 $5x + 3(x + 1) = 14$

4 $5(x + 1) = 20$

5 $2(x + 5) = 6(x + 1)$

<u>6</u> $28 = 4(3x + 1)$

<u>7</u> $4 + 2(x + 1) = 12$

<u>8</u> $7x + (x + 2) = 22$

<u>9</u> $8x + 3(2x + 1) = 7$

10 $4x - 2 = 1 + (2x + 3)$

11 $7x + x = 4x + (x + 1)$

12 $3(x + 2) + 4(2x + 1) = 6x + 20$

13 $6x + 4 + 5(x + 6) = 56$

14 $2 + 3(x + 8) = 4(2x + 1)$

Solve the equation $4 - (2 - x) = 5$.

$4 - (2 - x) = 5$ Remember that $-(2 - x)$ means $(-1) \times (2 - x)$

$4 - 2 + x = 5$ $(-1) \times (2) = -2$ and $(-1) \times (-x) = +x$

$2 + x = 5$

$x = 3$

Solve the following equations:

15 $2-(x-4)=2$

16 $3-(3x+1)=1$

17 $5-(3-x)=10$

18 $6x-2(x-4)=1$

19 $x-4(3-x)=3$

20 $2(5-x)-3(4-2x)=6$

21 $3(2x-4)-2(x-5)=10$

22 $5(1-x)-3(1-3x)=10$

23 $2(x+7)-3(x-5)=21$

24 $2(x-3)+x-(1-x)=1$

Puzzle

Hindu problem solving

The ancient Hindus were fond of doing number puzzles. A mathematician named Aryabhata who lived in India during the sixth century CE liked this kind of puzzle:

> If 5 is added to a certain number, the result divided by 2, that result multiplied by 6, and then 8 subtracted from that result, the answer is 34. Find the number.

Aryabhata solved this problem using the method of inversion, i.e. he worked backwards and did the inverse, or opposite steps as he went along. Adding and subtracting are inverse steps. Dividing and multiplying are inverse steps.

Let us set out Aryabhata's problem using a diagram.

We will set out the problem on the left starting at the top.

On the right we will start at the bottom and do the inverse steps:

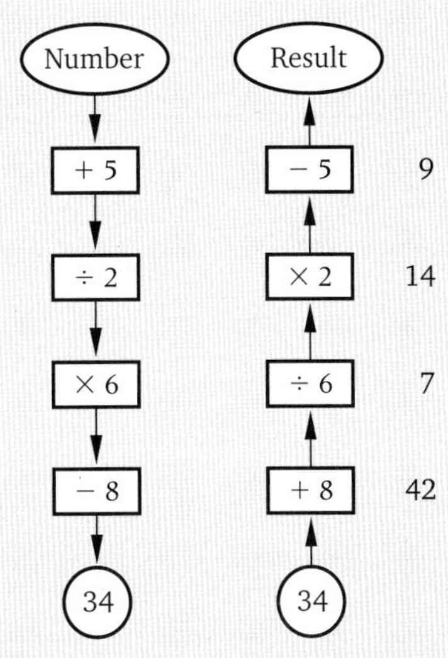

Try this method yourself on questions **1**, **2** and **4** of the next exercise.

Problems to be solved by forming equations

Exercise 19j

The width of a rectangle is x cm. Its length is 4 cm more than its width. The perimeter is 48 cm. What is the width?

The width is x cm so the length is $(x+4)$ cm.

The perimeter is the distance all around the rectangle; from the diagram this is $x+(x+4)+x+(x+4)$.

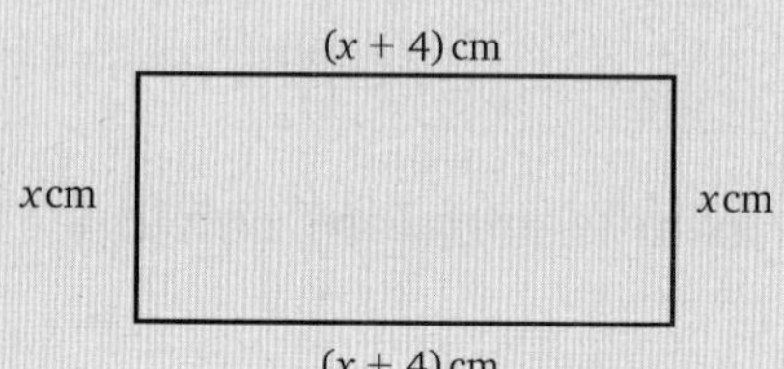

You also know this is 48 cm

so $\quad x+(x+4)+x+(x+4)=48$

Removing the brackets and collecting like terms gives

$$4x+8=48$$

Take 8 from each side $\quad 4x=40$

Divide each side by 4 $\quad x=10$

Therefore the width is 10 cm.

A choc-ice costs x cents and a cone costs 3 cents more. One choc-ice and two cones together cost 54 cents.

How much is a choc-ice?

A choc-ice costs x cents and a cone costs $(x+3)$ cents.

It follows that 2 cones cost $2\times(x+3)$ cents

so the cost of a choc-ice and two cones is $x+2(x+3)$ cents

But you know that the total cost is 54 cents

so $\quad x+2(x+3)=54 \quad$ Now multiply out the bracket

$x+2x+6=54 \quad$ Collect like terms

$3x+6=54 \quad$ Take 6 from each side

$3x=48 \quad$ Divide each side by 3

$x=16$

Therefore a choc-ice costs 16 cents.

Solve the following problems by forming an equation in each case. Explain, either in words or on a diagram, what your letter stands for and always end by answering the question asked.

1 I think of a number, double it and add 14. The result is 36. What is the number?

Start by letting the number be x. Next write down what double this is and then add 14. You can now form an equation in x.

2 I think of a number and add 6. The result is equal to twice the first number. What is the first number?

3 In triangle ABC, AB = AC. The perimeter is 24 cm. Find AB.

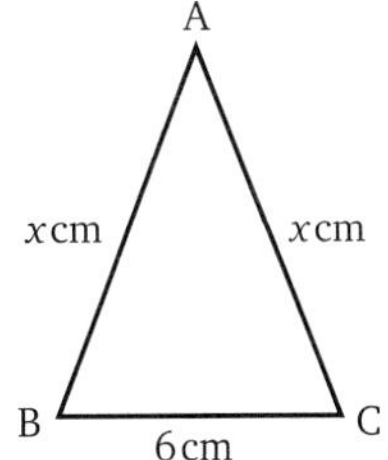

4 A bun costs x cents and a cake costs 3 cents more than a bun. Four cakes and three buns together cost 159 cents. How much does one bun cost?

Find the cost of 1 cake, then the cost of 4 cakes. Add on the cost of 3 buns. The total cost is given, so you can form an equation in x and solve it to find x.

5 A bus started from the terminus with x passengers. At the first stop another x passengers got on and 3 got off. At the next stop, 8 passengers got on. There were then 37 passengers. How many passengers were there on the bus to start with?

Mixed exercises

Exercise 19k

Select the letter that gives the correct answer.

1 The solution of the equation $2x - 5 = 7$ is $x =$

A 4 B 5 C 6 D 7

2 The solution of the equation $4x - 3 = 2x + 3$ is $x =$

A 1 B 2 C 3 D 4

3 I think of a number, double it and add 5. The result is 19. What number did I think of?

A 6 B 7 C 8 D 9

4 I think of a number, treble it and subtract 9. The answer is 12.
What number did I think of?

A 6 **B** 7 **C** 8 **D** 9

5 The solution of the equation $7 - 2x = 3$ is $x =$

A 2 **B** 3 **C** 4 **D** 5

6 The value of x that satisfies the equation $5(x - 1) - 3 = 3(x + 2)$ is

A 5 **B** 6 **C** 7 **D** 8

Exercise 19l

1 Solve the equation $4x - 5 = 3$.

2 Solve the equation $4(x + 3) = 16$.

3 Solve the equation $3x - 2 = 4 - x$.

4 When I think of a number, double it and add three, I get 11.
What number did I think of?

5 Solve the equation $3x - 4 - x + 6 = 8$.

6 Solve the equation $3 - 4(5 - x) = 3$.

Exercise 19m

1 Solve the equation $2x - 9 = 2$.

2 Solve the equation $2x + 8 + 3x - 6 = 4$.

3 Solve the equation $5 - 3x + 2 + 7x = 11$.

4 I think of a number and double it and subtract 3 and I get 7.
What number did I think of?

5 When shopping, Mrs Jones spent $x in the first shop, the same amount in the second shop, $2 in the third and $8 in the last. The total amount she spent was $18. Form an equation. How much did she spend in the first shop?

6 In a quadrilateral ABCD, angle A is $x°$, angle B is twice the size of angle A, angle C is 40° less than angle A and angle D is 25° more than angle A. Find the size of angle D.

Puzzle

1 May bought a certain number of 19 c stamps and a certain number of 28 c stamps. Altogether she paid $3.19 for these stamps. How many of each did she buy?

2 Lance wrote down a lot of plus sevens and minus fours. Altogether he wrote 22 digits. When he came to add them all up the total was zero. How many plus sevens were there?

Investigation

P is any point on a diagonal of a 6 cm × 4 cm rectangle.

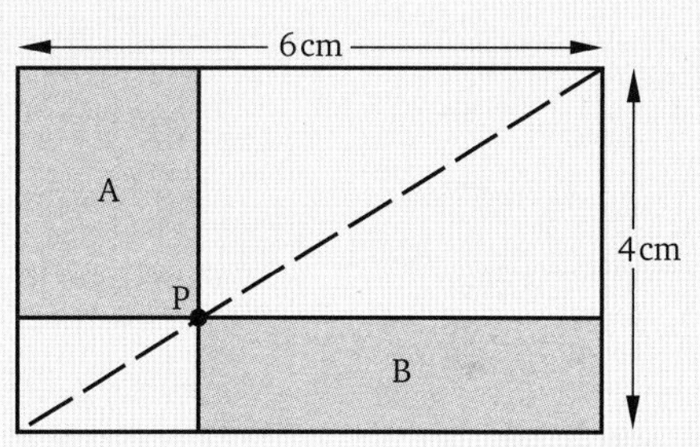

Investigate the relationship between the area of rectangle A and the area of rectangle B.

Which of these is true?

area A $>$ area B

area A = area B

area A $<$ area B

In this chapter you have seen that...

✔ an equation means the equality of two expressions

✔ you can do whatever you like with an equation as long as you do the same to both sides

✔ to solve an equation, aim to have the letter terms on one side of the equals sign and the number terms on the other side

✔ you can check your solution by replacing the letter by the number in each side independently: they will be equal if your answer is correct.

✔ you can solve problems by forming an equation.

20 Sequences

At the end of this chapter you should be able to...

1 find any term of a sequence when you know the expression for the nth term

2 find an expression for the nth term of a sequence from the pattern seen in the first few terms.

Did you know?

Throughout the ages tools have been used in mathematics. Use your encyclopedia to find out about the following tools, and match them to the possible uses given.

Tool	**Uses**
Vernier caliper	Drawing arcs
Dice	Drawing similar figures
Napier's bones	Scientific computation
Pantograph	Measuring small objects
Pair of compasses	Multiplication
Abacus	Early Peruvian computation
Quipu	Random-number generation
Slide rule	Manual four-function calculation

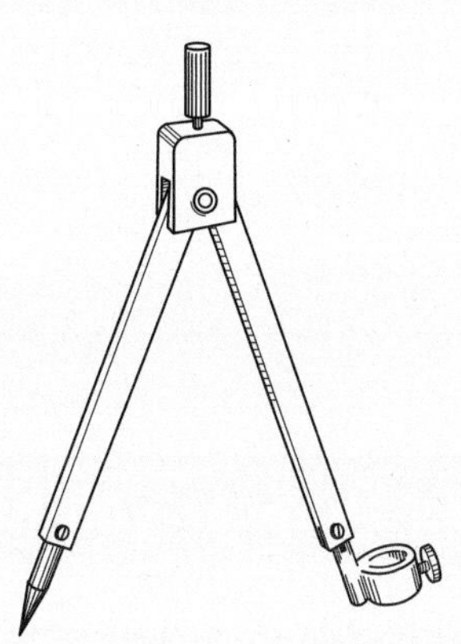

You need to know...

✔ the meaning of an algebraic expression
✔ how to form an expression from a written description
✔ how to substitute numerical values into an expression
✔ how to work with directed numbers.

Key words

even numbers, expression, nth term, odd numbers, sequence, term of a sequence, variable

Sequences

A sequence is a collection of numbers or objects in a particular order.

The set of numbers {5, 11, 8, 2} is not in any particular order and is not a sequence.

However 2, 5, 8, 11, ... is a sequence. There is a first term, a second term, a third term, and so on. The pattern is 'add 3 to get the next number'.
We can now continue the sequence: 2, 5, 8, 11, 14, 17, 20, 23, ...

If we want the 40th term, we could continue adding threes until we get to that term. However, it is quicker if we can use a general expression with a *variable* for the position number of the term. Then we can substitute the value we want for the variable to find any particular term.

For this sequence, the nth term is given by $3n - 1$.

The 40th term is therefore the value of $3n - 1$ when $n = 40$,

giving

$$\begin{aligned} 40\text{th term} &= 3 \times 40 - 1 \\ &= 120 - 1 \\ &= 119 \end{aligned}$$

Exercise 20a

1 This table shows a sequence of shapes.

Shape number	1	2	3	4	5
Number of asterisks	*	* * *	* * * * * *		

a Draw the 4th and 5th shapes in the sequence.

b How many asterisks are there in the 8th shape?

2 This table shows a sequence of shapes made with rectangles that each measure 1 cm by 2 cm.

Shape	▭	▭▭	▭▭▭		
Shape number	1	2	3	4	5
Area of shape (cm^2)	2	4	6		

a Draw shapes numbers 4 and 5. Hence complete the last row of the table.

b Find the area of the 20th shape without drawing the shape.

3 This table shows a sequence of shapes made from sticks.

Shape	Area of shape	Number of sticks used
☒	1 square unit	6
☒☒	2 square units	11
☒☒☒	3 square units	16

a Copy the table and add two more rows. Fill in the rows with the shapes, their area and the number of sticks used.

b A shape in this sequence has an area of 8 square units. How many sticks are used to make it?

c A shape in this sequence uses 51 sticks. What is the area of this shape?

4 This table shows a pattern of dots that form triangles.

Pattern	○	○ ○ ○	○ ○ ○ ○ ○ ○	○ ○ ○ ○ ○ ○ ○ ○ ○ ○			
Pattern number	1	2	3	4	5	6	7
Number of dots	1	3	6	10			
Sum of dots in the pattern number and the pattern before it		4	9	16			

a Copy the table and fill in the blank cells.

b What is the relationship between the number in the second row and the number below it in the fourth row?

The nth term of a sequence is $20 - 2n$. Find:

a the first three terms **b** the 20th term.

a The 1st term is when $n = 1$, i.e. $20 - 2 = 18$

The 2nd term is when $n = 2$, i.e. $20 - 2 \times 2 = 20 - 4 = 16$

The 3rd term is when $n = 3$, i.e. $20 - 2 \times 3 = 20 - 6 = 14$

b The 20th term is when $n = 20$ giving $20 - 2 \times 20$

$20 - 40 = -20$

5 The nth term of a sequence is $2n$. Find the first three terms and the 10th term.

6 The nth term of a sequence is $2n - 1$. Find the first three terms and the 12th term.

7 The nth term of a sequence is $1 + 2n$. Find the first three terms and the 8th term.

8 The nth term of a sequence is $20 - 2n$. Find the first three terms and the 6th term.

9 The nth term of a sequence is $1 - n$. Find the first three terms and the 20th term.

In questions **10** to **16**, one of the terms of a sequence is given and the expression for the nth term. Check that the given term is correct and write down the first four terms and the tenth term.

10 nth term $= 2 + 2n$, 6th term $= 14$

11 nth term $= 3n - 1$, 8th term $= 23$

12 nth term $= n + 5$, 9th term $= 14$

13 nth term $= 3n - 2$, 6th term $= 16$

14 nth term $= \frac{1}{2n}$, 22nd term $= \frac{1}{44}$

15 nth term $= \frac{1}{n+1}$, 7th term $= \frac{1}{8}$

16 nth term $= 4 - n$, 5th term $= -1$

Finding an expression for the nth term of a sequence

In the *sequence* 2, 6, 10, 14, 18, ... , the first term is 2, the second term is 6, the third term is 10, and so on.

If we use n for the position number of a term, we can arrange the terms in a table, i.e.

n	1	2	3	4	5
nth term	2	6	10	14	18

We can see that each term is 4 more than the term before it. We can use this fact to find nth term in terms of n.

Rewriting the table to give the nth term in terms of the first term, 2, and the difference between the terms, 4, gives

n	1	2	3	4	5
nth term	2	$2 + 1(4)$	$2 + 2(4)$	$2 + 3(4)$	$2 + 4(4)$

Comparing the value of the nth term with the value of n, we can see that the nth term is equal to 2 plus one fewer number of 4s than the value of n, i.e.

$$\begin{aligned} n\text{th term} &= 2 + (n - 1)4 \\ &= 2 + 4n - 4 \\ &= 4n - 2 \end{aligned}$$

Exercise 20b

A sequence is 6, 10, 14, 18, …

Find an expression for the nth term.

The 1st term = 6, 2nd term = 10, 3rd = 14, and so on.
Using n for the position number of a term, arrange the terms in a table:

n	1	2	3	4	…
nth term	6	10	14	18	

The first term is 6, the second term is 6 + 4, the third term is 6 + 2(4), the fourth term is 6 + 3(4), and so on.

We can put this information in a table:

n	1	2	3	4	5	…
nth term	6	6 + 4	6 + 2(4)	6 + 3(4)	6 + 4(4)	…

Now we can see clearly that we add one fewer number of 4s than the term number. So we can write that the nth term is $6 + 4(n - 1)$

$$\begin{aligned} &= 6 + 4n - 4 \\ &= 4n + 2 \end{aligned}$$

Check: when $n = 1$, $4n + 2 = 4 + 2 = 6$

when $n = 2$, $4n + 2 = 8 + 2 = 10$

when $n = 3$, $4n + 2 = 12 + 2 = 14$

In questions **1** to **4**, find an expression for the nth term. Check your expression by using it to find the first three terms.

1

n	1	2	3	4	5
nth term	2	3	4	5	6

2

n	1	2	3	4	5
nth term	4	5	6	7	8

3

n	1	2	3	4	5
nth term	2	4	6	8	10

4

n	1	2	3	4	5
nth term	0	1	2	3	4

5 For each sequence given in questions **1** to **4**, write down, in words, the rule for generating the sequence.

6 The terms of a sequence are generated by starting with 2 and adding 3 each time.

a Write the first five terms in a table like those given in questions **1** to **4**.

b Find an expression for the nth term.

7 The terms of a sequence are generated by starting with 10 and subtracting 2 each time.

a Write the first five terms in a table like those given in questions **1** to **4**.

b Find an expression for the nth term.

8 The terms of a sequence are generated by starting with 5 and adding 5 each time.

a Write the first five terms in a table like those given in questions **1** to **4**.

b Find an expression for the nth term.

9 The terms of a sequence are generated by starting with 2 and subtracting $\frac{1}{2}$ each time.

a Write the first five terms in a table like those given in questions **1** to **4**.

b Find an expression for the nth term.

Questions **10** and **11** describe how the terms of a sequence are generated. For each question repeat parts **a** and **b** of question **6**.

10 Double the position number and add 1.

11 Subtract 5 from the position number.

In each of questions **12** to **20** find an expression for the nth term and write down the next three terms of the sequence.

12 3, 8, 13, 18, ...

13 20, 18, 16, 14, ...

14 3, 6, 9, 12, ...

15 3, 7, 11, 15, ...

16 $1, \frac{1}{2}, \frac{1}{3}, \frac{1}{4}, \ldots$

17 $\frac{1}{2}, \frac{1}{4}, \frac{1}{6}, \frac{1}{8}, \ldots$

18 60, 54, 48, 42, ...

19 100, 50, 25, 12.5, ...

20 $\frac{1}{3}, \frac{1}{5}, \frac{1}{7}, \frac{1}{9}, \ldots$

Exercise 20c

Select the letter that gives the correct answer.

1 The nth term of a sequence is $2n + 1$. The 8th term is

A 17 **B** 18 **C** 19 **D** 20

2 The nth term of a sequence is $16 - n$. The 9th term is

A 6 **B** 7 **C** 8 **D** 9

3 The nth term of a sequence is $1 - n$. The 5th term is

A -4 **B** -3 **C** -2 **D** -1

4 21 is a term in the sequence given by the expression $2n + 3$.

Which term in the sequence is this?

A 7th **B** 8th **C** 9th **D** 10th

5 Starting with 11 and adding 4 each time, an expression for the nth term in this sequence is

A $6n + 5$ **B** $4n + 7$ **C** $4n + 11$ **D** $4n + 8$

6 The terms of a sequence are generated by starting with 20 and subtracting 3 each time.

An expression for the nth term in this sequence is

A $20 - 3n$ **B** $20 - 2n$ **C** $23 - n$ **D** $23 - 3n$

Investigation

Can you determine how many handshakes there would be if each member in a class of thirty decides to shake hands with every other member of the class?

Consider the following table and fill in the blank spaces.

Number of people, n	Number of handshakes, h	Difference in number of handshakes
1	0	0
2	1	1
3	3	2
4	6	3
5	10	4
6		
7		
8		
9		
*		
*		
*		
20	190	19

How many handshakes will there be for a class of 30?

How many handshakes will there be for 100 persons?

In this chapter you have seen that...

- ✔ a sequence is a set of numbers in the order 1st term, 2nd term, 3rd term, and so on
- ✔ when you have an expression for the nth term in terms of n, you can use it to find any term in the sequence
- ✔ when you know the first few terms in a sequence you can use a table to help find the pattern and use the pattern to find an expression for the nth term in terms of n.

21 Consumer arithmetic

At the end of this chapter you should be able to...

1 work out best buys
2 find the sales tax given the percentage tax
3 work out discounts given the percentage reduction
4 express profit and loss as a percentage of the cost price
5 find the simple interest on a sum of money given the interest rate and the time
6 calculate the amount of a sum of money given the interest rate and the time.

Did you know?

Marjorie Lee Browne (1914–79) was one of the first two black women to receive a doctorate in mathematics in the USA. Her father was considered to be a 'whiz' at mental arithmetic. He first stimulated her interest in maths as a child and later he learned maths from her.

You need to know...

✔ how to work with decimals and fractions
✔ how to work with percentages
✔ how to substitute numbers into expressions
✔ how to correct a number to a given place value.

Key words

amount, cost price, discount, interest, loss, per annum, principal, profit, rate per cent, sales tax, selling price, simple interest

Cash

The currency used in many Caribbean countries is dollars.

These are the dollar bills in circulation in Trinidad and Tobago. Other countries use a $1 coin instead of a note.

Exercise 21a

1 What is the smallest number of bills in the currency of your country needed to make a total of $1000?

2 How many $50 bills are needed to make $1000?

3 Give two possible combinations of $50, $20 and $10 bills that can be used to make $1000.

4 Brittney had two $100 bills, four $50 bills and one $10 bill. She needed to make up a total of $1000. When she went to the bank they offered $10 and $20 bills. Give two possible combinations of bills that Brittney could add to the bills she had already to make a total of $1000.

Best buys

These two jars of coffee contain different amounts of coffee and cost different amounts of money.

You can find which of these two jars is the better value for money (or best buy). There are two ways you can do this.

The first way is to work out the cost of the *same weight* for each jar.

The smaller jar holds 200 g and costs \$2.75.

The larger jar holds 1 kg and costs \$13.45.

To compare the cost of coffee with the smaller jar, you can find the cost of 200 grams. $1\,\text{kg} = 5 \times 200\,\text{g}$, so 200 g of coffee in the larger jar costs $\$13.45 \div 5 = \$2.69$.

Now you can see that the cost of 200 g of coffee is less in the larger jar than in the smaller jar. So the larger jar is better value for money.

The second way is to find the mass of coffee that the *same amount of money* will buy.

The smaller jar costs \$2.75 for 200 g, so \$1 will buy $200\,\text{g} \div 2.75 = 73\,\text{g}$ to the nearest gram.

The larger jar costs \$13.45 for 1 kg, so \$1 will buy $1\,\text{kg} \div 13.45 = 1000\,\text{g} \div 13.45 = 74\,\text{g}$ to the nearest gram.

Now you can see that \$1 will buy more coffee in the larger jar than the smaller jar. So the larger jar is better value for money.

Exercise 21b

1

3 for \$5.55

175 c each

You can compare these prices by either finding the cost of 3 of the single peppers or by finding the cost of one of the peppers in the pack. Whichever way you choose, remember to show your working.

Peppers are sold in packs of three or singly.
Which is the better value?
Give a reason for your answer.

2 Cans of cola are sold in packs of 4 cans and in packs of 6 cans.

Which pack is better value for money?
Give a reason for your answer.

3 These are two different bags of paper clips.
Which bag is better value for money?
Explain your answer.

You can compare the number of clips per cent or the cost of one clip.

4

Which pack of tomatoes is better value for money?
Give a reason for your answer.

5 String is sold in rolls of two sizes.
Jane said that the larger roll is better value for money.
Is Jane correct?
Give a reason for your answer.

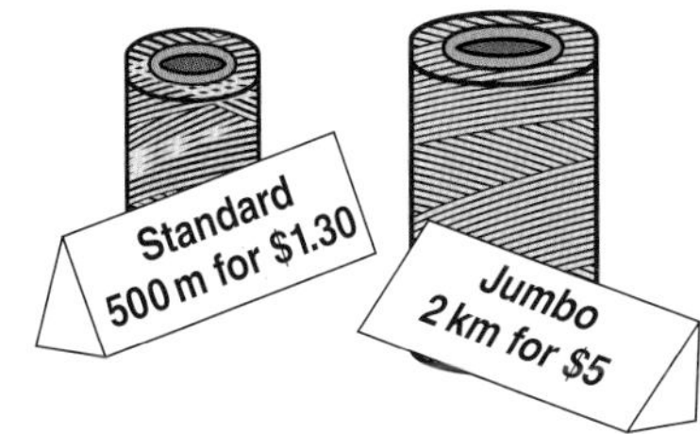

6 Cheese is sold from the delicatessen counter where it is priced at $3.52 per 500 g.
Cheese is also sold in prepacks weighing 200 g and costing $1.30 a pack.
Which way of buying cheese is better value?
Explain your answer.

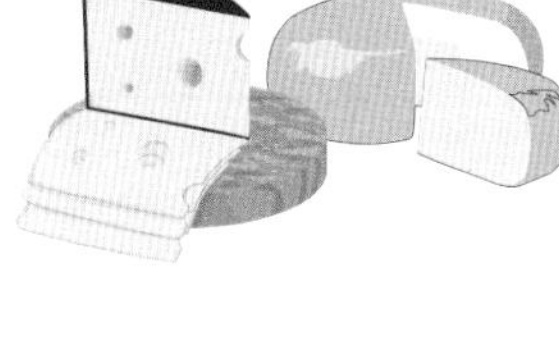

7 **a** What is the cost of 25 g from the smaller jar of coffee?
b What is the cost of 25 g from the larger jar?
c Which jar is the better value for money?
d An even larger jar contains 250 g of coffee and costs $3.70.
Is this better value for money than either of the other two?
Give a reason for your answer.

$1.20

$2.90

8

$1.50

$3

Which jar is better value?

Sales tax

The government is forever looking for ways of extracting money from us to pay for its spending. One such way is to put a tax on almost everything that is sold. This *sales tax* is usually a fixed percentage of the selling price. It is also called value added tax (VAT) in some countries.

Exercise 21c

A cell phone is priced at \$500 plus a sales tax of 12%.

Find: **a** the sales tax **b** the price to be paid for the cell phone.

a The sales tax = 12% of \$500

$= \$500 \times \frac{12}{100}$

$= \$500 \times 0.12$

$= \$60.00$

b The price to be paid = \$500 + \$60.00

$= \$560.00$

In questions **1** to **3** find the total purchase price of the item. Take the rate of sales tax as 15%

1 An electric cooker marked \$1600 + sales tax

2 A calculator costing \$20 + sales tax

3 A van marked \$21 000 + sales tax

4 The price tag on a television gives \$655 plus sales tax at 15%. What does the customer have to pay?

5 In March, Nicki looked at a camera costing \$320 plus sales tax. The sales tax rate at that time was $17\frac{1}{2}$%. How much would the camera have cost in March? Nicki decided to wait until June to buy the camera but by then the sales tax had been raised to 22%. How much did she have to pay?

6 An electric cooker was priced in a showroom at \$1100 plus value added tax (VAT) at 15%.

a What was the price to the customer?

Later in the year value added tax was increased to 17.5%. The showroom manager placed a notice on the cooker that read:

Due to the increase in VAT this cooker will now cost you \$1296.63.

b Was the manager correct?

c If your answer is 'Yes', state how the manager calculated the new price. If your answer is 'No', give your reason and find the correct price.

Discount

Stores often have promotions or sales when they offer a reduction of some prices. This is called a *discount*. Sometimes the discount is an amount of money. For example '\$20 off when you spend \$200'. Sometimes the discount is a percentage of the price. For example, 'Sale: 10% off all sale items'.

Exercise 21d

The online store goodbuys.com is offering a discount of 10% on all items.

Keron orders a table priced at \$500. What is the price of the table after the discount is applied?

$$10\% \text{ of } \$500 = \$500 \times \frac{10}{100}$$
$$= \$500 \times 0.1 = \$50$$

Therefore the discounted price is \$500 – \$50 = \$450.

In a sale, a shop offers a discount of 20%. What would be the cash price for each of the following articles?

1 A dress marked \$105

2 A lawn mower marked \$460

3 A pair of shoes marked \$64

4 A set of garden tools priced \$290.00

5 Light fittings marked \$168 each

In a sale, a department store offers a discount of 50% on the following articles. Find their sale price:

6 A pair of curtains marked \$153

7 A leather football marked \$129.20

8 A boy's jacket marked \$85.80

9 A girl's dress marked \$64.50

10 In order to clear a large quantity of goods a shopkeeper puts them on sale at a discount of $33\frac{1}{3}\%$. Find the cash price of

a a shirt marked \$36.60

b a skirt marked \$66.60.

Profit and loss

When a store buys items, the price it pays is called the *cost price* (CP). The store then sells the items at a price called the *selling price* (SP).

When the selling price is greater than the cost price, the store makes a *profit*. When the selling price is less than the cost price, the store makes a *loss*.

For example, SportCom purchased some pairs of trainers for \$150 a pair. They sold them for \$250 a pair. Therefore the profit on each pair is \$250 – \$150 = \$100.

Some pairs of trainers did not sell at the full price, so SportCom sold them for \$120 a pair. Therefore the store made a loss on those trainers of \$150 – \$120 = \$30.

Profit and loss are often given as percentages. The percentage profit or loss is always found as a percentage of the cost price. So the percentage profit on the trainers sold at full price is \$100 as a percentage of \$150, which is

$$\frac{100}{150} \times 100\% = 66.66...\% = 66.7\% \text{ correct to 1 decimal place.}$$

The percentage loss on the trainers sold at \$120 is \$30 as a percentage of \$150, which is

$$\frac{30}{150} \times 100\% = 20\%$$

Exercise 21e

In questions **1** to **6** find the percentage profit or loss.

1 A calculator costing \$80 and sold for \$120

2 A food mixer costing \$500 and selling for \$750

3 A car that cost \$3000 and was sold for \$2000

4 A concert ticket that cost \$75 and was sold for \$50

5 A chair costing \$250 that was sold for \$150

6 A computer desk that cost \$90 and was sold for \$180

7 Monique bought a cell phone for \$1500 and sold it two years later for \$800. What was Monique's loss?

8 Kyle bought an old chair for \$10. He renovated the chair and sold it for \$50. What profit did Kyle make?

A second-hand car dealer bought a car for \$3500 and sold it for \$4340. Find his percentage profit.

$$\begin{aligned}\text{Profit} &= \text{SP} - \text{CP} \\ &= \$4340 - \$3500 = \$840 \\ \%\ \text{profit} &= \frac{\text{profit}}{\text{CP}} \times 100\% \\ &= \frac{\$840}{\$3500} \times 100\% = 24\%\end{aligned}$$

Therefore the percentage profit is 24%.

Find the percentage profit:

9 CP \$12, profit \$3

10 CP \$28, profit \$8.40

<u>11</u> CP \$16, profit \$4

<u>12</u> CP \$55, profit \$5.50

A retailer bought a leather chair for \$375 and sold it for \$285. Find his percentage loss.

$$\text{Loss} = \text{CP} - \text{SP}$$

$$= \$375 - \$285 = \$90$$

$$\%\ \text{loss} = \frac{\text{loss}}{\text{CP}} \times 100\%$$

$$= \frac{\$90}{\$375} \times 100\% = 24\%$$

Therefore the percentage loss is 24%.

Find the percentage loss:

13 CP \$20, loss \$4

14 CP \$125, loss \$25

<u>15</u> CP \$64, loss \$9 .60

<u>16</u> CP \$160, loss \$38.40

An article costing \$30 is sold at a profit of 25%. Find the selling price.

Method 1 Find the profit then add it to the cost.

$$\text{Profit} = 25\%\ \text{of}\ \$30 = \frac{25}{100} \times \$30 = \$7.50$$

$$\text{SP} = \$30 + \$7.50$$

Therefore the selling price is \$37.50

Method 2 First find the SP as a percentage of the CP.

SP = 125% of CP.

$$\therefore \qquad \text{SP} = \frac{125}{100} \times \$30$$

Therefore the selling price is \$37.50

Find the selling price:

17 CP \$50, profit 12%

18 CP \$64, profit $12\frac{1}{2}\%$

<u>19</u> CP \$29, profit 110%

20 CP \$36, loss 50%

21 CP \$75, loss 64%

<u>22</u> CP \$128, loss $37\frac{1}{2}\%$

Finding simple interest

Everybody wishes to borrow something at one time or another. Perhaps you want to borrow a video camera to record a wedding, a dress to wear to an important event or even a bicycle for a few minutes. In the same way, the time will come when you will wish to borrow money to buy a motorcycle, a car, furniture or even a house.

The cost of hiring or borrowing money is called the *interest*. The sum of money borrowed (or lent) is called the *principal* and the interest is usually an agreed *percentage* of the sum borrowed.

For example, if \$100 is borrowed for a year at an interest rate of 12% per year, then the interest due is $\frac{12}{100}$ of \$100, i.e. \$12.

The interest due on \$200 for one year at 12% would be $\$200 \times \frac{12}{100} = \$24$, and on \$$P$ for one year at 12% would be $\$P \times \frac{12}{100}$.

If we double the period of the loan, we double the interest due, and so on. The interest on \$$P$ borrowed for T years at 12% would therefore be $\$P \times \frac{12}{100} \times T$.

If the interest rate was R% instead of the given 12%, the interest, I, would be

$$\$P \times \frac{R}{100} \times T.$$

When interest is calculated this way it is called *simple interest*.

Therefore $$I = \frac{PRT}{100}$$

where I is the simple interest in \$s
P is the principal in \$s
R is the rate per cent per year
T is the time in years.

Unless stated otherwise, R% will always be taken to mean R% each year or *per annum*.

When we put money in a savings account, it is called *investing*. That money is being borrowed by the bank and they pay us interest.

Exercise 21f

Find the simple interest on:

1 $100 for 2 years at 10%

2 $100 for 2 years at 12%

3 $100 for 3 years at 8%

4 $100 for 4 years at 13%

5 $100 for 7 years at 11 %

6 $200 for 2 years at 10%

7 $200 for 5 years at 8%

8 $300 for 4 years at 12%

9 $400 for 6 years at 9%

10 $600 for 7 years at 11%

$100 is the principal, 2 years is the time and 10% is the rate.
so $I = \frac{100 \times 10 \times 2}{100}$.

The answers to the following questions are exact in dollars and cents.

Find the simple interest on:

11 $350 for 5 years at 7%

12 $125 for 4 years at 12%

13 $642 for 7 years at 11%

14 $1740 for 8 years at 8%

15 $724 for 3 years at 6%

16 $484 for 3 years at 7%

17 $372 for 7 years at 14%

18 $94 for 6 years at 9%

19 $648 for 5 years at 13%

20 $926 for 9 years at 14%

Find the simple interest on $134.66 for 5 years at 12%, giving your answer correct to the nearest cent.

$$I = \frac{PRT}{100} \text{ where } P = 134.66,\ R = 12 \text{ and } T = 5$$

$$\therefore \quad \text{simple interest} = \$\frac{134.66 \times 12 \times 5}{100}$$

$$= \$80.796$$

$$= \$80.80 \text{ correct to the nearest cent}$$

Find, giving your answers correct to the nearest cent, the simple interest on:

21 $526.52 for 2 years at 12%

22 $94.56 for 4 years at 8%

23 $142.16 for 5 years at 11%

24 $813.40 for 4 years at 13%

25 $627.83 for 3 years at 14%

26 $555.45 for 5 years at 9%

27 $123.72 for 4 years at 8%

28 $543.89 for 7 years at 9%

29 $826.92 for 6 years at 7%

30 $717.47 for 4 years at 17%

Find, giving your answers correct to the nearest cent, the simple interest on:

31 $154.40 for 4 years at $8\frac{1}{2}$%

32 $273.80 for $4\frac{1}{2}$ years at 9%

Write $8\frac{1}{2}$ as 8.5.

33 $527.49 for 3 years at $12\frac{3}{4}\%$

34 $436.15 for $7\frac{1}{2}$ years at $11\frac{1}{4}\%$

35 $84.72 for $4\frac{1}{4}$ years at $13\frac{1}{2}\%$

36 $73.58 for $5\frac{3}{4}$ years at $9\frac{3}{4}\%$

37 $364.88 for $2\frac{3}{4}$ years at $8\frac{1}{4}\%$

38 $2034.48 for $1\frac{1}{2}$ years at $7\frac{1}{5}\%$

39 $613.27 for $3\frac{1}{4}$ years at $15\frac{1}{2}\%$

40 $454.92 for $6\frac{1}{4}$ years at $18\frac{1}{4}\%$

Find, giving your answers correct to the nearest cent, the simple interest on:

41 $320 for 100 days at 12%

42 $413 for 150 days at 8%

43 $1000 for 300 days at 9%

44 $282.50 for 214 days at 16%

45 $613.94 for 98 days at $14\frac{1}{2}\%$

46 $729.32 for 22 days at 11%

T must be in years so change the number of days to a fraction of a year. Use 365 as the number of days in a year.

100 days $= \frac{100}{365}$ yrs

Puzzle

Four married couples met at a party.

Everyone shook hands with everyone else except each husband with his own wife.

How many handshakes were there?

Amount

If I borrow $250 for 3 years at 11% simple interest, the *sum* of the *interest* and *principal* is the total I must repay to clear the debt. This sum is called the *amount* and is denoted by *A*$,

i.e. $$A = P + I$$

In this case $$I = \frac{250 \times 11 \times 3}{100}$$

$$= 82.50$$

So the simple interest = $82.50

$\therefore$ amount = $250 + $82.50

= $332.50

Exercise 21g

Find the amount of:

1 $350 for 5 years at 10%

2 $420 for 2 years at 8%

3 $650 for 4 years at 12%

4 $513 for 4 years at $13\frac{1}{2}$%

5 $820 for 8 years at 14%

6 $970 for 7 years at 9%

7 $492 for 5 years at $8\frac{1}{2}$%

8 $654.20 for 4 years at 9%

9 $738 for $3\frac{1}{2}$ years at 9%

10 $186 for $4\frac{1}{4}$ years at 12%

11 $285 for 9 years at 6%

12 $826.50 for 6 years at 8%

13 $192.63 for 5 years at 11%

14 $564.27 for $6\frac{1}{2}$ years at 12%

15 $718.55 for $4\frac{1}{4}$ years at $13\frac{1}{2}$%

16 $318 for $5\frac{3}{4}$ years at $11\frac{1}{2}$%

Mixed exercises

Exercise 21h

1 A grocery store is offering $10 of all bills above $100. Zane's shopping came to $130 before the discount. Find the percentage discount on Zane's bill.

2 The cost price of a tie is $45 and the sale price is $60. Find the percentage profit.

3 A shirt is sold for $75 at a loss of $40. Find:

a the cost price b the percentage loss.

4 Find the simple interest on $50 000 invested for 10 years at 2%.

5 Find the simple interest on $537 for 5 years at 11%.

6 Find the amount of $737 for 8 years at 12%.

Exercise 21i

Select the letter that gives the correct answer.

1 A shop gives a discount of 20% on all items in a sale. The full price of a soccer ball was $120. What would it cost in the sale?

A $94.50 B $96 C $105.80 D $106.48

2 The price of a desk is $540 plus sales tax of 10%. The full purchase price is

A $594 B $599 C $605 D $610

3 A watch is priced at $455 plus sales tax at 15%. The full purchase price is

A $470.00 **B** $521.50 **C** $523.25 **D** $535.75

4 The simple interest on $682 invested for 3 years at 4% is

A $76.42 **B** $78.64 **C** $81.84 **D** $86.84

5 Correct to the nearest cent, the simple interest on $85 invested for $2\frac{1}{2}$ years at 5% is

A $8.63 **B** $9.62 **C** $8.50 **D** $10.63

6 If $950 is invested for 5 years at 4% it amounts to

A $1040 **B** $1080 **C** $1110 **D** $1140

In this chapter you have seen that...

- ✔ discounts can be a fixed amount of money or a percentage of the selling price
- ✔ profit or loss is calculated as a percentage of the cost price
- ✔ sales tax is a percentage of the selling price
- ✔ you can find the simple interest on a sum of money by using the expression for I: $I = \frac{PRT}{100}$
- ✔ the 'amount' is the sum of the principal and the interest.

REVIEW TEST 3: CHAPTERS 14–21

In questions **1** to **13** choose the letter for the correct answer.

1 What percentage of 14 is 42?

A $\frac{1}{3}\%$ B 3% C $33\frac{1}{3}\%$ D 300%

2 $\frac{4}{25}$ as a percentage is

A 0.16% B 4% C 16% D 160%

3 In a sale, all marked prices are reduced by 10%. The sale price of goods marked \$250 is

A \$25 B \$125 C \$225 D \$240

4 Given $3x - 8 = 4$, $x =$

A 0 B $1\frac{1}{3}$ C 3 D 4

5 The simple interest on \$200 for 3 years at 5% is

A \$10 B \$15 C \$30 D \$60

6 The area of rectangle is $4.5\,\text{cm}^2$. The length of the rectangle is 9 cm. The width is

A 0.05 cm B 0.5 cm C 5 cm D 50 cm

7 A sequence starts 3, 5, 7, 9, 11,... The nth term is

A $3n$ B $n + 2$ C $1 + 2n$ D $3n - 1$

8 How many lines of symmetry does a rectangle have?

A 1 B 2 C 3 D 4

9 The solution of the equation $2 - 3(4 - x) = 5$ is

A −5 B 3 C 4 D 5

10 A clock bought for \$200 was sold at a profit of 20%. The profit was

A \$20 B \$40 C \$240 D \$400

11 A car bought for \$10 000 was sold a year later for \$7000. The percentage loss is

A 10% B 30% C 70% D 300%

12 Triangle PQR is translated 2 units horizontally and one unit vertically. The diagram showing this is

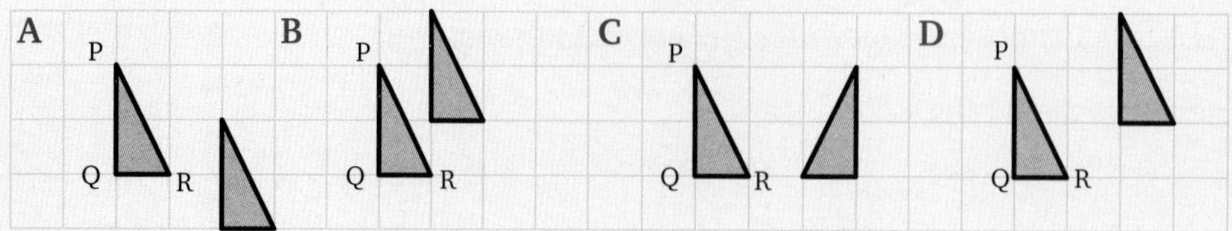

13 A pair of trainers is marked as $245 plus sales tax of 15%. The price is

A $37.50 **B** $245 **C** $265 **D** $ 281.75

14 A room is 3.06 m long. Its length is 1.35 m more than its width. What is the perimeter of the room?

15 Given that 1 kg = 2.2 lb, calculate which is cheaper, 3 kg of meat for $16.50 or 5 lb for $18 (show all working).

16 Copy this diagram on to 1 cm squared paper.
On your diagram draw

a the reflection of triangle ABC in a horizontal line one square below BC.

b the translation of triangle ABC by one square vertically upwards and two squares to the left.

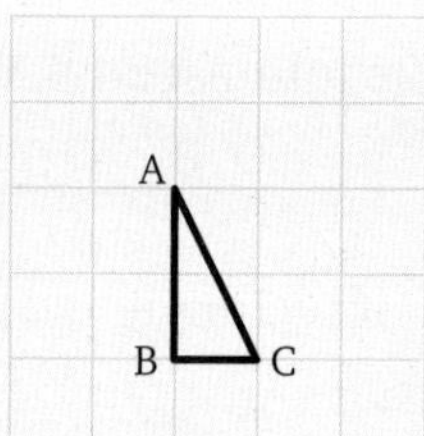

17 Find the area of this figure.

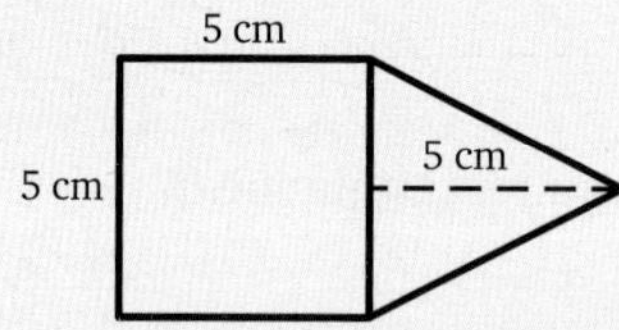

18 Express $37\frac{1}{2}\%$ as

a a fraction in its lowest terms **b** a decimal

19 The two equal sides of an isosceles triangle are each x cm long. The third side is 52 cm long. The perimeter of the triangle is 120 cm. Find the length of one of the equal sides.

REVIEW TEST 4: CHAPTERS 1–21

Choose the letter for the correct answer.

1 The smallest prime number is

A 1 B 2 C 7 D 9

2 $\frac{0.3}{100}$ has the same value as

A 0.003% B 0.03% C 0.3% D 3%

3 X = {odd numbers from 2 to 5}

Y = {prime numbers from 2 to 5}

The element not common to both X and Y is

A 2 B 3 C 4 D 5

4 From the numbers 1 to 10, the largest prime number exceeds the smallest prime number by

A 8 B 7 C 6 D 5

5 An item bought for $120 is sold to make a profit of 20%. The selling price is

A $96 B $125 C $140 D $144

6 In an exam marked out of 120 marks a student requires a minimum of 80% to attain a grade 'A'. The minimum mark required for a grade 'A' is

A 80 B 96 C 100 D 120

7 Two sets of 'flashing lights' start together and then flash at intervals of 5 seconds and 6 seconds respectively. They will flash together at intervals of

A 6 seconds B 11 seconds C 15 seconds D 30 seconds

8

rectangle

16 cm

square

8 cm

The square and the rectangle shown in the diagram above have the same area. The width of the rectangle is

A 8 cm B 6 cm C 4 cm D 2 cm

9 If 10 is the mean of x, 10, 12 and 14, then x =

A 10 B 8 C 6 D 4

10 A box contains 9 bulbs of which 3 are defective. If one bulb is chosen at random then the probability that it is not defective is

A $\frac{1}{9}$ **B** $\frac{1}{3}$ **C** $\frac{2}{3}$ **D** $\frac{8}{9}$

11 R = {equilateral triangles}

I = {isosceles triangles}

The diagram illustrating R and I is

A

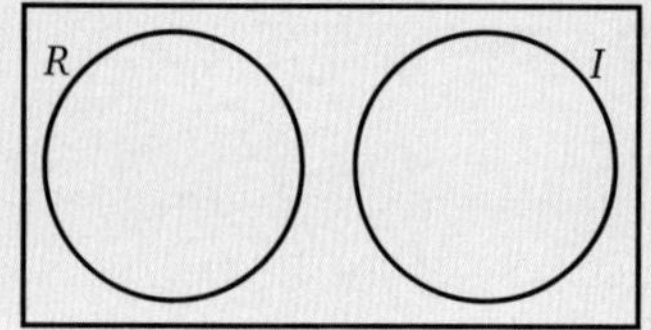

B

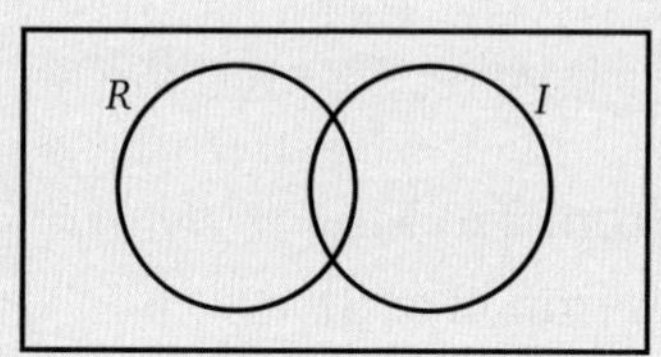

C

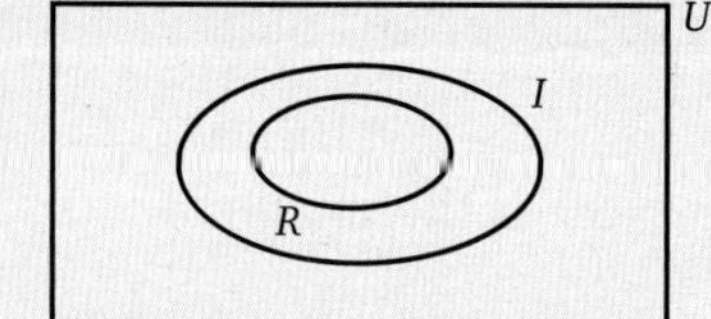

D

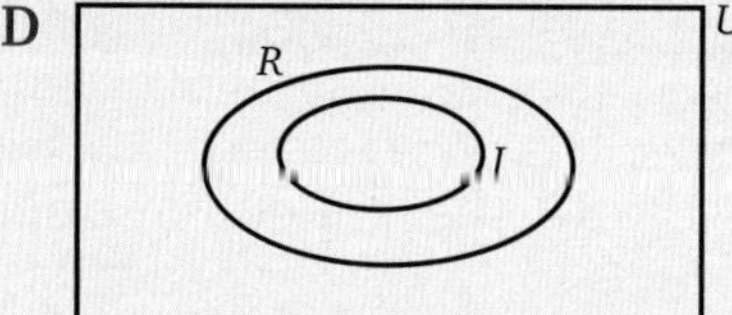

12 $\frac{2}{7} \div \frac{6}{7} =$

A $\frac{1}{3}$ **B** $\frac{3}{7}$ **C** $\frac{7}{3}$ **D** 3

13 A liquid weighs 800 g per litre. The number of litres that weigh 1 kg is

A 1.25 **B** 1.8 **C** 8 **D** 12.5

14

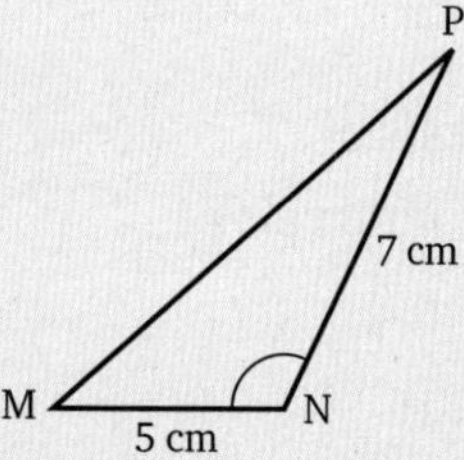

In the triangle MNP shown above, MN = 5 cm, NP = 7 cm and $\hat{N}$ is obtuse. Which of the following statements are true?

i MP is greater than 7 cm.

ii Triangle MNP is isosceles.

iii Angle M is greater than angle P.

A i and ii only **B** i and iii only **C** ii and iii only **D** i, ii and iii

15 $0.1 \div 0.01 =$

A 10 000 **B** 1000 **C** 100 **D** 10

16 $\frac{5}{8}$ written as a decimal is

A 0.5 B 0.625 C 0.8 D 0.875

17 The median of the set of numbers 6, 1, 2, 3, 7 and 5 is

A 2 B 2.5 C 3 D 4

18 The value of $2^3 + 3^2$ is

A 12 B 17 C 36 D 72

19 $\frac{2}{3} + \frac{1}{6} =$

A $\frac{2}{18}$ B $\frac{3}{9}$ C $\frac{3}{6}$ D $\frac{5}{6}$

20

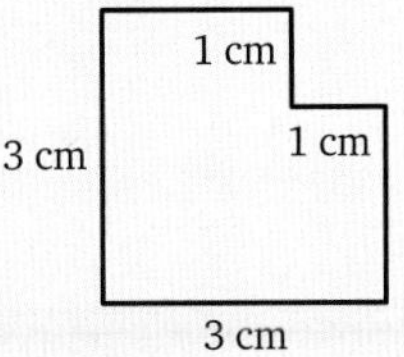

The area of this figure is

A 9 cm² B 8 cm² C 5 cm² D 4 cm²

21 $2(x + 3) = 9$, x is

A $1\frac{1}{2}$ B 3 C 6 D $7\frac{1}{2}$

22 $\frac{4x}{3} \times \frac{9}{2x} =$

A $6x$ B $\frac{8x^2}{27}$ C 6 D $7x$

23

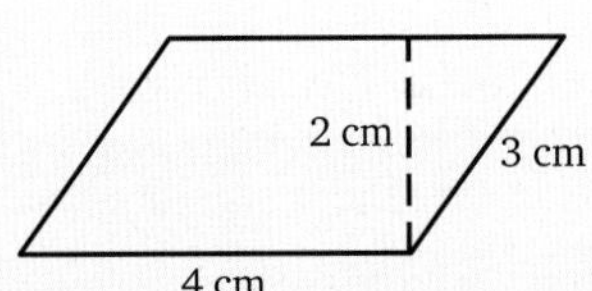

The area of this parallelogram is

A 4 cm² B 6 cm² C 8 cm² D 12 cm²

24 160 miles in kilometres is about

A 320 km B 256 km C 240 km D 100 km

25 The value of $-2 - (-4) + (-3)$ is

A -9 B -7 C -1 D 5

26 The expression $3(4 - x) - (7 - x)$ simplifies to

A $5 - 2x$ B $5 - 4x$ C $-2x$ D $5 + 2x$

27 10% of 20 differs from 0.5 of 2 by

A 1 B 2 C 4 D 5

28 $P = \{1, 2, 3, \ldots 10\}$. In the set P, the largest odd number exceeds the largest prime number by

A 0 B 1 C 2 D 3

29 The solution of the equation $2x - 3(4 - x) = 3$ is

A 2 B 3 C 4 D 5

30 The nth term of a sequence is given by $\frac{n}{2}(n + 3)$. The 20th term is

A 100 B 200 C 230 D 460

Glossary

acute angle	an angle less than 90°
algebraic fraction	a fraction with variables in the numerator and/or the denominator
amount	the sum of the interest and the principal (the original money invested or borrowed)
angle	a measure of turning
angles at a point	a group of angles round a point that make a complete revolution, e.g.
angles on a straight line	a group of angles that together make a straight line, e.g.
anticlockwise	turns in the opposite sense to the hands of a clock
approximation	an estimate of the value of a calculation or quantity
area	the amount of surface covered
arithmetic average	the sum of a set of values divided by the number of values
bar chart	a diagram of bars, each representing a quantity. The height of the bar represents the number (frequency) of that quantity
base	the line from which the perpendicular height of a plane figure is measured
cancel	dividing top and bottom of a fraction by common factors
capacity	the amount of space inside a container
centimetre	a measure of length
centre	(of a circle) the point that is the same distance from any point on the circumference (edge)
circle	a curve made by moving one point at a fixed distance from another, e.g. ○
clockwise	turns in the same sense as the hands of a clock
coefficient	the number multiplied by a variable
common factor	a number that divides exactly into two or more other numbers
complementary angles	two angles that add up to 90°
composite number	a number that can be written as the product of two or more prime numbers
congruent	exactly the same shape and size
consecutive	one after the other, e.g. 12 and 13 are consecutive integers, but 12 and 14 are not
construction	drawing a figure exactly as specified

cube	a solid with six faces, each of which is a square, e.g.
cuboid	a solid with six faces, each of which is a rectangle, e.g.
data	a collection of facts
decimal	a fraction expressed by numbers on the right of a point, e.g. $0.2 = \frac{2}{10}$
degree	the unit of measure for an angle (1 turn = 360°) or for temperature, e.g. °F or °C
denominator	the bottom of a fraction
depreciates	reduces in value
diagonal	a line, which is not a side, from one corner to another in a figure
digit	one of the figures 0, 1, 2, 3, 4, 5, 6, 7, 8, 9
diameter	a line across a circle going through the centre
difference	the value of the larger number minus the smaller number
dimension	a measurable length in an object
directed number	the collective name for positive and negative numbers
discount	the amount an item is reduced by
disjoint sets	sets that have no common elements
divisible	divides exactly
edge	where two faces meet
element	a member of a set
empty set	a set with no members
equation	two expressions connected by an equal sign
equilateral triangle	a triangle whose sides are all the same length
equivalent fraction	measures the same part of a quantity
estimate	an approximate value
even number	a number that is divisible by 2
expression	a collection of algebraic terms connected with plus and minus signs, without an equal or inequality sign
face	a surface on a solid
factor	a number or letter that divides exactly into another number or algebraic expression
finite set	a set whose members are limited in number
foot	a measure of length

fraction	part of a quantity
frequency table	a table listing the number of each quantity or group of quantities
frequency	the number of times that a value or group of values occurs
gram	a measure of mass
hexagon	a six-sided polygon
highest common factor	the largest number that divides exactly into two or more other numbers
horizontal	parallel to the surface of the Earth
hundredweight	a measure of mass
image	a shape after it is reflected or translated
improper fraction	a fraction whose numerator is larger than its denominator
inch	a measure of length
index (pl indices)	a superscript to a number that tells you how many of those numbers are multiplied together
infinite set	a set with an unlimited number of members
integer	a positive or negative whole number
interest	the money paid for the use of money lent or borrowed
intersection of sets	the set of elements common to two or more sets
inverse	the reverse of an operation
isosceles triangle	a triangle with two equal sides
kilogram	a measure of mass
kilometre	a measure of length
kite	a quadrilateral with two pairs of adjacent sides that are equal, e.g. ◊
like terms	terms that contain the same combination of letters, e.g. $3xy^2$ and $7xy^2$ but not xy^2 and xy
line of symmetry	a line through a figure such that the parts of the figure on each side of the line are identical
line segment	a line with a beginning and an end
litre	a measure of capacity
lowest common multiple	the lowest number that two or more other numbers divide into exactly
mass	the quantity of matter in an object
mean	the sum of a set of values divided by the number of values

median	the middle item of a set of items arranged in order of size
member	an item that belongs to a set of items
metre	a measure of length
mile	a measure of length
millilitre	a measure of capacity
millimetre	a measure of length
mirror line	a line in which an object is reflected
mixed number	the sum of a whole number and a fraction
mixed operation	a calculation involving two or more of addition, subtraction, multiplication and division
mode	the most frequent item in a set
multiple	a particular number multiplied by any other number is a multiple of that particular number
natural number	a counting number, i.e. 1, 2, 3, 4, …
negative	a number less than zero
net	a flat shape that can be folded to make a solid
null set	a set with no members
number line	a straight line with numbers marked on it with zero in the middle
number pattern	a pattern of numbers with a rule for getting the next number in the pattern
numerator	the top of a fraction
object	a shape before it is reflected or translated
obtuse angle	an angle whose size is between 90° and 180°
odd number	a whole number that is not divisible by 2
operation	a way of combining two numbers by, for example, addition, subtraction, multiplication or division
ounce	a measure of mass
pair of compasses	an instrument used for drawing circles or parts of circles
parallel	two lines that are always the same distance apart
parallelogram	a four-sided figure whose opposite sides are parallel
pentagon	a five-sided polygon
per annum	each year
percentage	out of a hundred, i.e. a fraction whose denominator is 100

percentage decrease	a decrease of a quantity expressed as a percentage of that quantity
percentage increase	an increase of a quantity expressed as a percentage of that quantity
perimeter	the total distance round the edge of a figure
perpendicular	at right angles to a line or surface
perpendicular height	the height of an object measured at right angles to an edge or surface
pictograph	a diagram showing the frequencies of values in the form of small pictures
place value	the position of a digit in a number that shows its value, e.g. in 247, the digit 4 has a place value of 4 tens
polygon	a plane figure bounded by straight line segments
positive	a number greater than zero
pound	a measure of mass
prime number	a number whose only factors are 1 and itself (1 is not a prime number)
principal	the amount of money lent or borrowed
prism	a solid with two identical ends and flat faces between them
product	the result of multiplying two or more numbers together
proper fraction	a fraction whose numerator is less than its denominator
protractor	an instrument for measuring angles
pyramid	a solid with a polygon as its base and sloping sides that meet at a point
quadrilateral	a figure bounded by four straight lines
radius	the distance from the centre of a circle to the edge
rate per cent	the annual (or other time span) interest paid as a percentage of the money lent or borrowed
rational number	a fraction whose numerator and denominator are integers
ray	a line with one end
rectangle	a quadrilateral whose angles are each 90°
rectangular grid	a grid of lines crossing each other at right angles
rectangular number	a number that can be shown as a rectangular array of dots
rectilinear solid	a solid whose edges are straight lines
recurring decimal	a decimal that never terminates but where the digits form a repeating pattern, e.g. 0.191919...
reflex angle	an angle whose size is between 180° and 360°, e.g. 
regular pentagon	a five-sided figure whose sides are all the same length
remainder	the amount left over when one number is divided by another

revolution	a complete turn
rhombus	a four-sided figure whose sides are all the same length, e.g. ◊
right angle	one quarter of a revolution (90°)
sequence	an ordered collection of items, e.g. 2, 4, 8, 16, …
set	a collection of items
solution	the correct answer to a puzzle or equation
solve	find the correct answer
square	a four-sided figure whose sides are all the same length and each of whose angles is a right angle
square centimetre	a measure of area
square kilometre	a measure of area
square metre	a measure of area
square millimetre	a measure of area
square number	a number that can be shown as a square array of dots
subset	a set whose members are also members of another set
supplementary angles	angles whose sum is 180°
symmetry	having congruent parts each side of a line or around a point
tessellation	an arrangement of flat shapes that cover a flat surface
tonne	a measure of mass
translation	a movement of an object without turning it or reflecting it
trapezium	a four-sided figure with one pair of unequal sides parallel
triangle	a three-sided figure
triangular number	a number that can be shown as a triangular array of dots, e.g. 6: ⠴
union of sets	the set containing all the different elements of two or more sets
units	the standard quantity used to measure, e.g. a metre, a litre, a square inch
universal set	the set containing all elements
unlike terms	terms containing different combinations of letters
variable	a quantity that can vary in value
Venn diagram	a diagram used to show the elements in two or more sets
vertex (pl vertices)	corner
vertically opposite	the pair of angles opposite each other where two lines cross
yard	a measure of length

Answers

CHAPTER 1

Exercise 1a page 3

1 a 327 b 15 234 c 20 000 400
2 a seven hundred and thirty-four
b nine thousand four hundred and eighty-eight
c three hundred and sixty thousand one hundred
d two million five hundred thousand
e three million six hundred and twenty thousand
3 a 9 b 6 c 7 d 8
4 a 3724, 5024, 5566, 6493
b 6643, 8492, 17 021, 24 721
c 534, 8451, 8876, 10 880
d 43 624, 734 921, 933 402, 2 000 843
5 a tens b hundreds c units
d thousands e ten thousands
6 a hundreds b units c thousands
d ten thousands
7 a 65 410 b 10 456
8 20 379
9 204 678
10 22 460
11 8543, 8534, 8453, 8435, 8354, 8345,
5843, 5834, 5483, 5438, 5384, 5348
4853, 4835, 4583, 4538, 4385, 4358
3854, 3845, 3584, 3548, 3485, 3458

Exercise 1b page 4

1	16	11	280	21	90 434	31	21 321
2	19	12	332	22	3087	32	36 209
3	27	13	717	23	9826	33	361 208
4	22	14	3295	24	211 005	34	379 302
5	39	15	5413	25	256 043	35	1 423 502
6	37	16	923	26	2 237 005	36	3 079 000
7	24	17	8529	27	1 467 452	37	800 233
8	25	18	14 147	28	10 117	38	7 132 919
9	218	19	642	29	143 041	39	29 203 794
10	202	20	19 346	30	1 035 049	40	112 505 480

Exercise 1c page 6

1 1250 c 2 790 c 3 $8099 4 18 287
5 856 cm 6 14 542 miles
7 a 15 506 miles b 12 144 miles c 15 601 miles
8 $32 600 000
9 1 c, 2 c, 4 c, 8 c, 16 c, 32 c, 64 c, 128 c, 256 c, 512 c; 1023 c

Exercie 1d page 8

1	11	12	3	23	406	34	331 000
2	12	13	11	24	218	35	50 201
3	14	14	8	25	1126	36	101 202
4	5	15	10	26	1926	37	7707
5	7	16	4	27	926	38	458 018
6	12	17	5	28	3893	39	149 999
7	15	18	6	29	781	40	1 091 000
8	9	19	14	30	23 071	41	23 940 000
9	8	20	8	31	169 824	42	51 994 500
10	6	21	211	32	22 123		
11	13	22	551	33	303 001		

Exercise 1e page 9

1	203c	5	17 287	9	6623 m
2	464	6	58 483	10	$15 760 000
3	7705	7	98 254	11	99 704 599
4	989	8	914 358		

Exercise 1f page 10

1	5	4	4	7	2	10	7
2	5	5	9	8	7	11	4
3	7	6	4	9	9	12	4

Exercise 1g page 11

1	17	8	3	15	65 000
2	5	9	6	16	2888
3	2	10	4	17	57 480 000
4	20	11	43	18	85 000
5	30	12	10 740	19	1 052 050
6	28	13	1535	20	3 855 500
7	13	14	1036		

Exercise 1h page 12

1 80c 4 9562 7 35c
2 3290 cm 5 269 kg 8 1 Jan, 31 Dec
3 318 6 a 17 b 20

Exercise 1i page 14

1	80	11	31 000	21	280
2	150	12	876 000	22	370
3	630	13	710 000	23	150
4	230	14	980 000	24	250
5	160	15	267 000	25	250
6	800	16	457 000 000	26	360
7	300	17	7 000 000	27	250
8	1200	18	35 000 000	28	10
9	1400	19	94 000 000		
10	3800	20	330		

Exercise 1j page 16

1	304	15	180 000	29	720 000
2	130	16	4 938 500	30	1620
3	249	17	5 405 400	31	10 200
4	423	18	8 086 000	32	35 840
5	144	19	79 000 000	33	156 000
6	324	20	31 750 000	34	520 200
7	1224	21	246 004 800	35	2 196 000
8	3264	22	493 150 000	36	73 640 700
9	1950	23	94 500 000	37	261 936 000
10	3228	24	22 802 000	38	3 232 000
11	5110	25	760	39	31 800 000
12	3960	26	2600	40	46 550 000 000
13	19 200	27	830		
14	32 328	28	47 000		

Exercise 1k page 17

1	559	6	25 758	11	1 203 000
2	35 100	7	84 254	12	204 940 120
3	38 920	8	67 624	13	224 858 480
4	243 000	9	2 763 180	14	1 248 425 280
5	14 600	10	26 544 000	15	15 715 384 320

Exercise 1l page 18

1 3024
2 1210
3 3534
4 1062
5 8004
6 14999
7 36252
8 16252
9 53070
10 85008
11 580569
12 425480
13 166413
14 156919
15 178112
16 238628
17 1778105
18 5183452
19 802782
20 5292822
21 5309850
22 3869370
23 1361160
24 4594866
25 25634364
26 11370320
27 74361792
28 29888196
29 24803373
30 59462592
31 25862112
32 166520726

Exercise 1m page 19

1 760988
2 1428
3 833
4 2916
5 2592
6 65376 g
7 111973500
8 a 200
b 1000
c 60000
9 457002
10 a $3309215
b $3310000

Exercise 1n page 21

1 29
2 6
3 18
4 14 r3
5 23
6 13
7 12 r1
8 6 r6
9 210
10 100 r1
11 160
12 73 r2
13 62 r3
14 74 r7
15 114 r2
16 235 r1
17 601
18 18250
19 3334 r2
20 40480
21 971432
22 843000
23 1572701 r1
24 2668200 r2
25 150085
26 30013
27 9111111 r1
28 580 r2
29 40005 r3
30 12100140
31 900900
32 350001
33 25 r6
34 8 r7
35 1 r96
36 27 r83
37 4 r910
38 5 r7
39 18 r6
40 278 r1
41 9 r426
42 85 r12
43 30 r77
44 5 r704

Exercise 1p page 22

1 22
2 7
3 21
4 17
5 2
6 5
7 1
8 10
9 3
10 6
11 8
12 22
13 13
14 17
15 6
16 8
17 10
18 8
19 5
20 9
21 21
22 14
23 12
24 13
25 32
26 9
27 16
28 14
29 14
30 30

Exercise 1q page 24

1 2
2 56
3 9
4 14
5 15
6 8
7 49
8 2
9 45
10 2
11 17
12 3
13 17
14 2
15 11
16 7
17 30
18 1
19 4
20 36
21 45
22 6
23 14
24 0
25 10
26 1
27 4
28 25
29 1
30 18

Exercise 1r page 25

1 61875c
2 47
3 14
4 1695c
5 $2162
6 1635
7 5515 c
8 2538
9 120
10 $162521
11 840 cm
12 Jane 220 c, Sarah 290 c, Claire 450 c
13 $10
14 $608
15 a 245 b 295
16 54
17 67
18 1831 or 1832, depending on when her birthday was
19 16
20 119

Exercise 1s page 27

1

8	1	6
3	5	7
4	9	2

2

4	9	2
3	5	7
8	1	6

3

2	14	7	11
15	3	10	6
9	5	16	4
8	12	1	13

5
1
6 4
3 2 5

6
4
2 3
6 1 5

7
2
3 5
6 1 4

8 a

s	10	11	12
v	9	12	15
$3s - v$	21	21	21

b 21, 21, 21
c equal

9 13, 16
10 4, 2
11 17, 21
12 32, 64
13 15, 18
14 4, 2
15 81, 243
16 36, 49
17 10000, 100000
18 45, 36
19 19, 23
20 37, 50

Exercise 1t page 29

1 $1 + 3 + 5 + 7 + 9 = 25 = 5 \times 5$
$1 + 3 + 5 + 7 + 9 + 11 = 36 = 6 \times 6$
$1 + 3 + 5 + 7 + 9 + 11 + 13 = 49 = 7 \times 7$
a 64 b 400
2 $2 + 4 + 6 + 8 + 10 = 30 = 5 \times 6$
$2 + 4 + 6 + 8 + 10 + 12 = 42 = 6 \times 7$
$2 + 4 + 6 + 8 + 10 + 12 + 14 = 56 = 7 \times 8$
12
3 4, 9, 36, 169
4 8, 6, 14, 72, 91, 323 (17×19), 403 (13×31)
5 2×6, 3×4
6 2×9, 3×6
7 2×18, 3×12, 4×9 or 6×6
8
9 36, 45, 55
10 1, 4, 9, 16; square numbers

11 triangular numbers
12 **a** 1, 4, 9
b 4, 6, 8, 9, 10, 12
c 1, 3, 6, 10
13 **a** 25, 36
b 24, 25, 26, 27, 28, 30, 32, 33, 34, 35, 36, 38, 39, 40
c 28, 36

Exercise 1u page 31

1 71814
2 7699917
3 68407600
4 16300
5 27608
6 43860720
7 1802
8 25
9 2
10 11
11 176 girls, 199 boys
12 square numbers

Exercise 1v page 31

1 D
2 B
3 A
4 B
5 C
6 B
7 D

CHAPTER 2

Exercise 2a page 34

1 $1 \times 18, 2 \times 9, 3 \times 6$
2 $1 \times 20, 2 \times 10, 4 \times 5$
3 $1 \times 24, 2 \times 12, 3 \times 8, 4 \times 6$
4 $1 \times 27, 3 \times 9$
5 $1 \times 30, 2 \times 15, 3 \times 10, 5 \times 6$
6 $1 \times 36, 2 \times 18, 3 \times 12, 4 \times 9, 6 \times 6$
7 $1 \times 40, 2 \times 20, 4 \times 10, 5 \times 8$
8 $1 \times 45, 3 \times 15, 5 \times 9$
9 $1 \times 48, 2 \times 24, 3 \times 16, 4 \times 12, 6 \times 8$
10 $1 \times 60, 2 \times 30, 3 \times 20, 4 \times 15, 5 \times 12, 6 \times 10$
11 $1 \times 64, 2 \times 32, 4 \times 16, 8 \times 8$
12 $1 \times 72, 2 \times 36, 3 \times 24, 4 \times 18, 6 \times 12, 8 \times 9$
13 $1 \times 80, 2 \times 40, 4 \times 20, 5 \times 16, 8 \times 10$
14 $1 \times 96, 2 \times 48, 3 \times 32, 4 \times 24, 6 \times 16, 8 \times 12$
15 $1 \times 100, 2 \times 50, 4 \times 25, 5 \times 20, 10 \times 10$
16 $1 \times 108, 2 \times 54, 3 \times 36, 4 \times 27, 6 \times 18, 9 \times 12$
17 $1 \times 120, 2 \times 60, 3 \times 40, 4 \times 30, 5 \times 24, 6 \times 20, 8 \times 15, 10 \times 12$
18 $1 \times 135, 3 \times 45, 5 \times 27, 9 \times 15$
19 $1 \times 144, 2 \times 72, 3 \times 48, 4 \times 36, 6 \times 24, 8 \times 18, 9 \times 16, 12 \times 12$
20 $1 \times 160, 2 \times 80, 4 \times 40, 5 \times 32, 8 \times 20, 10 \times 16$

Exercise 2b page 34

1 1, 2, 3, 6, 9, 18
2 1, 2, 4, 5, 10, 20
3 1, 2, 3, 4, 6, 8, 12, 24
4 1, 3, 9, 27
5 1, 2, 3, 5, 6, 10, 15, 30
6 1, 2, 3, 4, 6, 9, 12, 18, 36
7 1, 2, 4, 5, 8, 10, 20, 40
8 1, 3, 5, 9, 15, 45
9 1, 2, 3, 4, 6, 8, 12, 16, 24, 48
10 1, 2, 3, 4, 5, 6, 10, 12, 15, 20, 30, 60
11 1, 2, 4, 8, 16, 32, 64
12 1, 2, 3, 4, 6, 8, 9, 12, 18, 24, 36, 72
13 1, 2, 4, 5, 8, 10, 16, 20, 40, 80
14 1, 2, 3, 4, 6, 8, 12, 16, 24, 32, 48, 96
15 1, 2, 4, 5, 10, 20, 25, 50, 100
16 1, 2, 3, 4, 6, 9, 12, 18, 27, 36, 54, 108
17 1, 2, 3, 4, 5, 6, 8, 10, 12, 15, 20, 24, 30, 40, 60, 120
18 1, 3, 5, 9, 15, 27, 45, 135
19 1, 2, 3, 4, 6, 8, 9, 12, 16, 18, 24, 36, 48, 72, 144
20 1, 2, 4, 5, 8, 10, 16, 20, 32, 40, 80, 160

Exercise 2c page 34

1 21, 24, 27, 30, 33, 36, 39
2 20, 25, 30, 35, 40, 45
3 28, 35, 42, 49, 56
4 55, 66, 77, 88, 99
5 26, 39, 52, 65

Exercise 2d page 35

1 2, 3, 5, 7, 11, 13
2 23, 29
3 31, 37, 41, 43, 47
4 5, 19, 29, 61
5 41, 101, 127
6 **a** F **b** F **c** T **d** T **e** F

Exercise 2e page 36

1 2^3
2 3^4
3 5^4
4 7^5
5 2^5
6 3^6
7 13^3
8 19^2
9 2^7
10 6^4
11 32
12 27
13 25
14 8
15 9
16 49
17 81
18 16
19 100
20 1000
21 10000
22 10
23 2^2
24 3^2
25 2^3
26 3^3
27 7^2
28 5^2
29 2^5
30 2^6

Exercise 2f page 37

1 **a** 6×10^1 **b** 6×10^2 **c** 6×10^0 **d** 6×10^3
2 **a** 300 **b** 2000 **c** 205 **d** 3060
3 $2^2 \times 7^2$
4 $3^3 \times 5^2$
5 $5^3 \times 13^2$
6 $2^2 \times 3^2 \times 5^2$
7 $2^3 \times 3^2 \times 5^2$
8 $2^2 \times 3 \times 11^2$
9 $3^2 \times 5 \times 7^4$
10 $5^2 \times 13^3$
11 $3^3 \times 5^2 \times 7^2$
12 $2^2 \times 3^2 \times 5^2$
13 108
14 225
15 112
16 36
17 180
18 126
19 153
20 371
21 370

Exercise 2g page 38

1 yes
2 no
3 yes
4 yes
5 no
6 yes
7 yes
8 no
9 yes
10 yes
11 yes

Exercise 2h page 40

1 $2^3 \times 3$
2 $2^2 \times 7$
3 $3^2 \times 7$
4 $2^3 \times 3^2$
5 $2^3 \times 17$
6 $2^2 \times 3 \times 7$
7 $2^3 \times 3^3$
8 $2^4 \times 3 \times 11$
9 $3^4 \times 5$
10 $2^4 \times 7^2$
11 $20 = 3 + 17; 7 + 13$
$22 = 3 + 19; 5 + 17; 11 + 11$
$24 = 5 + 19; 7 + 17; 11 + 13$
$26 = 3 + 23; 7 + 19; 13 + 13$
$28 = 5 + 23; 11 + 17$
$30 = 7 + 23; 11 + 19; 13 + 17$

Exercise 2i page 40

1 3
2 8
3 12
4 14
5 25
6 11
7 21
8 13
9 5
10 4
11 15
12 2

Exercise 2j page 41

1	15	**4**	36	**7**	48	**10**	108
2	24	**5**	36	**8**	60	**11**	36
3	15	**6**	60	**9**	36	**12**	168

Exercise 2k page 41

1	50 c	**4**	50 cm	**7**	480, 20
2	$10.80	**5**	78 s	**8**	18
3	120 m	**6**	30 steps; 2		

Exercise 2l page 43

1	D	**3**	D	**5**	C	**7**	C
2	D	**4**	B	**6**	D		

CHAPTER 3

Exercise 3b page 47

1 {the last four letters of the alphabet}
2 {the months whose names begin with J}
3 {the 6th to 8th months of the year}
4 {the Windward Islands}
5 {three islands in the Leeward Islands}
6 {even numbers less than 13}
7 {the first six whole numbers}
8 {the first six prime numbers}
9 {the whole numbers from 15 to 50 inclusive}
10 {multiples of 5 from 15 to 35 inclusive}
11 {boys' names}
12 {outerwear}
13 {breakfast cereals}
14 {Caribbean plants}
15 {plays by Shakespeare}
16 {11, 12, 13, 14, 15}
17 {a, b, c, d, e, f, g, h}
18 {a, c, e, h, i, m, s, t}
19 {Grenada, St Vincent, St Lucia, Dominica}
20 {Antigua, St Kitts, Montserrat, Guardaloupe}
22 {Arctic, Antarctic, Pacific, Atlantic, Indian}
24 {2, 3, 5, 7, 11, 13, 17, 19}
25 {2, 4, 6, 8, 10, 12, 14, 16, 18}
26 {21, 23, 25, 27, 29}
27 {12, 15, 18, 21, 24, 27, 30}
28 {21, 28, 35, 42, 49}
29 {St George's, Kingstown, Castries, Roseau}
30 {Guyana, Trinidad, Jamaica, Barbados, Grenada, St Vincent, St Lucia, Dominica, Antigua, St Kitts, Montserrat}

Exercise 3c page 48

1 apple ∈ {fruit}
2 shirt ∈ {clothing}
3 dog ∈ {domestic animals}
4 geography ∈ {school subjects}
5 carpet ∈ {floor coverings}
6 hairdressing ∈ {occupations}

Exercise 3d page 49

1 orange ∉ {animals}
2 cat ∉ {fruit}
3 table ∉ {trees}
4 shirt ∉ {subjects/study}
5 Anne ∉ {boys' names}
6 chisel ∉ {buildings}
7 cup ∉ {bedroom furniture}
8 cherry ∉ {Japanese cars}
9 aeroplane ∉ {foreign countries}
10 curry ∉ {breeds of dogs}
11 porridge ∈ {breakfast cereals}
12 electricity ∉ {building materials}
13 water ∉ {metals}
14 spider ∈ {living things}
15 Saturday ∈ {days of the week}
16 salmon ∈ {fish}
17 August ∉ {days of the week}
18 Spain ∈ {European countries}
19 Brazil ∉ {Asian countries}

Exercise 3e page 51

1	Yes	**2**	No	**3**	Yes	**4**	Yes	**5**	Yes
6	Yes	**7**	student's own answer			**8**	No		

Exercise 3f page 51

2 **a, c, d**

Exercise 3g page 52

1 {x, y}, {w, x}, {y, z}, {w, y}, {x, z}, {w, z}
2 {A, L}, {A, L, K, B}, {A, L, K}, {A, L, B}
3 $A = \{1, 3, 5, 7, 9\}$ $B = \{2, 4, 6, 8, 10\}$
$C = \{2, 3, 5, 7\}$
5 **a, b, c, d**

Exercise 3h page 53

1 {whole numbers}
2 {letters of the alphabet}
3 {rivers}
4 {pupils}
5 {cats}
6 {birds}
13 {geometrical instruments}
14 {dwellings}
15 {vehicles}
16 {footwear}
17 {sportsmen and sportswomen}

Exercise 3i page 56

1 {Peter, James, John, Andrew, Paul}
2 {3, 4, 6, 8, 9, 12, 16}
3 {a, b, c, d, e, i, o, u}
4 {a, b, c, x, y, z}
5 {p, q, r, s, t}
6 {1, 2, 3, 5, 7}
7 {5, 6, 7, 8, 10, 11, 12, 13}
8 {1, 2, 3, 4, 5, 6, 10, 12}
9 {a, c, h, l, m, o, r, s}
10 {a, b, c, e, g, h, i, l, m, r, t}

Exercise 3j page 57

1
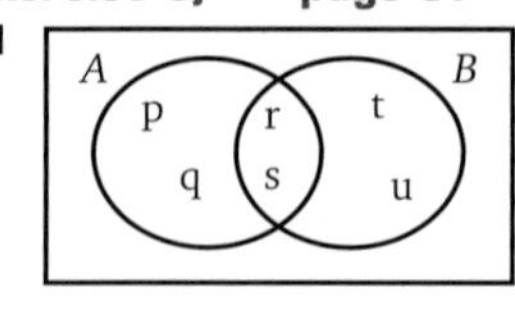

4
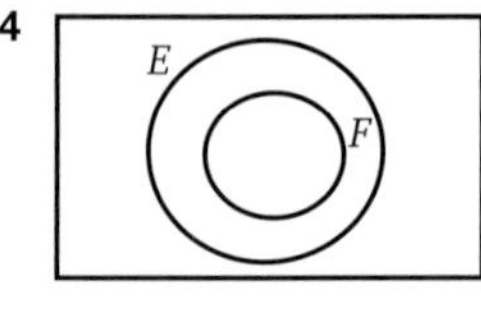

2
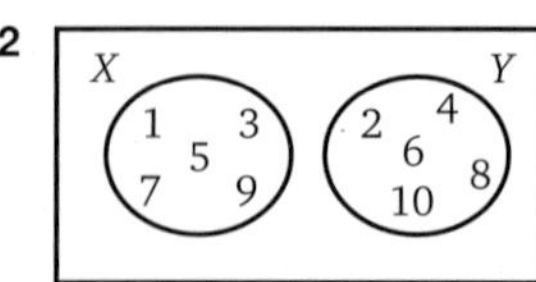

5
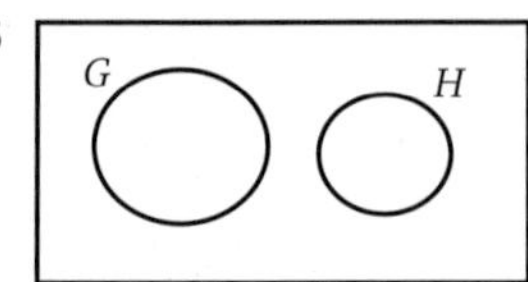

3
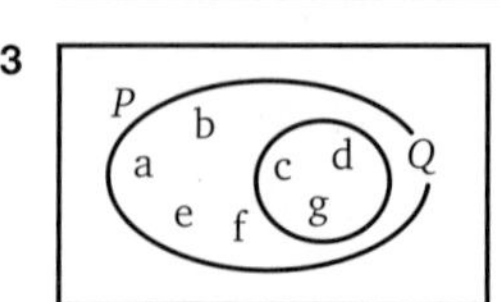

6
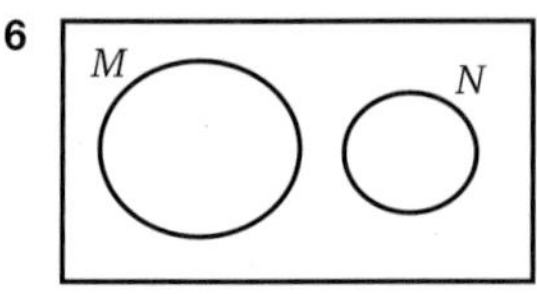

7

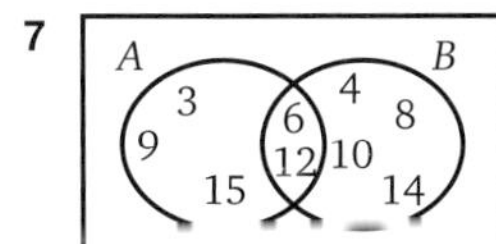

9

X Y
M J S
C L Y

8

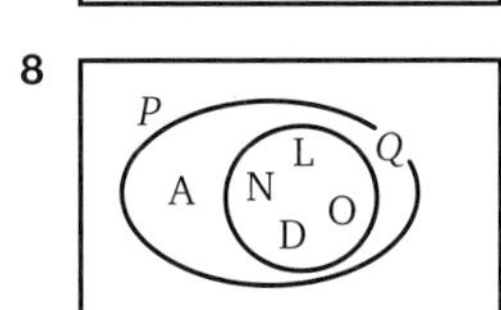

10

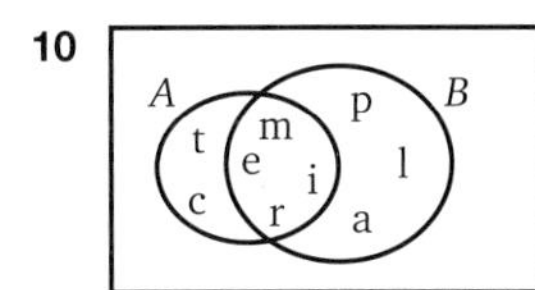

Exercise 3k **page 58**

1	{6, 9}	**6**	{3, 5, 7, 11}
2	{4, 12, 20}	**7**	{8, 16}
3	{Alice, Zane}	**8**	{2}
4	{o}	**9**	{e, t, w}
5	{cabbage, tomato}	**10**	{m, e, i, r}

Exercise 3l **page 59**

1	{3, 5, 7}	**6**	{8, 16}
2	{Dino, John}	**7**	{2, 4}
3	{o, u}	**8**	{t, i, n}
4	{oak, elm}	**9**	{r, t, m, e}
5	{boxer}	**10**	{3, 5, 7}

Exercise 3m **page 60**

1 D **2** B **3** B **4** A **5** A

CHAPTER 4

Exercise 4a **page 65**

2 **a** 2 **b** 1 **c** 4 **d** 3

3 **a** ray **b** line **c** line segment

Exercise 4b **page 66**

parallelogram	**a** 2 pairs	**b** the opposite side	**c** none
rhombus	**a** 4	**b** both pairs of opposite sides	**c** none
kite	**a** 2 pairs	**b** none	**c** none
trapezium	**a** none	**b** the shortest and longest side	**c** none

Exercise 4c **page 66**

5 yes

Exercise 4d **page 69**

2 **a** **i** 2 **ii** 2 **iii** 4 cm by 3 cm

3 **a** 6

4 **a** 5 **b** 8 **c** 5

5 **a** 5 **b** 9 **c** 6

Exercise 4e **page 70**

1 B **2** A **3** C **4** B **5** D **6** C

CHAPTER 5

Exercise 5a **page 74**

1	$\frac{1}{6}$	**5**	$\frac{2}{6}$	**9**	$\frac{1}{2}$	**13**	$\frac{3}{7}$
2	$\frac{3}{8}$	**6**	$\frac{7}{10}$	**10**	$\frac{3}{10}$	**14**	$\frac{2}{6}$
3	$\frac{1}{3}$	**7**	$\frac{1}{4}$	**11**	$\frac{5}{12}$	**15**	$\frac{4}{8}$
4	$\frac{5}{6}$	**8**	$\frac{3}{4}$	**12**	$\frac{1}{4}$	**16**	$\frac{1}{6}$

Exercise 5b **page 75**

1 **a** $\frac{1}{60}$ **b** $\frac{9}{60}$ **c** $\frac{30}{60}$ **d** $\frac{45}{60}$

2	$\frac{5}{7}$	**7**	$\frac{35}{180}$	**11**	$\frac{150}{500}$
3	$\frac{11}{31}$	**8**	$\frac{3}{31}$	**12**	$\frac{45}{120}$
4	$\frac{51}{365}$	**9**	$\frac{17}{61}$	**13**	$\frac{37}{3600}$
5	$\frac{35}{100}$	**10**	$\frac{5}{21}$	**14**	$\frac{35}{80}$
6	$\frac{90}{500}$				

15 **a** $\frac{10}{32}$ **b** $\frac{8}{32}$ **c** $\frac{25}{32}$

16 $\frac{2}{5}, \frac{3}{5}$

17 **a** $\frac{20}{62}$ **b** $\frac{10}{62}$ **c** $\frac{48}{62}$

18 **a** $\frac{12}{37}$ **b** $\frac{8}{37}$ **c** $\frac{29}{37}$

19 **a** $\frac{9}{14}$ **b** $\frac{3}{14}$

Exercise 5c **page 77**

7	6	**16**	6	**25**	300
8	4	**17**	16	**26**	110
9	21	**18**	18	**27**	40
10	36	**19**	18	**28**	1000
11	18	**20**	30	**29**	90
12	4	**21**	10	**30**	8000
13	15	**22**	10	**31**	55
14	12	**23**	100	**32**	500
15	100	**24**	8	**33**	10 000

34 **a** $\frac{12}{24}$ **c** $\frac{4}{24}$ **e** $\frac{10}{24}$
b $\frac{8}{24}$ **d** $\frac{18}{24}$ **f** $\frac{9}{24}$

35 **a** $\frac{6}{45}$ **c** $\frac{27}{45}$ **e** $\frac{42}{45}$
b $\frac{20}{45}$ **d** $\frac{15}{45}$ **f** $\frac{9}{45}$

36 **a** $\frac{27}{36}$ **c** $\frac{6}{36}$ **e** $\frac{21}{36}$
b $\frac{20}{36}$ **d** $\frac{10}{36}$ **f** $\frac{24}{36}$

37 **a** $\frac{12}{72}$ **c** $\frac{12}{14}$ **e** $\frac{12}{18}$
b $\frac{12}{16}$ **d** $\frac{12}{15}$ **f** $\frac{12}{24}$

38 **b** $\frac{2}{3} = \frac{6}{9}$ **e** $\frac{7}{10} = \frac{70}{100}$

Exercise 5d **page 80**

1 **a** **b**

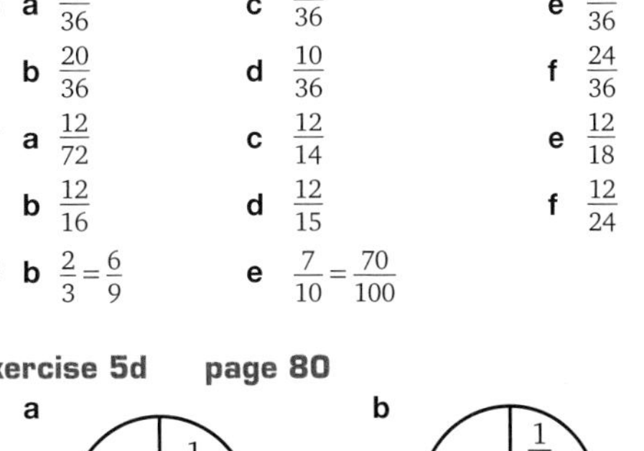

c **d**

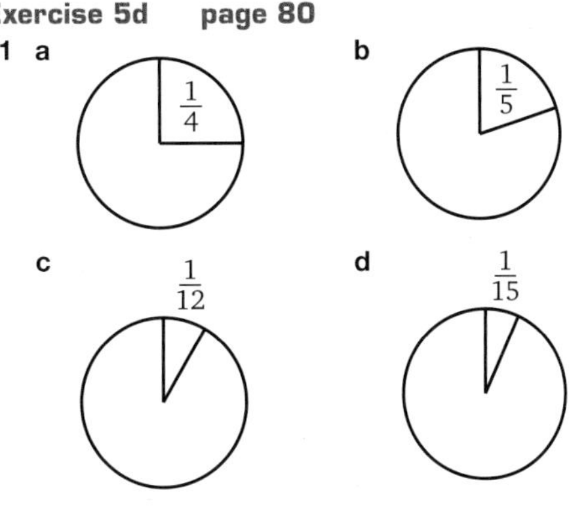

2 $\frac{1}{2}$ **11** $\frac{6}{7}$ **20** $\frac{3}{11}$ **29** $<$
3 $\frac{5}{6}$ **12** $\frac{3}{5}$ **21** $\frac{7}{9}$ **30** $>$
4 $\frac{4}{5}$ **13** $\frac{3}{4}$ **22** $\frac{9}{11}$ **31** $<$
5 $\frac{2}{9}$ **14** $\frac{3}{11}$ **23** $\frac{2}{5}$ **32** $<$
6 $\frac{3}{8}$ **15** $\frac{5}{7}$ **24** $\frac{3}{5}$ **33** $>$
7 $\frac{3}{4}$ **16** $\frac{5}{11}$ **25** $\frac{5}{8}$ **34** $<$
8 $\frac{3}{7}$ **17** $\frac{4}{11}$ **26** $<$ **35** $>$
9 $\frac{5}{6}$ **18** $\frac{2}{7}$ **27** $>$ **36** $<$
10 $\frac{3}{8}$ **19** $\frac{5}{8}$ **28** $<$ **37** $>$

38 $\frac{7}{30}, \frac{1}{2}, \frac{3}{5}, \frac{2}{3}$
39 $\frac{4}{10}, \frac{5}{8}, \frac{13}{20}, \frac{3}{4}$
40 $\frac{1}{3}, \frac{1}{2}, \frac{7}{12}, \frac{5}{6}$
41 $\frac{3}{8}, \frac{2}{5}, \frac{1}{2}, \frac{7}{10}, \frac{17}{20}$
42 $\frac{1}{2}, \frac{17}{28}, \frac{5}{7}, \frac{3}{4}, \frac{11}{14}$
43 $\frac{2}{5}, \frac{1}{2}, \frac{14}{25}, \frac{3}{5}, \frac{7}{10}$
44 $\frac{5}{6}, \frac{7}{9}, \frac{2}{3}, \frac{11}{18}, \frac{1}{2}$
45 $\frac{3}{4}, \frac{7}{10}, \frac{13}{20}, \frac{3}{5}, \frac{1}{2}$
46 $\frac{3}{4}, \frac{17}{24}, \frac{2}{3}, \frac{7}{12}, \frac{1}{6}$
47 $\frac{4}{5}, \frac{23}{30}, \frac{11}{15}, \frac{7}{10}, \frac{2}{3}$
48 $\frac{3}{4}, \frac{5}{8}, \frac{19}{32}, \frac{1}{2}, \frac{7}{16}$
49 $\frac{5}{6}, \frac{4}{5}, \frac{3}{4}, \frac{7}{12}, \frac{1}{2}$

Exercise 5e page 82

1 $\frac{1}{3}$ **7** $\frac{1}{3}$ **13** $\frac{1}{5}$ **19** $\frac{3}{5}$ **25** $\frac{4}{5}$
2 $\frac{3}{5}$ **8** $\frac{2}{3}$ **14** $\frac{2}{5}$ **20** $\frac{2}{5}$ **26** $\frac{4}{7}$
3 $\frac{1}{3}$ **9** $\frac{1}{2}$ **15** $\frac{2}{7}$ **21** $\frac{5}{9}$ **27** $\frac{1}{3}$
4 $\frac{1}{2}$ **10** $\frac{1}{4}$ **16** $\frac{1}{3}$ **22** $\frac{7}{11}$ **28** $\frac{9}{11}$
5 $\frac{1}{3}$ **11** $\frac{2}{7}$ **17** $\frac{1}{2}$ **23** $\frac{3}{4}$ **29** $\frac{3}{4}$
6 $\frac{1}{2}$ **12** $\frac{3}{10}$ **18** $\frac{1}{5}$ **24** $\frac{3}{11}$ **30** $\frac{4}{5}$

Exercise 5f page 83

1 $\frac{3}{4}$ **8** $\frac{2}{5}$ **15** $\frac{1}{2}$ **22** $\frac{15}{23}$ **29** $\frac{9}{17}$
2 $\frac{1}{2}$ **9** $\frac{11}{21}$ **16** $\frac{9}{10}$ **23** $\frac{8}{9}$ **30** $\frac{12}{19}$
3 $\frac{5}{11}$ **10** $\frac{1}{2}$ **17** $\frac{3}{4}$ **24** $\frac{2}{3}$ **31** $\frac{13}{30}$
4 $\frac{10}{13}$ **11** $\frac{11}{13}$ **18** $\frac{11}{19}$ **25** $\frac{4}{5}$ **32** $\frac{5}{9}$
5 $\frac{19}{23}$ **12** $\frac{4}{5}$ **19** $\frac{1}{2}$ **26** $\frac{2}{5}$ **33** $\frac{1}{2}$
6 $\frac{3}{7}$ **13** $\frac{6}{7}$ **20** $\frac{2}{5}$ **27** $\frac{23}{31}$ **34** $\frac{25}{99}$
7 $\frac{3}{5}$ **14** $\frac{9}{17}$ **21** $\frac{6}{11}$ **28** $\frac{11}{14}$

Exercise 5g page 84

1 $\frac{13}{15}$ **3** $\frac{11}{30}$ **5** $\frac{29}{30}$ **7** $\frac{25}{42}$
2 $\frac{23}{40}$ **4** $\frac{29}{35}$ **6** $\frac{39}{56}$ **8** $\frac{20}{21}$

9 $\frac{19}{42}$ **16** $\frac{33}{100}$ **23** $\frac{13}{15}$ **30** 1
10 $\frac{41}{42}$ **17** $\frac{19}{20}$ **24** $\frac{3}{4}$ **31** $\frac{39}{40}$
11 $\frac{82}{99}$ **18** $\frac{5}{8}$ **25** $\frac{19}{20}$ **32** $\frac{13}{18}$
12 $\frac{47}{90}$ **19** $\frac{8}{9}$ **26** $\frac{17}{24}$ **33** $\frac{17}{20}$
13 $\frac{7}{10}$ **20** $\frac{13}{18}$ **27** $\frac{19}{20}$ **34** $\frac{17}{18}$
14 $\frac{13}{16}$ **21** $\frac{13}{20}$ **28** $\frac{11}{12}$ **35** $\frac{19}{30}$
15 $\frac{17}{21}$ **22** $\frac{13}{22}$ **29** $\frac{6}{7}$ **36** $\frac{2}{3}$

Exercise 5h page 86

1 $\frac{2}{3}$ **7** $\frac{5}{13}$ **13** $\frac{18}{55}$ **19** $\frac{3}{16}$
2 $\frac{1}{2}$ **8** $\frac{3}{5}$ **14** $\frac{1}{9}$ **20** $\frac{4}{15}$
3 $\frac{5}{17}$ **9** $\frac{5}{21}$ **15** $\frac{3}{26}$ **21** $\frac{1}{8}$
4 $\frac{11}{20}$ **10** $\frac{5}{21}$ **16** $\frac{1}{12}$ **22** $\frac{1}{4}$
5 $\frac{2}{5}$ **11** $\frac{7}{15}$ **17** $\frac{9}{100}$ **23** $\frac{1}{6}$
6 $\frac{3}{7}$ **12** $\frac{1}{3}$ **18** $\frac{19}{56}$ **24** $\frac{4}{15}$

Exercise 5i page 87

1 $\frac{3}{8}$ **7** $\frac{3}{5}$ **13** $\frac{1}{18}$ **19** $\frac{1}{8}$
2 $\frac{5}{7}$ **8** $\frac{17}{18}$ **14** $\frac{1}{12}$ **20** $\frac{1}{3}$
3 $\frac{1}{16}$ **9** $\frac{17}{50}$ **15** $\frac{1}{5}$ **21** $\frac{19}{100}$
4 $\frac{5}{12}$ **10** $\frac{1}{2}$ **16** $\frac{1}{16}$ **22** $\frac{1}{4}$
5 $\frac{9}{50}$ **11** $\frac{3}{4}$ **17** $\frac{2}{9}$ **23** $\frac{5}{18}$
6 $\frac{5}{12}$ **12** $\frac{1}{2}$ **18** $\frac{7}{20}$ **24** $\frac{1}{30}$

Exercise 5j page 88

1 $\frac{13}{15}, \frac{2}{15}$ **2** $\frac{11}{15}, \frac{4}{15}$
3 a $\frac{1}{3}$ **b** $\frac{1}{12}$
4 a $\frac{3}{8}$ **b** $\frac{7}{8}$
5 a $\frac{11}{40}$ **b** $\frac{19}{20}$ **c** $\frac{7}{40}$

Exercise 5k page 90

1 $2\frac{1}{4}$ **6** $3\frac{1}{2}$ **11** $13\frac{5}{8}$ **16** $12\frac{5}{6}$
2 $4\frac{3}{4}$ **7** $6\frac{3}{4}$ **12** $11\frac{6}{7}$ **17** $13\frac{2}{3}$
3 $6\frac{1}{6}$ **8** $5\frac{1}{8}$ **13** $13\frac{4}{9}$ **18** $13\frac{2}{5}$
4 $5\frac{3}{10}$ **9** $25\frac{2}{5}$ **14** $15\frac{1}{6}$ **19** $24\frac{1}{3}$
5 $9\frac{7}{9}$ **10** $10\frac{4}{11}$ **15** $7\frac{10}{11}$ **20** $4\frac{9}{10}$

Exercise 5l page 91

1 $\frac{13}{3}$ **2** $\frac{33}{4}$ **3** $\frac{17}{10}$ **4** $\frac{98}{9}$

5 $\frac{57}{7}$ **9** $\frac{11}{3}$ **13** $\frac{19}{5}$ **17** $\frac{19}{10}$
6 $\frac{33}{5}$ **10** $\frac{11}{2}$ **14** $\frac{43}{9}$ **18** $\frac{20}{3}$
7 $\frac{20}{7}$ **11** $\frac{37}{5}$ **15** $\frac{35}{4}$ **19** $\frac{59}{8}$
8 $\frac{25}{6}$ **12** $\frac{22}{9}$ **16** $\frac{73}{7}$ **20** $\frac{101}{10}$

Exercise 5m page 92

1 $5\frac{1}{7}$ **4** $2\frac{1}{2}$ **7** $13\frac{2}{3}$ **10** $10\frac{7}{10}$
2 $9\frac{5}{6}$ **5** $16\frac{2}{5}$ **8** $7\frac{1}{9}$ **11** $7\frac{2}{5}$
3 $4\frac{8}{11}$ **6** $7\frac{1}{4}$ **9** $8\frac{1}{6}$ **12** $6\frac{1}{2}$

Exercise 5n page 93

1 $5\frac{3}{4}$ **11** $10\frac{13}{16}$ **21** $11\frac{1}{2}$
2 $3\frac{5}{6}$ **12** $6\frac{1}{3}$ **22** $17\frac{3}{7}$
3 $5\frac{23}{40}$ **13** $11\frac{3}{14}$ **23** $17\frac{3}{16}$
4 $9\frac{4}{9}$ **14** $8\frac{1}{16}$ **24** $21\frac{1}{18}$
5 $5\frac{29}{36}$ **15** $12\frac{1}{16}$ **25** $15\frac{2}{5}$
6 $4\frac{1}{6}$ **16** $11\frac{9}{10}$ **26** $15\frac{4}{5}$
7 $4\frac{9}{20}$ **17** $8\frac{3}{10}$ **27** $14\frac{51}{100}$
8 $3\frac{3}{14}$ **18** $18\frac{1}{2}$ **28** $17\frac{13}{32}$
9 $7\frac{7}{10}$ **19** $10\frac{1}{10}$ **29** $22\frac{2}{7}$
10 $13\frac{17}{21}$ **20** $11\frac{1}{10}$ **30** $22\frac{1}{2}$

Exercise 5p page 94

1 $1\frac{5}{8}$ **10** $3\frac{11}{35}$ **19** $3\frac{9}{35}$ **28** $2\frac{1}{2}$
2 $1\frac{13}{15}$ **11** $2\frac{2}{15}$ **20** $6\frac{2}{33}$ **29** $\frac{7}{9}$
3 $1\frac{1}{6}$ **12** $3\frac{1}{4}$ **21** $3\frac{3}{28}$ **30** $1\frac{1}{2}$
4 $\frac{3}{4}$ **13** $3\frac{3}{10}$ **22** $1\frac{5}{8}$ **31** $2\frac{5}{6}$
5 $5\frac{5}{12}$ **14** $2\frac{4}{63}$ **23** $\frac{3}{4}$ **32** $2\frac{7}{8}$
6 $1\frac{1}{2}$ **15** $3\frac{7}{24}$ **24** $1\frac{27}{35}$ **33** $3\frac{9}{10}$
7 $1\frac{5}{14}$ **16** $2\frac{25}{28}$ **25** $1\frac{3}{8}$ **34** $\frac{2}{3}$
8 $2\frac{3}{10}$ **17** $1\frac{3}{4}$ **26** $2\frac{7}{10}$ **35** $1\frac{1}{6}$
9 $1\frac{7}{10}$ **18** $3\frac{7}{20}$ **27** $3\frac{1}{2}$ **36** $2\frac{16}{21}$

Exercise 5q page 95

1 a $1\frac{5}{21}$ **c** $\frac{35}{72}$ **e** $\frac{11}{12}$
b $\frac{11}{24}$ **d** $2\frac{1}{6}$
2 a $2\frac{1}{4}$ **b** $3\frac{1}{5}$
3 a $\frac{3}{7}$ **b** $\frac{17}{30}$
4 a $\frac{1}{2}, \frac{3}{5}, \frac{13}{20}, \frac{7}{10}$ **b** $\frac{7}{12}, \frac{2}{3}, \frac{3}{4}, \frac{5}{6}$ **c** $\frac{3}{5}, \frac{7}{10}, \frac{71}{100}, \frac{17}{20}$
5 a $<$ **b** $>$ **c** $>$
6 a $\frac{3}{11}$ **b** $\frac{7}{22}$

Exercise 5r page 96

1 C **2** C **3** D **4** B **5** C **6** A

Exercise 5s page 96

1 a $\frac{43}{140}$ **c** $\frac{1}{8}$ **e** 0
b $\frac{17}{45}$ **d** $3\frac{1}{12}$ **f** 5
2 a $1\frac{3}{8}$ **b** $2\frac{2}{5}$ **c** $\frac{5}{16}$
3 a $<$ **b** $<$
4 a $\frac{1}{2}, \frac{3}{5}, \frac{3}{4}, \frac{5}{6}$ **b** $\frac{1}{2}, \frac{5}{9}, \frac{2}{3}, \frac{5}{6}$
5 a $\frac{7}{60}$ **b** $\frac{1}{3}$ **c** $\frac{38}{79}$
6 a $\frac{17}{19}$ **b** $\frac{13}{19}$

Exercise 5t page 97

1 a $1\frac{1}{6}$ **c** $\frac{1}{12}$ **e** $\frac{11}{12}$
b $\frac{5}{8}$ **d** $2\frac{9}{20}$ **f** $3\frac{2}{3}$
2 a $4\frac{3}{8}$ **b** $\frac{1}{8}$ **c** $2\frac{4}{7}$
3 a $\frac{5}{24}$ **b** $\frac{1}{10}$ **c** $\frac{5}{12}$
4 a $>$ **b** $<$
5 a $\frac{5}{11}, \frac{1}{2}, \frac{23}{44}, \frac{13}{22}$ **b** $\frac{5}{9}, \frac{7}{12}, \frac{2}{3}, \frac{3}{4}$
6 a $\frac{1}{5}$ **b** $\frac{8}{15}$ **c** $\frac{1}{3}$

CHAPTER 6

Exercise 6b page 101

1 $\frac{3}{8}$ **10** $\frac{14}{27}$ **19** $\frac{3}{4}$ **28** $\frac{1}{5}$
2 $\frac{10}{21}$ **11** $\frac{3}{20}$ **20** $\frac{6}{7}$ **29** $\frac{1}{7}$
3 $\frac{2}{15}$ **12** $\frac{3}{35}$ **21** $\frac{5}{48}$ **30** $\frac{3}{16}$
4 $\frac{7}{16}$ **13** $\frac{1}{6}$ **22** $\frac{11}{20}$ **31** $\frac{3}{20}$
5 $\frac{3}{7}$ **14** $\frac{4}{7}$ **23** $\frac{4}{11}$ **32** $\frac{2}{3}$
6 $\frac{4}{63}$ **15** $\frac{7}{18}$ **24** $\frac{4}{11}$ **33** 4
7 $\frac{6}{35}$ **16** $\frac{2}{3}$ **25** $\frac{2}{9}$ **34** $\frac{1}{18}$
8 $\frac{6}{25}$ **17** $\frac{1}{9}$ **26** $\frac{2}{31}$ **35** $\frac{3}{22}$
9 $\frac{5}{24}$ **18** $\frac{15}{28}$ **27** $\frac{2}{3}$ **36** $\frac{1}{6}$

Exercise 6c page 102

1 $\frac{3}{5}$ **3** $\frac{3}{4}$ **5** $\frac{1}{2}$
2 2 **4** $11\frac{1}{5}$ **6** $\frac{1}{2}$

7 $\frac{7}{8}$
8 2
9 $16\frac{1}{3}$
10 $\frac{17}{21}$
11 14
12 4
13 30
14 $16\frac{1}{2}$
15 $7\frac{1}{2}$
16 9
17 10
18 10
19 20
20 60
21 5
22 $6\frac{1}{3}$
23 7
24 15
25 $29\frac{1}{4}$
26 9
27 14
28 12
29 3
30 8

Exercise 6d page 103

1 23
2 30
3 $12\frac{1}{2}$
4 $37\frac{1}{2}$
5 110
6 $13\frac{1}{2}$
7 36
8 $8\frac{1}{2}$
9 120
10 $18\frac{1}{3}$
11 14
12 44

Exercise 6e page 103

1 6
2 6
3 3
4 16
5 10
6 6
7 5
8 8
9 30
10 15
11 12 m
12 25 dollars
13 15 litres
14 33 miles
15 21 gallons
16 8 m
17 10 dollars
18 28 litres
19 15 miles
20 88 gallons
21 50 c
22 8 c
23 30 c
24 12 c
25 292 days
26 9 h
27 1 day
28 $3
29 60 c
30 21 h

Exercise 6f page 105

1 14
2 20
3 21
4 15
5 12
6 10
7 21
8 45
9 99
10 30
11 18
12 16
13 49
14 99
15 39
16 63
17 38
18 $\frac{3}{4}$
19 $1\frac{1}{5}$
20 $\frac{1}{12}$
21 $1\frac{1}{2}$
22 $\frac{2}{5}$
23 1
24 $2\frac{1}{3}$
25 $\frac{2}{3}$
26 $1\frac{1}{2}$
27 $1\frac{2}{5}$
28 $\frac{2}{3}$
29 $\frac{3}{8}$

Exercise 6g page 106

1 $10\frac{1}{2}$
2 $\frac{5}{6}$
3 $5\frac{1}{3}$
4 6
5 $2\frac{8}{11}$
6 $6\frac{2}{3}$
7 $\frac{9}{10}$
8 $4\frac{5}{6}$
9 $1\frac{4}{5}$
10 4
11 6
12 $2\frac{2}{3}$
13 12
14 6
15 $5\frac{3}{5}$
16 6
17 $1\frac{3}{7}$
18 $3\frac{1}{3}$
19 $1\frac{1}{2}$
20 12

Exercise 6h page 107

1 1
2 $2\frac{1}{2}$
3 $1\frac{2}{3}$
4 $\frac{2}{3}$
5 $\frac{8}{15}$
6 $2\frac{2}{3}$
7 $5\frac{1}{10}$
8 $2\frac{1}{4}$
9 $1\frac{1}{2}$
10 $\frac{9}{32}$
11 $\frac{9}{20}$
12 $\frac{4}{5}$

Exercise 6i page 108

1 $\frac{3}{5}$
2 $\frac{7}{12}$
3 $\frac{1}{5}$
4 $\frac{3}{14}$
5 $\frac{13}{15}$
6 $\frac{5}{24}$
7 $1\frac{5}{8}$
8 $\frac{41}{42}$
9 $\frac{1}{16}$
10 $\frac{1}{3}$
11 $\frac{2}{21}$
12 $\frac{7}{10}$
13 $\frac{21}{34}$
14 $1\frac{1}{2}$
15 $\frac{1}{22}$
16 $\frac{9}{22}$
17 $\frac{5}{21}$
18 $\frac{5}{18}$
19 $\frac{2}{33}$
20 $1\frac{2}{25}$
21 $\frac{1}{21}$
22 $1\frac{1}{4}$
23 $\frac{1}{4}$
24 $\frac{1}{3}$
25 $\frac{1}{9}$
26 $4\frac{2}{9}$
27 $1\frac{3}{8}$
28 $2\frac{7}{30}$
29 $\frac{11}{16}$
30 $1\frac{8}{9}$
31 T
32 F
33 T
34 T
35 F
36 F
37 T
38 F
39 F
40 T

Exercise 6j page 109

1 $4\frac{3}{4}$
2 $1\frac{1}{8}$
3 $\frac{3}{4}$
4 4
5 $2\frac{1}{14}$
6 $\frac{17}{18}$
7 22
8 $\frac{13}{15}$
9 3
10 $3\frac{7}{8}$
11 $6\frac{1}{4}$
12 2
13 $1\frac{7}{10}$
14 $2\frac{2}{7}$
15 $2\frac{2}{5}$
16 $\frac{17}{20}$
17 $4\frac{1}{14}$
18 $4\frac{5}{8}$
19 $3\frac{13}{16}$
20 $4\frac{1}{2}$
21 $1\frac{1}{12}$
22 $\frac{7}{12}$
23 $4\frac{1}{8}$
24 $3\frac{1}{12}$
25 $\frac{7}{8}$
26 $1\frac{3}{8}$
27 $3\frac{1}{20}$
28 $1\frac{1}{2}$
29 $5\frac{3}{7}$
30 $\frac{1}{2}$
31 $3\frac{1}{2}$
32 1
33 $2\frac{1}{4}$
34 0
35 $\frac{1}{5}$
36 $\frac{3}{8}$
37 $\frac{1}{16}$
38 $4\frac{2}{7}$
39 $2\frac{6}{7}$
40 2

Exercise 6k page 110

1 30 kg
2 $\frac{7}{20}$ litres
3 3 km
4 $58\frac{1}{2}$ min
5 22
6 $1\frac{1}{2}$

Exercise 6l page 111

1 C **2** C **3** D **4** C **5** D **6** B

Exercise 6m page 112

1 a 15 **b** $11\frac{1}{3}$
2 a $1\frac{2}{3}$ **b** $4\frac{11}{18}$
3 a $<$ **b** $<$
4 a $1\frac{1}{12}$ **b** 9

5 $\frac{1}{3}, \frac{2}{5}, \frac{7}{15}$ **6** 2

7 **a** $6\frac{1}{4}$ **b** $2\frac{6}{11}$

8 125 s

9 **a** 24   **b** 21

10 **a** $3\frac{1}{8}$ **b** $5\frac{4}{9}$ **c** $6\frac{1}{6}$

11 $12\frac{1}{8}$ km; $\frac{77}{97}$ **12** 6

Exercise 6n page 113

1 **a** $2\frac{25}{36}$ **b** 0

2 **a** $\frac{1}{4}$ **b** $\frac{4}{5}$

3 25 days   **4** $\frac{17}{20}, \frac{3}{4}, \frac{7}{10}$

5 **a** $6\frac{1}{4}$ **b** $17\frac{11}{12}$

6 $\frac{8}{11}$ **7** $1\frac{6}{7}$ **8** $2\frac{2}{5}$

9 **a** $7\frac{1}{3}$ **b** $9\frac{1}{5}$ **c** $10\frac{3}{5}$

10 a, b and c   **11** 18 min   **12** $1\frac{4}{7}$ kg, $\frac{6}{11}$

CHAPTER 7

Exercise 7a page 116

1	$\frac{3}{4}$	**6**	$\frac{1}{2}$	**11**	$\frac{1}{3}$	**16**	6	**21**	6
2	$\frac{1}{2}$	**7**	$\frac{1}{2}$	**12**	$\frac{1}{3}$	**17**	9	**22**	4
3	$\frac{1}{4}$	**8**	$\frac{1}{2}$	**13**	$\frac{3}{4}$	**18**	9	**23**	8
4	$\frac{1}{2}$	**9**	1	**14**	$\frac{3}{4}$	**19**	3	**24**	9
5	$\frac{1}{4}$	**10**	$\frac{1}{4}$	**15**	$\frac{2}{3}$	**20**	6	**25**	12

Exercise 7b page 117

1	N	**3**	N	**5**	N	**7**	$\frac{3}{4}$
2	W	**4**	E No	**6**	$\frac{3}{4}$	**8**	$\frac{1}{2}$

Exercise 7c page 119

1	1	**5**	4	**9**	2	**13**	4
2	2	**6**	2	**10**	1		
3	3	**7**	3	**11**	1		
4	1	**8**	4	**12**	3		

Exercise 7d page 120

1	obtuse	**6**	reflex	**11**	reflex
2	acute	**7**	acute	**12**	obtuse
3	reflex	**8**	acute	**13**	obtuse
4	acute	**9**	obtuse	**14**	obtuse
5	obtuse	**10**	acute	**15**	acute

Exercise 7e page 121

1	180°	**5**	90°	**9**	90°	**13**	180°	**17**	45°	**22**	120°	**27**	180°	**32**	300°
2	90°	**6**	270°	**10**	120°	**14**	90°	**18**	120°	**23**	30°	**28**	300°	**33**	210°
3	270°	**7**	180°	**11**	270°	**15**	180°	**19**	60°	**24**	60°	**29**	330°	**34**	150°
4	180°	**8**	270°	**12**	270°	**16**	30°	**20**	45°	**25**	120°	**30**	150°	**35**	210°
								21	30°	**26**	210°	**31**	210°		

Exercise 7f page 123

1	36°	**8**	54°	**15**	345°
2	60°	**9**	80°	**16**	330°
3	75°	**10**	11°	**17**	240°
4	137°	**11**	325°	**18**	345°
5	150°	**12**	332°	**19**	282°
6	20°	**13**	250°	**20**	213°
7	115°	**14**	218°	**21**	145°

Exercise 7g page 126

1	30°	**13**	1	**37**	350°
2	60°	**14**	10	**38**	260°
3	90°	**15**	2	**39**	25°
4	120°	**16**	6	**40**	300°
5	150°	**17**	3	**41**	45°
6	180°	**18**	7	**42**	5°
7	3	**19**	6	**43**	25°
8	2	**20**	8	**44**	80°
9	4	**21**	1	**45**	160°
10	12	**22**	12	**46**	105°
11	5	**35**	60°		
12	9	**36**	140°		

Exercise 7i page 129

4	150°	**6**	35°	**8**	140°
5	20°	**7**	65°	**9**	160°

Exercise 7j page 130

1 180°   **2** 180°

Exercise 7k page 131

1	120°	**4**	100°	**7**	80°	**10**	140°
2	155°	**5**	20°	**8**	15°	**11**	90°
3	10°	**6**	130°	**9**	135°	**12**	50°

13 *e* and *f*
14 *m* and *k*, *j* and *d*
15 *d* and *f*, *f* and *e*, *e* and *g*, *g* and *d*
16 *f* and *g*
17 *f* and *g*, *g* and *d*, *d* and *e*, *e* and *f*
18 *n* and *d*, *d* and *p*, *p* and *m*, *m* and *n*

19	50°, 130°, 130°	**20**	60°, 120°, 120°
21	180°, 60°	**24**	180°, 155°
22	105°, 180°	**25**	80°, 100°, 100°
23	45°, 135°, 135°	**26**	165°, 180°

Exercise 7l page 135

1	110°	**5**	180°	**9**	310°
2	60°	**6**	150°	**10**	60°
3	110°	**7**	100°		
4	80°	**8**	120°		

Exercise 7m page 136

1	120°	**5**	150°, 60°
2	120°, 60°	**6**	50°
3	120°	**7**	40°
4	310°	**8**	120°, 60°, 120°, 60°

Exercise 7n page 138

1 B 2 C 3 A 4 C 5 D 6 A

Exercise 7p page 139

1 240°
2 W
3 354°
4 140°, 40°
5 50°
6 30°
7 35°

REVIEW TEST 1 page 141

1 C
2 A
3 D
4 A
5 A
6 C
7 D
8 C
9 A
10 C
11 B
12 B

13 a $\frac{1}{9}$ **b** $2 \times 2 \times 5 \times 7$

14 $x = 50°, y = 130°, z = 70°$

15 a 12

b 13: yes, it is a factor of 12 740; 9: no, for 12 740 to divide by 9 it would need to divide by 3 and by 3 again

16 a $\frac{19}{32}$ litres **b** $\frac{1}{4}$

17 a i 1, 2, 3, 6 **ii** 1, 2, 3, 4, 6, 7, 9, 12, 14, 18, 21, 36, 42

b

A: 3, 6, 12
A and B: 2, 4
B: 8

18 a 9, 16, 36, 169

b 5 and 11; they are the only two prime numbers.

CHAPTER 8

Exercise 8b page 145

1 $\frac{1}{5}$
2 $\frac{3}{50}$
3 $1\frac{3}{10}$
4 $\frac{7}{10\,000}$
5 $\frac{1}{1000}$
6 $6\frac{2}{5}$
7 $\frac{7}{10}$
8 $2\frac{1}{100}$
9 $1\frac{4}{5}$
10 $1\frac{7}{10}$
11 $15\frac{1}{2}$
12 $8\frac{3}{50}$
13 $\frac{73}{100}$
14 $\frac{81}{1000}$
15 $\frac{207}{1000}$
16 $\frac{29}{10000}$
17 $\frac{67}{100000}$
18 $\frac{17}{100}$
19 $\frac{71}{1000}$
20 $\frac{3001}{10000}$
21 $\frac{207}{10000}$
22 $\frac{63}{100}$
23 $\frac{31}{1000}$
24 $\frac{47}{100}$
25 $\frac{1}{4}$
26 $\frac{9}{125}$
27 $\frac{19}{50}$
28 $\frac{61}{2000}$
29 $\frac{3}{20}$
30 $\frac{1}{40}$
31 $\frac{7}{20}$
32 $\frac{1}{625}$
33 $\frac{11}{250}$
34 $\frac{1}{8}$
35 $\frac{12}{25}$
36 $\frac{5}{8}$

Exercise 8c page 146

1 0.07
2 0.9
3 1.1
4 0.002
5 0.4
6 2.06
7 0.04
8 7.8
9 7.08
10 0.0006
11 4.005
12 0.0029

Exercise 8d page 147

1 10.8
2 7.55
3 0.039
4 3.98
5 5.83
6 14.04
7 7.6
8 12.24
9 3.68
10 9.12
11 0.2673
12 2.102
13 0.001 76
14 0.131
15 4.698
16 0.3552
17 4.6005
18 20.7
19 6.798
20 27.374
21 2.38
22 17.301
23 15.62
24 13.52
25 16.81

Exercise 8e page 148

1 2.5
2 7.8
3 18.5
4 0.41
5 0.0321
6 16.87
7 2.241
8 0.191
9 71.4
10 6.65
11 41.45
12 6.939
13 3.06
14 2.94
15 3.13
16 2.66
17 2.4
18 7.882
19 6.118
20 2.772
21 11.1974
22 0.000 197
23 0.0067
24 0.0013
25 0.005 27
26 0.059 27
27 5.27
28 5.927
29 7.24
30 729.4
31 0.729 94
32 0.13
33 57.6
34 8.3
35 0.149
36 6.81

Exercise 8f page 149

1 10.32
2 6.92
3 2.98
4 6.6
5 4.4
6 100.28
7 99.72
8 0.286
9 0.234
10 77.62
11 39.88
12 36.52
13 202.84
14 17.76
15 0.59
16 0.007
17 0.382
18 6.64
19 38.82
20 7.81
21 22.6 cm
22 5.3 m
23 $24.77
24 $21.04
25 1
26 53.2 mm
27 $9.25
28 5.9 cm

Exercise 8g page 152

1 72 000
2 82.4
3 0.24
4 460
5 3278
6 430
7 6.02
8 32.06
9 72 810
10 0.000 063
11 0.703
12 374

Exercise 8h page 153

1 2.772
2 7.626
3 0.000 024
4 0.014
5 2.7
6 0.068
7 0.026
8 0.0158
9 0.0426
10 1.34
11 0.003 74
12 0.0092

Exercise 8i page 153

1 0.16
2 16
3 7.8
4 0.000 78
5 1420
6 6.8
7 0.0163
8 0.002
9 0.14
10 78 000
11 0.24
12 63
13 3.2
14 0.079
15 0.078
16 0.24
17 11 100
18 0.000 38
19 0.0038
20 380 000
21 0.000 24
22 0.000 003
23 4.1
24 10.04
25 4.2 m
26 $152
27 0.138, 1380
28 0.16
29 0.1746
30 0.0038

Exercise 8j page 154

1 B
2 B
3 C
4 C
5 B
6 D

Exercise 8k page 154

1 $\frac{3}{10}$
2 0.14
3 27.32
4 0.000 62
5 \$10.58
6 1.5
7 $\frac{1}{125}$
8 27.79
9 85.04
10 0.0086
11 6.28
12 2.98
13 280
14 \$2.52

CHAPTER 9

Exercise 9a page 157

1 0.006
2 0.01
3 0.018
4 0.06
5 0.0003
6 0.000 04
7 0.24
8 0.000 48
9 0.0008
10 0.000 000 6
11 0.018
12 0.008

Exercise 9b page 158

1 0.18
2 0.0024
3 0.018
4 0.000 56
5 0.0108
6 0.000 021
7 0.035
8 4.8
9 0.0064
10 0.0018
11 0.042
12 0.72
13 0.84
14 0.036
15 8.1
16 0.0088
17 0.077
18 0.28
19 0.1502
20 1.6
21 1.4
22 0.000 912
23 240
24 63
25 0.112
26 2.048
27 22.4
28 0.0022
29 0.03
30 0.014 08
31 0.64
32 0.8
33 0.64
34 0.0008
35 6.4
36 0.08
37 0.000 000 006 4
38 800
39 0.64
40 0.008
41 0.0432
42 12.4

Exercise 9c page 159

1 6.72
2 12.48
3 0.0952
4 1253.2
5 434
6 0.4536
7 33
8 0.000 278 8
9 7476
10 118.4
11 8.97
12 198
13 64.8
14 0.111 52
15 0.002 592
16 2.56
17 2.56
18 2.56
19 0.0784
20 0.1054
21 1.722
22 17.29
23 22.96
24 0.031 02

Exercise 9d page 160

1 0.2
2 1.6
3 0.21
4 2.6
5 0.1
6 0.19
7 0.224
8 3.8
9 21.3
10 2.51
11 1.64
12 0.15
13 0.019
14 0.000 13
15 0.002 18
16 0.042
17 0.002
18 0.000 06
19 0.81
20 1.06
21 0.308
22 0.1092
23 0.0057
24 0.0453
25 0.0019
26 0.09
27 0.1043
28 0.000 015
29 0.9
30 0.0106
31 0.019
32 0.77
33 2.107
34 0.62
35 0.037
36 0.78
37 1.2
38 1.85
39 0.415
40 0.15
41 0.72
42 0.000 04
43 0.8875
44 1.75
45 4.55
46 0.000 155
47 2.35
48 0.0124
49 0.125
50 0.038 75
51 0.52
52 1.905
53 3.6
54 0.05
55 0.0025
56 0.6028
57 0.853 75
58 2.45
59 0.575
60 0.055 75
61 3.65 cm
62 4.075 m
63 7.15 kg
64 3.2 cm
65 \$4.50

Exercise 9e page 162

1 1.1
2 0.15
3 0.12
4 0.45
5 0.51
6 3.2
7 0.0041
8 0.036
9 0.53
10 0.26
11 0.56
12 0.7
13 0.32
14 0.26
15 0.024
16 0.000 23
17 3.2
18 0.43
19 0.21
20 0.000 713
21 0.52
22 3.12
23 0.84
24 0.005 68

Exercise 9f page 162

1 0.25
2 0.375
3 0.6
4 0.3125
5 0.04
6 2.8
7 0.625
8 0.4375
9 0.12
10 0.031 25

Exercise 9g page 163

1 $\frac{1}{5}$
2 $\frac{3}{10}$
3 $\frac{4}{5}$
4 $\frac{3}{4}$
5 $\frac{3}{5}$
6 $\frac{7}{10}$
7 $\frac{9}{10}$
8 $\frac{1}{20}$
9 0.9
10 0.25
11 0.8
12 0.375
13 0.03
14 0.75
15 0.625
16 0.07

Exercise 9h page 164

1 \$325
2 4.4 cm
3 3.8 kg
4 16.8 cm
5 4216 c or \$42.16
6 0.24
7 3.25 m
8 50.4 m

Exercise 9i page 166

1 0.233…
2 0.002 727…
3 0.571 428 571…
4 0.143 33…
5 0.004 285 714 28…
6 0.1222…
7 0.444…
8 0.666…
9 0.1818…
10 0.714 285 714…
11 0.777…
12 1.142 857 142 8…

Exercise 9j page 167

1 $0.2\dot{3}$
2 $0.00\dot{2}\dot{7}$
3 $0.\dot{5}7142\dot{8}$
4 $0.14\dot{3}$
5 $0.00\dot{4}2857\dot{1}$
6 $0.1\dot{2}$
7 $0.\dot{4}$
8 $0.\dot{6}$
9 $0.\dot{1}\dot{8}$
10 $0.\dot{7}1428\dot{5}$
11 $0.\dot{7}$
12 $1.\dot{1}4285\dot{7}$

Exercise 9k page 168

1	0.33	**11**	14	**21**	0.363	**31**	1.8
2	0.32	**12**	6	**22**	0.026	**32**	42.6
3	1.27	**13**	27	**23**	0.007	**33**	1.01
4	2.35	**14**	3	**24**	0.070	**34**	0.0094
5	0.04	**15**	4	**25**	0.001	**35**	0.735
6	0.69	**16**	7	**26**	0.084	**36**	1.64
7	0.84	**17**	110	**27**	0.084	**37**	1.6
8	3.93	**18**	6	**28**	0.325	**38**	2
9	0.01	**19**	74	**29**	0.033	**39**	3.50
10	4.00	**20**	4	**30**	4.000	**40**	3.5

Exercise 9l page 169

1	0.17	**13**	4.1	**25**	0.006
2	0.93	**14**	57.4	**26**	0.018
3	0.35	**15**	2.6	**27**	0.417
4	2.03	**16**	0.9	**28**	0.021
5	2.85	**17**	7.3	**29**	0.038
6	0.16	**18**	1.2	**30**	0.001
7	0.04	**19**	2.1	**31**	0.028
8	0.05	**20**	0.9	**32**	0.031
9	0.24	**21**	9.7	**33**	0.016
10	0.04	**22**	0.6	**34**	0.019
11	0.22	**23**	1.7	**35**	0.039
12	0.95	**24**	27.3	**36**	0.037

Exercise 9m page 170

1	0.625	**11**	0.429	**21**	0.214
2	0.075	**12**	0.444	**22**	0.235
3	0.1875	**13**	0.167	**23**	0.462
4	0.6	**14**	0.667	**24**	0.190
5	0.36	**15**	0.818	**25**	0.158
6	0.14	**16**	0.857	**26**	0.176
7	0.0625	**17**	1.143	**27**	0.267
8	1.375	**18**	0.111	**28**	0.389
9	0.52	**19**	0.333	**29**	0.136
10	0.0375	**20**	0.364	**30**	0.121

Exercise 9n page 172

1	0.2	**13**	800	**25**	0.8
2	0.02	**14**	360	**26**	900
3	8	**15**	0.012	**27**	0.31
4	20	**16**	0.01	**28**	0.16
5	4500	**17**	100	**29**	24.5
6	12	**18**	2.3	**30**	3.2
7	0.16	**19**	21	**31**	1.2
8	6	**20**	0.012	**32**	41
9	60	**21**	0.001 71	**33**	7
10	5	**22**	52 000	**34**	1.2
11	13	**23**	0.004	**35**	9
12	120	**24**	60	**36**	0.08

Exercise 9p page 172

1	6.33	**6**	41.67	**11**	0.02
2	8.43	**7**	0.03	**12**	2.9
3	16.67	**8**	0.93	**13**	8.2
4	28.17	**9**	1.03	**14**	0.087
5	0.72	**10**	0.71	**15**	1.3333
16	32.9	**21**	36	**26**	4
17	20.3	**22**	3.9	**27**	0.72
18	0.032	**23**	0.167	**28**	0.2571
19	283.333	**24**	1.1	**29**	0.57
20	1.7	**25**	2.3	**30**	2.5

Exercise 9q page 174

1	0.144	**8**	0.14	**15**	4
2	1.6	**9**	6.72	**16**	4
3	0.0512	**10**	4.2	**17**	10
4	128	**11**	12.24	**18**	0.12
5	2.88	**12**	84	**19**	0.125
6	5.76	**13**	0.3	**20**	0.7
7	0.000 126	**14**	0.16	**21**	12

Exercise 9r page 174

1	$0.2, \frac{1}{4}$	**5**	$\frac{7}{8}, \frac{8}{9}, 0.9$	**9**	$\frac{3}{7}, \frac{5}{11}, \frac{6}{13}$
2	$\frac{2}{5}, \frac{4}{9}$	**6**	$\frac{3}{4}, \frac{17}{20}$	**10**	$\frac{8}{11}, 0.\dot{7}$
3	$\frac{4}{9}, \frac{1}{2}$	**7**	$0.35, \frac{9}{25}, \frac{3}{8}$	**11**	$0.\dot{3}, \frac{5}{12}$
4	$\frac{3}{11}, 0.3, \frac{1}{3}$	**8**	$\frac{4}{7}, 0.59, \frac{3}{5}$	**12**	$0.45, \frac{9}{19}, \frac{1}{2}$

Exercise 9s page 175

1	C	**4**	D
2	C	**5**	B
3	B	**6**	A

Exercise 9t page 175

1 $\frac{3}{50}$

2 **a** 0.0624 **b** 0.52

3 1.7 **4** 6.4 cm **5** 0.048 **6** 0.24

7 $55.68

8 **a** 8 **b** 7.8 **c** 7.782

Exercise 9u page 176

1 $0.\dot{7}1428\dot{5}$

2 **a** 0.064 **b** 0.000 64

3	16.28	**6**	2.05
4	$\frac{31}{50}$	**7**	$\frac{7}{9}$
5	7.4437	**8**	25

Exercise 9v page 176

1	0.16	**5**	14.63
2	9.186 (9.1857)	**6**	$2.03
3	0.0036	**7**	2
4	$\frac{19}{2000}$	**8**	0.666 …

CHAPTER 10

Exercise 10a page 180

1 146–150 cm, 7; 151–155 cm, 14; 156–160 cm, 17; 161–165 cm, 22; 166–170 cm, 12

2 35–39 kg, 4; 40–44 kg, 22; 45–49 kg, 18; 50–54 kg, 17; 55–59 kg, 7; 60–64 kg, 2; 65–69 kg, 1; 70–74 kg, 1

3 11–20, 1; 21–30, 2; 31–40, 10; 41–50, 15; 51–60, 16; 61–70, 20; 71–80, 10; 81–90, 6; 91–100, 2

Exercise 10c page 183

1 a lowest = 2009; highest: 2014
b 2014
c 2014, 2018
d 2015, 2016

2 a A **c** 2011, 2012, 2013
b 2009

3 a 1993–94 **d** 1995–96
b defence **e** 1995–96
c 1994–95

Exercise 10d page 184

1 b Tuesday
c all of the material blasted during the week had already been taken away
d Monday to Friday, when most lorries left the quarry

2 b Dominica **c** Barbados

Exercise 10e page 185

1 a 10, 14, 10, 22 **c** Very effective
b Danger

2 a French **b** 18, 15, 11, 12, 16: total 72

3 a Consumption is rising each year
b Impression is given by the volume in the bottle which goes up more quickly than the height of the bottle.

Exercise 10g page 189

1	8	**5**	16	**9**	6.2
2	7	**6**	28	**10**	3.5
3	15	**7**	3	**11**	50
4	29	**8**	40	**12**	0.62

13	63	**28**	110 c
14	96	**29**	92
15	16.5	**30**	9
16	63	**31**	233, 193
17	74	**32**	106, 238
18	1.35	**33**	11.8 hours, 5.6 hours
19	0.875	**34**	68; reduces it to 67
20	5.8	**35**	158 cm; increases it to 159 cm
21	2 mm	**36**	63 610, 12 722, 8294
22	86 kg, 81 kg	**37**	136.4 kg
23	1837 miles	**38**	160.6 cm
24	2583 km	**39**	55.6 kg
25	72 mm	**40**	26
26	131.6 hours	**41**	285 cm
27	134	**42**	2652

Exercise 10h page 193

1	12	**5**	5.9	**9**	155 cm
2	9	**6**	26.4	**10**	31, 3
3	1.8	**7**	1	**11**	36, 6
4	56	**8**	8		

Exercise 10i page 195

1	5	**5**	3.2	**9**	1.885
2	42	**6**	12	**10**	15
3	17	**7**	98		
4	16	**8**	36		

Exercise 10j page 197

1	B	**4**	C
2	A	**5**	D
3	C	**6**	C

Exercise 10k page 198

1	**a** 23	**b** 21	**c** 21
2	**a** 71	**b** 66, 67	**c** 69
3	**a** 45	**b** 43	**c** 45
4	**a** 43	**b** 13	**c** 32
5	**a** 28	**b** 27	**c** 27
6	77, 72, 73		
7	**a** 157 cm	**b** 157 cm	**c** 157 cm
8	**a** 54	**b** 52	**c** 52
9	83, 84, 83.5		
10	**a** 0	**b** 0	**c** 1.5
11	**a** 3	**b** 3.5	**c** 3.77

CHAPTER 11

Exercise 11a page 201

1	+10°	**14**	12°	**28**	−1 min
2	−7	**15**	4°	**29**	+$50
3	−3°	**16**	−3°	**30**	− $5
4	+5°	**17**	2°	**31**	+5 paces
5	−8°	**18**	−2°	**32**	−5 paces
6	0°	**19**	1°	**33**	+200 m
7	2° below zero	**20**	3°	**34**	−5 m
8	3° above zero	**21**	−7°	**35**	−3 °C
9	4° above zero	**22**	−2°	**36**	+21 °C
10	10° below zero	**24**	−5 s	**37**	+150 m
11	8° above zero	**25**	+5 s	**38**	−3 °C
12	freezing point	**26**	+50 c	**39**	+25 c
13	10°	**27**	−50 c	**40**	6 paces in front

Exercise 11b page 204

1	>	**9**	>	**17**	0, −3
2	>	**10**	<	**18**	5, 8
3	>	**11**	<	**19**	−7, −11
4	<	**12**	>	**20**	16, 32
5	>	**13**	10, 12	**21**	$\frac{1}{6}, \frac{1}{36}$
6	<	**14**	−10, −12	**22**	−4, −2
7	>	**15**	−2, −4	**23**	−8, −16
8	>	**16**	2, 4	**24**	−2, −3

Exercise 11c page 205

1	−3	**9**	−12	**17**	2	**25**	4
2	3	**10**	−1	**18**	−3	**26**	6
3	−2	**11**	5	**19**	−3	**27**	3
4	−2	**12**	−2	**20**	−1	**28**	0
5	2	**13**	−2	**21**	3	**29**	−3
6	7	**14**	−1	**22**	−6	**30**	−5
7	1	**15**	4	**23**	−10		
8	2	**16**	6	**24**	−5		

Exercise 11d page 206

1	2	**8**	6	**15**	−6	**22**	13
2	−3	**9**	−14	**16**	7	**23**	−6
3	7	**10**	10	**17**	−3	**24**	8
4	3	**11**	−14	**18**	2	**25**	1
5	−9	**12**	0	**19**	−4		
6	3	**13**	0	**20**	5		
7	−3	**14**	6	**21**	13		

Exercise 11e page 207

1	1	**15**	1	**29**	−3	**43**	−2
2	−5	**16**	9	**30**	−19	**44**	1
3	9	**17**	−1	**31**	2	**45**	2
4	8	**18**	0	**32**	3	**46**	−12
5	2	**19**	2	**33**	0	**47**	3
6	7	**20**	16	**34**	0	**48**	18
7	4	**21**	5	**35**	−1	**49**	−2
8	10	**22**	−4	**36**	0	**50**	1
9	15	**23**	−8	**37**	9	**51**	2
10	2	**24**	19	**38**	−7	**52**	−15
11	5	**25**	−4	**39**	−4	**53**	−9
12	−12	**26**	−4	**40**	3	**54**	−6
13	5	**27**	4	**41**	−10	**55**	−8
14	−9	**28**	−3	**42**	−3		

Exercise 11f page 209

1	−15	**9**	−5	**17**	−24	**25**	−24
2	−8	**10**	+18	**18**	+8	**26**	−24
3	+14	**11**	+27	**19**	+3	**27**	+45
4	+4	**12**	−16	**20**	−8	**28**	−20
5	12	**13**	−35	**21**	−6	**29**	−28
6	+12	**14**	+24	**22**	+15	**30**	+36
7	−	**15**	−15	**23**	−18		
8	+16	**16**	−45	**24**	+20		

Exercise 11g page 211

1	−2	**8**	1	**15**	$-4\frac{2}{5}$	**22**	36	**29**	4
2	5	**9**	−3	**16**	−2	**23**	−9	**30**	$-\frac{1}{4}$
3	−4	**10**	−5	**17**	−2	**24**	5	**31**	−4
4	2	**11**	$-1\frac{1}{4}$	**18**	−9	**25**	−10	**32**	$-1\frac{1}{2}$
5	−1	**12**	$-1\frac{2}{3}$	**19**	3	**26**	0	**33**	$1\frac{1}{4}$
6	4	**13**	$3\frac{3}{5}$	**20**	$-1\frac{1}{8}$	**27**	0	**34**	36
7	−3	**14**	−1	**21**	−2	**28**	13	**35**	$-6\frac{1}{4}$

Exercise 11h page 213

1	D	**4**	A
2	C	**5**	B
3	B	**6**	D

Exercise 11i page 213

1	−2	**5**	5	**9**	−3
2	50	**6**	$-\frac{1}{2}$	**10**	−36
3	$\frac{1}{2}$	**7**	2	**11**	$\frac{1}{2}$
4	−1	**8**	$1\frac{1}{3}$	**12**	$\frac{1}{2}$

CHAPTER 12

Exercise 12a page 216

1	$x-3$	**3**	$x-6$	**5**	$2x$	**7**	$7x$
2	$x+1$	**4**	$x-5$	**6**	$4x$	**8**	$6x$

9 A number n is multiplied by 3
10 9 is added to an unknown number
11 5 is subtracted from an unknown number
12 8 is added to an unknown number
13 An unknown number is multiplied by 8
14 An unknown number is subtracted from 7
15 An unknown number is added to 12
16 An unknown number is divided by 6

Exercise 12b page 217

1	$10x$	**3**	$2x$	**5**	$8y$	**7**	1
2	$4x$	**4**	2	**6**	7	**8**	0

Exercise 12c page 218

1	$7x + 7$	**7**	$4x + 2y$	**13**	$10x + 8y$
2	$5x + 5$	**8**	$4x + 8y$	**14**	$11x + 3y$
3	$4x + 1$	**9**	$8x + 3$	**15**	$15x$
4	$5c + 10a$	**10**	$8x + 8$	**16**	$4x + y + 8z$
5	$8x + 2y$	**11**	$3x + 6$	**17**	$9x + y + 3$
6	$8x + 8y$	**12**	$19x + 3y$	**18**	11

Exercise 12d page 219

1	$2x + 2$	**5**	$8 + 10x$	**9**	$18 + 12x$
2	$9x + 6$	**6**	$12 + 10a$	**10**	$5x + 5$
3	$5x + 30$	**7**	$5a + 5b$	**11**	$14 + 7x$
4	$12x + 12$	**8**	$16x + 12$	**12**	$24 + 16x$

Exercise 12e page 219

1	$6x + 4$	**5**	$5x + 23$
2	$10x + 18$	**6**	$5x + 5$
3	$3x + 7$	**7**	$3x + 5$
4	$4x + 17$	**8**	$9x + 8$

Exercise 12f page 220

1	z^3	**22**	$6 \times a \times a \times b$
2	a^2	**23**	$2 \times x \times x \times x$
3	b^5	**24**	$3 \times a \times a \times a \times a \times b \times b$
4	y^5	**25**	$6xz$
5	s^3	**26**	$6x^3$
6	z^6	**27**	$12a^2$
7	$a \times a \times a$	**28**	$6a^3$
8	$x \times x \times x \times x \times x$	**29**	$2a^2bc$
9	$b \times b$	**30**	$24x^2y$
10	$a \times a \times a \times a \times a$	**31**	z^4
11	$x \times x \times x \times x \times x \times x \times x$	**32**	$6z^2$
12	$z \times z \times z \times z$	**33**	$24x^2$
13	$2a$	**34**	$16x$
14	$4x^2$	**35**	$4s^3$
15	$12a$	**36**	x^6
16	a^2b	**37**	y^2z^2
17	$15xz^2$	**38**	$10xyz$
18	$5a^2b^2$	**39**	a^7
19	$3 \times z \times z$	**40**	$8x^4$
20	$2 \times a \times b \times c$	**41**	$axyz$
21	$4 \times z \times y \times y$	**42**	s^7

Exercise 12g page 221

1	2	**12**	1	**23**	$\frac{2}{3a}$
2	$\frac{22}{5}$ or $4\frac{2}{5}$	**13**	$\frac{2}{5}$	**24**	1
3	$\frac{5}{8}$	**14**	$\frac{7}{6}$ or $1\frac{1}{6}$	**25**	$\frac{x}{4}$
4	$\frac{z^2}{6}$	**15**	$\frac{9}{7}$ or $1\frac{2}{7}$	**26**	$\frac{7}{4}$ or $1\frac{3}{4}$
5	$\frac{3ab}{10}$	**16**	2	**27**	$\frac{20}{3b}$
6	$\frac{4}{3}$ or $1\frac{1}{3}$	**17**	4	**28**	1
7	3	**18**	$\frac{2}{5}$	**29**	$\frac{ay}{4}$
8	$\frac{y^2}{24}$	**19**	$\frac{3c}{2y}$	**30**	$\frac{y}{2x}$
9	$\frac{c^2}{10}$	**20**	$\frac{3}{10z}$	**31**	$\frac{4}{b}$
10	6	**21**	$\frac{r^2}{24}$	**32**	$\frac{2x}{3y}$
11	$\frac{x^2}{4}$	**22**	$\frac{5z}{2}$		

Exercise 12h page 223

1	**a** 5	**b** −3	**c** −9
2	**a** 7	**b** 0	**c** −4
3	**a** 20	**b** 10	**c** 1
4	**a** 1	**b** −1	**c** 7
5	**a** 10	**b** 13	**c** 1
6	**a** 2	**b** 0	**c** 10
7	**a** 10	**b** 1	**c** −4
8	**a** 5	**b** −1	**c** −7
9	**a** 8	**b** 50	**c** 8
10	**a** 8	**b** 27	**c** −8

11 $\frac{3}{4}$ **13** $3\frac{1}{4}$ **15** 15 **17** 16 **19** 20
12 24 **14** 190 **16** 30 **18** $-1\frac{1}{6}$ **20** −23

Exercise 12i page 224

1 D **2** D **3** B **4** D **5** C **6** C

Exercise 12j page 224

1 $4x + 13$ **2** $60abc$ **3** 1 **4** −24 **5** a^6

Exercise 12k page 225

1 $7 + 2x$ **2** $16x + 14$ **3** x multiplied by itself five times **4** $3x - 10$ **5** 18

Exercise 12l page 225

1 $22 - x + y$ **2** −1 **3** $1\frac{3}{5}$ **4** 23 **5** $24x^2y$

CHAPTER 13

Exercise 13b page 231

1 PR, PQ
2 **a** XY **b** XZ **c** $\hat{X}$

Exercise 13c page 233

1 60° **2** 85° **3** 55° **4** 110° **5** 40° **6** 30° **7** 55° **8** 60° **9** 75° **10** 25° **11** 50° **12** 90° **13** 120° **14** 55° **15** 65°

Exercise 13d page 234

1 60°, 50° **2** 65°, 45° **3** 70° **4** 65°, 115° **5** 85°, 30° **6** 45° **7** 60° **8** 60°, 30° **9** 90°, 45°

Exercise 13e page 237

1 110° **2** 60° **3** 70° **4** 40° **5** 70° **6** 55° **7** 90° **8** 35° **9** 110° **10** 95°

Exercise 13f page 238

1 4.2 cm, 57°, 83°
2 4.6 cm, 97°, 48°
3 6.5 cm, 70°, 40°
4 8.5 cm, 97°, 33°
5 3.8 cm, 52°, 83°
6 4.8 cm, 79°, 53°
7 4.3 cm, 53°, 62°
8 5.7 cm, 53°, 75°
9 6.4 cm, 38°, 69°
10 6.2 cm, 44°, 80°

Exercise 13g page 239

1 34°, 106° **2** 34°, 98° **3** 35°, 80° **4** 37°, 90° **5** 40°, 84° **6** 45°, 83° **7** 37°, 90° **8** 47°, 75° **9** 33°, 90° **10** 52°, 69°

Exercise 13h page 239

1 3.6 cm, 5.4 cm
2 34°, 101°
3 4.6 cm, 49°
4 7.8 cm, 50°
5 119°, 26°
6 13.4 cm, 17.8 cm
7 8.9 cm, 30°
8 5.9 cm, 5 cm
9 127°, 21°
10 Equilateral
11 Two possible triangles: $\hat{C}$ = 56°, AC = 6 cm; $\hat{C}$ = 124°, AC = 2.6 cm
12 $\hat{R}$ = 71°, PR = 4.8 cm; $\hat{R}$ = 109°, PR = 1.2 cm

Exercise 13i page 241

1 50° **2** 80° **3** 110° **4** 50° **5** 60° **6** 40° **7** 90° **8** 60° **9** 120° **10** 90° **11** 110° **12** 65° **13** 60°, 120° **14** 80°, 70° **15** 80°, 115° **16** 50°, 130°

Exercise 13k page 246

11 70° **12** 70° **13** 65° **14** 40° **15** 90° **16** 110° **17** 45° **18** 70° **19** 60° **20** 20° **21** 75° **22** 86° **27** 55°, 70° **28** 45°, 135° **29** 80°, 80° **30** 50°, 80° **31** 40°, 140° **32** 20°, 70°

Exercise 13l page 249

1 B **2** D **3** C **4** C **5** C **6** D

Exercise 13m page 251

1 85°, 45° **2** 45°, 135° **3** 55°, 125° **4** $\hat{C}$ = 70° **5** AC = 4.1 cm

Exercise 13n page 251

1 60°, 30° **2** 65°, 65°, 60° **3** 80°, 140° **4** 7.1 cm (base) **5** 96°, 136°, 58°; 360°

REVIEW TEST 2 page 253

1 C **2** B **3** A **4** D **5** C **6** D **7** D **8** D **9** A **10** A **11** C **12** C **13** B **14** 0.28125 cm **15** 33
16 **a** $n + 2$ **b** $3m + 6$ **c** $\frac{1}{9}$
17

Frequency
12
10
8
6
4
2
0
41-45 46-50 51-55 56-60 61-65 66-70
Marks

18 **a** 12.38 (2 d.p.) **b** 15 **c** 13.5
19 PQR = 52°, PRQ = 73°

CHAPTER 14

Exercise 14a page 256

1	$\frac{1}{5}$	**13**	$\frac{5}{8}$	**25**	$\frac{41}{50}$	**37**	3.5
2	$\frac{9}{20}$	**14**	$\frac{5}{4}$	**26**	$\frac{7}{8}$	**38**	0.487
3	$\frac{1}{4}$	**15**	$\frac{7}{10}$	**27**	$\frac{1}{16}$	**39**	0.92
4	$\frac{18}{25}$	**16**	$\frac{3}{4}$	**28**	$\frac{3}{2}$	**40**	0.65
5	$\frac{1}{3}$	**17**	$\frac{12}{25}$	**29**	0.47	**41**	1.2
6	$\frac{1}{8}$	**18**	$\frac{69}{100}$	**30**	0.12	**42**	2.31
7	$\frac{1}{40}$	**19**	$\frac{3}{8}$	**31**	0.055	**43**	0.857
8	$\frac{1}{2}$	**20**	$\frac{4}{75}$	**32**	1.45	**44**	0.08
9	$\frac{13}{20}$	**21**	$\frac{7}{40}$	**33**	0.583	**45**	0.03
10	$\frac{14}{25}$	**22**	$\frac{19}{20}$	**34**	0.58	**46**	1.8
11	$\frac{37}{100}$	**23**	$\frac{3}{20}$	**35**	0.3	**47**	0.053
12	$\frac{2}{3}$	**24**	$\frac{2}{25}$	**36**	0.025	**48**	0.541

Exercise 14b page 257

1	50%	**11**	75%	**21**	50%	**31**	25%
2	70%	**12**	45%	**22**	22%	**32**	74%
3	65%	**13**	140%	**23**	83%	**33**	125%
4	$33\frac{1}{3}$ %	**14**	$62\frac{1}{2}$ %	**24**	172%	**34**	341%
5	52.5%	**15**	$266\frac{2}{3}$ %	**25**	62.5%	**35**	7.5%
6	25%	**16**	60%	**26**	90%	**36**	36%
7	15%	**17**	35%	**27**	4%	**37**	16%
8	16%	**18**	124%	**28**	55%	**38**	139%
9	37.5%	**19**	$87\frac{1}{2}$ %	**29**	264%	**39**	635%
10	$38\frac{1}{3}$ %	**20**	160%	**30**	84.5%	**40**	18.25%

Exercise 14c page 258

1 **a** $\frac{3}{10}$ **b** $\frac{17}{20}$ **c** $\frac{17}{40}$ **d** $\frac{21}{400}$

2 **a** 0.44 **b** 0.68 **c** 1.7 **d** 0.165

3 **a** 40% **b** 85% **c** $12\frac{1}{2}$ % **d** $113\frac{1}{3}$ %

4 **a** 20% **b** 62% **c** $84\frac{1}{2}$ % **d** 178%

	Fraction	Percentage	Decimal
	$\frac{3}{4}$	75%	0.75
5	$\frac{4}{5}$	80%	0.8
6	$\frac{3}{5}$	60%	0.6
7	$\frac{7}{10}$	70%	0.7
8	$\frac{11}{20}$	55%	0.55
9	$\frac{11}{25}$	44%	0.44
10	$\frac{8}{25}$	32%	0.32

Exercise 14d page 259

1	52%	**6**	12%	**11**	3%
2	13%	**7**	43%	**12**	252
3	36%	**8**	68%	**13**	1400
4	92%	**9**	20%		
5	88%	**10**	38%		

14 **a** 2% **b** 10% **c** 66% **d** 22%

Exercise 14e page 261

1	25%	**10**	20%	**19**	20%
2	60%	**11**	30%	**20**	40%
3	$33\frac{1}{3}$%	**12**	50%	**21**	60%
4	$33\frac{1}{3}$%	**13**	200%	**22**	25%
5	75%	**14**	$62\frac{1}{2}$%	**23**	72%
6	60%	**15**	10%	**24**	$333\frac{1}{3}$%
7	15%	**16**	$66\frac{2}{3}$%	**25**	72%
8	25%	**17**	25%	**26**	42%
9	10%	**18**	$37\frac{1}{2}$%		

Exercise 14f page 262

1	48	**13**	333	**25**	320 m^2
2	96 g	**14**	198 kg	**26**	45 km
3	55.5 cm	**15**	1.44 m	**27**	5 km
4	286 km	**16**	\$1.50	**28**	149 cm^2
5	16 c	**17**	0.34 km	**29**	14 c
6	3.08 kg	**18**	1.6 litres	**30**	\$53.43
7	252	**19**	\$75	**31**	48 c
8	989 g	**20**	198 m	**32**	6 g
9	4.73 m	**21**	90 g	**33**	2.1 m
10	206.4 cm^2	**22**	2.94 mm	**34**	\$10
11	2.52 m	**23**	18 cm	**35**	2 kg
12	14.4 m^2	**24**	9 m^2	**36**	14 mm

Exercise 14g page 263

1	40%	**4**	20%	**7**	75%	**10**	1960
2	70%	**5**	30%	**8**	$66\frac{2}{3}$%		
3	20%	**6**	75%	**9**	65%		

11 **a** $46\frac{2}{3}$% **b** $53\frac{1}{3}$%

12 **a** 52 **b** 28

13 **a** 12 **b** 18

14 **a** 7 **b** 343

15 5760 **16** 78 **17** \$62.40 **18** 112

Exercise 14h page 265

1	D	**4**	C
2	B	**5**	C
3	B	**6**	B

Exercise 14i page 265

1 **a** $\frac{9}{25}$ **b** 0.36

2 **a** 62.5% **b** 133.3% **c** 250%

3 $12\frac{1}{2}$% **4** 289 m^2 **5** \$1440

Exercise 14j page 266

1 **a** $12\frac{1}{2}\%$ **b** $37\frac{1}{2}\%$ **c** 50%
2 **a** 28.6% **b** 27.9% **c** 122.2%
3 **a** $\frac{1}{8}$ **b** 0.125
4 90 c
5 54

CHAPTER 15

Exercise 15a page 270

1 **a** metres **b** centimetres **c** metres **d** kilometres **e** centimetres **f** millimetres
3 **a** 4 **b** 2 **c** 5 **d** 1 **e** 10
4 (to the nearest millimetre)
a 20 **b** 10 **c** 4 **d** 16 **e** 24
9 40 cm
10 900 cm

Exercise 15b page 271

1	200	**9**	3000	**17**	1900
2	5000	**10**	2 000 000	**18**	3500
3	30	**11**	500	**19**	270
4	400	**12**	7000	**20**	190 000
5	12 000	**13**	150	**21**	38
6	150	**14**	23	**22**	9200
7	6000	**15**	4600	**23**	2300
8	100 000	**16**	3700	**24**	840

Exercise 15c page 273

1	12 000	**9**	4000	**17**	5 200 000
2	3000	**10**	2 000 000	**18**	600
3	5000	**11**	3000	**19**	11 300
4	1 000 000	**12**	4000	**20**	2500
5	1 000 000	**13**	1500	**21**	7300
6	13 000	**14**	2700	**22**	300 000
7	6000	**15**	1800	**23**	500
8	2 000 000	**16**	700	**24**	800

Exercise 15d page 274

1	136	**6**	3020	**11**	3500	**16**	1020
2	35	**7**	502	**12**	2008	**17**	1250
3	1050	**8**	5500	**13**	5500	**18**	3550
4	48	**9**	202	**14**	2800	**19**	2050
5	207	**10**	8009	**15**	3250	**20**	1010

Exercise 15e page 274

1	30	**15**	3.8	**29**	1.01
2	6	**16**	0.086	**30**	0.000 085
3	1.5	**17**	0.56	**31**	5.142
4	25	**18**	0.028	**32**	48.171
5	1.6	**19**	0.19	**33**	9.008
6	0.072	**20**	0.086	**34**	9.088
7	0.12	**21**	3.45	**35**	12.019
8	8.8	**22**	8.4	**36**	4.111
9	1.25	**23**	11.002	**37**	1.056
10	2.85	**24**	2.042	**38**	5.003
11	1.5	**25**	4.4	**39**	0.2505
12	3.68	**26**	5.03	**40**	0.850 55
13	1.5	**27**	7.005		
14	5.02	**28**	4.005		

Exercise 15f page 275

1	5.86	**13**	3250	**25**	748
2	1.035	**14**	3115	**26**	0.922
3	3001.36	**15**	15 100	**27**	1150
4	3051	**16**	2550	**28**	73.6
5	5.647	**17**	1046.68	**29**	2642
6	4.65	**18**	308.73	**30**	19 850
7	440	**19**	2580	**31**	35 420
8	55	**20**	2362	**32**	910
9	1820	**21**	2.22	**33**	448.2
10	2456	**22**	1606.4	**34**	5
11	5059	**23**	1089.6		
12	1358	**24**	5972		

Exercise 15g page 278

1	13 540	**5**	32	**9**	22.77
2	45 792	**6**	10.6	**10**	16 240
3	13.563	**7**	15 366		
4	12.55	**8**	24.448		

Exercise 15h page 278

1	9.72 m	**5**	1080 mm	**9**	33.2 cm
2	1840 g	**6**	4 kg	**10**	5.3 kg
3	748 kg	**7**	2.2 kg		
4	4.11 g	**8**	15 m		

Exercise 15i page 280

1	68 in	**11**	3 ft
2	14 ft	**12**	2 ft 5 in
3	1809 yd	**13**	7 ft 2 in
4	35 in	**14**	3 yd
5	100 in	**15**	4 yd 1 ft
6	4320 yd	**16**	1 mile 240 yd
7	17 ft	**17**	6 ft 3 in
8	123 in	**18**	33 yd 1 ft
9	28 ft	**19**	10 ft
10	118 in	**20**	17 miles 80 yd

Exercise 15j page 281

1	38 oz	**5**	162 lb	**9**	1 ton 10 cwt
2	28 oz	**6**	1 lb 8 oz	**10**	1 cwt 8 lb
3	67 oz	**7**	1 lb 2 oz		
4	64 cwt	**8**	2 lb 4 oz		

Exercise 15k page 282

1	6 lb	**9**	8 oz	**17**	11 lb
2	6 ft	**10**	1 lb	**18**	2 m
3	2 kg	**11**	16 km	**19**	2 m
4	3 m	**12**	32 km	**20**	4 kg
5	3 lb	**13**	24 km	**21**	1st cloth
6	15 ft	**14**	160 km	**22**	37.5 miles
7	7 lb	**15**	120 km	**23**	8 oz
8	$2\frac{2}{3}$ m	**16**	64 km	**24**	15 cm
25	4 in	**26**	**a** 25 mm	**b**	15 mm
27	15 cm	**28**	in the market		

Exercise 15l page 286

1 **a** September **b** Thursday **c** 17th **d** 13th
2 13
3 4
4 **a** Dennis **b** Johanne **c** 2023

5 **a** 17 **b** P. Baldrick **c** 2021
6 **a** 3 hours 10 min **b** 18 days 18 hours
7 **a** 308 seconds **b** 210 min
8 **a** $\frac{1}{3}$ **b** $\frac{1}{100}$
9 **a** 10. 25 **b** 11.10 **c** 45 min
10 **a** 21 min **b** 1734
11 **a** 1 hour 45 min **b** 8 hours 40 min
c 2 hours 10 min
12 2 hours 40 min
13 **a** 20 min **b** 8.05 p.m.
14 **a** 6 hours 30 min **b** 8 hours 29 min
c 8 hours **d** 27 hours 3 min
15 1715
16 **a** 2 hours 22 min and 2 hours 17 min
b Astleton and Morgan's Hollow; shortest journey time

Exercise 15m page 289

1 **a** 12 °C **b** 27 °F
c the one in part **a**; it is above the freezing point of water, the other is below
2 **a** 105 °F **b** 40 °C **c** 20 °C **d** 68 °F
3 **a** 50 °F **b** 40 °F **c** 27 °C **d** 2 °C
4 $38.\dot{3}$ °C **5** 18 °F
6 17.6 °F; more precise

Exercise 15n page 291

1 C **4** C
2 D **5** B
3 A **6** B

Exercise 15p page 291

1	2.36 m	**5**	4.25 km	**9**	4 lb
2	20 mm	**6**	3600 kg	**10**	30 cm
3	5000 g	**7**	2.35 kg		
4	0.5 g	**8**	2000 mg		

Exercise 15q page 292

1	5780 kg	**5**	1.56 t	**9**	600 m
2	354 p	**6**	2 years 50 days	**10**	80 km
3	0.35 t	**7**	90 min		
4	0.0155 cm	**8**	2.05 km		

CHAPTER 16

Exercise 16a page 295

1, 3, 4 and **6**

Exercise 16b page 299

1 2 **3** 0 **5** 2
2 1 **4** 1 **6** 2

Exercise 16c page 301

1 6 **2** 6 **3** 0 **4** 3

Exercise 16d page 304

1

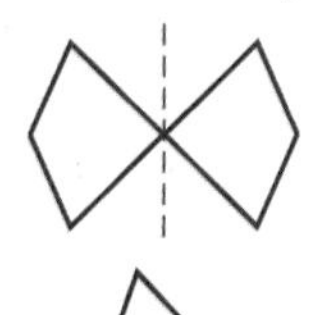

2

3

4

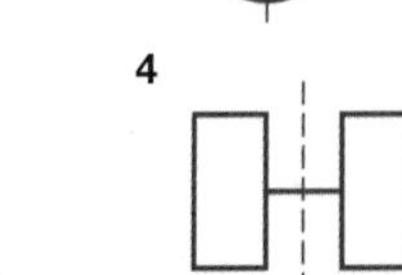

5

6

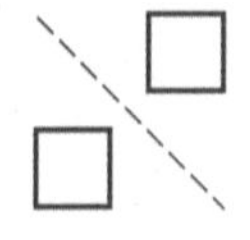

7

8

9

10

11

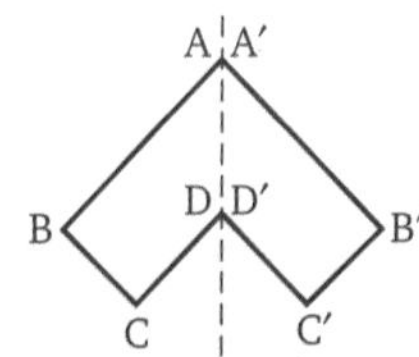

12

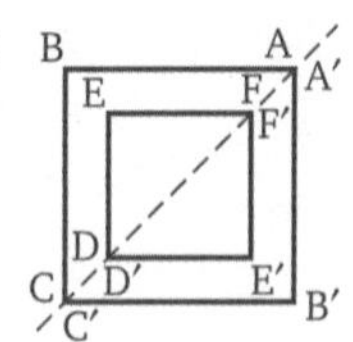

13

14

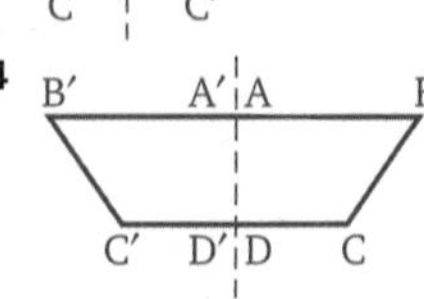

15

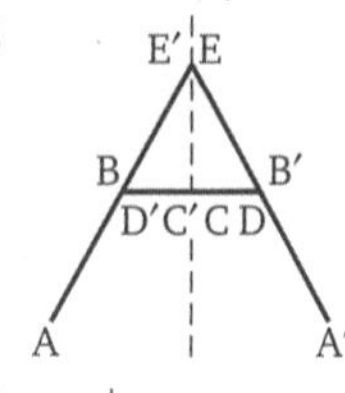

16

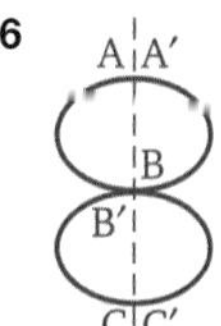

17

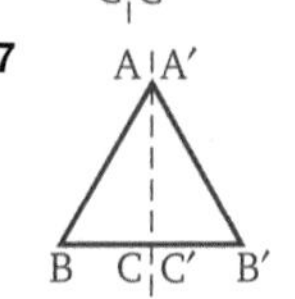

18

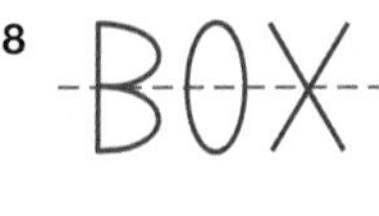

19 Q9 A and A′, Q11: A, A′; D D′, Q12: A, A′; F, F′; D, D′; C, C′, Q13: B and B′, Q14: A, A′ and D, D′, Q15: E, E′ and C, C′, Q16: A, A′; B B′; C, C′, Q17: A, A′; C, C′.
They all lie on the axis of symmetry.
20 Equal distances; perpendicular lines.
21 Equal distances; perpendicular lines.

Exercise 16e page 307

1 *a* and *c*
2 Translation *e* and *b*
Reflection *a* and *c*
Neither *d*

3

4

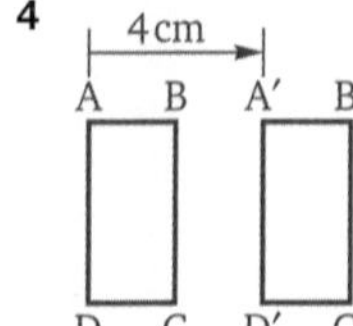

5

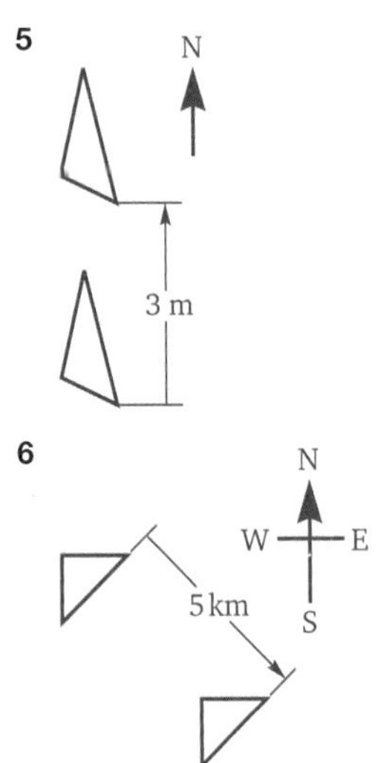

6

7 a

b

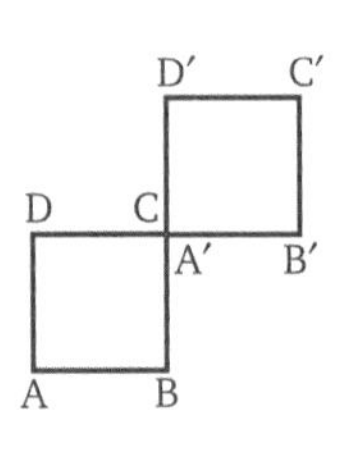

Exercise 16f page 308

1 D
2 D
3 C
4 D
5 D
6 B
7 D

CHAPTER 17

Exercise 17a page 312

1 11
2 16
3 11
4 20
5 26
6 20
7 21
8 **a** A **b** B
9 45
10 43
11 55
12 40
13 37
14 76
15 62
16 26

Exercise 17b page 316

1 $4\,cm^2$
2 $64\,cm^2$
3 $100\,cm^2$
4 $25\,cm^2$
5 $2.25\,cm^2$
6 $6.25\,cm^2$
7 $0.49\,m^2$
8 $1.44\,cm^2$
9 $\frac{1}{4}\,km^2$
10 $\frac{9}{16}\,m^2$
11 $30\,cm^2$
12 $48\,cm^2$
13 $27\,m^2$
14 $280\,cm^2$
15 $3.96\,mm^2$
16 $1470\,km^2$
17 $2.85\,m^2$
18 $30.24\,cm^2$
19 $22\,800\,cm^2$
20 $36\,000\,mm^2$

Exercise 17c page 316

1 $120\,cm^2$
2 $36\,m^2$
3 $149\,m^2$
4 $208\,mm^2$
5 $52\,m^2$
6 $87\,cm^2$
7 $544\,mm^2$
8 $90\,cm^2$
9 $43\,m^2$
10 $228\,cm^2$

Exercise 17d page 318

1 8 cm
2 32 cm
3 40 cm
4 20 cm
5 6 cm
6 10 cm
7 2.8 m
8 4.8 cm
9 2 km
10 3 m
11 22 cm
12 28 cm
13 24 m
14 68 cm
15 8 mm
16 154 km
17 6.8 m
18 22.2 cm
19 670 cm
20 780 mm

Exercise 17e page 319

1 2 cm, $8\,cm^2$
2 2 cm, $10\,cm^2$
3 5 m, $15\,m^2$
4 9 mm, $54\,mm^2$
5 5 cm, 22 cm
6 10 m, 44 m
7 9 km, 26 km
8 9 mm, 32 mm
9 25 cm, $125\,cm^2$
10 80 cm, 202 cm

Exercise 17f page 319

1 **a** 24 cm **b** $28\,cm^2$
2 **a** 24 cm **b** $24\,cm^2$
3 **a** 48 mm **b** $80\,mm^2$
4 **a** 32 m **b** $15\,m^2$
5 **a** 272 cm **b** $1664\,cm^2$
6 84 cm2
7 128 cm2
8 $78\,cm^2$
9 $90\,cm^2$
10 $184\,cm^2$
11 $91\,cm^2$
12 $198\,cm^2$
13 $432\,cm^2$
14 $4.84\,m^2$

Exercise 17g page 322

1 4
2 9
3 6
4 6
5 45
6 500

Exercise 17h page 324

1 **a** 30 000 **b** 120 000 **c** 75 000 **d** 820 000 **e** 85 000
2 **a** 1400 **b** 300 **c** 750 **d** 2600 **e** 3250
3 **a** 560 **b** 56 000
4 **a** 4 **b** 25 **c** 0.5 **d** 0.25 **e** 7.34
5 **a** 0.55 **b** 14 **c** 0.076 **d** 1.86 **e** 2970
6 **a** 7.5 **b** 0.43 **c** 0.05 **d** 0.245 **e** 176

Exercise 17i page 325

1 $50\,000\,cm^2$
2 $1800\,mm^2$
3 $175\,000\,cm^2$
4 $14\,000\,cm^2$
5 $8\,m^2$
6 $15\,000\,cm^2$
7 $37\,500\,cm^2$
8 $180\,mm^2$
9 $120\,000\,m^2$
10 $22\,500\,m^2$

Exercise 17j page 325

1 **a** $8250\,m^2$ **b** 370 m
2 **a** $7000\,m^2$ **b** 340 m
3 **a** $8400\,m^2$ **b** 380 m
4 **a** $312\,m^2$ **b** 76 m
5 $5\,m^2$
6 1200
7 $12\,m^2$, $9
8 $9000\,cm^2$
9 100
10 96

Exercise 17k page 326

1 C
2 B
3 A
4 C
5 D
6 B

CHAPTER 18

Exercise 18a page 330

1 $3240\,mm^2$
2 $43.2\,cm^2$
3 $4.56\,m^2$
4 $1\frac{1}{8}\,m^2$
5 $4\frac{1}{3}\,cm^2$
6 $21.6\,cm^2$
7 $320\,cm^2$
8 $552\,cm^2$
9 $672\,cm^2$
10 $2870\,mm^2$

Exercise 18b page 331

1	0.4 cm	**6**	1.5 m
2	5 cm	**7**	1.25 cm
3	10 m	**8**	3 m
4	4 mm	**9**	7 m
5	5 cm	**10**	6 cm

Exercise 18c page 332

1	84 cm^2	**11**	26.4 cm^2
2	600 cm^2	**12**	352 cm^2
3	37.2 cm^2	**13**	63 cm^2
4	0.0288 m^2	**14**	11.25 cm^2
5	12.8 m^2	**15**	130 cm^2
6	1736 m^2	**16**	48 cm^2
7	24.48 cm^2	**17**	36 cm^2
8	7 cm^2	**18**	180 cm^2
9	38.88 cm^2	**19**	12 cm, 6 cm, 7 cm, 12 cm
10	28.8 cm^2		

Exercise 18d page 336

1	48 cm^2	**14**	44 cm^2
2	1.56 m^2	**15**	64 cm^2
3	80 cm^2	**16**	540 cm^2
4	3.2 cm^2	**17**	33 cm^2
5	100 cm^2	**18**	75 cm^2
6	399 cm^2	**19**	70 cm^2
7	2.4 cm, 12 cm, 25 cm	**20**	24.4 cm^2
8	24 cm^2	**21**	82.5 cm^2
9	14.4 cm^2	**22**	30 cm^2
10	40 cm^2	**23**	96 cm^2
11	32.4 m^2	**24**	21 cm^2
12	22.2 cm^2	**25**	8.32 cm^2
13	45 cm^2		

Exercise 18e page 338

1	8 cm	**5**	3 cm	**9**	0.4 cm
2	6 cm	**6**	36 cm	**10**	6 cm
3	6 cm	**7**	3 cm	**11**	8 cm
4	20 cm	**8**	$2\frac{2}{3}$ cm	**12**	4 cm

Exercise 18f page 340

1	78 cm^2	**6**	75 cm^2
2	22.5 cm^2	**7**	18 cm^2
3	20 cm^2	**8**	68 cm^2
4	54 cm^2	**9**	38.5 cm^2
5	60 cm^2	**10**	48 cm^2

Exercise 18g page 342

1	180 cm^2	**4**	48 cm^2
2	20 cm^2	**5**	14 cm
3	10 cm^2 or 1000 mm^2	**6**	6.5 cm

Exercise 18h page 342

1	A	**4**	D
2	B	**5**	A
3	B	**6**	A

CHAPTER 19

Exercise 19a page 346

1	$x - 3 = 4$, 7	**5**	$2x = 8$, 4
2	$x + 1 = 3$, 2	**6**	$7x = 14$, 2
3	$3 + x = 9$, 6	**7**	$3x = 15$, 5
4	$x - 5 = 2$, 7	**8**	$6x = 24$, 4

Exercise 19b page 348

1	8	**7**	6	**13**	10	**19**	5
2	9	**8**	6	**14**	3	**20**	12
3	2	**9**	5	**15**	8	**21**	12
4	7	**10**	7	**16**	10	**22**	3
5	4	**11**	3	**17**	9	**23**	2
6	5	**12**	1	**18**	12	**24**	9

Exercise 19c page 349

1	2	**10**	4	**19**	5	**28**	23
2	9	**11**	4	**20**	11	**29**	4
3	3	**12**	8	**21**	16	**30**	7
4	13	**13**	12	**22**	12	**31**	9
5	3	**14**	10	**23**	10	**32**	9
6	3	**15**	11	**24**	9	**33**	4
7	7	**16**	10	**25**	17	**34**	4
8	0	**17**	6	**26**	5	**35**	4
9	1	**18**	11	**27**	16	**36**	2

Exercise 19d page 350

1	2	**7**	$\frac{1}{3}$	**13**	6	**19**	9
2	3	**8**	3	**14**	1	**20**	2
3	$2\frac{1}{2}$	**9**	$1\frac{2}{5}$	**15**	$\frac{1}{6}$	**21**	$\frac{3}{4}$
4	3	**10**	20	**16**	2	**22**	$1\frac{1}{5}$
5	4	**11**	2	**17**	$1\frac{4}{5}$	**23**	5
6	$2\frac{1}{4}$	**12**	$\frac{1}{2}$	**18**	$3\frac{1}{2}$	**24**	$\frac{1}{7}$

Exercise 19e page 350

1	4	**10**	13	**19**	2
2	12	**11**	8	**20**	$1\frac{2}{3}$
3	2	**12**	16	**21**	11
4	1	**13**	6	**22**	0
5	$1\frac{1}{5}$	**14**	$3\frac{1}{3}$	**23**	5
6	3	**15**	5	**24**	20
7	8	**16**	$\frac{2}{7}$	**25**	30
8	16	**17**	$2\frac{2}{3}$	**26**	30
9	$5\frac{1}{2}$	**18**	7	**27**	$\frac{1}{5}$

Exercise 19f page 351

1	4	**10**	7	**19**	2	**28**	3
2	3	**11**	5	**20**	2	**29**	$2\frac{1}{5}$
3	2	**12**	3	**21**	$1\frac{2}{3}$	**30**	$\frac{1}{3}$
4	6	**13**	5	**22**	$\frac{1}{2}$	**31**	6
5	3	**14**	2	**23**	4	**32**	$\frac{1}{4}$
6	0	**15**	3	**24**	0	**33**	5
7	6	**16**	3	**25**	2	**34**	$\frac{6}{7}$
8	5	**17**	0	**26**	$3\frac{1}{3}$		
9	$2\frac{2}{3}$	**18**	$1\frac{4}{5}$	**27**	$2\frac{3}{7}$		

Exercise 19g page 352

1	$4x - 8 = 20$, 7	**6**	$2x + 6 = 24$, 9
2	$6x - 12 = 30$, 7	**7**	$2x + 6 = 20$, 7
3	$3x + 6 = 21$, 5	**8**	$2x + 10 = 24$, 7
4	$x + 8 = 10$, 2	**9**	$3x - 9 = 18$, 9
5	$3x + 7 = 28$, 7	**10**	$2x + 9 = 31$, 11 cm

Exercise 19h page 353

1 $5x+15$
2 $3x+12$
3 $7x-11$
4 $8x+12$
5 $6x-14$
6 $12x-6$
7 $2x+1$
8 $x+3$
9 $8x-7$
10 $5x+2$
11 $5x+1$
12 $8x-3$

Exercise 19i page 354

1 2
2 0
3 $1\frac{3}{8}$
4 3
5 1
6 2
7 3
8 $2\frac{1}{2}$
9 $\frac{2}{7}$
10 3
11 $\frac{1}{3}$
12 2
13 2
14 $4\frac{2}{5}$
15 4
16 $\frac{1}{3}$
17 8
18 $-1\frac{3}{4}$
19 $7\frac{1}{2}$
20 2
21 3
22 2
23 8
24 2

Exercise 19j page 356

1 11
2 6
3 9 cm
4 21 c
5 16

Exercise 19k page 357

1 C
2 C
3 B
4 B
5 A
6 C

Exercise 19l page 358

1 2
2 1
3 $1\frac{1}{2}$
4 4
5 3
6 5

Exercise 19m page 358

1 $5\frac{1}{2}$
2 $\frac{2}{5}$
3 1
4 5
5 \$4
6 75°

CHAPTER 20

Exercise 20a page 361

1 a 4th shape

```
   *
  * *
 * * *
* * * *
```

5th shape

```
    *
   * *
  * * *
 * * * *
* * * * *
```

b 36

2 a last row of the table:
2 4 6 8 10
b 40 cm^2

3 a row 4: 4 square units, 21 sticks
row 5: 5 square units, 26 sticks
b 41
c 10 square units

4 a missing numbers in second row: 15, 21, 28
missing numbers in third row: 1, 25, 36, 49
b the number in the fourth row is the square of the number above it in the second row

5 2, 4, 6, … 20
6 1, 3, 5, … 23
7 3, 5, 7, … 17
8 18, 16, 14, … 8
9 0, –1, –2, … –19
10 4, 6, 8, 10, … 22
11 2, 5, 8, 11, … 29
12 6, 7, 8, 9, … 15
13 1, 4, 7, 10, … 28
14 $\frac{1}{2}, \frac{1}{4}, \frac{1}{6}, \frac{1}{8}, \dots \frac{1}{20}$
15 $\frac{1}{2}, \frac{1}{3}, \frac{1}{4}, \frac{1}{5}, \dots \frac{1}{11}$
16 3, 2, 1, 0, … –6

Exercise 20b page 364

1 $n+1$
2 $n+3$
3 $2n$
4 $n-1$
5 Add one to the term number, add three to the term number, double the term number, subtract one from the term number

6 a

n	1	2	3	4	5
nth term	2	5	8	11	14

b nth term is $3n-1$

7 a

n	1	2	3	4	5
nth term	10	8	6	4	2

b nth term is $12-2n$

8 a

n	1	2	3	4	5
nth term	5	10	15	20	25

b nth term is $5n$

9 a

n	1	2	3	4	5
nth term	2	$1\frac{1}{2}$	1	$\frac{1}{2}$	0

b nth term is $\frac{1}{2}(5-n)$

10 a

n	1	2	3	4	5
nth term	3	5	7	9	11

b nth term is $2n+1$

11 a

n	1	2	3	4	5
nth term	–4	–3	–2	–1	0

b nth term is $n-5$

12 $5n-2$, 23, 28, 33
13 $2(11-n)$, 12, 10, 8
14 $3n$, 15,18,21
15 $4n-1$, 19, 23, 27
16 $\frac{1}{n}, \frac{1}{5}, \frac{1}{6}, \frac{1}{7}$
17 $\frac{1}{2n}, \frac{1}{8}, \frac{1}{10}, \frac{1}{12}$
18 $6(11-n)$, 36, 30, 24
19 $100 \times \left(\frac{1}{2}\right)^n$, 6.25, 3.125, 1.5625
20 $\frac{1}{2n+1}, \frac{1}{11}, \frac{1}{13}, \frac{1}{15}$

Exercise 20c page 366

1 A 2 B 3 A 4 C 5 B 6 D

CHAPTER 21

Exercise 21a page 369

1 10
2 20
3 For example 19 \$50s, 2 \$20s, 1 \$10 or 2 \$50s, 40 \$20s, 10 \$10
4 For example 28 \$20s, 3 \$10s or 14 \$20s, 31 \$10s

Exercise 21b page 370

1 Single peppers; 175 c against 185 c
2 Pack of 6; \$2.40 per can against \$2.50 per can
3 The larger bag; 1.25 c per clip against 1.4 c per clip
4 1 kg pack ; 1.3 c per gram against 1.5 c per gram
5 Yes; 1 km costs \$2.50 against \$2.60
6 Prepacks; \$6.50 per kg against \$7.04 per kg
7 **a** 40 c **b** 36.25 c **c** 200 g jar
d No, it costs 37 c for 25 g which is dearer than the 200 g jar
8 950 g jar; 16 c per 50 g against 17 c per 50 g

Exercise 21c page 372

1 \$1840
2 \$23
3 \$24 150
4 \$753.25
5 \$376, \$390.40
6 **a** \$1265 **b** No **c** The manager added $2\frac{1}{2}\%$ to the original sale price. The manager should have added $17\frac{1}{2}\%$ to the pre-sales tax price.

Exercise 21d page 373

1 \$84
2 \$368
3 \$51.20
4 \$232
5 \$134.40
6 \$76.50
7 \$64.60
8 \$42.90
9 \$32.25
10 **a** \$24.40 **b** \$44.40

Exercise 21e page 374

1 50% profit
2 50% profit
3 33.3% loss
4 33.3% loss
5 40% loss
6 100% profit
7 \$700
8 \$40
9 25%
10 30%
11 25%
12 10%
13 20%
14 20%
15 15%
16 24%
17 \$56
18 \$72
19 \$60.90
20 \$18
21 \$27
22 \$80

Exercise 21f page 377

1 \$20
2 \$24
3 \$24
4 \$52
5 \$77
6 \$40
7 \$80
8 \$144
9 \$216
10 \$462
11 \$122.50
12 \$60
13 \$494.34
14 \$1113.60
15 \$130.32
16 \$101.64
17 \$364.56
18 \$50.76
19 \$421.20
20 \$1166.76
21 \$126.36
22 \$30.26
23 \$78.19
24 \$422.97
25 \$263.69
26 \$249.95
27 \$39.59
28 \$342.65
29 \$347.31
30 \$487.88
31 \$52.50
32 \$110.89
33 \$201.76
34 \$368.00
35 \$48.61
36 \$41.25
37 \$82.78
38 \$219.72
39 \$308.93
40 \$518.89
41 \$10.52
42 \$13.58
43 \$73.97
44 \$26.50
45 \$23.90
46 \$4.84

Exercise 21g page 379

1 \$525
2 \$487.20
3 \$962
4 \$790.02
5 \$1738.40
6 \$1581.10
7 \$701.10
8 \$889.71
9 \$970.47
10 \$280.86
11 \$438.90
12 \$1223.22
13 \$298.58
14 \$1004.40
15 \$1130.82
16 \$528.28

Exercise 21h page 379

1 7.69% (2 d.p.)
2 $33\frac{1}{3}\%$
3 **a** \$115 **b** 34.8% (1 d.p.)
4 \$10 000
5 \$295.35
6 \$1444.52

Exercise 21i page 379

1 B
2 A
3 C
4 C
5 D
6 D

REVIEW TEST 3 page 381

1 C
2 C
3 C
4 D
5 C
6 B
7 C
8 B
9 D
10 B
11 B
12 D
13 D
14 9.54 m
15 3 kg for \$16.50 is \$2.5 per lb while 5 lb for \$18 is \$3.6 per lb so the former is the cheaper.
16 **a**

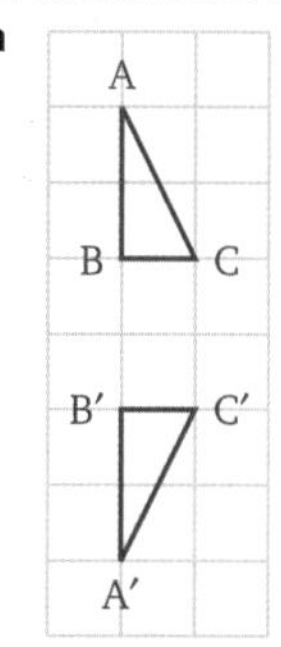

b

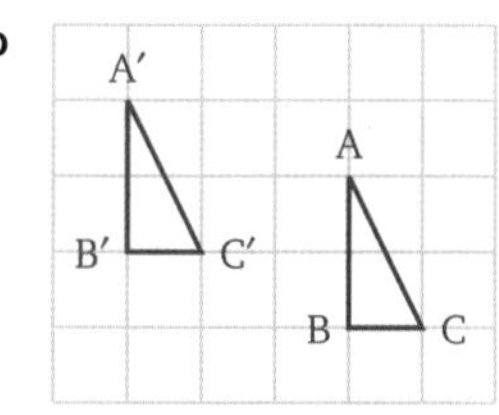

17 $37\frac{1}{2}\text{cm}^2$
18 **a** $\frac{3}{8}$ **b** 0.375
19 34 cm

REVIEW TEST 4 page 383

1 B
2 A
3 A
4 D
5 D
6 B
7 D
8 C
9 D
10 C
11 C
12 A
13 A
14 B
15 D
16 B
17 D
18 B
19 D
20 B
21 A
22 C
23 C
24 B
25 C
26 A
27 A
28 C
29 B
30 C

Index